ORIGINS OF THE BLACK ATLANTIC

"This excellent set of essays gathered and introduced by Laurent Dubois and Julius Scott will become a classic of its kind—useful to scholars, teachers, and readers of history as long as we want to understand the world of race and class we live in."
— Marcus Rediker, author of *The Slave Ship: A Human History*

"Any course on Atlantic revolutions would benefit from this anthology. It provides an important counter-weight to more Euro-centric accounts of the Age of Revolution by showing how enslaved people understood and re-imagined their role within the societies that had enslaved them."
— John D. Garrigus, author of *Before Haiti: Race and Citizenship in French Saint-Domingue*

"Laurent Dubois and Julius Scott have put together an up-to-date collection of the most interesting literature on the formation of the Black Atlantic, which could easily form the core of a course on the subject. They have been particularly careful to find literature that reveals the dynamic nature of Afro-Atlantic culture and its engagement with the political and cultural dimensions of the Americas."
— John K. Thornton, author of *Africa and Africans in the Making of the Atlantic World, 1400–1800*

Between 1492 and 1820, about two thirds of the people who crossed the Atlantic to the Americas were Africans. With the exception of the Spanish, all the European empires settled more Africans in the New World than they did Europeans. The vast majority of these enslaved men and women worked on plantations, and their labor was the foundation for the expansion of the Atlantic economy during the seventeenth and eighteenth centuries.

In *Origins of the Black Atlantic*, Laurent Dubois and Julius S. Scott bring together some of the key contributions to this growing area of scholarship, showing a range of methodological approaches, that can be used to understand and reconstruct the lives of these enslaved people.

Laurent Dubois is Professor of History at Duke University. He is the author of *A Colony of Citizens: Revolution & Slave Emancipation in the French Caribbean, 1787–1804*.

Julius S. Scott is Lecturer in the History department at the University of Michigan. He is also part of their Center for Afroamerican and African Studies.

REWRITING HISTORIES focuses on historical themes where standard conclusions are facing a major challenge. Each book presents papers (edited and annotated when necessary) at the forefront of current research and interpretation, offering students an accessible way to engage with contemporary debates.

Series editor **Jack R. Censer** is Professor of History at George Mason University.

REWRITING HISTORIES
Series editor: Jack R. Censer

ORIGINS OF THE BLACK ATLANTIC

Edited by
Laurent Dubois
and
Julius S. Scott

Routledge
Taylor & Francis Group

NEW YORK AND LONDON

First published 2010
by Routledge
711 Third Ave, New York, NY 10017

Simultaneously published in the UK
by Routledge
2 Park Square, Milton Park, Abingdon, Oxon OX14 4RN

Routledge is an imprint of the Taylor & Francis Group, an informa business

© 2010 Taylor & Francis

Typeset in Palatino by RefineCatch Limited, Bungay, Suffolk

Library of Congress Cataloging in Publication Data
Origins of the Black Atlantic / edited by Laurent Dubois and
Julius Scott.
p. cm.—(Rewriting histories)
Includes bibliographical references and index.
1. Blacks—America—History.   2. Blacks—America—
Historiography.   3. Slavery—America—History.   4. Slave trade—
America—History.   5. Slave insurrections—America—History.
6. America—Race relations.   7. America—Civilization—African
influences.   I. Dubois, Laurent, 1971–   II. Scott, Julius Sherrard, 1955–
E29.N3075 2010
973'.0496073—dc22
2009018688

ISBN10: 0–415–99445–4 (hbk)
ISBN10: 0–415–99446–2 (pbk)

ISBN13: 978–0–415–99445–3 (hbk)
ISBN13: 978–0–415–99446–0 (pbk)

CONTENTS

SERIES EDITOR'S PREFACE

Rewriting history, or revisionism, has always followed closely in the wake of history writing. In their efforts to re-evaluate the past, professional as well as amateur scholars have followed many approaches, most commonly as empiricists, uncovering new information to challenge earlier accounts. Historians have also revised previous versions by adopting new perspectives, usually fortified by new research, which overturn received views.

Even though rewriting is constantly taking place, historians' attitudes towards using new interpretations have been anything but settled. For most, the validity of revisionism lies in providing a stronger, more convincing account that better captures the objective truth of the matter. Although such historians might agree that we never finally arrive at the "truth," they believe it exists and over time may be better approximated. At the other extreme stand scholars who believe that each generation or even each cultural group or subgroup necessarily regards the past differently, each creating for itself a more usable history. Although these latter scholars do not reject the possibility of demonstrating empirically that some contentions are better than others, they focus upon generating new views based upon different life experiences. Different truths exist for different groups. Surely such an understanding, by emphasizing subjectivity, further encourages rewriting history. Between these two groups are those historians who wish to borrow from both sides. This third group, while accepting that every congery of individuals sees matters differently, still wishes somewhat contradictorily to fashion a broader history that incorporates both of these particular visions. Revisionists who stress empiricism fall into the first of the three camps, while others spread out across the board.

Today the rewriting of history seems to have accelerated to a blinding speed as a consequence of the evolution of revisionism. A variety of approaches has emerged. A major factor in this process has been the enormous increase in the number of researchers. This explosion has reinforced and enabled the retesting of many assertions. Significant ideological shifts have also played a major part in the growth of revisionism. First, the crisis of Marxism, culminating in the events in Eastern Europe in 1989, has given rise to doubts about explicitly Marxist accounts. Such doubts have spilled over into the entire field of social history which has been a dominant subfield of the discipline for several decades. Focusing on society and its class divisions implied that these are the most important elements in historical analysis. Because Marxism was built on the same claim, the whole basis of social history has been questioned, despite the very many studies that directly had little to do with Marxism. Disillusionment with social history simultaneously opened the door to cultural and linguistic approaches largely developed in anthropology and literature. Multiculturalism and feminism further generated revisionism. By claiming that scholars had, wittingly or not, operated from a white European/American male point of view, newer researchers argued that other approaches had been neglected or misunderstood. Not surprisingly, these last historians are the most likely to envision each subgroup rewriting its own usable history, while other scholars incline towards revisionism as part of the search for some stable truth.

"Rewriting Histories" will make these new approaches available to the student population. Often new scholarly debates take place in the scattered issues of journals which are sometimes difficult to find. Furthermore, in these first interactions, historians tend to address one another, leaving out the evidence that would make their arguments more accessible to the uninitiated. This series of books will collect in one place a strong group of the major articles in selected fields, adding notes and introductions conducive to improved understanding. Editors will select articles containing substantial historical data, so that students—at least those who approach the subject as an objective phenomenon—can advance not only their comprehension of debated points but also their grasp of substantive aspects of the subject.

This extraordinary collection of articles is, in fact, the result of two stages of the rewriting of history. Over thirty years ago, when national histories provided, almost unchallenged, the organizing principle for the modern Western history, scholars began to develop various world systems to provide new explanatory models. Included in this revisionism was the Atlantic World whose origins date back to Columbus. This paradigm immediately included both whites and blacks, but periodization and other factors made Europeans at home and abroad appear the most significant actors. Nonetheless, even this early paradigm brought much greater visibility to the lives of Native Americans and blacks. This book represents a new effort to inscribe within this Atlantic World, not just blacks, but a system of blacks, a world within a world. One after another, these articles powerfully promote the idea of black connection and agency.

INTRODUCTION

Laurent Dubois and Julius S. Scott

"Pericles on democracy, Paine on the Rights of Man, the Declaration of Independence, the Communist Manifesto," wrote C.L.R. James in *The Black Jacobins*, "these are some of the political documents which, whatever the weakness of wisdom of their analysis, have moved men and will always move them. . . . " But there was another set of writings that, according to James, had been unjustly excluded from this canon: the writings of Toussaint Louverture. The circumstances in which these writings were produced, argued James, were remarkable. Louverture wrote, and thought, in the midst of slave revolution, imperial war, and social transformation, and did so without the benefit of a "liberal education," dictating to secretaries "until their devotion and his will had hammered them into adequate shape." Nevertheless, he wrote in "the language and accent" of French philosophers and revolutionaries who were "masters of the spoken and written word." And, in the end, he "excelled them all," for unlike them he didn't have "to pause, to hesitate, to qualify." "Toussaint could defend the freedom or the blacks without reservation, and this gave to his declaration a strength and a single-mindedness rare in the great documents of the time."[1]

If James' work has become a touchstone for so many subsequent historians, it is because through such passages and the broader narrative they frame, it issued a profound challenge to the way the history of political thought and action had traditionally been told. Without using the term, James pioneered what we now call an "Atlantic" approach to the history of Europe and the Americas. At the core of his work was a simple, but vital, claim: that the enslaved whose labor built much of the Atlantic world were also thinkers and political actors, and that at certain moments they transformed and expanded the meaning of democracy. For James, the history of the Haitian Revolution was part of a larger epic of political struggle, and by telling it he hoped to reconfigure the reader's vision of the past, and therefore of the possibilities inherent in the future.

Especially since its republication in 1963, James' work has inspired and informed the work of decades of scholarship on Caribbean,

1

African-American and Atlantic history. It was, of course, part of a larger tradition that included the prior writings of W.E.B. DuBois and those of his contemporary Eric Williams, a part of whose work is presented in this collection. But his work probably best crystallizes the challenge and the vision that shapes the work we present in this collection. In the essays that follow, some of them widely read and cited and others less well known, historians struggle to reconstruct, analyze, narrate, and interpret how enslaved people in the Americas thought, acted, and transformed the world in which they lived.

The Atlantic world was deeply shaped by slavery and the slave trade and by the plantation complex it sustained. Between 1492 and 1820, about two-thirds of the people who crossed the Atlantic to the Americas were Africans. With the exception of the Spanish, all the European empires settled more Africans in the New World than they did Europeans. The vast majority of these enslaved men and women worked on plantations, and their labor was the foundation for the expansion of the Atlantic economy during the seventeenth and eighteenth centuries. In a 1993 book, Paul Gilroy famously deployed the term "Black Atlantic" – previously used by the art historian Robert Farris Thompson – to describe the cultural and political space that emerged out of this experience of mass displacement, exile, oppression and struggle. Now, many scholars have come to recognize that, outside of Europe, the Atlantic was, in its demography, its economic structure, and its political, cultural and intellectual formation, largely a "Black Atlantic."[2]

Until relatively recently, and with some important exceptions, comparatively little attention was paid to the perspectives, daily experiences, hopes and especially the political ideas of the enslaved who played such a central role in the making of the Atlantic world. Over the past decades, however, enormous scholarly energy has been focused on the study of the history of slavery and emancipation in the Atlantic world. This work has ranged from micro-history to synthetic surveys, and it has increasingly made connections across regions and empires in exploring the many connections that existed between enslaved communities in the Americas. It has also propelled the development of new methods and approaches aimed at uncovering the actions, experiences, and ideas of the enslaved and formerly enslaved.

These articles in this collection all seek, in one way or another, to comprehend how the enslaved and formerly enslaved imagined, reformulated, and transformed the political and legal contexts in which they lived. They showcase a range of methodological approaches that can be used to understand and reconstruct such politics out of often fragmentary and scattered sources. They do so in two major ways. The first is by grounding their analysis in rich exploration of a local context, grounded in the social, economic and cultural dimensions of this context. They therefore show how locating politics in a particular

2

historical and geographical moment can both help us to better understand its broader contexts and to expand our understanding of who is involved in and shaping political discourses and events. At the same time, they excel at highlighting the complicated connections, itineraries, and trajectories taken by people, ideas, objects, images, rumors, and hopes in a highly connected, if differentiated, Atlantic world. In combining these approaches, bridging the specificity of the local with an equivalent attention to the particular forms of trans-Atlantic and often trans-cultural movement, they provide us with a layering understanding of the shape of this broader world and of its political history.

Through their geographical and chronological range, they also highlight the complexity and variation of anti-slavery activity, and of its multiple sources. Though they range as far north as New York and as far south as Brazil, our selections cluster around the Greater Caribbean, which was at the center of the plantation complexes of the French, Spanish and British empires. Many of the pieces, however, elucidate the complex connections between political changes and ideas in different regions, connecting developments in parts of the Americas with one another and with Europe and Africa. They explore both the parallels and differences between imperial contexts, showcasing how particular systems' juridical traditions and institutions, as well as forms of imperial governance, were mobilized by anti-slavery actors. As a group, then, they offer a set of effective methods for making connections and re-thinking the sites of political thought in the Atlantic world, and help to turn our attention to the ways in which the enslaved and newly emancipated themselves shaped the Atlantic not only as laborers but also as political thinkers and actors.

This "Black Atlantic" was incredibly complex and diverse. It brought together a wide array of African groups from West and Central Africa, and the process of enslavement itself inflected and sometimes transformed what it meant to belong to these groups. In the following pages, historians repeatedly grapple with the question of how the African origins of particular individuals and communities shaped their perspectives and actions in the Americas, with many insisting that such analysis is central to any understanding of the broader Atlantic world. At the same time, of course, the Black Atlantic was shaped by ongoing processes of creolization, in which both the African-born and the American-born who were enslaved adapted and invented as they confronted their masters and one another in changing and often unstable social and political contexts. The great challenge of doing Atlantic history comes in part from the difficulty of interpreting and balancing how all these varied contexts shape any particular story. The articles in this collection, we feel, present successful and inspiring models for just how this can be done, and therefore can serve to inspire and propel the further research and writing that need to be done in this area.

Such a collection cannot, of course, hope to be exhaustive in its range. Given how much rich work has been produced in this field, it has been extremely difficult for us to decide what to include here, and we offer what follows with an understanding that it will inevitably leave important issues and worthwhile contributions out. We have, however, sought to present a combination of older and newer work so that readers will get a sense of the genealogy of certain approaches as well as an appreciation of the diversity and range of methods used by historians to explore the perspectives and actions of people of African descent in the Atlantic world. We have also sought to present a mix of classic and well-known articles with slightly lesser-known contributions, as well as seeking to make a few difficult-to-access works readily available.

Inspired by the earlier work of scholars such as James and Williams, the scholars represented here have effectively expanded and fleshed out the methodological tools and theoretical perspectives through which the experiences and thought of the enslaved can be comprehended and illuminated. They have opened up new avenues of research and analysis, creatively bringing together an impressive range of perspectives and sources. In many ways, their work has been the fruit of direct or indirect collaboration, for they have all profited from the expanding knowledge of slavery and the slave trade in which they participated. The current production in the field of Atlantic history today is stunningly rich and varied. The essays here have, in many ways, successfully done what they set out to do, transforming how historians think about the place of the enslaved in the Atlantic world, and inspiring other historians to follow in their footsteps.

Our title suggests that the stories told here represent a kind of foundation for a larger history of Black Atlantic culture and politics that has flourished and changed in the nineteenth and twentieth centuries, and which scholars such as Paul Gilroy and many others have explored in the past decades. This world, one of intense cultural exchange and invention as well as ongoing political struggle, is the continuation of a centuries-long process that this collection aims to illuminate. The contexts explored here are multiple and diverse, they represent plural origins rather than any kind of unified foundation. But they also show that, for centuries, people of African descent in the Atlantic have made and remade both themselves and the societies in which they lived.

There is perhaps no better visual representation of this process than the famous painting of Jean-Baptiste Belley presented on the cover of this book. Produced by the artist Anne-Louis Girodet in 1797, the painting has been the subject of ongoing debate among scholars. Some have emphasized the ways in which it exoticizes and sexualizes Belley, while others see it as a dignified and impressive portrait, unique for the way in which it foregrounded a well-known individual of African descent. For all its aesthetic and ideological ambiguities, the painting does clearly stand as a testament to Belley's remarkable story. Born in West Africa in the 1740s, Belley survived the Middle Passage and slavery in Saint-Domingue. By 1791, when enslaved insurgents rose up in the northern plain of the colony, he was a free man. In 1793 slavery was abolished in the colony by two French commissioners, and Belley – who had distinguished himself protecting the commissioners during a battle in the city – was elected part of a group of representatives sent to represent Saint-Domingue in the French National Convention in Paris. He and his colleagues travelled to France via Philadelphia, where he was attacked by a mob of white exiles from Saint-Domingue infuriated by the fact that he was wearing a tri-color cockade, the symbol of the French Republic. Once in Paris, he joined with other representatives to argue in favor of the general abolition of slavery throughout the French Empire. The National Convention agreed, and after it voted to abolish slavery a joyful Belley shouted: "I was a slave during my childhood. Thirty-six years have passed since I became free through my own labor, and purchased myself. Since then, in the course of my life, I have felt worthy of being French." The tri-color flag of France, he continued, would fly over Saint-Domingue "as long as there is a drop of blood in our veins." For the next four years, Belley served in parliament, defending the project of emancipation against its many enemies. In 1795, he confronted a particularly virulent and racist attack against emancipation by another representative by telling another part of his own story. "I was born in Africa," he announced, and denounced the racism that refused to accept the equality and citizenship of blacks in the French colonies. Girodet's portrait transformed him into a living avatar of the "Black Spartacus" prophesied in the Abbé Raynal's *Histoire des Deux Indes*, in a passage written by Dénis Diderot that warned that if slavery was not abolished, the slaves would ultimately produce a leader who would lead them to vengeance and freedom. But Belley's story, like that of Toussaint Louverture, ultimately ended tragically, for he was imprisoned by Napoleon Bonaparte's government and died there in 1805.[3]

In his life, Belley experienced first-hand all the forces that shaped the world of the Black Atlantic that the essays in this book illuminate: the horrors of the slave trade and plantation slavery, the struggles for both individual and collective freedom that shaped the political and social lives of many people of African descent, and the possibilities and limitations of revolutionary change. But perhaps the most striking thing about the way he was captured in 1797 by Girodet is the way that he looks away, and upwards, towards an unseen and uncertain future.

5

NOTES

1 C.L.R. James, *The Black Jacobins: Toussaint L'Ouverture and the San Domingo Revolution* (New York: Vintage, 1963), 197–198.
2 Paul Gilroy, *The Black Atlantic* (Cambridge, MA: Harvard University Press, 1988); Robert Farris Thompson, *Flash of the Spirit: African and Afro-American Art and Philosophy* (New York: Vintage, 1984).
3 For details on Belley's life, see Laurent Dubois, *Avengers of the New World: The Story of the Haitian Revolution* (Cambridge, MA: Harvard University Press, 2004), 157, 168–170, 195–196, 285; for compelling interpretations of the painting, see Darcy Grimaldo Grigsby, *Extremities: Painting Empire in Post-Revolutionary France* (New Haven, CT: Yale University Press, 2002), chap. 1; and Helen Weston, "Representing the Right to Represent: The Portrait of Citizen Belley, Ex-Representative of the Colonies, by A.L. Girodet," *Res* 26 (Autumn 1994): 83–100.

Part I

PEOPLE AND IDEAS IN CIRCULATION

The Atlantic plantation system was based on confining and containing the African captives who provided the labor that made the system function. But people of African descent were remarkably mobile, and despite ongoing attempts to limit their ability to communicate with other individuals and communities, they were highly connected. This section gathers together some of the key work that has enabled scholars to understand how inter-connected communities of African descent in the Atlantic were. They show how, by moving beyond regionally-focused studies, we see how both free and enslaved people of African descent took advantage of the sinews that held together Atlantic empires to pursue individual and collective freedom through escape and revolt.

Barry Gaspar's essay examines an early revolutionary decade in the eighteenth century, that of the 1730s. During this period, a remarkable series of insurrections and plots developed in different parts of the Americas. In North America the most famous and influential of these were the Stono Revolt of 1739 and the 1741 plot in New York. These took place, though, after a series of uprisings in the British Caribbean. Indeed, as Peter Linebaugh and Marcus Rediker have recently written about this decade: "The magnitude of the upheaval was, in comparative terms, extraordinary, encompassing more than eighty separate cases of conspiracy, revolt, mutiny and arson – a figure probably six or seven times greater than the number of similar events that occurred in either the dozen years before 1730 or the dozen after 1742." These actions on the part of the enslaved, they note, have tended to be studied as "isolated events" rather than "in relation to each other," and suggest that they have "both a coherence and a collective causal power."[1] Gaspar's little-known 1981 article, however, importantly established the links between events in the Caribbean. It presents some of the material and ideas published in his book *Bondsmen and Rebels*, which used the Antigua plot of 1736 to examine the functioning of a slave society. But, published in a short-lived and little-known journal of Caribbean Studies, *Cimarrons*, published in Guadeloupe, until now it has been difficult to access for most researchers. Gaspar's article was remarkably pioneering in its emphasis on the connections between events during this period.

In his bicentennial 1976 article, Richard Sheridan explores a little-known plot discovered among slaves in Jamaica in 1776. The article combines a fine-grained analysis of the plot, based on the interrogations of those involved with a careful rendering of the various contexts necessary to understand it. Sheridan situates the plot within the long history of enslaved action on the island, from the resistance of the maroons starting in the late seventeenth century through the 1831 "Baptist War" just before emancipation. As importantly, he places the revolt in a larger geographical context, interpreting it in relation to the events of 1776 in North America. The connection was both pragmatic, since the plotters noticed the departure of troops incited by events in North America and, he argues, ideological, since they found inspiration in the revolutionary political rhetoric circulating at the time. At the same time, Sheridan is meticulous about situating the revolt within the particular circumstances of the plantations on which it emerged. The result is a model of multi-layered analysis of slave resistance.

Neville Hall's article on "Maritime Maroons" turns its attention to a pivot within the Caribbean, the islands of the Danish West Indies, a series of islands (including St. John, St. Croix and St. Thomas) east of Puerto Rico. Rather than focusing on particular events of resistance, as Gaspar and Sheridan do, it seeks to identify and document a long-standing set of forms of escape from bondage practiced by the enslaved. While these islands had their own plantation economies, they also played a central role as sites of trade, often contraband, helping to sustain the development of other parts of the Caribbean. As Hall points out, meanwhile, as small islands they had relatively little protected space for escaped slaves (maroons) to constitute communities, as they did most famously in Jamaica and Surinam. In these places, he notes, permanent escape often meant what he calls "maritime marronage": escaping by finding work as a sailor on a ship, or stowing away on one, to find a haven either on the high seas or in another port, in another empire, where old masters were further away and easier to shake. Hall's article is a model both for the way that it helps illuminate and define a particular form of resistance that had previously been overlooked and for the way it brings together a wide range of sources—official documents, newspapers, and poetry—to present a detailed and rigorous account of its practice and impact.

All of these works influenced the often-cited and germinal work of Julius Scott, who in his 1986 dissertation "A Common Wind" insisted on the important place of black sailors, both free and enslaved, in the transmission of information and ideas during the era of the Haitian Revolution. In this selection of the work, Scott lays out his vision of a world connected by these sailors, one in which news traveled with remarkable, sometimes miraculous, speed between communities who were aware of and inspired by actions in other parts of the Altantic world. Scott's work crystallizes a series of earlier insights by historians and pushed them further, illuminating the forms of communication and dialogue that framed the politics of the enslaved in the Atlantic world during this period. His own insight has been taken up by many subsequent historians, including Jeffrey Bolster as well as Peter Linebaugh and Marcus Rediker.[2]

NOTES

1   Peter Linebaugh and Marcus Rediker, *The Many-Headed Hydra* (Boston: Beacon Press, 2000), 193.
2   Jeffrey Bolster, *Black Jacks: African-American Seamen in the Age of Sail* (Cambridge, MA: Harvard University Press, 1997).

1

A DANGEROUS SPIRIT OF LIBERTY

Slave Rebellion in the West Indies in the 1730s

David Barry Gaspar

In regard to slave unrest in North America, Herbert Aptheker noted that "uprisings and plots came in waves, as though anger accumulated and vented itself and then a period of rest and recuperation was needed before the next upsurge". One such wave came in the 1730s, when there was also notable slave unrest in the West Indies.[1] If what Aptheker says is true, then it must mean that exceptional unrest required the conjunction of a number of conducive elements, such as gave rise to the Stono Rebellion in South Carolina in September 1739.[2] A climate conducive to slave unrest must also have existed in the West Indies where, according to a report from Jamaica in 1737, the "negros in many of the British plantations" had "of late been possessed of a dangerous spirit of liberty" having "actually risen in Antigua" and "threatened to do it in the rest of the sugar plantations".[3]

Slave unrest in the British sugar islands during the 1730s peaked with the intensification of the First Maroon War in Jamaica, and the Antigua slave plot of 1736; but in the Danish island of S. John a slave revolt also broke out in 1733. By examining these three major episodes of collective resistance against the background of intensifying slave unrest in those particular islands, and by looking also at unrest elsewhere in the West Indies, this paper attempts to justify the generalization that during the 1730s slave resistance intensified in the West Indies.

* * *

Running away was the most common form of slave resistance throughout the slave colonies of the Americas. Wherever mountains, jungle or swamps provided a suitable environment, fugitives or maroons established communities, ranging in size from Palmares in Brazil with a population of more than ten thousand, to much smaller groups existing on the borders of plantations as in the American South, or even in the interior of tiny islands such as Antigua during the later seventeenth century before the sugar plantations had achieved their maximum territorial expansion.[4] The most famous maroons in the British West Indies were those in Jamaica,[5] and the earliest of them were the former slaves of the Spanish who lost the island to the English in 1655.

After five years of guerilla style resistance in which they were aided sometimes by their former slaves now operating as independent guerillas, the Spanish withdrew from the island in 1660. By this time, three groups of black guerillas had emerged. One of these had made peace with the English and helped them to drive out the Spanish; but all attempts to encourage the others "to live peaceable under His Majesty's obedience and in due submission to the government of the island" failed, and they continued to harass the English settlements, later settling in the north-western part of the island where, as time went by, they were joined by revolting slaves and runaways to form the Windward band of Maroons.[6]

Jamaica was much larger than Barbados, St. Kitts or Antigua (three of the older English island colonies), and greatly increased the acreage available for sugar cultivation among the islands, but planting there developed slowly until late in the century. At first supplies of slaves came from the older English colonies, mainly Barbados, but later slaves were transported direct from Africa. From 550 in 1662 the slave population surged to 9,500 in 1673 and 45,000 by 1703. By 1720 the island had surpassed Barbados as the leading English sugar colony.[7] As the number of slaves increased slaveowners were confronted with the pressing problem of how to control them.

The first significant slave revolt of the seventeenth century broke out in 1673 on the remote north coast, in the parish of St. Ann. There, 200 mostly Coromantee slaves (Akan-speaking slaves from the Gold Coast) on Major Selby's plantation killed him and about thirteen other whites, and then attacked several smaller estates in the vicinity, seizing arms and ammunition, before disappearing into the nearby mountains. These rebels became the core of the Leeward band of Maroons, and after their revolt many slaves ran away to join them. On the north coast again, in 1675, there was another revolt; yet another followed in 1678, and a year-long one a few years later (1685–1686), which began once again on the north coast with the revolt of 150 slaves and later spread to the south. A revolt in 1690 involved 400 mostly Coromantee slaves from Sutton's plantation in Clarendon parish, one of the largest and best developed plantations.

Other revolts broke out in 1696, 1702 and 1704. In 1722, to prevent expansion of new settlements on the north-east coast, the Windward Maroons embarked upon a systematic plundering of those already established. By the mid 1720s, revolts and desertion of slaves who joined the

Maroons had contributed to the growth in size of the two main groups. The Leeward Maroons occupied the exceptionally rugged country of the west-central interior including the "Cockpit Country", while in the north-eastern mountains that included the Blue Mountains (highest in Jamaica, rising to 7,402 feet) and the John Crow Mountains were the Windward Maroons.[8] George Metcalf estimated that the "entire Maroon population in the 1730s cannot have numbered much more than a thousand".[9]

The intensification of the Maroon conflict round about the mid 1720s continued into the 1730s when, according to one historian, Jamaica was for a time "an armed camp".[10] In 1730, Governor Robert Hunter, after several unsuccessful attempts to overcome the rebels, described the critical situation to the assembly. "The Slaves in rebellion" he declared, "from the increase of their numbers by the late desertions from several settlements, or from the bad success of common parties, are grown to that height of insolence that your frontiers that are no longer in any sort of security, must be deserted, and then the danger must spread and came nearer if not prevented".[11] Orlando Patterson contends that a notable decline in the white population about this time can be traced largely to fear of the Maroons, but harsh treatment of indentured servants and economic instability also contributed to it.[12] Fearful of a general uprising, Governor Hunter took the opportunity again in 1732 to warn the legislature that now more than ever they needed to find effective ways of subduing the Maroons, "your slaves in rebellion, animated by their success, and others (as it is reported) ready to join them on the first favourable opportunity". Hunter urged them to consider "more solid measures than have been hitherto resolved upon for your security; all former attempts against these slaves having been either unsuccessful or to very little purpose".[13]

Parties sent out against the Windward Maroons in 1732 achieved some success, taking three main settlements including Nanny Town, but the following year the rebels recaptured it. The war dragged on. By 1734 the number of slaves believed to be deserting to the Maroons had grown alarmingly, and two years later, in an address to the king outlining conditions in Jamaica, the legislature claimed that the "slaves in rebellion which have already cost so many lives and so much expense continue as insolent, troublesome, and we believe as numerous as ever".[14] Also in 1736, John Gregory, President of the Council searching about for a way to end the Maroon War, stated that he had tried "to propose a treaty to such as have been out for the space of five years promising them liberty and lands to cultivate if they would submit on condition that they would clear the woods of such as resolve to stand out, and entertain no more amongst them". However, he had been unable "to procure any that would venture to carry the message to them though upon promise of reward". Gregory went so far as to suggest that the home government could help by purchasing the freedom of 200 slaves "such as we should judge could be best depended upon, and put them under a British establishment as to their pay", their main job being to hunt down the Maroons. But the Council of Trade and Plantations did not support the idea although they agreed that "negroes inured to the heat of the climate may be better able to bear the fatigues attending any expedition through the woods". Should "this black regiment be inclined to favour those of their own colour", they argued, "they would prove a party of much more dangerous consequence than those of the mountains. How little confidence may be placed in any negroes", they pointed out significantly, "and how little they ought to be trusted with arms appears too plainly from the late rebellion in Antigua, where those were chiefly concerned who had the greatest share of trust and confidence from their masters".[15]

In attempting to subdue the Maroons the authorities used Mosquito Coast Indians, bloodhounds, British regiments and local militia, all to no avail. Finally, they signed treaties with the two Maroon groups in 1739–40 which, inter alia, recognized the rebels' freedom and rights to land, but most important from the point of view of the future of slave resistance in Jamaica, was the Maroons' undertaking "to take, kill, suppress, or destroy . . . all rebels wheresoever they be unless they submit to the same terms", and to capture and return any runaways. These agreements drove a deep wedge between the slaves not in open rebellion and the Maroons who had now become part of the island machinery for policing runaways and quelling rebellions.[16] In securing their freedom the Maroons had deprived the slaves of opportunity to seek their own in flight or rebellion, and it is not surprising that the slaves became dangerously restive once they understood what they were now up against; but after a conspiracy to revolt was discovered and the ringleaders brutally punished as an example to others, the restless mood seems to have subsided.[17]

Although no major slave revolts or plots were reported in Jamaica during the 1730s, yet the slaves were notably restless and continued to run away to the Maroons, encouraged undoubtedly by the success with which the rebels in the mountains eluded capture. By joining up with the Maroons, themselves originally runaways and regarded as such by the whites, runaways became part of a larger sustained slave revolt begun in 1655 and dominated by a Maroon dimension. Indeed, it has been suggested that "all sustained slave revolts must acquire a Maroon dimension since the only way in which a slave population can compensate for the inevitably superior military might of their masters is to resort to guerilla warfare with all its implications of flight, strategic retreat to secret hideouts, and ambush".[18]

To take the contrasting case of Antigua, for example. There, the disturbances among the slaves during the 1670s were prompted largely by the existence of maroons in the as yet unsettled interior, especially in the region about the low Shekerley Hills (highest elevation just over

1,000 feet)[19] in the south-west corner of the island. But the topography of the area did not support the development of maroon-type resistance and the maroons were routed without too much difficulty. The absence therefore of a significant maroon dimension after the 1670s limited the intensity and style of slave resistance in Antigua.[20]

In Jamaica, maroon activity and revolts, plots, and general slave unrest were interrelated phenomena. Because they reinforced one another the first Maroon War can be regarded as a sustained slave revolt of a particular type – the maroon type.[21]

The first thing to be taken into account therefore in explaining the strong rebelliousness among the Jamaica slaves in the 1730s would be the activities of the Maroons who continually demonstrated that runaways joining them could preserve their freedom. But because the Maroon War intensified in the 1730s, the particular set of conditions favoring the conflict before that are also relevant in that they created a foundation for slave rebelliousness of the decade. Patterson, who has carefully analyzed the Maroon War, cites the following contributing factors; the master-slave ratio, the ratio of creole (local) to foreign (African) born slaves, the opportunities for leadership and political organization slavery allowed, the rugged interior of Jamaica suitable for sustained maroon activity, absenteeism, large-scale plantation agriculture and the harsh treatment of slaves, and finally, the lack of social commitment on the part of the whites.[22] The discussion which follows considers these.

By the late seventeenth century, the slave population outnumbered the whites with the result that there were not enough whites to properly control them. By 1739 the ratio of slaves to whites was about 10 to 1. There were 117, 411 slaves compared with 11,540 whites. Richard Sheridan has suggested that the First Maroon War "was both cause and effect of the growing disparity between the whites and blacks, for the war itself made frontier settlements unsafe, and thus discouraged immigration, while slaves were emboldened to revolt by the paucity of white masters".[23] While it is difficult to prove how the slaves' numerical superiority helped develop a situation conducive to revolt, comparative information on slave revolts in the Americas and in antiquity suggests a strong connection between a low master-slave ratio and insurrection. One thing seems certain. To help set the stage for revolt, the low master-slave ratio would have to carry some positive meaning for the slaves, and the establishment of that awareness would have to be one of the key functions of the slave leaders.

Perhaps more important than the ratio of masters to slaves was the ratio of Creole to African born slaves[24] most of whom were Coromantee and Papaw, the latter coming from Dahomey or Whydah on the Slave Coast. Between 1655 and 1740 Africans made up "no less than four-fifths" of the slave population, according to Patterson; "recruited from outside the system" and unacculturated to Jamaican slavery, they were probably more likely to rebel than the Creoles who were born and socialized in the island or some other. It is probably not coincidental that many of the seventeenth century uprisings involved Africans, particularly Coromantees.

Whether African or Creole, a slave could rise to a position of leadership and use it to engage in political organization of the sort which encouraged group solidarity and which might be the foundation for collective resistance. Whenever plots or revolts occurred, some of which were well planned, there were always slave leaders available to play an active role, whether they had been leaders already in Africa, or had assumed the role in Jamaica assigned by masters, or by the slave themselves using their own criteria. In the Americas, slave leaders generally derived their sanctions from economic, religious and ethnic sources.[25]

The role of the rugged terrain in the interior of Jamaica has already been referred to, and according to Patterson it was of less importance than absenteeism, "perhaps the most important" factor of all. But this assessment of the role of absenteeism is based upon the assumption that attorneys and overseers who ran the plantations for the proprietors, uninfluenced by proprietorial self-interest, would probably have treated the slaves badly and bred dissatisfaction leading to unrest. If it is true that absenteeism encouraged such tendencies, then these would certainly have been reinforced by the harsh treatment of slaves inherent in the operation of large plantations where most slaves were simply part of the machinery of production and dispensable so long as new supplies of slaves were forthcoming from Africa. Furthermore, on such large units the potential for rebellion could be increased if the slaves felt safety in numbers.

All of these factors referred to combined to encourage slave unrest before 1740, but the lack of social commitment among whites – as for example, reluctance to serve in the militia – also played a part, preventing the focussing of their energies in a well coordinated effort to pacify the maroons and rebellious slaves.[26] With special regard to the 1730s, however, the recession in the sugar industry during that decade should also be taken into account. Muscovado sugar prices on the English market declined relative to prices of English exports to the colonies, turned the terms of trade in favor of the mother country for the greater part of the decade and imposed hardship on the islands.[27]

In 1736, the Jamaica legislature, in an address to the King on the "distressed and unhappy condition to which this colony is at present reduced", lamented that the recession coming on top of the difficulties with the Maroons and other problems would not only "prevent the hopes and prospects of any further accession of strength to the island and . . . discourage entirely the undertaking of any new settlements among us but also . . . deprive those who are already settled of the means of carrying on and improving their estates, discharging the debts which they have been obliged to contract in settling them, and paying the taxes necessarily imposed . . . for their own defence and the security of the public". They feared that the recession threatened "no less than the utter ruin and desolation of this once flourishing island".[28]

Whether this account of distress in Jamaica was exaggerated, in those difficult years throughout the British sugar islands, many small holders "went to the wall . . . while small to middling planters found themselves in reduced circumstances".[29] Frank Wesley Pitman noted a growing threat of slave rebellion in Jamaica, "practically every year", attributable in part possibly to "the condition of both the sugar and provision markets" which "inclined overseers to make greater demands upon the slaves for labor and cut down their supplies of food and clothing".[30] The adverse internal effects of the recession especially in regard to harsh treatment and deterioration of the slaves' living conditions are important in explaining heightened slave unrest. Also of some importance would be natural disasters such as the hurricane of September 1734 which did damage in more than half of the island.

Yet, all of these conditions that encouraged slave unrest in the 1730s resulted in the slaves seizing freedom when they could because they were above everything else ideologically persuaded that freedom was a desirable goal. The desire for freedom, universal among slaves in slave societies throughout the Americas, helped create a constant potential for revolt.

In tiny Antigua further east along the Caribbean island chain, slave resistance lacked an effective maroon dimension by the 1730s because every usable acre of land had been converted to sugar cultivation, and the hilly district of the south-west corner where runaways had sought refuge in the seventeenth century had been penetrated. This made for a qualitative difference between slave resistance in Antigua and Jamaica. While the Antigua slaves may not have run away as frequently and threatened life and property in a long war against the whites, in less dramatic ways, they did express their opposition to slavery. Where large numbers of Jamaica slaves could grasp freedom and defend it by joining the Maroons, Antigua slaves could not, and the only way to collectively achieve freedom was to seize the whole island,[31] an operation requiring careful planning.

In October 1736 Antigua whites discovered that their slaves were plotting to destroy them.[32] The discovery caused much anxiety and abruptly brought "a general Stop to all Business". Later, the trial judges described the plot as an island-wide affair, in preparation since November 1735, if not earlier.[33] "Most of the free Negroes, and free Mulattos were Actually engaged in it" claimed councillor Vallentine Morris, alarmed by the plot's extent and long secrecy, and "the Negro Women by their Insolent behaviour and Expressions had the Utter Extirpation of the whites as much at heart, as the Men, and would undoubtedly have Done as much Mischief by Butchering all the Women and Children". Morris added that "the Universality of this Conspiracy is but one of many Circumstances that Distinguish it from that which happened many Years Since in Barbados; for that formerly in Martinique like that Now in Jamaica were open Rebellions and therefore much less Dangerous".[34]

The plot was masterminded by Court, alias Tackey (in Akan meaning Chief), a Coromantee slave aged about 35 belonging to Thomas Kerby, justice of the peace and Speaker of the Assembly. His chief accomplice was Tomboy, the Creole slave of Thomas Hanson. They planned a general insurrection to begin on the night of October 11 during the annual ball held in St. John's, the capital town, to commemorate the king's coronation. A carpenter by trade, Tomboy was to have secured the job of building seats for the ballroom so that he could plant gunpowder in the cellar for blowing up the island gentry during the ball. The blast itself was intended as a signal for several groups of armed slaves to enter the town and kill the whites while others on the outskirts prevented relief reaching them. Other slaves were to be deployed to seize the forts and shipping in the Harbor, while those still on the plantations were to march to town leaving a scene of destruction wherever they passed. Unfortunately for the slaves, however, the ball was postponed until the end of the month, and this gave the authorities time to uncover the plot.[35] In all 88 slaves were executed; 5 were broken on the wheel, 6 gibbetted and 77 burned alive; 47 others were banished.

The list of slaves executed and banished does not distinguish African from island born, and the names themselves are not a reliable enough clue, but the evidence shows that the plot, while originating with Court and other Coromantees, ultimately evolved into a coalition between Coromantees and Creoles who were the most numerous ethnic group of slaves. Court had drawn Tomboy and other Creoles into the plot because he saw he did not have enough Coromantees to undertake the massive operation of seizing the whole island. The revolt was thus originally conceived as an ethnic, Coromantee affair, the Creoles being later invited in for tactical reasons. That feature indeed, as well as the large scale of the plot and especially the amount of planning that went into it, suggest that it was a more advanced type of slave rebellion than the Jamaica maroon type about the same time, although both were African led and inspired. But because of these distinguishing characteristics the Antigua affair was less likely to succeed, as indeed were most long-planned, elaborate rebellions. The longer the conspiracy stage and the greater the problems to be overcome, the greater the chance of discovery.

From the trial judges' general report and other primary evidence related to the plot's causes, it would appear that the preconditions included the slaves' desire for freedom, population imbalance, absenteeism, general slave resistance, and the lax enforcement of slave controls. These established a strong potential for collective rebellion that was reinforced by the recession of the 1730s, sickness, natural disasters, and slave leadership able and willing to make use of that potential.[36]

First on the judges' list of causes was the slaves' desire for freedom, a constant factor requiring no elaboration here. As far as slaves outnumbering whites is concerned, they had already done so by the start of the eighteenth century, and as the sugar revolution advanced the ratio of slaves to whites increased. From Christmas 1720 to Christmas 1729, the number of slaves imported was 12,278 or 1,364 a year; in 1730 alone, 2,288 arrived. By 1736 the ratio of slaves to whites stood at about 8 to 1; slaves made up more than 88 percent of a total population that included at least 24,000 slaves and not more than about 3,000 whites. In the rural areas, of course, on the plantations, the ratio of slaves to whites would have been even greater; so too, would have been the ratio of slaves to militia-men in the island.[37]

What about absenteeism as one of the plot's causes? It is difficult to trace the role of absenteeism, although it can be said that it would have contributed, though probably not significantly, to the small size of the white population.[38] As in Jamaica the slaves' numerical superiority helped develop among the slaves a sense of potential advantage, bolstering hopes for a successful insurrection. Their large numbers may also help to explain why enforcement of slave controls was so lax; there were not enough whites to do the enforcing. But more important though, on this point, was that the style of slave resistance in Antigua during the early decades of the eighteenth century did not generally appear to seriously threaten life and property, although from time to time bands of runaways had to be dealt with. Overall, it seems Antigua slaveowners did not strictly supervise their slaves.

Lax enforcement of the slave laws, perhaps the single most important general cause of the plot, encouraged a groundswell of slave resistance that erupted in a localized plot in 1728–29.[39] In 1732 there were "fresh Complaints of Runaway Negroes in Shackerley's Mountains and the Road Mountains who daily increase in Numbers". Nearly 50 runaways were executed or hunted down and killed between 1730 and 1735. Less numerous were executions for other crimes, but it is significant that they happened "during a period of widespread slave insubordination encouraged by negligent supervision, notably in St. John's town". The police system was so lax by the mid 1730s that the slaves were able to hold frequent meetings to recruit followers and lay plans for their revolt. A slave told Robert Arbuthnot, one of the trial judges, that he thought the slaves had of late been given too much freedom. The most striking evidence of this permissiveness was the ritual "ikem dance" or "Military dance and Shew" which Court held at two o'clock in the afternoon, Sunday October 3, 1736 at Mrs Dunbar Parke's plantation near St. John's, by which to determine the amount of support he could expect, at the same time binding his followers to their duty. At that time, "Near Two Thousand" blacks were assembled, yet no attempt was made to break up the meeting.[40] Such permissiveness made the mobilization of the rebels easier.

As in many other slave revolts and conspiracies, the leaders of the Antigua plot came from the ranks of the privileged slaves. Of the ten main ringleaders, Court was a waiting man, and Tomboy a carpenter; of the rest, there were two carpenters, one carpenter/fidder, one waiting man, one cooper, one mason, two drivers, and another slave of unknown occupation. Of these only Court was Coromantee, eight were Creoles and another either a Creole or he had come to Antigua as a child. Many of the Creoles had "been lately baptized and several of them could read and write". The trial judges thought these men had behaved outrageously in planning the destruction of whites because "none of them (could) justly complain of the hardship of Slavery; their lives being as easy as those of our white Tradesmen and Overseers, and their manner of living much more Plentiful, than that of our Common Whites, who were looked upon by some of them, for their Poverty and Distress with Contempt".[41] These were the slaves then who became the leaders of a plot involving restless slaves from all over the island whose discontent and frustration under slavery worsened as a result of recession and natural disasters.

The hardship which the recession imposed on the slaves must have been greater in Antigua than in Jamaica, because "unlike the Jamaican slaves who grew much of their own food, the Antiguans were fed largely on imported supplies, the price of which had increased". In 1731, the lieutenant governor and council noted that many slaves ran away because they were treated badly and underfed. And one frustrated slave did complain in 1736 that slaves were forced to live on "a Bit and Six herrings a Week". Further hardship followed crop disease, drought, an epidemic of "black leprosy and joint evil", excessive rain and earthquakes.[42] In the end, it was left to the leaders of the plot, and the obeahmen, to persuade the slaves that the time was right for a successful revolt.

The discovery of the plot gave the whites a good scare and many, fearing further trouble, left the island. But if they fled to neighboring St. Bartholomew, Anguilla and St. Martin, they would have had reason not to stay because there too the slaves were restless. Governor Mathew of the Leeward Islands reported that "The Contagion of rebellion is spread further among these islands than I apprehend is discovered. By an enclosed affidavit of John Hanson, it actually has taken effect in St. Bartholomew, and is discovered in Anguilla and St. Martins". Hanson reported an uprising among the St. Bartholomew slaves on December 15, 1736 in which eleven white men were killed, and a plot in the French quarter of St. Martin which was discovered and eight slaves condemned to death. He also mentioned that according to reports the slaves in Anguilla had planned an uprising for December 26, 1736.[43] But Governor Mathew's claim that a "contagion" of rebellion had spread among the slaves in the islands around the British Leewards does not necessarily imply the slaves were collaborating. It seems possible, however, that they had heard of the failure of the plot in Antigua perhaps from slave seamen, and far from being discouraged by it, resolved to make their own attempt. Slave seamen travelled back and forth between the islands, and they or any travellers for that matter, could have been the carriers of news that reached the slaves.[44] So, it is also not impossible that the Antigua plot may have been influenced by the troubles with the Jamaica Maroons and the slave revolt in the Danish island of St. John in 1733.

Through the Danish West India Company, the Danes occupied St. John during the early eighteenth century. Small, mountainous, and fertile, the island attracted sugar planters from the other Danish island of St. Thomas settled in the seventeenth century, but many of these planters did not move over but hired overseers to run their St. John properties. The number of plantations in the island rose from 39 in 1720–1721 to 87 in 1728 by which time the slave population stood at 677, according to Walderman Westergaard. There were 109 plantations and 1,087 slaves in this developing sugar island by 1733.[45]

The slave revolt began on the morning of November 23 when twelve or fourteen slaves belonging to the Company were allowed to enter the fort with bundles of wood in which they had concealed cane bills or knives, and once inside they killed the soldiers and later gave the signal for a general uprising throughout the island. A soldier who escaped from the fort and some other refugees went over to St. Thomas where they raised the alarm. While the authorities there prepared to send aid, fearing that if the rebels were not subdued early their own slaves might also revolt, St. John became a scene of fear, destruction, and bloodshed. Probably entertaining fears similar to the St. Thomas authorities, the English in the neighboring island of St. Kitts, closest of the four main British Leewards, sent aid. "Stratagems, attempts at poisoning, and the armed forces of Danes and English had failed alike to dislodge or exterminate the desperate slaves", Westergaard wrote, but finally with the help of the French at Martinique, the revolt was put down after nine months in August 1734. A list of February 1734 indicated that 146 slaves, male and female, were at the time implicated in the revolt. A number of slaves and whites were killed, and 27 rebels were reported tried and executed; 48 plantations were damaged or destroyed.[46]

In his account of the revolt Westergaard did not dwell on its causes, but it is probable that harsh treatment of the slaves, a high ratio of slaves to whites, and absenteeism played important roles. But what probably made revolt among the slaves highly predictable was a succession of natural disasters. The year 1733 was marked by months of drought, a hurricane which severely damaged crops, buildings and shipping, an insect plague that confronted the slaves with the possibility of famine, and an early winter storm that seriously affected the crop of maize, the slaves' main source of food. Westergaard observed that the "most persistent motive that led to general unrest among the slaves was lack of food". That motive was strong late in 1733; and the governor's proclamation of a body of repressive measures in September, which were meant to check the slaves' rebellious activities intensified by hard times, did little to alleviate their distress.[47] Indeed, these new regulations may well have triggered the revolt. Instead of pacifying the restless slaves, it inflamed their rebelliousness.

The St. John slave revolt went further than the conspiracy stage, but it is not clear why this happened. Probably the planning stage was sufficiently short so that there was not enough time for the whites to become suspicious, or for some faithful slave to betray the plans. Still, like the attempt in Antigua three years later, the odds against success in the long run were enormous, because it would have been difficult for the slaves to hold the island against the armed might of the Europeans.

In S. John, Jamaica, Antigua, St. Bartholomew, St. Martin and Anguilla during the 1730s, slave unrest crystallized into open revolt or conspiracy to revolt. There was also a report of an attempted uprising in St. Kitts in 1734, months after the St. John revolt, when six houses were set on fire. And there may have been another attempt a few years later, for the South Carolina merchant, Robert Pringle, in a letter to a friend in St. Kitts in 1739, mentioned that he was "much Concern'd to hear . . . of your being alarm'd for fear of an Insurrection of the Negroes but hope their wicked Designs will prove abortive and turn to their own Confusion".[48] A number of long-run conditions, such as the slaves' desire for freedom, or harsh conditions of slavery, nurtured a constant potential for revolt, but so far as the British sugar colonies were concerned, probably the most important precipitant of growing unrest in the 1730s was the recession in the sugar industry. In Antigua it gave the slaves a critical additional incentive to lay plans for the complicated operation of seizing the whole island. While the recession did hit Barbados most severely, and along with it came hurricane and drought,[49] no major revolt or conspiracy was reported there, although the slaves may have been more restive than usual. On the North American mainland also, resistance appears to have reached a new level of intensity. Plots were discovered and crushed in 1730 in Virginia, South Carolina, and Louisiana, but during the remainder of the decade it was in South Carolina that slave unrest seemed most pronounced, the "turmoil of discontent" there reaching a climax in the Stono Rebellion of 1739.[50] According to Peter Wood, whites in that colony "whose anxieties about controlling slaves had been growing for some time, saw their fears of open violence realized, and this in turn generated new fears".[51]

It can be said, finally, that mounting slave unrest during the 1730s was evident not only in the West Indies but also in North America, and erupted into significant episodes of collective resistance justifying whites' fears, latent or open, that if slaves were given the opportunity they would attempt to destroy the slave system or at least achieve individual or collective freedom however precarious.

NOTES

1 Herbert Aptheker, *American Negro Slave Revolts* (New York, 1974), 3; Peter H. Wood, " 'I Did the Best for My Day': The Study of Early Black History During the Second Reconstruction, 1960 to 1976," *William and Mary Qtly. (WMQ)*, 3rd Series, vol. XXXV, No. 2 (April 1978), 216. Wood drew attention to the fact that while there has been much work recently on slave resistance in particular slave societies, "yet there have been no successful longitudinal studies, analyzing periods of intensified slave resistance throughout the Atlantic community, such as the late 1730s or the early 1790s."

2 These may have included the high ratio of slaves to whites, epidemics, growing slave resistance, publication of a Security Act in mid-August 1739 to tighten surveillance of slaves, the possibility of securing refuge among the Spaniards at St. Augustine in Florida, and the arrival of news about the outbreak of war between England and Spain. For discussions of the rebellion and its background see Peter H. Wood, *Black Majority: Negroes in Colonial South Carolina From 1670 through the Stono Rebellion* (New York, 1975), 219–326; Aptheker, *Slave Revolts*, 179–189.

3 W. Noel Sainsbury et al, eds., *Calendar of State Papers (C.S.P.)*, Colonial Series, America and West Indies (London, 1862–), XLIII, 191–2, quoted in Richard B. Sheridan, *Sugar and Slavery: An Economic History of the British West Indies 1623–1775* (Baltimore, 1973), 430.

4 Barbara Klamon Kopytoff, "The Early Political Development of Jamaican Maroon Societies," *WMQ*, 3rd Series, vol. XXXV, No. 2 (April, 1978), 287; David Barry Gaspar, "Runaways in Seventeenth Century Antigua, West Indies," unpublished paper. For a comparative survey of maroon societies, see Richard Price, ed., *Maroon Societies: Rebel Slave Communities in the America* (New York, Doubleday Anchor, 1973).

5 Older histories of the Jamaica Maroons include Robert C. Dallas, *The History of the Maroons from their Origin to the Establishment of their Chief Tribe at Sierra Leone*, 2 vols. (London, 1803); Edward Long, *The History of Jamaica . . .*, 3 vols. (London, 1774), vol. II, 338–350. More recent studies include, Barbara Klamon Kopytoff, "Jamaica Maroon Political Organization: the Effects of the Treaties," *Social and Economics Studies (SES)*, vol. 25, No. 2 (June, 1976), 87–105; "The Early Political Development of Jamaicans Maroon Ethnicity," *Caribbean Qtly.*, XXII (1976), 33–50. Orlando Patterson, "Slavery and Slave Revolts: A Socio-Historical Analysis of the First Maroon War, 1655–1740," *SES*, vol. 19, No. 3 (Sept., 1970), 289–325.

6 Patterson, "Slavery and Slave Revolts," 294–297, 299–300.

7 Richard S. Dunn, *Sugar and Slaves: The Rise of the Planter Class in the English West Indies, 1624–1713* (Chapel Hill, N.C., 1972), 21, chpt. 5; Patterson, "Slavery and Slave Revolts," 297. Barbados is 166 square miles in area, St. Kitts 68, Antigua 108, and Jamaica 4,411.

8 Dunn, *Sugar and Slaves*, 259–262; Patterson, "Slavery and Slave Revolts," 297–301; Patterson, *The Sociology of Slavery: An analysis of the Origins, Development and Structure of Negro Slave Society in Jamaica* (London, 1967), 266–271; Alan Eyre, *A New Geography of the Caribbean* (London, 1962), 69; Kopytoff, "Jamaican Maroon Societies," 290, 293–294. Kopytoff has asserted that "despite the nearly identical background and the common setting" in which the two Maroon groups emerged, their political organization was different. *Ibid.*, 288. See *ibid* for a full discussion of this subject.

9 George Metcalf, *Royal Government and Political Conflict in Jamaica, 1729–1783* (London, 1965), 38; but see also Patterson, "Slavery and Slave Revolts," 303.

10 Sheridan, *Sugar and Slavery*, 221.

11 Hunter to Assembly, C.O. 137/18 of *Journals of the House of Assembly, Jamaica* (J.H.A.), vol. 3, 708, quoted in Patterson, "Slavery and Slave Revolts," 304.

12 Patterson, "Slavery and Slave Revolts," 304.

13 Hunter to Assembly, J.H.A., vol. 3, 46–47, quoted in *ibid.*, 305.

14 Patterson, "Slavery and Slave Revolts," 306–308; *C.S.P.*, XLIII, 1737, No. 156ii, 79.

15 *C.S.P.* XLIII, 1737, No. 156i, 78–79; No. 198, 101.

16 Sheridan, *Sugar and Slavery*, 221; Patterson, "Slavery and Slave Revolts," 311–312. See also Kopytoff, "Jamaican Maroon Political Organization."

17 Patterson, "Slavery and Slave Revolts," 312–313.

18 *Ibid.*, 316–317.

19 Eyre, *Geography of the Caribbean*, 65.

20 Gaspar, "Runaways in Seventeenth Century Antigua."

21 Patterson, "Slavery and Slave Revolts," 316–319; Michael Craton, *Sinews of Empire: A Short History of British Slavery* (London, 1974), 228; "Jamaican Slavery" in Stanley L. Engerman and Eugene D. Genovese eds., *Race and Slavery in the Western Hemisphere: Quantitative Studies* (Princeton, 1975), 271.

22 Patterson, "Slavery and Slave Revolts," 318–325. See also *Sociology of Slavery*, 273–283, in which the author deals with the general causes of slave rebellion in Jamaica for the longer period up to the nineteenth century; and for an assessment of these see Sidney W. Mintz, "Review Article: Slavery and the Slaves," *Caribbean Studies*, VIII (Jan. 1969), 65–70.

23 *The Development of the Plantations to 1750* (Barbados, 1970), 42, 49.

24 Mintz, "Slavery and the Slaves," 69.

25 Monica Schuler, "Ethnic Slave Rebellions in the Caribbean and the Guianas," *Journal of Social History*, vol. 3, No. 4 (1970), 382.

26 See the discussion in Patterson, "Slavery and Slave Revolts," 322–324. The author summarized his socio-historical analysis of the First Maroon War and the slave unrest that accompanied it in the following hypothesis: "Large-scale, monopolistic slave systems with a high rate of absenteeism will, geographical conditions permitting exhibit a high tendency towards slave revolts." *Ibid.*, 325.

27 Sheridan, *Sugar and Slavery*, 426–432.

28 *C.S.P.* XLIII, 1737, No. 156ii, 79.

29 Sheridan, *Sugar and Slavery*, 429.

30 *The Development of the British West Indies, 1700–1763* (New York, 1967), 115.

31 The same most probably applied to the slaves in Barbados and the rest of the small sugar islands which were not very mountainous or covered with jungle. Dunn, *Sugar and Slaves*, 261–262.

32 David Barry Gaspar, "The Antigua Slave Conspiracy of 1736; A Case Study of the Origins of Collective Resistance," *WMQ*, 3rd Series, vol. XXXV (April, 1978), 308–323; "Bondsmen and Rebels: Slave Resistance and Social Control in Antigua, 1632–1763" (unpublished ms), chpts. 1, 2, 3.

33 "Extract of a Letter from Antigua, Oct. 24 (1736)," *Gentleman's Magazine: and Historical Chronicle*, VII (1737), 59; *Judges' General Report* (hereafter *General Report*) in Gov. William Mathew to Board of Trade, Jan. 17, 1737, C.O. 152/22, W94, Public Record Office, England.

34 Address before the Antigua Council, Jan. 24, 1737, C.O. 9/10.

35 *General Report*; Mathew to Board of Trade, May 26, 1737, C.O. 152/23, X7; "An Act for attaining several Slaves who abscond and are fled from Justice and for the Banishment of other(s) concerned in the conspiracy," April 11, 1737, C.O. 8/6.

36 Gaspar, "The Antigua Slave Conspiracy."

37 *Ibid.*, 312–314.

38 *Ibid.*, 313.

39 In January 1729 Antigua authorities claimed they had unearthed a plot originating among the slaves of councillor, Colonel Mathaniel Crump, to kill him and his family "and Cutt off every White Inhabitant." Fourteen slaves were eventually found guilty; four were executed and ten banished. Gov. Londonderry to Board of Trade, April 5, 1729, *C.O. 152/17, T25*; Mins. of Council in Assembly, Feb. 28, Mar. 8, Mar. 25, Mar. 31, Apr. 29, 1729, *C.O. 9/6*; Council Mins., Mar. 31, Apr. 11, 1737, *C.O. 9/11*; "An Act for the Banishment of Several Negroe Slaves Concern'd in the late Conspiracy," Mar. 8, 1729, *C.O. 8/6*.

40 Gaspar, "The Antigua Slave Conspiracy," 315–316.

41 *Ibid.*, 317–322; *General Report*.

42 Gaspar, "The Antigua Slave Conspiracy," 316–317; Sheridan, *Sugar and Slavery*, 256, 428.

43 Mathew to Board of Trade, Jan. 17, 1737, *C.O. 152/22, W88*.

44 The Ibo, Olaudah Equiano, for example, who came to the New World as a slave in 1756, worked aboard the vessels of his master, the Quaker Robert King of Philadelphia who was a leading merchant in Montserrat, one of the British Leewards. Equiano visited many Caribbean islands, and related his experiences in some of them. Paul Edwards ed., *Equiano's Travels* (London, 1967), 75–90. A number of slaves from Antigua worked on boats and small vessels operating among the islands, and on larger craft sailing to places outside the Caribbean. See the account of vessels belonging to Antigua, Aug. 8, 1718 – May 8, 1720, encl. No. 62 in Gov. Hamilton to Board of Trade, Aug. 22, 1720, *C.O. 152/13, Q51*. In 1722 several white seamen petitioned the Antigua legislative to forbid slaves from working as seamen. Assembly Mins., Jan. 19, 1722, *C.O. 9/5*. Antiguans must have long recognized that their slaves were in contact with slaves in other neighboring islands. In banishing the slaves involved in the 1728–9 conspiracy, the assembly firmly recommended that "their banishment ought to be to some place from whence they cannot carry on a Correspondence with the Negros of this Island." Mins. of Council in Assembly, Feb. 28, 1719, *C.O. 9/6*.

45 Waldemar Westergaard, *The Danish West Indies under Company Rule, 1671–1754* . . . (New York, 1917), 165–166.

46 *Ibid.*, 168–178.

47 *Ibid.*, 166–168.

48 Wood, *Black Majority*, 222; Robert Pringle to Francis Guichard, Feb. 5, 1739, *Pringle Letterbook*, quoted in *ibid*.

49 Sheridan, *Sugar and Slavery*, 428.

50 Aptheker, *Slave Revolts*, 179–189.

51 Wood, *Black Majority*, 308.

2

THE JAMAICAN SLAVE INSURRECTION SCARE OF 1776 AND THE AMERICAN REVOLUTION[1]

Richard Sheridan

The American War of Independence had military, political, and social repercussions outside the territory of the thirteen colonies. Military campaigns were waged in the Ohio and Great Lakes country and in Canada. Privateering and naval forces engaged in captures and conflicts in Atlantic, Gulf, and Caribbean waters. Amphibious forces conquered and re-conquered islands in the Caribbean Sea. France and Spain became allies of the United States in the struggle against Great Britain, while disaffection in the British colonies extended to the Jamaica House of Assembly which passed a petition and memorial in support of the American colonies. American loyalists migrated to Nova Scotia, Canada, the Bahamas, the West Indies, and Britain, while many of the black slaves who fell into the hands of British forces were sent to the West Indies. Trade embargo and wartime blockade curtailed shipments of foodstuffs from North America to the British sugar islands, resulting in the starvation of thousands of slaves. Slaves who were prone to rebel in both peace and war found their opportunities enhanced by the unsettled conditions of wartime. The interesting thing is that the slaves in one parish in Jamaica planned an island-wide insurrection that was timed to break out after a British military unit was dispatched to North America. Moreover, there is some evidence to suggest that the slaves in Jamaica were inspired to revolt by the revolutionary ideology of the Americans.

Though by no means negligible, slave insurrections in the Old South did not compare in size, frequency, intensity, or general historical significance with those of the Caribbean or South America, writes Eugene D. Genovese.[2] The greatest slave revolt in modern times occurred in the prosperous French colony of St. Domingue where nearly half a million blacks gained their freedom after defeating the armies of France, England, and Spain. Brazil, the Guianas, Cuba, Jamaica, and other Caribbean territories had slave populations that resisted their bondage by such means as malingering, petty theft, sabotage, arson, poisoning, running away, suicide, and armed resistance. Violent protest was nearly endemic in seventeenth- and eighteenth-century Jamaica where outbreaks occurred on an average of every five years and involved about 400 slave participants. Orlando Patterson maintains that, with the possible exception of Brazil, no other slave society in the New World experienced such continuous and intense servile revolts as those that occurred in Jamaica.[3]

Patterson distinguishes between three types of rebellions in the slave society of Jamaica: (1) purely spontaneous revolts usually restricted to either one estate or to a few neighbouring properties, (2) planned revolts involving or meant to involve either all slaves or restricted to one group of slaves, and (3) revolts involving slaves who had already absconded or who lived in rebel hideouts. The years 1739–40 marked a watershed in the relationship between the planters and the already absconded slaves, or Maroons. By the treaties of those years, the Maroons received tracts of land and extraterritorial rights and bound themselves to remain at peace and to assist the whites in suppressing slave rebellions and in resisting foreign invasions. Whereas the Maroons had previously been indifferent to or encouraged English slaves to join their ranks, they were now by the terms of the treaties compensated for apprehending and bringing in runaway slaves.[4]

The Maroons were originally Spanish slaves who found refuge in the rugged interior at the English conquest of Jamaica in 1655. One group of Maroons was induced to surrender to the English under the condition of pardon, but another group raided frontier settlements and murdered and harrassed the whites until about 1670 when they retreated to the north-eastern section of the island. Meanwhile, English settlers purchased numbers of slaves who were imported from Africa and other Caribbean colonies. Patterson writes that the year 1673 witnessed the first serious rebellion of some 300 English Negroes who formed the nucleus of what later became known as the Leeward band of Maroons. Other revolts, generally of a spontaneous nature, occurred in subsequent years with a concentration in the period from 1700 to 1722.[5]

The first Maroon war involved the whites in a fifteen-year (1725–1740) struggle against two groups of insurgents, one in the north-east or windward part of the island, the other in the north-west or Leeward part. The Maroon leaders were chiefly Coromantee slaves of originally Akan-speaking stock who came from the Gold Coast. The war was a major undertaking on the part of the whites, involving local militia units, British regiments, seamen from warships, black freedmen, baggage Negroes, and Mosquito-coast Indians. According to Patterson, "The rebels relied not only on their guerilla skills in compensating for the vastly superior weaponry of the whites, but also on a sophisticated intelligence system in which many of the slaves still on the plantations functioned, providing them with information about the plans of the whites."[6]

After long years of losses from ambushes, skirmishes, disease, and incompetent leadership, the whites sued for peace. The first treaty of March 1739 was signed between the whites and the Leeward Maroons commanded by Colonel Cudjoe. In 1740 similar terms were agreed to between the whites and Captain Quao, leader of the Windward Maroons. The Maroon towns and their populations in 1749 were enumerated by Edward Long, the Jamaica planter-historian, as follows: Trelawny Town in St. James parish, 276; Accompong's in St. Elizabeth, 85; Crawford or Charles Town in St. George, 233; Nanny or Moore Town in Portland, 70. The first two towns were to leeward, the last two to windward.[7]

No insurrection of any consequence occurred for many years after the Maroon treaties. According to Long, rebellions were frustrated by the Maroons "who scoured the woods, and apprehended all straggling and vagabond slaves, that from time to time deserted their owners." But in 1760, at a time when the Maroons were less active, the slaves on several plantations in the parish of St. Mary rebelled, broke into a fort and acquired arms and gunpowder. They then marched from plantation to plantation killing the whites and gaining black recruits. Long claimed that the conspiracy was conducted with such great secrecy under the able leadership of Tackey that while almost all of the Coromantee slaves throughout the island were privy to it, the whites found no grounds for suspicion. The goal of the rebels was "the entire extirpation of the white inhabitants; the enslaving of all such Negroes as might refuse to join them; and the partition of the island into small principalties in the African mode; to be distributed among their leaders and head men."[8] Before the rebels were defeated some 60 whites were killed and between 300 and 400 slaves were killed or committed suicide. At least 600 other rebels were executed or transported.[9]

Coromantee headmen on seventeen estates in St. Mary's parish entered into a conspiracy to rise in armed rebellion sometime in July 1765. But owing to the impetuosity of one conspirator, the rising broke out prematurely and was suppressed by the whites before it had spread beyond the locality of its origin. One year later the Coromantees struck again, killing nineteen whites in Westmoreland parish at the west end of the island. In 1769 a number of slaves were involved in a plot to burn the city of Kingston and kill all its white inhabitants.[10]

In his studies of Jamaican slavery, Patterson attributes the numerous slave revolts to the following general factors: (1) the ratio of masters to slaves, (2) the ratio between creole and African slaves, (3) the quality of slaves bought by the planters, (4) the character of the Jamaican whites, (5) the treatment and maintenance of the slaves, and (6) the impact of certain social, religious and political forces in the period from 1770 to 1832.[11]

In her writings on slave revolts in the Caribbean area, Monica Schuler distinguishes between the more or less constant factors of geography and the challenge of existing Maroon settlements, and the variable factors of "hard work and harsh punishment—circumstances which often coincided with absentee proprietorship; crises such as famine, epidemic, hurricanes, European wars; type of leadership available; military and numerical strength of the slaves vis-a-vis their masters; and ethnic and religious cohesiveness."[12] Both Patterson and Schuler find it remarkable that almost every one of the slave rebellions during the seventeenth and eighteenth centuries were instigated and carried out mainly by Coromantee or Akan slaves who came from the Gold Coast where the Ashanti Federation had a highly developed military regime which was skilled in jungle warfare.[13]

The Jamaican slave insurrection scare of 1776 had certain elements in common with previous threatened and actual outbreaks, but it also differed in certain remarkable features. The conspiracy occurred in a part of the island that was of relatively recent settlement where there was a high ratio of blacks to whites and of African to creole slaves, where the Coromantees and other warlike peoples were forced to labor on plantations, where a number of prominent planters were absentees or minors, where there is evidence that harsh treatment was meted out to slaves. Previous insurrections had been planned to occur at times when the whites were thought to be most vulnerable, such as the Christmas holiday. The intended revolt of 1776 was also planned to take advantage of white weakness, but in this instance it was the removal of a military unit that was to signal the uprising. Though some of the Coromantees were implicated in the conspiracy, the leaders were chiefly creoles whose level of acculturation was relatively high and who possessed skills and were entrusted with subordinate supervisory responsibilities. Finally, the leaders of the conspiracy were apparently informed of the progress of the American Revolution and may have been influenced to revolt by its idealogical content as well as the opportunity afforded by the removal of a military unit.

The economy and society of Jamaica experienced a remarkable growth from the Maroon treaties of 1739–40 to the outbreak of the American Revolution in 1775. The white population increased from about 10,000 to 18,000, the free coloreds and blacks from an unknown number to 4,000 and the black slaves from nearly 100,000 to 200,000. The greater part of the island's resources was concentrated on sugar production, which increased from 16,000 to 50,000 tons, while the number of sugar plantations increased from 429 to 775.[14] Besides the sugar plantations or estates, there were numerous cattle ranches or pens, and small holdings devoted to ginger, pimento, cotton, coffee, and provisions. Indeed, the years from 1763 to 1775 marked a brief golden age for the plantocracy of Jamaica, a time of good harvests, generally high sugar prices, and a planter-dominated government which gave evidence of strength and initiative.[15]

The conspiracy took place in the parish of Hanover in the northwest corner of Jamaica. Five parishes—Hanover, St. James, Trelawny, Westmoreland, and St. Elizabeth—comprise the western county of Cornwall which outgrew the two other counties of Middlesex (nine parishes) and Surry (five parishes) after the Maroon treaties. Governor Sir William Trelawny reported in 1770 that the county of Cornwall was so much improved as to make three-sevenths of the whole produce of the island, that there was a great number of new plantations within ten miles of the sea, and that commerce had increased at the free ports of Montego Bay in St. James parish and Lucea (or St. Lucea) in Hanover parish.[16] The slave population of Hanover increased from 3,339 in 1734 to 13,571 in 1768. In 1772 the parish had 75 sugar plantations besides other settlements. The parish had "advanced surprisingly," wrote Edward Long, "and contains more sugar-works than some of three times the extent."[17] The neighboring parish of St. James had, in 1774, 12,557 slaves and only 478 whites, or a ratio of 26 to 1, which was probably similar to that of Hanover.[18] Africans probably outnumbered creole slaves because of the recent settlement and rapid growth of the parish.[19]

Upon orders from Lord George Germaine, the Secretary of State in England, the Fiftieth Regiment sailed from Jamaica to strengthen General William Howe's army in North America on July 3, 1776. The removal of this regiment from the fort at Lucea in Hanover parish and the sailing of the convoy from Montego Bay was intended to signal the insurrection of the slaves and spread death and destruction throughout the island. Though the plot was discovered prior to the time of the rising, white fear and frenzy led to the mobilization of military and naval forces, declaration of martial law, embargo of shipping, seizure and examination of suspected conspirators, summary trials, executions and transportation of those found quilty. For nearly seven weeks the whites were in a state of apprehension and anxiety as the examination of ringleaders revealed further discoveries of the intended insurrection, allegedly extending to the Maroon Negroes at Trelawny Town. Savage punishment of the conspirators, followed by measures to strengthen the military defense of the island against both external and internal enemies probably acted as a deterrent to further conspiracies during the long wartime period of hardship and famine.[20]

The plot was discovered on Monday, July 15th, when a slave boy was discovered to be drawing the balls from his overseer's pistols and filling them with cotton and oil. One white resident said that the insurrection was planned to take place on July 11th, while another was informed it was set for July 22nd. One of the conspirators who was examined said that he and his confederates "were Encouraged in this Undertaking by the Soldiers going away from the Fort at Lucea and all the Ships Sailing for Great Britain."[21] Upon discovering the plot, the horse and foot militia of Hanover was called out to suppress the rebellious blacks. Similarly, General Palmer, the militia general in neighboring St. James, mustered the companies under his command and appointed a guard to be kept at Montego Bay and patrols throughout the parish. He also dispatched a company of light infantry to go to the relief of the Hanover militia.[22]

The first word of the extent of the plot was revealed on Saturday, July 20th. Colonel John Grizell of the Hanover militia wrote that day that the slaves on almost every plantation to the west of Lucea in the parish "are deeply Concerned in the Intended Insurrection, the Number of the Troop is small and the Duty severe, Our apprehensions are great upon the occasion as we know not where it will end." He was pleased to inform General Palmer that approximately forty of the ringleaders had already been apprehended. Major James Lawrence of the St. James light infantry wrote the same day that "Already forty Eight Ring leaders are detained Prisoners at St. Lucea and by some who have turned King's Evidence among them We have reason to presume that We shall have in Custody by tomorrow night as many more." Retribution was speedy for Governor Sir Basil Keith was informed by the magistrates of Hanover parish on the same day.

> We have try'd—found Guilty and Executed Yesterday the follow-ing Conspirators, Blue Hole Harry, and Leander of the Spring Estate, Charles of the Baulk, Peter of Batchelors Hall, Prince belonging to John Priest of Lucea, and Quamino to Sir Simon Clarke, these are the Chief Ring-leaders and the most Active in Promoting the Intended Insurrection and We propose proceeding tomorrow in trying the Other Chiefs.

The magistrates informed the governor that militia aid had been received from the parishes of St. James and Westmoreland and that a detachment of regulars stationed at Montego Bay had come to guard the fort at Lucea. They requested that a frigate be sent "to Cruize between this Port and Montego Bay, and the Marines now and then landed (if but for a few hours) it would strike more Terror probably than all Our Militia force will make upon the present Occasion."[23]

Four days later came news of the discovery of more conspirators. Sir Simon Clarke, a leading planter, wrote from Lucea that "at least 20 or 30 more principal Negroes are impeached, the number before being about 100; in short there appears no end to this horrid affair." It was learned, he added, that a considerable quantity of gunpowder and arms had been hidden by the conspirators at Lucea, but upon investigating the hiding place it was found that the guns and ammunition had been removed.[24] This alarming intelligence reached St. Jago de la Vega or Spanish Town, the seat of government, the same day. On the following day Governor Keith called a council of war and forthwith ordered a state of martial law to be declared throughout the island. Additional naval and military forces were dispatched to the scene of the conspiracy. On July 26th the

Race Horse armed vessel arrived at Lucea with a company of regulars and supplies of gunpowder. Three days later there arrived at the same port the sloop *Atalanta* of fourteen guns, bringing a quantity of arms.[25]

Clarke was concerned about persuading the governor and admiral of the need to place an embargo on shipping. He feared that if news of the conspiracy reached England before it was totally suppressed, the credit of the island would be impaired by the apprehension that internal unrest would invite an invasion by the French and Spaniards, as well as the capture of Jamaican vessels by American privateers. As long as the threat of insurrection continued, an embargo was considered necessary to insure that all available manpower and every ship would be on hand for mobilization in the event of internecine warfare. When Governor Keith brought this matter before his privy council on July 25th, it was unanimously agreed that the state of the island absolutely required a general embargo to be placed on all merchant ships and vessels bound for Europe. This action delayed the convoy which was scheduled to sail on the 26th of that month with part of the island's sugar and rum crops.[26]

The conspiracy took on a more ominous complexion by the confession of one of the ring leaders on Sunday, July 28th. Pontack, a slave belonging to Blue Hole Estate in the parish of Hanover, said at his examination on that date that he had seen two of "Cudjoe's Negroes" from the Maroon settlement at Trelawny Town three or four weeks before, and that they recommended to another ring leader to make haste, take the Country to themselves, and drive the white people entirely out of it, assuring him at the same time, that they (the said Cudjoe Negroes Billy and Asherry) would find Guns, Powder, and Shot, for the Negroes belonging to the different Estates, and likewise added, that they were angry too much with the white people, because they had taken from them their bread, by appointing Rangers to go after Runaways which they had always considered, as a right of their own.[27]

General Palmer, who had dealings with the Trelawny Town Maroons and their white superintendent John James, corroborated Pontack's testimony that the Maroons were dissatisfied with the Ranger's Law which had the effect of depriving them of head money for the return of runaway slaves. On the other hand, Governor Keith received a letter from Superintendent James who offered to pledge his life for the affection and fidelity of the Maroons. Only one of the Maroons was brought to trial for alleged complicity in the conspiracy, and he was acquitted for want of sufficient proof. Yet as the report of the committee of the Assembly of Jamaica to investigate the conspiracy, pointed out, strong suspicion remained among the whites that the Maroons were concerned in some general plan for instigating the slaves to rebellion.[28]

The intended insurrection kept Jamaica and especially Hanover parish in a high state of anxiety until late August of 1776. Though the conspiracy was found to be confined largely to one parish, rumors of island-wide revolt were contagious and actual slave disturbances in other parishes were reported. The rector of the parish of Vere on the south side of the island wrote to the governor that "two Negro Slaves had been lately tried there, and convicted of endeavouring to procure Fire Arms with evil Intentions, and had been executed for the same." From the eastern part of the island came a letter to the governor from a Colonel Gwyn who had received information from a mulatto man that the Maroon Negroes at Moore Town intended to revolt, "and that they had invited the Coromantee Negroes in the Neighbourhood to join them: that upon this alarming Information he immediately Ordered out all the Blue Mountain Valley Troop, also the Port Morant and Plantain Garden River Troop to meet him at Bath, together with the Foot Militia in that Quarter." It was later learned that the evidence of the mulatto men "was all a Made up Story, not containing a Syllable of Truth."[29] Notwithstanding this false alarm, the situation remained dangerous to public order. Governor Keith informed Lord Germaine on 6th August that "there is now an apparent Spirit of insolence among the Slaves, over the whole Island, and in several Parishes there have been executions and Punishments for open Acts of Rebellion, since the commencement of this alarm, so that I may truly say, we are now in the most imminent Danger, and the most pressing Necessity."[30]

As late as August 21st forty more Negroes were impeached by Adam who had been sentenced to be hanged in chains, but it was suspected that he was endeavouring to prolong his life by false impeachment. The embargo on shipping was lifted on August 3rd and martial law taken off on the 29th instant, the day that the magistrates of Hanover parish cautiously declared it as their opinion that the danger from the late conspiracy was at an end.[31] In his letter to Lord Germaine of October 29, 1776, Governor Keith enclosed "A List of the Negroes Tried in the Parish of Hanover for intending to rise in Rebellion and being concerned in Rebellious Conspiracies &c. from the 20th July to the 18th of September 1776." The number tried amounted to 135; 17 were executed, 45 transported, 11 administered severe corporal punishment, and 62 acquitted. A planter who lived near Lucea wrote of the conspiracy that "some have been burnt alive, some hanged, some gibbeted, and others transported."[32]

Having summarized the major occurrences of the intended insurrection of 1776, it remains to analyze the causes of the conspiracy, explore the geographical area where it took place, explain the strategy and tactics that were intended to be employed, comment on the leadership and organization of the movement, and compare the conspiracy of 1776 with other conspiracies in Jamaica and elsewhere. It should be noted that the greater part of the information came from the impeached slaves and especially four of the ring leaders who were examined by the magistrates of the parish. Considering the stress and hysteria generated by the conspiracy, it is not surprising that the evidence is not always consistent.

Indeed, on one occasion the magistrates were so baffled by conflicting testimony that they were not able to proceed with the trial of the blacks for several days.[33]

As Monica Schuler writes, "Many factors contributed to the 'right' environment for resistance, factors deriving from the situation of masters and slaves." Factors of more or less importance in the conspiracy of 1776 include hard labor, harsh punishment, absentee proprietorship, scarcity of food, military strength, rugged terrain and the enticing presence of Maroons, political crisis, common ethnic origin, the ratio of blacks to whites and of foreign born to creole slaves. Various combinations of these and other factors determined the type of resistance to which the slaves resorted. Hard labor and harsh punishment were cited as strong motives by several slaves who were examined by the magistrates of Hanover parish. Negro Adam said that Coromantee Sam who belonged to the Baulk estate informed him "that he had been ill used by the Overseer and that the Hardships on Negroes were too great and that if all the rest of the Negroes' Hearts were like his the Matter would have been finished long ago."[34]

Both Orlando Patterson and Monica Schuler contend that most of the conspiracies and revolts in the period of this study began on estates belonging to absentee proprietors. It is maintained that absenteeism resulted in gross mismanagement of estates by attorneys and overseers who forced the slaves to work far beyond their strength to produce large profits for their principals and commissions and salaries for themselves.[35] The "Account Produce" volume for the year 1775 shows that of the forty-seven impeached estates, eleven (or 23 percent) were owned by absentees, minors, or deceased persons, and that of the 8,618 slaves on the impeached estates, 2,439 (or 28 percent) were on estates owned by absentees, minors, or deceased persons. Although absenteeism was less prevalent in Hanover parish than it was in Jamaica as a whole, it is nevertheless true that the leadership of the conspiracy was concentrated on the estates of absentees. Pontack said at his examination that he met the driver of one estate who expressed great displeasure against his overseer for keeping him and his fellow slaves so long at their labor and preventing them from going to supper on time. It is of interest that this estate was owned by an absentee and that the same overseer was complained of by another slave who was examined by the magistrates.[36]

Food shortages and hunger brought misery and disaffection to the slaves. Having been dependent upon North American supplies to meet a substantial part of their food requirements, the slaves in Jamaica and other British sugar colonies were dealt a severe blow by the interruption of trade at the outbreak of the American Revolution. Severe scarcity had led to an embargo on the exportation of provisions from Jamaica by January 1776. One absentee proprietor was informed in late July 1776 that "The present unhappy disputes subsisting between America and Great

Table 2.1 List of the Impeached Estates in the Parish of Hanover and the Number of Blacks on them, 28th July 1776

Proprietors	Estates	Blacks	Proprietors	Estates	Blacks
William Anglin	Paradise	218	Philip Haughton Junr. dec'd	Venture	130
Estate of John Blagrove	Magotty	340	Benjamin Harding dec'd	Blue Hole	148
John & Thom. Buckner	Hopewell	166	Cunninghame & Harding	Harding Hall	146
George Brissett	Cacoon	164	Richard Haughton James & Co.	Davis's Cove	176
Richard Brissett	Georgia	246	Haughton James	Haughton Tower	244
James Bean	Beans	102	Montague James	Spring	580
William Brown	....			Green Island	160
William Clarke	Claremont			Hog River	186
Edward Chambers	Prosper			....	
	Batchelors Hall	777	James Kerr	Dundee	231
	Richmond		Peter McKenzie, dec'd.	Flint River	260
Sir Simon Clarke	Wood Church		James Lewis	Boggy Hill	102
	Fatt Hog Quarter	353	Dugald Malcolm	Pitt River	368
James Crooke	Couzens Cove	186	Neill Malcolm	Retrieve	346
Isaac Wm. Cresse	Cresse Field		Neill Malcolm & Co.	Unity	155
	Eaton	294	Malcolm & Nevison	....	7
	Kew		Hutchinson Mure	Caldwal	196
Philip Dehany	Barbican	644	Benjamin Mowatt	Pedro	106
	Fountain		John Priest	....	10
Heirs of Rich'd Haughton	Esher	170	Samuel Riley	Rileys	134
Dias Fernandes & Co.	Red Hill	90	Wm. Samuells	Couzens's Cove	127
John Grizell	....	153	George Spence	Top River	190
Gilling & Walker	....	15	Tryall Estate	....	226
Richard Haughton & Co.	Baulk	202			
Samuel Haughton & Co.	Orange Cove	270	Total blacks impeached		8,618

Source: "List of the Impeached Estates in the Parish of Hanover and the Number of Negroes on them Inclosed in the Letter from the Magistrates, as of the 28th July 1776." In Sir Basil Keith's (No. 9) of 6th August 1776. P.R.O. London, C.O. 137/71, f. 272.

Britain affects this island greatly particularly in the Articles of Provisions and Lumber, the Prices of which are advanced at least 100 percent."[37] Supplies of food became scarce in consequence of drought, a state of martial law, and the need to feed additional soldiers and sailors. "We are likewise labouring under the Dreadful apprehension of Scarcity from the long Drowth which has prevailed over three fourths of the Island," wrote Governor Keith to Lord Germaine on August 6, 1776.[38]

What significance should be attached to political unrest centered on the American Revolution as a factor in the planned insurrection is difficult to say. While it is true that for a slave society Jamaica had a highly permissive political environment which included radical thought and expression, it is nevertheless reasonable to believe that the slaves needed no borrowed ideology and motivation but only favorable circumstances to rise against their oppressors.[39]

One prominent Jamaican who linked the conspiracy with revolutionary ideology was the Reverend John Lindsay, D.D., Rector of the parish of St. Catherine and Spanish Town. In a letter to Dr. William Robertson, the famous historian and Principal of Edinburgh University, he said that while slave insurrections were not uncommon, the conspiracy of 1776 was unique in its involvement of both the creole and house slaves. "In our late constant disputes," wrote Lindsay, "at our tables (where by the by every Person has his own waiting man behind him) we have I am afraid been too careless of Expressions, especially when the topic of American rebellion has been by the Disaffected amongst us, dwelt upon and brandished of with strains of Virtuous Heroism."[40]

Most Englishmen and Irishmen in Jamaica were early partisans of John Wilkes, the English radical leader, according to Dr. Lindsay. In the American controversy they were on the side of rebellion and violently opposed to the Tory ministry in England. The following long extract from Lindsay's letter conveys his view of how the slaves were affected by the radical rhetoric of white Jamaicans:

> And here I give data to the first seeds of this present Conspiracy. For what mind of a Slave will not recoil and burn into Resentment; when he shall have been the frequent witness of Sedition and Ingratitude in the Conduct of his Master—when he shall hear the Obligation of a subject to his Lord spurn'd at—the Blood spilt by Rebells extoll'd as precious drops of Record—Obedience to Laws and Authority upon all these Occasions mentioned with a strong Idea of Slavery. And Men toasted into Immortal Honours for Encountering Death in every form, rather than submit to Slavery let its Chains be ever so gilded. Dear Liberty has rang in the heart of every *House-bred Slave*, in one form or other, for these Ten years past—While we only talk'd about it, they went no farther than their private reflections upon us & it: but as soon as we came to

blows, we find them fast at our heels. Such has been the seeds sown in the minds of our Domestics by our Wise-Acre Patriots.[41]

Stephen Fuller, the agent for Jamaica in England, suggested that the American Revolution may have been partly responsible for the slave revolt scare of 1776.[42]

The scene of the conspiracy was the parish of Hanover where the land was taken up chiefly by sugar plantations and the only town was the little seaport of Lucea. The magistrates of the parish said that the conspiracy had spread rather by the connection of one estate to another than from any general plan of rebellion. Table I shows the proprietors, names, and number of slaves on the forty-seven impeached estates. George Spence, the leading magistrate, wrote that the impeached estates amounted to nearly one-half of those in the parish. Since they were all connected by an "uninterrupted line or Chain" extending about twenty-five miles from east to west, the conspirators were enabled to act the more decisively because they could plan the uprising in a joint and uniform manner. The rugged lands in interior parts of the parish afforded hideouts for runaway slaves.[43]

The conspirators held meetings, chose their leaders, assigned to individuals such tasks as recruiting supporters and gathering arms and ammunition, agreed on the hour and the day of the rising and the manner in which the signal was to be given. Coromantee Sam testified that he and thirty-eight slaves had conspired together to rise in rebellion. At their several meetings they appointed captains and officers, each to act in his separate districts. He recalled three meetings held on Sundays in the open street on Lucea Bay. At the first meeting two slaves were appointed to manage matters to windward of Lucea, two towards Glasgow estate and Westmoreland parish, and two others to leeward of Lucea. Malcolm at the Baulk estate was to take the guns out of the great house at that estate, draw the lead balls and substitute ashes for gunpowder, re-insert the balls and return the guns to the place from whence they were taken and Charles and George were to kill their mistresses, "and that their Design in General was to kill all the White people they could."[44]

Peter, a slave at the Point estate, was asked by his rebel friends to engage as many slaves as he could among the estates to windward of Lucea Bay. In his examination he recalled his visits to twelve estates and the conversations he had with forty-five slaves. On his visit to Kew estate, for example, he was rebuffed by Johnny, "a Cooper Negro," but was promised support by Bacchus, Harry, Hamilton, and Ned, "but at the same time told him they could not promise to get any Guns or Powder." At Tryal estate he said that Quashy, Ned, Guy, and Jupiter had agreed to rise, and they promised to speak to the rest of the Negroes on that estate. Only two of the forty-five slaves that Peter talked with refused to take part in the uprising.[45]

The rebels were much concerned to store adequate supplies of arms and ammunition, as well as taking measures to keep the white peoples' guns from firing. Adam testified that on one visit he met Congo Leander of the Spring estate who showed him "a Certain Quantity of Gunpowder Contained in a Tuskin, Calabash or Goard [sic] which they were to make Use of in their intended Insurrection." When Adam asked what other supplies of powder and guns they had, Congo Leander replied, "Never Fear, their Friends had Gunpowder and Guns enough, and that they would supply themselves further by breaking into the White Peoples' Houses on the several Estates." According to Pontack, the two Maroon Negroes who took part in the conspiracy promised to find guns, powder, and shot for the slaves belonging to the different estates. The plan was for the estate Negroes to run into the woods when the signal was sounded, while the Maroons (or "Cudjoe's Negroes") were to set fire to the cane-fields while the whites were away from their estates in pursuit of the runaways. Then when the whites were employed in extinguishing the cane fires, both the Maroon and estate Negroes "were instantly to repair to the Towns, break open the Stores, and houses, and from thence supply themselves plentifully, with Gun Powder &c."[46]

Coromantee Sam's version of the planned insurrection differed markedly from that of Pontack. He testified that the rebels agreed that signals should be given in the following manner: "First by discharging a Gun at Batchelors Hall by Mingo which was to be Answered by Another at Fat Hog Quarter by Cook Quamin and this to be Answered by Adam at Richmond and after that to be followed by firing at the Baulk Estate by Charles and that they were then to Rise in General Rebellion and Attack the several Estates and put to death all the White people they could."[47]

Apart from its links with the American Revolution, the intended insurrection of 1776 was remarkable for its leadership by creole headmen and the cooperation displayed by creoles and Africans who were organized along ethnic lines. George Scott, one of the magistrates in Hanover parish, wrote that the movement took its rise and was persecuted by the more sensible of the creoles and the old and most trusted of the Africans. It was wisely concerted and truly formidable, he wrote, being in the hands of chiefs or headmen only who rarely trusted more than two upon any estate, who were to answer for the rest of the slaves.[48] Sir Simon Clarke wrote that almost all of the slaves were "under the degree of Captains and Lieutenants among them, and are indeed the most valuable Negroes in general, on the Estates to which they belong, Creoles, Coromantees and Eboes are principally concerned."[49]

It was of concern to Governor Keith that the chief conspirators were creoles "who never were before engaged in Rebellions, and in whose fidelity we had always most firmly relied, that they were invited to this attempt, by the particular circumstances of the times; well knowing, there were fewer Troops in the Island, then [sic] had been at any time within their Memory."[50]

The Organization, as revealed by Coromantee Sam, was tripartite with a headman or king and his lieutenants for the three groups of rebels. Prince who was owned by John Priest of Lucea Bay was to be the headman or king of the creoles, and Coromantee Sam who belonged to the heirs of Jonathan Haughton was to be the headman or king of the Coromantees. The numerous slaves who were implicated in the conspiracy included creoles. Coromantees, Eboes, and Congoes. That they were trusted and skilled slaves is indicated by their occupations which included drivers, coopers, distillers, millwrights, penkeepers, cartmen, carpenters, and cooks.[51]

The part played by household slaves who were presumably creoles in the conspiracy was described by Dr. Lindsay. He told of an overseer's waiting man who was discovered to have "drawn the Charges, filled them up with dust, and instead of Powder in the Pan had substituted Black Sand" in his master's pistol. Upon learning of the tampered pistol, the owner of the estate privately sent for a few neighbouring gentlemen to come to help him investigate the matter. Upon their arrival he called his servant to get wine and punch for the gentlemen's refreshment. In bringing in the punch the servant "hit the Bowl on the edge of a Marble slab, which breaking & spilling the Punch on the floor display'd a Quantity of Arsnic [sic] which he had mix'd with the cup." Lindsay wrote of the servant that

> He wanted to poison these Gentlemen to come at their Arms: He had combined with many hundreds from the Neighbouring Estates to effect a General Massacre of Whites throughout the Island. That even the Creole Negroes, who were the savers of their Master's Mistress in the Rebellion 1760, were now engaged against them; that the Creoles had taken the Coromantees and Ebo Negroes in the Conspiracy with them: had chosen a King of each People to lead them on. That he himself was to begin the Massacre (on the Evening of July 25th, when the Fleet always sails for England) by Murdering his Master and firing a Gun—which as a signal was to be answered by four Neighbouring Estates, a Gun to be repeated from each, that the havoc was begun: that having made away with every white person on the Estates, they were to March down to the Town (St. Lucea) which was to be set on fire by the conspirators there, and as the Inhabitants should run to the fields and streets for shelter, the Country Negroes were to fall upon them.[52]

The white reaction to the intended insurrection can be traced in the *Journals of the Assembly of Jamaica* for the session which began on October 22, 1776. The conspiracy was responsible, in part or in whole, for speeches, addresses, petitions, debates, reports, and the introduction of bills which were designed to prevent any such occurrences in the future. At the beginning of the session the Assembly gratefully acknowledged Governor Keith's vigilance and activity in suppressing the intended insurrection of the slaves in Hanover parish. Following this address to the governor, committees were appointed to bring in bills for a variety of purposes. Six of the bills which were enacted into law were more or less related to the conspiracy. Fines were levied for failing to provide a sufficient number of white people on plantations; forts, fortifications and barracks were inspected; the militia act was strengthened; measures were taken to control runaway slaves; parties were raised and given supplies for suppressing any rebellion in the island; and an act was passed for the better order and government of the Maroons.[53] That these laws resulted in stricter control of the slaves is suggested by the assertion of one planter of Hanover parish who wrote on May 14, 1777, that no harm could then be done since there was always a strong guard of white people at all suspected places.[54]

On November 5, 1776, a petition of the justices, vestrymen, freeholders, and other inhabitants of the parish of Hanover was presented to the Assembly. The petitioners claimed to have incurred very heavy expenses for their own militia and in calling in the assistance of the regulars and militia of the neighboring parishes and maintaining them. Their appeal to the Assembly for relief was referred to a committee which was appointed to inquire into the truth of the allegations and report the facts, with their opinion, relative to the cause of the intended insurrection. After some deliberation, the committee reported to the Assembly on December 17, 1776. It recommended that all reasonable expenses that had been incurred for the suppression of the intended insurrection be paid by the public. The principal cause, it said, was the removal of the troops which encouraged the chief conspirators to rise against their white masters. The committee recommended that the governor "be particularly attentive to the appointment of proper persons, for the superintendancy of the negro-towns, and obliging them to keep strict discipline among the maroons." Some of the slaves were reported to have kept mares and horses which enabled them to ride twelve or fifteen miles in a night's time and spread their plots and conspiracies. Conspiracies might have been prevented or confined to a narrow circle by banning slave ownership of riding animals and by strict enforcement of the laws against harboring runaway slaves. The committee reflected with horror on a recent attempt at Montego Bay to poison the water at the market by making use of arsenic. They deplored the careless manner in which arsenic was kept at almost every apothecary's shop and the general manner in which that pernicious drug was sold in the community.[55]

Setting the Jamaican slave insurrection scare of 1776 in a broader setting involves a comparison of its main features with those of other plots and revolts in Jamaica and elsewhere. Though no other incidents were reported during the period of the American Revolution, a plot was discovered in

Jamaica in 1784 which involved mainly the Coromantee slaves. In the eastern Caribbean, a conspiracy to revolt was discovered at St. Kitts in 1778. It was stated in evidence that the conspirators intended "to murder the Inhabitants, to deliver the Island to the French, or any Person who would make them free."[56] Wartime food shortages and the possibility that famine would induce the slaves to revolt generated fear among the whites, as it did with the manager of a plantation in Antigua who wrote to his owner in England, "You have more than five hundred Negroes to feed, who will eat your Cattle and Mules, if they have nothing else to eat, and cut my Throat, if I attempt to prevent them."[57] Britain's naval and military power together with law and habit went far to deter violent slave resistance in the West Indies, writes Elsa Goveia.[58]

Jamaican plots and rebellions in the period from 1770 to 1832 were caused partly by the impact upon the slaves of certain social, religious, and political forces and events that were current at that time, writes Orlando Patterson. These included the American and French revolutions, Haitian slave revolt, British abolitionist movement, closing of the Atlantic slave trade in 1807, and the coming to the island of nonconformist missionaries. Monica Schuler says that these new forces had wide repercussions on the lives and attitudes of slaves and naturally influenced the manner in which they reacted to their bondage.[59]

Though the period from 1795 to 1832 witnessed a second Maroon war and numerous conspiracies, the greatest of the Jamaican slave rebellions took place in 1831–1832 on the eve of emancipation. It broke out two days after Christmas 1831 and lasted for less than two weeks. Yet during that brief span, it involved an estimated 20,000 slaves and a much larger number of sympathizers; 207 slaves were killed in action and over 500 executed; and property loss amounted to L1,132,400. Fourteen whites were killed.[60] Mary Record writes that the rebellion was precipitated by such classic ingredients of revolt as "political excitement stirred by rumours of emancipation, economic stress, a revolutionary philosophy circulating among the slaves and the presence of a group of whites whom the slaves could identify as their allies."[61]

As with the conspiracy of 1776, the blacks at the time of the 1831 revolt overheard their white masters making inflammatory statements. But instead of voicing their support for the rebels in the sister colonies of North America, the Jamaican whites now threatened armed revolt rather than submit to slave emancipation which was being debated in the House of Commons. As with the trouble in 1776, that of 1831 took place in the western parishes of St. James, Hanover, Westmoreland, St. Elizabeth, and Trelawny. But instead of the uprising being timed to follow the withdrawal of a British regiment, numerous predicated missions, nominative-agreement and independent religious meetings were the catalyzing influence. As with the conspiracy of 1776, the revolt of 1831 was led by the creoles, especially those who had achieved some degree of status within slave society. In 1831, however, the slaves believed that the planters were withholding the liberty which the British Parliament had bestowed on them. As in 1776, the rebellion of 1831 centered in areas of sugar monoculture where the system of color and status was most highly developed, and where the slaves were oppressed by heavy work loads, insufficient food, harsh punishment, and a high mortality rate. Barry Higman writes of the 1831 rebellion that it "was predominantly rural, yet the 'urban' character of the western parishes was obviously even greater in the towns. It seems that in the towns the slaves more often attained a quasi-freedom or manumized themselves, whereas the rural slaves could see few advantages in such freedom within the fixed structure of rural slavery."[62]

The rebellion of 1831 happened more than two decades after the closing of the Atlantic slave trade when the ratio of creoles to Africans in the servile population of Jamaica had increased substantially. Creole leadership of the revolt was not shared with the Coromantees and Eboes, nor were the Maroons involved as in the conspiracy of 1776. Above all, liberty was the fundamental goal of the blacks in both the conspiracy of 1776 and the rebellion of 1831.[63]

In the thirteen colonies the Revolutionary War was waged for white freedom and black slavery. In all of the colonies and especially the plantation south there were large numbers of slaves who were ready to bear arms in exchange for freedom. In the main, however, their offer was not accepted. It was Washington's opinion that the freeing of some slaves for performing military service would engender discontent among those who remained in slavery. Nevertheless, many blacks fought on the side of the revolution who were freemen at the beginning of the war or as slaves who passed as freemen. One British measure which horrified the southern whites was Governor Dunmore's declaration that all indentured servants, Negroes, and others who were able and willing to bear arms would be made free.[64]

Fear of servile insurrection was apparently widespread in communities where the blacks outnumbered the whites. During 1775 and 1776 there were disturbances among the slaves and alarms in the provinces of Georgia, South Carolina, North Carolina, Virginia, Pennsylvania, New Jersey, and New York. One plot which had some features in common with that of this study occurred in Beaufort, Pitt, and Craven counties, North Carolina in July 1775. Nearly forty slaves were apprehended. Upon examination there was revealed "a deep laid Horrid Tragick Plan laid for destroying the inhabitants of this province without respect of persons, age or sex." Several of the slaves had in their possession arms and ammunition. The plotters confessed that they planned to rise up on the night of July 8th and destroy the whites, family by family, as they proceeded to the back country where there were loyalists who had agreed to help them settle in a free government of their own.[65]

The problem of slavery in the Age of Revolution was one of great perplexity and anguish. The inconsistency of holding black slaves while resisting British tyranny was apparent to a growing number of American writers and political leaders. They smarted under the biting sarcasm of Thomas Day, the English critic, who wrote that "If there be an object truly ridiculous in nature, it is an American patriot, signing resolutions of independency with the one hand, and with the other brandishing a whip over his affrighted slaves."[66] Even in Jamaica there were planters and merchants who were critical of the slave trade and slavery. In 1774, for example, a debating society in Kingston met on several occasions to debate the merits and demerits of the slave trade; it was determined by the majority "that the trade to Africa for slaves was neither consistent with sound policy, the laws of nature, nor morality."[67]

Slave unrest in Jamaica and the United States was symptomatic of the dilemma confronting the two slave societies. Edward Brathwaite contends that the physical and psychological barriers between masters and slaves and the debasement of the labor force stood in the way of effective resistance to British mercantilism and the transformation of Jamaican society and economy in a cooperative and humane direction. He believes that the American Revolution presented the opportunity to achieve measures of social and cultural integration. Unfortunately, the slave insurrection scare of 1776 was not seen by the Jamaican whites as an opportunity to ameliorate the peculiar institution and lower and eventually remove the barriers between masters and slaves.[68]

NOTES

1 Research for this article was supported in part by the National Institutes of Health Grant LM-01539 from the National Library of Medicine.
2 Eugene D. Genovese, *Roll, Jordan, Roll: The World the Slaves Made* (New York, Pantheon Books 1974), pp. 588–589.
3 Orlando Patterson, *The Sociology of Slavery: An Analysis of the Origins, Development and Structure of Negro Slave Society in Jamaica* (London, MacGibbon and Kee, 1967), pp. 273–274.
4 *Ibid.*, pp. 266–267.
5 *Ibid.*, pp. 267–268; Orlando Patterson, "Slavery and Slave Revolts: A Socio-Historical Analysis of the First Maroon War, 1655–1740," *Social and Economic Studies*, vol. 19, no. 3 (September 1970), pp. 289–301.
6 Patterson, "Slavery and Slave Revolts," p. 303.
7 *Ibid.*, pp. 310–313; Edward Long, *The History of Jamaica* (3 vols., London, 1774), vol. II, pp. 349–350.
8 Long, *History of Jamaica*, II, 447.
9 Patterson, *Sociology of Slavery*, p. 271.
10 Long, *History of Jamaica*, II, 465–469; Patterson, *Sociology of Slavery*, pp. 271–272.
11 Patterson, *Sociology of Slavery*, pp. 273–276; Patterson, "Slavery and Slave Revolts," pp. 318–325.
12 Monica Schuler, "Ethnic Slave Rebellions in the Caribbean and the Guianas," *Journal of Social History*, vol. 3, no. 4 (Summer 1970), pp. 381–382; Monica Schuler, "Akan Slave Rebellions in the British Caribbean," *Savacou: A Journal of*

the Caribbean Artists Movement, Kingston and London, vol. I, no. 1 (June 1970), pp. 8–31.

13 Patterson, *Sociology of Slavery*, p. 276; Schuler, "Ethnic Slave Rebellions," pp. 375, 378, 383–385; Schuler, "Akan Slave Rebellions," pp. 8–31.

14 Richard Sheridan, *Chapters in Caribbean History* (Barbados, Caribbean Universities Press, 1973), p. 41.

15 George Metcalf, *Royal Government and Political Conflict in Jamaica 1729–1783* (London, Longmans, 1965), p. 167.

16 David MacPherson, *Annals of Commerce* (4 vols., Edinburgh, 1805), vol, III, p. 505.

17 Long, *History of Jamaica*, II, 212; Douglas Hall, *Free Jamaica 1838–1865: An Economic History* (New Haven, Yale University Press, 1959), p. 82.

18 British Museum Additional MS. 12,435. *E. C. Long Papers*, ff. 3–6: "A List of Sugar Estates and other Properties in the Parish of Saint James as they were in the Month of September 1774."

19 Data to compute comprehensive ratios of creole to African slaves are not extant for the period of this study and only scattered planation records have survived. On Worthy Park estate in St. John's parish, Middlesex county, the proportion of creole-born slaves probably rose from about 25 percent to 65 percent from 1730 to 1780. Michael Craton and James Walvin, *A Jamaican Plantation: The History of Worthy Park 1670–1970* (University of Toronto Press, 1970), p. 149. York estate in St. James's parish had a total of 488 slaves in 1778, of which 246, or slightly more than one-half, were creole born. *Gale/Morant Papers*, 3/c/1, Exeter University Library, England.

20 Public Record Office, London, *Colonial Office* 137/71, ff. 230–231: Governor Sir Basil Keith to Lord George Germaine, Jamaica, 6 August 1776.

21 *Ibid.*, C.O. 137/71, ff. 248, 252, 254: lre. from T. S. Salmon to Judge Martin, 20 July 1776; lre. from George Scott to John Allen, 21 July 1776; Examination of Sam a Negro belonging to the heirs of Jonathan Haughton in the Parish of Hanover, 19 July 1776.

22 *Ibid.*, C.O. 137/71, f. 236: lre. from General John Palmer of St. James parish to Governor Keith, 20 July 1776.

23 *Ibid.*, C.O. 137/71, ff. 238–239, 242–243, 250–251: lre. from Colonel John Grizell to General Palmer, 19 July 1776; lre from Major James Lawrence to General Palmer, 20 July 1776; lre. from the Magistrates of Hanover parish to Governor Keith, 20 July 1776.

24 *Ibid.*, C.O. 137/71, ff. 252–257: lre. from Sir Simon Clarke to Benjamin Lyon, 23 July 1776.

25 *Ibid.*, C.O. 137/71, ff. 304–305: Minutes of a Council of War held at St. Jago de la Vega, 24 July 1776; *ibid.*, ff. 259, 275: lres, from the Magistrates of Hanover parish to Governor Keith, 26 and 29 July 1776.

26 *Ibid.*, C.O. 137/71, ff. 256–257: lre. from Sir Simon Clarke to Benjamin Lyon, 23 July 2776; *ibid.*, f. 306: Minutes of the Privy Council, 25 July 1776.

27 *Ibid.*, C.O. 137/71, ff. 276–278: Examination of Pontack a Negro belonging to Bluehole Estate in the Parish of Hanover, 28 July 1776.

28 *Ibid.*, C.O. 137/71, f. 308: Minutes of the Privy Council, 31 July 1776; *ibid.*, ff. 272–273: lre. from General Palmer to Governor Keith, 1 August 1776; *Journals of the Assembly of Jamaica*, vol. VI, pp. 692–693: Report of the committee to investigate the cause of the late insurrection in Hanover parish, 17 December 1776. Concerning the Maroon grievances, Charles, a slave belonging to Bluehole estate, said that he heard the Maroon named Asherry say "that the white People no longer sent them after runaways, that they had not got Rangers of their own, to go and look for them, and that by this ill usage, the bread was taken out of their mouths, but that they were determined to make the County

come good again." Examination of Charles a Negroe belonging to Bluehole Estate in the Parish of Hanover, 29 July 1776, *C.O.* 137/71, f. 288.

29 P.R.O. London, *C.O.* 137/71, ff. 309, 358: Minutes of the Privy Council, 31 July and 6 August 1776.

30 *Ibid., C.O.* 137/71, f. 230: lre. from Governor Keith to Lord Germaine, 6 August 1776.

31 *Ibid., C.O.* 137/71, ff. 314, 360, 362: Minutes of the Privy Council, 3, 21 and 27 August 1776; *ibid.*, f. 357: lre, from the Magistrates of Hanover parish to Governor Keith, 29 August 1776.

32 *Ibid., C.O.* 137/71, ff. 397–398; *The Scots Magazine*, vol. XXXIX (August 1777), p. 449: A letter from a planter at Roxburg, in Lucea bay, Jamaica, signed "J. P.", dated 14 May 1777.

33 *Ibid., C.O.* 137/71, f. 342: lre. from General Palmer to Governor Keith, 8 August 1776.

34 Schuler, "Ethnic Slave Rebellions," p. 380; Patterson, *Sociology of Slavery*, pp. 273–283; P.R.O. London, *C.O.* 137/71, ff. 234–235: Examination of Negro Adam, 17 July 1776.

35 Patterson, *Sociology of Slavery*, pp. 43–44, 278; Schuler, "Ethnic Slave Rebellions," p. 381.

36 Jamaica Public Record Office, Spanish Town, *Account Produce*, vols. 6–8; Richard B. Sheridan, *Sugar and Slavery: An Economic History of the British West Indies 1623–1775* (Baltimore, Johns Hopkins University Press, 1974), pp. 222–233, 385–387; P.R.O. London, *C.O.* 137/71, ff. 262, 278: Examinations of Peter and Pontack, 23 and 28 July 1776.

37 P.R.O. London, *C.O.* 137/71: lre, from Governor Keith to the Earl of Dartmouth, 18 January 1776; Bristol Archives Office, *Woolnough Papers, Ashton Court Collection*: AC/WO 16(27), 89–101: Messrs. Dalhouse & Stephens to John Hugh Smith, Jamaica, 23 July 1776. I am indebted to Dr. Selwyn H. H. Carrington for this reference.

38 P.R.O. London, *C.O.* 137/71, f. 230; see also the author's forthcoming article in the *William and Mary Quarterly*, entitled, "The Crisis of Slave Subsistence in the British West Indies during and after the American Revolution."

39 For a discussion of the protest of the Assembly of Jamaica against Parliamentary tyranny and the petition and memorial of 1774 in support of the American colonies, see Edward Brathwaite, *The Development of Creole Society in Jamaica 1770–1820* (Oxford, Clarendon Press, 1971), pp. 68–79.

40 National Library of Scotland, MS. 3942, *Robertson-Macdonald Letters*, ff. 259–263: lre, from Dr. J. Linsay to the Revd. the Principal Dr. Wm Robertson in Edinburgh, dated St. Jago de la Vega, Jamaica, 6 August 1776. I am indebted to Mr. Thomas I. Rae, Keeper of Manuscripts at the National Library of Scotland, for permission to quote extracts from the Robertson-Macdonald Letters.

41 *Ibid.*, ff. 260–261.

42 Patterson, *Sociology of Slavery*, p. 279, citing P.R.O. London, *C.O.* 138/27: Fuller to Lords, 27 October 1776.

43 P.R.O. London, *C.O.* 137/71, f. 258: lre, from the Magistrates of Hanover parish to Governor Keith, 25 July 1776; *ibid.*, ff. 268–269; lre, from George Spence to Governor Keith, 28 July 1776.

44 *Ibid., C.O.* 137/71, ff. 252–253: The Examination of Sam A Negro belonging to the heirs of Jonathan Haughton in the Parish of Hanover, 19 July 1776.

45 *Ibid., C.O.* 137/71, ff. 262–265: The Examination of Peter of the Point Estate the property of Philip Dehany Esqr., 23 July 1776.

46 *Ibid., C.O.* 137/71, f. 234: The Examination of Adam the Property of Edward Chambers Esquire, 17 July 1776; *ibid.*, ff. 276–277: Examination of Pontack, 28 July 1776.

47 *Ibid., C.O.* 137/71, f. 253: Examination of Sam, 29 July 1776.

48 *Ibid., C.O.* 137/71, f. 254: lre. from George Scott to Governor Keith, 21 July 1776.

49 *Ibid., C.O.* 137/71, f. 256: lre. from Sir Simon Clarke to Benjamin Lyon, 23 July 1776.

50 *Ibid., C.O.* 137/71, ff. 228–229: lre from Governor Keith to Lord Germaine, 6 August 1776.

51 *Ibid., C.O.* 137/71, f. 253: Examination of Sam 19 July 1776.

52 National Library of Scotland, MS. 3942, *Robertson-Macdonald Letters*, f. 262: lre. from Dr. J. Lindsay to Dr. William Robertson, 6 August 1776.

53 *Journals of the Assembly of Jamaica*, vol. VI, pp. 634–660.

54 Lre. signed "J. P." in *The Scots Magazine*, XXXIX (August 1777), p. 449.

55 *Journals of the Assembly of Jamaica*, vol. VI, pp. 692–693.

56 Patterson, *Sociology of Slavery*, p. 272; P.R.O. London, *C.O.* 152/58: lre, from Governor William Mathew Burt to Lord Germaine, 28 April 1778, cited in Elsa V. Goveia, *Slave Society in the British Leeward Islands at the End of the Eighteenth Century* (New Haven, Yale University Press, 1965), p. 95.

57 Somerset Record Office, Taunton, *Tudway Papers*, DD/TD, c/2209: lre, from Main Swete Walrond to Clement Tudway, Antigua, 28 March 1776.

58 Goveia, *Slave Society*, pp. 252–254.

59 Patterson, *Sociology of Slavery*, pp. 279–281; Schuler, "Ethnic Slave Rebellions," p. 385.

60 Patterson, *Sociology of Slavery*, p. 273; Noel Deerr, *The History of Sugar* (2 vols., London, Chapman and Hall, 1949–50), vol. II, pp. 325–326; Barry W. Higman, *Slave Population and Economy in Jamaica at the Time of Emancipation.* Unpublished Ph.D. dissertation, University of the West Indies, Mona, Jamaica, 1970, pp. 428–429.

61 Mary Record, "The Jamaica Slave Rebellion of 1831," *Past and Present*, vol. 40 (1968), p. 108.

62 Higman, *Slave Population and Economy*, p. 433.

63 *Ibid.*, pp. 428–439; Record, "Jamaica Slave Rebellion," pp. 108–125.

64 Benjamin Quarles, *The Negro in the American Revolution* (Chapel Hill, University of North Carolina Press, 1961), pp. 19, 51, 62; Duncan J. MacLeod, *Slavery, Race and The American Revolution* (Cambridge, Cambridge University Press, 1974), pp. 152–158.

65 Herbert Aptheker, *American Negro Slave Revolts* (New York, International Publishers, 1963), pp. 202–204. In his study of slave resistance in Virginia, Gerald W. Mullin presents a model which seeks to uncover the psychological implications of the rebellious slave's goals, and the significance of these goals for the slave and his society. Gerald W. Mullin, *Flight and Rebellion: Slave Resistance in Eighteenth-Century Virginia* (New York, Oxford University Press, 1972), pp. 35–47, 157–160.

66 Quoted in David Brion Davis, *The Problem of Slavery in the Age of Revolution 1770–1823* (Ithaca and London, Cornell University Press, 1975), pp. 398–399.

67 Thomas Southey, *Chronological History of the West Indies* 3 vols., London, Frank Cass and Co. Ltd., 1968), vol. II, pp. 420–421.

68 Brathwaite, *Creole Society in Jamaica*, pp. 306–311.

3

MARITIME MAROONS

Grand Marronage from the Danish West Indies

Neville A.T. Hall

The islands of St. Croix, St. Thomas, and St. Jan—now the Virgin Islands of the United States—were Denmark's outpost of empire in the Caribbean. Denmark was a late entrant in the seventeenth-century scramble for West Indian colonies. Its colonization of St. Thomas, beginning in 1671, and of St. Jan in 1718, occurred at a time when England, France, and Holland had long since broken, de facto and de jure, Spain's monopoly in the hemisphere and were consolidating their New World gains. Denmark's choice was limited in the extreme; its acquisition of St. Thomas and St. Jan was determined not by choice but by lack of feasible alternatives. St. Croix, bought from France in 1733, was the last of the Lesser Antilles to come under European rule, and the purchase has the dubious distinction of bringing to a close the first century of non-Hispanic colonization in the Caribbean. The acquisition completed Denmark's territorial empire in the New World. Apart from two British occupations during the Napoleonic Wars, in 1801 and again from 1807 to 1815, the islands remained in Denmark's possession until 1917, when they were sold to the United States.[1]

The geological origins of the Lesser Antilles fall between the Eocene and Pliocene intervals of the Tertiary Period, when tectonic activity produced the collision of the floors of the Atlantic Ocean and Caribbean Sea that created an inner arc of volcanic islands to which the Danish West Indies belonged. These islands, unlike those of the outer arc such as Antigua or Barbuda, are characterized by serrated ridges and rugged peaks. St. Thomas and St. Jan rise respectively to 517 meters (1,700 feet) and 396 meters (1,300 feet). St. Croix has a range of hills along its northern coast rising to 367 meters (1,200 feet) in its northwestern corner but contains in its center and south an area of flat and fairly well-watered land totaling about 100 square kilometers (39 square miles) that is particularly well adapted to agriculture. This fact, combined with its greater area of 217 square kilometers (84 square miles), determined that neither

St. Thomas, with an area of 72 square kilometers (28 square miles), nor St. Jan, 52 square kilometers (20 square miles), ever rivaled St. Croix in sugar production.[2]

Sugar integrated these tropical islands into the economy of their metropolitan center, and it was notoriously labor intensive. Although the use of white indentured workers was attempted,[3] African slave labor soon became the exclusive basis of the monocrop culture of each island. As Table 3.1 demonstrates, the eighteenth century was a period of almost unvaryingly upward growth in the number of slaves, which peaked at the turn of the nineteenth century, coincident with Denmark's decision in 1792 to abolish the transatlantic slave trade in 1802 and with consequent feverish importations during that ten-year grace period.[4] Relatively and absolutely, the increments of growth were largest for St. Croix. As the nineteenth century progressed, however, all the Danish islands experienced a gradual decline of slave populations as rates of mortality exceeded those of birth.[5]

But even as their numbers dwindled, slaves remained in the majority, a position held almost from the outset of each island's exploitation. Even after 1835, when freedmen, having obtained their civil liberties, were enumerated with whites in the category "free," slaves never lost numerical superiority vis-à-vis nonslaves. St. Thomas, however, had become an exception in this regard by 1835, and the explanation inheres in that island's large number of freedmen, who then composed well above 70 percent of the entire population.[6]

The increase of freedmen was closely related to the expansion of mercantile activity in St. Croix's port towns of Christiansted and Frederiksted and, most dramatically, in St. Thomas's port of Charlotte Amalie. That growth also greatly enlarged the number of slaves in those towns. By 1838, slaves composed some 26 percent of Charlotte Amalie's population. Many were women, engaged mostly as domestics and constituting, in St. Croix, some 62 percent of the urban slave population in 1839.[7] The data for male slaves do not permit quantification of their employment, although it is a fair assumption that most were occupied in maritime work—loading and unloading vessels, driving the wains that delivered or removed cargo, and laboring in warehouses or as crew in interisland or other seagoing traffic. As market centers the towns drew slaves from the countryside to sell fruit, vegetables, poultry, grass, and firewood.[8] At least in St. Thomas and St. Croix, almost the entire slave population was thus in constant contact with the port towns.

The sex distribution of slaves reflected, for the eighteenth century, a general preference for males in plantation America, since planters assumed that females were less able to withstand the rigors of labor. Indeed, the Danish Slave Trade Abolition Commission, in order to redress the imbalance and promote self-sustaining growth, exempted female slaves imported after 1792 from the usual taxes.[9] For St. Croix, for

Table 3.1 Slave, White, and Freedman populations of the Danish West Indies, 1688–1846

	St. Croix			St. Thomas			St. Jan		
Year	Slaves	Whites	Freedmen	Slaves	Whites	Freedmen	Slaves	Whites	Freedmen
1688				422	317				
1691				547	389				
1715				3,042	555				
1733				**	**		1,087	208	**
1755	8,897	1,303*	**	3,949	325	138	2,031	213*	**
1770	18,884	1,515		4,338	428	67	2,302	118	
1789	22,488	1,952	953	4,614	492	160	2,200	167	16
1797	25,452	2,223	1,164	4,769	726	239	1,992	113	15
1815	24,330	1,840	2,480	4,393	2,122	2,284	2,306	157	271
1835	19,876	6,805*		5,315	8,707*		1,943	532*	
1846	16,706	7,359*		3,494	9,579*		1,790	660*	

* These figures include freedmen as well as whites.

** No data.

Note: Between 1688 and 1715, neither St. Jan nor St. Croix had been acquired by the Danes. St. Jan was acquired in 1718 and was Danish at the time of the slave uprising there in 1733.

Sources: Forskellige Oplysninger, VI, General Toldkammer, Rigsarkiv, Copenhagen; Oxholm's "Statistik Tabelle over de danske Amerikanske Eilande St. Croix, St. Thomas og St. Jan, 1797," Dokumenter vedkommende Kommissionen for Negerhandelen, ibid.; "Viisdomsbog," Diverse Dokumenter, Vestin-diske Sager, ibid.; Originale Forestillinger fra Kommissionen angaaende Negernes Stilling, ibid.; Westergaard, Danish West Indies; J. O. Bro-Jørgensen, Vore Gamle Tropekolonier (Copenhagen, 1966); Hans West, Beretning om det dansk eilande St. Croix i Vestindien (Copenhagen, 1791).

Table 3.2 Sex distribution of the slave population of St. Croix, 1792–1840

Year	Female	Male	Total	Ratio of Females per 100 Males
1792*	7,364	8,579	15,943	85.8
1804	10,475	11,601	22,076	90.2
1815	12,250	12,080	24,330	101
1835	10,423	9,453	19,876	110
1840	9,714	8,891	18,605	109

* Figures do not include disabled and runaway slaves, numbering 96 and 2,082 respectively.

Sources: Oxholm's "General Tabelle for St. Croix, 1792," Dokumenter vedkommende Kommissionen for Negerhandelen, General Toldkammer, Rigsarkiv; Forskellige Oplysninger, VI, *ibid.;* "Extract af General Tabellerne over Folkmængden paa de danske vestindiske Øer, den 1ste Oktober 1835," Originale Forestillinger fra Kommissionen angaaende Negernes Stilling, *ibid.;* G.W. Alexander, *Om den moralske Forpligtelse til og den hensigtsmæssige af strax og fuldstændigt at ophæve Slaveriet i de dansk-vestindiske Kolonier* (Copenhagen, 1843).

example, the bias against females and its reversal over time is indicated by a comparison of the sex composition of that island's slave population of 1792 (when abolition was announced), 1804 (when the trade had just ended), 1815, 1835, and 1840, eight years before emancipation. Table 3.2 shows a dramatic half-century shift from a ratio of 85.8 female slaves to 100 males in 1792 to a ratio of 109 to 100 in 1840.

This change does not appear to have resulted in larger numbers of females than males among the slaves who escaped from the islands. Maroons from the Danish West Indies, as from Jamaica, Surinam, and Brazil, were preponderantly male.[10] The reason was not that women were physically less resilient or robust than men, but, more probably, that men were more likely to have acquired skills needed to survive in forests, swamps, or at sea, while, in addition, women were rendered less mobile by pregnancy or the responsibilities of maternity. In the Danish West Indies, moreover, women began to predominate in the slave population at a time when the creolization of that population was well advanced. (See Table 3.3.) By the nineteenth century, creole slave women were arguably further deterred from deserting by attachments of family, sentiment, or a sense of place.

Table 3.3 Creoles and Africans in the slave population of the Danish West Indies, 1804–1805

	Creoles	Africans	Total	% Creoles
St. Croix	11,530	10,546	22,076	52.2
St. Thomas	2,096	1,248	3,344	62.7
St. Jan	1,521	896	2,417	62.9
Total	15,147	12,690	27,837	54.4

Source: Raw data from Forskellige Oplysninger, V, General Toldkammer, Rigsarkiv.

The three islands lie within sight of each other just east of Puerto Rico and at the northern end of the eastern antillean chain as it curves gently westward in the vicinity of 18 degrees north latitude. Under Danish administration, they constituted a wedge, as it were, between Spanish Puerto Rico with its dependencies to the west and Britain's Virgin Islands to the east. This factor of insular proximity in a patchwork of national properties had an important bearing on how *grand marronage* from the Danish West Indies developed. There were significant differences from the pattern in the rest of the hemisphere, where aggregates of single fugitives created discrete communities that threatened the plantation system militarily and economically. Irrespective of their location, the viability of such communities, as Richard Price has noted, was a function of topography.[11] Natural barriers such as jungle, swamp, and hardly penetrable mountain fastnesses enabled maroon communities to develop in isolation and successfully defend themselves against attack. Slaves on the Danish islands enjoyed none of these advantages. The extensive cutting of forests to make way for sugar plantations removed nature's only benefaction from which maroons could profit. The experience of the Danish West Indies therefore provides empirical foundation for a theorem: that in small islands where geographical factors were hostile to the formation of permanent maroon communities, *grand marronage* tended to mean maritime *marronage*.

Grand marronage was the most viable of alternatives to servitude short of the supreme act of rebellion. From the beginning of Danish colonization to the time of emancipation in 1848, this form of resistance was continuous, indicating that its incidence was not significantly affected by the degree of acculturation or creolization of the slave population or by the changing proportions of male and female slaves. The numbers involved, however, were never very great. Hans West, a Danish pedagogue in St. Croix, reported 1,340 slaves at large in 1789, when the slave population stood at 22,448—a mere 5.9 percent.[12] P. L. Oxholm, a military engineer who later became governor-general, identified 96 deserters in 1792, only 0.5 percent[13] of St. Croix's 18,121 slaves. In St. Thomas the 86 known deserters in 1802 constituted 2.7 percent of the slave population of 3,150.[14]

The evidence indicates that *grand marronage* commenced shortly after the settlement of St. Thomas and the beginnings of that island's development as a plantation colony, which Waldemar Westergaard dates at 1688.[15] During the governorship of Johan Lorentz in the 1690s, proclamations were issued on the subject of runaways,[16] and the Privy Council of St. Thomas resolved early in 1706 to take action against *grand marronage*. Accordingly, it was ordered on October 2 that all trees on the island from which slaves could make canoes were to be cut down; a proclamation of December 30 offered a reward of fifty *Rigsdaler* for the return of any slave dead or alive who had escaped to Puerto Rico.[17]

The proclamations of 1706 demonstrate two factors that had an important bearing on the phenomenon of *marronage* immediately and over time: environment and geography. In the early years of settlement, before the apotheosis of sugar, the primeval forest provided superb cover and supplied wood for canoes in which slaves could seek freedom in nearby islands. The "marine underground" to Puerto Rico and Vieques (Crab Island), and farther afield to islands in the northern Leewards and elsewhere, ultimately became a major route of escape.

When the expansion of the plantations removed the forest cover, in St. Thomas and St. Jan by the 1730s and a generation or so later in St. Croix,[18] the best chances for permanent escape lay overseas, although, as we shall see, the islands' towns, as their populations grew, also provided havens. J. L. Carstens, who was born in St. Thomas in 1705 and died there in 1747, noted in his memoirs that in those early years runaways occupied the island's coastal cliffs, where they sheltered in almost inaccessible caves. Those first maroons chose well, with a keen strategic eye, for the cliffs could not be scaled from the seaward side and vegetation obstructed the landward approaches. Such refugees went naked and subsisted on fish, fruit, small game such as land turtles, or stolen provender. Slave hunts, organized three times a year, could neither loosen their grip on freedom nor dislodge them from the cliffs.[19]

Regrettably, Carstens recorded nothing of the size and social organization of this early community or its relationship with plantation slaves. It was the only such community that St. Thomas ever had, and it did not last long. The Danish authorities could ill afford to stand idly by, especially when St. Thomas was not yet self-sustaining.[20] During the War of the Spanish Succession they began to organize the *klappe jagt* or slave hunt more effectively, using planters, soldiers, and trusty slaves.[21] The forests then became less safe, while at the same time the agricultural exploitation of St. Thomas, peaking in the 1720s,[22] reduced the vegetational cover. As a result, slaves turned to the sea. Their line of escape led west, with favorable northeast trade winds and currents, toward Puerto Rico and other islands, none of which lay more than sixty kilometers from St. Thomas. Slaves had opportunities to become familiar with the surrounding waters on fishing expeditions for sea turtles around Vieques, and the same boats they manned on their masters' behalf could be used to make a break for Puerto Rico.[23] In 1747, nineteen slaves deserted from St. Croix, and the following year forty-two seized a sloop there and sailed to comparative freedom among the Spaniards.[24]

Puerto Rico, which became their preferred destination, was sparsely populated before the *Cédula de Gracias* of 1815, and its authorities, perhaps for this very reason, looked leniently if not encouragingly on runaways from the Danish islands. As early as 1714, Gov. Don Juan de Rivera organized eighty deserters from Danish and other islands into a community at San Mateo de Cangrejos east of San Juan, gave them public land, and required them to function as an auxiliary militia.[25] The Spanish government ratified these arrangements in *cédulas* of 1738 and 1750, and in the latter decreed freedom for runaways who embraced Catholicism.[26] Eugenio Fernández Méndez has argued that the Spanish acted largely from religious motives.[27] But there was also an element of calculating realpolitik: in addition to providing manpower, maroons were potential sources of useful intelligence in the event of hostilities. It is instructive to note that slaves from South Carolina found an equally agreeable haven in Spanish Florida in the early eighteenth century and were used by the Spaniards in border incursions that kept the British colony in a state of apprehension.[28]

Early legislative prescriptions against *grand marronage* authorized such physical deterrents as leg amputations, hamstring attenuation, and leg irons or neck collars.[29] Such measures hampered but did not prevent escape by water. Later laws elaborated rules for access to and use of boats. Even before 1750, legislation limited the size of canoes and barges that whites could keep and specified conditions of ownership.[30] Although mutilations and hardware such as neck irons fell out of use pari passu with the disappearance of the forests,[31] regulation of boats persisted until the very end of the era of slavery. The ordinance of October 2, 1706, was the forerunner of many, the necessity for which was proof of the problem they sought to eradicate. But despite a flurry of laws in the 1740s and 1750s, probably inspired by the beginning of the agricultural exploitation of St. Croix, *grand marronage* could not be suppressed.

Reimert Haagensen, who lived in St. Croix in the 1750s, noted in an account of that island that planter families were being ruined by the running away of slaves in groups of as many as twenty to twenty-five in a single night. He instanced occasions when slaves seized boats by surprise attack and forced their crews to sail to Puerto Rico. Many plantation owners, Haagensen complained, had *"capital staaende iblandt de Spanske, bvoraf dog ingen Interesse svares."*[32] It was commonly supposed in the Danish islands that a year in the service of the Spanish crown brought freedom. This Haagensen said he could neither confirm nor deny; but he had personal knowledge of slaves who had escaped to Spanish territory, lived well and in freedom, and sent back messages of greeting to their former masters and slave companions.[33] Similarly, C.G.A. Oldendorp, a Moravian missionary inspector, writing in the 1760s, noted that Maron-bjerg—Maroon Mountain, in the northwestern corner of St. Croix—was no longer a secure retreat, and that as a result the proximity of Puerto Rico and the promise of freedom there acted as powerful stimulants. The still largely African-born slave population demonstrated the same levels of inventiveness and daring that Haagensen observed in the previous decade. Slaves secretly built canoes large enough to accommodate whole families, commandeered when they could not build, forced sailors to take them to Puerto Rico, and, when all else failed, bravely swam out to sea in hope of accomplishing the same objective.[34]

Legislation dealing with *marronage* at the end of the eighteenth century and in the early years of the nineteenth shows a continuing preoccupation with the problem. Gov.-Gen. Ernst von Walterstorff attempted to introduce a boat registry in St. Croix in 1791 and insisted that all canoes must have bungs that were to be put away, along with oars and sails, when the canoes were not in use. All craft were to be stamped with the royal arms and bear a registration number as well as the owner's name; none was to be sold or rented outside the towns' harbors.[35] In 1811 the police chief of Christiansted announced a fine of ten *pistoles* for employing slaves on the wharves or on boats in the harbor without a police permit.[36] The Danish West Indian government in 1816 expressed concern at the persistence of escapes by boat and contemplated introducing regulatory measures such as prohibition of boat ownership except in towns.[37] Finally, as late as 1845, three years before emancipation, Adam Søbøtker, the acting governor-general, promulgated a decree permitting plantations to keep only flat-bottomed boats, as slaves were unlikely to try to escape in such craft.[38] By then, however, the marine underground had other destinations than Puerto Rico, as will be shown below.

Over time, legislation to cauterize the hemorrhage proved only minimally effective. The failure of preventative measures prompted a search for other solutions. The absence of a formal extradition convention had enabled runaways to Puerto Rico to cock their snooks at former owners, a form of salutation that Haagensen for one found less than amusing.[39] The establishment of such a convention, it was thought, would resolve the difficulty. Accordingly, a series of cartels between Spain and Denmark in 1742, 1765, 1767, and 1776 established that deserters would have to be claimed within one year by their owners; that the latter would pay the expenses of their slaves' maintenance for that period; that reclaimed fugitives would not be punished; that those who embraced Catholicism would be allowed to remain in Puerto Rico; and, finally, that a Catholic church and residence for its priest would be built in St. Thomas at Denmark's expense.[40]

These diplomatic initiatives, however, proved disappointing. The cartels applied to future deserters but not to slaves already in Puerto Rico. The Spanish authorities, moreover, were less than expeditious in dealing with claims. The Danish West India Company filed a claim in 1745 for the return of some 300 deserters known to be in San Mateo de Cangrejos, but twenty-one years passed before it was adjusted.[41] Less than a decade after the 1767 convention, Gov.-Gen. Peder Clausen was engaged in a brisk correspondence with Don Miguel de Muesos, captain general of Puerto Rico. Several slaves had decamped from St. Thomas early in 1775, but the envoy sent to claim them was met by Spanish professions of ignorance of their whereabouts.[42] *Grosso modo*, the Spaniards showed little inclination to cooperate in the matter of runaways. Occupation of the Danish West Indies in the early years of the nineteenth century by Spain's wartime ally

England appears to have made little difference. The British lieutenant governor of St. Croix in 1811, Brig. G. W. Harcourt, issued a proclamation asserting that slaves had been carried off in Puerto Rican boats and declared that such boats found illegally four weeks thereafter in any harbor except Christiansted and Frederiksted would be seized and confiscated.[43] Two months later, the British authorities invited persons who had recently lost slaves and believed them to be in Puerto Rico to submit information on the slaves' age, sex, appearance, and time of desertion.[44]

As late as 1841, the "long-standing difficulties" with Puerto Rico were the subject of exchanges between the Danish West Indian governor-general and King Christian VIII, each hoping that the new Puerto Rican captain general, Mendez Vigo, would be more disposed to "friendly conclusions" than some of his predecessors had been.[45] An incident reported by Van Dockum in the early 1840s reveals the nature of the difficulties. Acting on information that two slaves had been spirited away to Vieques in boats from that island, the authorities in St. Croix sent the frigate on patrol duty in the West Indies to reclaim them. When the frigate arrived at Isabel Segunda, the main town of Vieques, that island's governor, though full of conviviality and consideration, would admit only that a boat had in fact taken slaves from St. Croix to Vieques.[46] It appears that the shortage of labor in the Spanish islands after the legal suspension of the slave trade in the 1820s bred illegal trafficking, often with the collusion of Spanish authorities.[47] The episode to which Van Dockum referred seems to have been an instance of labor piracy willingly embraced by the slaves of St. Croix as an avenue of *grand marronage*.

Taking refuge in forested hills and fleeing to Puerto Rico or Vieques were the most dramatic early acts of *grand marronage*. While slaves continued to escape by water, the disappearance of primeval vegetation prompted others to find ways of deserting without leaving the islands. Sugar served their need and turn. Harvesting began in late December or early January when the canes approached maturity and had grown high enough to conceal even the tallest person. Until the end of the "crop" or reaping season in July, therefore, each unreaped field provided an artificial forest in which slaves could continue to conceal themselves over a six-month period. The work of these months of harvest made the most strenuous and exacting demands on slaves' endurance. This was also the dry season, before high summer brought the heavy showers associated with the movement of the intertropical convergence zone. A slave thus had multiple inducements: he could find cover, escape the period of hardest labor, and keep dry. A Danish official in the late eighteenth century noted that the expansion of plantations on St. Croix made it difficult for runaway slaves to find shelter in forests that were disappearing or in fields that no longer contained scrub. The alternative, he observed, rendered them secure but posed a constant fire hazard: "Fleeing to the cane fields in which the cane and leaves can exceed a man's height, they put down poles of about a meter and a half and make a bower over these with the leaves of the nearest canes plaited together. In this way they form a little hut about four and a half feet high by six to seven feet around. Having cleared the ground in the hut of dry leaves and left an opening, they then use the place to lie up, to store whatever ground provisions they can, and as a fireplace."[48] The existence of maroon hideouts in the cane fields was authenticated by discoveries of corner posts, ashes, and coal. A causal link between such hideouts and cane fires was also established by remnants of pork and other meat abandoned to and partially consumed by fires out of control.[49]

Another variant of *grand marronage* was desertion to the coastal towns. Christiansted and Frederiksted in St. Croix, and Charlotte Amalie in St. Thomas, grew in population and commercial importance in the prosperous years of the late eighteenth century: plantations flourished, trade expanded, and Charlotte Amalie was established as a free port.[50] For slaves on islands as small as the Danish West Indies, towns offered advantages of comparative anonymity; a prospect of work on the wharves, in warehouses, and aboard coastal or other vessels; the likelihood of finding a sympathetic reception and succor in the areas of these towns designated by law for free persons of color; concealment, incongruously enough, by whites; and the chance of using the town as a staging post in what might become a step-migration to freedom.

Anonymity was enormously enhanced when a slave on the run shipped from one Danish island to another. One cannot quantify this type of *marronage*, but it was known to have taken place, and as the bustle of free-port commerce in Charlotte Amalie arguably rendered that town a more impersonal place than either Christiansted or Frederiksted, it must be presumed that the tendency would have been toward St. Thomas. Newspaper advertisements appear to support such a hypothesis, although there is also evidence of *marronage* from Charlotte Amalie to St. Jan and St. Croix. Most notorious was the case of Jane George, who in an advanced state of pregnancy escaped from St. Thomas in a canoe with a white man early in September 1815 paddling for St. Jan or St. Croix.[51] Another runaway, James Dougharty, an artisan apprentice, headed for St. Jan in 1822. A reward of $20 was offered for information, "as it [was] not likely [he] had walked all the way."[52] By and large, however, advertisements for maroons in St. Thomas over the first fifteen years of the publication of the *Sankt Thomæ Tidende* (1815–1830) show approximately twice as many desertions to St. Thomas as to St. Croix or St. Jan from St. Thomas.

The variety of employment in the growing towns facilitated *grand marronage* into them, and the anonymity they offered was compounded by the notorious laxity of the Danish West Indian police,[53] so that it was possible for runaways to sustain a livelihood in wharf-related work or itinerant vending without too great a risk of discovery.[54] Fugitives enjoyed the normally supportive presence of freedmen in their legally prescribed areas of residence, the Free Guts. With freedmen, urban slaves, and poor whites, deserters composed a demimonde of the marginalized. Governor-General Clausen in St. Croix in the 1770s and Lt. Gov. Thomas de Maleville in St. Thomas in the 1780s expressed only more explicitly than most the sense of community that prevailed among runaways and freedmen in the Guts.[55] Poor whites involved in petty retail trading or artisan trades were known to consort with and provide shelter for runaways. The latter were potential sources of stolen goods and, if they had an artisanal skill, could be hired out to earn an income for their protectors. Throughout the late eighteenth and early nineteenth centuries, therefore, one finds legislation aimed at curtailing the mutually reinforcing liaison of fugitives and their patrons, especially in the towns. The preamble to an ordinance issued by Gov.-Gen. Adrian Bentzon in 1817 spoke of the long history of this liaison; the ordinance prescribed severe penalties for whites and free persons of color who either hired or hid slaves on the run.[56] As late as 1831, Adam Søbøtker, acting as governor-general, was still vainly attempting to curb that sort of collusion.[57]

For runaways, the coastal towns were above all a porthole of opportunity to a wider world. *Marronage* overseas to foreign destinations, before the significant growth of the towns, had been limited to Vieques and Puerto Rico. However, as towns grew, they attracted an increasing number of vessels from distant ports, widening the escape hatch for slaves. The schooners, brigs, sloops, yawls, and snows that called at these towns, especially Charlotte Amalie as it became a Caribbean entrepôt, brought St. Domingue/Haiti and Jamaica in the Greater Antilles, the islands of the Leewards and Windwards, the North American continent, and even Europe within reach, though after 1802 Denmark ruled itself out as a haven for escapees. A Supreme Court decision that year in the case of the slave Hans Jonathan decreed that the free soil of the mother country did not confer freedom on the enslaved.[58]

Access to avenues of flight depended in some measure on the collusion of masters of vessels. Service at sea in the eighteenth and early nineteenth centuries was such as to suggest a parallel between masters of vessels and slave masters, between ships and regimented slave plantations, between crews and enslaved estate labor. Ship masters, not surprisingly, had their own problems of *marronage* in the form of desertion. It was not unusual for crewmen, singly or in numbers, to jump ship in West Indian waters. One Swedish sloop, the *William*, Capt. Joseph Almeida, lost five hands in St. Thomas harbor on February 5, 1827.[59] Such incidents meant that additional or substitute crews were often needed, and since the white population of Caribbean coastal towns was too small to meet the need, it was unlikely that runaway slaves who offered themselves would be interrogated closely, if at all, about their status. Black crewmen were therefore commonplace. Many of Almeida's men were Africans of unspecified status, and slave shiphands were by no means extraordinary. One such, Jan Maloney, deserted from a vessel of British registry in St. Thomas in 1819.[60]

In 1778 regulations were adopted to obstruct this avenue of *grand marronage* by forbidding shipboard employment of any slave without a sailor's pass and written permission from his owner. Significantly, it was considered necessary to reissue these regulations in 1806.[61] The 1833 royal proclamation of Frederik VII, by offering the extravagant reward of 1,500 *pistoles* for information on masters of vessels secretly exporting slaves, suggests that the problem still persisted even at that late date.[62] The size of the reward indicated the seriousness with which the problem was viewed, particularly at a time when the slave population of the Danish islands was steadily declining.[63]

Some ship captains, even before the end of the eighteenth century, were free persons of color. One such was Nicholas Manuel, whose ship, the *Trimmer*, plied between St. Thomas and Jeremie, St. Domingue, in 1796.[64] In such a vessel, arguably, a slave could find the maritime equivalent of a house of safety in a Free Gut. The legislation directed at captains thus took into account a potential collaborator, the colored shipmaster, while it also expressed the paranoia prevailing after the revolution in St. Domingue and accompanying disturbances in the French West Indies. Vulnerability to revolutionary contamination from these trouble spots was a recurring concern of Danish West Indian authorities, who lived in constant fear that their slaves would emulate the St. Domingue example. The years from 1791 to about 1807 were therefore punctuated by measures to establish a *cordon sanitaire* against St. Domingue. These involved, inter alia, the confiscation of any boats arriving from St. Domingue/Haiti and the imposition of a fine of 1,000 *Rigsdaler*.[65] Yet there is evidence to suggest that such prophylaxis achieved only indifferent results. The traffic to St. Domingue/Haiti, especially from St. Thomas, continued, and in the early 1840s Governor-General von Scholten felt moved to remark on the "significant" number of "unavoidable" desertions to that island.[66]

Legislation could not prevent desertions, for the movement of interisland maritime traffic depended to a degree on slave crews, and the law permitted slaves with seamen's passes to be so engaged, making a pragmatic virtue out of necessity, considering the shallowness of the white labor pool.[67] Engaged as crews in their island of origin, slaves embraced the opportunity to escape on reaching a foreign port. Jamaica was one such destination in the western Caribbean at which goods from the emporium that was St. Thomas were arriving well before the end of the eighteenth century. Both the *Royal Gazette* and the *Jamaica Courant* carried information that confirms that slaves considered any port a station in the maritime underground. The St. Thomas sloop *Martha*, Capt. John Simmons Blyden, arrived in Kingston in August 1788 and promptly lost

Jack, a sailor aged twenty-five, and Tony, twenty-three, described as a "waiting man and occasional fiddler." Another St. Thomas sloop, the *Hope,* Capt. John Winfield, lost George, aged nineteen, at about the same time.[68] Joe, twenty-five, jumped ship in Kingston from the schooner *Eagle,* registered in St. Croix, in May 1806.[69] Not all the deserting slave seamen from the Danish West Indies appear to have made it to freedom. Some like Sam, a St. Thomas creole who arrived in Kingston on a sloop commanded by Captain Capp in 1797, were apprehended.[70] No doubt a reasonable competence in an English creole tongue must have helped a slave negotiate the narrows of early freedom in a strange English-speaking island, and in this regard slaves from St. Croix may have enjoyed an advantage. In that island, step by step with the creolization of the slave population, there developed an English-based creole lingua franca, whereas in St. Thomas it was Dutch-based.[71] Having an employable skill in addition to seafaring would also have helped. Another Sam, for example, who deserted from a Danish island schooner in Kingston late in 1793, was a hairdresser by trade. Since he was American-born and spoke good English,[72] he stood a doubly good chance of getting past the exit turnstiles of this station in the maritime underground.

In the Caribbean, the same flows of trade that took vessels to St. Domingue/Haiti or farther away to Jamaica also took Danish West Indian vessels to the Lesser Antilles in the opposite direction. These flows presented like opportunities to slaves for employment as crew, and such employment, legitimate or illegitimate, created chances for desertion to the Leewards, Windwards, and elsewhere. That traffic, moreover, complemented the trade originating to leeward of St. Thomas and St. Croix, thereby widening the possibilities for maritime *marronage.* This branch of eastern Caribbean intercourse in the early nineteenth century was part of the expanding seaborne commerce into St. Thomas[73] and opened a major escape route for runaways to St. Thomas from islands in the northern Leewards and from as far away as Curaçao and Barbados.[74] Danish slaves were not slow to exploit the situation. One reported example from St. Thomas in 1819 indicates that eight slaves—seven men and one woman—probably crew on the seventeen-ton interisland schooner *Waterloo,* stole the ship when it arrived in St. Vincent in the British Windwards.[75]

This episode is remarkable for its daring and also for the fact that it is the only incident of running away to the non-Danish islands of the eastern Caribbean, excluding Tortola, that the newspapers report. Though one of the best sources for the study of all forms of *marronage,* the Danish West Indian newspapers are in fact less helpful than one would like on maritime *marronage* to the foreign islands of the eastern Caribbean—perhaps understandably so, for the logical place in which to advertise for deserters was the terminus a quo or point of escape. The Danish West Indian papers therefore report desertions from other islands more fully than desertions from the Danish islands. The local advertisement placed in the *Sankt Thomæ Tidende* by James Hazel, owner of the above-mentioned *Waterloo*, was thus unusual. Recovery of his lost schooner and slaves would have been better served by insertions in the foreign press. But perhaps the size of his loss—schooner, cargo, and eight slaves—obliged him to issue, in modern police parlance, an all points bulletin.[76]

From the inception of Danish colonization, slaves showed their capacity for creating possibilities for *grand marronage* overseas from each new set of circumstances. They responded ingeniously to the openings presented by the islands' ecology, the proximity of the Spanish islands, and the growing volume of traffic to and from the Danish ports. But of all the circumstances affecting *grand marronage*, none appears to have had a more quickening effect than emancipation in the neighboring British Leeward Islands, particularly Tortola. Desertions to Tortola began to increase from 1839, the year after the post-emancipation period of apprenticeship ended in the British West Indies.[77] Especially in St. Jan, no more than a cannon shot's distance from Tortola, the urge to run away then appears to have become irresistible.

Slaves were well aware that once they set foot on Tortola their freedom was secure, for the effect of the British Emancipation Act of 1833 was to confer on them on arrival the free status that the West Indian slave James Somerset had acquired in England in 1772 only after litigation at the highest level. For example, in reporting the incident of the early 1840s involving the two slaves from St. Croix, Van Dockum noted that before proceeding to Vieques they had requested to be taken to Tortola, where they went ashore. The authorities in Vieques used this fact to explain why they could not return persons who were in law free men.[78] The difficulties that British West Indian emancipation posed for the Danish authorities were practically insurmountable. Louis Rothe, an observant judge of probate who came to St. Croix in the 1840s, noted that desertions from St. Jan were almost impossible to control—and not only because of the proximity of Tortola. Overlooked by precipitous cliffs, St. Jan's innumerable bays made coastal patrols for the most part ineffective. Moreover, the patrols were too few to police bays that, even when contiguous, did not permit observation of one from another. Deserters crossed the straits by boats and improvised rafts from St. Jan. Boats also originated from Tortola; some even came by appointment to fetch a slave or group of slaves. In Tortola, Rothe observed, "all classes receive them with open arms and emissaries await with tempting offers of money and free transportation to larger islands, and promises of high wages and little work." For the years 1840 to 1846, he reported desertion by 70 slaves.[79] Though the total seems insignificant, it was more than double the number of runaways from St. Thomas over the same period.[80] If Rothe was correct—and he admitted that no official records were kept—an important fact emerges. St. Jan's slave population declined from 1,970 in 1840 to 1,790 in

1846.[81] The 70 slaves therefore represented nearly 40 percent of the decline over that period.[82]

As the 1840s began, the Danish West Indian government sought to close this route to freedom by using frigates on the naval station. Governor-General von Scholten's orders were apparently to shoot to kill, although his long-term objective, as expressed in a letter to Christian VIII, was to reduce the attractions of desertion by progressive amelioration of conditions for slaves.[83] In 1840, a slave woman attempting to reach Tortola by canoe was killed by naval fire. Two others in the party, a mother and child, were apprehended, but two escaped by swimming.[84] In Denmark, the newspaper *Fædrelandet* observed in righteous indignation that "blood ought not to be shed to compensate for an inability to reconcile the slaves to their existence" and found a sinister significance in the recent erection of "an enormous prison" in St. Croix.[85] Von Scholten and the authorities were for the moment impervious to such voices of humanitarian protest, but it was another matter when pursuit of slaves involved firing upon them in ill-defined territorial waters claimed by the British. An ensuing British protest led to an investigation in 1841 by a senior Danish naval officer, Hans Birch Dahlerup. Formal charges were brought against a Lieutenant Hedemann for the killing of the woman and violation of British waters. The investigation ended in a court martial in Copenhagen and two months' imprisonment for Hedemann—"more to satisfy England and its then powerful abolitionist lobby," Dahlerup concluded, "than for the offence with which he was charged."[86]

The year 1845 was a particularly successful one for slaves bidding for freedom in Tortola. The administration's preoccupation, if not panic, was by then plain. Acting Governor-General Søbøtker reported to the crown in tones of anguish a sequence of escapes. On October 26, six slaves—five men and a woman[87]—from plantations on St. Croix's north side, got hold of a fishing canoe and made it to Tortola, although police and fire corps went in immediate pursuit. The Tortolan authorities returned the boat but not the people. Of particular interest is the fact that the leadership of this escape was attributed to a seasoned maritime maroon who some years previously had deserted from Dutch Saba and had been recaptured and resold in St. Croix.[88]

Less than a month after this incident the most spectacular episode of *grand marronage* from St. Jan to Tortola occurred. On the night of November 15, thirty-seven slaves, including six from one plantation, deserted from southside St. Jan in two English boats sent from Tortola for that purpose. The maroon patrol, such as it was, was based on the island's north side, closest to Tortola, leaving the south side unguarded. For some time planters in St. Jan had been allowed to get their supplies of salt from Tortola in boats from that island, but they were less than vigilant in this instance. No satisfaction was to be expected, Søbøtker felt, as the government of the British Leeward Islands was unlikely to make reparations and would take no action against the two Tortolan boatmen who were accessories. "The established principle since emancipation," he pointed out, "was that no one who had helped an unfree person to gain freedom could be punished for it." The best the frustrated Søbøtker could do was to issue stern warnings to plantation owners, increase night patrols by his inadequate militia, and make new regulations respecting planters' ownership of boats.[89]

Grand marronage by Danish West Indian slaves lasted from the beginning of colonization, when the slave population was exclusively African-born, until slavery's end in 1848, when it was largely creole. In the decade or so before that date, emancipation in the British West Indies, particularly in neighboring Tortola, stimulated desertions on a scale that, especially in St. Jan, threatened to destabilize the slave system. In the 1840s such desertions, though they may have robbed the slave population of its potentially most revolutionary leadership, nevertheless prefigured and arguably acted as a catalyst for the successful rebellion of 1848.

Later commentators, like earlier observers, rationalized *grand marronage* in a variety of ways, some self-serving, others perceptive. These included depravity, overwork, fear of punishment or impending trial, arbitrary owners, the attractions of a work-free Sunday on other islands, and scarcity of food.[90] Whenever the occasion arose, officials were given to asserting, in an access of obtuseness or arrogant self-satisfaction, that fugitives would willingly return if only they could enjoy more discretionary time.[91] One of the thirty-seven who fled to Tortola in 1845 seized a boat and did indeed return to St. Jan early in 1846. The records do not disclose his reasons but do report him as having said that others were equally ready to return, "which was not improbable," the authorities smugly concluded, "having regard to the prevailing destitution in Tortola."[92] But there is no evidence that these escapees came back to St. Jan, nor did this one swallow make a summer. On the occasion of the 1759 slave conspiracy in St. Croix, the examining magistrate, Engebret Hesselberg, made the surprisingly enlightened observation that "the desire for freedom is an inseparable part of the human condition."[93] Oldendorp, no libertarian himself, concurred, although with less generosity of spirit. "It is extraordinarily difficult," he noted, "to convince the . . . Negroes that the rights their masters exercise over them are their due rights. They follow their uncontrollable nature and consider every means of gaining their freedom justified. . . . [T]hey run away from their masters . . . and seek violent means of escaping from their service."[94]

By running away as they had always done, and in the numbers they did to Tortola, slaves reinforced the truth of Hesselberg's observation. In the 1840s they began to press the issue of their freedom by bringing the metropolitan authorities urgently to consider concrete measures for emancipation. Their initiatives helped embolden liberal opinion in Denmark, already critical of absolute monarchy and colonial policy and favorably disposed to emancipation on economic as well as humanitarian grounds.[95] The newspaper *Fædrelandet*, organ of the opposition, declared it "impossible for all practical purposes to place limits on the longing for freedom."[96]

Indeed, when a deserted slave spoke into the record, he gave poignant endorsement to *Fædrelandet*'s sentiments. Such a man was William F. A. Gilbert, the only escaped slave from the Danish West Indies from whom we have a personal written testament. We do not know when or how he reached Boston, Massachusetts, but it was from that city on August 12, 1847, a year before emancipation, that he addressed to Christian VIII an impassioned plea not only on his own behalf but for every member of his race who had ever been or was still oppressed by slavery:

> To His Supreme Magistrate, King Christian VIII, Copenhagen, Denmark. Sir: I taken my pen in hand a runaway slave, to inform your excelcy of the evil of slavery. Sir Slavery is a bad thing and if any man will make a slave of a man after he is born free, i, should think it anoutrage becose i was born free of my Mother wom and after i was born the Monster, in the shape of a man, made a slave of me in your dominion now Sir i ask your excelcy in the name of God & his kingdom is it wright for God created man Kind equal and free so i have a writ to my freedom I have my freedom now but that is not all Sir. i want to see my Sisters & my Brothers and i now ask your excelcy if your excelcy will grant me a free pass to go and come when ever i fail dispose to go and come to Ile of St. Croix or Santacruce the west indies Sir i ask in arnist for that pass for the tears is now gushing from mine eyes as if someone had poar water on my head and it running down my Cheak. Sir i ask becose i have some hopes of geting it for i see there your Nation has a stablished Chirches and Schools for inlightning the Slave. that something the American has not done all though she is a republican my nam is Frederick Augustus Gilbert now i has another name thus

> Wᵐ F. A. Gilbert

> Sir, when i see such good sines i cannot but ask for such a thing as liberty and freedom for it is Glorius. Sir i make very bold to write to a King but i cannot helpit for i have been a runaway slave i hope your excelcy will for give me if i is out in order Please to sind you answer to the Deinish Council in Boston

> His withered hands he holds to view
> With nerves once firmly strung,
> And scarcely can believe it true

That ever he was yong,
And as he thinks o'er all his ills,
Disease, neglect, and scorn,
Strange pity of himself he feels
That slave is forlane

William F. A. Gilbert.[97]

NOTES

1 Useful introductory material on the Danish West Indies published in English can be found in Isaac Dookhan, *A History of the Virgin Islands of the United States* (Epping, Eng., 1974); Jens Larsen, *Virgin Islands Story* (Philadelphia, 1950); Florence Lewisohn, *St. Croix under Seven Flags* . . . (Hollywood, Fla., 1970); and Waldemar Westergaard, *The Danish West Indies under Company Rule (1671–1754)* . . . (New York, 1917).

2 See John Macpherson, *Caribean Lands: A Geography of the West Indies*, 3d ed. (Kingston, Jamaica, 1973), 3, 123, and P. P. Sveistrup, "Bidrag til de Tidligere Dansk-Vestindiske Øers Økonomiske Historie, med særligt Henblik paa Sukker-production og Sukkerhandel," *National Økonomiske Tidsskrift for Samfundsspørgsmaal Økonomi og Handel*, LXXX (1942), 65, 87.

3 J. L. Carstens, "En almindelig Beskrivelse om Alle de danske Amerikanske eller West-Indiske Eylande," ed. H. Nielsen, *Danske Magazin*, III, No. 8, pts. 3 and 4 (1960–1970), 260–261.

4 Svend E. Green-Pedersen, "The Economic Considerations behind the Danish Abolition of the Negro Slave Trade," in Henry A. Gemery and Jan S. Hogendorn, eds., *The Uncommon Market: Essays in the Economic History of the Atlantic Slave Trade* (New York, 1979), 407–408, and "Slave Demography in the Danish West Indies and the Abolition of the Danish Slave Trade," in David Eltis and James Walvin, eds., *The Abolition of the Atlantic Slave Trade: Origins and Effects in Europe, Africa, and the Americas* (Madison, Wis., 1981), 234.

5 Green-Pedersen, "Slave Demography," in Eltis and Walvin, eds., *Abolition of the Atlantic Slave Trade*, 245.

6 N.A.T. Hall, "The 1816 Freedman Petition in the Danish West Indies: Its Background and Consequences," *Boletín de Estudios Latinoamericanos y del Caribe*, No. 29 (1980), 56.

7 N.A.T. Hall, "Slavery in Three West Indian Towns: Christiansted, Fredericksted and Charlotte Amalie in the Late Eighteenth and Early Nineteenth Century," in B. W. Higman, ed., *Trade, Government and Society in Caribbean History, 1700–1920: Essays Presented to Douglas Hall* (Kingston, Jamaica, 1983), 18.

8 *Ibid.*, 23.

9 Green-Pedersen, "Economic Considerations," in Gemery and Hogendorn, eds., *Uncommon Market*, 408.

10 Richard Price, ed., *Maroon Societies: Rebel Slave Communities in the Americas* (New York, 1973), 9.

11 *Ibid.*, 3.

12 That number is not to be taken at face value since West made no distinction between *petit* and *grand marronage*. West, *Beretning*, "Mandtal Optaget for 1789."

13 Oxholm's General Tabell, St. Croix, 1792, Dokumenter vedkommende Kommissionen for Negerhandelens bedre Indretning og Ophævelse, samt Efterretninger om Negerhandelen og Slaveriet i Vestindien, 1783–1806, General Toldkammer, Rigsarkiv.

14 Recapitulation of the State of the Different Quarters of the Island of St. Thomas, May 13, 1802, Den Engelske Okkupation 1801, 1807, General Toldkammer, Rigsarkiv.

15 Westergaard, *Danish West Indies*, 121.

16 Copies of Orders Issued during Governorships, 1672–1727, Bancroft Papers, Z-A 1, 3, University of California, Berkeley.

17 Kongelig Secretaire Schwartkopp's Report, Oct. 13, 1786, *ibid.*, Z-A 1, 48.

18 In the case of St. Croix, contemplated legislation in 1783 against illegal felling of trees was justified on the basis that "since almost all the forests have been cut down, illegal felling of trees is of greater importance than previously" (Udkast og Betænkning angaaende Neger Loven med bilag 1783–1789, No. 24, Pt. 1, Article 48, General Toldkammer, Rigsarkiv).

19 Carstens, "En almindelig Beskrivelse," ed. Nielsen, *Danske Magazin*, III, No. 8, Pts. 3 and 4 (1960–1970), 225, 259.

20 N.A.T. Hall, "Empire without Dominion: Denmark and Her West Indian Colonies, 1671–1848" (seminar paper, University of the West Indies, Mona, 1983), 3–10.

21 Bro-Jørgensen, *Vore Gamle Tropekolonier*, 225.

22 Westergaard, *Danish West Indies*, 160.

23 *Ibid.*, 161.

24 Arturo Morales Carrión, *Albores Históricos del Capitalismo en Puerto Rico* (Barcelona, Spain, 1972), 83.

25 Luis M. Diaz Soler, *Historia de la Esclavitud Negra en Puerto Rico* (Rio Piedras, Puerto Rico, 1974), 233, 236.

26 Cayetano Coll y Toste, ed., *Boletin Histórico de Puerto Rico* (San Juan, Puerto Rico, 1914), I, 16, 20.

27 Fernández Méndez, *Historia Cultural de Puerto Rico, 1493–1968* (San Juan, Puerto Rico, 1971), 165.

28 Peter H. Wood, *Black Majority: Negroes in Colonial South Carolina from 1670 through the Stono Rebellion* (New York, 1974), 305–307.

29 Westergaard, *Danish West Indies*, 162. See also C.G.A. Oldendorp, *Geschichte der Mission der evangelischen Brüder* (Barby, Germany, 1777), I, 496, and Neville Hall, "Slave Laws of the Danish Virgin Islands in the Later Eighteenth Century," New York Academy of Sciences, *Annals*, CCXCII (1977), 174–186.

30 Gov.-Gen. Walterstorff's Placat of Nov. 21, 1791, quoting earlier proclamations of 1742, 1744, 1750, and 1756, Bancroft Papers, Z-A 1, 52.

31 Oldendorp mentions amputations for which the definitive slave code of 1733 made provision (*Geschichte*, I, 396). But by the 1780s there were already voices critical of the code's provisions as barbaric. See, for example, Judge Colbiørnsen's Opinion, Sept. 3, 1785, Miscellaneous Papers, Udkast og Betænkning, General Toldkammer, Rigsarkiv, and General Toldkammer Skrivelse to Danish West Indian Government, Dec. 23, 1782, Kommissions Forslag og Anmærkning angaaende Negerloven, Bind 1, 1785, *ibid.*

32 "Capital invested among the Spaniards that yields no interest" (Haagensen, *Beskrivelse over Eylandet St. Croix i America i Vestindien* [Copenhagen, 1758], 42).

33 *Ibid.*, 43.

34 Oldendorp, *Geschichte*, I, 396–397. Oldendorp did not say whether he knew of any slaves who managed to reach Puerto Rico or adjacent islands by swimming.

35 Gov.-Gen. Walterstorff's Placat, Nov. 21, 1791, Bancroft Papers, Z-A 1, 52.

36 *St. Croix Gazette*, Mar. 12, 1811.

37 Akter Vedkommende Slaveemancipation, Frikulørte 1826, 1834, Dansk Vestindisk Regerings Deliberations Protocoller, Apr. 30, 1816, General Toldkammer, Rigsarkiv.

38 Søbøtker to Christian VIII, Dec. 13, 1845, Record Group 55, Box 9, National Archives, Washington, D.C.

39 Haagensen, *Beskrivelse*, 43.

40 Oldendorp, *Geschichte*, I, 396–397; E. V. Lose, *Kort Udsigt over den danskeluther-ske Missions Historie paa St. Croix, St. Thomas og St. Jan* (Copenhagen, 1890), 22–23; Diaz Soler, *Historia de la Esclavitud*, 234–236; Morales Carrión, *Albores Históricos*, 67; Kommissions Forslag, Bind 2, fols. 74, 89, General Toldkammer, Rigsarkiv.

41 Westergaard, *Danish West Indies*, 161. Diaz Soler is of the view that the settlement of the claim under the 1767 convention was facilitated by the demise of the Danish West India Company, whose illicit trading with Puerto Rico had always been an obstacle to negotiations (*Historia de la Esclavitud*, 234).

42 Clausen to de Muesos, July 4, 1775, Bancroft Papers, Z-A 1, 43.

43 *St. Croix Gaz.*, Feb. 8, 1811.

44 *Ibid.*, Apr. 9, 1811.

45 Von Scholten to Christian VIII, Jan. 13, 1841, in which reference is also made to an unfiled letter of Nov. 18, 1840, Originale Forestillinger fra Kommissionen angaaende Negernes Stilling i Vestindien med Resolutioner, General Told-kammer, Rigsarkiv. See also Christian VIII to von Scholten, Oct. 7, Dec. 4, 1840, Aug. 1, 1841, Privatarkiv 6795, Rigsarkiv.

46 C. Van Dockum, *Livserindringer* (Copenhagen, 1893), 74–77.

47 Andrés Ramos Mattei, *La Hacienda Azucarera: Su Crecimiento y Crisis en Puerto Rico (Siglo XIX)* (San Juan, Puerto Rico, 1981), 23–24. Demand for labor inspired the decree of 1849 establishing an obligatory work regimen for free labor in Puerto Rico. See *ibid.*, 24, and Labor Gomez Acevedo, *Organización y Reglamentación del Trabajo en el Puerto Rico del Siglo XIX* (San Juan, Puerto Rico, 1970), 449–453.

48 Etats Raad Laurbergs Erinderinger, Jan. 12, 1784, Kommissions Forslag, Bind 2, fols. 10–11, General Toldkammer, Rigsarkiv. Cf. *ibid.*, Bind 1, fol. 326.

49 It is possible that cane field deserters were simply engaging in short-term absenteeism. The length of absence and the construction of shelter that made absence of that duration possible would suggest, more plausibly, an intention to remain at large and ultimately leave the island.

50 Hall, "Slavery in Three West Indian Towns," in Higman, ed., *Trade, Government and Society*, 19–20.

51 *Sankt Thomæ Tidende*, Sept. 16, 1815.

52 *Ibid.*, Mar. 5, 1822.

53 Hall, "Slave Laws," N.Y. Acad. Sciences, *Annals*, CCXCII (1977), 184.

54 Hall, "Slavery in Three West Indian Towns," in Higman, ed., *Trade, Government and Society*, 27, 29, 30.

55 Clausen's Placat, 39, July 29, 1775, Udkast og Betænkning . . . No. 27, General Toldkammer, Rigsarkiv; de Maleville's Anmærkning, Apr. 7, 1784, and de Maleville's Betænkning, Oct. 19, 1787, Kommissions Forslag, Bind 2, fols. 33, 84, *ibid.*

56 Bentzon's Ordinance of Sept. 11, 1817, Forskellige Oplysninger, V, fol. 315, General Toldkammer, Rigsarkiv.

57 Søbøker's Proclamation of July 22, 1831, *ibid.*, VI, fol. 216.

58 A. S. Ørsted, "Beholdes Herredømmet over en vestindisk Slave, naar han betræder dansk-europæisk Grund," *Arkiv for Retsvidenskaben og dens Anvendelse*, I (1824), 459–485.

59 *Sankt Thomæ Tidende*, Feb. 9, 1827.

60 *Ibid.*, Mar. 9, 1819.

61 *Dansk Vestindisk Regerings Avis*, May 15, 1806.

62 *Sankt Thomæ Tidende*, Mar. 9, 1833.

63 Green-Pedersen, "Slave Demography," in Eltis and Walvin, eds., *Abolition of the Atlantic Slave Trade*, 245. See also Alexander, *Om den moralske Forpligtelse*, 5–7.

64 Calendar of Records, High Court of Vice Admiralty, Jamaica, 1796, fol. 17, Jamaica Government Archives, Spanish Town. Freedmen sometimes also owned their own vessels. The brothers Jacob and August Dennerey jointly owned a boat in St. Thomas in 1820. See Hall, "1816 Petition," *Boletín de Estudios Latinoamericanos*, No. 29 (1980), 70.

65 General Toldkammer Skrivelse to Dansk Vestindisk Regering, Nov. 23, 1793, and Dansk Cancelli to General Toldkammer, Aug. 8, 1807, enclosure 4, Oct. 29, 1805, Akter Vedkommende Slaveemancipation Frikulørte 1826, 1834, General Toldkammer, Rigsarkiv. For further examples of boat legislation directed at St. Domingue/Haiti see N.A.T. Hall, "Forslag til Ordning af Vestindisk Forfatningsforhold Angaaende Negerne med Mere," Bureau of Libraries, Museums and Archaeological Services–Department of Conservation and Cultural Affairs, Occasional Paper No. 5 (1979), 3, 7, n. 16.

66 Von Scholten's comments on G. W. Alexander's "Anmærkninger til Kongen af Danmark m.h.t. de danske Øer" [n.d.], Akter Vedkommende Slaveemancipation 1834–1847, II, General Toldkammer, Rigsarkiv.

67 The scarcity of white labor was a continuous problem, especially for plantations, forcing von Scholten to pass deficiency legislation in the 1830s. See Hall, "Empire without Dominion," 26.

68 *Royal Gazette*, Supplement, Aug. 8–15, 1788.

69 *Jamaica Courant*, May 17, 1806.

70 *Royal Gaz.*, Dec. 2–9, 1797.

71 Hall, "Empire without Dominion," 18.

72 *Royal Gaz.*, Nov. 7, 1793.

73 The total tonnage of shipping into St. Thomas, 1821–1830, doubled that of the previous decade. There was an annual average of 2,890 vessels with a total tonnage of 177,441. See Westergaard, *Danish West Indies*, 252.

74 Hall, "Slavery in Three West Indian Towns," in Higman, ed., *Trade, Government and Society*, 30.

75 *Sankt Thomæ Tidende*, Apr. 10, 1819.

76 The newspapers of the Leewards, Windwards, Barbados, and elsewhere in the eastern and southern Caribbean can be expected to be good sources for *marronage* from the Danish West Indies. It has not been possible at this writing to consult such sources.

77 Louis Rothe, "Om Populations Forhold i de danske vestindiske Colonier og fornemlig paa St. Croix" [n.p.], Neger Emancipation Efter Reskript af 1847, General Toldkammer, Rigsarkiv.

78 Van Dockum, *Livserindringer*, 74–77.

79 Rothe, "Om Populations Forhold" [n.p.], Neger Emancipation Efter Reskript, General Toldkammer, Rigsarkiv.

80 *Ibid.*

81 The figures for 1840 are derived from Alexander, *Om den moralske Forpligtelse*, 7. Those for 1846 are from Sveistrup, "Bidrag," *National Økonomiske Tidsskrift*, LXXX (1942), 78–79.

82 Rothe did not make any attempt to quantify the effects of *grand marronage* from St. Jan, but he did state that *marronage* to Tortola would have a "conclusive influence upon the structure of [St. Jan's] slave population" ("Om Populations Forhold" [n.p.], Neger Emancipation Efter Reskript, General Toldkammer, Rigsarkiv).

83 Von Scholten to Christian VIII, Jan. 15, 1841, Originale Forestillinger fra Kommissionen angaaende Negernes Stilling, General Toldkammer, Rigsarkiv.

84 Alexander, *Om den moralske Forpligtelse*, 15.

85 *Fædrelandet*, Dec. 15, 22, 1840.
86 Dahlerup, *Mit Livs Begivenheder* (Copenhagen, 1909), II, 270, 289, and "Skizzer fra et kort Besøg paa vore vestindiske Øer i Sommeren 1841," *Nyt Archiv for Sovæsnet*, I (1842), 1.
87 Statistics on the sex distribution of deserters or groups of deserters are not abundant, but the available data do point to a heavy preponderance of males. For example, of the 86 deserters in St. Thomas in 1802 (see above, n. 14), 73 were male and 13 female. The 7 men and 1 woman in the incident in 1819 (see above, n. 75) represent a not dissimilar proportion. The party of 5 in 1840 (see above, n. 84), assuming the two escapees were men, appears to be almost evenly balanced. But that distribution, on the basis of other evidence, can be considered unusual.
88 Søbøtker to Christian VIII, Nov. 11, 1845, no. 3, Copies of Letters Sent to the King, Record Group 55, Box 9, fols. 2–3, Natl. Archs.
89 For letters reporting the incident see Nov. 28, Dec. 13, 1845, Jan. 27, 28, 1846, nos. 4–7, *ibid.*
90 For examples see Gardelin's Placat, Sept. 5, 1733, Udkast og Betænkning . . . No. 4, General Toldkammer, Rigsarkiv; Walterstorff to General Toldkammer, July 20, 1802, Akter Vedkommende Slaveemancipation, Frikulørte, 1826, 1824, *ibid.*; Laurbergs Erindringer, Jan. 12, 1784, Kommissions Forslag, Bind 2, *ibid.*; and von Scholten to Christian VIII, May 14, 1842, Originale Forestillinger fra Kommissionen, *ibid.*; Søbøtker to Christian VIII, Jan. 28, June 12, 1846, nos. 7, 19, Record Group 55, Box 9, Natl. Archs.; and Haagensen, *Beskrivelse*, 35.
91 Von Scholten to Christian VIII, May 14, 1842, Originale Forestillinger fra Kommissionen, General Toldkammer, Rigsarkiv.
92 Søbøtker to Christian VIII, Jan. 28, 1846, no. 7, Record Group 55, Box 9, Natl. Archs.
93 "Species Facti over den paa Eilandet St. Croix Intenderede Neger Rebellion Forfattet efter Ordre af Byfoged Engebret Hesselberg" [n.p.], Udkast og Betænkning . . . No. 3, General Toldkammer, Rigsarkiv.
94 Oldendorp, *Geschichte*, I, 394.
95 For a detailed discussion of opposition liberal and other positions on the emancipation debate in Denmark see Grethe Bentzen, "Debatten om det Dansk-Vestindisk Negerslaveri 1833–1848 med særligt Henblik paa de igennem Tidsskriftpressen og Stænderdebatterne udtrykt Holdninger" (M.A. thesis, Aarhus University, 1976).
96 *Fædrelandet*, Jan. 5, 1841.
97 Henlagte Sager, Vestindisk Journal, No. 141, 1848, General Toldkammer, Rigsarkiv.

4

"NEGROES IN FOREIGN BOTTOMS"

Sailors, Slaves, and Communication

Chapter 2 of *A Common Wind: Currents of
Afro-American Communication in the Era of the
Haitian Revolution*

Julius S. Scott

After planters and merchants forced them off the land in the late 1600s, Caribbean buccaneers took to the sea as pirates. As slavery expanded in the next century, sailing vessels remained a refuge for the disaffected. By the 1790s, residents of the region recognized a close symbolic connection between experience at sea and freedom. In typical fashion, when Tom King, a Kingston slave "well-known in this Town, Spanish-Town, and Port Royal," slipped away in November 1790, his owner warned that King, "having been at sea may attempt to pass for a Free Man."[1]

In the same spirit as King's owner, many slaveholding whites in the eighteenth-century Caribbean commonly observed that "it was a very dangerous thing to let a negro know navigation." Olaudah Equiano, a slave who became a sailor in the 1760s and 1770s and eventually worked his way to freedom, felt that his mobile occupation placed him on a more equal footing with his owner, and he did not hesitate to "tell him my mind."[2] Whites often accused non-plantation and skilled black workers of insolence, but slaves who looked to the sea for either employment or escape posed special problems of control, as did those masterless blacks and browns who arrived in vessels from foreign colonies. Whether runaways like Tom King or sailors like Equiano, many slaves found it in their interest to orient themselves toward the sea and the world beyond the horizon. The movement of ships and seamen not only offered opportunities for developing skills or escaping, but provided the medium of long-distance communication and allowed interested Afro-Americans to follow developments in other parts of the world.

(i)

Deep sea sailors from European vessels made up a highly visible segment of the Caribbean underground, where they formed local connections, kept people abreast of developments overseas, and often ran afoul of local authorities. In the late eighteenth century, these seamen arrived in the colonies in substantial numbers, especially considering local population levels. By the late 1780s, roughly 21,000 British mariners travelled to the West Indian colonies each year. In 1788, Jamaica's trade alone employed close to 500 ships and well over 9,000 seamen. More than twice as many French sailors arrived in Saint-Domingue in 1789, when 710 vessels brought 18,460 mariners to the booming French colony. In a small but growing city like Cap Français, this dockside constituency represented a sizable percentage of the population. By multiplying numbers of ships in the harbor "in normal times" by average crew sizes, Moreau de Saint-Méry estimated that about 2,550 seamen occupied Cap Français at any given time. In a city whose official population was barely above 12,000 in 1788, sailors outnumbered both white and free colored residents.[3]

While the population of arriving seamen saw considerable turnover, individual sailors might remain in the islands for considerable periods of time. Depending upon the time of year, the state of the market, prices, and other factors, ships' masters and supercargoes often required several weeks to put together a full cargo for the return voyage; preparing the vessels for sea compounded these inevitable delays. Disease, one of the many occupational hazards of life before the mast, also lengthened the stay of many seamen. In Jamaica for example, sailors made up 84 percent of the persons—301 of 359—checking into the Island Hospital in Kingston in 1791; the following year, they comprised 78 percent of the hospital's patients.[4] Finally, some of the sailors undoubtedly decided to linger in the colonies rather than subject themselves again to the rigid discipline and absolute authority of ship captains.

The behavior of seamen left to their own devices ashore caused steady complaint among Caribbean officials and presented a social control problem for police authorities throughout the region. Jamaican newspapers decried the "riotous and disorderly" conduct of sailors in Port Royal, Kingston, and the port cities of the north coast, and carried frequent accounts of clashes between transient Jack Tars and local militia units. Kingston's Town Guard, whose primary task consisted of controlling the movements of slaves after dark, routinely turned out to round up groups of rowdy sailors accused of disturbing the peace, whom the guardsmen shepherded to the parish jail or confined aboard royal vessels at anchor in Port Royal.[5] Collective resistance to such displays of authority, however, became a vital part of the ethos of the Anglo-American merchant seaman, as Jamaican authorities knew only too well. When a town magistrate in St. Ann's Bay sentenced one of their number to jail for "harassing" a local resident, "a mob of sailors" collected in front of the guilty official's home, "determined to rescue the prisoner from the constable." The frightened magistrate sounded the alarm, summoning the Light Infantry which finally dispersed the gathering crowd and enabled "a file of men" to escort the prisoner to jail.[6]

Like the many laws designed to regulate the conduct of slaves, legislation directed against British seamen in the West Indies aimed at maintaining their loyalty through a combination of half-hearted "reforms" and rigid restrictions. Legal pressure increased in times of international tension such as the late 1780s and 1790s, when navies expected merchant marines to provide a reserve of able-bodied and experienced seamen to man the warships. A royal proclamation of 1788, for example, prohibited British seamen in the West Indies "from serving foreign Princes and States." In the early 1790s, Jamaica's House of Assembly brought forward measures "for the better order and government of the sea-port towns in this island," one of which promised to prevent "cheats, frauds, and abuses, in paying seamen's wages." With the declaration of war against France in 1793, however, the resistance of merchant sailors to service in the Royal Navy forced the Assembly to adopt another approach. "The Seamen having fled into the Country the moment they discovered by the public Papers ... that War had taken place," the Assembly drafted a tougher bill "to prevent their deserting from the ships or vessels to which they belong, and also to prevent their being harbored or concealed by persons keeping tippling or punch houses, and retailing rum and other spiritous liquors." Three years later, however, exasperated military officers continued to complain that "Crimping Houses and [other] Suspected places" where sailors congregated still protected deserters.[7]

Legislators seldom expressed openly the full range of their motives in putting such legislation into effect, but laws regulating the behavior of seamen undoubtedly aimed at driving a wedge between the mariners from Europe and local blacks and browns and at preventing any mutual sharing of interest or information. Subject to arbitrary punishments (including the lash) and often pressed or tricked into merchant vessels against their will, sailors might have easily found some common cause with local slaves. The language of these statutes usually cited the necessity of maintaining public order after hours. Grenada's "Police Act" of 1789 singled out for stiff penalties male slaves, free coloreds, and sailors who "to the ruin of their own health and morals, and to the evil example and seduction of others" gambled and caroused in the island's gaming houses by night.[8]

Controlling other activities which brought together slaves and sailors from abroad, however, presented greater difficulty. Sailors provided a natural market for the produce grown by slaves in their garden plots— "yams, cocoas, plantains, bananas, fruits, &c."—which they swapped for the salted beef, linens, shoes, or other goods which made up the "private adventures" of the seamen—portions of their ships' cargo which they were allowed to trade on their own account. Irish merchant James Kelly, who inherited a wharf on the north coast of Jamaica early in the nineteenth century, observed with fascination the operation of this system of internal marketing and the interaction which grew up around it. "Sailors and Negroes are ever on the most amicable terms," he remarked, describing a "mutual confidence and familiarity" and "a feeling of independence in their intercourse" which contrasted sharply with the "degradation" blacks suffered in their everyday relationships with local whites.[9] Contact between sailors and West Indian blacks also had enduring cultural consequences. Many popular sea shanties, maritime work songs which travelled with sailors on British ships to all parts of the globe in the nineteenth century, bear striking resemblances to Caribbean slave songs; in fact, considerable evidence exists to show that the very practice of shantying may have its roots in the interaction of sailors and black dockworkers on the shorelines of the West Indian islands. One theory of the origins and development of pidgin and creole languages in the Caribbean region likewise emphasizes contact and borrowing between European sailors and African slaves.[10]

The commerce of Saint-Domingue brought to that colony an extraordinarily diverse group of European sailors. Like their British counterparts in Jamaica, many of these seamen participated actively in the local underground and economy. In 1790, French Minister of the Marine La Luzerne reported that Saint-Domingue teemed with French mariners but also "Majorcans, Minorcans, Italians, Maltese, and other seafarers" laying over "in the course of a longer voyage" or "attracted to Saint-Domingue by the hope of a better lot." By this time, the island's port cities had long experience with accommodating these sailors. One observer in the 1770s counted no less than fifteen hundred *"cabarets"* and "Billiards," small drinking and gambling joints which catered to an unending stream of "twelve thousand Navigators and seafarers" who frequented these establishments and "make them profitable."[11]

Though municipal governments passed ordinances in response to the complaints of colonists about the sailors leading masterless lives in *"cabarets*, in dark gambling houses, or among the slaves," these laws registered little effect. In the Cap, for example, bar owners, slaves, and the authorities alike simply ignored regulations passed in 1780 limiting the number of such establishments and setting down rules for their operation. Bars remained open long after the appointed hour of closing, and owners violated other provisions by exceeding the restrictions on the amount of rum which they could dispense and by refusing to clear slaves from their places of business. A special division of the police force of Cap Français charged with keeping the sailors in line and with finding "all deserted mariners" was similarly ineffective.[12]

As in the British islands, extensive contact between seamen and local slaves and free coloreds occurred in the daylight hours as well as after dark. According to contemporary observers in Cap Français, sailors traditionally set up stands along the wharves on Sundays and holidays to barter and trade with all comers, including slaves. This so-called "white market," almost as old as the city itself, survived despite official opposition because sailors violently resisted several attempts to close it down. Perhaps as a result of interaction with sailors, certain aspects of the language and culture of the slaves of Saint-Domingue suggest an orientation toward the world of the sea. Mingled with French, Spanish, and African components, several "sea terms also found their place" in the island's distinctive *créole* language. In addition, African women in Saint-Domingue sometimes referred to each other as "sailors," a custom which Moreau de Saint-Méry traced back to the old buccaneers who used the term as a way of confirming their solidarity.[13]

The constant yet shifting stream of itinerant seafaring folk provided the masterless underground in the colonies with a crucial transatlantic connection. As developments in Europe began to affect the future of slavery in the colonies, these sailors brought with them reports of great interest to both slaves and their owners. By 1790, British sailors arrived with news that an antislavery movement was gathering momentum in England, while French seamen wearing tricolored cockades had even more exciting stories to tell of political developments in France.

(ii)

As outposts of European empires, each of the American colonies operated, at least in theory, within autarkic commercial schemes designed to keep colonial trade inside the imperial system and to protect this trade from the meddling of outsiders, thereby enhancing the state treasury. But from the beginning, fraud, bribery, smuggling, and other forms of illegal commerce linked the colonies of the European powers in the Caribbean region together despite the numerous official barriers. By the end of the eighteenth century, the British Navigation Acts, the French *exclusif,* and the Spanish *flota* system had gradually given way to modified approaches which precariously balanced the competing interests of free trade and imperial revenue. These concessions to local practice reflect the Caribbean reality of a regional community where geographic proximity was often more important than national boundaries. The easing of commercial restrictions had the effect of increasing intercolonial communication.

Denmark created the first Caribbean "free port" in 1724, opening St. Thomas to the ships of every nation as a place where seafaring folk from all over the region could come together to exchange goods and information without the intrusion of mercantilist regulations. Before 1800 all the colonial powers followed suit and experimented with similar measures to attract the shipping of their rivals and undercut smugglers by taking away part of the incentive for illegal intercolonial trade. The slow movement toward less restricted, if not "free," trade picked up steam after 1763. In 1766, the first of the British Free Port Acts provided French and Spanish ships controlled access to ports in Jamaica and Dominica. The next year the French followed suit, opening Môle Saint-Nicolas to foreign shipping, and they extended these provisions to include Cap Français, Port-au-Prince, and Cayes in 1784. Meanwhile the Spanish crown, following the devastating defeats of the Seven Years' War, began to institute similar reforms along the lines suggested by the Bourbon reformers in France. After first breaking the Sevilla-Cádiz monopoly on trade with the Indies, the new policies allowed Spanish ports in the colonies (with the exception of those belonging to the Captaincy-General of Caracas) to trade directly with one another in 1778.[14]

Even though they exclude the large number of ships which continued to engage in contraband trade after 1780 and record only how many vessels took advantage of these new regulations, official trade figures testify to the extent to which seagoing commerce bound the Caribbean community together. Jamaica's entry into the free port system, devised primarily to attract the trade of the French and Spanish, brought ships from Cuba, from the Spanish and French colonies on Hispaniola, and from as far south as the island of Curaçao and the port of Coro on the coast of Venezuela. These foreign vessels, while never constituting a majority of entering ships, nevertheless represented a significant percentage. In the last quarter of 1787, Jamaican customs agents registered eighty-nine British ships and sixty-four foreign vessels. During the next six months, eighty-six more Spanish vessels and seventy-two French vessels, over fifty of them from Saint-Domingue, called at Kingston alone. In the early 1790s, Jamaican newspapers recorded the daily arrivals of foreign vessels, but were careful to hide specifics in order to protect them from reprisals in their home territories, where such activity might still be considered illegal. Even during the war year of 1793, almost 350 foreign vessels successfully eluded the privateers to land at Jamaica.[15]

The kinds of goods which flowed into the British colonies from this regional trade touched the everyday lives of people throughout the social structure and therefore probably attracted general interest. Jamaica's commercial connection with the Spanish in Cuba brought to the island vitally needed livestock, fresh beef, and specie. Ships arriving from Saint-Domingue, on the other hand, provided foodstuffs for the consumption of slaves and the king's soldiers and sailors. In 1790 and 1791, "frequent supplies" of plantains arrived from Hispaniola to ease the effects of high prices induced by shortages of "that most valuable article of food for Negroes" in the British island. At the same time, military authorities noted that "regular arrivals" of cocoa from Saint-Domingue, which continued even after the slave rebellion in 1791, enriched the breakfasts of the troops and were thought to reduce their rates of mortality and morbidity.[16]

In Saint-Domingue geographic factors, combined with the chronic inability of the French merchant fleet to satisfy the colony's rising demand for all types of commodities, lent both motive and opportunity to merchants and planters to develop extensive contacts with the English,

Spanish, Dutch, and Danish. In lean times, colonists in smaller ports often depended on contacts with foreign territories for their very survival. In the 1770s French colonists were taking matters into their own hands in order to battle shortages of grain and livestock; they outfitted vessels to travel to North America for flour and to Cuba and the Spanish Main for horses and mules. When British cruisers cut off the western and southern ports from French ships during the American Revolution, Jérémie and Cayes relied on ships coming from Dutch Curaçao to ward off impending famine.[17] But these activities involved more than simply emergency measures or wartime expedients. Illicit commerce had always flourished in peacetime and continued after the peace of 1783. For decades, Saint-Domingue vessels took indigo and cotton worth thousands of pounds sterling to Jamaica in clear violation of the letter and spirit of the *exclusif*. Two-thirds of this amount came from the ports lying between Jérémie and Cap Tiburon, just 33 leagues, or half a day's sail, from Jamaica's east coast.[18]

Saint-Domingue's many good harbors attracted foreign shipping as well. In spite of the measures of 1767 and 1784 opening the Môle, the Cap, Port-au-Prince, and Cayes, merchants still pressed local officials to loosen restrictions against foreign shipping even more. Bowing to this mounting pressure by extending free trade regulations to Jacmel and Jérémie in 1789, the French governor-general was quickly dismissed.[19] Foreigners valued the opportunity to trade to Saint-Domingue as much as the French colonists valued the presence of their ships. As the revolutionary era approached, foreign colors flew proudly in Saint-Domingue's ports. In 1788, more than one thousand foreign vessels, the vast majority of them small ships averaging between sixty and seventy-five tons in weight, called at these ports. Of this number, 259 were Spanish traders from all parts of the Americas which exchanged bullion for European manufactures and slaves. The following year 283 Spanish ships came to trade in the French colony. Moreau de Saint-Méry's extraordinarily detailed description of the French colony in 1789 placed 140 vessels at anchor in the harbor of Cap Français when commerce was normal, 60 of which would bear foreign registry.[20] To the west and south, Port-au-Prince and Cayes more closely resembled free ports than colonial cities in the fall of 1790, with vessels registered in the United States, Jamaica, Curaçao, St. Croix, and St. Thomas far outnumbering French vessels. From January to September, customs figures counted 272 foreign arrivals at Port-au-Prince, an average of more than one per day, and 80 even at smaller and more remote Cayes.[21]

Though foreign trade produced clear advantages, the movement of ships in this short-distance trade increased inter-island mobility, and many observers expressed concern about the many strangers who arrived aboard these vessels. Soon after Jamaica opened its first free ports in 1766, for instance, French, Spanish, Dutch, and Portuguese seamen, merchants, and commercial agents began to appear in large numbers in the island's port cities. Residents worried about the loyalty of these strangers. Far from solving the island's problems of provisioning, argued Rose Fuller in 1773, the Free Port Act had only succeeded in lending an air of legality to the annoying presence of "many Foreigners" who had no intention of becoming naturalized British citizens, did nothing to support the government of the island, and therefore represented possible dangers to the island's security.[22]

White Jamaicans registered stronger reactions to the presence of foreigners of color. In 1782, Jamaica's Grand Jury of the Quarter Sessions called attention to the many people of color from Dutch Curaçao, like Jamaica a hub of trade, and other foreign territories living on the island. A "multitude of this description" had settled in Kingston, while "others [roamed] at large." The Grand Jury proposed that the legislature oblige these foreign Negroes to carry tickets to be produced on demand or, better, that "they should have a label round their necks describing who and what they are." In addition, they recommended that captains of foreign ships post a bond promising "to take away such people as they may bring into port."[23] By the 1790s, foreign blacks and browns continued to be fixtures in Jamaican port cities where they attracted the suspicion of municipal authorities. In July 1791, officials in Montego Bay took "Hosa, a Spanish Negro" off a Spanish sloop and placed him in the workhouse as a runaway slave over his protestations that he was free. The following year, "two Spanish mulattos" received one month's hard labor in the Kingston workhouse after a row with a local "free negro."[24] The revolution of slaves in Saint-Domingue would soon provide a major pretext for authorities in both the British and Spanish colonies to take much stronger measures to discourage the immigration of foreign blacks.

(iii)

The regional trade in re-shipped African slaves, a specialized branch of intercolonial Caribbean free trade, allowed ships and people to travel to places where they were otherwise prohibited. Because trading slaves provided a convenient cover for ships engaging in illegal commerce, this trade brought foreign shipping to the otherwise restricted Spanish territories. The British showed the way. From early in the eighteenth century, Jamaica was the center of a thriving network of contraband trade which included a substantial illegal trade in African labor to French and Spanish ports. Moreover, under British control the *asiento* to provide Spanish America with slaves enabled smugglers posing as slave traders to unload a wide variety of illegal goods. Occasionally, free seamen even resorted to passing themselves off as slaves in order to land and barter with the locals.[25] The rising demand for slaves throughout the Caribbean justified the free port system and the general loosening of commercial restrictions which occurred after 1763.

When the end of the American Revolution brought peace to the Caribbean, all the colonial powers once again turned their attention to questions of economic development. Awed with the opulent success of Saint-Domingue, policymakers in other parts of the Caribbean set about making their ports as attractive to ships loaded with cargoes of Africans. In 1789, news concerning these latest commercial loopholes buzzed everywhere. The French in Saint-Domingue were not the only ones devising new schemes for increasing their black labor force.[26] The newly appointed governor of the Dutch entrepôt of St. Eustatius left word in Dominica in May that he brought "orders to fortify, and to open the Port for the importation of negroes in foreign bottoms." News that a Spanish royal decree of 28 February 1789 allowed foreign vessels of less than three hundred tons to land and sell cargoes of slaves at ports in Cuba, Santo Domingo, Puerto Rico, and Caracas sparked even greater interest. In addition to granting foreign vessels opportunities to trade directly with the Spanish, the decree of *comercio libre* allowed Spanish ships to travel to foreign colonies for the purpose of purchasing slaves.[27]

Under these new dispensations, the movement of small vessels either carrying slaves or produce for their purchase was the most active form of intercolonial commerce linking the Greater Antilles in the years immediately prior to and after the outbreak of the revolution in Saint-Domingue, and commercial activity picked up in other Caribbean sub-regions as well. In the Greater Antilles, Jamaica continued to be the major transshipping point for this trade, and the French and later the Spanish depended greatly on the ability of the British to provide slaves for their colonies. In the 1770s, merchants from Saint-Domingue outfitted vessels with rum and molasses and headed for Jamaica, where they traded for slaves over the objections of the island's sugar planters. French agents engaged in putting together black cargoes for the return voyage were already familiar sights in Kingston and other ports.[28] Small Spanish ships operating out of Cuban ports also made hundreds of such voyages. Whereas Havana could receive foreign slavers under the *cédula* of 1789, merchants and planters in cities like Santiago de Cuba relied on locally registered vessels to travel to foreign ports to make slave purchases. Between September 1789 and June 1791, ships from Santiago de Cuba made 157 authorized trips abroad in search of slaves. They visited Saint-Domingue and even called as far away as Curaçao, but nine of ten made their purchases in Jamaica.[29] Along the coast of Caracas, nearby Curaçao served the same function as did Jamaica for its French and Spanish neighbors, though on a considerably smaller scale. Many of the 3,300 African laborers whom traders brought to Caracas in the first two-and-a-half years of *comercio libre* came through the Dutch entrepôt.[30]

Merchants, planters, and government authorities welcomed this free trade in slaves, but with reservations. Despite rules restricting foreign slavers to twenty-four hours in Spanish ports, officials soon reported that this supposed commerce in slaves smacked of the age-old abuses of the *asiento* system. Suspicious vessels arrived with only a few slaves to sell, and even some of these proved to be sailors posing as slaves in order to land contraband goods. Similarly, when small Spanish boats came to Jamaica's north coast to trade livestock for slaves, the British suspected them of engaging in mischief, particularly because their crews frequently included free black or brown sailors.[31] Lingering uneasiness about the kinds of slaves which their competitors offered for sale also tempered French and Spanish enthusiasm for the new methods of obtaining Africans. French planters experimenting with buying slaves from British smugglers in the early 1770s worried that Jamaicans had already bought "all the good Negroes" and that those remaining, while cheaper in price, might very well be unhealthy "rejects" or, worse, "mischievous or corrupt characters" transported for crimes. The voracious appetites of the French planters for more slaves in the 1780s caused some observers to fear that indiscriminate slave buying might make Saint-Domingue a repository for refractory creolized slaves from all over the Caribbean. A French memorialist expressed this sentiment in 1789. Not only was Saint-Domingue's dependence on the neighboring British colony for much of its labor supply unhealthy for the nation's commerce, he argued; furthermore, "the Slaves which our rivals furnish are almost always the refuse of their colonies."[32]

Certainly, many of the English-speaking slaves whose names appear in newspaper notices announcing auctions for captured runaways were plantation dissidents from Jamaica end other places. In March 1789, officials at Petit-Goave announced the sale of a 40-year-old "English" slave claiming to have escaped from a watchmaker in Port-au-Prince. In September, Moïse, another English-speaker recently sold to an owner in Cap Dame-Marie, was apprehended by police in Port-au-Prince. Attracted by the relative anonymity of the capital city, Moïse may also have been attempting to secure a passage to Jamaica. In early December officials auctioned three more English-speaking runaways, Williams and Joseph Phillips in Port-au-Prince, and an intriguing character calling himself "Sans-Peur" ("Without Fear") at Cap Français.[33] Slaves from English-speaking territories were not the only foreign slaves represented in these notices. In addition, they recorded slaves from Curaçao and others who spoke Portuguese and probably came from Brazil.[34]

Experience justified the French planters' concern with the influx of foreign creole slaves. Slaves from other colonies, especially from the British territories, engaged in rebellious activity in Saint-Domingue before 1790, and they played a pivotal role again during the revolutionary years. Plymouth, who led a band of maroons in the 1730s, came to Saint-Domingue from one of the British colonies. Mackandal, leader of another outlying group of rebels in the 1760s, escaped from Jamaica, as did Boukmann, the religious figure credited with organizing the initial revolt which signalled the oncoming revolution in August 1791. And Henry Christophe, a rebel commander who later became independent Haiti's second president, was born on the British island of St. Kitts.

On the Venezuelan coast, Spanish officials registered similar misgivings about some of the slaves introduced through the island of Curaçao. The arrival in September 1790 of a shipment of 31 slaves, nine of whom were said to have been "educated" in the Dutch colony, prompted *intendente* Juan Guillelmi to act to prohibit the creoles from landing. He explained that "it has been observed that creole slaves brought up in foreign colonies are harmful to these provinces."[35] Five years later, a runaway slave from Curaçao led the largest revolt of slaves and free coloreds in Venezuelan history. But even as Guillelmi spoke, portents of revolution in the French colonies had already forced colonial officials to examine anew the issues of black mobility, communication, and sea travel in the Caribbean.

(iv)

If commercial and political networks connected the islands with each other and significantly affected their development, the same web of contact linked the West Indies to British North America. Beginning long before 1776 and continuing into the decades following the independence of the thirteen colonies, ships transported goods and people between the Caribbean and the Atlantic coast of the northern continent. Just as residents of the Caribbean felt the effects of the American Revolution, the black rebellions in the Caribbean at the end of the eighteenth century frightened slaveholders and inspired slaves in the United States as much as in the islands.

In the seventeenth and eighteenth centuries, commerce between the mainland and the Caribbean islands shaped the history of both regions. Beginning in the 1600s, the temperate zone of North America and the tropical areas to the south took separate but complementary paths of development. By the next century, the North Americans supplied flour, dried fish, salted beef, lumber, horses and other livestock, and the dry provisions which allowed the sugar, cotton, and tobacco planters of the islands to specialize in the cultivation of these and other tropical staples. This trade represented such a vital element in the economic structures of both regions that its continuation and control became one of the most contentious issues leading to the rupture of the thirteen colonies with Great Britain. On the eve of the American Revolution, John Adams referred to the precious West India trade as "an essential link in a vast chain, which has made New England what it is, the southern provinces what they are, [and] the West India islands what they are," and predicted that "tearing and rendering" would result inevitably from the British effort to control that trade.[36]

From the perspective of North Americans like Adams, this "essential link" encompassed the non-British Caribbean islands as well as the British possessions. Beginning around 1700, especially close relations built up between the thirteen colonies and Saint-Domingue and the other French West Indies. As North American supply outstripped demand in the British islands, French ports presented valuable outlets for surplus goods while offering Yankee traders cheaper rum and molasses in return. As the British moved after 1763 to close off this flourishing but illicit trade, the French countered by liberalizing trade regulations in order to continue to attract North American vessels. During the American Revolution, these commercial connections proved especially valuable to the rebels, who bought powder and ammunition in French ports which allowed them to sustain the rebellion. After 1783, commerce with the Caribbean and in particular with Saint-Domingue expanded greatly. Trade figures demonstrate vividly the extent of mutual dependence as the post-revolutionary era in North America began to give way to the age of the French Revolution. By 1790, the value of United States trade with Saint-Domingue, a colony of barely more than half a million inhabitants, exceeded that of trade to all the rest of the Americas combined, and was second only to Great Britain's share in the overall foreign trade of the new nation. More than 500 North American ships engaged in the trade with Saint-Domingue, and the French West Indies produced two-thirds of all the coffee and sugar consumed in the United States. For their part, the French islands consumed one-fourth of all flour, three-fourths of all salted beef, sixty percent of the dried fish, eighty percent of the pickled fish, and seventy-three percent of the livestock exported from the American states. North American commercial interests in the Caribbean region continued into the Napoleonic era; between 1790 and 1814, one-third of all United States exports went to the Caribbean and South America.[37]

Social, political, and cultural contacts between north and south naturally resulted from this expanding commercial network. Before the Revolution, blacks were among the thousands of sailors who worked the North America–West Indies trade. Black New Englanders like Massachusetts native Paul Cuffe, who would later acquire his own vessel and become active in the colonization of Sierra Leone, made voyages to the Gulf of Mexico and the West Indies in the 1770s.[38] Caribbean blacks moved in the other direction as well. "I, who always much wished to lose sight of the West Indies," wrote Olaudah Equiano of his experiences and travels as a seaman in the 1760s, "was not a little rejoiced at the thoughts of seeing any other country." During that memorable decade, Equiano made friends in Savannah, witnessed demonstrations over the repeal of the Stamp Act in Charleston, and heard George Whitefield preach in Philadelphia.[39] Occasionally black visitors from the south chose to remain and begin new lives on the continent. In 1762, for instance, a carpenter from Saint-Domingue sued successfully for his and his family's freedom in the New York vice-admiralty court.[40]

In the 1770s, several hundred blacks and mulattos from Saint-Domingue participated directly in the war for North American independence, and they took back with them experiences in fighting for liberty which they may have applied to their later struggles. As a result of a 1778 commercial treaty between the United States and the French West Indies, French forces joined the Americans in military engagements against the British in the West Indies. In 1779, however, French admiral D'Estaing sailed from Saint-Domingue to Savannah with several battalions of black and mulatto troops in an effort to break up the British siege. Though the poorly coordinated attack failed to dislodge the British, observers credited one of these detachments from Saint-Domingue with covering the retreat of the American forces, thereby averting a major defeat. The lasting impact of this engagement on the minds of the black and brown soldiers proved of greater importance than their heroism in 1779. Considering that these troops, numbering at least six hundred and perhaps twice that many, included among their ranks Henry Christophe, André Rigaud, Martial Besse, and other leaders of Saint-Domingue's fight for freedom, a nineteenth-century student of their role at Savannah has argued presuasively that "this legion . . . formed the connecting link between the siege of Savannah and the wide development of republican liberty" in the New World.[41]

The aftermath of the American Revolution brought thousands of black and white loyalists from the mainland to the Caribbean in the early 1780s. This emigration from southern ports in 1782 foreshadowed the exodus from Saint-Domingue after the slave rebellion a decade later. When the British fled Savannah in July 1782, they allocated ample room aboard their vessels for Tory inhabitants and "their effects"—mostly slaves—and large numbers of both slaves and free people ended up in Jamaica. On August 15, an unspecified number of white loyalists landed in Jamaica along with some 1,400 blacks. It is estimated that four hundred white families and perhaps as many as 3,500 additional slaves, making a total near 5,000, reached Jamaica as a result of the evacuation of Savannah alone. Jamaica also received more than half of the 5,327 blacks, both free and enslaved, who left aboard British vessels during the hurried evacuation of Charleston in December 1782. Smaller contingents of black loyalists ended up in the Bahamas and other British islands.[42]

The fates of these highly visible refugees varied as widely as their backgrounds. A 1786 petition to the Jamaica House of Assembly boasted of those Americans in Kingston who were "opulent and industrious [and] practice commerce," but the authors complained in the same breath that many of the new arrivals were "extremely indigent and wholly supported at the expense of the parish." The petitioners urged repeal of a

1783 act exempting the North Americans from paying taxes as a means of driving out these undesirables.[43]

Black North American immigrants to the Caribbean region show a similar, if not quite so stark, diversity. Currents of Afro-North American thought followed the ex-slaves to the islands. For example, even a "successful" free black immigrant like George Liele could prove a troublesome presence in Jamaica. Liele, a Baptist minister, was responsible for introducing the Baptist faith to Jamaica and enlisted hundreds of black converts. Because of his race and his religion, he suffered to an extreme degree the persecution which the planter class directed at all Protestant evangelical believers in the late eighteenth century.[44] By the 1790s, other black immigrants in Jamaica appear in runaway slave notices and in workhouse records. Two North Americans followed different routes to arrive at the Kingston workhouse late in 1791. Solomon Dick, who claimed to be free, was arrested under vagrancy laws, while Daniel had escaped some three years earlier from his owner, a French planter living near Fort Dauphin in Saint-Domingue, and was apparently one of the many English-speaking slaves who escaped from the French colony to Jamaica in the late 1780s and early 1790s.[45]

At the same time, whites in the eastern Caribbean registered various complaints about the presence of North American blacks in that sub-region. When a Nevis merchant reported that slave sailors had appropriated his small sloop late in 1790, he described two members of the crew as "Virginians," including Long Jem, an "arch dog."[46] Another telling illustration comes from September 1791, when a Dominica slaveowner expressed his thanks to a resident of Charleston who had recently returned a runaway slave who was "secreted" in the Carolina capital. If only the British government would reciprocate, he sighed, as there were presently "not less than four hundred slaves, the property of the people of Carolina, brought off at the evacuation," making their home on the British island.[47] Inevitably, some of the black North Americans who had been shipped to the islands against their will desired to return to the less tropical and more familiar environment they had left behind. Young Daniel, "a native of Virginia" was "so much attached to his country," warned his owner after Daniel disappeared, that "he will endeavour to get on board some vessel for America."[48]

(v)

If ships and boats sailing among the island colonies of the Caribbean brought the region together commercially, their movement also aided those seeking to escape the rigorous social control of these slave societies. The prospect of attaining a masterless existence at sea or abroad lured every description of mobile fugitive in the region, from runaway slaves to military deserters to deep sea sailors in the merchant marines of the

European empires. While huge oceangoing vessels and warships continued to symbolize the power of planters and merchants, smaller vessels designed for local use became vehicles for hardy souls willing to brave the elements and the possibility of stiff punishment to seize their opportunity. For all the colonial powers, the mobility of these unauthorized seaborne travellers presented social dilemmas at home as well as diplomatic problems abroad.

Though advocates of free trade tried to undercut the contrabandists and interlopers, they still found ways to elude Spanish *guarda-costas*, British patrol boats, and customs officers to land and sell their goods. Illegal trade continued to thrive among Cuba, Jamaica, and Saint-Domingue in the 1780s in spite of the measures which each power took to stifle this trade. Most of the hard currency which circulated in Saint-Domingue in the years leading up to the revolution, for example, consisted of *pesos fuertes* earned in the illicit trade with Cuba. While Spanish boats from Cuba slipped into Saint-Domingue with fresh meats and bullion, British boats from Jamaica engaged in illegal trade with the Cubans. All kinds of people participated in unlawful commerce. In July 1790, Jamaican officials asked that the Spanish release several British sailors in a Cuban jail for illicit trading.[49] Mariners from outlawed vessels filled the jails in other colonies as well. In 1789, the British demanded the release of a crew of contrabandists taken off the coast of Puerto Rico and held in Caracas. The long exposed coast of the mainland invited scores of illegal traders. After disease and desertion decimated the Spanish fleet anchored at Puerto Cabello in 1793, officials in the capital considered a plan to raise 2,000 sailors by rounding up vagrant seamen and emptying prisons of many of the mariners found guilty of trading illegally. Especially in the western provinces, where free people of color were most numerous, many of these imprisoned sailors were listed as *"de color."*[50]

Deserters from military service often ran to foreign colonies to escape their pursuers. To stem frequent unauthorized travel from Cuba, officials issued licenses in order to control militiamen from taking advantage of their position to leave the island. During the war later in the decade, the crown extended amnesty to deserted soldiers and sailors both in other Spanish possessions and in foreign territories. In like fashion, shipwrecked British sailors fled to Cuba, where they could "call themselves Americans with a view of avoiding the British Service," rather than return to Jamaica.[51]

Finally, runaway slaves were prominent among this varied group which took advantage of commercial interaction to find both work and shelter on the seas or in foreign colonies. The commonplace ease of inter-island travel, slave access to transportation, and intercolonial rivalries combined to make both short- and long-distance, colony-to-colony slave flight possible. Most often, these seaborne runaways sought territories where plantations did not yet dominate the economy or where political considerations lessened the possibility that they would be returned to their original owners. But even a fully developed slave society like Jamaica received its share of runaway slaves from other colonies. When Parliament inquired in 1788 about whether any Jamaican slaves practiced Catholicism, officials cited several black immigrants "who were brought from Guadeloupe" during the Seven Years' War, and "some Runaways from the neighbouring Spanish and French Islands." Jamaican newspapers frequently listed black vagrants in parish workhouses claiming to be residents of other Caribbean islands. In the spring of 1792, for example, William, a Barbadian, languished in the Kingston workhouse while Sam, from Curaçao, was imprisoned in St. Elizabeth parish.[52]

For Jamaican and other British officials, however, slaves leaving the island presented a greater challenge than incoming deserters. From the late seventeenth century through the era of the French Revolution, the Spanish colonies attracted the largest number of maritime refugees from slavery. Even before 1700, runaways fleeing slavery in the British dominions began to arrive in canoes and ask for asylum in Spanish territories. The crown's early decision to protect black fugitives in both Florida and Cuba as refugees from Protestant heresy in search of instruction in Catholicism initiated a policy of welcoming slaves fleeing foreign colonies which lasted, though sometimes shakily, for a century. In the 1730s, the Spanish reconfirmed this policy of extending religious asylum to runaways, and word of the possibility of freedom quickly spread to distant slave communities through slaves working on trading vessels.[53]

In the 1750s, runaways to Spanish colonies created diplomatic stresses in Spain, as other nations began to raise legitimate questions about the religious justification for Spanish policy toward slave fugitives. In 1752, the Dutch demanded the return of runaways who had deserted to Puerto Rico from their colonies on St. Maarten and St. Eustatius, but the French ambassador called attention at the same time to slaves from Guadeloupe, a colony under a Catholic king, who had also found their way to that Spanish island.[54] Five years later, the governor of French Martinique reported that slaves had departed his island for Puerto Rico, and in 1760 the captain-general at Havana discovered a group of "French Negroes," most likely runaways from Saint-Domingue, at large "in the vicinity of the Moro Castle."[55] At the same time, the movement of slaves from the French islands in the eastern Caribbean to Trinidad, part of the captaincy-general of Caracas, gave that island a reputation as a sanctuary similar to Puerto Rico.[56]

The peace following the end of the Seven Years' War threatened to reduce this mobility, because the Bourbon reformers in Spain reassessed Spanish policy regarding slaves and other fugitives from foreign colonies and directed colonial officials to begin returning them. On Hispaniola, tensions between French and Spanish officials eased considerably in 1764 after the Spanish governor allowed a detachment of the *maréchaussée* (mounted militia) from Saint-Domingue to cross the border in pursuit of a band of runaways which had inhabited the mountainous stretches separating the colonies since 1728.[57] In July 1767, Spain and Denmark moved to cut off movement between Puerto Rico and the Danish islands of St. Croix, St. Thomas, and St. John in a treaty calling for the reciprocal return of runaway slaves and other fugitives travelling between Spanish and Danish territories.[58] But such delimitations were piecemeal and always subject to the vagaries of international politics. As Spain and Denmark finalized their agreement, the British argued in vain that a similar arrangement be applied to the many runaways from Jamaica in Cuba and those from the British Virgin Islands in Puerto Rico, where a British frigate arrived in 1770 in a futile effort to reclaim the most recent cohort of black fugitives from St. Kitts.[59] Black desertion from the British islands continued through the era of the American Revolution. By 1790, absentee lobbyists in London termed the losses of British slaves to Trinidad "very considerable," and reported that runaways to Puerto Rico "are supposed now to amount to some Thousands, including their descendents."[60]

(vi)

While seaborne black runaways from the Windward and Leeward Islands headed for Trinidad and Puerto Rico, Cuba's shores beckoned slaves from the islands farther west. On the north coast of Jamaica, black desertion to Spanish Cuba was a well-established custom by the 1790s. The earliest "boat people" leaving Jamaica for Cuba appear in the records in 1699, when twenty slaves arrived by canoe and were granted religious asylum in the Spanish colony. In 1718, the Jamaica Assembly first began to tackle the problem of "Negroes going off the Island to the French or Spanish Colonies" by ordering that such unauthorized emigrants be "tried by Two Justices and Three Freeholders, and suffer such Pains and Punishments (according to the Nature of their Crime) as they shall think fit."[61] Judicial measures of this nature, however, assumed that Jamaica slaveowners would first be able to recover their slaves from the Cubans, an extremely difficult task during this century of unceasing tension between Spain and England. Hundreds of English-speaking slaves travelled to Cuba in the rebellious 1730s, and in 1751, barely a year after the publication of a royal *cédula* reaffirming that Jamaican runaways embracing Catholicism would be protected by the Spanish in Cuba, reports stated that black Jamaicans were escaping to the protection of Catholic priests. Through the 1760s and the 1770s, the Assembly stepped up efforts to stem the tide of out-migration, levelling stiffer punishments upon slave runaways and their free abettors. By 1789, slaves attempting to leave the island could by law receive the death penalty. In addition, free coloreds aiding such escapes risked banishment from the island, and guilty whites suffered prohibitive fines.[62]

After reaching the shores of Cuba some of these runaway slaves found and became a part of whole communities of deserters of many descriptions and nations. An outlaw society near Bayamo, for example, amounted to a multinational guild of traders in illegal goods and all kinds of fugitives. The governor of Santiago de Cuba, capital of the Bayamo district, reported in 1771 that "deserters from the army, escaped convicts, and other fugitives," including runaway slaves, arrived in eastern Cuba in small vessels to take off hides, livestock, and dyewoods for sale in the British and French colonies. Investigating officials found the area's small unguarded harbors "full of ships engaged in illicit trade—French, English, and ours." Six years later, Bayamo's governor voiced concern about these same interlopers. Heavily armed, they resisted the government troops sent out against them, and their numbers were growing. "The refuge of all the troublemakers of the district," these outlying communities of illegal traders "welcomed" deserters from the army and militia and "thieves, vagabonds, foreigners, American-born runaway slaves, and all of those pursued by Justice." Jamaican planters often blamed illicit traders for seducing their slaves to run away to foreign colonies, and the observations of Cuban officials suggest that at least some of the black fugitives to the Spanish island arrived aboard the vessels of renegades engaged in illegal commerce.[63]

The long struggle between north coast planters and runaway slaves continued on the eve of the Haitian Revolution, as Jamaican slaves were still braving the elements in search of freedom in Cuba. In the spring of 1788, Richard Martin of St. Mary's parish reported to the Assembly that eleven of his slaves had absconded in a canoe and had arrived in Cuba aboard a Spanish brigantine which had picked them up *en route*. On a trip to the Spanish island shortly thereafter, Martin to his surprise encountered several other recent runaways from Jamaica boasting their new freedom under the Catholic church in the coastal towns of Trinidad and Puerto del Principe. Havana officials confirmed that Martin's slaves were "at present in this City instructing themselves in the Catholic religion, which was their object in coming here," adding that "the laws of Spain . . . put it beyond the power of this Government to deliver them up."[64] The following April, yet another small group of slaves left St. Ann's Bay for Cuba. A week later, they appeared off the eastern coast of the Spanish island in the company of a local fisherman. In June their owner, John Wilcox McGregor, hired a vessel and travelled to Cuba in pursuit, where he soon found them working in the employ of the governor and "town-major" in Santiago de Cuba. After the runaways claimed freedom under Spanish law, McGregor was "Struck with amazement" when Juan Baptista Vaillant, governor of Santiago de Cuba, blocked his attempts to recover his workers. Surely, he pleaded, Vaillant was not so credulous as to take seriously the "Sham pretences" which his and other Jamaican slaves were using to escape slavery. "Every set of people in

Bondage," McGregor implored, "will use every Artifice and try every Subterfuge, to obtain Emancipation." Equally infuriated with Spanish conduct, Governor Effingham excoriated this "most Jesuitical excuse which their Governors have made these many years." Just months after a remarkably similar incident in which he had a difficult time negotiating the release of British sailors accused of trading in contraband, the governor petitioned the King's ministers to bring diplomatic pressure to bear, as "on the North Side of this Island, some have been I am told Actually Ruin'd by such Losses repeated."[65]

Interestingly, some north coast planters every bit as concerned as McGregor about the desertion of their slaves to the Spanish seemed considerably less anxious to have them back. Blacks who had tasted freedom or had travelled the seas and seen other colonies were likely to attempt another escape. More importantly, hearing returned slaves recount their experiences abroad might tempt fellow workers to elope to Cuba or some other Spanish colony. On one occasion, these considerations led to an incident in which some rather complicated dynamics came into play. After several planters from Trelawny and St. Ann's succeeded in finding and bringing back to Jamaica a group of runaway slaves living in Bayamo, their prisoners agreed to (or were forced to) make public statements about the cruel treatment they had received at the hands of the Spanish. They then threw themselves upon the mercy of their captors and "earnestly supplicated that any other punishment, short of death, might be inflicted upon them rather than go back to Cuba." Apparently satisfied that they had made their point, the planters proceeded to "punish" the deserters by sending them back to Cuba with a warning never to return to Jamaica.[66]

Despite the remonstrances of British planters and officials, royal orders to Spanish governors in the Indies continued to encourage the immigration of runaway slaves from foreign colonies as late as the summer of 1789. In November of that year Jamaica's House of Assembly petitioned London asking that diplomatic pressure be applied in order to keep Spanish officials from "protecting the slaves eloping from this island, and refusing to deliver them up." At the same time, the frenzied search for local solutions intensified. Having discovered "a conspiracy . . . in a much larger number of negroes to desert this island, and take refuge in . . . Cuba," the Assembly attacked the problem in a different fashion, by restricting canoes "to a size not exceeding fourteen feet in length"—still large enough for fishing, but also sufficiently small to make "adventuring" at sea hazardous.[67]

During that eventful spring, however, Spanish policy shifted decisively. In May 1790 the Crown abruptly reversed its position of the previous year and issued new orders to governors in the colonies that they no longer protect foreign fugitives seeking shelter in Spanish territory. By mid-summer word of this change in policy reached the colonies. Soon governors at Cuba refused to accept foreign runaways, and Spanish officials in Trinidad announced that incoming fugitives would be arrested and sold abroad.[68] The British at Jamaica received the news with guarded skepticism, but gave it high public profile nevertheless, knowing that the slaves' network of communication provided the most effective way of informing them of the change in Spanish policy. In the absence of a public statement from the Spanish governors themselves, the Assembly settled for publishing private official correspondence, a move which, reported the governor in March 1791, "has given an alarm at least to our Negroes which has been of some use." Later in the year British officials were confident that, "as the measure appears now to be generally known among the Slaves, it will . . . have the good effect of checking their desertion in future."[69]

Other governments seized this opportunity to bring an end to slaves absconding to the Spanish. In the spring of 1791, the governments of Spain and Holland, "moved by the reiterated complaints of desertion in their colonies in America and desiring to remove the causes for desertion, and to make further complaints of desertion impossible," agreed to a "plan for the mutual return of deserters and fugitives." The Convention of 1791 was designed to cut off the communication between Puerto Rico and St. Eustatius, western Venezuela and Curaçao, and the Orinoco and the Dutch colonies along the Guiana coast.[70]

The intense diplomatic pressure which other European governments were bringing to bear against the Spanish in 1789 and 1790, and the threat of war with the British, clearly influenced the reversal of Spain's century-old practice regarding black fugitives from foreign colonies. But the British accepted too much of the credit. By the middle of 1790, the French Revolution had already begun to shape Spanish policy. Closing the door to slaves from other territories represented a first step in the attempt to guard the colonies against the spread of French revolutionary ideas. The action of Spanish officials in 1790 prefigured the concern which strangers—especially strangers of color—would cause as the Haitian Revolution developed.[71]

(vii)

Seagoing vessels of different sizes and functions sailed back and forth along the coasts of colonies throughout the Americas. The canoes which brought runaway slaves from Jamaica to Cuba had a variety of uses, from fishing to piloting to transport. Other open vessels which the English called "wherries" and "long boats" carried passengers from port to port or ferried freight and fresh water between the merchantmen at anchor and the wharves. Single-masted "shallops" and "droggers," larger decked boats ranging in size from twenty to one hundred tons burden, transported sugar casks, puncheons of rum, and other heavy articles, while smaller "plantain boats" carried cargoes of fresh fruit for local consumption. In the coastal waters of Saint-Domingue, as off Jamaica, small boats of every size and description "swarmed like bees" in the years prior to the revolution, according to one contemporary observer. Because incoming deep water vessels tended to focus on only the major ports, the bustling "interior traffic and navigation" controlled by the smaller boats linked the many coastal cities of the French colony to each other. In Jamaica, where the center of agricultural activity was located at a considerable distance from the seat of government and the island's major deep water port, this coastwise commerce in small vessels not only aided north coast planters in getting their produce to market, but also brought provisions and food to support the population of the towns.[72]

Already saddled with collecting duties and trying to detect the smuggled goods and contraband, customs officials often left the small locally registered boats to accomplish their errands with a minimum of supervision. When officials did move to exercise more control over the coasters, they met with considerable resistance. In 1787, Jamaican customs officers attempted without success to implement a Parliamentary statute which called for registration of every ship of fifteen tons burden or above. Soon owners of plantain boats and piloting vessels complained of interminable delays in moving fruits, wood, and lime into Kingston and Port Royal and petitioned the Assembly to return to the old system of allowing these boats to move freely without having to clear customs. The Assembly's inquiry showed, however, that many owners took advantage of the system. For instance, while the exemption from customs clearance officially applied only to plantain boats of ten tons or smaller, owners of much larger vessels simply registered as plantain boats in order to avoid the customs. Moreover, examinants from the customs cited other reasons besides inconvenience for the resistance of boat owners, having "the strongest reasons to believe that illicit practices are carried on, to a very great degree, in all kinds of small vessels." These practices included trips to foreign colonies for prohibited goods. While the Assembly agreed that irregularities did exist and applauded the efforts of customs officers to detect them, the members could not come up with a feasible set of regulations which would not at the same time damage the efficiency of the system.[73]

All over the Caribbean region, the vital work of coastal commerce involved slaves and free people of color at every level, from loading and unloading to navigation. A French traveller to Havana in 1788 observed that "almost all the commission merchants there were free Negroes," whose responsibilities often included "superintending the loading of cargo for a whole ship."[74] In Jamaica, owners of plantain boats, some of whom were free blacks and browns, customarily hired black crews and captains to operate and navigate them. Other types of coastal vessel also made extensive use of black mariners. Newspaper advertisements made frequent reference to blacks employed as fishermen, as "sailor negroes," or as being "used to the Drogging business;" sometimes these skilled seaborne slaves were offered for sale as part of a package which included the wharves and boats which they worked. Barbados' governor Parry reported in 1786 that "the Numbers of Negro slaves employed in navigating the Trading Vessels in these Seas . . . seem to me to increase so much as to require the attention of the British Legislature, as it throws so many English Seamen out of employment."[75]

On both sides of the Atlantic, service at sea had always sheltered the masterless, from runaway slaves and indentured servants to fugitives from the law. In the insular slave societies of the Caribbean, the mystique of the sea existed to an even stronger degree than elsewhere. Life aboard one of the modest vessels which plied the coasts or engaged in small-scale intercolonial commerce presented an attractive alternative to the life of regimental hierarchy to be found aboard a larger ship or ashore on a standard sugar plantation. While a Jamaican editorialist could lament the "vicissitudes of Fortune" which plummeted one Francis Duchesne "from a life of ease and affluence" to "a wretched existence in the humble character of a foremast-man on board a drogger," considerable evidence suggests that both free blacks and slaves valued the opportunity to go to sea or to work in the coastal trade.[76] Olaudah Equiano, who began a long career at sea aboard a drogger in Montserrat in the 1760s, relished his occupation for several reasons. Working as a sailor enabled him to see other islands, meet new people, and deepen his understanding of regional politics; to "get a little money" by doing some trading on his own account; and, most importantly, to look his owner in the eye and demand respect. Both because of the ever-present opportunities for escape and because he could bid his services to other merchants, Equiano jealously defended his "liberty," resolving that he would desert his master before being "imposed upon as other negroes were."[77]

Like Equiano, other black workers on the shoreline hammered out a semi-independent status which their employers were forced to recognize. When the midday winds blew too strongly for the coastal boats to put to sea, Jamaica wharfinger James Kelly allowed his "wharf Negroes" to "go where they were inclined" with the implicit understanding that he "could, with confidence, count on their attendance" once the winds shifted. Often, however, black maritime workers used their privileged positions to make both individual and collective escape attempts. Caribbean newspapers are replete with accounts of such instances. In August 1790 a "well known" slave sailor in Grenada named William disappeared from the drogger which employed him, as did three slave pilots "all well acquainted" on the southern coast of Jamaica who absconded in a canoe in November 1792.[78] Late in 1790, a crew of slaves aboard the *Nancy*, a small sloop which moved goods among the closely situated islands near St. Kitts, mutinied against their captain and took over the vessel. This crew of four reflected in microcosm a broad segment of the Atlantic world: the leader of the rebellion was a native of the British island of Nevis, and his co-conspirators consisted of a sailor "of the congo nation" and two "Virginians." In a desperate attempt to recover his property, owner Jeremiah Neale recognized the wide range of options available to the black "pirates," and published detailed descriptions of the vessel and its rebellious crew in newspapers from Jamaica to Grenada.[79]

Aware that the proximity of the sea constantly beckoned slave dissidents from the plantations, owners of runaway slaves sternly warned ship captains and sailors that they would be prosecuted for admitting deserted slaves aboard their vessels, warnings which many captains apparently chose to ignore. Slaves with experience at sea were often successful in making escapes from estates and finding new jobs (and shelter) aboard ships. References to runaways as having seen service "on board some type of vessel" were commonplace in newspaper notices for runaways. Early in 1792, Bob, a Jamaica slave who had "been occasionally employed as a fisherman and as a sailor negro," left his owner, who expected that "he will endeavour to get on board some vessel." More than a year later, Bob landed in the workhouse at Black River after being apprehended aboard a shallop whose captain, incidentally, was also black.[80] Even slaves without experience at sea could pick up some key nautical terms or perhaps a verse or two of a popular sea shanty, and pass themselves off as free sailors. Captains looking to put together crews were often not disposed to inquire carefully after their background. Daniel, a young brown man learning the carpenter trade in Kingston, was seen attempting to flee Jamaica "on board his Majesty's Ship the Diana at Port Royal" in November 1791.[81]

As if the desire for freedom were not sufficiently compelling of itself, some slaves had more complex individual motives for seeking passages aboard seagoing vessels. Emy left her employer in St. Andrew parish and travelled to Kingston "in a drogger or a plantain boat" in order to visit her husband in neighboring St. Thomas. Even the religious awakenings of the late eighteenth century encouraged slaves to think about experiencing the wider world represented by ships and boats. Spiritual considerations led Jemmy, a precocious youngster who had "associated at times . . . with some of those description of people called *Methodists*" to try to "get on board some vessel, and thereby effect his escape from the island." Another slave named Adam, like the apostle Peter "a fisherman by trade," was described by his owner as "a great smatterer in religious topics." After embracing the Baptist faith, Adam was "always preaching or praying." Late in 1790, perhaps Adam decided to broaden his ministry and become "a fisher of men:" he boarded a merchantman gathering an outward cargo with the intent to "sail out with her when she is completely loaded."[82]

Like the daring runaway slaves whose exploits quickly became topics of conversation in slave communities, many "sailor Negroes" achieved considerable notoriety. This was partially a function of their mobile jobs; descriptions of sailors and other blacks in maritime professions which appear in runaway notices refer repeatedly to the fact that they were "well known" in the areas in which they worked. In Jamaica, some black sailors earned legendary status, while many others were colorful and familiar local fixtures. Bermuda-born Joe Anderson, "a stout ... sailor negro," successfully eluded his owner by jumping aboard a ship at Port Antonio on the north coast in 1779, despite being shackled with "an iron collar, rivetted, and about 5 or 6 links of chain." For the next fourteen years, Anderson continually managed to evade the grasp of his persistent master, finding work and shelter "all that time on board of vessels." By 1793, though still pursued, Anderson was "well known in Kingston" and continued to ply his trade. The people who frequented the working-class haunts in the west end of Kingston near the harbor, as they recounted the legend of Joe Anderson, must also have known the elder statesman called "Old Blue." This "tall ... long-visaged sailor negro" enjoyed a reputation as long and distinctive as his graying beard. When he was not "skulking about the west of town," Blue worked aboard droggers and plantain boats to make ends meet, or found jobs ashore "at some of the leeward parishes." By night, one could find him spinning stories and hoisting glasses with fellow seamen in local grog shops. Apparently drinking was among Old Blue's favorite pastimes; his owner revealed that the runaway sailor was "not unfrequently intoxicated."[83]

Besides being the refuge for masterless characters and runaways, the coastal trade was a vital source of information about happenings elsewhere in the region. In British Honduras, officials accused the Spanish in neighboring settlements of "enticing away the slaves of British Settlers under a pretence of granting them freedom," and cited one example of an official's aid disguising himself as a Spanish sailor and wandering "among the negro houses very late at night" trying to convince them to desert.[84] But largely through black and brown sailors, Jamaican slaves learned of the possibility of making a successful escape to Cuba. Sometimes they received more direct encouragement. The five runaway slaves whom John McGregor followed to Cuba in June 1789 consisted of a "Compleat Washer Woman," a "Ship and House Carpenter," and "three Sailor Negroes." When McGregor's slaves arrived on the coast of Cuba, they were accompanied by a sixth fugitive, a "French Negro" who had also been working in local vessels off St. Ann's Bay. McGregor was convinced that this foreign-born sailor, with the added appeals of the "low trading Spaniards" from Cuba who frequented Jamaica's north coast, had induced his slaves to desert. McGregor may very well have been correct. Testifying before Spanish officials, the alleged culprit told of having been taken off a French ship during the American Revolution and sold as a slave in Jamaica; he had fled in order to regain his freedom.[85] In 1790, a black dockworker in Kingston revealed that crewmembers of the "Two Brothers" shallop had "asked him to go with them to the Spanish Country where he should have his freedom." Officials identified the three sailors as a "Curracoa brown man," a "Spanish negro" who spoke no English, and "an old negro man named Edinburgh." The following day, the vessel disappeared, and officials surmised that this motley crew of "Foreigners" had "raised upon the captain and carried the vessel to some Foreign Port."[86]

During the 1790s, both before and after the outbreak of the revolution in Saint-Domingue, people involved in all of the various forms of sea-borne activity—sailors from the large deep water vessels and those from the small boats engaged in intercolonial trade; runaway slaves and other deserters; and "sailor Negroes"—assumed center stage. Whether at sea or on land, masterless people played a vital role in spreading rumors, reporting news, and transmitting political currents as antislavery movements and finally a republican revolution gathered momentum in Europe. The strongest evidence of their influence would come later, when officials all over Afro-America moved to suppress this uncontrollable communication of ideas by circumscribing the boundaries of human mobility in the region.

NOTES

1 *Kingston Daily Advertiser*, 4 February 1791.
2 [Olaudah Equiano], *The Life of Olaudal Equiano, or Gustavus Vassa the African, Written by Himself* (London, 1837; reprint ed., New York, 1969), pp. 137, 141.
3 Minutes of the West India Planters and Merchants, London, 19 May 1789, West India Committee Archives (microfilm, 17 reels), M-915, Institute of Commonwealth Studies, London, reel 3 (hereinafter Minutes of WIPM); Robert Charles Dallas, *The History of the Maroons, From their Origin to the Establishment of their Chief Tribe at Sierra Leone* (London, 1803), I, pp. 6–7; William Walton, Jr., *Present State of the Spanish Colonies; including a Particular Report of Hispañola, or the Spanish Part of Santo Domingo*, 2 vols. (London, 1810), I, pp. 298–299; Médéric Louis Elie Moreau de Saint-Méry, *Description topographique, physique, civile, politique et historique de la partie française de l'isle Saint Domingue* (Paris, 1958 [1797]), I, pp. 479–480.
4 "Account of the Sick admitted into the Island Hospital, in Kingston," printed in *Royal Gazette*, 26 January 1793.
5 *Royal Gazette*, 7 July 1792.
6 *Royal Gazette*, 5 May 1792.
7 John Orde to Lord Sydney, 11 May 1788, Colonial Office (hereafter C.O.) 71/14, Public Records Office (hereafter PRO); *Journals of the Assembly of Jamaica*, IX, pp. 93, 115, 336, 345–347; John Ford to Philip Stephens, 14 April 1793, ADM 1/245, PRO; Council to Hyde Parker, 1 July 1797, C. O. 137/98, PRO.
8 Cited in Edward L. Cox, *Free Coloreds in the Slave Societies of St. Kitts and Grenada, 1763–1833* (Knoxville, 1984), pp. 94–95.
9 James Kelly, *Voyage to Jamaica, and Seventeen Years' Residence in that Island: Chiefly Written with a View to Exibit Negro Life and Habits*, 2d ed. (Belfast, 1838), pp. 17, 29–30.

10 Roger D. Abrahams, *Deep the Water, Shallow the Shore: Three Essays on Shantying in the West Indies* (Austin and London, 1974), pp. 3–21; John E. Reinecke, "Trade Jargons and Creole Dialects as Marginal Languages," *Social Forces* 17 (October 1938), pp. 107–118; Loreto Todd, *Pidgins and Creoles* (London and Boston, 1974), pp. 32–33.

11 *Mémoire envoyé le 18 juin 1790, au Comité des Rapports de l'Assemblée Nationale, par M, de la Luzerne* (Paris, 1790), p. 27, in Révolutions de Saint-Domingue Collection, John Carter Brown Library (hereafter RSD); Michel-René Hilliard d'Auberteuil, *Considérations sur l'état présent de la colonie française de Saint-Domingue* (Paris, 1776), II, 42n.

12 Hilliard d'Auberteuil, *Considérations*, II, pp. 55–56; Moreau de Saint-Méry, *Description*, I, pp. 469, 475.

13 Moreau de Saint-Méry, *Description*, I, pp. 57, 81–82, 315–316.

14 Armytage, Frances, *The Free Port System in the British West Indies: A Study in Commercial Policy, 1766–1822* (London, 1953), pp. 54–55; Léon Deschamps, *Les colonies pendant la Révolution, la Constituante et la réforme coloniale* (Paris, 1898), pp. 21–22; *resumen* of the report of the Regente de la Real Audiencia de Santo Domingo on the commerce of Saint-Domingue up to 1788, Santo Domingo, 25 September 1793, Archivo General de Indias (hereafter AGI), Santo Domingo, leg. 1031; John Lynch, *Spanish Colonial Administration, 1782–1810: The Intendant System in the Viceroyalty of Río de la Plata* (London, 1958), pp. 1–24.

15 Armytage, *Free Port System*, pp. 10, 64; Alured Clarke to Lord Sydney, 30 May 1788, C. O. 137/87, PRO; *Royal Gazette*, 31 March 1792; "Number of Ships which have Entered and Cleared, in the Island of Jamaica, during the year 1793," n. d., C. O. 137/91, PRO.

16 Jamaica Assembly, *Report from the Committee of the Honourable House of Assembly, Appointed to Inquire into the State of the Colony, as to Trade, Navigation, and Culture* (St. Jago de la Vega, 1800), pp. 5–6; *Kingston Daily Advertiser*, 3 January 1791; Philip Affleck to Stephens, 14 January 1792, ADM 1/244, PRO.

17 Hilliard d'Auberteuil, *Considérations*, I, p. 279; Maurice Begouën-Démeaux, *Memorial d'une famille du Havre; Stanislas Foäche (1737–1806)* (Paris, 1951), p. 99.

18 Hilliard d'Auberteuil, *Considérations*, I, pp. 281–282; Balcarres to Commander-in-Chief, 31 July 1800, C. O. 137/104, PRO.

19 Clarke to Sydney, 12 July 1789, "Ordonnance concernant la liberté du Commerce pour la Partie du Sud de Saint-Domingue," 9 May 1789, C. O. 137/88, PRO; Affleck to Stephens, 14 September 1789, Admiralty Records (hereafter ADM) 1/244, PRO.

20 Bryan Edwards, *The History, Civil and Commercial of the British Colonies in the West Indies* 4th ed., 3 vols, (London, 1807), III, p. 219; Walton, *Present State of the Spanish Colonies*, I, p. 300; Moreau de Saint-Méry, *Description*, I, pp. 479–480. His figures do not include the numbers of slave ships.

21 *Affiches américaines* (Port-au-Prince), 11 september 1790.

22 [Rose Fuller], *Additional Reflections; Serving as a Supplement to a Paper relative to the Consequences of the Free Port Act on the Island of Jamaica transmitted to the Earl of Dartmouth in 1773* (Jamaica, 1774), n. p., MS 368, National Library of Jamaica, Kingston (hereinafter NLJ).

23 *Kingston Daily Advertiser*, 3 February 1791.

24 *Cornwall Chronicle and Jamaica General Advertiser* (Montego Bay), 2 July 1791, file in AAS; *Royal Gazette*, 17 March 1792.

25 George H. Nelson, "Contraband Trade under the Asiento," *American Historical Review* 51 (October 1945), p. 59.

26 See the copy of Saint-Domingue's "Ordonnance concernant la liberté du Commerce," 9 May 1789, C. O. 137/88, PRO.

27 John Orde to Lord Sydney, 31 May 1789, C. O. 71/15, PRO; James Ferguson King, "Evolution of the Free Slave Trade Principle in Spanish Colonial Administration," *Hispanic American Historical Review* 22 (February 1942), pp. 44, 51; Juan Guillelmi to Antonio Valdés, Caracas, 14 June 1789, AGI, Caracas, leg. 114.

28 Hilliard d'Auberteuil, *Considérations*, I, p. 279; [Fuller], *Additional Reflections*, n. p.

29 Juan Baptista Vaillant to Diego de Gardoqui, Cuba, 22 June 1791, "Estado que manifiesta el Total de Negros bozales introducidos de las Colonias Extrangeras en este Puerto consequente à la R1. Gracia de 28 de febrero de 1789," Santiago de Cuba, 22 June 1791, AGI, Santo Domingo, leg. 1256.

30 Esteban Fernández de León to Gardoqui, Caracas, 6 July 1792, AGI, Caracas, leg. 503.

31 Guillelmi to Pedro de Lerena, Caracas, 25 October 1790, AGI, Caracas, leg. 115; Manuel Gilavert to Luis de las Casas, Batabanó, AGI, Cuba, leg. 1468.

32 "Mme. Lory à M. de la Tranchandière, 20 mars 1773," reprinted in Gabriel Debien, *Plantations et esclaves à Saint-Domingue* (Dakar, 1962), p. 46; *Mémoire sur la commerce de la France et de ses colonies* (Paris, 1789), pp. 60–61, RSD.

33 *Affiches américaines*, 11 mars, 9 septembre, 4 décembre 1790; *Affiches américaines* (Supplément) (Cap Français), 4 décembre 1790.

34 See *Affiches américaines* (Supplément), 13 février, 16 octobre 1790, and Jean Fouchard and Gabriel Debien, "Aspects de l'esclavage aux Antilles françaises: le petit marronage à Saint-Domingue autour du Cap (1790–1791)," *Cahiers des Amériques Latines: Série "Sciences de l'homme"* 3 (Janvier–Juin, 1969): 31–67, p. 57.

35 Quoted in Miguel Acosta Saignes, *La trata de esclavos en Venezuela* (Caracas, 1961), p. 39.

36 Quoted in Charles W. Toth, ed., *The American Revolution in the West Indies* (Port Washington, N.Y. and London, 1975), ix. For the development and differentiation of north and south, see Richard Pares, *Yankees and Creoles; The Trade Between North America and the West Indies before the American Revolution* (Cambridge, 1956), pp. 1–24.

37 Rayford W. Logan, *The Diplomatic Relations of the United States with Haiti, 1776–1891* (Chapel Hill, 1941), pp. 7–31; Ludwell Lee Montague, *Haiti and the United States, 1714–1938* (Durham, 1940), pp. 29–32; John H. Coatsworth, "American Trade with European Colonies in the Caribbean and South America, 1790–1812," *William and Mary Quarterly*, 3d ser., 24 (April 1967), pp. 243, 245–246.

38 Lorenzo Johnston Greene, *The Negro in Colonial New England* (New York, 1942), pp. 114–117, discusses blacks in seagoing trades. For Cuffe see Sheldon H. Harris, *Paul Cuffe: Black America and the African Return* (New York, 1972), pp. 18–19.

39 [Equiano], *Life of Equiano*, pp. 142–155.

40 John Franklin Jameson, ed., *Privateering and Piracy in the Colonial Period: Illustrative Documents* (New York, 1923), p. 586.

41 T. G. Steward, *How the Black St. Domingo Legion Saved the Patriot Army in the Siege of Savannah, 1779* (Washington, 1899), p. 13; Logan, *Diplomatic Relations of the United States with Haiti*, p. 25.

42 Wilbur H. Siebert, *The Legacy of the American Revolution to the British West Indies and Bahamas: A Chapter out of the History of the American Loyalists* (Columbus, 1913), pp. 14–16; James W. St. G. Walker, *The Black Loyalists: The Search for a Promised Land in Nova Scotia and Sierra Leone 1783–1870* (London, 1976), pp. 8–10; Benjamin Quarles, *The Negro in the American Revolution* (Chapel Hill,

1961), pp. 163–167; Lowell J. Ragatz, *The Fall of the Planter Class in the British Caribbean, 1763–1833* (London, 1928), p. 194.

43 Brathwaite, *Establishment of Creole Society*, pp. 89–91.

44 See Carter G. Woodson, *The History of the Negro Church* (Washington, 1921), pp. 42–47.

45 *Royal Gazette*, 29 October 1791.

46 *Gallagher's Weekly Journal Extraordinary* (Dominica), 21 December 1790, copy in C. O. 71/18, PRO.

47 "Extract of a letter from Dominica," *Royal Gazette*, 17 December 1791.

48 *Royal Gazette*, 25 May 1793.

49 *Resumen* of the report of the *regente* of the Audiencia de Santo Domingo, 25 September 1793, AGI, Santo Domingo, leg. 1031; Vaillant to Las Casas and enclosures, Cuba, 22 July 1790, AGI, Cuba, leg. 1434.

50 Guillelmi to Valdés, Caracas, 17 July, 24 August 1789, AGI, Caracas, leg. 114; Gabriel Aristizábal to León, Puerto Cabello, 11 October 1793, León to Gardoqui, Caracas, 11 December 1793, AGI, Caracas, leg. 505.

51 Vaillant to Las Casas, Cuba, 21 June 1791, AGI, Cuba, leg. 1434; Conde de Santa Clara to Ministro de Guerra, La Habana, 7 July 1797, AGI, Cuba, leg. 1526; J. Brice to Las Casas, La Habana, 24 February 1794, AGI, Cuba, leg. 1469.

52 Great Britain, Board of Trade, *Report of the Lords of the Committee of Council appointed for the consideration of all matters relating to trade and foreign plantations*, 6 pts. ([London], 1789), pt. III, Jamaica, n. p. (hereinafter *Privy Council Report* [1789]); *Royal Gazette*, 14 April 1792.

53 Jane Landers, "Spanish Sanctuary: Fugitives in Florida, 1687–1790," *Florida Historical Quarterly* 62 (January 1984), p. 297; John J. TePaske, "The Fugitive Slave: International Rivalry and Spanish Slave Policy, 1687–1764," in Samuel Proctor, ed., *Eighteenth-Century Florida and Its Borderlands* (Gainesville, 1975), pp. 3–4; Orlando Patterson, *The Sociology of Slavery: An Analysis of the Origins, Development and Structure of Negro Slave Society in Jamaica* (London, 1967), p. 263; Peter H. Wood, *Black Majority: Negroes in Colonial South Carolina from 1670 through the Stono Rebellion* (New York, 1974), pp. 306–307.

54 H. H. Wassender to Joseph de Carvajal y Lancaster, Madrid, 13 October 1752, "Expediente sobre unos Negros, que de la Ysla de Guadalupe se pasaron a la de Puerto Rico, y reclama el embasador de Francia," (1752), AGI, Sección de Indiferente General, legajo 2787 (hereinafter AGI, Indiferente General).

55 See the *expediente* regarding fugitives to and from the Danish islands dated 9 May 1768, Madrid, AGI, Indiferente General, leg. 2787.

56 Angel Sanz Tapia, *Los militares emigrados y los prisioneros franceses en Venezuela durante la guerra contra la Revolución: Un aspecto fundamental de la época de la preëmancipación* (Caracas, 1977), pp. 42–43.

57 Gabriel Debien, "Le marronage aux Antilles françaises au XVIIIème siècle," *Caribbean Studies* 6 (October, 1966): 3–41, pp. 5–6.

58 *Expediente*, 10 April 1768, AGI, Indiferente General, leg. 2787.

59 *Expediente*, 9 May 1768, Miguel de Muesas to Julien de Arriaga, Puerto Rico, 15 May 1770, AGI, Indiferente General, leg. 2787.

60 Minutes of WIPM, 6 April 1790, reel 3.

61 Patterson, *Sociology of Slavery*, p. 263; Appendix, Act 66 (1718), reprinted in *Privy Council Report* (1789), pt. III, Jamaica, n. p.

62 Governor Trelawny to Board of Trade, 4 July 1751, C. O. 137/25, PRO; Acts of 1768, 1771, and 1777, reprinted in *Privy Council Report* (1789), pt. III, Jamaica, n. p.; *New Act of Assembly of the Island of Jamaica* (1789), articles LXIV, LXV, LXVI.

63 Juan Antonio Ayanz de Vreta to Pasqual de Cisneros, Cuba, 6 September 1771,

Juan Germin Lleonar to Cisneros, Bayamo, 7 September 1777, AGI, Indiferente General, leg. 2787.

64 *Journals of the Assembly of Jamaica*, VIII, pp. 457, 460; Joseph de Ezpeleta to Alured Clarke, 25 March 1789 (translation), C. O. 137/88, PRO.

65 *Journals of the Assembly of Jamaica*, VIII, pp. 514–515; John Wilcox McGregor to Vaillant, 7 June 1789, Lord Effingham to Grenville, 13 June, 9 October 1790, C. O. 137/88, PRO.

66 Jamaica Assembly, *Further Proceedings of the Honourable House of Assembly of Jamaica, Relative to a Bill Introduced into the House of Commons, for Effectually Preventing the Unlawful Importation of Slaves* (London, 1816), p. 98.

67 *Journals of the Assembly of Jamaica*, VIII, pp. 519, 565–566, 596; Stephen Fuller to Committee of Correspondence (Jamaica), 30 January 1791, "Mr. Stephen Fuller's Account as Agent from the 31st December 1789 to the 31st December 1790," FLB.

68 Antonio Porlier to Pedro de Lerena, Aranjuez, 14 June 1790, AGI, Indiferente General, leg. 2787; Joaquin Garcia to Porlier, Santo Domingo, 25 July 1790, AGI, Santo Domingo, leg. 953; Las Casas to Porlier, La Habana, 7 August 1790, AGI, Cuba, leg. 1490.

69 Effingham to Grenville, 19 March 1791, Henry Dundas to Effingham, 8 August 1791, C. O. 137/89, PRO. If this news did have such an effect, it was short-lived. Jamaican slaves continued to desert to Cuba during the 1790s, and as late as 1798 Spanish officials recognized their claims to freedom. See Isidro Joseph de Limonta to Santa Clara, Cuba, 26 August 1798, AGI, Cuba, leg. 1499–A; Santa Clara to Ministro de Gracia y Justicia, La Habana, 5 October 1798, AGI, Cuba, leg. 1528.

70 "Convención entre el Rey Nuestro Señor y los Estados Generales de las Provincias Unidas, para la reciproca restitución de desertores y fugitivos," 23 June 1791, AGI, Indiferente General, leg. 2787.

71 Chapter Four will examine more closely the resolution of 1790 within the context of the early French Revolution in the Caribbean.

72 *Resumen* of the report of the *regente*, Santo Domingo, 25 September 1793, AGI, Santo Domingo, leg. 1031.

73 *Journals of the Assembly of Jamaica*, VIII, pp. 287–288, 294–301.

74 J. P. Brissot de Warville, *New Travels in the United States of America, 1788*, trans. Mara Soceanu Vamos and Durand Echeverria, ed. Durand Echeverria (Cambridge, 1964), p. 64.

75 *Journals of the Assembly of Jamaica*, VIII, pp. 295, 298. For examples of advertisements, see *Royal Gazette*, 26 May 1787, 28 January 1792, 24 August 1793, and *The Charribbean Register, or Ancient and Original Dominica Gazette* (Roseau, Dominica), 26 March 1791, copy in C. O. 71/20, PRO. Parry is quoted in Ruth Anna Fisher, "Manuscript Materials Bearing on the Negro in British Archives," *Journal of Negro History* 27 (January 1942), p. 88.

76 Jesse Lemisch, "Jack Tar in the Streets: Merchant Seamen in the Politics of Revolutionary America," *William and Mary Quarterly*, 3d ser., 25 (July 1968), pp. 374–377; *Savanna-la-Mar Gazette* (Jamaica), 15 July 1788, file in AAS.

77 [Equiano], *Life of Equiano*, pp. 110, 131, 137, 141–142.

78 Kelly, *Voyage to Jamaica*, pp. 30–31; *St. George's Chronicle and New Grenada Gazette*, 13 August 1790; *Royal Gazette*, 24 November 1792.

79 *Gallagher's Weekly Journal Extraordinary* (Roseau, Dominica), 21 December 1790, copy in C. O. 71/18, PRO; *St. George's Chronicle and New Grenada Gazette*, 17 December 1790; *Kingston Daily Advertiser*, 14 February 1791.

80 *Royal Gazette*, 14 January 1792, 29 September 1792, 20 April 1793.

81 *Royal Gazette*, 12 November 1791. For other examples of slaves who may have

boarded vessels under similar circumstances, see *Royal Gazette*, 21 April 1792, 14 September 1793.

82 *Royal Gazette*, 23 February, 13 April 1793; *Kingston Daily Advertiser*, 7 January 1791.

83 *Royal Gazette*, 24 March 1792, 11 May 1793.

84 Colonel Hunter to Governor of Yucatan, [November 1790], C. O. 123/13, cited in Sir John Alder Burdon, ed., *Archives of British Honduras*, 3 vols. (London, 1931–35), I, 190n.

85 Vaillant to McGregor, 1 September 1790, "Narration of Facts . . . by John Wilcox McGregor of the Island of Jamaica," London, 1 September 1790, C. O. 137/88, PRO; "Testimonio de las Diligencias originales obradas sobre la aprehensión de seis negros . . . que profugaron de uno de los Pueblos de la Colonia Británica," 1789, AGI, Indiferente General, leg. 2787.

86 *Kingston Daily Advertiser*, 1 January 1791.

Part II

ATLANTIC GENERATIONS

Some historians have been able to reconstruct, in remarkable detail, the itineraries and struggles of individuals in the Atlantic world, and used biographies of individuals or of a series of individuals to illuminate the larger context in which they lived. The selections in this section showcase the ways in which individual stories can ground and illuminate our understanding of the shape of the Atlantic world. In some cases these individual or collective biographies help illuminate a particular context, while in others they help us understand the relationship between different generations within a shifting Atlantic context.

Richard Gray's article uses the story of one obscure man, Lourenço da Silva de Mendouça, to call up a largely hidden world of intellectual engagement and activism on the part of people of African descent within the Portuguese empire during the late seventeenth century. Lourenço da Silva, born in Brazil (probably into slavery) appeared in the papal court in the early 1680s to protest against slavery on behalf of an organized community in Lisbon (where he played a leadership role in a black confraternity) and, more broadly, on behalf of those kept in bondage in the Catholic world. He based his protest on a sixteenth-century papal decree outlawing the slavery of indigenous people, whose existence he had carefully noted on a piece of paper that he brought with him to Rome. The piece of paper, notes Gray "illuminates his world," and it illuminates a broader tradition of anti-slavery thought and discussion within the black communities of the Portuguese Atlantic as well (p. 105). As remarkable, perhaps, is the fact that da Silva's petition succeeded in convincing the papacy to condemn Atlantic slavery and to order the royal governments of Spain and Portugal to take steps to end the trade. This command was rejected and ignored, but remains, in Gray's words "among the most notable statements on human rights ever to have been published by the papacy" (p. 101).

Da Silva was one of large group of what Ira Berlin famously dubbed "Atlantic Creoles" in his widely cited 1996 article. In this essay, Berlin presents a group biography of a category of men and women who spoke multiple languages and inhabited multiple cultural worlds, acting as go-betweens between Europeans and Africans and who take advantage of this situation. Their stories help to illuminate the complex forms of circulation and negotiation that took place in the Atlantic world. Berlin's masterful essay examines how Atlantic creoles lived, worked, and sometimes thrived in cities on the African coast, as well as in North American cities like New Amsterdam (later New York) and New Orleans and European ports such as Lisbon. These figures, he argues, allow us to better understand "the slow, painful process whereby Africans became African-Americans" in a process that was never unidirectional, but rather one shaped by "cultural strategies that were manufactured and remanufactured" over time (p. 117). "Black life in North America," Berlin writes, "originated not in Africa or America but in the netherworld between the continents" (p. 118). And Atlantic creoles were particularly important in shaping North American societies, he argues, because these societies were so marginal. "In the seventeenth century," he writes, "few New World societies were more marginal than those of mainland North America" which therefore drew "liminal peoples" (p. 124). These societies, he argues, drawing on earlier work on Roman slavery to make an influential distinction, were "societies with slaves" rather than "slave societies." Their experiences were also very different than those of enslaved Africans who would follow them in the expanding plantation zones of eighteenth-century North America.

For Emily Clark and Virginia Meacham Gould, the biographies of several generations of women from one New Orleans family illuminate the history of what they call "Afro-Catholicism" in the city. Combining the detailed reconstruction of individual lives with a larger analysis of the demography and institutional history of Louisiana, they argue that women played a central role in establishing and defining Catholicism in the city. They describe a "process of religious creolization" that stretches over two centuries, and enabled "thousands of women of African descent in New Orleans" to use their "religious affiliation to transform themselves from nearly powerless objects of coercion into powerful agents" (p. 160). The particular form of Catholicism took in New Orleans, they show, was the result of interlaced Atlantic factors—the particular contours of the slave trade and the African origins of those who arrived there, the presence of Ursuline nuns as the major missionary force in the city, the threat posed to Catholicism by other religions after Louisiana became part of the U.S., and perhaps most importantly the spiritual and social action and choices made by generations of women both within their families and within religious institutions. The article represents both a powerful gendered interpretation of religious history in New Orleans and a potent example of how historians can bring together a series of methods in analyzing long-term historical processes through a detailed social and institutional lens.

THE PAPACY AND THE ATLANTIC SLAVE TRADE

Lourenço da Silva, the Capuchins, and the Decisions of the Holy Office

Richard Gray

Lourenço da Silva de Mendouça[1] was an extraordinary figure to arrive as an envoy at the papal curia in the 1680s. Of Afro-Brazilian origin, he represented no powerful institution, temporal or religious. He came armed with some vague recommendations from Lisbon and Madrid; together with these, a scrap of paper alone contained a hint of his secret purpose. We do not know how he reached Rome, nor how long he stayed there. We know frustratingly little about his previous career, and nothing about his subsequent fortunes. Yet his visit and protests led the highest organs of the church to deliver a judgement on 20 March 1686 which is among the most notable statements on human rights ever to have been published by the papacy.

It has previously been assumed that the Catholic church, as an institution, played no part in challenging European attitudes concerning the Atlantic slave trade. In his erudite and witty survey of this theme, Charles Boxer concludes that the contribution of the papacy to the humanitarian attack on slavery "was precisely nil before the year 1839 — and very little between that date and 1888, when slavery was finally abolished in Brazil", though Boxer does draw attention to "a very few maverick individuals who *did* condemn the African slave trade as being inherently unjustifiable, unchristian and immoral".[2] It is significant that, just as Lourenço's first-hand testimony in Rome was needed to jolt the papacy into action, so these other individual Catholic writers based their condemnation not merely on abstract principles, but on their personal knowledge of the evils arising from the actual operation of the slave trade. Mercado, one of the first moralists to discuss at some length the ethics of this trade, described in detail some of the horrendous crimes being committed on the Guinea coast. He concluded that the slave trade, as practised there, was mortally sinful, since many of the Africans were enslaved by crime and violence.[3] Another prominent critic of the Atlantic slave trade was the Jesuit, Alonso de Sandoval, who suggested extensive reforms based on his long experience with African slaves at Cartagena in South America. These reforms, Boxer concludes, "were so far-reaching that, if implemented, they would in effect have made [the slave trade] quite impracticable and so resulted in its abandonment or abolition".[4] Yet, as a direct result of Lourenço's mission, the Holy Office approved a set of propositions which, had they been implemented, would have had precisely the same effect.

Lourenço da Silva himself claimed royal ancestry. The first petition which he presented to Innocent XI begins with the proud statement that he was of "the royal blood of the kings of Congo and Angola".[5] None of the other scanty evidence definitely confirms this claim; all we know with reasonable certainty is that he was a Mulatto, probably born in Brazil,[6] presumably of slave origins. Yet his claim is not impossible. Even before the battle of Ambuila, which in 1665 destroyed the central power of the kingdom of Kongo, succession to the throne there had often been disputed. It is therefore by no means unlikely that some of the royal contestants had been sold into slavery. Indeed "some eight or more years" before the battle of Ambuila, a Capuchin missionary had been given a young boy of noble birth, whom subsequently he had taken back to Italy.[7]

Lourenço's claim of royal connections, however remote they may have been, is also consistent with the fact that he was a recognized Black leader when he eventually emerged in Portugal. We do not know how or when he reached Lisbon, but on 15 February 1681 an affidavit signed by Gaspar da Costa de Mezquita, an apostolic notary in Lisbon, described how Lourenço was recognized as the "competent procurator of all the Mulattos throughout this kingdom, as in Castile and Brazil, so that he might obtain a papal brief concerning a certain matter for which they are petitioning".[8] Over a year later, on 23 September 1682, "Don Lourenço", then resident at the court of Madrid, was formally appointed procurator of the Confraternity of Our Lady Star of the Negroes. In this office, he was empowered to establish branches of the confraternity "in any city, town or place whatsoever within the kingdoms of his majesty, as also throughout the whole of Christendom in any kingdom or dominion".[9]

In Kongo and Angola, and especially in Brazil and Portugal, lay confraternities or brotherhoods played an important role in the lives of Christians of African origin. Their activities and aspirations were an essential factor leading to Lourenço's mission to Rome. Modelled on the lay confraternities which have been termed "the most characteristic expressions of late medieval Christianity",[10] these Black confraternities served a variety of religious and social purposes. In both Portugal and Brazil, Blacks were able to participate in governing their own confraternities, for the crown saw these associations as a useful means of social control. Their constitutions and privileges were carefully recorded and jealously guarded. Participation in their governing councils conferred social prestige on a few Blacks and Mulattos, and for their members at large the confraternities acted as mutual aid societies. When funds permitted, members were assisted when they were sick or in prison. Membership entailed a wide range of religious obligations, including daily prayers and monthly confession and communion. Their regular activities were focused on their own chapels or, in the case of poorer groups, on the altar that they shared in a parish church or in the chapel of a more prosperous confraternity. At a local, interpersonal level, this formal worship provided a powerful focus for a common identity. Above all, members were assured of the last rites of the church and of a respectable burial, for all confraternities guaranteed the attendance of their members at the funeral of a fellow. Black confraternities were slower to develop in Brazil than in Portugal, but by the second half of the seventeenth century they were becoming significant there, and by the eighteenth century most towns in Brazil had a multiplicity of Black confraternities.[11]

Although the confraternities mainly voiced the concerns and furthered the interests of a small, élite minority, they also provided a model and rallying-point for less fortunate Blacks. By defending specifically Black and Mulatto causes, they proclaimed a measure of dignity, self-respect and hope for Blacks as a whole. As "the only form of communal life legally permitted" to slaves and freed Blacks in colonial Brazil, the confraternities offered a respectable alternative to the revolutionary *quilombos* or settlements formed by runaway slaves. To the Whites, they "represented moderation, authority and stability".[12]

In Africa itself, the confraternities played a significant role in the local response to the Capuchin mission in Kongo and Angola.[13] In Luanda, the Confraternity of Our Lady of the Rosary drew its membership from Blacks and slaves. In 1658, soon after its foundation, its members requested from Rome a formal recognition of its privileges. Their request illustrates how the members of these confraternities appropriated Christian values and applied them to the conditions in which they found themselves. The petitioners in Luanda sought to protect themselves against the pretensions of Whites "since", as they maintained, "in the service of God we must all be equal".[14] Across the Atlantic, in Bahia the Confraternity of Our Lady of the Rosary was at first limited to Blacks of Angolan origin and it became a recognized mouthpiece for Black rights.[15]

In Lisbon people of African descent had belonged to another Confraternity of Our Lady of the Rosary almost two centuries before Lourenço was recognized to be one of the leaders of the Mulattos there. In the sixteenth century the confraternity had flourished. It established branches in at least half a dozen other centres, held elaborate ceremonies and also sought to maintain the rights of free Blacks and of slaves seeking manumission.[16] Its rule and privileges were renewed by João IV in 1646 and were extended by Pedro II in 1688, for people of African descent were still a prominent feature of the Lisbon scene.[17] Almost certainly Lourenço was a leading member of this Lisbon confraternity. In his petition to Innocent XI, he claimed to be "procurator-general of the congregations of the Blacks and Mulattos of Our Lady of the Rosary and of many other institutions".[18] We do not know if he had been or was still in touch with the confraternity in Bahia, but his concerns were remarkably repeated there a few years later when Paschoal Dias, a freed Black, was entrusted by the confraternity in Bahia to undertake a similar journey to Rome to submit a petition on behalf of Christian slaves, representing the "miserable state" in which they found themselves.[19]

The Confraternity of Our Lady Star of the Negroes, of which Lourenço da Silva was appointed procurator in Madrid in 1682, also enjoyed influential connections. It was recognized at the Spanish royal court, and the initiative in Lourenço's appointment was taken by Lorenzo de Re, a Knight of the Order of Christ, Master of the King's Music, a native of Lima then resident in the court of Madrid. Giacinto Rogio Monzon, an apostolic notary and chief notary of the royal chapel, declared that Lorenzo de Re, who was as well known to him as "an elder brother", claimed also to be a member of this confraternity,[20] but we know nothing else about it. Confraternities for Blacks had existed in Spain from the late sixteenth century, the oldest being founded in Cadiz in 1593; and another was started by twenty-four Blacks in Madrid in the middle of the eighteenth century,[21] but in Antonio Rumeu's work on Spanish brotherhoods there is no reference to that of Our Lady Star of the Negroes. Lourenço da Silva's appointment supplied him, however, with an additional, avowed reason for his visit to Rome. He was presenting himself before the pope, the cardinal datary or other curial officials, wrote Monzon, in order to obtain confirmation of the indulgences and other privileges bestowed upon the confraternity.

The affidavits which Lourenço brought with him to Rome from Lisbon and Madrid, therefore, clearly marked him as a respectable and leading representative of these Blacks of the African diaspora. But what was the real quest which took him to Rome? What was "the certain matter" concerning which he was hoping to petition the pope and which "many Mulattos from various parts" had come to discuss with the Lisbon notary, Gaspar da Costa, as he stated with reticence in his affidavit?[22] The only clue we have is a scrap of paper, approximately 12 centimetres by 6.5 centimetres, which is now bound together with these affidavits. Da Costa's affidavit had been folded tightly, apparently to enclose this "secret" document, the outer page of the affidavit (folio 493) being soiled along the folds, presumably as a result of Lourenço's travels in the two years it had taken him to reach Rome from Lisbon. On the little piece of paper, there is a note in Portuguese, written in quite a fair hand: "There is a book by João Bottero [sic] which at page 119 states that Paul IV in 1533 sent a brief so that the Indians in the West Indies should not be slaves".[23]

The date is inaccurate; the pope involved is wrongly identified. In Book III of Part IV of the *Relationi universali* of Giovanni Botero there is a reference to a bull issued by Paul III in favour of the Indians, and Botero goes on to state that in 1543 the emperor ordered that Indians should not be made to work in the mines.[24] But the note treasured by Lourenço is of very great interest. It illuminates his world. It reveals that he came to Rome dominated by one passionate hope, and it proves conclusively that the petition which he presented to Innocent XI, although turned into sophisticated language by a Roman cleric,[25] sprang spontaneously from the overriding concerns of Lourenço and his fellow Blacks. He was in no way a front man for a bunch of humanitarian do-gooders.

It is possible that Lourenço had himself consulted Botero's work. More probably he had been given this information by someone else, perhaps even in the office of the notary in Lisbon. Somewhere in his wanderings and discussions, the fact had emerged that on one occasion, some hundred and fifty years earlier, a papal document had condemned a form of slavery. Armed with this apparently vital precedent, Lourenço had come to Rome to demand justice. The scrap of paper establishes that he, and he alone, initiated in Rome what was to be by far the most significant debate ever held within the curia concerning the iniquities of the Atlantic slave trade. Others in Rome, notably the Capuchins, were to take up and elaborate the charges, but the note and affidavits make it clear that Lourenço and his petition were not initially put forward by any pressure group in Rome itself. The crucial first initiative came from Lourenço, and from the Blacks with whom he had discussed the matter in Lisbon and elsewhere. His petition reveals, therefore, some of the deepest concerns of a harassed yet Christianized slave élite.

The principal thrust of Lourenço's petition was directed against the institution of perpetual slavery, especially when it involved Christians or, as the petition put it, those whom God had created and "with holy baptism had directed towards the enjoyment of eternal glory". He vividly described the cruelties inflicted on slaves, stating that they were punished by being burnt "with sealing-wax, lard, resin, pitch and other materials". (The Portuguese verb *pingar* was, indeed, commonly used to describe a punishment that consisted "of letting drops of hot molten fat or wax fall upon a slave's naked flesh".[26]) As a result of these and other cruelties, similar, Lourenço stated, to those used by the tyrants who persecuted the primitive church, "innumerable souls of these Christian Blacks" were lost. When these people, "overworked and subject to ill-treatment and punishments, see that not only they but also their children, even though they are white, are condemned to remain enslaved, they kill themselves in desperation". All this, Lourenço concluded, was the result of "the diabolic abuse of such slavery". His petition went on to remind the pope that his predecessors had issued various briefs on this matter, but they had been ignored. "In the name of all those oppressed", he requested that "those wretches who are involved in the sale and purchase of these unhappy Christians" should be placed under the severest excommunication, release from which would be reserved to the pope himself. Lourenço thought that by the publication of such a decree and by sending it to the inquisitors and bishops of the whole of Christendom, the pope would "liberate all these Christians, and increase in numbers all the more those who otherwise are being completely annihilated".[27]

Lourenço's petition was thus almost exclusively concerned with the fate of his fellow Christians, but his emphasis on the iniquity of perpetual slavery may have accurately reflected the deepest anguish of all Africans entrapped in the Atlantic slave systems. He did not attempt to question the institution of slavery itself. Indeed many of those African peoples who by the late seventeenth century were exposed to the Atlantic slave trade accepted within their own societies various degrees of servitude. Yet seldom, if ever, was the status of slavery in African societies rigidly perpetuated over the generations. A slave's descendants in Africa could hope eventually to escape from the stigma and disadvantages of their origins. It was precisely the absence of such a hope which was the feature most bitterly criticized by Lourenço, in what must be one of the earliest recorded representations by the victims of the established pattern of Atlantic slavery. Significantly, the institution of perpetual slavery had also been one of the principal aspects of the Atlantic slave trade denounced by one of its first critics, Fernando Oliveira, in his *Arte do guerra do mar* published in 1555. Here Oliveira maintained that there was absolutely no moral justification for the children of African Christian slaves to be brought up as slaves. Lourenço made no reference to this work, but this is hardly surprising since Charles Boxer believes that Oliveira's book was "never quoted by contemporaries ... and obviously it was ignored at Rome ... its enlightened author was clearly a voice crying in the wilderness".[28]

The crucial significance of Lourenço's petition lay, however, not in his own somewhat limited concerns but in its immediate impact on curial officials. His intervention had the effect of raising far wider and more fundamental problems. His first-hand account of the cruelties inflicted on slaves caught the attention of the cardinals assembled at Propaganda Fide, the curial Congregation with responsibility for mission territories, to which Innocent XI had referred Lourenço's petition. Other earlier reports from missionaries to the Congregation had denounced aspects of the slave trade,[29] but it seems as if Lourenço's presence in Rome and his impassioned plea presented at first hand had now suddenly opened the cardinals' eyes to the horrors which were being perpetrated on the outer fringes of their world. Archbishop Edoardo Cibo, the Secretary of Propaganda Fide, in placing the matter before the meeting of its General Congregation of 6 March 1684, made it quite clear that he accepted the facts as stated by Lourenço. Prior to this meeting, he had interrogated two Spaniards and a Portuguese who had been missionaries "in those parts". They confirmed Lourenço's description and added further horrific details of the punishments meted out to recalcitrant slaves. They described how the slaves were savagely whipped, tortured by being greased and grilled "as meat is roasted by our cooks", and "other tyrannies so evil that many of these Negroes suffocate themselves . . . or hurl themselves into the sea to drown when they are free to do so". The missionaries also considered that the purchase of slaves involved Christian merchants in "iniquity and injustice". Often the slaves had been stolen from their mothers and taken by force to the ships, where they were brought by traders to "be sold as cattle". In other cases, the merchants bought them from Christians who went into the bush to hunt them "as game is hunted in Europe", killing those who resisted and keeping the others promiscuously so that "like animals they would be made to breed and produce greater profits".[30]

The focus had thus shifted from the fate of Christian slaves to cover a whole range of injustices committed by Christian traders and masters. The cardinals of the Congregation of Propaganda Fide decided to take immediate action. Later the same day, strongly worded letters were despatched to the nuncios in Madrid and Lisbon which clearly reflect the impact of Lourenço's petition:

> New and urgent appeals on the part of the Negroes of the Indies to his holiness, and by him remitted to this holy Congregation, have caused no little bitterness to his holiness and their eminences on seeing that there still continues in those parts such a detestable abuse as to sell human blood, sometimes even with fraud and violence. This involves a disgraceful offence against Catholic liberty, by condemning to perpetual slavery not only those who are bought and sold, but also the sons and daughters who are born to them, although they have been made Christians.
>
> To this is added an even greater grief on hearing how they are then so cruelly tormented that this results in the loss of innumerable souls, who are rendered desperate by such maltreatment perpetrated by those same Christians who should indeed protect and defend them; and, by the hatred which this conceives, the progress of the missionaries in spreading the holy faith remains impeded.

The nuncios were therefore instructed earnestly to request the rulers of Spain and Portugal to order their officials overseas to prohibit under the severest penalties "such inhumanity as contrary to natural and civil law and much more to the gospel and sacred canons",[31] though, as will be seen, in responding to these instructions the nuncios were severely handicapped.

Perhaps partly because Lourenço claimed a royal Kongolese origin, the attention of Propaganda in this matter was particularly focused on that kingdom, and the discussion of his petition was listed under the heading "Congo". It was precisely in this area that the Capuchins were then undertaking what appeared to be one of their most promising missions, and of all Catholic missions in the seventeenth century those of the Capuchins were most readily open to the supervision and assistance of Propaganda Fide. On the same day that Archbishop Cibo wrote to the nuncios, he wrote also to the "prefect and missionaries of Congo", condemning the cruelty and evil inherent in the slave trade,[32] and in Rome the next move in the debate opened by Lourenço's initiative was in fact taken by the Capuchins.

A year after the meeting at which the cardinals had considered Lourenço's petition, they were again confronted with the issue of the Atlantic slave trade. At their meeting on 12 March 1685 they considered a long, undated memorandum which had been submitted to them by Capuchin missionaries. Like Lourenço's petition, this also is a fascinating document of fundamental importance. It is of startling originality, for it decisively broke away from the limits within which the ethics of the Atlantic slave trade had previously been discussed by the papacy. No longer was the argument concerned with the situation confronting Christians, but with rights arising from a common humanity.

The memorandum was signed by Giambattista Carampelli da Sabbio, who had been procurator-general of the Capuchins since 1678.[33] Some insight into his standing and influence in the papal curia is provided in an unpublished account written by a Capuchin missionary, Giovanni Belotti da Romano, who in May 1680 had arrived in Rome charged with affairs concerning the Congo mission. With the help of Cardinal Alderano Cibo, secretary of state and the distinguished elder brother of Edoardo, secretary of Propaganda, Fra Giambattista had no difficulty in arranging "very quickly" an audience for Fra Giovanni with Innocent XI, who the same evening ordered Edoardo Cibo to give Fra Giovanni "every satisfaction".[34] The following year, Fra Giambattista had defended his order in a celebrated case in the Congregation of Bishops and Regulars, which had the effect of bringing him even closer to Innocent XI, "who admitted him into a close friendship".[35]

It was fortunate that the Capuchins' memorandum was backed by Fra Giambattista's authority and influence, for among its other principal authors were, most probably, two Capuchin missionaries whose standing had recently been placed in doubt. One was a Spaniard, Francisco de Jaca, the other a Frenchman, Epiphane de Moirans. Both had been excommunicated in Havana in 1681 and subsequently arrested for behaviour which had resulted, so reported the local authorities, "in the gravest scandals". They had preached that "the owners of Negro slaves should liberate them and their children and pay them for their labours", and they had refused to give absolution to those who did not promise to do this.[36] Both Capuchins had written defences of their position. Fray Francisco's statement is a vibrant denunciation of the abuses and injustices that he had witnessed; Père Epiphane was a competent canon lawyer and his statement marshals at length the case against the Atlantic slave trade. He quotes from a formidable range of authorities, but he also draws vividly on his own experiences. He had lost no opportunities to collect relevant data, and while he had been in Lisbon, he had discussed the situation in Africa with Capuchins serving in the Congo mission.[37] Transported from Havana to Cadiz, they eventually managed to come to Rome. With the support of Fra Giambattista, Fray Francisco de Jaca presented a petition to Propaganda on behalf of the American Indians, and undoubtedly they had helped to draft the Capuchins' memorandum on Black slavery, which was considered immediately after Fray Francisco's petition at the General Congregation of 12 March 1685.

The strategy of the Capuchins' memorandum was crystal clear. They made no attempt to question the institution of slavery itself, accepted by Aristotle and enshrined in Roman law. Instead they insisted implicitly on the distinction between "just" enslavement, which resulted from the punishment of certain crimes or capture in a "just" war, and other forms of unjust servitude. In the conditions prevailing in Africa and the Americas, this was a vital, if theoretical, distinction. The thrust of their memorandum was directed against the fraudulent and unjust ways in which slaves were obtained in Africa, against traders who made no attempt to ascertain whether slaves had been justly enslaved or not, against the dangers and horrors of the middle passage and against the owners of slaves who held them, together with their children, under inhuman conditions in the Americas. Faced with these evils, the Capuchins requested the cardinals to condemn these abuses specifically listed in eleven propositions. The first three condemned both the enslavement by violence and fraud of innocent "Negroes and other natives", and also their purchase and sale even when they were sold together with those who had justly been deprived of their liberty. The next three made it necessary for anyone purchasing slaves to ascertain beforehand whether the reasons for their servitude were just, for owners to emancipate innocent slaves, and for both owners and traders to pay them compensation. In addition to these drastic limitations to the slave trade as it was practised, the seventh proposition forbade the owners of slaves to endanger, wound or kill them on their private authority.

If implemented, the effect of these propositions would have been even more drastic than the reforms earlier advocated by the Jesuit, Alonso de Sandoval. And it was equally significant that the Capuchins' plea was grounded solely in humanitarian concern or, as they themselves put it, they were motivated only "by Christian charity".[38] Whereas earlier papal documents[39] had merely condemned the sale of Christians, the Capuchins made no distinction between persons on the ground of religion. None of these seven propositions made the slightest distinction between Christian and other slaves, and only the remaining four were concerned with the questions of instructing slaves before and after baptism, of keeping them in concubinage, of manumission and of the sale of slaves to heretics. Taken as a whole, the memorandum was a skilful and radical plea for justice against a massive violation of basic human rights.

The Congregation of Propaganda Fide, although powerful and autonomous in other respects, did not, however, have the authority to decide theological or ethical issues. The eleven propositions submitted by the Capuchins were therefore forwarded the same day to the assessor of the Holy Office with the request that they should be examined and that suitable resolutions should be taken.[40] For over a year, nothing more was heard of the matter. Such a delay was by no means unusual. Indeed Francesco Ingoli, the first secretary of Propaganda Fide, had in vain attempted to wrest this power from the Holy Office, precisely because he had experienced similar problems and delays.[41]

It was at this stage that Lourenço da Silva made a further, decisive intervention. At the General Congregation of Propaganda Fide held on 14 January 1686, a petition was submitted to the cardinals on behalf of "the Blacks and Mulattos born of Christian parents both in Brazil and in the city of Lisbon". The petition was not presented by Lourenço in person, nor did it mention his name. He is, however, referred to by name as being responsible for it in the letters subsequently sent to the nuncios and bishops.[42] This time the petition was focused solely on the fate of these Christians in Brazil and Lisbon, all of them baptized, but held by "White Christians who make contracts to sell them in different places . . . like so many animals". Desperately the petitioners appealed to a common identity based, not on pigment which was insidiously to obliterate other values, but on religion, on "the seal of holy baptism, not being of Jewish race nor pagans, but only following the Catholic faith, like any and every Christian, as is known to all". The petition referred to the argument that Whites were entitled by a papal brief, granted "for a limited and long past time", to conduct "similar Negro peoples into the Catholic faith and to retain them for that time as slaves".[43] But, the petition robustly argued, it was not thereby conceded that these Negroes "nor their children, nor their children's children should remain slaves in perpetuity". Shrewdly the petition mobilized religious and racial prejudice by mentioning that some of these Christian slaves were even purchased and held by "occult Jews". The petition appealed therefore to the papacy to declare that:

> no one who has received the water of holy baptism should remain a slave, and all those who have been born or would be born to Christian parents should remain free, under pain of

excommunication . . . remembering that God sent His own Son to redeem humanity and that He was crucified.[44]

Ignoring the particular concern of this petition with the fate of baptized slaves, Archbishop Cibo nevertheless seized the opportunity to remind the cardinals that in order to prevent "similar illicit contracts" the Capuchins had submitted eleven propositions which had been sent to the Holy Office, but "no one knew what decisions had been taken about them".[45] The cardinals decided to write again to the Holy Office. The Capuchins had drafted their propositions with care, and on 20 March 1686 the Holy Office formally declared its complete agreement with every proposition.[46] No longer was it the case of a lone Jesuit or maverick Capuchins measuring themselves against the slave trade. The highest tribunal of the Roman curia had now promulgated a set of formidable and rigorous condemnations, covering a whole range of abuses. The debate initiated by Lourenço had been brought to a triumphant conclusion. His own somewhat limited concerns had been swept up into a far wider challenge. The doubts and hesitations expressed by the defenders of the status quo had been set aside. The Atlantic slave trade as it was actually operating had been officially condemned in the clearest possible way.

The sequel, however, was almost total anticlimax. Archbishop Cibo quickly sent the resolutions of the Holy Office to the bishops of Angola, Cadiz, Valencia, Seville and Malaga, and also to the nuncios in Spain and Portugal, with orders that these decisions should be enforced by the priests and missionaries in their dioceses.[47] The archbishop did not, however, order the nuncios to request the intervention of the Spanish and Portuguese crowns, as he had done under the initial impact of Lourenço's first petition. Nor was the papal power of excommunication specifically invoked as Lourenço had requested. Perhaps something of the urgency felt so acutely in 1684 under the immediate shock of the horrific disclosures had been lost. The Atlantic slave trade, for all its evils and abuses, was a remote phenomenon only occasionally impinging directly on the consciousness of the authorities in Rome. Even in Propaganda Fide it was but one issue among the many other problems which demanded the immediate attention of the cardinals and their officials.

Moreover the crowns of Spain and Portugal vigorously resisted any diminution of their patronal rights over ecclesiastical affairs. In 1684 when responding to Propaganda's first letter on the subject, the nuncios in both Madrid and Lisbon had underlined the difficulties of any reform and the need to rely on royal officials.[48] Indeed exactly at the same time as Rome was considering the protests of Lourenço and the propositions of the Capuchins, the Council of the Indies in Spain was curtly rebutting the attempted intervention of the nuncio in a complicated case involving a contract with a Dutch slave trader.[49] The Holy Office could define questions of ethics, but the enforcement of its decisions depended on clerics and laity whose immediate ecclesiastical, and ultimate political, loyalties lay elsewhere.

The *patronato* was but one indication of the way in which the church had been moulded by the social and economic structures of Europe and of European expansion overseas. In the seventeenth, as in other centuries, the church was not only the church of the poor and the oppressed, of those whom Lourenço and the Capuchins represented. It was also the church of the privileged and of the conquistadores. This aspect of reality was voiced right at the beginning of this particular debate on the slave trade. Among the documents considered by Propaganda Fide before the General Congregation of 6 March 1684 was an anonymous memorandum headed "Instructions for Mgr Cybo". Reflecting the reactions of an experienced and worldly-wise ecclesiastic, it may well have been the work of Archbishop Cibo's elder and distinguished brother. The second-born son of an aristocratic family whose power had recently increased, Cardinal Alderano Cibo had entered the conclave of 1676 as a *papabile*.[50] A close friend of the man who was in fact elected, he was immediately made secretary of state, a post he held throughout the pontificate of Innocent XI. As we have seen, when Fra Giovanni da Romano visited Rome, Cardinal Cibo showed a keen interest in the work of the Capuchin missionaries. It is therefore very probable that he had seen Lourenço's first petition before it was forwarded to Propaganda, and the tone of the memorandum is one of advice from a superior ecclesiastic, accustomed to corresponding with the nuncios.

These anonymous "Instructions" began by throwing considerable doubts on the facts as presented by Lourenço. Pointing out that a slave cost six hundred or more Spanish dollars, the author maintained that this would normally be sufficient to induce owners to care for slaves "as if they were sons". If, however, "a slave acted in a bestial way against his master, it was necessary to punish him severely in the most forceful manner by scalding him, as with cattle, otherwise he would kill his master as had happened on many occasions". Such treatment, this representative of the voice of the rich maintained, would, however, be an exception rather than the rule. The author agreed that the nuncio in Lisbon could be asked to make representations so that those who stole Blacks in Africa unjustly would be severely punished and excommunicated. Responding to Lourenço's specific request, he also envisaged ways in which the children of baptized slaves could be set at liberty, if the price paid for their fathers was reduced in anticipation of this reform. But he underlined "America's great need for Negroes, whether for cultivating the land or for work in the mines, for no other people could survive that heat and labour", and he warned that any reform would be difficult as the king of Spain received "very large sums from the tolls levied on such sales".[51]

This anonymous memorandum was a cool and realistic evaluation of the forces ranged against Lourenço, the Capuchins and the Holy Office.

Yet, under the impact of Lourenço's protest, the cardinals and secretary of Propaganda Fide had gone far beyond these instructions and had sought to launch a radical attack on the abuses of the slave trade. The document, however, helps to explain why they failed and why the vested interests involved continued to ignore their strictures. Only when Christians came to question the status of slavery itself, as some Quakers were beginning to do during the last quarter of the seventeenth century, would the attack on the slave trade gradually become widespread. The resolutions of the Holy Office were in practice largely ignored; they were not, however, forgotten. On several occasions during the eighteenth century and as late as 1821, Propaganda Fide referred enquirers, and itself appealed, to the principles enunciated in 1686;[52] but this was no consolation for the descendants of those for whom Lourenço and the Capuchins had campaigned.

NOTES

1 This is the form given in the only document in Portuguese which mentions him. Archives of Propaganda Fide, Rome, Scritture riferite nei Congressi, Series Africa, Angola, Congo, etc. (hereafter S.C. Africa), 1, fo. 486, affidavit signed by Gaspar da Costa de Mezquita, Lisbon, 15 Feb. 1681. In the Italian documents, Mendouça is rendered Mendoza.

2 C. R. Boxer, *The Church Militant and Iberian Expansion, 1440–1770* (Baltimore, 1978), pp. 32–6.

3 J. F. Maxwell, *Slavery and the Catholic Church* (Chichester, 1975), pp. 67–8.

4 Boxer, *Church Militant*, p. 35.

5 Archives of Propaganda Fide, Scritture originale riferite nelle Congregazioni generali (hereafter S.O.C.G.), 490, fo. 140, undated petition.

6 S.C. Africa, 1, fo. 487. This Italian version (the original is missing) of an affidavit signed by Giacinto Rogio Monzon, Madrid, 23 Sept. 1682, states that Lourenço was "moreno naturale del Brasile" [a dark-coloured native of Brazil]. The affidavit signed by Gaspar da Costa (fo. 486) states that he was "homem pardo e natural deste Reino de Portugal" [a Mulatto and native of this kingdom of Portugal — which, of course, included Brazil].

7 S.O.C.G., 250, fos. 439–40, Luis de Pistoia to prefect, 18 July 1665.

8 S.C. Africa, 1, fo. 486.

9 *Ibid.*, fo. 487, Monzon's affidavit, 23 Sept. 1682.

10 J. Bossy, *Christianity in the West, 1400–1700* (Oxford, 1985), p. 58.

11 A. J. R. Russell-Wood, "Black and Mulatto Brotherhoods in Colonial Brazil: A Study in Collective Behavior", *Hispanic Amer. Hist. Rev.*, liv (1974), pp. 567–602. See also A. J. R. Russell-Wood, *The Black Man in Slavery and Freedom in Colonial Brazil* (London, 1982).

12 Russell-Wood, "Black and Mulatto Brotherhoods in Colonial Brazil", pp. 597–9.

13 Giovanni Antonio Cavazzi de Montecuccolo, *Istorica descrisione de' tre' regni: Congo, Matamba et Angola* (Bologna, 1687), pp. 342–4, 493. See also R. Gray, "Come vero prencipe catolico: The Capuchins and the Rulers of Soyo in the Late Seventeenth Century", *Africa*, liii (1983), p. 45.

14 S.O.C.G., 250, fo. 248, petition dated 29 June 1658.

15 A. J. R. Russell-Wood, *Fidalgos and Philanthropists: The Santa Casa da Misericordia of Bahia, 1550–1755* (London, 1968), p. 142.

16 A. C. de C. M. Saunders, *A Social History of Black Slaves and Freedmen in Portugal, 1441–1555* (Cambridge, 1982), pp. 150–6.

17 A. Brasio, *Os pretos em Portugal* (Lisbon, 1944), pp. 87–90. When Fra Girolamo Merolla da Sorrento arrived at Lisbon in November 1682 on his way to the Congo, he was befriended by a Black from Kongo who, Merolla claimed, said that he merely wished to repay "the obligation which we Kongolese owe to the Italian Capuchins": Girolamo Merolla da Sorrento, *Breve, e succinta relatione del viaggio nel regno di Congo* (Naples, 1692), p. 16.

18 S.O.C.G., 490, fo. 140, undated petition. Compare also the statement by the Lisbon notary that Lourenço was "procurador bastante de todos os homems pardos" [competent procurator of all the Mulattos]: S.C. Africa, 1, fo. 486.

19 Archives of Propaganda Fide, Scritture riferite nei Congressi, Series America Meridionale, 1, fo. 309, affidavit of Francisco da Foncequa, Bahia, 2 July 1686.

20 S.C. Africa, 1, fo. 487, Monzon's affidavit, 23 Sept. 1682.

21 A. Rumeu de Armas, *Historia de la prevision social en España: cofradias, gremios, hermandades, montepios* (Madrid, 1944), pp. 272–4.

22 S.C. Africa, 1, fo. 486.

23 *Ibid.*, fo. 490.

24 G. Botero, *Relationi universali* (Venice, 1640 edn.), p. 557. This is the only reference in Part IV which could possibly have given rise to Lourenço's note. For a discussion of Paul III's bull *Sublimis Deus* of 2 June 1537, see Maxwell, *Slavery and the Catholic Church*, pp. 68–70.

25 The last six lines of the petition were evidently added by a second hand (S.O.C.G., 490, fo. 140ᵛ) and the wording of the petition suggests the hand of someone practised in curial correspondence.

26 Saunders, *Black Slaves and Freedmen in Portugal*, p. 268.

27 S.O.C.G., 490, fos. 140ʳ⁻ᵛ, undated petition.

28 Boxer, *Church Militant*, p. 33.

29 For example, those which resulted in the letter of Cardinal Barberini of 6 Oct. 1660, referred to by Cavazzi, *Istorica descrizione de' tre' regni*, pp. 690–1.

30 S.O.C.G., 490, fos. 136ᵛ–137ʳ, summary of Archbishop Cibo's statement. See also notes based on his interview with the Spanish and Portuguese missionaries (fos. 138ʳ⁻ᵛ).

31 Archives of Propaganda Fide, Lettere della S. Congregazione (hereafter Lettere), 73, fos. 9ᵛ–10, Cibo to Millini, 6 Mar. 1684; fos. 10ᵛ–11ᵛ, letter in similar terms to nuncio in Lisbon.

32 The actual impact of this letter in Kongo itself was disastrously different from that intended by the cardinals and Archbishop Cibo: see R. Gray, "Fra Girolamo Merolla da Sorrento, the Congregation of Propaganda Fide and the Atlantic Slave Trade", in U. Marazzi (ed.), *La conoscenza dell' Asia e dell'Africa in Italia nei secoli xviii e xix* (Istituto Universitario Orientale, Collana "Matteo Ripa", Naples, 1984), I, ii, pp. 803–11.

33 Born into a prosperous family in the province of Brescia, Fra Giambattista had entered the University of Padua to study law. While a student there, he became aware of a religious vocation and was accepted into the Capuchin novitiate in 1641. He became "one of the most learned members who then adorned the Capuchin order". Valdemiro da Bergamo, *I conventi ed i Cappuccini Bresciani* (Milan, 1891), p. 165.

34 The MS. entitled "Le Giornate Apostoliche ... dal P. F. Giovanni Belotti da Romano" is held in the General Archives of the Capuchins. It is described in T. Filesi and Isidoro de Villapadierna, *La "Missio Antiqua" dei Cappuccini nel Congo (1645–1835)* (Rome, 1978), pp. 222–3. The account of Fra Giovanni's visit to Rome is on fos. 786–811. I am most grateful to Father Isidoro for showing me this account and for innumerable other acts of kindness and guidance.

35 Valdemiro da Bergamo, *Conventi ed i Cappuccini Bresciani*, p. 168.

36 Archives of Propaganda Fide, Acta 53, fos. 112–16, n. 34, 31 May 1683. See also J. M. Lenhart, "Capuchin Champions of Negro Emancipation in Cuba, 1681–1685", *Franciscan Studies*, vi (1946), pp. 195–217.

37 J. T. López Garcia, *Dos defensores de los esclavos negros en el siglo xvii* (Maracaibo and Caracas, 1982), p. 192. This book contains the defences written by the two Capuchins.

38 S.O.C.G., 492, fos. 196[r-v], memorandum submitted by Joannes Baptista a Sabbio.

39 For example, the brief of 7 Oct. 1462: see Maxwell, *Slavery and the Catholic Church*, pp. 51–6.

40 Lettere, 74, fo. 97[v], Cibo to Piazza, 12 Mar. 1685.

41 J. Metzler, "Controversia tra Propaganda e S. Uffizio circa una commissione teologica 1622–1658", *Annales Pont. Universitas Urbanianae* (1968–9), pp. 47–62.

42 Lettere, 75, fos. 20[r-v], Cibo to the bishop of Angola, etc. The letters are undated. Probably they were sent on 26 Mar. 1686, as were the previous letters in this file. The letter immediately following them is dated 26 Apr. 1686. The cardinals in the General Congregation held on 26 Mar. 1686, after the decisions of the Holy Office had been received, considered a further request from "Lorenzo de Silva de Mendoza, a humble petitioner, [who] having come to Rome for important affairs concerning the Blacks, and having consumed what he had in an illness, and on account of his long stay in Rome", humbly requested the cardinals to grant him "some charitable subsidy to enable him to return to his country in the Indies". Sadly one must report that this request was merely noted by the cardinals. S.O.C.G., 495a, fos. 392–393[v].

43 Probably this is a reference to the briefs of Nicholas V of 1452 and 1454: see Maxwell, *Slavery and the Catholic Church*, p. 53.

44 S.O.C.G., 495a, fo. 58. At the head of the undated petition a clerk has written "Seconda reclamazione a N[ro] Sig[e] et alla S[ts] M[re] Chiesa reclamando Giustizia" (second complaint to the holy father and to holy mother church demanding justice).

45 S.O.C.G., 495a, fo. 62, summary of the secretary's statement.

46 The Capuchins' propositions and the reply of the Holy Office are to be found in *Collectanea S. Congregationis de Propaganda Fide seu decreta instructiones rescripta pro apostolicis missionibus*, i (Rome, 1907), item 230. Cardinal J. J. Hamer, O.P., when secretary of the Doctrinal Congregation, informed me by letter dated 16 Dec. 1981 that the Archives of the Congregation (formerly the Holy Office) "do not evidence any minutes or other notes" concerning their decisions of 20 Mar. 1686.

47 Lettere, 75, fos. 20[r-v]. See n. 42 above with regard to the date of these letters.

48 S.O.C.G., 495a, fos. 56–57[v], letters from nuncios to Cardinal Altieri, dated 20 Apr. 1684, 1 May 1684.

49 I. A. Wright, "The Coymans Asiento, 1685–1689", *Bijdragen voor Vaderlandsche Geschiedenis en Oudheidkunde*, vi (1924), pp. 23–62.

50 L. von Pastor, *History of the Popes*, xxxii, English trans. (London, 1940), p. 3.

51 S.O.C.G., 490, fos. 141[r-v], undated memorandum headed "Instructions for Mgr Cybo". Similar arguments in defence of the slave trade were advanced by the Jesuit António Vieira: see Boxer, *Church Militant*, p. 35.

52 T. Filesi, "L'epilogo della 'Missio Antiqua' dei Cappuccini nel regno del Congo (1800–1835)", *Euntes Docete*, xxiii (1970), pp. 434–5. See also G. Saccardo, "La schiavitu e i Cappuccini", *L'Italia Francescana*, liii (1978), pp. 75–113, reprinted in G. Saccardo, *Congo e Angola con la storia dell' antica missione dei Cappuccini*, 3 vols. (Venice, 1983), iii, pp. 263–305.

6

FROM CREOLE TO AFRICAN

Atlantic Creoles and the Origins of African-American Society in Mainland North America

Ira Berlin

In 1727, Robert "King" Carter, the richest planter in Virginia, purchased a handful of African slaves from a trader who had been cruising the Chesapeake. The transaction was a familiar one to the great planter, for Carter owned hundreds of slaves and had inspected many such human cargoes, choosing the most promising from among the weary, frightened men and women who had survived the transatlantic crossing. Writing to his overseer from his plantation on the Rappahannock River, Carter explained the process by which he initiated Africans into their American captivity. "I name'd them here & by their names we can always know what sizes they are of & I am sure we repeated them so often to them that every one knew their name & would readily answer to them." Carter then forwarded his slaves to a satellite plantation or quarter, where his overseer repeated the process, taking "care that the negros both men & women I sent . . . always go by the names we gave them." In the months that followed, the drill continued, with Carter again joining in the process of stripping newly arrived Africans of the signature of their identity.[1]

Renaming marked Carter's initial endeavor to master his new slaves by separating them from their African inheritance. For the most part, he designated them by common English diminutives—Tom, Jamey, Moll, Nan—as if to consign them to a permanent childhood. But he tagged some with names more akin to barnyard animals—Jumper, for example—as if to represent their distance from humanity, and he gave a few the names of some ancient deity or great personage like Hercules or Cato as a kind of cosmic jest: the most insignificant with the greatest of names. None of his slaves received surnames, marks of lineage that Carter sought to obliterate and of adulthood that he would not admit.[2]

The loss of their names was only the first of the numerous indignities Africans suffered at the hands of planters in the Chesapeake. Since many of the skills Africans carried across the Atlantic had no value to their new owners, planters disparaged them, and since the Africans' "harsh jargons" rattled discordantly in the planters' ears, they ridiculed them. Condemning new arrivals for the "gross bestiality and rudeness of their manners, the variety and strangeness of their languages, and the weakness and shallowness of their minds," planters put them to work at the most repetitive and backbreaking tasks, often on the most primitive, frontier plantations. They made but scant attempt to see that slaves had adequate food, clothing, or shelter, because the open slave trade made slaves cheap and the new disease environment inflated their mortality rate, no matter how well they were tended. Residing in sex-segregated barracks, African slaves lived a lonely existence, without families or ties of kin, isolated from the mainstream of Chesapeake life.[3]

So began the slow, painful process whereby Africans became African-Americans. In time, people of African descent recovered their balance, mastered the circumstances of their captivity, and confronted their owners on more favorable terms. Indeed, resistance to the new regime began at its inception, as slaves clandestinely maintained their African names even as they answered their owner's call.[4] The transition of Africans to African-Americans or creoles[5]—which is partially glimpsed in the records of Carter's estate—would be repeated thousands of times, as African slavers did the rough business of transporting Africa to America. While the transition was different on the banks of the Hudson, Cooper, St. Johns, and Mississippi rivers than on the Rappahannock, the scenario by which "outlandish" Africans progressed from "New Negroes" to assimilated African-Americans has come to frame the history of black people in colonial North America.[6]

Important as that story is to the development of black people in the plantation era, it embraces only a portion of the history of black life in colonial North America, and that imperfectly. The assimilationist scenario assumes that "African" and "creole" were way stations of generational change rather than cultural strategies that were manufactured and remanufactured and that the vectors of change moved in only one direction—often along a single track with Africans inexorably becoming creoles. Its emphasis on the emergence of the creole—a self-sustaining, indigenous population—omits entirely an essential element of the story: the charter generations, whose experience, knowledge, and attitude were more akin to that of confident, sophisticated natives than of vulnerable newcomers.[7] Such men and women, who may be termed "Atlantic creoles"[8] from their broad experience in the Atlantic world, flourished prior to the triumph of plantation production on the mainland—the tobacco revolution in the Chesapeake in the last third of the seventeenth century, the rice revolution in the Carolina lowcountry in the first decades of the eighteenth century, the incorporation of the northern colonies into the Atlantic system during the eighteenth century, and finally the sugar revolution in the lower Mississippi Valley in the first decade of the nineteenth century. Never having to face the cultural imposition of the likes of Robert "King" Carter, black America's charter generations took a different path—despite the presence of slavery and the vilification of slave masters and their apologists. The Atlantic creole's unique experience reveals some of the processes by which race was constructed and reconstructed in early America.

Black life in mainland North America originated not in Africa or America but in the netherworld between the continents. Along the periphery of the Atlantic—first in Africa, then in Europe, and finally in the Americas—African-American society was a product of the momentous meeting of Africans and Europeans and of their equally fateful encounter with the peoples of the Americas. Although the countenances of these new people of the Atlantic—Atlantic creoles—might bear the features of Africa, Europe, or the Americas in whole or in part, their beginnings, strictly speaking, were in none of those places. Instead, by their experiences and sometimes by their persons, they had become part of the three worlds that came together along the Atlantic littoral. Familiar with the commerce of the Atlantic, fluent in its new languages, and intimate with its trade and cultures, they were cosmopolitan in the fullest sense.

Atlantic creoles originated in the historic meeting of Europeans and Africans on the west coast of Africa. Many served as intermediaries, employing their linguistic skills and their familiarity with the Atlantic's diverse commercial practices, cultural conventions, and diplomatic etiquette to mediate between African merchants and European sea captains. In so doing, some Atlantic creoles identified with their ancestral homeland (or a portion of it)—be it African, European, or American—and served as its representatives in negotiations with others. Other Atlantic creoles had been won over by the power and largesse of one party or another, so that Africans entered the employ of European trading companies and Europeans traded with African potentates. Yet others played fast and loose with their diverse heritage, employing whichever identity paid best. Whatever strategy they adopted, Atlantic creoles began the process of integrating the icons and ideologies of the Atlantic world into a new way of life.[9]

The emergence of Atlantic creoles was but a tiny outcropping in the massive social upheaval that accompanied the joining of the peoples of the two hemispheres. But it represented the small beginnings that initiated this monumental transformation, as the new people of the Atlantic made their presence felt. Some traveled widely as blue-water sailors, supercargoes, shipboard servants, and interpreters—the last particularly important because Europeans showed little interest in mastering the languages of Africa. Others were carried—sometimes as hostages—to foreign places as exotic trophies to be displayed before curious publics, eager for firsthand knowledge of the lands beyond the sea. Traveling in more dignified style, Atlantic creoles were also sent to distant lands with commissions to master the ways of newly discovered "others" and to learn the secrets of their wealth and knowledge. A few entered as honored guests, took their places in royal courts as esteemed councilors, and married into the best families.[10]

Atlantic creoles first appeared at the trading *feitorias* or factories that European expansionists established along the coast of Africa in the fifteenth century. Finding trade more lucrative than pillage, the Portuguese crown began sending agents to oversee its interests in Africa. These official representatives were succeeded by private entrepreneurs or *lançados*, who established themselves with the aid of African potentates, sometimes in competition with the crown's emissaries. European nations soon joined in the action, and coastal factories became sites of commercial rendezvous for all manner of transatlantic traders. What was true of the Portuguese enclaves (Axim and Elmina) held for those later established or seized by the Dutch (Fort Nassau and Elmina), Danes (Fredriksborg and Christiansborg), Swedes (Karlsborg and Cape Apolina), Brandenburgers (Pokoso), French (St. Louis and Gorée), and English (Fort Kormantse and Cape Coast).[11]

The transformation of the fishing villages along the Gold Coast during the sixteenth and seventeenth centuries suggests something of the change wrought by the European traders. Between 1550 and 1618, Mouri (where the Dutch constructed Fort Nassau in 1612) grew from a village of 200 people to 1,500 and to an estimated 5,000–6,000 at the end of the eighteenth century. In 1555, Cape Coast counted only twenty houses; by 1680, it had 500 or more. Axim, with 500 inhabitants in 1631, expanded to between 2,000 and 3,000 by 1690.[12] Small but growing numbers of Europeans augmented the African fishermen, craftsmen, village-based peasants, and laborers who made up the population of these villages. Although mortality and transiency rates in these enclaves were extraordinarily high, even by the standards of early modern ports, permanent European settlements developed from a mobile body of the corporate employees (from governors to surgeons to clerks), merchants and factors, stateless sailors, skilled craftsmen, occasional missionaries, and sundry transcontinental drifters.[13]

Established in 1482 by the Portuguese and captured by the Dutch in 1637, Elmina was one of the earliest factories and an exemplar for those that followed. A meeting place for African and European commercial ambitions, Elmina—the Castle São Jorge da Mina and the town that surrounded it—became headquarters for Portuguese and later Dutch mercantile activities on the Gold Coast and, with a population of 15,000 to 20,000 in 1682, the largest of some two dozen European outposts in the region.[14]

The peoples of the enclaves—both long-term residents and wayfarers—soon joined together genetically as well as geographically. European men took African women as wives and mistresses, and, before long, the off-spring of these unions helped people the enclave. Elmina sprouted a substantial cadre of Euro-Africans (most of them Luso-Africans)—men and women of African birth but shared African and European parentage, whose combination of swarthy skin, European dress and deportment, knowledge of local customs, and multilingualism gave them inside under-standing of both African and European ways while denying them full acceptance in either culture. By the eighteenth century, they numbered several hundred in Elmina. Farther south along the coast of Central Africa, they may have been even more numerous.[15]

People of mixed ancestry and tawny complexion composed but a small fraction of the population of the coastal factories, yet few observers failed to note their existence—which suggests something of the disproportion-ate significance of their presence. Africans and Europeans alike sneered at the creoles' mixed lineage (or lack of lineage) and condemned them as knaves, charlatans, and shameless self-promoters. When they adopted African ways, wore African dress and amulets, and underwent ritual cir-cumcision and scarification, Europeans declared them outcasts (*tangomãos*, renegades, to the Portuguese). When they adopted European ways, wore European clothing and crucifixes, employed European names or titles, and comported themselves in the manner of "white men," Africans denied them the right to hold land, marry, and inherit property. Yet, although *tangomãos* faced reproach and proscription, all parties conceded that they were shrewd traders, attested to their mastery of the fine points of intercultural negotiations, and found advantage in dealing with them. Despite their defamers, some rose to positions of wealth and power, compensating for their lack of lineage with knowledge, skill, and entre-preneurial derring-do.[16]

Not all *tangomãos* were of mixed ancestry, and not all people of mixed ancestry were *tangomãos*. Color was only one marker of this culture-in-the-making, and generally the least significant.[17] From common experience, conventions of personal behavior, and cultural sensibilities compounded by shared ostracism and mercantile aspirations, Atlantic creoles acquired interests of their own, apart from their European and African antecedents. Of necessity, Atlantic creoles spoke a variety of African and European languages, weighted strongly toward Portuguese. From the seeming babble emerged a pidgin that enabled Atlantic creoles to communicate widely. In time, their pidgin evolved into creole, borrowing its vocabulary from all parties and creating a grammar unique unto itself. Derisively called *"fala de Guine"* or *"fala de negros"*—"Guinea speech" or "Negro Speech"—by the Portuguese and "black Portuguese" by others, this creole language became the lingua franca of the Atlantic.[18]

Although jaded observers condemned the culture of the enclaves as nothing more than "whoring, drinking, gambling, swearing, fighting, and shouting," Atlantic creoles attended church (usually Catholic), married according to the sacraments, raised children conversant with European norms, and drew a livelihood from their knowledge of the Atlantic commercial economy. In short, they created societies of their own, *of* but not always *in*, the societies of the Africans who dominated the interior trade and the Europeans who controlled the Atlantic trade.

Operating under European protection, always at African sufferance, the enclaves developed governments with a politics as diverse and complicated as the peoples who populated them and a credit system that drew on the commercial centers of both Europe and Africa. Although the trading castles remained under the control of European metropoles, the towns around them often developed independent political lives—separate from both African and European domination. Meanwhile, their presence created political havoc, enabling new men and women of commerce to gain prominence and threatening older, often hereditary elites. Intermarriage with established peoples allowed creoles to construct lineages that gained them full membership in local elites, something that creoles eagerly embraced. The resultant political turmoil promoted state formation along with new class relations and ideologies.[19]

New religious forms emerged and then disappeared in much the same manner, as Europeans and Africans brought to the enclaves not only their commercial and political aspirations but all the trappings of their cultures as well. Priests and ministers sent to tend European souls made African converts, some of whom saw Christianity as both a way to ingratiate themselves with their trading partners and a new truth. Missionaries sped the process of christianization and occasionally scored striking successes. At the beginning of the sixteenth century, the royal house of Kongo converted to Christianity. Catholicism, in various syncretic forms, infiltrated the posts along the Angolan coast and spread northward. Islam filtered in from the north. Whatever the sources of the new religions, most converts saw little cause to surrender their own deities. They incorporated Christianity and Islam to serve their own needs and gave Jesus and Mohammed a place in their spiritual pantheon. New religious practices, polities, and theologies emerged from the mixing of Christianity, Islam, polytheism, and animism. Similar syncretic formations influenced the agricultural practices, architectural forms, and sartorial styles as well as the cuisine, music, art, and technology of the enclaves.[20] Like the stone fortifications, these cultural innovations announced the presence of something new to those arriving on the coast, whether they came by caravan from the African interior or sailed by caravel from the Atlantic.

Outside the European fortifications, settlements—the town of Elmina as opposed to Castle São Jorge da Mina, for example—expanded to provision and refresh the European-controlled castles and the caravels and carracks that frequented the coast. In time, they developed economies of their own, with multifarious systems of social stratification and occupational differentiation. Residents included canoemen who ferried goods between ships and shore; longshoremen and warehousemen who unloaded and stored merchandise; porters, messengers, guides, inter-preters, factors, and brokers or *make-laers* (to the Dutch) who facilitated trade; inn keepers who housed country traders; skilled workers of all sorts; and a host of peddlers, hawkers, and petty traders. Others chopped wood, drew water, prepared food, or supplied sex to the lonely men who visited these isolated places. African notables occasionally established residence, bringing with them the trappings of wealth and power: wives, clients, pawns, slaves, and other dependents. In some places, small manufactories grew up, like the salt pans, boatyards, and foundries on the outskirts of Elmina, to supply the town and service the Atlantic trade. In addition, many people lived outside the laws; the rough nature and transient population of these crossroads of trade encouraged roguery and brigandage.[21]

Village populations swelled into the thousands. In 1669, about the time the English were ousting the Dutch from the village of New Amsterdam, population 1,500, a visitor to Elmina noted that it contained some 8,000 residents. During most of the eighteenth century, Elmina's population was between 12,000 and 16,000, larger than Charleston, South Carolina—mainland North America's greatest slave port at the time of the American Revolution.[22]

The business of the creole communities was trade, brokering the movement of goods through the Atlantic world. Although island settle-ments such as Cape Verde, Principé, and São Tomé developed indigenous agricultural and sometimes plantation economies, the comings and goings of African and European merchants dominated life even in the largest of the creole communities, which served as both field headquarters for great European mercantile companies and collection points for trade between the African interior and the Atlantic littoral. Depending on the location, the exchange involved European textiles, metalware, guns, liquor, and beads for African gold, ivory, hides, pepper, beeswax, and dyewoods. The coastal trade or cabotage added fish, produce, livestock, and other perishables to this list, especially as regional specialization developed. Everywhere, slaves were bought and sold, and over time the importance of commerce-in-persons grew.[23]

As slaving societies, the coastal enclaves were also societies with slaves. African slavery in its various forms—from pawnage to chattel bondage—was practiced in these towns. Both Europeans and Africans held slaves, employed them, used them as collateral, traded them, and sold them to outsiders. At Elmina, the Dutch West India Company owned some 300 slaves in the late seventeenth century, and individual Europeans and Africans held others. Along with slaves appeared the inevitable trappings of slave societies—overseers to supervise slave labor, slave catchers to retrieve runaways, soldiers to keep order and guard against insurrections, and officials to adjudicate and punish transgressions beyond a master's reach. Freedmen and freedwomen, who had somehow escaped bondage, also enjoyed a considerable presence. Many former slaves mixed Africa and Europe culturally and sometimes physically.[24]

Knowledge and experience far more than color set the Atlantic creoles apart from the Africans who brought slaves from the interior and the Europeans who carried them across the Atlantic, on one hand, and the hapless men and women on whose commodification the slave trade rested, on the other. Maintaining a secure place in such a volatile social order was not easy. The creoles' genius for intercultural negotiation was not simply a set of skills, a tactic for survival, or an attribute that emerged as an "Africanism" in the New World. Rather, it was central to a way of life that transcended particular venues.

The names European traders called Atlantic creoles provide a glimpse of the creole's cosmopolitan ability to transcend the confines of particular nations and cultures. Abee Coffu Jantie Seniees, a leading African merchant and politico of Cape Coast on the Gold Coast in the late seventeenth century, appears in various European accounts and account books as "Jan Snees," "Jacque Senece," "Johan Sinesen," and "Jantee Snees." In some measure, the renderings of his name—to view him only from the perspective of European traders—reflect phonic imperialism or, more simply, the variability of transnational spelling. Seniees probably did not know or care how his trading partners registered his name, which he may have employed for commercial reasons in any case. But the diverse renderings reveal something of Abee Coffu Jantie Seniees's ability to trade with the Danes at Fredriksborg, the Dutch at Elmina, and the English at Cape Coast, as well as with Africans deep in the forested interior.[25]

The special needs of European traders placed Atlantic creoles in a powerful bargaining position, which they learned to employ to their own advantage. The most successful became principals and traded independently. They played one merchant against another, one captain against another, and one mercantile bureaucrat against another, often abandoning them for yet a better deal with some interloper, all in the hope of securing a rich prosperity for themselves and their families. Success evoked a sense of confidence that observers described as impertinence, insolence, and arrogance, and it was not limited to the fabulously wealthy like Jantie Seniees or the near sovereign John Claessen (the near-ruler of Fetu) who rejected a kingship to remain at trade, or the merchant princes John Kabes (trader, entrepreneur, and dominant politico in Komenda) and John Konny (commanding ruler in Pokoso).[26] Canoemen, for example, became infamous among European governors and sea captains for their independence. They refused to work in heavy surf, demanded higher wages and additional rations, quit upon insult or abuse, and abandoned work altogether when enslavement threatened. Attempts to control them through regulations issued from Europe or from local corporate headquarters failed utterly. "These canoemen, despicable thieves," sputtered one Englishman in 1711, "think that they are more than just labour."[27]

Like other people in the middle, Atlantic creoles profited from their strategic position. Competition between and among the Africans and European traders bolstered their stock, increased their political leverage, and enabled them to elevate their social standing while fostering solidarity. Creoles' ability to find a place for themselves in the interstices of African and European trade grew rapidly during periods of intense competition among the Portuguese, Dutch, Danes, Swedes, French, and English and an equally diverse set of African nationals.

At the same time and by the same token, the Atlantic creoles' liminality, particularly their lack of identity with any one group, posed numerous dangers. While their middling position made them valuable to African and European traders, it also made them vulnerable: they could be ostracized, scapegoated, and on occasion enslaved. Maintaining their independence amid the shifting alliances between and among Europeans and Africans was always difficult. Inevitably, some failed.

Debt, crime, immortality, or official disfavor could mean enslavement— if not for great men like Jantie Seniees, Claessen, Kabes, or Konny—at least for those on the fringes of the creole community.[28] Placed in captivity, Atlantic creoles might be exiled anywhere around the Atlantic—to the interior of Africa, the islands along the coast, the European metropoles, or the plantations of the New World. In the seventeenth century and the early part of the eighteenth, most slaves exported from Africa went to the sugar plantations of Brazil and the Antilles. Enslaved Atlantic creoles might be shipped to Pernambuco, Barbados, or Martinique. Transporting them to the expanding centers of New World staple production posed dangers, however, which American planters well understood. The characteristics that distinguished Atlantic creoles—their linguistic dexterity, cultural plasticity, and social agility—were precisely those qualities that the great planters of the New World disdained and feared. For their labor force they desired youth and strength, not experience and sagacity. Indeed, too much knowledge might be subversive to the good order of the plantation. Simply put, men and women who understood the operations of the Atlantic system were too dangerous to be trusted in the human tinderboxes created by the sugar revolution. Thus rejected by the most prosperous New World regimes, Atlantic creoles were frequently exiled to marginal slave societies where would-be slaveowners, unable to compete with the great plantation magnates, snapped up those whom the grandees had disparaged as "refuse" for reasons of age, illness, criminality, or recalcitrance. In the seventeenth century, few New World slave societies were more marginal than those of mainland North America.[29] Liminal peoples were drawn or propelled to marginal societies.

During the seventeenth century and into the eighteenth, the Dutch served as the most important conduit for transporting Atlantic creoles to mainland North America. Through their control of the sea, they domin-ated the commerce of the Atlantic periphery. Stretching mercantile theory to fit their commercial ambitions, the Dutch traded with all comers, commissioned privateers to raid rival shipping, and dealt openly with pirates. The Dutch West India Company, whose 1621 charter authorized it to trade in both the Americas and west Africa, cast its eye on the lucra-tive African trade in gold, ivory, copper, and slaves even as it began to barter for furs and pelts in the North Atlantic and for gold and sugar in the South Atlantic. In 1630, the Dutch captured Portuguese *capitanias* in northeastern Brazil, including Pernambuco, the site of the New World's first sugar boom. About the same time, the West India Company estab-lished bases in Curaçao and St. Eustatius. To supply their new empire, the Dutch turned to Africa, supplementing their outposts at Mouri on the Gold Coast and Gorée in Senegambia by seizing the Portuguese enclaves of Elmina and Axim in 1637, Luanda and Principé in 1641, and São Tomé in 1647. They then swept the Angolan coast, establishing trading factories at Cabinda, Loango, and Mpinda.[30]

Although ousted from the Gold Coast, the Portuguese never abandoned their foothold in central Africa, and they and their Brazilian succes-sors regrouped and counterattacked. In 1648, the Portuguese recaptured Luanda and forced the Dutch to evacuate Angola. They expelled the Dutch from Pernambuco in 1645 and completed the reconquest of Brazil in 1654.

Still, the short period of Dutch dominance—roughly, 1620 to 1670—had a powerful impact on the Atlantic world. During those years, the Dutch took control of Portuguese enclaves in Africa, introduced their commercial agents, and pressed their case for Dutch culture and Calvinist religion on the ruling Kongolese Catholics and other remnants of Portuguese imperialism. Although unsuccessful for the most part, the Dutch estab-lished ties with the Atlantic creoles and preserved these linkages even after the Portuguese reconquest, keeping alive their connections along the African coast and maintaining their position as the most active agents in slavery's transatlantic expansion during the seventeenth century.[31]

The Dutch transported thousands of slaves from Africa to the New World, trading with all parties, sometimes directly, sometimes indirectly through their base in Curaçao. Most of these slaves came from the interior of Angola, but among them were Atlantic creoles whose connec-tions to the Portuguese offended the Dutch. Following the Portuguese restoration, those with ties to the Dutch may have found themselves in similar difficulties. During the Dutch invasions, the subsequent wars, and then civil wars in which the Portuguese and the Dutch fought each other directly and through surrogates, many creoles were clapped into slavery. Others were seized in the Caribbean by Dutch men-of-war, privateers sailing under Dutch letters of marque, and freebooting pirates.[32] While such slaves might be sent anywhere in the Dutch empire between New

Netherland and Pernambuco, West India Company officers in New Amsterdam, who at first complained about "refuse" slaves, in time made known their preference for such creoles—deeming "Negroes who had been 12 or 13 years in the West Indies" to be "a better sort of Negroes."[33] A perusal of the names scattered through archival remains of New Netherland reveals something of the nature of this transatlantic transfer: Paulo d'Angola and Anthony Portuguese, Pedro Negretto and Francisco Negro, Simon Congo and Jan Guinea, Van St. Thomas and Francisco Cartagena, Claes de Neger and Assento Angola, and—perhaps most telling—Carla Criole, Jan Creoli, and Christoffel Crioell.[34]

These names trace the tumultuous experience that propelled their owners across the Atlantic and into slavery in the New World. They suggest that whatever tragedy befell them, Atlantic creoles did not arrive in the New World as deracinated chattel stripped of their past and without resources to meet the future. Unlike those who followed them into slavery in succeeding generations, transplanted creoles were not designated by diminutives, tagged with names more akin to barnyard animals, or given the name of an ancient notable or a classical deity. Instead, their names provided concrete evidence that they carried a good deal more than their dignity to the Americas.

To such men and women, New Amsterdam was not radically different from Elmina or Luanda, save for its smaller size and colder climate. A fortified port controlled by the Dutch West India Company, its population was a farrago of petty traders, artisans, merchants, soldiers, and corporate functionaries, all scrambling for status in a frontier milieu that demanded inter-cultural exchange. On the tip of Manhattan Island, Atlantic creoles rubbed elbows with sailors of various nationalities, Native Americans with diverse tribal allegiances, and pirates and privateers who professed neither nationality nor allegiance. In the absence of a staple crop, their work—building fortifications, hunting and trapping, tending fields and domestic animals, and transporting merchandise of all sorts—did not set them apart from workers of European descent, who often labored alongside them. Such encounters made a working knowledge of the creole tongue as valuable on the North American coast as in Africa. Whereas a later generation of transplanted Africans would be linguistically isolated and de-skilled by the process of enslavement, Atlantic creoles found themselves very much at home in the new environment. Rather than losing their skills, they discovered that the value of their gift for intercultural negotiation appreciated. The transatlantic journey did not break creole communities; it only transported them to other sites.[35]

Along the edges of the North American continent, creoles found slaves' cultural and social marginality an asset. Slaveholders learned that slaves' ability to negotiate with the diverse populace of seventeenth-century North America was as valuable as their labor, perhaps more so. While their owners employed creoles' skills on their own behalf, creoles did the same for themselves, trading their knowledge for a place in the still undefined social order. In 1665, when Jan Angola, accused of stealing wood in New Amsterdam, could not address the court in Dutch, he was ordered to return the following day with "Domingo the Negro as interpreter," an act familiar to Atlantic creoles in Elmina, Lisbon, San Salvador, or Cap Françis.[36]

To be sure, slavery bore heavily on Atlantic creoles in the New World. As in Africa and Europe, it was a system of exploitation, subservience, and debasement that rested on force. Yet Atlantic creoles were familiar with servitude in forms ranging from unbridled exploitation to corporate familialism. They had known free people to be enslaved, and they had known slaves to be liberated; the boundary between slavery and freedom on the African coast was permeable. Servitude generally did not prevent men and women from marrying, acquiring property (slaves included), enjoying a modest prosperity, and eventually being incorporated into the host society; creoles transported across the Atlantic had no reason to suspect they could not do the same in the New World.[37] If the stigma of servitude, physical labor, uncertain lineage, and alien religion stamped them as outsiders, there were many others—men and women of unblemished European pedigree prominent among them—who shared those taints. That black people could and occasionally did hold slaves and servants and employ white people suggested that race—like lineage and religion—was just one of many markers in the social order.

If slavery meant abuse and degradation, the experience of Atlantic creoles provided strategies for limiting such maltreatment—contrary to notions that they were libidinous heathens without family, economy, or society—and even for winning to freedom. Freedom meant not only greater independence but also identification with the larger group. Although the routes to social betterment were many, they generally involved reattachment to a community through the agency of an influential patron or, better yet, an established institution that could broker a slave's incorporation into the larger society.[38] Along the coast of Africa, Atlantic creoles often identified with the appendages of European or African power—be they international mercantile corporations or local chieftains—in hopes of relieving the stigma of otherness—be it enslavement, bastard birth, paganism, or race. They employed this strategy repeatedly in mainland North America, as they tried to hurdle the boundaries of social and cultural difference and establish a place for themselves. By linking themselves to the most important edifices of the nascent European-American societies, Atlantic creoles struggled to become part of a social order where exclusion or otherness—not subordination—posed the greatest dangers. To be inferior within the sharply stratified world of the seventeenth-century Atlantic was understandable by its very ubiquity; to be excluded posed unparalleled dangers.

The black men and women who entered New Netherland between

1626 and the English conquest in 1664 exemplified the ability of people of African descent to integrate themselves into mainland society during the first century of settlement, despite their status as slaves and the contempt of the colony's rulers. Far more than any other mainland colony during the first half of the seventeenth century, New Netherland rested on slave labor. The prosperity of the Dutch metropole and the opportunities presented to ambitious men and women in the far-flung Dutch empire denied New Netherland its share of free Dutch immigrants and limited its access to indentured servants. To populate the colony, the West India Company scoured the Atlantic basin for settlers, recruiting German Lutherans, French Huguenots, and Sephardic Jews. These newcomers did little to meet the colony's need for men and women to work the land, because, as a company officer reported, "agricultural laborers who are conveyed thither at great expense . . . sooner or later apply themselves to trade, and neglect agriculture altogether." Dutch officials concluded that slave labor was an absolute necessity for New Netherland. Although competition for slaves with Dutch outposts in Brazil (whose sugar economy was already drawing slaves from the African interior) placed New Netherland at a disadvantage, authorities in the North American colony imported all the slaves they could, so that in 1640 about 100 blacks lived in New Amsterdam, composing roughly 30 percent of the port's population and a larger portion of the labor force. Their proportion diminished over the course of the seventeenth century but remained substantial. At the time of the English conquest, some 300 slaves composed a fifth of the population of New Amsterdam, giving New Netherland the largest urban slave population on mainland North America.[39]

The diverse needs of the Dutch mercantile economy strengthened the hand of Atlantic creoles in New Netherland during the initial period of settlement. Caring only for short-term profits, the company, the largest slaveholder in the colony, allowed its slaves to live independently and work on their own in return for a stipulated amount of labor and an annual tribute. Company slaves thus enjoyed a large measure of independence, which they used to master the Dutch language, trade freely, accumulate property, identify with Dutch Reformed Christianity, and— most important—establish families. During the first generation, some twenty-five couples took their vows in the Dutch Reformed Church in New Amsterdam. When children arrived, their parents baptized them as well. Participation in the religious life of New Netherland provides but one indicator of how quickly Atlantic creoles mastered the intricacies of life in mainland North America. In 1635, less than ten years after the arrival of the first black people, black New Netherlanders understood enough about the organization of the colony and the operation of the company to travel to the company's headquarters in Holland and petition for wages.[40]

Many slaves gained their freedom. This was not easy in New

Netherland, although there was no legal proscription on manumission. Indeed, gaining freedom was nearly impossible for slaves owned privately and difficult even for those owned by the company. The company valued its slaves and was willing to liberate only the elderly, whom it viewed as a liability. Even when manumitting such slaves, the company exacted an annual tribute from adults and retained ownership of their children. The latter practice elicited protests from both blacks and whites in New Amsterdam. The enslavement of black children made "half-freedom," as New Netherland authorities denominated the West India Company's former slaves who were unable to pass their new status to their children, appear no freedom at all.[41]

Manumission in New Netherland was calculated to benefit slave owners, not slaves. Its purposes were to spur slaves to greater exertion and to relieve owners of the cost of supporting elderly slaves. Yet, however compromised the attainment of freedom, slaves did what was necessary to secure it. They accepted the company's terms and agreed to pay its corporate tribute. But they bridled at the fact that their children's status would not follow their own. Half-free blacks pressed the West India Company to make their status hereditary. Hearing rumors that baptism would assure freedom to their children, they pressed their claims to church membership. A Dutch prelate complained of the "worldly and perverse aims" of black people who "wanted nothing else than to deliver their children from bodily slavery, without striving for piety and Christian virtues."[42] Although conversion never guaranteed freedom in New Netherland, many half-free blacks secured their goal. By 1664, at the time of the English conquest, about one black person in five had achieved freedom in New Amsterdam, a proportion never equalled throughout the history of slavery in the American South.[43]

Some free people of African descent prospered. Building on small gifts of land that the West India Company provided as freedom dues, a few entered the landholding class in New Netherland. A small group of former slaves established a community on the outskirts of the Dutch settlement on Manhattan, farmed independently, and sold their produce in the public market. Others purchased farmsteads or were granted land as part of the Dutch effort to populate the city's hinterland. In 1659, the town of Southampton granted "Peeter the Neigro" three acres. Somewhat later John Neiger, who had "set himself up a house in the street" of Easthampton, was given "for his own use a little quantity of land above his house for him to make a yard or garden." On occasion, free blacks employed whites.[44]

By the middle of the seventeenth century, black people participated in almost every aspect of life in New Netherland. They sued and were sued in Dutch courts, married and baptized their children in the Dutch Reformed Church, and fought alongside Dutch militiamen against the colony's enemies. Black men and women—slave as well as free—traded on their own and accumulated property. Black people also began to develop a variety of institutions that reflected their unique experience and served their special needs. Black men and women stood as god-parents to each other's children, suggesting close family ties, and rarely called on white people—owners or not—to serve in this capacity. At times, established black families legally adopted orphaned black children, further knitting the black community together in a web of fictive kinship.[45] The patterns of residence, marriage, church membership, and godparentage speak not only to the material success of Atlantic creoles but also to their ability to create a community among themselves.

To be sure, the former slaves' prosperity was precarious at best. As the Dutch transformed their settlement from a string of trading posts to a colony committed to agricultural production, the quality of freedpeople's freedom deteriorated. The Dutch began to import slaves directly from Africa (especially after the Portuguese retook Brazil), and the new arrivals—sold mostly to individual planters rather than to the company—had little chance of securing the advantages earlier enjoyed by the company's slaves.[46]

The freedpeople's social standing eroded more rapidly following the English conquest in 1664, demonstrating the fragility of their freedom in a social order undergirded by racial hostility. Nonetheless, black people continued to enjoy the benefits of the earlier age. They maintained a secure family life, acquired property, and participated as communicants in the Dutch Reformed Church, where they baptized their children in the presence of godparents of their own choosing. When threatened, they took their complaints to court, exhibiting a fine understanding of their legal rights and a steely determination to defend them. Although the proportion of the black population enjoying freedom shrank steadily under English rule, the small free black settlement held its own. Traveling through an area of modest farms on the outskirts of New York City in 1679, a Dutch visitor observed that "upon both sides of this way were many habitations of negroes, mulattos and whites. These negroes were formerly the property of the (West India) company, but, in consequence of the frequent changes and conquests of the country, they have obtained their freedom and settled themselves down where they thought proper, and thus on this road, where they have ground enough to live on with their families."[47]

Dutch vessels were not the only ones to transport Atlantic creoles from Africa to North America. The French, who began trading on the Windward Coast of Africa soon after the arrival of the Portuguese, did much the same. Just as a creole population grew up around the Portuguese and later Dutch factories at Elmina, Luanda, and São Tomé, so one developed around the French posts on the Senegal River. The Compagnie du Sénégal, the Compagnie des Indes Occidentales, and their successor, the

Compagnie des Indes—whose charter, like that of the Dutch West India Company, authorized it to trade in both Africa and the Americas—maintained headquarters at St. Louis with subsidiary outposts at Galam and Fort d'Arguin.[48]

As at Elmina and Luanda, shifting alliances between Africans and Europeans in St. Louis, Galam, and Fort d'Arguin also ensnared Atlantic creoles, who found themselves suddenly enslaved and thrust across the Atlantic. One such man was Samba, a Bambara,[49] who during the 1720s worked for the French as an interpreter—*maître de langue*—at Galam, up the Senegal River from St. Louis. "Samba Bambara"—as he appears in the records—traveled freely along the river between St. Louis, Galam, and Fort d'Arguin. By 1722, he received permission from the Compagnie des Indes for his family to reside in St. Louis. When his wife dishonored him, Samba Bambara called on his corporate employer to exile her from St. Louis and thereby bring order to his domestic life. But despite his reliance on the company, Samba Bambara allegedly joined with African captives in a revolt at Fort d'Arguin, and, when the revolt was quelled, he was enslaved and deported. Significantly, he was not sold to the emerging plantation colony of Saint Domingue, where the sugar revolution stoked a nearly insatiable appetite for slaves. Instead, French officials at St. Louis exiled Samba Bambara to Louisiana, a marginal military outpost far outside the major transatlantic sea lanes and with no staple agricultural economy.[50]

New Orleans on the Mississippi River shared much with St. Louis on the Senegal in the 1720s. As the headquarters of the Compagnie des Indes in mainland North America, the town housed the familiar collection of corporate functionaries, traders, and craftsmen, along with growing numbers of French *engagés* and African slaves. New Orleans was frequented by Indians, whose canoes supplied it much as African canoemen supplied St. Louis. Its taverns and back alley retreats were meeting places for sailors of various nationalities, Canadian *coureurs de bois*, and soldiers—the latter no more pleased to be stationed on the North American frontier than their counterparts welcomed assignment to an African factory.[51] Indeed, soldiers' status in this rough frontier community differed little from that on the coast of Africa.

In 1720, a French soldier stationed in New Orleans was convicted of theft and sentenced to the lash. A black man wielded the whip. His work was apparently satisfactory, because five years later, Louis Congo, a recently arrived slave then in the service of the Compagnie des Indes, was offered the job. A powerful man, Congo bargained hard before accepting such grisly employment; he demanded freedom for himself and his wife, regular rations, and a plot of land he could cultivate independently. Louisiana's Superior Council balked at these terms, but the colony's attorney general urged acceptance, having seen Congo's *"chef d'oeuvre."* Louis Congo gained his freedom and was allowed to live with his wife (although she was not free) on land of his own choosing. His life as Louisiana's executioner was not easy. He was assaulted several times, and he complained that assassins lurked everywhere. But he enjoyed a modest prosperity, and he learned to write, an accomplishment that distinguished him from most inhabitants of eighteenth-century Louisiana.[52]

Suggesting something of the symmetry of the Atlantic world, New Orleans, save for the flora and fauna, was no alien terrain to Samba Bambara or Louis Congo. Despite the long transatlantic journey, once in the New World, they recovered much of what they had lost in the Old, although Samba Bambara never escaped slavery. Like the Atlantic creoles who alighted in New Netherland, Samba Bambara employed on the coast of North America skills he had learned on the coast of Africa; Louis Congo's previous occupation is unknown. Utilizing his knowledge of French, various African languages, and the ubiquitous creole tongue, the rebel regained his position with his old patron, the Compagnie des Indes, this time as an interpreter swearing on the Christian Bible to translate faithfully before Louisiana's Superior Council. Later, he became an overseer on the largest "concession" in the colony, the company's massive plantation across the river from New Orleans.[53] Like his counterparts in New Amsterdam, Samba Bambara succeeded in a rugged frontier slave society by following the familiar lines of patronage to the doorstep of his corporate employer. Although the constraints of slavery eventually turned him against the company on the Mississippi, just as he had turned against it on the Senegal River, his ability to transfer his knowledge and skills from the Old World to the New, despite the weight of enslavement, suggests that the history of Atlantic creoles in New Amsterdam—their ability to escape slavery, form families, secure property, and claim a degree of independence—was no anomaly.

Atlantic creoles such as Paulo d'Angola in New Netherland and Samba Bambara in New Orleans were not the only products of the meeting of Africans and Europeans on the coast of Africa. By the time Europeans began to colonize mainland North America, communities of creoles of African descent similar to those found on the West African *feitorias* had established themselves all along the rim of the Atlantic. In Europe—particularly Portugal and Spain—the number of Atlantic creoles swelled, as trade with Africa increased. By the mid-sixteenth century, some 10,000 black people lived in Lisbon, where they composed about 10 percent of the population. Seville had a slave population of 6,000 (including a minority of Moors and Moriscos).[54] As the centers of the Iberian slave trade, these cities distributed African slaves throughout Europe.[55]

With the settlement of the New World, Atlantic creoles sprouted in such places as Cap Français, Cartagena, Havana, Mexico City, and San Salvador. Intimate with the culture of the Atlantic, they could be found speaking pidgin and creole and engaging in a familiar sort of cultural brokerage. Men drawn from these creole communities accompanied Columbus to the New World; others marched with Balboa, Cortés, De Soto, and Pizarro.[56] Some Atlantic creoles crisscrossed the ocean several times, as had Jerónimo, a Wolof slave, who was sold from Lisbon to Cartagena and from Cartagena to Murica, where he was purchased by a churchman who sent him to Valencia. A *"mulâtress"* wife and her three slaves followed her French husband, a gunsmith in the employ of the Compagnie des Indes, from Gorée to Louisiana, when he was deported for criminal activities.[57] Other Atlantic creoles traveled on their own, as sailors and interpreters in both the transatlantic and African trades. Some gained their freedom and mixed with Europeans and Native Americans. Wherever they went, Atlantic creoles extended the use of the distinctive language of the Atlantic, planted the special institutions of the creole community, and propagated their unique outlook. Within the Portuguese and Spanish empires, Atlantic creoles created an intercontinental web of *cofradias* (*confradias* to the Spanish), so that, by the seventeenth century, the network of black religious brotherhoods stretched from Lisbon to São Tomé, Angola, and Brazil.[58] Although no comparable institutional link-ages existed in the Anglo- and Franco-American worlds, there were numerous informal connections between black people in New England and Virginia, Louisiana and Saint Domingue. Like their African counter-parts, Atlantic creoles of European, South American, and Caribbean ori-gins also found their way to mainland North America, where they became part of black America's charter generations.

The Dutch were the main conduit for carrying such men and women to the North American mainland in the seventeenth century. Juan (Jan, in some accounts) Rodrigues, a sailor of mixed racial ancestry who had shipped from Hispaniola in 1612 on the *Jonge Tobias*, offers another case in point. The ship, one of the several Dutch merchant vessels vying for the North American fur trade before the founding of the Dutch West India Company, anchored in the Hudson River sometime in 1612 and left Rodrigues either as an independent trader or, more likely, as ship's agent. When a rival Dutch ship arrived the following year, Rodrigues promptly shifted his allegiance, informing its captain that, despite his color, "he was a free man." He served his new employer as translator and agent collecting furs from the native population. When the captain of the *Jonge Tobias* returned to the Hudson River, Rodrigues changed his allegiance yet again, only to be denounced as a turn-coat and "that black rascal." Barely escaping with his life, he took up residence with some friendly Indians.[59]

Atlantic creoles were among the first black people to enter the Chesapeake region in the early years of the seventeenth century, and they numbered large among the "twenty Negars" the Dutch sold to the English at

Jamestown in 1619 as well as those who followed during the next half century.[60] Anthony Johnson, who was probably among the prizes captured by a Dutch ship in the Caribbean, appears to have landed in Jamestown as "Antonio a Negro" soon after the initial purchase. During the next thirty years, Antonio exited servitude, anglicized his name, married, began to farm on his own, and in 1651 received a 250-acre headright. When his Eastern Shore plantation burned to the ground two years later, he petitioned the country court for relief and was granted a substantial reduction of his taxes. His son John did even better than his father, receiving a patent for 550 acres, and another son, Richard, owned a 100-acre estate. Like other men of substance, the Johnsons farmed independently, held slaves, and left their heirs sizable estates. As established members of their communities, they enjoyed rights in common with other free men and frequently employed the law to protect themselves and advance their interests. When a black man claiming his freedom fled Anthony Johnson's plantation and found refuge with a nearby white planter, Johnson took his neighbor to court and won the return of his slave along with damages from the white man.[61]

Landed independence not only afforded free people of African descent legal near-equality in Virginia but also allowed them a wide range of expressions that others termed "arrogance"—the traditional charge against Atlantic creoles. Anthony Johnson exhibited an exalted sense of self when a local notable challenged his industry. Johnson countered with a ringing defense of his independence: "I know myne owne ground and I will worke when I please and play when I please." Johnson also understood that he and other free black men and women were different, and he and his kin openly celebrated those differences. Whereas Antonio a Negro had anglicized the family name, John Johnson—his grandson and a third-generation Virginian—called his own estate "Angola."[62]

The Johnsons were not unique in Virginia. A small community of free people of African descent developed on the Eastern Shore. Their names, like Antonio a Negro's, suggest creole descent: John Francisco, Bashaw Ferdinando (or Farnando), Emanuel Driggus (sometimes Drighouse; probably Rodriggus), Anthony Longo (perhaps Loango), and "Francisco a Negroe" (soon to become Francis, then Frank, Payne and finally Paine).[63] They, like Antonio, were drawn from the Atlantic littoral and may have spent time in England or New England before reaching the Chesapeake. At least one, "John Phillip, A negro Christened in *England* 12 yeeres since," was a sailor on an English ship that brought a captured Spanish vessel into Jamestown; another, Sebastian Cain or Cane, gained his freedom in Boston, where he had served the merchant Robert Keayne (hence probably his name). Cain also took to the sea as a sailor, but, unlike Phillip, he settled in Virginia as a neighbor, friend, and sometimes kinsman of the Johnsons, Drigguses, and Paynes.[64]

In Virginia, Atlantic creoles ascended the social order and exhibited a sure-handed understanding of Chesapeake social hierarchy and the complex dynamics of patron-client relations. Although still in bondage, they began to acquire the property, skills, and social connections that became their mark throughout the Atlantic world. They worked provision grounds, kept livestock, and traded independently. More important, they found advocates among the propertied classes—often their owners—and identified themselves with the colony's most important institutions, registering their marriages, baptisms, and children's godparents in the Anglican church and their property in the county courthouse. They sued and were sued in local courts and petitioned the colonial legislature and governor. While relations to their well-placed patrons—former masters and mistresses, landlords, and employers—among the colony's elite were important, as in Louisiana, the creoles also established ties among themselves, weaving together a community from among the interconnections of marriage, trade, and friendship. Free blacks testified on each other's behalf, stood as godparents for each other's children, loaned each other small sums, and joined together for after-hours conviviality, creating a community that often expanded to the larger web of interactions among all poor people, regardless of color. According to one historian of black life in seventeenth-century Virginia, "cooperative projects . . . were more likely in relations between colored freedmen and poor whites than were the debtor-creditor, tenant-landlord, or employee-employer relations that linked individuals of both races to members of the planter class."[65] The horizontal ties of class developed alongside the vertical ones of patronage.

Maintaining their standing as property-holding free persons was difficult, and some Atlantic creoles in the Chesapeake, like those in New Netherland, slipped down the social ladder, trapped by legal snares—apprenticeships, tax forfeitures, and bastardy laws—as planters turned from a labor system based on indentured Europeans and Atlantic creoles to raw Africans condemned to perpetual slavery. Anthony Johnson, harassed by white planters, fled his plantation in Virginia to establish the more modest "Tonies Vineyard" in Maryland. But even as they were pushed out, many of the Chesapeake's charter generations continued to elude slavery. Some did well, lubricating the lifts to economic success with their own hard work, their skills in a society that had "an unrelenting demand for artisanal labor," and the assistance of powerful patrons. A few of the landholding free black families on Virginia's Eastern Shore maintained their propertied standing well into the eighteenth century. In 1738, the estate of Emanuel Driggus's grandson—including its slaves—was worth more than those of two-thirds of his white neighbors.[66]

Atlantic creoles also entered the lowcountry of South Carolina and Florida, carried there by the English and Spanish, respectively. Like the great West Indian planters who settled in that "colony of a colony," Atlantic creoles were drawn from Barbados and other Caribbean islands, where a full generation of European and African cohabitation had allowed them to gain a knowledge of European ways. Prior to the sugar revolution, they worked alongside white indentured servants in a variety of enterprises, none of which required the discipline of plantation labor. Like white servants, some exited slavery, as the line between slavery and freedom was open. An Anglican minister who toured the English islands during the 1670s noted that black people spoke English "no worse than the natural born subjects of that Kingdom."[67] Although Atlantic creole culture took a different shape in the Antilles than it did on the periphery of Africa or Europe, it also displayed many of the same characteristics.

On the southern mainland, creoles used their knowledge of the New World and their ability to negotiate between the various Native American nations and South Carolina's European polyglot—English, French Huguenots, Sephardic Jews—to become invaluable as messengers, trappers, and cattle minders. The striking image of slave and master working on opposite sides of a sawbuck suggests the place of blacks during the early years of South Carolina's settlement.[68]

Knowledge of their English captors also provided knowledge of their captors' enemy, some two hundred miles to the south. At every opportunity, Carolina slaves fled to Spanish Florida, where they requested Catholic baptism. Officials at St. Augustine—whose black population was drawn from Spain, Cuba, Hispaniola, and New Spain—celebrated the fugitives' choice of religion and offered sanctuary. They also valued the creoles' knowledge of the countryside, their ability to converse with English, Spanish, and Indians, and their willingness to strike back at their enslavers. Under the Spanish flag, former Carolina slaves raided English settlements at Port Royal and Edisto and liberated even more of their number. As part of the black militia, they, along with other fugitives from Carolina, fought against the English in the Tuscarora and Yamasee wars.[69]

Florida's small black population mushroomed in the late seventeenth and early eighteenth centuries, as the small but steady stream of fugitives grew with the expansion of lowcountry slavery. Slaves from central Africa—generally deemed "Angolans"—numbered large among the new arrivals, as the transatlantic trade carried thousands of Africans directly to the lowlands. Although many were drawn from deep in the interior of Africa, others were Atlantic creoles with experience in the coastal towns of Cabinda, Loango, and Mpinda. Some spoke Portuguese, which, as one Carolinian noted, was "as near Spanish as Scotch is to English," and subscribed to an African Catholicism with roots in the fifteenth-century conversion of Kongo's royal house. They knew their catechism, celebrated feasts of Easter and All Saint's Day or Hallowe'en, and recognized Christian saints.

These men and women were particularly attracted to the possibilities of freedom in the Spanish settlements around St. Augustine. They fled from South Carolina in increasing numbers during the 1720s and 1730s, and, in 1739, a group of African slaves—some doubtless drawn from the newcomers—initiated a mass flight. Pursued by South Carolina militia-men, they confronted their owners' soldiers in several pitched battles that became known as the Stono Rebellion.[70] Although most of the Stono rebels were killed or captured, some escaped to Florida, from where it became difficult to retrieve them by formal negotiation or by force. The newcomers were quickly integrated into black life in St. Augustine, since they had already been baptized, although they prayed—as one Miguel Domingo informed a Spanish priest—in Kikongo.[71]

Much to the delight of St. Augustine's Spanish rulers, the former Carolina slaves did more than pray. They fought alongside the Spanish against incursions by English raiders. An edict of the Spanish crown promising "Liberty and Protection" to all slaves who reached St. Augustine boosted the number of fugitives—most from Carolina—especially after reports circulated that the Spanish received runaways "with great Honors" and gave their leaders military commissions and "A Coat Faced with Velvet." In time, Spanish authorities granted freedom to some, but not all, of the black soldiers and their families.[72]

Among the unrewarded was Francisco Menéndez, a veteran of the Yamasee War and leader of the black militia. Frustrated by the ingrati-tude of his immediate superiors, Menéndez petitioned the governor of Florida and the bishop of Cuba for his liberty, which he eventually received. In 1738, when a new governor established Gracia Real de Santa Teresa de Mose, a fortified settlement north of St. Augustine, to protect the Spanish capital from the English incursions, he placed Menéndez in charge. Under Captain Menéndez, Mose became the center of black life in colonial Florida and a base from which former slaves—sometimes joined by Indians—raided South Carolina. The success of the black militia in repelling an English attack on Mose in 1740 won Menéndez a special commendation from the governor, who declared that the black captain had "distinguished himself in the establishment, and cultivation of Mose." Not one to lose an opportunity, the newly literate Menéndez promptly requested that the king remunerate him for the "loyalty, zeal and love I have always demonstrated in the royal service" and petitioned for a stipend worthy of a militia captain.[73]

To secure his reward, Menéndez took a commission as a privateer, with hopes of eventually reaching Spain and collecting his royal reward. Instead, a British ship captured the famous "Signior Capitano Francisco." Although stretched out on a cannon and threatened with emasculation for alleged atrocities during the siege of Mose, Menéndez had become too valuable to mutilate. His captors gave him 200 lashes, soaked his wounds in brine, and commended him to a doctor "to take Care of his Sore A-se." Menéndez was then carried before a British admiralty court on New Providence Island, where "this Francisco that Cursed Seed of Cain" was ordered sold into slavery. Even this misadventure hardly slowed the irrepressible Menéndez. By 1752, perhaps ransomed out of bondage, he was back in his old position in Mose.[74]

Meanwhile, members of the fugitive community around St. Augustine entered more fully into the life of the colony as artisans and tradesmen as well as laborers and domestics. They married among themselves, into the Native American population, and with slaves as well, joining as husband and wife before their God and community in the Catholic church. They baptized their children in the same church, choosing godparents from among both the white and black congregants. Like the Atlantic creoles in New Amsterdam about a century earlier, they became skilled in identifying the lever of patronage, in this case royal authority. Declaring themselves "vassals of the king and deserving of royal protection," they continually placed themselves in the forefront of service to the crown with the expectations that their king would protect, if not reward, them. For the most part, they were not disappointed. When Spain turned East Florida over to the British in 1763, black colonists retreated to Cuba with His Majesty's other subjects, where the crown granted them land, tools, a small subsidy, and a slave for each of their leaders.[75]

In the long history of North American slavery, no other cohort of black people survived as well and rose as fast and as high in mainland society as the Atlantic creoles. The experience of the charter generations contrasts markedly with what followed: when the trauma of enslavement, the violence of captivity, the harsh conditions of plantation life left black people unable to reproduce themselves; when the strange language of their enslavers muted the tongues of newly arrived Africans; and when the slaves' skills and knowledge were submerged in the stupefying labor of plantation production. Rather than having to face the likes of Robert Carter and the imposition of planter domination, Paulo d'Angola, Samba Bambara, Juan Rodrigues, Antonio a Negro, and Francisco Menéndez entered a society not markedly different from those they had left.[76] There, in New Netherland, the Chesapeake, Louisiana, and Florida, they made a place for themselves, demonstrating confidence in their abilities to master a world they knew well. Many secured freedom and a modest prosperity, despite the presumption of racial slavery and the contempt of their captors.

The charter generations' experience derived not only from who they were but also from the special circumstances of their arrival. By their very primacy, as members of the first generation of settlers, their experience was unique. While they came as foreigners, they were no more strange to the new land than were those who enslaved them. Indeed, the near simultaneous arrival of migrants from Europe and Africa gave them a shared perspective on the New World. At first, all saw themselves as outsiders. That would change, as European settlers gained dominance, ousted native peoples, and created societies they claimed as their own. As

Europeans became European-Americans and then simply Americans, their identification with—and sense of ownership over—mainland society distinguished them from the forced migrants from Africa who continued to arrive as strangers and were defined as permanent outsiders.

The charter generations owed their unique history to more than just the timing of their arrival. Before their historic confrontation with their new owner, the men and women Robert Carter purchased may have spent weeks, even months, packed between the stinking planks of slave ships. Atlantic creoles experienced few of the horrors of the Middle Passage. Rather than arriving in shiploads totaling into the hundreds, Atlantic creoles trickled into the mainland singly, in twos and threes, or by the score. Most were sent in small consignments or were the booty of privateers and pirates. Some found employment as interpreters, sailors, and *grumetes* on the very ships that transported them to the New World.[77] Although transatlantic travel in the seventeenth and eighteenth centuries could be a harrowing experience under the best of circumstances, the profound disruption that left the men and women Carter purchased physically spent and psychologically traumatized was rarely part of the experience of Atlantic creoles.

Most important, Atlantic creoles entered societies-with-slaves, not, as mainland North America would become, slave societies—that is, societies in which the order of the plantation shaped every relationship.[78] In North America—as in Africa—Atlantic creoles were still but one subordinate group in societies in which subordination was the rule. Few who arrived before the plantation system faced the dehumanizing and brutalizing effects of gang labor in societies where slaves had become commodities and nothing more. Indeed, Atlantic creoles often worked alongside their owners, supped at their tables, wore their hand-me-down clothes, and lived in the back rooms and lofts of their houses. Many resided in towns, as did Paulo d'Angola, Samba Bambara, and Francisco Menéndez. The proportion of the mainland's black population living in places such as New Amsterdam, Philadelphia, Charleston, St. Augustine, and New Orleans was probably higher during the first generations of settlement than it would ever be again. Urban slaves, for better or worse, lived and worked in close proximity to their owners. The regimen imposed the heavy burdens of continual surveillance, but the same constant contact prevented their owners from imagining people of African descent to be a special species of beings, an idea that only emerged with the radical separation of master and slave and the creation of the worlds of the Big House and the Quarters. Until then, the open interaction of slave and slaveowner encouraged Atlantic creoles, and others as well, to judge their enslavement by its older meaning, not by its emerging new one.

The possibility of freedom had much the same effect. So long as some black people, no matter how closely identified with slavery, could still wriggle free of bondage and gain an independent place, slavery may have carried the connotation of otherness, debasement, perhaps even transgression, iniquity, and vice, but it was not social death. The success of Atlantic creoles in rising from the bottom of mainland society contradicted the logic of hereditary bondage and suggested that what had been done might be undone.

The rise of plantation slavery left little room for the men and women of the charter generations. Their efforts to secure a place in society were put at risk by the new order, for the triumph of the plantation régime threatened not inequality—which had always been assumed, at least by Europeans—but debasement and permanent ostracism of the sort Robert "King" Carter delivered on that Virginia wharf. With the creation of a world in which peoples of African descent were presumed slaves and those of European descent free, people of color no longer had a place. It became easy to depict black men and women as uncivilized heathens outside the bounds of society or even humanity.[79]

Few Atlantic creoles entered the mainland after the tobacco revolution in the Chesapeake, the rice revolution in lowcountry Carolina, and the sugar revolution in Louisiana. Rather than being drawn from the African littoral, slaves increasingly derived from the African interior. Such men and women possessed little understanding of the larger Atlantic world: no apprenticeship in negotiating with Europeans, no knowledge of Christianity or other touchstone of European culture, no acquaintance with western law, and no open fraternization with sailors and merchants in the Atlantic trade—indeed, no experience with the diseases of the Atlantic to provide a measure of immunity to the deadly microbes that lurked everywhere in the New World. Instead of speaking a pidgin or creole that gave them access to the Atlantic, the later arrivals were separated from their enslavers and often from each other by a dense wall of language. Rather than see their skills and knowledge appreciate in value, they generally discovered that previous experience counted for little on the plantations of the New World. Indeed, the remnants of their African past were immediately expropriated by their new masters.

In the stereotypes that demeaned slaves, European and European-American slaveholders inadvertently recognized the difference between the Atlantic creoles and the men and women who followed them into bondage, revealing how the meaning of race was being transformed with the advent of the plantation. Slaveholders condemned creoles as roguish in the manner of Juan Rodrigues the "black rascal," or arrogant in the manner of Antonio a Negro, who knew his "owne ground," or swaggering in the manner of "Signior Capitano Francisco," who stood his ground against those who threatened his manhood. They rarely used such epithets against the postcreole generations that labored on the great plantations. Instead, slaveholders and their apologists scorned such slaves as crude primitives, devoid of the simple amenities of refined society. The failings of plantation slaves were not those of calculation or arrogance, but of stark ignorance and dense stupidity. Plantation slaves were denounced, not for a desire to convert to Christianity for "worldly and perverse aims" as were the half-free blacks in New Netherland or because they claimed the "True Faith" as did the Carolinians who fled to St. Augustine, but because they knew nothing of the religion, language, law, and social etiquette that Europeans equated with civilization. The unfamiliarity of the post-Atlantic creole cohort with the dynamics of Atlantic life made them easy targets for the slaveholders' ridicule. Like the Virginia planters who slammed Africans for the "gross bestiality and rudeness of their manners," an eighteenth-century chronicler of South Carolina's history declared lowcountry slaves to be "as great strangers to Christianity, and as much under the influence of Pagan darkness, idolatry and superstition, as they were at their first arrival from Africa." Such a charge, whatever its meaning on the great lowcountry rice plantations, could have no relevance to the runaways who sought the True Faith in St. Augustine.[80]

In time, stereotypes made were again remade. During the late eighteenth century, planters and their apologists rethought the meaning of race as more than a century and a half of captivity remolded people of African descent. As a new generation of black people emerged—familiar with the American countryside, fluent in its languages, and conversant in its religions—the stereotype of the artful, smooth-talking slave also appeared. Manipulative to the point of insolence, this new generation of African-Americans peopled the slave quarter, confronted the master on their own terms, and, in the midst of the Revolution, secured freedom. African-Americans reversed the process of enslavement—among other things, taking back the naming process (although not the names) that "King" Carter had usurped.[81]

Their story—whereby Africans became creoles—was a great one and one that Americans would repeat many times in the personages of men as different as David Levinsky, the Godfather, or Kunta Kinte—as greenhorns became natives. Historians, like novelists and film makers, have enjoyed retelling the tale, but in so doing, they lost the story of another founding generation and its transit from immigrant to native. While the fathers (and sometimes the mothers) of European America, whether Puritan divines or Chesapeake adventurers, would be celebrated by their posterity, members of black America's charter generations disappeared into the footnotes of American history. Generations of Americans lived in the shadow of John Winthrop and William Byrd, even Peter Stuyvesant and Jean Baptiste Bienville, but few learned of Paulo d'Angola, Samba Bambara, Juan Rodrigues, Antonio a Negro, and Francisco Menéndez. If Atlantic creoles made any appearance in the textbook histories, it would be as curiosities and exceptions to the normal pattern of American race relations, examples of false starts, mere tokens.

The story of how creoles became Africans was lost in a chronicle that presumed American history always moved in a single direction. The assimiliationist ideal could not imagine how the diverse people of the Atlantic could become the sons and daughters of Africa. The possibility that a society-with-slaves was a separate and distinct social formation, not a stage in the development of slave society, was similarly inconceivable in a nation in which wealth and power rested upon plantation slavery.

The causes of creole anonymity ran deep. While Carter initiated newly arrived Africans to the world of the plantation, the descendants of the charter generations struggled to maintain the status they had earlier achieved. To that end, many separated themselves from the mass of Africans on whom the heavy weight of plantation bondage fell. Some fled as a group, as did the creole community in St. Augustine that retreated with the Spanish from Florida to Cuba following the British takeover in 1764.[82]

Others merged with Native American tribes and European-American settlers to create unique biracial and triracial combinations and established separate identities. In the 1660s, the Johnson clan fled Virginia for Maryland, Delaware, and New Jersey. John Johnson and John Johnson, Jr., the son and grandson of Anthony Johnson, took refuge among the Nanticoke Indians and so-called Moors, among whom the Johnson name has loomed large into the twentieth century. Near one Nanticoke settlement in Delaware stands the small village of "Angola," the name of John Johnson's Virginia plantation and perhaps Anthony Johnson's ancestral home. Similar "Indian" tribes could be found scattered throughout the eastern half of the United States, categorized by twentieth-century ethnographers as "tri-racial isolates."[83]

Others moved west to a different kind of autonomy. Scattered throughout the frontier areas of the eighteenth century were handfuls of black people eager to escape the racially divided society of plantation America. White frontiersmen, with little sympathy for the nabobs of the tidewater, sometimes sheltered such black men and women, employing them with no questions asked. People of African descent also found refuge among the frontier banditti, whose interracial character—a "numerous Collection of outcast Mulattos, Mustees, free Negroes, all Horse-Thieves," by one account—was the subject of constant denunciation by the frontier's aspiring planters.[84]

While some members of the charter generations retreated before the expanding planter class, a few moved toward it. At least one male member of every prominent seventeenth-century free black family on the Eastern Shore of Virginia married a white woman, so the Atlantic creoles' descendants would, perforce, be lighter in color. Whether or not this was a conscious strategy, there remains considerable, if necessarily incomplete, evidence that these light-skinned people employed a portion of their European inheritance—a pale complexion—to pass into white society.[85]

Retreat—geographic, social, and physical—was not the only strategy members of the charter generations adopted in the face of the emergent plantation régime. Some stood their ground, confronting white authorities and perhaps setting an example for those less fortunate than themselves. In 1667, claiming "hee was a Christian and had been severall years in England," a black man named Fernando sued for his freedom in a Virginia court. The case, initiated just as tidewater planters were consolidating their place atop Virginia society, sent Virginia lawmakers into a paroxysm that culminated in the passage of a new law clarifying the status of black people: they would be slaves for life and their status would be hereditary. In succeeding years, such Atlantic creoles—men and women of African descent with long experience in the larger Atlantic world—would continue as Fernando continued to bedevil planters and other white Americans in and out of the court room, harboring runaway slaves, providing them with free papers, and joining together matters slaveholders viewed as subversive. In 1671, New York authorities singled out Domingo and Manuel Angola, warning the public "that the free negroes were from time to time entertaining sundry of the servants and negroes belonging to the Burghers ... to the great damage of their owners." It appears that the warning did little to limit black people from meeting, for several years later New York's Common Council again complained about "the frequent randivozing of Negro Slaves att the houses of free negroes without the gates hath bin occasion of great disordr." As slaveholders feared, the line between annoyance and subversion was a thin one. Atlantic creoles were among the black servants and slaves who stood with Nathaniel Bacon against royal authority in 1676.[86]

The relentless engine of plantation agriculture and the transformation of the mainland colonies from societies-with-slaves to slave societies submerged the charter generations in a régime in which African descent was equated with slavery. For the most part, the descendants of African creoles took their place as slaves alongside newly arrived Africans. Those who maintained their freedom became part of an impoverished free black minority, and those who lost their liberty were swallowed up in an oppressed slave majority.[87] In one way or another, Atlantic creoles were overwhelmed by the power of the plantation order.

Even so, the charter generations' presence was not without substance. During the American Revolution, when divisions within the planter class gave black people fresh opportunities to strike for liberty and equality, long-suppressed memories of the origins of African life on the mainland bubbled to the surface, often in lawsuits in which slaves claimed freedom as a result of descent from a free ancestor, sometimes white, sometimes Indian, sometimes free black, more commonly from some mixture of these elements.[88] The testimony summoned by such legal contests reveals how the hidden history of the charter generations survived the plantation revolution and suggests the mechanisms by which it would be maintained in the centuries that followed. It also reveals how race had been constructed and reconstructed in mainland North America over the course of two centuries of African and European settlement and how it would be remade.

NOTES

1 Carter to Robert Jones, Oct. 10, 1727 [misdated 1717], Oct. 24, 1729, quoted in Lorena S. Walsh, "A 'Place in Time' Regained: A Fuller History of Colonial Chesapeake Slavery through Group Biography," in Larry E. Hudson, Jr., ed., *Working toward Freedom: Slave Society and the Domestic Economy in the American South* (Rochester, N. Y., 1994), 14.

2 For the names of Carter's slaves see the Carter Papers, Alderman Library, University of Virginia, Charlottesville. The naming of Chesapeake slaves is discussed in Allan Kulikoff, *Tobacco and Slaves: The Development of Southern Cultures in the Chesapeake, 1680–1800* (Chapel Hill, 1986), 325–26, and John Thornton, "Central African Names and African-American Naming Patterns," *William and Mary Quarterly*, 3d Ser., 50 (1993), 727–42. For surnames see Walsh, "A 'Place in Time' Regained," 26–27 n. 18. The pioneering work on this subject is Peter H. Wood, *Black Majority: Negroes in Colonial South Carolina from 1670 through the Stono Rebellion* (New York, 1974), 181–86. Henry Laurens, the great South Carolina slave trader and planter, followed a similar routine in naming his slaves; Philip Morgan, "Three Planters and Their Slaves: Perspectives on Slavery in Virginia, South Carolina, and Jamaica, 1750–1790," in Winthrop D. Jordan and Sheila L. Skemp, eds., *Race and Family in the Colonial South* (Jackson, Miss., 1987), 65.

3 Gerald W. Mullin, *Flight and Rebellion: Slave Resistance in Eighteenth-Century Virginia* (New York, 1972), chaps. 1–3; Kulikoff, *Tobacco and Slaves*, esp. 319–34; Russell R. Menard, "The Maryland Slave Population, 1658 to 1730: A Demographic Profile of Blacks in Four Counties," *WMQ*, 3d Ser., 32 (1975), 29–54; Lois Green Carr and Walsh, "Economic Diversification and Labor Organization in the Chesapeake, 1650–1820," in Stephen Innes, ed., *Work and Labor in Early America* (Chapel Hill, 1988), 144–88. Quotation in Hugh Jones, *The Present State of Virginia, from Whence Is Inferred a Short View of Maryland and North Carolina*, ed. Richard L. Morton (Chapel Hill, 1956), 36–38, and Philip Alexander Bruce, *Institutional History of Virginia in the Seventeenth Century . . .*, 2 vols. (New York, 1910), 1:9. See a slightly different version in "The Journal of the General Assembly of Virginia," June 2, 1699, in W. N. Sainsbury et al., eds., *Calendar of State Papers, Colonial Series, America and West Indies*, 40 vols. (London, 1860–1969), 17:261.

4 In the summer of 1767, when two slaves escaped from a Georgia plantation, their owner noted that one "calls himself GOLAGA," although "the name given him [was] ABEL," and the other "calls himself ABBROM, the name given him here BENNET." For evidence that the practice had not ended by 1774 see Lathan A. Windley, comp., *Runaway Slave Advertisements: A Documentary History from the 1730s to 1790*, 4 vols. (Westport, Conn., 1983), 4:22 (*[Savannah] Georgia Gazette*, June 3, 1767), 62 (ibid., Apr. 19, 1775).

5 "Creole" derives from the Portuguese *crioulo*, meaning a person of African descent born in the New World. It has been extended to native-born free people of many national origins, including both Europeans and Africans, and of diverse social standing. It has also been applied to people of partly European but mixed racial and national origins in various European colonies

and to Africans who entered Europe. In the United States, creole has also been specifically applied to people of mixed but usually non-African origins in Louisiana. Staying within the bounds of the broadest definition of creole and the literal definition of African American, I use both terms to refer to black people of native American birth; John A. Holm, *Pidgins and Creoles: Theory and Structure*, 2 vols. (Cambridge, 1988–1989), 1:9. On the complex and often contradictory usage in a single place see Gwendolyn Midlo Hall, *Africans in Colonial Louisiana: The Development of Afro-Creole Culture in the Eighteenth Century* (Baton Rouge, 1992), 157–59, and Joseph G. Tregle, Jr., "On that Word 'Creole' Again: A Note," *Louisiana History*, 23 (1982), 193–98.

6 See, for example, Mullin, *Flight and Rebellion*, and Mullin, *Africa in America: Slave Acculturation and Resistance in the American South and the British Caribbean, 1736–1831* (Urbana, Ill., 1992), 268, which examines the typology of "African" and "creole" from the perspective of resistance. See also the 3 stages of black community development proposed by Kulikoff, "The Origins of Afro-American Society in Tidewater Maryland and Virginia, 1700–1790," *WMQ*, 3d Ser., 35 (1978), 226–59, esp. 229, and expanded in his *Tobacco and Slaves*, chaps. 8–10. Although the work of Sidney Mintz and Richard Price, which has provided the theoretical backbone for the study of African acculturation in the New World, begins by breaking with models of cultural change associated with "assimilation" and, indeed, all notions of social and cultural change that have a specific end point, it too frames the process as a progression from African to creole; *Anthropological Approach to the Afro-American Past: A Caribbean Perspective*, Institute for the Study of Human Issues Occasional Papers in Social Change (Philadelphia, 1976). Others have followed, including those sensitive to the process of re-Africanization. See, for example, Wood, *Black Majority*; Kulikoff, *Tobacco and Slaves*; Ira Berlin and Ronald Hoffman, eds., *Slavery and Freedom in the Age of Revolution* (Charlottesville, 1983); and Berlin, "Time, Space, and the Evolution of Afro-American Society on British Mainland North America," *American Historical Review*, 85 (1980), 44–78. Thornton's work represents an important theoretical departure. He distinguishes between the African and the Atlantic experiences, maintaining the "Atlantic environment was . . . different from the African one." He extends the Atlantic environment to the African littoral as well as the Americas, in *Africa and Africans in the Making of the Atlantic World, 1440–1680* (Cambridge, 1992), quotation on 211.

7 The use of charter groups draws on T. H. Breen, "Creative Adoptions: Peoples and Cultures," in Jack P. Greene and J. R. Pole, eds., *Colonial British America: Essays in the New History of the Early Modern Era* (Baltimore, 1984), 203–08. Breen, in turn, borrowed the idea from anthropologist John Porter.

8 "Atlantic creole," employed herein, designates those who by experience or choice, as well as by birth, became part of a new culture that emerged along the Atlantic littoral—in Africa, Europe, or the Americas—beginning in the 16th century. It departs from the notion of "creole" that makes birth definitive (see n. 5 above). Circumstances and volition blurred differences between "African" and "creole" as defined only by nativity, if only because Africans and creoles were connected by ties of kinship and friendship. They worked together, played together, intermarried, and on occasion stood together against assaults on their freedom. Even more important, men and women could define themselves in ways that transcended nativity. "African" and "creole" were as much a matter of choice as of birth. The term "Atlantic creole" is designed to capture the cultural transformation that sometimes preceded generational change and sometimes was unaffected by it. Insightful commentary on the process of creolization is provided by Mintz, "The Socio-Historical Background to Pidginization and Creolization," in Dell Hymes, ed., *Pidginization*

and Creolization of Languages: Proceedings of a Conference Held at the University of the West Indies, Mona, Jamaica, April 1968 (Cambridge, 1971), 481–96.

9 For ground-breaking works that argue for the unity of working peoples in the Atlantic world see Peter Linebaugh, "All the Atlantic Mountains Shook," *Labour/Le Travailleur*, 10 (1982), 82–121, and Linebaugh and Marcus Rediker, "The Many-Headed Hydra: Sailors, Slaves, and the Atlantic Working Class in the Eighteenth Century," *Journal of Historical Sociology*, 3 (1990), 225–52. Thornton, *Africa and Africans in the Making of the Atlantic World*, adopts a similar perspective in viewing the making of African-American culture. A larger Atlantic perspective for the formation of black culture is posed in Paul Gilroy, *The Black Atlantic: Modernity and Double Consciousness* (Cambridge, Mass., 1993).

10 A. C. de C. M. Saunders, *A Social History of Black Slaves and Freedmen in Portugal, 1441–1555* (Cambridge, 1982), 11–12, 145, 197 n. 52, 215 n. 73 (for black sailors and interpreters in the African trade); P.E.H. Hair, "The Use of African Languages in Afro-European Contacts in Guinea, 1440–1560," *Sierra Leone Language Review*, 5 (1966), 7–17 (for black interpreters and Europeans' striking lack of interest in mastering African languages); George E. Brooks, *Landlords and Strangers: Ecology, Society, and Trade in West Africa, 1000–1630* (Boulder, Colo., 1993), chap. 7 (particularly for the role of *grumetes*), 124, 136–37; Wyatt Mac-Gaffey, "Dialogues of the Deaf: Europeans on the Atlantic Coast of Africa," in Stuart B. Schwartz, ed., *Implicit Understandings: Observing, Reporting, and Reflecting on the Encounters between Europeans and Other Peoples in the Early Modern Era* (Cambridge, 1994), 252 (for hostages); Kwame Yeboa Daaku, *Trade and Politics on the Gold Coast, 1600–1720: A Study of the African Reaction to European Trade* (Oxford, 1970), chap. 5, esp. 96–97 (for ambassadors to the United Provinces in 1611); Anne Hilton, *The Kingdom of Kongo* (Oxford, 1985), 64; Paul Edwards and James Walvin, "Africans in Britain, 1500–1800," in Martin L. Kilson and Robert I. Rotberg, eds., *The African Diaspora: Interpretive Essays* (Cambridge, Mass., 1976), 173–205 (for African royalty sending their sons to be educated in Europe). See also Shelby T. McCloy, "Negroes and Mulattos in Eighteenth-Century France," *Journal of Negro History*, 30 (1945), 276–92. For the near-seamless, reciprocal relationship between the Portuguese and the Kongolese courts in the 16th century see Thornton, "Early Kongo-Portuguese Relations, 1483–1575: A New Interpretation," *History in Africa*, 8 (1981), 183–204.

11 For an overview see Thornton, *Africa and Africans in the Making of the Atlantic World*, chap. 2, esp. 59–62. See also Daaku, *Trade and Politics on the Gold Coast*, chap. 2; Brooks, *Landlords and Strangers*, chaps. 7–8 (see the Portuguese crown's penalties against *lançados* for illegal trading, 152–54); Philip D. Curtin, *Economic Change in Precolonial Africa: Senegambia in the Era of the Slave Trade* (Madison, Wis., 1975), chap. 3; Ray A. Kea, *Settlements, Trade, and Polities in the Seventeenth-Century Gold Coast* (Baltimore, 1982); John Vogt, *Portuguese Rule on the Gold Coast, 1469–1682* (Athens, Ga., 1979); C. R. Boxer, *Four Centuries of Portuguese Expansion, 1415–1825: A Succinct Survey* (Johannesburg, 1961); and Boxer, *The Dutch Seaborne Empire, 1600–1800* (New York, 1965). *Lançados* comes from a contraction of *lançados em terra* (to put on shore); Curtin, *Economic Change in Precolonial Africa*, 95. As the influence of the Atlantic economy spread to the interior, Atlantic creoles appeared in the hinterland, generally in the centers of trade along rivers.

12 Kea, *Settlements, Trade, and Polities*, chap. 1, esp. 38.

13 Ibid.; Vogt, *Portuguese Rule on the Gold Coast*; Harvey M. Feinberg, *Africans and Europeans in West Africa: Elminans and Dutchmen on the Gold Coast during the Eighteenth Century*, American Philosophical Society, *Transactions*, 79, No. 7 (Philadelphia, 1989). For mortality see Curtin, "Epidemiology and the Slave Trade," *Political Science Quarterly*, 83 (1968), 190–216, and K. G. Davies, "The

Living and the Dead: White Mortality in West Africa, 1684–1732," in Stanley L. Engerman and Eugene D. Genovese, eds., *Race and Slavery in the Western Hemisphere: Quantitative Studies* (Princeton, 1975), 83–98.

14 Kea, *Settlements, Trade, and Polities*, chap. 1, esp. 38–50, 133–34; Vogt, *Portuguese Rule on the Gold Coast*; Feinberg, *Africans and Europeans in West Africa*. Eveline C. Martin, *The British West African Settlements, 1750–1821: A Study in Local Administration* (New York, 1927), and Margaret Priestley, *West African Trade and Coast Society: A Family Study* (London, 1969), describe the English enclaves in the 18th and 19th centuries, casting light on their earlier development.

15 Brooks, *Landlords and Strangers*, chaps. 7–9, esp. 188–96, and Brooks, "Luso-African Commerce and Settlement in the Gambia and Guinea-Bissau Region," *Boston University African Studies Center Working Papers* (1980), for the connection of the Luso-Africans with the Cape Verde Islands; Daaku, *Trade and Politics on the Gold Coast*, chaps. 5–6; Vogt, *Portuguese Rule on the Gold Coast*, 154; Feinberg, *Africans and Europeans in West Africa*, 32, 88–90; Curtin, *Economic Change in Precolonial Africa*, 95–100, 113–21 (for Afro-French). For the development of a similar population in Angola see Joseph C. Miller, *Way of Death: Merchant Capitalism and the Angolan Slave Trade, 1730–1830* (Madison, Wis., 1988), esp. chaps. 8–9, and Miller, "A Marginal Institution on the Margin of the Atlantic System: The Portuguese Southern Atlantic Slave Trade in the Eighteenth Century," in Barbara L. Solow, ed., *Slavery and the Rise of the Atlantic System* (Cambridge, Mass., 1991), 125, 128–29. By the mid-17th century, the hierarchy of Kongolese Catholics was largely mixed African and European ancestry or *pombeiros*; Hilton, *Kingdom of Kongo*, 140–41, 154. See also Allen F. Isaacman, *Mozambique: The Africanization of a European Institution: The Zambezi Prazos, 1750–1902* (Madison, Wis., 1972). The number of such individuals in west Africa is difficult to estimate. Brooks, in his study of the Grain Coast and its interior, estimates "hundreds of Portuguese and Cabo Verdean traders were admitted to western African communities by the close of the fifteenth century." Probably the same could be said for other portions of the African coast at that time. By the middle of the 16th century, Atlantic creoles were more numerous. In 1567, when the English adventurer John Hawkins launched a raid on an African settlement on the Cacheu River, he was repulsed by a force that included "about a hundred" *lançados*; Brooks, *Landlords and Strangers*, 137, 230–31. By the 19th century, the Afro-Europeans had become to a "remarkable extent soundly and politically integrated" and "occupied their own 'quarter' of the town" of Elmina; Larry W. Yarak, "West African Coastal Slavery in the Nineteenth Century: The Case of Afro-European Slaveowners of Elmina," *Ethnohistory*, 36 (1989), 44–60, quotation on 47; J. T. Lever, "Mulatto Influence on the Gold Coast in the Early Nineteenth Century: Jan Nieser of Elmina," *African Historical Studies*, 3 (1970), 253–61.

16 Daaku, *Trade and Politics on the Gold Coast*, chaps. 4–5; Brooks, *Landlords and Strangers*, chaps. 7–9, esp. 188–96; Curtin, *Economic Change in Precolonial Africa*, 95–100. See also Miller's compelling description of Angola's Luso-Africans in the 18th and 19th centuries that suggests something of their earlier history, in *Way of Death*, 246–50. Brooks notes the term *tangomãos* passed from use at the end of the 17th century, in "Luso-African Commerce and Settlement in the Gambia and Guinea-Bissau," 3.

17 Speaking of the Afro-French in Senegambia in the 18th century, Curtin emphasizes the cultural transformation in making this new people, noting that "the important characteristic of this community was cultural mixture, not racial mixture, and the most effective of the traders from France were those who could cross the cultural line between Europe and Africa in their commercial relations," in *Economic Change in Precolonial Africa*, 117.

18 Holm, *Pidgins and Creoles*; Thornton, *Africa and Africans in the Making of the Atlantic World*, 213–18; Saunders, *Black Slaves and Freedman in Portugal*, 98–102 (see special word—*ladinhos*—for blacks who could speak "good" Portuguese, 101); Brooks, *Landlords and Strangers*, 136–37. See also Robert A. Hall, Jr., *Pidgin and Creole Languages* (Ithaca, 1966); David Dalby, "The Place of Africa and Afro-America in the History of the English Language," *African Language Review*, 9 (1971), 280–98; Hair, "Use of African Languages in Afro-European Contacts in Guinea," 5–26; Keith Whinnom, "Contacts De Langues et Emprunts Lexicaux: The Origin of the European-Based Pidgins and Creoles," *Orbis*, 14 (1965), 509–27, Whinnom, "Linguistic Hybridization and the 'Special Case' of Pidgins and Creoles," in Hymes, ed., *Pidginization and Creolization of Languages*, 91–115, and Whinnom, "The Context and Origins of Lingua Franca," in Jürgen M. Meisel, ed., *Langues en Contact—Pidgins—Creoles* (Tübingen, 1975); and J. L. Dillard, "Creole English and Creole Portuguese: The Early Records," in Ian F. Hancock, ed., *Readings in Creole Studies* (Ghent, 1979), 261–68. For another theory on the origins of the west African pidgin see Anthony J. Naro, "The Origins of West African Pidgin," in Claudia Corum, T. Cedric Smith-Stark, and Ann Weiser, eds., *Papers from the Ninth Regional Meeting*, Chicago Linguistic Society (1973), 442–49.

19 Daaku, *Trade and Politics on the Gold Coast*, chaps. 3–4; Feinberg, *Africans and Europeans in West Africa*, chap. 6, quotation on 86; Kea, *Settlements, Trade, and Polities*, esp. pt. 2; Curtin, *Economic Change in Precolonial Africa*, 92–93.

20 Vogt, *Portuguese Rule on the Gold Coast*, 54–58; Daaku, *Trade and Politics on the Gold Coast*, 99–101; Thornton, "The Development of an African Catholic Church in the Kingdom of Kongo, 1491–1750," *Journal of African History*, 25 (1984), 147–67; Hilton, *Kingdom of Kongo*, 32–49, 154–61, 179, 198; MacGaffey, *Religion and Society in Central Africa: The BaKongo of Lower Zaire* (Chicago, 1986), 191–216, and MacGaffey, "Dialogues of the Deaf," 249–67. Pacing the cultural intermixture of African and Europe was the simultaneous introduction of European and American plants and animals, which compounded and legitimated many of the cultural changes; Alfred W. Crosby, *Ecological Imperialism: The Biological Expansion of Europe, 900–1900* (Cambridge, 1986).

21 The history of one element of this population, the canoemen, is discussed in Peter C. W. Gutkind, "The Boatmen of Ghana: The Possibilities of a Pre-Colonial African Labor History," in Michael Hanagan and Charles Stephenson, eds., *Confrontation, Class Consciousness, and the Labor Process: Studies in Proletarian Class Formation* (Westport, Conn., 1986), 123–66, and Gutkind, "Trade and Labor in Early Precolonial African History: The Canoemen of Southern Ghana," in Catherine Coquery-Vidrovitch and Paul E. Lovejoy, eds., *The Workers of African Trade* (Beverly Hills, Calif., 1985), 25–49; Robert Smith, "The Canoe in West African History," *J. African Hist.*, II (1970), 515–33; and Robin Law, "Trade and Politics behind the Slave Trade: The Lagoon Traffic and the Rise of Lagos," ibid., 24 (1983), 321–48. See also Daaku, *Trade and Politics on the Gold Coast*, 103–04, 121–22. For an overview of the coastal towns see Kea, *Settlements, Trade, and Polities*, esp. chap. 2; Daaku, *Trade and Politics on the Gold Coast*, chap. 4; and Curtin, *Economic Change in Precolonial Africa*, 119–20, for the relation between European trading communities and African towns. Since Africans would not rent outsiders more land than needed for a house or a store, food production and other services remained in African hands; Brooks, *Landlords and Strangers*, 189–90. For bandits see Kea, " 'I Am Here to Plunder on the General Road': Bandits and Banditry in the Pre-Nineteenth Century Gold Coast," in Donald Crummey, ed., *Banditry, Rebellion, and Social Protest in Africa* (London, 1986), 109–32.

22 Feinberg, *Africans and Europeans in West Africa*, 84–85 (for Elmina); Joyce D.

Goodfriend, *Before the Melting Pot: Society and Culture in Colonial New York City, 1664–1730* (Princeton, 1992), 13 (for New Amsterdam); Peter A. Coclanis, *The Shadow of a Dream: Economic Life and Death in the South Carolina Low Country, 1670–1920* (New York, 1989), 115 (for Charleston).

23 Kea, *Settlements, Trade, and Polities*, esp. chap. 6.

24 Feinberg, *Africans and Europeans in West Africa*, 65, 82–83; Kea, *Settlements, Trade, and Polities*, 197–202, 289–90. On the Cape Verde Islands, free blacks obtained the right to hold public office in 1546. Racial distinctions did not appear until the emergence of a plantation society in the mid-16th century, when the preoccupation with skin color and hair texture emerged along with racially exclusionary policies; Brooks, *Landlords and Strangers*, 158–59, 186–87; Dierdre Meintel, *Race, Culture, and Portuguese Colonialism in Cabo Verde* (Syracuse, N.Y., 1984), 96–103.

25 Kea, *Settlements, Trade, and Polities*, 233–35, 315–16, 319–20. Daaku notes that "difficulties arise in establishing the exact nationalities" of Gold Coast traders, as European "writers tended to 'Europeanize' the names of some of the Africans with whom they traded and those in their service, while some of the Africans fancifully assumed European names," in *Trade and Politics on the Gold Coast*, 96.

26 Daaku, *Trade and Politics on the Gold Coast*, chaps. 5–6; David Henige, "John Kabes of Komenda: An Early African Enterpreneur and State Builder," *J. African Hist.*, 18 (1977), 1–19.

27 Gutkind, "Boatmen of Ghana," 131–39, quotation on 137, and Gutkind, "Trade and Labor in Early Precolonial African History," 40–41 (for canoemen who pawned themselves and later became successful traders).

28 For enslavement of canoemen for violation of Portuguese regulations see Gutkind, "Trade and Labor in Early Precolonial African History," 27–28, 36. Okoyaw, a canoeman who pawned himself to the Royal African Company in 1704 to redeem a debt, agreed in return "to attend Dayly the Company's Work"; cited in Kea, *Settlements, Trade, and Polities*, 243. Because there was no established system of commercial law, creditors might seize the slaves or even the fellow townsmen of their debtors to satisfy an obligation; Curtin, *Economic Change in Precolonial Africa*, 302–08.

29 The northern North American colonies often received "refuse" slaves. For complaints and appreciations see Goodfriend, "Burghers and Blacks: The Evolution of a Slave Society at New Amsterdam," *New York History*, 59 (1978), 139; Sainsbury et al., eds., *Calendar of State Papers, Colonial Series, 1708–1709*, 24:110; Lorenzo J. Greene, *The Negro in Colonial New England, 1620–1776* (New York, 1942), 35; Jeremias van Rensselaer to Jan Baptist van Rensselaer, ca. 1659, in A.J.F. Van Laer, ed., *Correspondence of Jeremias Van Rensselaer, 1651–1674* (Albany, 1932), 167–68, 175; William D. Pierson, *Black Yankees: The Development of an Afro-American Subculture in Eighteenth-Century New England* (Amherst, Mass., 1988), 4–5; Edgar J. McManus, *Black Bondage in the North* (Syracuse, N. Y., 1973), 18–25, and McManus, *A History of Slavery in New York* (Syracuse, N. Y., 1966), 23–39; James G. Lydon, "New York and the Slave Trade, 1700 to 1774," *WMQ*, 3d Ser., 35 (1978), 275–79, 281–90; Darold D. Wax, "Negro Imports into Pennsylvania, 1720–1766," *Pennsylvania History*, 32 (1965), 254–87, and Wax, "Preferences for Slaves in Colonial America," *J. Negro Hist.*, 58 (1973), 374–76, 379–87; and Sharon V. Salinger, *"To Serve Well and Faithfully": Labour and Indentured Servitude in Pennsylvania, 1682–1800* (Cambridge, 1987), 75–78.

30 Boxer, *The Dutch in Brazil, 1624–1654* (Oxford, 1957); Johannes Menne Postma, *The Dutch in the Atlantic Slave Trade* (Cambridge, 1990), chaps. 2–3, 8; Cornelis C. Goslinga, *The Dutch in the Caribbean and on the Wild Coast, 1580–1680* (Gainesville, Fla., 1971).

31 Boxer, *Four Centuries of Portuguese Expansion*, 48–51, and Boxer, *Dutch in Brazil*; P. C. Emmer, "The Dutch and the Making of the Second Atlantic System," in Solow, ed., *Slavery and the Rise of the Atlantic System*, 75–96, esp. 83–84; Thornton, *Africa and Africans in the Making of the Atlantic World*, 64–65, 69–77. Albert van Danzig, ed. and trans., *The Dutch and the Guinea Coast, 1674–1742: A Collection of Documents from the General State Archives at the Hague* (Accra, 1978), provides insight into the operation of the Dutch West India Company and the role of the Dutch on the Gold and Slave coasts.

32 Thornton, *The Kingdom of Kongo: Civil War and Transition, 1641–1718* (Madison, Wis., 1983), esp. 72–74, chaps. 6–7 passim; Hilton, *Kingdom of Kongo*, chaps. 6–7; Ernst Van Den Boogaart and Pieter C. Emmer, "The Dutch Participation in the Atlantic Slave Trade, 1596–1650," in Henry A. Gemery and Jan S. Hogendorn, eds., *The Uncommon Market: Essays in the Economic History of the Atlantic Slave Trade* (New York, 1979), 353–71. The best survey of the Dutch trade is Postma, *Dutch in the Atlantic Slave Trade*.

33 Goslinga, *Dutch in the Caribbean and on the Wild Coast*; Van Laer, ed., *Correspondence of Jeremias Van Rensselaer*, 167–68, 175, quotation on 167; Elizabeth Donnan, ed., *Documents Illustrative of the History of the Slave Trade to America*, 4 vols. (Washington, D. C., 1930–1935), 3:421; Goodfriend, "Burghers and Blacks," 139.

34 Names are drawn from E. B. O'Callaghan, comp., *The Documentary History of the State of New-York*, 4 vols. (Albany, 1849–1851); O'Callaghan, ed., *Documents Relative to the Colonial History of the State of New-York*, 15 vols. (Albany, 1853–1887) (hereafter *N. Y. Col. Docs.*); O'Callaghan, comp., *Laws and Ordinances of New Netherland, 1638–1674* (Albany, 1868); O'Callaghan, ed., *Calendar of Historical Manuscripts in the Office of the Secretary of State, 1630–1664* (Albany, 1865); Berthold Fernow, ed., *The Records of New Amsterdam from 1653 to 1674*, 7 vols. (New York, 1897); Fernow, ed., *Minutes of the Orphanmasters Court of New Amsterdam, 1655–1663*, 2 vols. (New York, 1907); Kenneth Scott and Kenn Stryker-Rodda, comps., *New York Historical Manuscripts: Dutch*, vols. 1–4 (Baltimore, 1974–); Charles T. Gehring, ed., *New York Historical Manuscripts: Dutch Land Papers* (Baltimore, 1980); New York Genealogical and Biographical Society, Collections, *Marriages from 1639 to 1801 in the Reformed Dutch Church of New York* (New York, 1890); I. N. Phelps Stokes, *Iconography of Manhattan Island, 1498–1909*, 6 vols. (New York, 1914–1928). A few names suggest the subtle transformation as the Atlantic creoles crossed the ocean and assumed a new identity that was unfamiliar to its hosts. For example, Anthony Jansen of Salee or Van Vaes, a man of tawny complexion—"mulatto," per below—who claimed Moroccan birth, became "Anthony the Turk," perhaps because Turks were considered fierce—as Anthony's litigious history indicates he surely was—but, more important, because he was alien in status and brown in pigment; Leo Hershkowitz, "The Troublesome Turk: An Illustration of Judicial Process in New Amsterdam," *N. Y. Hist.*, 46 (1965), 299–310. But if names of new arrivals in New Netherland reflect their lived experience rather than an owner's designation, they also have nothing of the ring of Africa: no Quaws, Phibbis, or any of the day names that Africans later carried. Such names would become familiar to northern slaveholders when the slave trade reached into the interior of Africa. In Portugal, the names slaves bore do not seem different from those of native Portuguese; Saunders, *Black Slaves and Freedmen in Portugal*, 89–90. The practice of attaching a national modifier to a given name was employed for others besides Africans. See Edmund S. Morgan, *American Slavery, American Freedom: The Ordeal of Colonial Virginia* (New York, 1975), 153–54.

35 Nothing evidenced the creoles' easy integration into the mainland society

better than the number who survived into old age. There are no systematic demographic studies of people of African descent during the first years of settlement, and perhaps because the numbers are so small, there can be none. Nevertheless, "old" or "aged" slaves are encountered again and again, sometimes in descriptions of fugitives, sometimes in the deeds that manumit—i. e., discard—superannuated slaves. Before the end of the 17th century, numbers of black people lived long enough to see their grandchildren.

36 Fernow, ed., *Records of New Amsterdam,* 5:337, cited in Goodfriend, *Before the Melting Pot*, 252 n. 25.

37 Suzanne Miers and Igor Kopytoff, eds., *Slavery in Africa: Historical and Anthropological Perspectives* (Madison, Wis., 1977); Paul E. Lovejoy, *Transformations in Slavery: A History of Slavery in Africa* (Cambridge, 1983); Patrick Manning, *Slavery and African Life: Occidental, Oriental, and African Slave Trades* (Cambridge, 1990); Thornton, *Africa and Africans in the Making of the Atlantic World*, chap 3; Claude Meillassoux, *The Anthropology of Slavery: The Womb of Iron and Gold* (Chicago, 1991); Martin A. Klein, "Introduction: Modern European Expansion and Traditional Servitude in Africa and Asia," in Klein, ed., *Breaking the Chains: Slavery, Bondage, and Emancipation in Modern Africa and Asia* (Madison, Wis., 1993), 3–26; Toyin Falola and Lovejoy, "Pawnship in Historical Perspective," in Falola and Lovejoy, eds., *Pawnship in Africa: Debt Bondage in Historical Perspective* (Boulder, Colo., 1994), 1–26. A dated but still useful critical review of the subject is Frederick Cooper, "The Problem of Slavery in African Studies," *J. African Hist.*, 20 (1979), 103–25.

38 Miers and Kopytoff, eds., *Slavery in Africa*, chap. 1, esp. 17.

39 Goodfriend, *Before the Melting Pot*, 10, chap. 6; Van Den Boogaart, "The Servant Migration to New Netherland, 1624–1664," in Emmer, ed., *Colonialism and Migration: Indentured Labour before and after Slavery* (Dordrecht, 1986), 58; O'Callaghan, ed., *N. Y. Col. Docs.*, 1:154.

40 Goodfriend, *Before the Melting Pot*, chap. 6; Goodfriend, "Burghers and Blacks," 125–44; Goodfriend, "Black Families in New Netherland," *Journal of the Afro-American Historical and Genealogical Society*, 5 (1984), 94–107; Morton Wagman, "Corporate Slavery in New Netherland," *J. Negro Hist.*, 65 (1980), 34–42; McManus, *Slavery in New York*, 2–22; Michael Kammen, *Colonial New York: A History* (New York, 1975), 58–60; Van Den Boogaart, "Servant Migration to New Netherland," 56–59, 65–71; Vivienne L. Kruger, "Born to Run: The Slave Family in Early New York, 1626 to 1827" (Ph. D. diss., Columbia University, 1985), chap. 2, esp. 46–48, chap. 6, esp. 270–77; Oliver A. Rink, *Holland on the Hudson: An Economic and Social History of Dutch New York* (Ithaca, 1986), 161 n. 33. Between 1639 and 1652, marriages recorded in the New Amsterdam Church represented 28% of the marriages recorded in that period—also note one interracial marriage. For baptisms see "Reformed Dutch Church, New York, Baptisms, 1639–1800," New York Genealogical and Biographical Society, *Collections*, 2 vols. (New York, 1901), 1:10–27, 2:10–38; for the 1635 petition see Stokes, *Iconography of Manhattan Island*, 4:82, and No. 14, Notulen W1635, 1626 (19–11–1635), inv. 1.05.01. 01. (Oude) Algemeen Rijksarchief, The Hague. A petition by "five blacks from New Netherland who had come here [Amsterdam]" was referred back to officials in New Netherland. Marcel van der Linden of the International Institute of Social History in Amsterdam kindly located and translated this notation in the records of the Dutch West India Company.

41 Petition for freedom, in O'Callaghan, ed., *Calendar of Historical Manuscripts*, 269. White residents of New Amsterdam protested the enslavement of the children of half-free slaves, holding that no one born of a free person should be a slave. The Dutch West India Company rejected the claim; O'Callaghan, ed.,

N. Y. Col. Docs., 1:302, 343; O'Callaghan, ed., *Laws and Ordinances of New Netherland*, 4:36–37. For the Dutch West India Company's "setting them free and at liberty, on the same footing as other free people here in New Netherland," although children remained property of the company, see Van Den Boogaart, "Servant Migration to New Netherland," 69–70.

42 For black men paying tribute to purchase their families see O'Callaghan, ed., *Calendar of Historical Manuscripts*, 45, 87, 105; O'Callaghan, ed., *N. Y. Col. Docs.*, 1:343; Goodfriend, "Burghers and Blacks," 125–44, and "Black Families in New Netherlands," 94–107; McManus, *Slavery in New York*, 2–22; Wagman, "Corporate Slavery in New Netherland," 38–39; quotation in Gerald Francis DeJong, "The Dutch Reformed Church and Negro Slavery in Colonial America," *Church History*, 40 (1971), 430; Kruger, "Born to Run," chap. 1, esp. 90–92; Henry B. Hoff, "Frans Abramse Van Salee and His Descendants: A Colonial Black Family in New York and New Jersey," *New York Genealogical and Biographical Register*, 121 (1990), 65–71, 157–61.

43 Goodfriend estimates that 75 of New Amsterdam's 375 blacks were free in 1664, in *Before the Melting Pot*, 61.

44 Kruger, "Born to Run," 50–55, 591–606, tells of the creation of a small class of black landowners as a result of gifts from the Dutch West India Company and direct purchase by the blacks themselves (quotation on 592); Goodfriend, *Before the Melting Pot*, 115–16, 253 n. 36; Peter R. Christoph, "The Freedmen of New Amsterdam," *J. Afro-Amer. Hist. Gen. Soc.*, 5 (1984), 116–17. See also Stokes, *Iconography of Manhattan Island*, 2:302, 4:70–78, 100, 104–06, 120–48, 265–66; Gehring, ed., *New York Historical Manuscripts*; and Van Den Boogaart, "Servant Migration to New Netherland," 56–59, 65–71. For the employment of a white housekeeper by a free black artisan see ibid., 69; Fernow, ed., *Minutes of the Orphanmasters Court*, 2: 46; and Roi Ottley and William J. Weatherby, eds., *The Negro in New York: An Informal Social History* (New York, 1967), 12.

45 O'Callaghan, ed., *Calendar of Historical Manuscripts*, 87, 105, 269 (for manumission, dubbed "half slaves"), 222 (adoption), 269 (land grants). See also Goodfriend, *Before the Melting Pot*, chap. 6, and Fernow, ed., *Records of New Amsterdam from 1653 to 1674*, 3:42, 5, 172, 337–40, 7, 11 (for actions in court); Goodfriend, "Burghers and Blacks," 125–44, and "Black Families in New Netherlands," 94–107; Van Den Boogaart, "Servant Migration to New Netherland," 56–59, 65–71; McManus, *Slavery in New York*, 2–22; DeJong, "Dutch Reformed Church and Negro Slavery in Colonial America," 430; Kruger, "Born to Run," 46–48; 270–78; Hoff, "Frans Abramse Van Salee and His Descendants"; Kammen, *New York*, 58–60. For blacks using Dutch courts early on see Rink, *Holland on the Hudson*, 160–61—e.g., in 1638, Anthony Portuguese sued Anthony Jansen for damages done his hog; soon after, one Pedro Negretto claimed back wages. For adoption of a black child by a free black family see Scott and Stryker-Rodda, eds., *The Register of Salmon Lachaire, Notary Public of New Amsterdam, 1661–1662* (Baltimore, 1978), 22–23; O'Callaghan, ed., *Calendar of Historical Manuscripts*, 222, 256; and Kruger, "Born to Run," 44–51.

46 Until New Netherland developed an agricultural base, slavery did not seem to take hold, and settlers admitted in 1649 that slaves imported at great cost "just dripped through the fingers" and "were sold for pork and peas"; O'Callaghan, ed., *N. Y. Col. Docs.*, 1:302. For the change that took place during the 1650s and the beginning of direct African importation in 1655 see O'Callaghan, ed., *Calendar of Historical Manuscripts*, 268, 289, 293, 307, 331. New York sharply limited manumission in 1712. Few slaves were freed before then. One careful enumeration counted 8 manumissions between 1669 and 1712; Kruger, "Born to Run," 593.

47 James B. Bartlett and J. Franklin Jameson, eds., *Journal of Jasper Danckaerts,*

1679–1680 (New York, 1913), 65. See also Goodfriend, *Before the Melting Pot*, 115–16 (land). After the English conquest, black people continued to present their children for baptism, although they changed to the Anglican church; ibid., 131.

48 Curtin, *Economic Change in Precolonial Africa*, 104–05, 121–27; Jean Mettas, *Répertoire des Expéditions Négrières Françaises au XVIIIe Siècle*, 2 vols: (Paris, 1984); Marcel Giraud, *A History of French Louisiana: The Reign of Louis XIV, 1698–1715*, trans. Joseph C. Lambert (Baton Rouge, 1974); Hall, *Africans in Colonial Louisiana*, chaps. 2–4. For the French slave trade see Robert Louis Stein, *The French Slave Trade in the Eighteenth Century: An Old Regime Business* (Madison, Wis., 1979).

49 The Bambaras had complex relations with the French. Although many Bambaras—usually captives of the tribe whom the French also deemed Bambaras (although they often were not)—became entrapped in the international slave trade and were sold to the New World, others worked for the French as domestics, boatmen, clerks, and interpreters in the coastal forts and slave factories. Their proud military tradition—honed in a long history of warfare against Mandingas and other Islamic peoples—made them ideal soldiers as well as slave catchers. Along the coast of Africa, "Bambara" became a generic word for soldier; Hall, *Africans in Colonial Louisiana*, 42, and Curtin, *Economic Change in Precolonial Africa*, 115, 143, 149, 178–81, 191–92; see the review of Hall in *Africa*, 64 (1994), 168–71.

50 The evidence of Samba's participation in the Fort D'Arguin insurrection is insubstantial and contradictory, but he got himself into enough trouble to be enslaved and deported; Hall, *Africans in Colonial Louisiana*, 109–10; Le Page du Pratz, *Histoire de la Louisiane*, 3 vols. (Paris, 1758), 3:305–17; Daniel H. Usner, Jr., "From African Captivity to American Slavery: The Introduction of Black Laborers to Colonial Louisiana," *La. Hist.*, 20 (1979), 37. On the Afro-French community in St. Louis and other enclaves on the Senegal see Curtin, *Economic Change in Precolonial Africa*, 113–21.

51 The first census of the French settlement of the lower Mississippi Valley comes from Biloxi in 1699. It lists 5 naval officers, 5 petty officers, 4 sailors, 19 Canadians, 10 laborers, 6 cabin boys, and 20 soldiers; Hall, *Africans in Colonial Louisiana*, 3, and esp. chap. 5. Usner makes the point in comparing the use of black sailors on the Mississippi and the Senegal, in "From African Captivity to American Slavery," 25–47, esp. 36, and more generally in *Indians, Settlers, and Slaves in a Frontier Exchange Economy: The Lower Mississippi Valley before 1783* (Chapel Hill, 1992). See also James T. McGowan, "Planters without Slaves: Origins of a New World Labor System," *Southern Studies*, 16 (1977), 5–20; John G. Clark, *New Orleans, 1718–1812: An Economic History* (Baton Rouge, 1970), chap. 2; and Thomas N. Ingersoll, "Old New Orleans: Race, Class, Sex, and Order in the Early Deep South, 1718–1819" (Ph. D. diss., University of California at Los Angeles, 1990), chaps. 2–3.

52 Hall, *Africans in Colonial Louisiana*, 131–32.

53 Ibid., 106–12; du Pratz, *Histoire de la Louisiane*, 3:305–17; Usner, "From African Captivity to American Slavery," 37, 42.

54 Charles Verlinden, *The Beginnings of Modern Colonization: Eleven Essays with an Introduction* (Ithaca, 1970), 39–40; Saunders, *Black Slaves and Freedmen in Portugal*, chap. 1, esp. 55; Ruth Pike, "Sevillian Society in the Sixteenth Century: Slaves and Freedmen," *Hispanic American Historical Review*, 47 (1967), 344–59, and Pike, *Aristocrats and Traders: Sevillian Society in the Sixteenth Century* (Ithaca, 1972), 29, 170–92; P.E.H. Hair, "Black African Slaves at Valencia, 1482–1516," *History in Africa*, 7 (1980), 119–31; Thornton, *Africa and Africans in the Making of the Atlantic World*, 96–97; A.J.R. Russell-Wood, "Iberian Expansion and the Issue of Black Slavery: Changing Portuguese Attitudes, 1440–1770,"

AHR, 83 (1978), 20. During the first two decades of the 16th century, about 2,000 African slaves annually entered Lisbon and were sold there. By the 1530s, most slaves brought to Lisbon were sent to the New World via Seville.

55 In the mid-16th century, black people entered the periphery of Europe; Verlinden, *Beginnings of Modern Colonization*, chap 2. England developed a small black population that grew with English involvement in the African trade; see James B. Walvin, *Black and White: The Negro and English Society, 1555–1945* (London, 1973), chap. 1, and F. O. Shyllon, *Black Slaves in Britain* (London, 1974), and *Black People in Britain 1555–1833* (London, 1977). For France see William B. Cohen, *The French Encounter with Africans: White Response to Blacks, 1530–1880* (Bloomington, 1980), and Sue Peabody, " 'There Are No Slaves in France': Law, Culture, and Society in Early Modern France, 1685–1789" (Ph. D. diss., University of Iowa, 1993).

56 J. Fred Rippy, "The Negro and the Spanish Pioneer in the New World," *J. Negro Hist.*, 6 (1921), 183–89; Leo Wiener, *Africa and the Discovery of America*, 3 vols. (Philadelphia, 1920–1922).

57 Saunders, *Black Slaves and Freedmen in Portugal*, 29; for sailors see 11, 71–72, 145, and Hall, *Africans in Colonial Louisiana*, 128. A sale of 6 slaves in Mexico in 1554 included one born in the Azores, another born in Portugal, another born in Africa, and the latter's daughter born in Mexico; Colin A. Palmer, *Slaves of the White God: Blacks in Mexico, 1570–1650* (Cambridge, Mass., 1976), 31–32; "Abstracts of French and Spanish Documents Concerning the Early History of Louisiana," *Louisiana Historical Quarterly*, 1 (1917), 111.

58 Saunders, *Black Slaves and Freedmen in Portugal*, 152–55; Russell-Wood, "Black and Mulatto Brotherhoods in Colonial Brazil," *Hisp. Amer. Hist. Rev.*, 54 (1974), 567–602, and Russell-Wood, *The Black Man in Slavery and Freedom in Colonial Brazil* (New York, 1982), chap. 8, esp. 134, 153–54, 159–60. See also Pike, *Aristocrats and Traders*, 177–79. In the 16th century, some 7% (2,580) of Portugal's black population was free; Saunders, *Black Slaves and Freedmen in Portugal*, 59.

59 Simon Hart, *The Prehistory of the New Netherland Company: Amsterdam Notarial Records of the First Dutch Voyages to the Hudson* (Amsterdam, 1959), 23–26, 74–75, quotations on 80–82; Thomas J. Condon, *New York Beginnings: The Commercial Origins of New Netherland* (New York, 1968), chap. 1, esp. 30; Rink, *Holland on the Hudson*, 34, 42; Van Cleaf Bachman, *Peltries or Plantations: The Economic Policies of the Dutch West India Company in New Netherland, 1623–1639* (Baltimore, 1969), 6–7.

60 Wesley Frank Craven's investigation determined that the first black people to arrive at Jamestown were prizes taken by a Dutch man-of-war in consort with an English ship somewhere in the eastern Caribbean. Craven maintains they were born in the West Indies and stolen from there. J. Douglas Deal suggests they may have been taken from a Portuguese or Spanish slaver. Craven, *White Red, and Black: The Seventeenth-Century Virginian* (Charlottesville, 1971), 77–81; Deal, *Race and Class in Colonial Virginia: Indians, Englishmen, and Africans on the Eastern Shore during the Seventeenth Century* (New York, 1993), 163–64. In 1708, a Virginia planter remembered "that before the year 1680 what negros were brought to Virginia were imported generally from Barbados for it was very rare to have a Negro ship come to this Country directly from Africa"; Donnan, ed., *Documents Illustrative of the Slave Trade*, 4:89.

61 Anthony Johnson's primacy and "unmatched achievement" have made him and his family the most studied members of the charter generation. The best account of Johnson and his family is found in Deal, *Race and Class in Colonial Virginia*, 217–50. Also useful are T. H. Breen and Stephen Innes, "*Myne Owne Ground*": *Race and Freedom on Virginia's Eastern Shore, 1640–1676* (New York, 1980), chap. 1; Ross M. Kimmel, "Free Blacks in Seventeenth-Century

Maryland," *Maryland Magazine of History*, 71 (1976), 22–25; Alden Vaughan, "Blacks in Virginia: A Note on the First Decade," *WMQ*, 3d Ser., 29 (1972), 475–76; James H. Brewer, "Negro Property Owners in Seventeenth-Century Virginia," ibid., 12 (1955), 576–78; Susie M. Ames, *Studies of the Virginia Eastern Shore in the Seventeenth Century* (Richmond, 1940), 102–05; John H. Russell, *The Free Negro in Virginia, 1619–1865* (Baltimore, 1913); and Russell, "Colored Freemen as Slave Owners in Virginia," *J. Negro Hist.*, 1 (1916), 233–42. Indirect evidence of the baptism of Johnson's children comes from the 1660s, when John Johnson replied to challenges to his right to testify in court by producing evidence of baptism. He may have been baptized as an adult.

62 Quotation in Breen and Innes, *"Myne Owne Ground,"* 6. The statement is generally attributed to Johnson but may have been uttered by Francis Payne. See Deal, *Race and Class in Colonial Virginia*, 266–67. For John Johnson's Angola see Kimmel, "Free Blacks in Maryland," 23.

63 Deal, *Race and Class in Colonial Virginia*, 205–406, 265–67 (for Payne), 305 n. 2 (for the Driggus name), and Deal, "A Constricted World: Free Blacks on Virginia's Eastern Shore, 1680–1750," in Lois Green Carr, Philip D. Morgan, and Jean B. Russo, eds., *Colonial Chesapeake Society* (Chapel Hill, 1989), 275–305; Breen and Innes, *"Myne Owne Ground,"* esp. chap. 4, 69 (names).

64 The nature of the slave trade in the Chesapeake was summarized by Maryland's governor in 1708: "before the year 1698, this province has been supplyd by some small Quantitys of Negro's from Barbados and other her Ma'tys Islands and Plantations, as Jamaica and New England Seaven, eight, nine or ten in a Sloope, and sometymes larger Quantitys, and sometymes, tho very seldom, whole ship Loads of Slaves have been brought here directly from Affrica by Interlopers, or such as have had Lycenses, or otherwise traded there." Most of the latter had arrived in the previous decade; Donnan, ed., *Documents Illustrative of the Slave Trade*, 4:21–23, 88–90; Menard, "From Servants to Slaves: The Transformation of the Chesapeake Labor System," *Southern Studies*, 16 (1977), 363–67; Deal, *Race and Class in Colonial Virginia*, 164–65; Breen and Innes, *"Myne Owne Ground,"* 70–71. On Phillip see Robert McColley, "Slavery in Virginia, 1619–1660: A Reexamination," in Robert H. Abzug and Stephen E. Mazlish, eds., *New Perspectives on Race and Slavery in America* (Lexington, Ky., 1986), 15–16, and Vaughan, "Blacks in Virginia," 470; on Cain see Deal, *Race and Class in Colonial Virginia*, 254–55, 317–19, and Robert C. Twombly and Robert H. Moore, "Black Puritan: The Negro in Seventeenth-Century Massachusetts," *WMQ*, 3d Ser., 24 (1967), 236.

65 Deal, *Race and Class in Colonial Virginia*, 205–405, quotation on 209, and Deal, "A Constricted World," 275–305; Michael L. Nicholls, "Passing Through This Troublesome World: Free Blacks in the Early Southside," *Virginia Magazine of History and Biography*, 92 (1984), 50–70.

66 Deal, *Race and Class in Colonial Virginia*, 225–35, quotation on 208, and Deal, "A Constricted World," 290; Breen and Innes, *"Myne Owne Ground,"* 79–82, 86, 90.

67 Morgan Godwyn, *The Negro's and Indian's Advocate* (London, 1680), 101, quoted in Breen and Innes, *"Myne Owne Ground,"* 70, 130 n. 8.

68 Wood, *Black Majority*, chaps. 1, 4, esp. 97, for a reference to a slave master who "worked many days with a Negro man at the Whip saw." See also Clarence L. Ver Steeg, *Origins of a Southern Mosaic: Studies of Early Carolina and Georgia* (Athens, Ga., 1975), 105–07.

69 Jane Landers, "Spanish Sanctuary: Fugitives in Florida, 1687–1790," *Florida Historical Quarterly*, 62 (1984), 296–302, and Landers, "Gracia Real de Santa Teresa de Mose: A Free Black Town in Spanish Colonial Florida," *AHR*, 95 (1990), 9–30; John J. TePaske, "The Fugitive Slave: Intercolonial Rivalry and Spanish Slave Policy, 1687–1764," in Samuel Proctor, ed., *Eighteenth-Century Florida and*

Its Borderlands (Gainesville, 1975), 2–12; I. A. Wright, comp., "Dispatches of Spanish Officials Bearing on the Free Negro Settlement of Gracia Real de Santa Teresa de Mose, Florida," *J. Negro Hist.,* 9 (1924), 144–93, quotation on 150; Zora Neale Hurston, "Letters of Zora Neale Hurston on the Mose Settlement, and Negro Colony in Florida," ibid., 12 (1927), 664–67; J. D. Duncan, "Slavery and Servitude in Colonial South Carolina, 1670–1776" (Ph. D. diss., Emory University, 1964), chap. 17, quotation on 664; and J. G. Dunlop, "William Dunlop's Mission to St. Augustine in 1688," *South Carolina Historical and Genealogical Magazine,* 34 (1933), 1–30. Several of the slaves who rejected freedom and Catholicism in St. Augustine and returned to South Carolina were rewarded with freedom, creating a competition between English and Spanish colonies that redounded to the fugitives' advantage. See Duncan, "Slavery and Servitude in Colonial South Carolina," 381–83.

70 Wood, *Black Majority*, chaps. 11–12; Thornton, "African Dimensions of the Stono Rebellion," *AHR*, 96 (1991), 1101–11, quotation on 1102. Thornton makes a powerful case for the Kongolese origins of the Stono rebels in their military organization and the nature of their resistance. For the pretransfer conversion of slaves from central Africa to Christianity see Thornton, "Development of an African Catholic Church in the Kingdom of Kongo," 147–50, and *Kingdom of Kongo*, 63–68; MacGaffey, *Religion and Society in Central Africa*, 198–211; and Hilton, *Kingdom of Kongo*, 179–98.

71 Thornton, "African Dimensions of the Stono Rebellion," 1107; Landers, "Gracia Real de Santa Teresa de Mose," 27; Michael Mullin, ed., *American Negro Slavery: A Documentary History* (New York, 1976), 84.

72 Landers, "Spanish Sanctuary," 296–302; Landers, "Gracia Real de Santa Teresa de Mose," 9–30; Duncan, "Servitude and Slavery in Colonial South Carolina," chap. 17, quotations on 659, 663.

73 Landers, "Gracia Real de Santa Teresa de Mose," 15–21, quotation on 20; Larry W. Kruger and Robert Hall, "Fort Mose: A Black Fort in Spanish Florida," *The Griot*, 6 (1987), 39–40.

74 Landers, "Gracia Real de Santa Teresa de Mose," 21–22, quotations on 22.

75 Ibid., quotations on 21, 23–30; Theodore G. Corbett, "Population Structure in Hispanic St. Augustine," *Florida Historical Quarterly*, 54 (1976), 265, and "Migration to a Spanish Imperial Frontier in the Seventeenth and Eighteenth Centuries: St. Augustine," *Hisp. Amer. Hist. Rev.*, 54 (1974), 420–21.

76 I have been unable to locate female analogues of Paulo d'Angola, Samba Bambara, Juan Rodrigues, Antonio a Negro, and Francisco Menéndez. Their absence does not, however, reflect the experience of Atlantic creoles, as small shards of evidence indicate that women played central roles in the production of creole culture, the transmission of language, the facilitation of trade, and the accumulation of capital. The best study derives from the 18th century. See George E. Brooks, Jr., "The *Signares* of Saint-Louis and Gorée: Women Entrepreneurs in Eighteenth-Century Senegal," in Nancy J. Hafkin and Edna G. Bay, eds., *Women in Africa: Studies in Social and Economic Change* (Stanford, Calif., 1976), 19–44. For an interpretation of 17th-century Chesapeake society that stresses the critical role of women in the shaping of race relations and the emergence of slavery see Kathleen Mary Brown, "Gender and the Genesis of a Race and Class System in Virginia, 1630–1750" (Ph. D. diss., University of Wisconsin, 1990).

77 Writing about the forced transfer of Africans to the New World, W. Jeffrey Bolster observes that "many of the slaves who left Africa with no maritime skills acquired rudimentary ones on the Middle Passage, along with some knowledge of European work-routines and social organization," in *Black Jacks: African-American Seamen in the Atlantic World, 1740–1865* (forthcoming).

78 For a useful distinction between societies with slaves and slave societies see Keith Hopkins, *Conquerors and Slaves: Sociological Studies in Roman History*, 2 vols. (Cambridge, 1978), 1:99, and Moses I. Finley, "Slavery," *International Encyclopedia of the Social Sciences* (New York, 1968), and *Ancient Slavery and Modern Ideology* (New York, 1980), 79–80.

79 Jordan, *White over Black: American Attitudes toward the Negro* (Chapel Hill, 1968), chaps. 1–6, traces the initial appearance of such notions among the transplanted English and their later triumph.

80 Quotations in Bruce, *Institutional History of Virginia in the Seventeenth Century*, 1:9, and Alexander Hewatt, *An Historical Account of the Rise and Progress of the Colonies of South Carolina and Georgia*, 2 vols. (London, 1779), 2:100.

81 Their story is told by Mullin, *Flight and Rebellion*, and *Africa in America*. On renaming see Berlin, *Slaves without Masters: The Free Negro in the Antebellum South* (New York, 1974), 51–52; Gary Nash, *Forging Freedom: The Formation of Philadelphia's Black Community, 1720–1840* (Cambridge, Mass. 1988), 79–88, and "Forging Freedom: The Emancipation Experience in the Northern Seaport Cities, 1775–1820," in Berlin and Hoffman, eds., *Slavery and Freedom in the Age of Revolution*, 20–27; and Cheryll Ann Cody, "Kin and Community among the Good Hope People after Emancipation," *Ethnohistory*, 41 (1994), 28–33.

82 Corbett, "Migration to a Spanish Imperial Frontier in the Seventeenth and Eighteenth Centuries," 420; Wilbur H. Siebert, "The Departure of the Spaniards and Other Groups from East Florida, 1763–1764," *Florida Historical Quarterly*, 19 (1940), 146; Robert L. Gold, "The Settlement of the East Florida Spaniards in Cuba, 1763–1766," ibid., 42 (1964), 216–17; Landers, "Gracia Real de Santa Teresa de Mose," 29. For the northward migration of free people of color from the Chesapeake region see Deal, *Race and Class in Colonial Virginia*, 188.

83 The accepted anthropological designation for these communities is "tri-racial isolates." Scholars have traced their origins to Virginia and North Carolina in the 17th century and then their expansion into South Carolina, Kentucky, and Tennessee with various branches moving north and south. A recent survey by Virginia Easley DeMarce provides an excellent overview; " 'Verry Slitly Mixt': Tri-Racial Isolate Families of the Upper South—A Genealogical Study," *National Genealogical Society Quarterly*, 80 (1992), 5–35.

84 Rachel N. Klein, *Unification of a Slave State: The Rise of the Planter Class in the South Carolina Backcountry, 1760–1808* (Chapel Hill, 1990), 18–21, 62–72.

85 For Johnson's whitening see Deal, *Race and Class in Colonial Virginia*, 258–69, esp. 277. See, for example, the case of Gideon Gibson, a mulatto slaveholder who during the mid-18th century was in the process of transforming himself from "black" to "white," in Jordan, *White over Black*, 171–74; Klein, *Unification of a Slave State*, 69–71; Robert L. Meriwether, *The Expansion of South Carolina, 1729–1765* (Kingsport, Tenn., 1940), 90, 96. As a group, free people of color were getting lighter in the Chesapeake during the late 17th century and into the 18th, perhaps as part of a conscious strategy of successful free men who married white women. See, for example, Deal, *Race and Class in Colonial Virginia*, 187, 276 n. 20, and Berlin, *Slaves without Masters*, 3–4.

86 Quotation from William W. Hening, comp., *The Statutes at Large: Being a Collection of All the Laws of Virginia*, 13 vols. (Richmond, 1800–1823) 2:260; Warren M. Billings, "The Cases of Fernando and Elizabeth Key: A Note on the Status of Blacks in Seventeenth-Century Virginia," *WMQ*, 3d Ser., 30 (1973), 467–74; Billings, ed., *The Old Dominion in the Seventeenth Century: A Documentary History of Virginia, 1606–1689* (Chapel Hill, 1975), 165–69; David W. Galenson, "Economic Aspects of the Growth of Slavery in the Seventeenth-Century Chesapeake," in Solow, ed., *Slavery and the Rise of the Atlantic System*, 271; Fernow, ed., *Records of New Amsterdam*, 6:146, 286; Herbert L. Osgood, ed.,

Minutes of the Common Council of the City of New York, 8 vols. (New York, 1905), 1:134, 276–77; J. B. Lyon, ed., *Colonial Laws of New York from 1664 to the Revolution*, 5 vols. (Albany, 1894–1896), 1:356–57; Goodfriend, *Before the Melting Pot*, 120–21. After warning Domingo and Manuel Angola not to repeat their behavior, the court ordered them to communicate its admonition to "the other remaining free negroes"; ibid.

87 Goodfriend, *Before the Melting Pot*, 116–17; Nicholls, "Passing Through This Troublesome World," 50–53; Deal, "A Constricted World," 275–305; Breen and Innes, "*Myne Owne Ground*," chaps. 4–5.

88 Berlin, *Slaves without Masters*, 33–34; Shane White, *Somewhat More Independent: The End of Slavery in New York City, 1770–1810* (Athens, Ga., 1991), 117–18; Nash and Jean R. Soderlund, *Freedom by Degrees: Emancipation in Pennsylvania and Its Aftermath* (New York, 1991), 115–36. Also see the papers of the Pennsylvania Society for Promoting the Abolition of Slavery (Historical Society of Pennsylvania), and the New York Manumission Society (New-York Historical Society), for the upsurge of suits for freedom. For naming patterns within free black families that reached from the Revolutionary era back to the mid-17th century see Deal, *Race and Class in Colonial Virginia*, 342.

7

THE FEMININE FACE OF AFRO-CATHOLICISM IN NEW ORLEANS, 1727–1852

Emily Clark and Virginia Meacham Gould

On the second Sunday before Easter in 1838, Henriette Delille, a free creole woman of African descent in New Orleans, walked the eight blocks from her home to the chapel of the St. Claude Street convent and school. She regularly traversed the distance between her house and the chapel, but this morning was special. It was the beginning of the paschal season during which adults were traditionally baptized in the Catholic church, and Delille was on her way to take part in this ancient annual ritual. Waiting for her at the chapel was a free black catechumen, fourteen-year-old Marie Therese Dagon. Standing with Dagon at the baptismal font was the immigrant French chaplain Etienne Rousselon, who would act that day as both priest and godfather.[1]

The biracial tableau of Marie Dagon's baptism reveals the distinctive profile of Catholic tradition in New Orleans and Delille's place in it. Delille belonged to a congregation of pious women of African descent who were pledged to the corporal and spiritual care of the city's enslaved and free women of color. The spiritual aspect of that mission expressed itself in catechizing and godparenting, and by this time Delille had demonstrated her dedication to the group's aims by sponsoring more than a dozen slaves and people of African descent.[2] While each of those sacraments would have been meaningful to Delille in its own way, the baptism of Marie Dagon held particular significance.

A young adult and a free woman, Dagon came to the sacrament of her own free will. She was almost certainly led to the act by Delille herself, as it was customary for women to act as godmother to those they catechized. The ceremony took place in a religious precinct endowed with special meaning for the free black Catholic community of New Orleans. The St. Claude Street school and convent, the sacred place where free girls of color were instructed and educated, had evolved from a century-old mission to instruct females of African descent. The baptism was enacted

159

within a space at the heart of female Afro-Catholic tradition in the city. Finally, the participation of Rousselon as both celebrant and godfather signaled a distinctive and crucial partnership between women of color and the Catholic church in the city.

Dagon's baptism manifested key features of Afro-Catholicism in early nineteenth-century New Orleans: the appropriation of Catholicism by the city's free black women, the women's determination to extend the embrace of their church, and the white male clergy's recognition of their role as partners in this mission. When Delille and Rousselon shared the role and obligation of godparenting, they enacted both the spiritual equality that existed between them and their joint commitment to the propagation of the faith. The baptism of Marie Dagon—the symbolic conjoining of a French priest and a pious woman of African descent in the sanctuary of the St. Claude Street chapel—shows the dynamic that shaped the distinctive relationship between people of African descent and the church in New Orleans and illuminates Delille's extraordinary place within it.

To understand how a woman descended from enslaved Africans came to stand as a spiritual equal beside a French priest in antebellum New Orleans, we must look back to the eighteenth century and the process of religious creolization that resulted in both the feminization and the Africanization of New Orleans's Catholic church. In colonial Louisiana, enslaved African women and their free and enslaved descendants participated in increasing numbers and with apparently growing devotion in Catholic ritual and worship. During the four decades following the Louisiana Purchase of 1803, their numerical dominance persisted and was joined to organizational innovation. By the 1830s, a large group of free women of color, led by Delille, leveraged the importance of their numbers and their piety to win acceptance and support for the first Catholic religious congregation created by and for African-American women. In 1842, Delille and a small band of companions took the first formal steps toward the formation of the canonical order the Soeurs de Sainte Famille—the Sisters of the Holy Family. The order built an educational and charitable enterprise to serve free and enslaved people of African descent that was unique in the antebellum South.[3] The establishment of the activist Sisters of the Holy Family represents an ironic culmination of a process of religious creolization that began with the crushing blow of initial enslavement.

Henriette Delille is a unique figure in the history of New Orleans and of American Catholicism, yet she and her female ancestors also exemplify a general process by which thousands of women of African descent in New Orleans became Catholic and eventually employed their religious affiliation to transform themselves from nearly powerless objects of coercion into powerful agents. This progression was highly sensitive to the particular contours of the city's colonial evolution. The development of Afro-Catholicism in New Orleans was particularly inflected by gender and the rhythm of the slave trade to Louisiana.

The evidence suggests a process of religious creolization that moved through four stages. First, West African women, perhaps predisposed by their particular religious and social traditions and responding to a unique female ministry in colonial New Orleans, were drawn into the orbit of Catholic ritual in the 1730s and 1740s. In this initial phase, enslaved females of all ages, though a minority in the general slave population, constituted the majority of slave baptisands.[4] In the next generation, a hiatus in the slave trade to Louisiana forestalled the revitalization of African religious retention, and males came to dominate most adult group baptisms. During the second half of the eighteenth century, people of African descent increasingly assumed ritual responsibility for induction into Catholicism by becoming godparents, marking a third phase in religious creolization. The final phase was characterized by the expansion and formalization of the leadership role of black women in religious instruction and benevolence. In the opening decades of the nineteenth century, women of color dominated Catholic congregations and led propagation efforts by initiating adult enslaved women from Africa and from Protestant areas of the United States into Catholicism. African women and their descendants' long tradition of participation and leadership culminated in the organization of the Sisters of the Holy Family In each of these four stages, Henriette Delille and her matrilineal ancestors were visible actors in the process of religious creolization, forming a line of Afro-Catholic women who led the faithful and perpetuated religious practice for more than a century.

Generation after generation, Delille's matrilineal ancestors enacted these four stages. Her first female ancestor in New Orleans arrived in the 1720s amid the first immigrant wave of Africans forcibly transported to Louisiana. Known in New Orleans as Nanette, she was Delille's great-great-grandmother. One of the hundreds of adult slaves baptized in St. Louis Church in New Orleans during the 1720s, 1730s, and 1740s, Nanette is typical of the first Africans inducted into the young colony's church.[5] The record of ritual inductions indicates that the predominance of Africans in the Catholic community and the prominence of women among them originated in these early decades, but it is only when we consider the vicissitudes in the Louisiana slave trade and the specific situation of Nanette and her daughters that we are offered clues as to how and why such a pattern took shape.

French slavers brought the first shipment of captive Africans to Louisiana in 1719, and over the next dozen years roughly 6,000 bound men, women, and children entered the colony through the slave trade.[6] Male imports substantially outnumbered females, and at the end of the 1720s there were three enslaved men for every two women. This first generation of enslaved women was significantly more likely than its male counterpart to participate in the ritual of baptism. Captive females constituted nearly half the baptisms of adult African slaves performed in the 1731–1733 period, though they represented only 40 percent of the population of adult enslaved Africans in the 1730s. A similar pattern appears among the baptisms of enslaved infants. During the same three-year period, 158 enslaved infant females were baptized compared with 127 infant males. Infant female baptisands constituted a majority of 55 percent, a figure striking in view of the normative birth rate of 104 males to every 100 females.[7]

The predominance of females in these baptismal statistics confounds simple explanations for the history of slave baptism in the city. Numerous historians have argued that Catholic baptism and other forms of Christian observance were imposed on the enslaved in an effort to exert social control. The tide of slave baptism that surged through New Orleans during the French regime from 1718 until 1763 could be attributed to anxious planters' avid compliance with the *Code Noir*'s stipulation that owners have their enslaved servants baptized.[8] Yet this is an unsatisfactory explanation for several reasons. If baptism under the *Code Noir* was intended as a tool to regulate slave behavior, it was not being promptly and efficiently deployed in Louisiana. There was often a significant lag between the arrival of enslaved Africans and their baptism; the norm was two to three years.[9] Nor was baptism successfully directed toward the bound Africans who were presumably the greatest threat to white order, that is, adult males. Finally, we find that the individuals most active in the promotion of slave baptism were not colonial officials modeling compliance with the law or major planters grappling with the management of their labor force but rather colonists associated with a religious confraternity pledged to slave catechesis. The confraternity and the women's religious order that sponsored it offer a more successful starting point for unraveling the circumstances that produced the gendered slave baptism pattern of the 1730s and 1740s.

New Orleans was unique among circum-Caribbean settlements of Catholic colonial powers in that its primary missionaries were not male priests but Ursuline nuns, members of an order dedicated to advancing Catholicism through an aggressive program of female catechesis.[10] The Ursulines were the first order of teaching nuns established in the Catholic church. Before their foundation in northern Italy in 1535, all nuns were cloistered contemplatives who conducted no ministries to the public. The Ursulines remained an obscure congregation until they spread to France at the end of the sixteenth century. In France, they grew rapidly and by 1700 counted some 10,000 nuns in more than 300 convents throughout the country. Their apostolate was a radical departure from past practice in several ways. It advocated the propagation of Catholicism through the catechesis and education of women, recognizing the essential role that mothers played in inculcating faith in their children and enforcing a regimen of pious observation in their families. It also provided a rationale for female education and insisted that, for this program to succeed, it must not be limited to elites but extended to all women, regardless of their social standing. The Ursuline plan was to catechize all women, train them to become catechizers themselves, and create an army of laywomen, each shouldering responsibility for ensuring the future of Catholicism through her own pious acts.[11]

The universalism that transcended established social boundaries in France framed the Ursuline nuns' approach to emerging racial boundaries in Louisiana. Twelve Ursuline missionaries arrived in New Orleans in 1727 and quickly established a school with boarding and day divisions. In the spring of 1728, there were "seven slave boarders to instruct for baptism and first communion, and a large number of day students and Negresses and Indian girls who come two hours each day for instruction."[12] The nuns' project was advanced in May 1730, when eight laywomen visited the Ursuline convent and asked the nuns to help them organize a women's confraternity. Between 1730 and 1744, the pious association grew to include eighty-five women and girls who called themselves the Children of Mary. Although a significant number of the confreresses were wealthy plantation mistresses and wives and daughters of the bureaucratic elite, many were drawn from the artisan and noncommissioned military classes, and some were impoverished widows and orphans.[13] Three members were listed without either the titles or the surnames with which white women were always recorded. "Marie Thérèse," "Marthe," and "Magdelaine" were almost certainly women of color and may have been slaves.[14]

The confraternity adopted a formal constitution, in which members pledged to honor the Virgin "not by their prayers alone, but by their morals, and by all the conduct of their lives." This promise was defined later in the constitution with some precision. "Confreresses," it stipulated, "should have a special zeal for . . . the instruction of their children and their slaves."[15] An analysis of sacramental records available for the years the confraternity was active shows that these laywomen acted on their constitutional promise. In the 1730s and 1740s, confreresses and their families were more involved in sponsoring slave baptism than any other group in colonial New Orleans and in numbers disproportionate to their representation in the slave-owning population as a whole.[16]

Nanette, the African captive who was Delille's ancestor, was destined to become an object of the female campaign of catechesis mounted by the Children of Mary. Nanette's service as a domestic in the household of the wealthy planter Claude Joseph Dubreuil brought her into intimate contact with two women who were among the more aggressive Children of Mary. Both Dubreuil's wife, Marie Payen Dubreuil, and his daughter-in-law Felicité de la Chaise Dubreuil were members of the confraternity.[17] The sacramental records of the 1730s and 1740s—peppered with the names of Dubreuil family bondpeople—bear witness to the Dubreuil women's zeal. Few of the Dubreuil's adult African slaves or their children were ignored—or spared. Indeed, Marie Payen and Félicité set the standard for their kin. Monsieur Dubreuil, his two sons, and his grandchildren frequently stood as godparents to adult slaves and their infants, both inside and outside their own households.[18]

Nanette's membership in the Dubreuil household explains her exposure to female Catholic catechetical efforts but does not speak to the nature of her response to it. She may simply have capitulated to the Dubreuil confreresses' imprecations or demands, judging resistance to be either futile, dangerous, or disadvantageous. In such circumstances, the likelihood of choice and agency in her baptism would have been minimal and the female nature of evangelization of no significance. Some evidence related to the specific nature of the slave trade to Louisiana, however, suggests an alternate reading.

The first significant immigration of captive Africans that brought Nanette to Louisiana was distinguished by the preponderance of Senegambians. Of the approximately 6,000 Africans carried to Louisiana between 1719 and 1731, some 4,000 originally inhabited the territory in West Africa lying between the Senegal and the Gambia Rivers and stretching from the inland headwaters of the rivers to the Atlantic littoral. There is good reason to assume that Nanette, like many of the captive women brought to Louisiana, was a member of the coastal Wolof ethnic group. Generally, slave traders acquired their male captives from inland territories, but they preferred women taken from the littoral. Coastal women, exposed through trade to European language and culture, were thought better suited for domestic service than less cosmopolitan inland women. At the same time, inland women lacked the strength that made their male compatriots attractive as field laborers.[19] Among the French, coastal Wolof women were particularly favored for domestic service and intimate companionship in both Africa and the American colonies. The eighteenth-century French missionary Jean Baptiste Labat recounts that Frenchmen living in Senegambia, to protect the interests of the slave trade, eschewed the colonial ambience of the fortress at St. Louis to live in huts with Wolof women. Le Page du Pratz, the overseer of the large plantation operated by the Company of the Indies in Louisiana, recommended that only Wolof women be selected for service in the home.[20]

Nanette's appearance in Louisiana during the first phase of African immigration makes it likely that she was Senegambian. Her position in the Dubreuil household as a *domestique* suggests Wolof origins. If she was among the many Wolof women who had mingled regularly with Europeans living along the West African littoral, she would not have been entirely unfamiliar with the French language and the Roman Catholic ritual pressed on her by the Dubreuil confreresses.[21] While familiarity with Catholicism and French would not necessarily have inclined

Nanette toward a fuller engagement with Catholicism, it could nonetheless have reduced two practical obstacles to conversion. Another feature of Senegambian womanhood in the era of the slave trade is more important to the story of religious creolization in Louisiana. Whether Wolof or not, Nanette came from a West African society in which women were sacred practitioners and mothers took responsibility for inducting their daughters into religious cults. Nanette came of age in a region where tradition dictated a gendered division of instruction and ritual initiation. In the cultures of Senegambian Africa, women took ritual responsibility for initiating their daughters, fathers for their sons.[22]

The gendered division of ritual responsibility in Nanette's African religious heritage is relevant not simply because it illuminates the roots of Henriette Delille's piety, but also because it was shared by a majority of the captives brought to Louisiana in the first stage of the colony's Africanization. Nanette bore four daughters who survived infancy to be baptized in Louisiana: Marianne in 1735, Fanchonette in 1737, Tonica in 1742, and Cecile in 1744.[23] Their baptisms and those of hundreds of other enslaved women and girls in the 1730s and 1740s likely reflect a confluence of complementary ritual traditions. The practice of maternally administered religious initiation in Senegambia harmonized with the mother-centered approach of the Ursulines and the Children of Mary. Mindful of their own cultural heritage, the first generation of enslaved women in Louisiana perhaps found in the daily female gatherings at the convent compound for catechism and the alien induction rite of Catholic baptism a way to sustain their accustomed religious roles. If so, their participation in these Christian rites represented something more than superficial acts of submission or meaningless mimicry. Their actions became, instead, the beginnings of a new religious tradition adapted to their new circumstances. Initially, their appropriation of Catholicism would have been largely performative, a constellation of ritual behaviors that could be read in two completely different ways. To the enslaved African women, baptism and the female sacred space and activity at the convent could represent fidelity to central, sustaining features of their traditional religion. For their part, when the nuns surveyed the African women who came to the convent with their daughters and stayed to be baptized, they saw devout women won to the true faith. This explanation of the baptismal statistics of early New Orleans, while recognizing the power differential between the European confreresses and the African objects of their evangelization, uncovers crucial elements of agency and the preservation of African cultural values otherwise obscured by the tide of apparent capitulation and conversion.

The episode of European evangelization and African appropriation that marked the 1730s and 1740s represents the first phase of the relationship between enslaved women and Catholicism. While it seems unlikely that the adult women who were baptized in the 1720s, 1730s, and 1740s initially experienced conversion to Christian belief, factors operating within both the European and the African communities supported the growth of religious practice among enslaved women and paved the way for belief to follow. A hiatus in the direct slave trade to Louisiana after 1743 enhanced the influence of European forms over the African legacy and shaped the subsequent development of Catholicism among African Americans in New Orleans.

Between 1719 and 1750, much of the first generation of enslaved Africans came to Louisiana and a second, creolized generation was born. No new shipments of Africans arrived in New Orleans between 1733 and 1737, when a census was taken, and except for a single slave ship in 1743, it appears that no vessel conveying Africans directly to Louisiana arrived until after 1776, when the Spanish re-instituted the slave trade. This interval of more than three decades produced a generation of enslaved people in New Orleans who, like Nanette's four daughters, were baptized as infants and came to maturity without significant contact with adult Africans who had been untouched by Catholic evangelization. The evangelizing work of the Ursulines and the Children of Mary, with their emphasis on female participation in catechesis and religious devotion, was thus unchallenged by direct African influences during the last three decades of the French period.[24]

During this period of stasis in the slave trade and religious creolization, African mothers and their creole daughters dominated the ranks of the city's baptisands. In the next generation, the women appear to have been influential in extending baptismal participation among enslaved males. The gender breakdown of adult slave baptism during two crucial periods in each of these two generations illustrates these trends. From 1731 to 1733, there were only two adult females for every three adult males among the city's slaves, yet women and men were baptized at roughly equal rates. The pattern was reversed during the second period, 1750–1762, when male baptismal rates outstripped male representation in the adult slave population and women's participation lagged. In eight of these thirteen years, men predominated by significant margins.

There are several possible explanations for this pattern. Men of the first generation of enslaved Africans may have resisted to greater effect than women all attempts by Europeans to evangelize them. They were physically strong and did not face the perils of childbirth, factors that lessened the appeal of the conversion as a survival strategy. And whereas the majority of enslaved women lived and worked in town as domestic servants, most men worked in the fields. This placed them beyond the surveillance of French masters and reduced their exposure to French cultural norms, especially on the larger plantations. Resistance may have played a part. The Senegambian captives who constituted most of Louisiana's laborers had a history of violent revolt both in the *captiveries* of African coastal entrepôts and aboard ship.[25] There was also, most obviously, no male missionary program to match the effort mounted by the Ursulines and the Children of Mary. The colony's chief cleric, Abbé L'Isle Dieu, observed to the minister of the marine in 1750 that Louisiana's female slaves had grown more productive, intelligent, and well behaved under the tutelage of the nuns. In an early example of unwitting gender analysis he went on to remark that Louisiana's male slaves might be improved "if two teaching brothers were assigned to them to instruct them, cultivate their reason, and civilize their morals by the principles and maxims of religion."[26] Both Senegambians and Catholics practiced a gendered division of piety and religious induction that cut both ways for the Catholic campaign for conversion among the enslaved of New Orleans. The ministry of eighteenth-century Ursulines was restricted to women, a positive factor for the evangelization of Senegambian women who were accustomed to responding to female sacred practitioners, but an obstacle to the proselytization of men.

In the end, fewer positive incentives and an ineffective evangelizing force probably combined to retard the progress of Catholic conversion among adult male slaves. The increase in adult male baptism in the 1750s can be explained as men's voluntary submission to the wishes, injunctions, or instruction of Christian female partners. Girls born in the 1730s and 1740s were more likely than boys to have been baptized, creating a disparity in religious affiliation among young creoles who would have become sexually active in the 1750s. The sexual unions of this generation may have been influenced by growing Christian practice as well. Sacramental marriage between enslaved people enjoyed significant growth in the 1750s: nearly a fifth of enslaved infants born in 1760 were born to married parents, compared to 12 percent in 1744.[27] Sacramental observance among the enslaved thus seems to have been advanced by both positive and negative forces. Without the arrival of fresh cohorts of enslaved Africans after 1743, the vitality of the male religious culture of the Senegambian interior would have waned, opening the way for converted women to prevail in an intimate campaign of evangelization.

Although enslaved men were baptized in increasing numbers, women of African descent continued to dominate in overall baptismal participation for the colonial population as a whole throughout the eighteenth century, usually in numbers disproportionate to their representation in the general population. In five of six sample periods (1731–1733, 1763, 1778, 1795, 1804–1805), females of African descent constituted the largest cohort of baptisands. While males of African descent consistently represent the second-largest group among the ranks of the baptized, they were often significantly outpaced by females, most notably in 1733, 1763, and 1804. Whites of both sexes never constituted more than 35 percent of the New Orleanians who joined the church.[28]

The configuration of infant baptisms suggests even more that the Ursuline female apostolate complemented the West African custom of gendered religious instruction and initiation. In each of four sample years during the colonial period, baptisms of enslaved infant females made up more than half the total, nourishing the perpetuation and growth of a feminine Afro-Catholic congregation in New Orleans.[29]

Baptism is important, but it tells us only that enslaved female Africans participated in a single rite of the Catholic church that ultimately resulted in their numerical domination of the New Orleans congregation. It speaks neither to the growth of belief nor to the ways that people of African descent employed the church as a means of advancing their own interests. Godparenting is a more reliable indication of these developments because priests required godparents to demonstrate more than a superficial commitment to the faith and because the bonds created by religious sponsorship could be turned to social purposes. Analysis of the sacramental records of New Orleans for the period under consideration reveals dramatic and sustained growth in the participation of people of African descent in this ritual function—a phenomenon that delineates phase three in our scheme.

In 1733, people of African descent, whether slave or free, served as godparents in only 2 percent of the baptisms of enslaved people that took place at St. Louis Church. By 1750, their participation had risen to 21 percent, but the most telling figure comes from 1765, which would represent the presence of the first full generation born in Louisiana, a generation whose creolization was not affected by new arrivals from Africa.[30] In that year, we see a striking jump in the frequency of people of African descent in godparenting—to 68 percent. In 1775, when the adult creole proportion of the New Orleans slave population was probably at its eighteenth-century peak, 89 percent of the godparents of slaves were people of African descent.[31]

The most cynical reading of the growth of slave godparenting would be to see it simply as evidence of the successful exercise of coercive social control by Europeans. The cleric who remarked that the Ursulines' instruction had made the colony's female slaves "more hard-working, wiser, and better regulated in their morals" speaks volumes to the nature of the Europeans' motive to catechize their bondpeople.[32] Yet conversion was not a simple matter of imposition, nor was Christianity, once embraced, the malleable instrument of social control that slaveholders may have hoped it would be. Rather, slaves in various times and places appear to have embraced Christianity to different degrees and put it to a variety of purposes, from self-defense to armed resistance.[33]

In New Orleans, the numerical dominance of people of African descent alone exercised a form of power over the Catholic church. Clergy engaged in a demanding cycle of sacramental ceremony that offered no financial or legal reward. By the middle of the eighteenth century, the Capuchin friars who staffed St. Louis Church were called several times a week to the sanctuary to baptize slave infants. Father Eustache began the week of March 3, 1765, with the baptism of a mulatto infant, Jean Baptiste. Two days later, a Tuesday, he baptized a slave infant named François. The following Sunday, he administered the sacrament to five infant slaves and was called back to the church the next Wednesday to baptize Charlotte, another infant slave. Later in the century, the priests were called out even more frequently to baptize both free and enslaved black infants. Father Olot had little rest during the first week of May 1790. He began on Sunday, May 2, with the baptisms of Mariana, a free Afro-Creole, and Carlos, a slave. Tuesday he ministered to Honorario, a slave, and Julia Bonne, a free quadroon. The next day he presided over the baptisms of two free blacks and on Friday at the induction of a slave named Simon.[34]

Individual baptisms of infants burdened the clergy by their frequency; large group baptisms of adult slaves performed at Easter and Pentecost required lengthy and complex ceremonial effort as a succession of cat-echumens, sometimes numbering more than 100, stepped forward indi-vidually to receive the sacrament, each accompanied by the requisite godparents. Each baptism had to be recorded in the register, and god-parents were invited to sign in witness to the promises they made. During the French period, the simple marks made by black slaves mingle with the signatures of free whites at the bottom of such entries, mute testimony to the respect accorded the slave godparents' religious role, if not their civil status.[35] The Spanish clergy of the later eighteenth century ended the practice of allowing godparents to sign personally in witness of their obligation, but the demands of group baptisms remained onerous by vir-tue of their sheer size. At the adult baptism on Easter Eve of 1790, 112 catechumens made their way to the font in a ceremony that must have lasted hours. In some cases, the unwieldy group baptisms of the 1790s were spread out over consecutive days to ease the clergy's burden.[36]

Baptism was not the only means through which the enslaved entered and influenced the workings of the New Orleans church. Services and sacred spaces had to accommodate a large congregation of slaves. Mass would have been prolonged by the number of bound people queuing to receive communion, African voices joined in congregational responses, and black women, men, and children swelled the sections of the sanctu-ary reserved for their use. As the Catholic community of African descent grew to predominate, it could not have been lost on the clergy that the future and vibrancy of their mission depended on the piety of the black majority who filled the pews.[37]

Godparenting was the most formal way people of African descent laid claim to the resources and spaces of one of the city's chief institutions and made them their own. It was also almost certainly adapted to other essential functions. Enslavement resulted in a violent rupture with family and community that necessitated the refabrication of identity and social affiliation. Godparenting was an effective form of fictive kinship that helped recreate community and familial bonds, knit together the fractured polity of the enslaved, and advanced both individual and group interests.[38]

In the absence of testimony from godparents themselves, discerning the degree to which religious belief motivated them to take on the role is almost impossible. Apparently, godparents at least exhibited external piety to the satisfaction of the clergy who presided over the sacrament. Catholic canon law requires that a godparent "be a Catholic who has been confirmed and has already received the sacrament of the Most Holy Eucharist and leads a life in harmony with the faith and the role to be undertaken" and take a "lasting interest in their spiritual child, and to take good care that he leads a truly Christian life."[39] As the eighteenth century advanced, those of African descent increasingly met these requirements in the eyes of the clergy of New Orleans.

The priests made their judgments on the basis of external acts, although gauging belief through behavior is difficult for any population, particularly for the enslaved. Yet, there is evidence that Catholicism and its rites did more than appease white masters and create fictive kin networks. A bondman of the Ursuline nuns, one Pierre, seems to have been anxious about the disposition of his daughter's immortal soul. Before he died in 1784, he instructed his daughter Anne to purchase her freedom from the nuns but to continue serving them and "come to die [in the convent] so that she would die like a good Christian." The piety of one woman was such that it brought the precious gift of freedom; the notarial document manumitting Julia and her three children in 1776 stated that she was being liberated because of her loyalty and love and "because she has become a good Catholic." More persuasive still of a true commitment to the faith is the testimony of the sacramental records that reveal people of African descent who acted frequently as godparents. Free blacks François and Françoise, perhaps husband and wife, sponsored four adult baptisands in 1760, 1761, and 1762. Angelique and Barthelemé, a slave couple, served as godparents in nine baptisms, sometimes together, sometimes individually.[40]

Henriette Delille's matrilineal ancestors were prominent among those who created the statistical upswing in godparenting by people of African descent in the 1750s and 1760s. During this phase of religious creolization, Delille's great-aunt Marianne and her great-grandmother Cecile sponsored numerous slaves—both infants and adults—at the baptismal font. Both women appeared regularly as godmothers throughout these decades, with a frequency that is distinctive. From an early age, Marianne exemplified a piety and devotion that history previously accorded only white women, and she did so as one of New Orleans first bound creoles. In an extraordinary act on May 28, 1746, then eleven-year-old Marianne sponsored the adult African Victor for baptism. Victor, like Marianne, was owned by Claude Dubreuil, and Marianne may well have catechized the older man. In addition, she regularly sponsored infants born into bondage in Dubreuil's household, including Marie Anne, baptized in 1746, and Agathe, in early 1747. As she grew older, she sponsored those outside her own household, standing as sponsor later in 1747 to a male infant, Jean Baptiste, owned by colonial *ordonnateur* Jacques de la Chaise, and in 1748 to the bound infant Elizabeth. Her younger sister, Cecile, Henriette Delille's great-grandmother, also began her career as a god-mother at an early age. She demonstrated her piety and devotion at age fourteen, on Pentecost Eve 1758, when she sponsored the baptism of an enslaved adult female named Therese. On two separate occasions in 1760, in May and in September, Marianne, still bound to Dubreuil, served as godmother to two separate infants. Her recently freed mother, the African Nanette, took her place as sponsor at the baptismal font in March the same year. The creole Marianne and her African-born mother continued to demonstrate their piety among the first and second generation of the city's bondwomen, standing as godmothers in baptisms in 1765 and 1775.[41] In the actions of Nanette and her daughters we read both a homage to the West African tradition of female sacred practice passed on through the maternal line and a reflection of the female religious leadership modeled by the Ursulines and their confraternity.

Sometime after 1776, a hiatus of more than three decades, slave ships resumed their commerce with New Orleans, and in the closing years of the eighteenth century the slave population of Louisiana underwent what one historian terms a "re-Africanization." From then until the closing of the international slave trade, new Africans arrived in New Orleans in substantial numbers. Once more, Senegambians figured significantly among the forced immigrants to Louisiana.[42] The dynamics of cultural encounter and evangelization were different, however. The most effective introduction of newly enslaved Africans to Catholicism now came through a large population of creole slaves who were second- and third-generation Catholics, as well as a substantial population of free Afro-Creoles who were active in the church.[43]

Changes in the economy of the colony further altered the morphology of conversion by making it a largely urban phenomenon. In the last quarter of the eighteenth century, the long-struggling economy of the Lower Mississippi Valley stabilized and began to take on the familiar contours of a slave society nourished by successful staple crop agriculture. As planta-tion slavery matured in the region, New Orleans grew into an urban commercial center. Together, these two factors enlarged the differences between urban and rural slave communities in Louisiana. Urban blacks, whether enslaved or free, lived in close proximity to Europeans and con-ducted business with them as small merchants and skilled tradespeople. In New Orleans, people of European and African descent were also accustomed to sharing not only the sacred space of the church, but also the recreational spaces of ballroom, tavern, and billiard hall.[44] Like other colonial urban blacks, the Afro-Creoles of New Orleans, particularly those who were free, were economically and culturally enmeshed in a web of European behaviors and institutions, an engagement that was likely strengthened by the thirty-year suspension of the slave trade in the middle decades of the eighteenth century. The ties between European culture and the enslaved men and women inhabiting the plantations that lined the Mississippi, on the other hand, were more tenuous. The fresh infusion of religious practices that accompanied the newly arrived Africans would have found the rural slave community more fertile ground for a revitalization of traditional religion.[45] And, indeed, the majority of these newcomers was destined to join the population working on the plantations. Thus, for a variety of reasons, the re-Africanization of Louisiana brought no surge of traditional African religious repatriation for the Afro-Creoles of late colonial New Orleans. There is no evidence that the city's Afro-Creoles, bound or free, abandoned the racially integrated dances at the city ballroom for the weekly Sunday festivals of traditional music and dance mounted by native-born Africans at Congo Square.[46] Nor does it appear that creoles of color were drawn away from the church by the reappearance of African religious alternatives. On the contrary, free and enslaved Afro-Creoles continued to bring their children to St. Louis Church for baptism, dominating the sacramental registers, and Afro-Creole women, particularly those who had gained their freedom, expanded their work of catechesis to include the African newcomers who remained in the city. The real threat to the survival of African culture that was joyfully celebrated each Sunday in Congo Square was not a local government decree that banned it, but the band of pious Afro-Creole women intent on Catholic conversion.

A close look at the adult group baptisms of 1781 reveals some interesting patterns that are typical of the late colonial period. A total of thirty-eight adult Africans were baptized that year, seventeen women and twenty-one men. Although slave women outnumbered slave men in New Orleans, among newly enslaved Africans, men substantially outnumbered women, so the male–female ratio probably corresponds to that of the population of new Africans in the city. Godparents of African descent participated in all but four of the baptisms. All four baptisands who had only white godparents were males. Nineteen baptisands were sponsored by slaves alone. Free Afro-Creoles were the next largest group of godparents, sponsoring fifteen of the baptisms. The women figured significantly, acting as godmothers in thirteen of the baptisms involving free people of color, slightly more than one-third of the total baptisms.[47]

A few speculative observations are in order. First, the association of white baptismal sponsorship with enslaved males suggests that white masters imposed the sacrament, perhaps as an aid to social control. It is also possible that some slaves chose white godparents in order to advance their status. The sponsorship of slaves by slaves can be read in two ways. Either it represents voluntary evangelization of slaves by slaves, or it suggests that white masters pressed their slaves into acting to see that new Africans accepted the sacrament. It is likely that both functions were at play. The sponsorship by free people of African descent seems less ambiguous. They, of all the groups, were more likely to be acting from genuine religious motives. There were no owners pressing them to acculturate new Africans; their participation in godparenting was entirely voluntary. The numerical strength of women among these free black godparents is organic to the evolution of female participation in the church over the preceding fifty years.

Once again, Henriette Delille's maternal ancestors put flesh on the statistical bones before us. By the time re-Africanization began in the 1770s, her great-great-grandmother, great-grandmother, and great-grandmother's sister had become free women. In the years that followed, this female clan sustained a high profile as godmothers. The African Nanette and her daughters Cecile and Marianne appear time and again in the sacramental records as godmothers. In 1781, Marianne served as godmother to two enslaved infants and a free boy of color. The same year, Nanette sponsored an infant female slave.[48] Cecile's daughter Henriette Laveau sustained the tradition, appearing as a godmother in both years in the 1780s that we surveyed.[49] Whatever role fear, coercion, or expediency may have played in their initial acts of induction in the 1740s, we know from these and subsequent events that Nanette and her female descendants were ultimately led into a close and lasting association with the church. By the 1780s, these free women of color would have been familiar faces to the priests and sacristans of St. Louis Church who had seen them stand time after time beside Catholic initiates at the baptismal font.

Delille's ancestors illustrate more than the development of Catholic piety among women of African descent in New Orleans. They exemplify the growth in the city's free black population in the last quarter of the eighteenth century. Spanish rule brought an alternation in the colony's slave laws that favored the expansion of a free black community. Under the French *Code Noir*, in order to grant an enslaved person's freedom, owners had to petition the Louisiana Superior Council. Manumission could be initiated only by an owner, and it was a public act that required time, effort, and a willingness to reveal the intimate relationships between white men and women of color that sometimes lay behind such proceedings. Predictably, few masters subjected themselves to the tedious and potentially embarrassing process. Spanish slave law required only a simple, privately executed notarial act of emancipation. In the first decade of the Iberian regime, Louisiana slaveowners took advantage of the new system to free hundreds of bondpeople, most of them women and children. Although Spanish slave law also provided for *coartación*, the right of self-purchase at a reasonable price, the majority of New Orleans' free people of color gained their liberty because they were the issue of intimate interracial liaisons. Such was the case of Nanette and several of her children. Nanette, Cecile, and Cecile's daughters were freed publicly by their owner, Claude Joseph Dubreuil *fils*, in 1770. Several records relating to the emancipation of Nanette's children identify them as half-siblings of Dubreuil *fils*.[50]

Among the Afro-Creoles of New Orleans, free women of color like Nanette and her daughters were bound by both faith and blood to the Catholic church of the French colonizers. Together with the city's other free Afro-Creole women, free women of color constituted a notable segment of the population. Numbering 161 in 1777, they represented 73 percent of the free black adult population and approximately 13 percent of the total free adult inhabitants. By 1795, the number of free women of color in the city had nearly doubled to 300. The women composed 66 percent of the free colored population and 14 percent of the total free adult population.[51] In the 1780s, captives newly arrived from Africa were the primary objects of catechesis by these free black women. With the turn of the century, this situation began to change as American-born slaves from the anglophone Upper South made their way to Louisiana.

We can detect the very beginnings of this transition in the large group baptism of Easter Eve 1805, two years after the Louisiana Purchase made New Orleans part of the young American republic. African-born baptisands still predominated at this date. Ninety-two enslaved adults, nearly all Africans with their nations noted next to their names, formally entered the embrace of Catholicism on that day; many were brought to the font by free women of African descent.[52] Two-thirds of the baptisands were women, many of them adolescents. Although white men owned two-thirds of all those baptized at this ceremony, free women of African descent represented the next largest group of slaveowners. Though they owned only 21 percent of the baptisands, they were the owners of nearly a third of the women who received the sacrament. Eighteen women and two men owned by the women stood before the baptismal font that day. The women appear to have been especially conscientious in securing the sacrament for their new African slaves, but they also attended to the anglophone bondwomen beginning to appear in the city. "Una negra, Criolla Inglesa," aged thirty-two years, stood at the font, her godmother, a free Afro-Creole named Marie Mendes, at her side.[53]

With the closure of the international slave trade in 1808, "American" or "English" bondpeople sold away from the Protestant Upper South began to replace Africans as the primary object of Catholic evangelizers in New Orleans. Spanish and French priests accustomed to noting an enslaved person's nationality reserved "creole" for those born in francophone Louisiana. Ana Maneta was sixteen years old and "de nacion Americana," according to the Capuchin friar who recorded her baptism in 1825. Most of the slaves labeled "American" by the city's priests were baptized as young adults, but there are also numerous cases of young children whose mothers are identified as "Americanas." Free Afro-Creole women are a notable constituency among the godparents of both groups. Among the seven adult female "Americanas" baptized in 1825 were Marie Françoise, aged fifteen and a native of Tennessee, and Ana Maneta, sponsored by the free Louisse Gamette and Maria Theresa Meunié. Luis Antonio, the three-year-old son of Jani, a "negra Americana" belonging to a Mr. Smith, was sponsored by the free Afro-Creole Henrieta Ducourneau. Female Catholic evangelizers paid special attention to "American" mothers with young children. The infants of Betsy, Esther, and Delsy were all baptized in 1825. Free Afro-Creole women also seem to have made certain that the older children of their "American" bondwomen were brought to the faith. Margueritte, the seventeen-year-old daughter of "Nancy de Charleston de Carolina Sud," was baptized in February 1825 under the watchful eye of her mistress, Adele Roseau, a free mulatta.[54]

The magnitude of the anglophone slave influx to Louisiana made conversion essential to the preservation of black influence in the New Orleans Catholic church. The number of bondpeople doubled in size between 1820 and 1830, rising from 7,355 to 14,440. Yet the arrival of Protestant slaves from the Upper South was not the only challenge that tested the faith and resourcefulness of New Orleans's Afro-Catholic community in the antebellum decades. White Catholic immigrants from Germany and Ireland began to trickle into the city in the 1820s and by the late 1830s had come to dominate the Catholic population.[55] Black Catholics faced the prospect of losing their hard-won place in the church if they could not retain their francophone core and expand it through the evangelization of Protestant or unconverted adults. Once again, a Delille ancestor played a prominent role in sustaining the Afro-Catholic Church. In a short interval between 1826 and 1828, Delille's mother, Maria Josefa Diaz, can be found in a spate of baptismal entries: she stood as godmother to an infant girl in November 1826 and the following May to an infant boy. Just seven months later, in December 1827, she served as godmother to an enslaved adult man. In August 1828, she stood at the baptismal font beside Josephine, an "adult negre esclave."[56]

By the 1820s, when Maria Josefa Diaz appears regularly as a godmother in the sacramental records, the Delille female lineage had enacted each of the phases of religious creolization we have posited. In the first phase, the African Nanette preserved the matrifocal feature of her West African religious heritage through the vehicle of a Catholic female institution and tradition. She and her daughters represented the cadre of Christianized women who modeled Afro-Catholicism in the next generation and drew adult males into the church in the 1750s. In the third phase, when people of African descent came to dominate as godparents in slave baptism, the Delille clan was again prominent. After the turn of the nineteenth century, Delille's mother was active in the effort to sustain the Catholic Church among people of African descent. When Henriette Delille was born to Maria Josefa Diaz in 1812, she inherited the legacy of four generations of active Catholic women.[57]

When the American journalist John F. Watson traveled south to New Orleans shortly after the Louisiana Purchase, he penned an unwitting testament to that legacy. Describing Holy Week celebrations in 1805, Watson evoked a scene dominated by motherhood and female piety. "Mothers bring their infants; some cry and occasion other disturbances; some are seen counting their beads with much attention and remain long on their knees." This impressive display of femininity and maternity was especially striking, in Watson's eyes, for its racial aspect. "Visit the churches when you will," he noted, "and the chief audience is formed of mulatresses and negresses."[58] By the turn of the nineteenth century, the church had come to depend upon the support and piety of free and enslaved women of African descent like Delille's family. Without them, the churches that Watson visited would have been nearly empty.

Women of African descent advanced from powerless to powerful in the church as New Orleans Catholics entered the nineteenth century. In the 1720s and 1730s, they had been considered little more than objects of proselytization. As creolization progressed and they assumed the authority of the church, they became evangelizers themselves and were ultimately the most significant agents for Catholic propagation in the city. Following the patterns in godparenting that emerged as the colonial period gave way to the early national and antebellum eras reveals the ascendance of Afro-Creole women as agents of the church. In the 1760s, they shared godparenting with men of African descent. After 1760, however, women took the lead and retained it. Though Afro-Creoles of both sexes fully participated in the rite, significantly more women than men could be found standing as godparents at the baptismal font. White male participation as sponsors in slave baptism rose slightly between the 1770s and 1825, as new Africans and anglophone slaves from the Upper South poured into the city, though the downward trend of white female participation continued. After 1825 when Afro-Creoles, both enslaved and free, were more rigidly segregated in the city and the church, white sponsorship of blacks fell to very low levels. By 1842, nearly 90 percent of the city's slaves and free people of color were sponsored by women of African descent, while free men of color sponsored approximately 70 percent. Free women of African descent all but replaced white women in the records and, in an unprecedented move, they replaced them as ministers to their community.[59]

The loyalty of the women became even more essential to the church as a result of a structural transformation in the relationship between the secular and religious realms in early national New Orleans. The Louisiana Purchase of 1803, like the French Revolution, separated church and state. Catholic religious as well as laity in the Diocese of New Orleans, like their brothers and sisters in France, suddenly found themselves without state support. In New Orleans, the numerical dwindling of the clergy and thus their ability to respond to their parishioners as well as the rapidly growing numbers of free people and bound people who were either unconverted or actively Protestant were substantially accelerated. By 1815, only a handful of priests and a few Ursulines remained, and their decline occurred in the context of a rapidly growing population, much of it black. The deterioration of the church was only addressed in 1812, when the reluctant French missionary priest Louis William Dubourg was sent to administer a church that lay in ruins throughout the vast Louisiana territory.[60]

Dubourg's appointment to the diocese of Louisiana was pivotal, not only because he began the slow process of restoring the church, but also because he looked to France to do so. He revived the link between Louisiana and the French Catholic Church when he traveled to Europe in 1815 in order to accept his appointment as bishop of New Orleans.[61] After a brief stay in Rome, Dubourg set about his mission, first crossing the Alps to France, where he stayed for most of the next two years seeking aid for his flock. French historians who write of the revival of the missionary effort in France in the nineteenth century all point out that Dubourg's visit to France, especially to the area around Lyon, could not have occurred at a more auspicious moment. Pauline Jaricot, a dévote or secular religious woman, and her brother Philias, a Sulpicien priest, had just begun a movement in Lyon that led to the foundation of l'Association de la Propagation de la Foi (Society for the Propagation of the Faith; SPF) and eventually to Le Rosaire Vivant (Living Rosary). Both organizations were devoted, in large part, to foreign missionary work. At the same time, La Mission Étrangère (Foreign Mission) had begun to reorganize in Paris. All three organizations, and especially the SPF, responded to Dubourg's appeal by sending missionaries and financial support to Louisiana.[62]

The resurgence of missionary fervor that Dubourg found in Lyon was representative of the revival of Catholic spirit that increasingly influenced France after the revolution. To be sure, many eighteenth-century French men and women had rejected Catholicism before the revolution, and many more were to do so during the revolution, while still others remained only nominally Catholic. But by the time Dubourg reached France in 1815, significant numbers of the population were caught up in the revivalism that swept through French cities, villages, and into the countryside. As revolutionary promises remained unfulfilled, well-known Catholic thinkers and founders of religious orders renounced liberalism and rationalism. Instead, they sought to return France to a complete and coherent system that proposed a vision of a global world order responsive to all the problems of humanity and of human society. This organic universalist Catholic system was not a new one; it reflected in fundamental ways the older ideals of the seventeenth and eighteenth centuries that were so evident in the mission the Ursulines brought with them to New Orleans.[63] And as this renewal of Catholic spirit gained vigor in the nineteenth century, it took a more activist form, with its largest constituency—women—energetically seeking to remold society.[64]

The changes that swept through most nineteenth-century French convents were practical ones. Many of the older orders of women religious, having survived in clandestine havens throughout France, began to sweep off their stoops and open their windows. At the same time, new smaller groups of pious women began to emerge, gathering together in houses, doing manual labor in order to support their charitable missions. All of these women, in one way or another, began to build their communities on familiar models. Yet even as they sought to re-establish themselves in communities as if the revolutionary period had only interrupted them, they did so in a new age. For one thing, the church was no longer associated with or supported by the state; thus women living in community were forced to be financially independent, and after their experiences during the revolution, many had learned to cherish their newfound autonomy and sought to protect it. Another change was the marriage of the older missionary outlook with the activist emphasis of new female congregations. Congregation after congregation of women religious in nineteenth-century France used their autonomy in order to reform society by inculcating faith to their French sisters and their children, through instruction of the ignorant, education of the illiterate, and the provision of care for the sick, the poor, and the orphaned. The emphasis of these new communities of women was on betterment of the human condition, and as the nineteenth century unfolded, the women began to extend their ministry beyond the borders of France.[65]

At this time, significant numbers of women began to leave France in order to transmit their revived activist consciousness in other places. Nine women who left France to spread their devotion in the New World came to New Orleans in 1817 in response to an appeal—issued by the Ursulines through Bishop Dubourg—for aid. Each of these female missionaries came from a different section of France, a different background, a different walk of life. What united them was their extraordinary and personal response to the ideals of the Catholic apostolic fervor then sweeping through France. One of the women, Sister Ste. Marthe Fontiere, brought the most radical form of French evangelical dedication to the poor with her to New Orleans. Before leaving France, Sister Ste. Marthe had been an Hospitaliere sister in Belley, where she cared for the sick and the poor.[66] After she left Belley, she became affiliated with the Ursulines, living in their convent in Bordeaux for three months while she awaited the ship that would transport her to the New World. It was there, in Bordeaux, that she received three months of novitiate training.[67] Yet even though Fontiere was received by the Ursulines in New Orleans and lived in their convent for some time, she did not enter the community. Instead, she associated herself with one of their apostolates in the city, taking over the instruction of slave women and the education of free girls of color.[68] In 1824, when the Ursulines moved to a new convent several miles down the Mississippi River, Sister Ste. Marthe remained in the city, establishing a convent and a school for the girls.[69]

Sister Ste. Marthe dedicated herself to the city's women of African descent, introducing the newer French religious fervor to the city's poorest but most pious constituency. The student records for her school are no longer extant; however, the oral tradition of the Sisters of the Holy Family and the history of the community written in the nineteenth century by Sister Mary Bernard Deggs has it that Henriette Delille was educated by Sister Ste. Marthe. Her presence is documented at the school for free girls of color through 1831. During the 1830s, responsibility for the school passed through several hands. The Ursulines took it on for two interludes between 1831 and 1838 and assigned two nuns to staff it. Mademoiselle Marie Jeanne Aliquot, a French laywoman, assumed the work in 1834 and bought a new facility to house the school on St. Claude Street. When she left the city in 1836, the Ursulines resumed the commitment, until they persuaded the Sisters of Our Lady of Mount Carmel to take over in 1838.[70]

Sister Ste. Marthe, Marie Aliquot, the Ursulines, and the Sisters of Our Lady of Mount Carmel who maintained the school for free girls of color in antebellum New Orleans found themselves in more and more contentious circumstances as the city shed the flexible racial boundaries of the colonial era and fell more closely into step with the racial segregation that characterized the American plantation South.[71] The situation only began to change when the French women who had maintained control over the institutions populated by women and girls of African descent were joined by the French priest Michael Portier. Within a short time of his arrival in the Crescent City, Portier had unintentionally posed what would be a more fundamental threat to the racial order when he organized a confraternity of free women of African descent. Founded with paternalistic enthusiasm, Portier's project quickly took on a life of its own and ultimately eluded both paternalistic and maternalistic white control.

The evidence we have of the early years of this association comes from an 1820 letter that Portier wrote to Father Cholleton, the director of the Grand Séminaire in Lyon. In that letter, Portier described what was the beginnings of the first confraternity of free Afro-Creole women: he wrote that he had a dozen young free women of color who were "fervent, like angels." Another sixty young women, he noted, surrounded him every night, and he read the Gospel to them and then explained it. The members of this congregation, he professed, were his consolation. "They wear a red ribbon and a cross and they promise to fight daily like valiant soldiers of Jesus Christ." Portier had the congregation assemble each Sunday and usually presided at their assembly. In that way, he assured Cholleton, he regulated the manner in which the young women practiced religion. Portier told the French priest that he had the happiness to see the young women as faithful as the seminarians in Lyon. He pointed out, however, that the student priests in Lyon lived in a seminary while the New Orleans flock lived in "Babylon," in the midst of scandals. These young women, he concluded, were "like angels; they teach the Blacks to pray, they catechize, they instruct, and they communicate . . . [the rest of the sentence is lost]."[72]

Sister Ste. Marthe and Portier, both missionaries who came from the generation of activist religious in postrevolutionary France, were no doubt welcomed by New Orleans women of African descent who had themselves long been engaged in the work of the church. Portier's letter paints a portrait of a dedicated group of followers. The women who joined his confraternity, however, were not rapt neophytes but daughters of a long Afro-Catholic tradition poised to turn Portier's patronage into a religious foundation of their own. In the 1830s, they took over the direction of their confraternity, and by 1836, led by Henriette Delille, they had a set of rules and regulations that named them the Sisters of the Congregation of the Presentation of the Blessed Virgin Mary. With that move into the publicly acceptable arena of religious activism, the free women of African descent in New Orleans, empowered themselves and acted on the universalist ideals brought by nineteenth-century French missionaries.[73]

The rules and regulations of this unique congregation required members to demonstrate piety and charity. The women were to "seek to bring back the Glory of God and the salvation of their neighbor by a charitable and edifying behavior." Each woman took a pledge to aid any of her sisters when necessary. Finally, the women promised to serve "the sick, the infirm, and the poor," who were the "first and dearest objects of the solicitude of the congregation." These lay sisters went into homes to visit the sick and to comfort the dying. They brought food to the hungry and warmth to the cold. They sought out the uninstructed so they might "teach the principal mysteries of religion and the most important points of Christian morality."[74]

There can be little doubt that Henriette Delille and the women who joined her in 1836, Juliette Gaudin and Josephine Charles, were founding members of the Sisters of the Presentation. They were influenced by the Ursulines through heritage and tradition, replicating in important ways the much earlier organization and mission of the Children of Mary confraternity sponsored by the nuns in the eighteenth century. But the eighteenth-century model of female religious activism had since been revitalized and transformed by an array of more insistently activist and universalist religious orders founded in postrevolutionary France. Three of these new orders, the Sisters of Charity, Sisters of the Sacred Heart, and Sisters of Our Lady of Mount Carmel, established communities in nineteenth-century New Orleans and provided Delille and her colleagues with a contemporary French model of women ministering to the sick, the needy, and the poor and instructing the uninstructed. Marthe Fontiere's personal and practical dedication to all New Orleans' women of African descent transcended in yet another way that of the Ursulines, who were willing to support the ministry but hoped it would flourish in other hands. The Sisters of the Presentation thus drew on two sources to create their new religious congregation. Delille's enterprise was grounded in the older Counter-Reformation French tradition of women evangelizing women promoted by the Ursulines and the Children of Mary and passed down to her and other Afro-Creoles in New Orleans through their matrilineal forebears. It was nourished and animated by the postrevolutionary French emphasis on women aiding other women with practical action and charity that Delille and her companions witnessed in their formative years.[75]

Delille and her companions were women who had few choices and little if any power as women of color in antebellum New Orleans. That changed when they redefined themselves as pious women and joined forces to meet the needs of others of African descent they saw around them. Yet, while the social implications of the congregation's actions are the first to strike the modern eye, the women themselves saw their project as an act of faith and piety. In 1836, Delille wrote her intentions in the form of a prayer in the front of one of her devotional books: "I believe in God. I hope in God. I love. I wish to live and die for God."[76] This simple prayer exemplifies the fulfillment of the tradition of pious Catholic devotion Delille received from her ancestors. It demonstrates the culmination of the process delineated in the preceding pages. But it also previewed what was to come.

By 1842, Delille, the great-great-granddaughter of the African bondwoman Nanette, began to move toward an even more activist ministry. Not satisfied with her role as a pious laywoman, she, along with Gaudin and Charles, adopted several key features of formal religious life. They moved into a house near St. Augustine's Church in New Orleans and began to define their mission to the city's slaves and free people of color. In 1852, the three women changed their dress—from blue to black— began to wear rosaries around their necks, and took private vows, committing themselves to the church and to those they called "our people." The religious order of women of color that emerged between 1836 and 1852 is recognized today as the Sisters of the Holy Family.[77]

Henriette Delille and her allies in the foundation of the Sisters of the Holy Family claimed French Catholic tradition in order to defy the social and racial conventions of antebellum New Orleans in numerous ways. Their chastity contested the sexualization of women of color and vitiated racist ideology that denied such women their claim to the feminine virtue that defined the ideal of American womanhood.[78] Their ministry to enslaved and free people of color, which came to include a school, an orphanage, nursing care for the sick and the elderly, and the provision of food and clothing for the destitute, transgressed and cast shame on the racially limited parameters of antebellum white benevolence. The institution they built conferred on them authority and power to shape the city's common welfare and denied whites a monopoly on the institutional life of New Orleans. Finally, by providing catechesis to the city's people of African descent, they ensured the continued dominance of the city's Catholic Church by African Americans and at the same time kept Protestantism at bay, effectively molding the religiosity of the city's black population.

In the 1730s, Marie Payen Dubreuil joined the confraternity of the Children of Mary that was pledged to evangelize the slaves of colonial New Orleans. One of the bondwomen of her household, an African known in Louisiana as Nanette, was subsequently baptized. A great-great-granddaughter of Nanette was Henriette Delille. In this simple narrative of catechesis and kinship, we can observe the larger movement delineated by statistics of baptism and population. The intergenerational transmission of Roman Catholicism to the people of African descent in New Orleans was a matrilineal process. It was initiated in 1727 by women who were mothers by faith alone, the Ursuline nuns, and aided by a confraternity of laywomen in the 1730s and 1740s. Enslaved African women seeking to preserve their religious traditions in an alien environment contributed the vital current of blood motherhood and brought their daughters into the ritual circle of the church. Increasingly, African American women undertook primary responsibility for the transmittal of their adopted faith, not only to their daughters, but also to all those of African descent in their city. And finally, they expressed their leadership through their own religious order. This evolution was probably nothing the first generation of European evangelizers ever imagined and contrasts markedly with the development of Catholicism elsewhere in the Caribbean and circum-Caribbean. Although the urban setting of New Orleans is an obvious point of difference from the plantation environment that characterized most other areas, the feminine nature of the initial missionary effort and the gradual assumption of leadership by laywomen of African descent during the colonial period and in the opening decades of the nineteenth century were key factors shaping the growth of an Afro-Catholic community. In a religious culture promoted by female catechesis rather than by male missionaries, leadership and responsibility for propagation of the faith were shared among a network of believers through the channel of motherhood. This method of religious diffusion was more organic to the existing West African cultural structures that enslaved women brought to Louisiana and provided more attractive opportunities for the adaptation of Catholic practices to community interests than the hierarchical model of conversion and evangelization controlled by a male priesthood.

Canon Peter L. Benoit, an English Mill Hill Father, discovered the primacy of the church in the Afro-Creole community in New Orleans when he visited there in 1875 in order to determine if there was a need for missionaries to minister to the city's freed blacks. Canon Benoit was sincere in his efforts, but his visit proved less than successful. Soon after his arrival in the Crescent City, Archbishop Napoléon Joseph Perché suggested to Benoit that there might be some need for his services in the English-speaking section of the city, where most of the blacks were Protestant. Benoit soon discovered for himself why Perché did not need Catholic missionaries to attract African Americans to their worship services in the French section of the city: "The Creoles or real French here are, I am sorry to say, as stingy here as in their own country. They support the theatres, and go to them well dressed. But they don't support their churches in the same way nor are they frequenters of the Sacraments."[79] But Benoit noted that the city's people of African descent living in the French section of the city had a different experience. While most African Americans in other cities were Baptist or Methodist, those in New Orleans were Catholic, and "the French clergy would not like to have them withdrawn from their churches because they are their chief support."[80] The missionary field of francophone Africans in postbellum New Orleans had already been successfully cultivated and had no need of Benoit's ministrations. Indeed, had it not been, the francophone church in the city would have withered from the indifference of the "stingy" white creoles of French descent. The francophone Catholic Church that Benoit encountered in postemancipation New Orleans quite simply owed its survival to the devout people of African descent who had come to it for generations through their women.

NOTES

1 Ursuline Convent Chapel Baptismal Register, 1837–1845, Apr. 1, 1838, Ursuline Convent of New Orleans Archives, New Orleans. The entry, in translation from the original French, reads: "On this first of April of eighteen hundred and thirty-eight, I baptized, in the Convent Chapel of St. Claude Marie Therese Dagon daughter of Charles Dagon and of Charlotte Diggs born the twenty-fifth of December of eighteen hundred and twenty-three. The godfather being the undersigned and the godmother being Henriette Delile. [signed] E. Rousselon, Chaplain of the Ursulines." The record does not explicitly state that Dagon was of African descent; however, it can be assumed as we have discovered no record in which a person of African descent served as a godparent to a white baptisand. Further, the St. Claude Street Chapel, no longer in existence, was a part of the St. Claude Street school for free girls of African descent. Translations of French sources are by the authors unless otherwise noted.

2 In September 1826, Delille made her debut as a godmother in the sacramental

records, sponsoring Fleurine, the 6-month-old daughter of Pelagie, the slave of Didier Livaudais; St. Louis Cathedral Baptismal Register of Slaves and Free People of Color, 1826–1827, Archives of the Archdiocese of New Orleans, New Orleans.

3 Another order for free women of color, the Oblates of Providence, was founded in Baltimore in 1828. Several features differentiate the two orders. The Oblates, who focused on teaching, undertook a narrower ministry than the Sisters of the Holy Family. The Sisters of the Holy Family, whose members were often light-skinned enough to "pass" for white, explicitly and continuously affirmed their identities as Afro-Creoles. By contrast, the black identity and origins of the Oblates were intentionally suppressed when one of its early leaders took its teaching ministry to the American Midwest. Finally, the impetus for the Oblates' formal foundation appears to have been external: a French priest, Jacques Joubert, organized a group of 3 women to teach and catechize free girls of color; Cyprian Davis, *The History of Black Catholics in the United States* (New York, 1990), 99. The foundation is described in Joubert, "The Original Diary of the Oblate Sisters of Providence, 1827–1842," Oblate Sisters of Providence Archives, Baltimore, 285 n. 2. See also John Thaddeus Posey, "An Unwanted Commitment: The Spirituality of the Early Oblate Sisters of Providence, 1829–1890" (Ph.D. diss., St. Louis University, 1993); William Leafonza Montgomery, "Mission to Cuba and Costa Rica: The Oblate Sisters of Providence in Latin America, 1900–1970" (Ph.D. diss., Catholic University of America, 1997); and Diane Batts Morrow, "The Oblate Sisters of Providence: Issues of Black and Female Agency in Their Antebellum Experience, 1828–1860" (Ph.D. diss., University of Georgia, 1996).

4 The pattern of female catechesis that we demonstrate in this section probably began in the late 1720s shortly after the Ursulines reached New Orleans in 1727. However, the sacramental records for the 1720s were lost in a fire that destroyed much of New Orleans in 1788. Baptismal records for the years 1734–1743 met the same fate; Earl C. Woods, Charles E. Nolan, and Dorenda Dupont, eds., *Sacramental Records of the Roman Catholic Church of the Archdiocese of New Orleans*, vol. 1: *1718–1750* (New Orleans, 1987), xiv.

5 Henriette Delille's African ancestor is called "Nanette" throughout this essay, though she appears in colonial records under both her baptismal name, "Marie Anne," and her diminutives, "Nanette" and "Manette," which were the familiar forms of the name Anne and were undoubtedly adopted to differentiate her from her daughter "Marianne." She is, for example, called "Marie Anne" in the marginal notation for her daughter Cecile's baptismal record, St. Louis Cathedral Baptism, 1744–1753, Archives of the Archdiocese of New Orleans, Dec. 31, 1744, but is "Nanette" in the estate inventory of her owner, Claude Joseph Dubreuil; inventory of the estate of Claude Joseph Dubreuil, May 29, 1773, Louisiana State Archives, New Orleans, box 30, document 274, file 13.

6 Gwendolyn Midlo Hall, *Africans in Colonial Louisiana: The Development of Afro-Creole Culture in the Eighteenth Century* (Baton Rouge, 1992), 60.

7 Baptismal statistics based on St. Louis Cathedral Baptisms, 1731–1733, and St. Louis Cathedral Baptisms, 1744–1753, Archives of the Archdiocese of New Orleans. Censuses nearest in date to 1731–1733 and 1750 are those of 1737 and 1763. Our figures are drawn from Paul Lachance, "Summary of Louisiana Census of 1737," based on "Recapitulation du recensement general de la Louisiane en 1737," Archives Nationales, Archives des Colonies, séries C (hereafter cited as AC), C13, C4:197, and "Summary of Louisiana Census of 1763," based on Jacqueline K. Voorhies, trans. and comp., *Some Late Eighteenth-Century Louisianians: Census Records, 1758–1796* (Lafayette, La., 1973), 103–05. Both summaries have subsequently been published in Hall, ed., *Databases for*

the *Study of Afro-Louisiana History and Genealogy, 1699–1860*, CD-Rom (Baton Rouge, 2000). In these sacramental records priests usually noted whether the baptisand was an "infant" (many of whom were under age 2) or an "adult" (who was able to consent and enjoyed a different rite).

8 "Le Code Noir ou Édit du Roi. Servant de Réglement pour le gouvernement & l'Administration de la Justice, Police, Discipline & le Commerce des Esclaves Nègres, dans la Province ou Colonie de la Louisiane. Donné à Versailles au mois de Mars 1724," in *Le Code Noir ou Recueil des reglemens rendus jusqu'à présent: concernant le Gouvernment, l'Administration de la Justice, la Police, la Discipline & le Commerce des Nègres dans les Colonies Françaises* (Paris, 1742), 321. Thomas N. Ingersoll, *Mammon and Manon in Early New Orleans: The First Slave Society in the Deep South, 1718–1819* (Knoxville, 1999), 112, 135, implies that baptism could function as a means of social control, yet notes planter opposition to slave catechesis on the basis of its subversive potential and points out an annotation in a manuscript copy of the *Code Noir* that declares that the injunction to have slaves baptized was ignored in Louisiana.

9 On the lag between slaves' arrival in the colony and their baptism, note, for example, that 151 adult Africans were baptized in 1746, 3 years after the most recent direct shipment of African captives to Louisiana; St. Louis Cathedral Baptisms and Marriages, 1744–1753.

10 The parochial priests assigned to New Orleans were Capuchin friars. They were few in number and did not pursue a program of catechesis among the enslaved of the city and its environs. There is some evidence that the Capuchins hoped to convert Indians, but such plans were not carried to fruition. Jesuits, known for a more proactive ministry to enslaved populations, were prohibited from evangelizing in the area; AC, C 13A, 10:43–46v, 11:217–19; Charles Edwards O'Neill, *Church and State in French Colonial Louisiana: Policy and Politics to 1732* (New Haven, 1966), 55, 70–77, 130, 162–73.

11 For full discussion of the Ursuline apostolate and descriptions of their schools see Elizabeth Rapley, *The Dévotes: Women and Church in Seventeenth-Century France* (Montreal, 1990), 3–22, 48–60, 74–75, 142–54, and Linda Lierheimer, "Female Eloquence and Maternal Ministry: The Apostolate of Ursuline Nuns in Seventeenth-Century France" (Ph.D. diss., Princeton University, 1994).

12 *The Letters of Marie Madeleine Hachard, 1727–28*, trans. Myldred Masson Costa (New Orleans, 1974), 59.

13 "Premiere Registre de la Congrégation des Dames Enfants de Marie," Ursuline Convent of New Orleans Archives, 3, 7. For a full discussion of the social makeup of the Children of Mary, see Emily Clark, " 'By All the Conduct of Their Lives': A Laywomen's Confraternity in New Orleans, 1730–1744," *William and Mary Quarterly*, 3d Ser., 54 (1997), 769–94, and "A New World Community: The New Orleans Ursulines and Colonial Society, 1727–1803" (Ph.D. diss., Tulane University, 1998), 74–79.

14 Sacramental records and other colonial documents typically inscribed only the given name of slaves, a practice that was apparently reserved only for people of color in the colony. See, for example, St. Louis Cathedral Baptisms, 1731–1733, and St. Louis Cathedral Baptisms, 1744–1753, for conventions used in sacramental records. At least two women of color were boarding at the Ursuline convent during the 1730s when the Children of Mary were active; "Records of the Superior Council," *Louisiana Historical Quarterly*, 4 (1921), 355, and ibid., 9 (1926), 310.

15 "Premiere Registre de la Congrégation des Dames Enfants de Marie," 7.

16 Clark, "By All the Conduct of Their Lives," 790–92.

17 "Premiere Registre de la Congrégation des Dames Enfants de Marie," 13–14.

18 See entries for Jan. 13, May 23, and Aug. 15, 1733, in St. Louis Cathedral

Baptisms, 1731–1733, and entries for Feb. 6, May 12, 2(?), Aug. 30, 31, Sept. 22, and Dec. 31, 1744, in St. Louis Cathedral Baptisms, 1744–1753.

19 Liliane Crété with Patricia Crété, *La Traite des Nègres sous l'Ancien Régime: Le Nègre, le Sucre, et la Toile* (Paris, 1998; orig. pub. 1989), 82. The preference for taking women from the Senegambian littoral and men from further inland was first described by David P. Geggus in "Sex Ratio, Age, and Ethnicity in the Atlantic Slave Trade: Data from French Shipping and Plantation Records," *Journal of African History*, 30 (1989), 23–44. See also Patrick Manning, *Slavery and African Life: Occidental, Oriental, and African Slave Trades* (Cambridge, 1990), 97–98; Michael Gomez, *Exchanging Our Country Marks: The Transformation of African Identities in the Colonial and Antebellum South* (Chapel Hill, 1998), 43; and Hall, *Africans in Colonial Louisiana*, 41–95, 275–315.

20 Labat, *Nouvelle rélation de l'Afrique occidentale contenant une description exacte du Sénégal et des Païs situés entre le Cap Blanc et la Riviere de Serrelione, jusqu'à plus de 300 lieues en avant dans les Terres*, 5 vols. (Paris, 1728), 2:209, 232–33; Le Page du Pratz, *Histoire de la Louisiane*, 3 vols. (Paris, 1757), 1:342, 343n, 344–45. Hall, "African Women in French and Spanish Louisiana: Origins, Roles, Family, Work, Treatment," in Catherine Clinton and Michele Gillespie, *The Devil's Lane: Sex and Race in the Early South* (New York, 1997), 249–50, asserts the primacy of Wolof women in early Louisiana.

21 See, for example, James Searing, *West African Slavery and Atlantic Commerce: The Senegal River Valley, 1700–1860* (Cambridge, 1993), 60, 66, 76. Searing describes the intensive interactions of the French sailors, merchants, and administrators with the coastal and river Africans who served as traders, cultural guides, and interpreters. French speakers as well as Catholics were to be found amongst these riverine and coastal populations. Boubacar Barry, *Senegambia and the Atlantic Slave Trade* (New York, 1998), 76, describes the commercial and social power wielded by the female Afro-European *signares* of St. Louis, at the mouth of the Senegal River. See also "Lettre du Conseil Supérieur," AC, C 6:11, Jan. 28, 1738, and La Courbe, *Premier Voyage du sieur de la Courbe fait a la coste d'Afrique en 1685* (Paris, 1913), 107, 109.

22 Assigning ethnicity and related cultural attributes to early 18th-century Senegambians is a difficult and contentious exercise, but if Nanette was from a coastal group, it is likely that she was a non-Muslim woman. From the 1670s and through the first half of the 18th century, Muslim factions waged war for political and religious control in Waalo, Futa Toro, Kajoor, Jolof, and the more inland and southern regions of Bundu and Futa Jallon. Muslims did not achieve lasting control of the northwestern areas of Waalo, Futa Toro, Kajoor, and Jolof until the second half of the 18th century. During the first phase of the Louisiana slave trade, 1719–1743, the northwestern areas of Senegambia remained in the hands of warlords who practiced traditional African religion and generally claimed succession to their positions matrilineally. A series of conflicts over succession in the early 18th century provided captives from these areas for the slave trade; Barry, *Senegambia and the Atlantic Slave Trade*, 28, 50–54, 81–105. Nanette's enslavement was likely a product of this succession of local conflicts among non-Muslim warlords. On religious behavior among non-Muslim women, see Arlette Gautier, *Les soeurs de Solitude: La Condition féminine dans l'Esclavage aux Antilles du XVII au XIX Siècle* (Paris, 1985), 45, and Abdoulaye-Bara Diop, *La Famille Wolof: Tradition et Changement* (Paris, 1985), 44–45, 51. Also see Peter Caron, " 'Of a Nation Which Others Do Not Understand': Bambara Slaves and African Ethnicity in Colonial Louisiana, 1718–60," *Slavery and Abolition*, 18 (1997), 98–121.

23 Nanette and her children are enumerated in the inventory of Claude Joseph Dubreuil's estate. They are identified as a family of domestics living in the

household and are protected by codicil to the will; inventory of the estate of Claude Joseph Dubreuil. The fire of 1788 destroyed the baptismal records of Nanette and her children Marianne, Fanchonette, Tuyanne, and Tonica. We infer the baptisms of Nanette and Marianne from the women's appearance in sacramental records as godmothers. See, for example, May 13, 1775, in St. Louis Cathedral Baptisms, 1772–1776; Mar. 23, May 25, and Sept. 7, 1760, in St. Louis Cathedral Baptisms, 1759–1762; Oct. 27, 1765, in St. Louis Cathedral Baptisms and Marriages, 1763–1766.

24 Hall, *Africans in Colonial Louisiana*, chap. 9.

25 Ibid., 68.

26 Quotation in AC 11A, 96:222v.

27 Clark, "New World Community," 136.

28 Statistics based on St. Louis Cathedral Baptisms, 1731–1733; St. Louis Cathedral Baptisms and Marriages, 1763–1766; "Libro donde se asientan las partidas de baptismos . . . 1777 que empezó hasta el año de 1781 que es el corriente"; St. Louis Cathedral Baptisms and Marriages, 1777–1786; "Libro quinto de bautizados negros y mulatos de la parroquia de San Luis de esta ciudad de la Nueva Orleans: contiene doscientos trienta y siete folios útiles, y da principio en primero de octubre de mil setecientos noventa y dos, y acaba [en 1798]"; St. Louis Cathedral Baptisms and Marriages, 1786–1796; St. Louis Cathedral Baptisms of Slaves and Free Persons of Color, 1801–1804; St. Louis Cathedral Baptisms of Slaves and Free Persons of Color, 1804–1805; St. Louis Cathedral Baptisms, 1802–1806; St. Louis Cathedral Baptisms of Slaves and Free People of Color, February 1824–February 1825; St. Louis Cathedral Baptisms of Slaves and Free People of Color, March 1820–December 1826; St. Louis Cathedral Baptisms, January 1822–March 1825; and St. Louis Cathedral Baptisms, April 1825–January 1827, all in Archives of the Archdiocese of New Orleans.

29 Statistics based on St. Louis Cathedral Baptisms, 1731–1733; St. Louis Cathedral Baptisms and Marriages, 1763–1766; "Libro donde se asientan las partidas de baptismos . . . 1777 que empezó hasta el año de 1781 que es el corriente"; and "Libro quinto de bautizados negros y mulatos."

30 For a discussion of creolization, see Edward Brathwaite, *The Development of Creole Society in Jamaica* (Oxford, 1971), 193–239, who notes that creolization is a process that radiates outward from the slave community, affecting the entire culture by degrees. The process, he explains, begins when all those in a society begin to share a common style and should be understood as prismatic with each separate group acculturating. He then adds that this concept is problematic in slaveholding societies where interculturation was channeled by the dominant class with the whip of legislation. The process, he argues, should not be understood as continual, but as one with highs and lows, ebbs and flows.

31 Statistics based on St. Louis Cathedral Baptisms, 1731–1733; St. Louis Cathedral Baptisms, 1744–1753; St. Louis Cathedral Baptisms and Marriages, 1763–1766; "Libro donde se asientan las partidas de baptismos . . . 1777 que empezó hasta el año de 1781 que es el corriente"; "Libro quinto de bautizados negros y mulatos," St. Louis Cathedral Baptisms of Slaves and Free Persons of Color, 1804–1805; St. Louis Cathedral Baptisms, 1802–1805; St. Louis Cathedral Baptisms of Slaves and Free People of Color, Mar. 9, 1824–Feb. 28, 1825; St. Louis Cathedral Baptisms of Slaves and Free People of Color, Mar. 1, 1825–Dec. 1, 1825; St. Louis Cathedral Baptisms of Slaves and Free People of Color, Dec. 4, 1825–Dec. 9, 1826; and St. Louis Cathedral Baptisms of Slaves and Free People of Color, January 1840–December 1842.

32 AC 11A, 96:222v.

33 For these arguments, see, among others, Sylvia R. Frey and Betty Wood, *Come*

187

Shouting to Zion: African American Protestantism in the American South and British Caribbean to 1830 (Chapel Hill, 1998), which discusses both the failure of Anglican missionaries and the ways in which the enslaved took control of their religious lives; John Thornton, *Africa and Africans in the Making of the Atlantic World, 1400–1800,* 2d ed. (Cambridge, 1998); Frey, *Water from the Rock: Black Resistance in a Revolutionary Age* (Princeton, 1991), 243–325, which places the appropriation of evangelical Christianity by slaves in the context of resistance; Gomez, *Exchanging Our Country Marks,* 263–90; and Mary Turner, *Slaves and Missionaries: The Disintegration of Jamaican Slave Society, 1787–1834* (Urbana, 1982), 71–95, which describes slave resistance to the efforts of white evangelical missionaries to replace African religious and social beliefs and habits with Christian models. Other recent scholarship that considers the agency of slaves in relation to Christianity in more general studies of slavery includes Ira Berlin, *Many Thousands Gone: The First Two Centuries of Slavery in North America* (Cambridge, Mass., 1998), esp. 42, 51, 73, 75, 138–39, 151, 171–73, 189–90, and Philip D. Morgan, *Slave Counterpoint: Black Culture in the Eighteenth-Century Chesapeake and Lowcountry* (Chapel Hill, 1998), esp. 424–25, 431–32.

34 St. Louis Cathedral Baptisms and Marriages, 1763–1766; "Libro quinto de bautizados negros y mulatos."

35 See, for example, the entry for the adult group baptism on Pentecost Eve 1762, in St. Louis Cathedral Baptisms and Marriages, 1759–1762.

36 "Libro quinto de bautizados negros y mulatos," June 3–6, 1797.

37 Thornton, *Africa and Africans in the Making of the Atlantic World,* 2d ed., 253–71, speaks to the conversion process of Africans in Africa and in the Americas, where Christianized Africans at times acted as evangelists to other slaves. See especially p. 323, where the Kongolese of St. Jan in the Danish West Indies, "as Christians of many generations' standing, took it upon themselves to baptize all newly arrived slaves, serving as godparents of sorts to them," in the 1750s. Mechal Sobel, *The World They Made Together: Black and White Values in Eighteenth-Century Virginia* (Princeton, 1989), 180–84, 189, 204–05, speaks to the influence of slave worship styles and piety on the ministers and white congregations of the First Great Awakening, as does Morgan, *Slave Counterpoint,* 429–30. Gomez, *Exchanging Our Country Marks,* 244–90, stresses the degree to which African belief and worship forms infused the Christianity practiced by slaves.

38 Kimberly S. Hanger, *Bounded Lives, Bounded Places: Free Black Society in Colonial New Orleans, 1769–1803* (Durham, N. C., 1997), 104–05; Clark, "New World Community," 140–45; Hall, *Africans in Colonial Louisiana,* 157–200.

39 Canon 874, in James A. Coriden, Thomas J. Green, and Donald E. Heintschel, eds., *The Code of Canon Law: A Text and Commentary* (New York, 1985), and Stanislaus Woywod, *A Practical Commentary on the Code of Canon Law,* rev. Callistus Smith (New York, 1957), 393, 395.

40 Acts of Juan Garic, 1776, New Orleans Notarial Archives, New Orleans; "Déliberations du Conseil," Archives of the Ursuline Convent of New Orleans, 59; Clark, "New World Community," 143.

41 Entries for May 28, June 29, 1746, Feb. 7, Mar. 5, 1747, June 11, 1748, in St. Louis Cathedral Baptisms and Marriages, 1744–1753; May 13, 1775, in St. Louis Cathedral Baptisms and Marriages, 1753–1759; Mar. 23, May 25, Sept. 7, 1760, in St. Louis Cathedral Baptisms and Marriages, 1759–1762; Oct. 27, 1765, in St. Louis Cathedral Baptisms and Marriages, 1763–1766; Mar. 4, July 23, 1775, in "Libro donde se asientan las partidas de baptismos . . . 1777 que empezó hasta el año de 1781 que es el corrente." Marianne was younger than the canonical age (16 yrs.) required for godparents, a stipulation regularly ignored according to the New Orleans records. Underage godmothers appear more often than underage godfathers.

42 See note 24 above.

43 Virginia Meacham Gould, "Free Women of Color and the Catholic Church in Spanish Louisiana," in *Religion in Louisiana*, ed. Charles Nolan, Bicentennial Series of the Louisiana Purchase (Lafayette, La., forthcoming).

44 Santiago Bernard Coquet and José Antonio Boniquet held the concession on a city-owned ballroom that was the scene in the 1790s of multiracial dances that became known as "tricolor balls"; Gilbert C. Din and John E. Harkins, *The New Orleans Cabildo: Colonial Louisiana's First City Government, 1769–1803* (Baton Rouge, 1996), 164, 173–75. Hanger, *Bounded Lives*, 148–49, chronicles a series of raids in the 1790s on taverns and billiard halls where whites, free blacks, and slaves were found fraternizing.

45 Hanger, *Bounded Lives*, 136–43, portrays the free Afro-Creoles of New Orleans as thoroughly assimilated to European culture even as they embraced a revolutionary insistence on racial equality that was rejected by those of unmixed European descent in the city. The church, she notes, was a primary venue for the assertion of their European cultural identities. Hanger also provides statistical evidence of the religious observance of the city's slaves, which confounds such generalizations as "the free colored generally [adhered] to orthodox Catholicism, the slaves frequently [retained] their original religious orientation"; Thomas Marc Fiehrer, "The African Presence in Colonial Louisiana: An Essay on the Continuity of Caribbean Culture," in Robert R. Macdonald, John R. Kemp, and Edward F. Haas, eds., *Louisiana's Black Heritage* (New Orleans, 1979), 23; Michael Mullin, *Africa in America: Slave Acculturation and Resistance in the American South and the British Caribbean, 1736–1831* (Urbana, 1992), 228–29. Gomez, *Exchanging Our Country Marks*, 269–70, also comments on the cultural distance between urban and rural blacks. On the shift in the economy of colonial Louisiana, see Berlin, *Many Thousands Gone*, 325, 338–44; John G. Clark, *New Orleans, 1718–1812: An Economic History* (Baton Rouge, 1970), 189–92; Hall, *Africans in Colonial Louisiana*, 276–81, 286, 308–10; and Daniel H. Usner, Jr., *Indians, Settlers, and Slaves in a Frontier Exchange Economy: The Lower Mississippi Valley before 1783* (Chapel Hill, 1992), 118–19, 148, 177–278, 281–82.

46 Berlin, *Many Thousands Gone*, 209, notes that the town council of Spanish colonial New Orleans, the Cabildo, promulgated a new slave law in 1777 that explicitly attempted to suppress expressions of African religion. While Berlin links this to manifestations of creole religion still imbued with African practice, the timing suggests that it may have been triggered by the activities of newly arrived Africans.

47 "Libro donde se asientan las partidas de baptismos . . . 1777 que empezó hasta el año de 1781 que es el corrente."

48 There are far too many examples to cite; thus we have included a sampling: Oct. 27, 1765, in St. Louis Cathedral Baptisms and Marriages, 1763–1766, and Feb. 26, June 12, 1781 (one a slave, one free), in "Libro donde se asientan las partidas de baptismos . . . 1777 que empezó hasta el ano de 1781 que es el corrente."

49 Aug. 9, 1781, in "Libro donde se asientan las partidas de baptismos . . . 1777 que empezó hasta el año de 1781 que es el corrente"; Feb. 19, 1784, in "Libro quinto de bautizados negros y mulatos."

50 One Marie Ann was first freed privately before the French colonial governor, Louis de Kerelec, and was later publicly emancipated by notarial act under the Spanish regime; Emancipation of Marie Ann, Acts of Andrés Almonester y Roxas, Jan. 10, 1770, Notarial Archives of New Orleans. Marianne and her children were freed in 1772. Cecile was freed two years later; Emancipation of Cecile, Acts of Fernando Rodriguez, 1772, Notarial Archives of New Orleans. Marianne's emancipation is recorded in Acts of Juan Garic, Feb. 11, Sept. 23,

1772, Notarial Archives of New Orleans. The Spanish process would obviously have been more attractive to men wishing to free their mixed-race children and mistresses. See Hanger, *Bounded Lives*, 24–25, 31–38.

51 See the census of New Orleans for 1795, Archivo General de Indias, papales de Cuba, legajo 216, Seville, Spain.

52 Apr. 13, 1805, in St. Louis Cathedral Baptisms of Slaves and Free Persons of Color, 1804–1805.

53 Ibid. Henriette Delille owned one slave, who was probably already baptized when Delille inherited her.

54 Ana Manetta was baptized on May 17, 1825, St. Louis Cathedral Baptisms of Slaves and Free Persons of Color, Mar. 1, 1825–Dec. 1, 1825; Marie Françoise on Jan. 23, 1825, St. Louis Cathedral Baptisms of Slaves and Free Persons of Color, Mar. 9, 1824–Feb. 28, 1825; Luis Antonio on Jan. 16, 1825, ibid.; Esther's son Baptiste was baptized on May 15, 1825, St. Louis Cathedral Baptisms of Slaves and Free Persons of Color, Mar. 1, 1825–Dec. 1, 1825; Betsy's son Louis on May 14, 1825, ibid.; and Delsy's daughter Adele on May 13, ibid.

55 John Frederick Nau, *The German People of New Orleans, 1850–1900* (Leiden, 1958), 4–5; Earl F. Niehaus, *The Irish in New Orleans, 1800–1860* (Baton Rouge, 1965), 28–36; Lachance, "The Foreign French," in *Creole New Orleans: Race and Americanization*, ed. Arnold R. Hirsch and Joseph Logsdon (Baton Rouge, 1992), 119.

56 St. Louis Cathedral Baptisms of Slaves and Free People of Color, Mar. 1825–Dec. 1826, and St. Louis Cathedral Baptisms of Slaves and Free People of Color, Sept. 1827–June 1829, Archives of the Archdiocese of New Orleans.

57 "Matricula," Archives, Sisters of the Holy Family.

58 Watson, "Notia of Incidents at New Orleans in 1804 and 1805," *The American Pioneer*, 2 (May 1843), 230, 234.

59 See footnote 31 for sources.

60 Annabelle M. Melville, *Louis William Dubourg: Bishop of Louisiana and the Floridas, Bishop of Montauban, and Archbishop of Besançon, 1766–1833*, 2 vols. (Chicago, 1986). Also see Father John Marie Tessier, diary, in Archives of the Sulpiciens, Baltimore, and the letters from Dubourg to Bishop John Carroll in the Archives of the Archdiocese of Baltimore and in the Archives of the Daughters of Charity at Emmitsburg, Pa.

61 In 1815, the Diocese of New Orleans included all of Louisiana, which in turn included the Illinois Territory.

62 The best account of Pauline Jaricot's work is recorded in her *positio*, archived in the Congregation for the Causes of Saints, Vatican City. It is in Jaricot's writings that one finds the best evidence of the early activities of the Propagation de la Foi and Le Rosaire Vivant. The records of Le Rosaire Vivant are housed in La Maison Dominicaine, Lyon. Also see Edward John Hickey, "The Society for the Propagation of the Faith: Its Foundation, Organization, and Success (1822–1922)" (Ph.D. diss., Catholic University of America, 1922), and David LaThoud, *Marie-Pauline Jaricot*, 2 vols. (Paris, 1938).

63 Ernest Sevrin, *Les Missions Religieuses en France sous la Restauration, 1815–1830*, vol. 1 (Saint Manot, 1948).

64 Patricia Wittberg, *The Rise and Fall of Catholic Religious Orders: A Social Movement Perspective* (Albany, 1994), 58–70.

65 Yvonne Turin, *Femmes et Religieuses au XIXe Siècle: Le Féminisme "en Religion"* (Paris, 1989); Elisabeth Dufourcq, *Les Aventurières de Dieu: Trois Siècles d'Histoire Missionnaire Française* (Paris, 1993); Claude Langlois, *Le Catholicisme au Féminin: Les Congrégations Françaises à Supérieure Générale au XIXe Siècle* (Paris, 1984).

66 "Des Annales des Soeurs Hospitalieres de Belley," Archives Départementales, Bourg-en-Bresse, France.

67 "Des Annales des Ursulines de Bordeaux," 1816, Archives of the Ursuline Convent, Lyon; André Dallemagne, *Histoire de Belley* (Belley, Fr., 1979), 81, 191–99, 229, 245.

68 Fontiere does not appear in the book of professions of the New Orleans Ursulines. The annals of the New Orleans Ursulines record that Sr. Ste. Marthe "resta quelques années ici habilée comme nous, travaillant à l'institut avec beaucoup de zèle. En 1823, elle sortit pour aller établir la maison comme sous le nom de St. Claude destinée à l'instruction des jeunes filles de couleur" ("stayed here several years dressed like us, working in the school with much zeal. In 1823, she left to establish the house known under the name of St. Claude, intended for the instruction of young girls of color"); "First Book of Annals [of the New Orleans Ursulines]," 72–73, Ursuline Convent of New Orleans Archives.

69 When the Ursulines moved to their new site, they allowed the bishop the use of their old convent compound in the city center subject to several obligations. The first of these enumerated demands was "that every Sunday and feast day an instruction or catechism will be given to the negresses of the country to replace that being given now on those days." It is possible that Sr. Ste. Marthe was the individual employed with the fulfillment of this obligation; "Déliberations du Conseil," Apr. 1, 1826. On the Ursuline stewardship of the school for free girls of color, see entries for Jan. 31, Feb. 10, Mar. [n.d.] 1836, Feb. 26, 1837, ibid.

70 Between 1831 and 1834, the Ursulines assigned two of their nuns to take over Sr. Ste. Marthe's school on a temporary basis. They were recalled by the convent council in 1834, but Sr. Ste. Francis de Sales chose to stay on with her sister Marie Jeanne Aliquot, who had bought the school building and property. Together they ran the school until 1836, when the Ursulines again assumed full responsibility for the institution and reimbursed Aliquot for the purchase price. Between 1836 and 1838, four Ursulines were involved as director and teachers at the school. The Ursulines spent an additional $10,000 to purchase a piece of property adjacent to the school in 1836 in order to provide living quarters for the members of their community assigned to the school; "First Book of Annals," 219–20; entries for Mar. 7, 1834, Jan. 31, May 2, 1836, in "Déliberations du Conseil." On the transfer to the Sisters of Mount Carmel, see the contract between Aliquot and the Ursuline Community of New Orleans, Feb. 16, 1836, and the contract between the Ursuline Community of New Orleans and the Community of the Order of Our Lady of Mount Carmel of New Orleans, Nov. 25, 1840, both in Acts of Theodore Seghers, Notarial Archives of New Orleans. See also Charles Nolan, *Bayou Carmel: The Sisters of Mount Carmel of Louisiana, 1833–1903* (Kenner, La., 1977), 18–21.

71 Hall, *Africans in Colonial Louisiana*, 239–40; Usner, *Indians, Settlers, and Slaves*, 276–78; Jerah Johnson, "Colonial New Orleans: A Fragment of the Eighteenth-Century French Ethos," in Hirsch and Logsdon, eds., *Creole New Orleans*, 23. For another view, see Ingersoll, *Mammon and Manon*, which argues that a rigid racial hierarchy was established by a controlling planter regime as early as the 1730s, operating continuously throughout the colonial period.

72 Portier to Cholleton, Sept. [n. d.] 1820, in Records of La Propagation de la Foi, Oeuvres Missionaires Pontificale, Lyon. Although Portier does not identify the gender of his confraternity members, they were undoubtedly female. Confraternities in this period were not mixed, and the overwhelming majority were for women. The activities of Portier's confraternity—catechesis and instruction—were traditionally assumed by women, as they had been by the 18th-century Children of Mary.

73 "Rules and Regulations of the Sisters of the Congregation of the Presentation of the Blessed Virgin Mary," Archives of the Sisters of the Holy Family.

74 Ibid.

75 Father Joseph Rosati to Sr. Xavier Clark, Apr. 19, 1927; Bishop Antoine Blanc to Mother Rose White, Feb. 7, 1838, both in Records and Letters of the Daughters of Charity, Daughters of Charity Archives, St. Joseph Provincial House, Emmitsburg, Pa. Ste Madeleine-Sophie Barat and Ste Philippine Duschesne, "Correspondance: Texte des manuscrits originaux présent avec une introduction, des notes et un index analytique, Premier partie (1818–1821) et Second partie (1821–1826), Periode de l'Amérique" (Rome, 1989). Records of the Sisters of Our Lady of Mount Carmel, Convent of the Sisters of Our Lady of Mount Carmel, New Orleans.

76 This prayer, written in French and signed by Delille, was inscribed in a French book of spirituality, J.-A. Poncet de La Rivière, *Madame la Comtesse de Carcado, l'Ame unie à Jésus-Christ dans le Très-S. Sacrement de l'autel, ou Préparations et actions de grâces . . .* (Paris, 1830). The inscribed book is housed in the Archives of the Sisters of the Holy Family.

77 The description of the changes that occurred in 1852 are found in loose notes of Sr. Mary Borgia Hart, Archives of the Sisters of the Holy Family. Sr. Mary began a history of the Sisters of the Holy Family in 1916, when Sr. Ann Fazende was still living. Sr. Ann was one of the novices who entered the community in 1852, when the women were finally allowed to take in novices.

78 Gould, "In Full Enjoyment of Their Liberty: Free Women of Color in the Gulf Ports of New Orleans, Mobile, and Pensacola, 1769–1860" (Ph.D. diss., Emory University, 1991).

79 Benoit, diary entry, Apr. 9, 1875, in Mill Hill Fathers' Archives, copy in the Josephite Archives in Baltimore. For an excellent account of religion in the era of Reconstruction and Jim Crow in Louisiana, see Dolores Egger Labbé, *"Jim Crow Comes to Church": The Establishment of Segregated Catholic Parishes in South Louisiana*, 2d ed. (New York, 1978; orig. pub. 1971).

80 Benoit, diary entry, Apr. 9, 1875.

Part III

AFRICA IN THE AMERICAS

In recent years scholars have increasingly argued that, given the centrality of Africans in the making of the Atlantic world, we need to understand a great deal more about the particular ways in which African political ideologies, agricultural techniques, culture, religion, and social organization shaped societies in the Americas. The three selections in this section showcase how an analysis that focuses on the connections between Africa and the Americas can help us better understand the perspective of the enslaved, focusing particularly on the ways in which the African experience of captives in the Americas shaped strategies and ideologies of anti-slavery revolt.

In John Thornton's article, the military history of the Haitian Revolution is re-interpreted as an extension of conflicts within Central Africa. Noting that the largest group of enslaved people, and indeed of residents, in Saint-Domingue on the eve of the revolution came from the Kongo region, Thornton asserts that many of them were in fact "African veterans" captured in late-eighteenth century wars, and that they brought across the Atlantic valuable experience and knowledge of military tactics (p. 209). By comparing accounts of warfare in the Kongo and Saint-Domingue, he suggests that the fact that the enslaved revolutionaries had access to this resource of knowledge about how to fight, and win, proved pivotal in the success of the insurrection of 1791.

In the chapter from João Reis' book *Slave Rebellion in Brazil*, it is religion that helps to shape tactics and perspectives on resistance in Bahia. Reis examines the presence of Muslim slaves in Bahia, and shows how some mobilized their institutions and their religious practices in organizing an uprising in 1835. The chapter is constructed around a series of remarkable archival documents from Bahia—Koranic texts that were written to be worn, and to protect fighters—which strikingly illuminate the presence of Islamic practice in the Americas. At the same time, Reis shows how both religious practice and the organization of the revolt were shaped by the specific contexts of the Brazilian slave society.

Kenneth Bilby's article, the fruit of decades of ethnographic research in Jamaica and Surinam, examines practices of oath-taking and treaty-making among maroon groups in these areas. Like Thornton and Reis, he shows how particular practices were carried across the Atlantic to be both mobilized and transformed in a new context shaped by slavery and marronage. Bringing together extensive fieldwork among the maroons with archival research, Bilby analyzes how different groups interpreted and legitimized the treaties they signed with European powers. These oaths combined "swearing on the past" by "drawing on the legitimating power of their African gods and ancestors" and "swearing to the future, by endorsing a new life of peace and prosperity that these pacts promised" (p. 254). Bilby's work, which builds on the insights of the pioneering work of Richard Price and is included in his remarkable recent book *True-Born Maroons*, highlights the powerful ways in which ethnographic work allows us to understand both historical processes and the narratives produced about them within maroon communities.[1]

NOTE

1   Richard Price, *First Time: The Historical Vision of an Afro-American People* (Baltimore: Johns Hopkins University Press, 1983). Kenneth Bilby, *True-Born Maroons* (Gainesville: University of Florida Press, 2005).

8

AFRICAN SOLDIERS IN THE HAITIAN REVOLUTION

John K. Thornton

The rebellious slaves of Haiti inflicted grievous military defeat on all who opposed them: the *colons* of the island and their militias, regular French regiments sent from Europe, a significant Spanish army from Santo Domingo, a British army with regular soldiers, and finally, a fully equipped French force fresh from Napoleon's victories in Europe led by the Emperor's own brother-in-law. For many who have recounted this story the victory is made all the more dramatic by the fact that the triumphant slaves, fresh from the debilitating labor of plantation agriculture in the tropics, were able to defeat experienced soldiers. As C.L.R. James put it: "The revolt is the only successful slave revolt in history ... The transformation of slaves, trembling in hundreds before a single white man, into a people able to organise themselves and defeat the most powerful European nations of their day, is one of the great epics of revolutionary struggle and achievement."[1]

Historians seeking to explain this military achievement have not agreed on the reasons for the slaves' remarkable capacities in war. Some have emphasized the heroism of the slaves, and have seen their military performance as a reflection of broader themes connecting a love of liberty and desperate war, or have stressed the individual genius of slave leaders, especially Toussaint Louverture.[2] Still other historians find this interpretation too romantic in the real world of war. Enthusiasm ultimately could not overcome cold steel, and even Toussaint had no military experience other than that of a coachman. Instead they suggest the divisions among the various colonial powers, or the dissension among the *colons* and between them and various factions of Frenchmen, hamstrung a war effort which should have easily defeated the slaves and returned them to the plantations. Most also stress the importance of the tropical climate and especially tropical diseases in decimating and debilitating European troops.[3] Varying assessments of the slaves' military capacity or that of their leaders were recently emphasized in Roger Buckley's criticism of David Geggus for having underestimated the military competence of both Toussaint Louverture and his soldiers.[4]

The crux of these differences often lies in the historians' understanding of the military capacity of the slaves. Most have assumed that the slaves had no military experience prior to the revolution, and rose from agricultural labour to military prowess in an amazingly short time. Romantics have tended to point to this rapid ascent as evidence either of the great capacities of revolutionary labourers or the brillance of Toussaint Louverture, but others have found it incredible and sought non-military explanations.

However, it is probably a mistake to see the slaves as simply agricultural workers, like the peasants of Europe, and this is the crucial element in explaining the situation in Haiti. A majority of slaves, especially those who fought steadily in the revolution, were born in Africa, and were not just agricultural labourers with no experience in war.

In fact, a great many of the slaves had served in African armies prior to their enslavement and arrival in Haiti. Indeed, African military service had been the route by which many, if not most, of the recently arrived Africans became slaves in the first place, since so many people had been enslaved as a result of war. Under these circumstances, their military performance may not be as remarkable as historians have assumed. As ex-soldiers and veterans of African wars, they may have needed little more than the opportunity to serve again, in a rather different sort of war in America.

In order to understand the importance of the slaves' military background, one must first understand that a majority of the inhabitants of Saint Domingue in 1791 had been born in Africa and had arrived within ten years of the start of the revolution. Import statistics assembled by historians of slavery in Saint Domingue show this tendency clearly: 60–70 percent of the adult slaves listed on inventories in the late 1780s and 1790s were Africa born.[5] Thus, a knowledge of the African background is essential in understanding anything that they did, and especially in knowing what skills or attitudes they had.

In addition to being African born, these slaves came overwhelmingly from just two areas of Africa: the Lower Guinea coast region of modern Bénin, Togo and Nigeria (also known as the "Slave Coast"), and the Angola coast area. Again the statistics of imports and inventories both converge to reveal this pattern which shaped the whole of the French slave trade. Indeed, French shippers were riding the crest of a great surge of exports from these two regions, a surge that was reflected in British shipping as well.[6] According to French shipping data, French ships transported over 224,000 slaves from Africa in the decade before the revolution, of which 116,000 (51%) came from the Angola coast, and 55,000 (25%) from Lower Guinea, making together over three-quarters of the total.[7]

Although one cannot discount the vagaries of European wars, blockades and demands in shaping the slave trade, the primary African cause of the surge seems to have been war. In Angola, this was the great civil war in the Kingdom of Kongo, which reached a high level of intensity in the period around 1780. In the Lower Guinea region it was the complex of wars between the Oyo Empire, the Kingdom of Dahomey and the smaller states of the coast, the Nagô region and the Mahi country. In both Angola and Lower Guinea, slaves were taken in great military actions in which armies mobilised and fought in battles, thus resulting in a high percentage of the captives being prisoners of war, and veterans.

The Kongo civil wars can be said to have begun in the aftermath of the battle of Mbwila (29 October 1665), when the death of King António I without a clear heir left the country open for a succession struggle. The struggle was not resolved easily, since the various contenders were able to operate against each other from fairly secure bases, and within a few years the pretenders coalesced into two great family based groups, the Kimpanzu and the Kimulaza. The wars had a number of active episodes interspersed with periods of relative peace, such as that period which followed the nominal restoration of the kingdom under King Pedro IV (1696–1718),[8] in which a compromise between the two families was worked out, apparently coupled with an agreement to share power through selecting kings alternately from the two lines.[9] In spite of this, a new episode of war broke out in the 1760s: it began with an attempt on the part of Pedro V to seize power out of turn, and the successful attempt at resistance by Alvaro XI, who drove his rival from the capital of São Salvador and was crowned in 1764. However, Pedro V fled to a base at Mbamba Lubota and continued to bid for the throne.[10] This war went on with varying degrees of intensity, and eventually partisans of Pedro recaptured São Salvador around 1779, but José I, Alvaro XI's Kimulaza successor, drove them out in a large and bloody battle in September 1781.[11] Although a brief period of peace followed, it broke down after 1785 when José's brother and successor Afonso V died under suspicious circumstances.[12] Squabbles broke out among his descendants and fighting recommenced, not really quieting down until Henrique I reestablished a shaky order in 1794.[13]

During this time, then, armies faced each other on a number of occasions, with the prisoners of war being sold in the outcome. Sometimes these armies were large: according to eyewitness testimony, some 30,000 troops stormed São Salvador under José I's command in 1781; the defenders must have also numbered in the tens of thousands.[14] Most of the slaves sold on the coast in those years were likely to have come from these engagements. They were carried from battlefields by the Vilis, a generic name for coast-based African merchants, to coastal ports ranging from Mbrize (Ambriz) in the south to Loango in the north.[15] Because the Vilis were not Christian, the Church, acting through Father de Castello de Vide who was the Apostolic Vicar in Kongo from 1780 to 1788, sought to persuade the kings of Kongo to expel the Vilis, or at least to make them sell slaves to Catholic (which actually meant Portuguese) Europeans.[16]

The European beneficiaries of this great surge were French merchants who fixed their operations along the coast north of the Zaire River, but regularly visited the Kongo coast as well. In the 1780s, French ships carried a total of over 116,000 slaves from this coast, mostly to Saint Domingue, while their closest competitors, the English, exported only 25,000.[17] This was also the period of the great growth of the slave population of Saint Domingue, and naturally enough the civil wars in Kongo really ended on the colony's coffee and sugar plantations.

At the same time as these people were carried from Angolan ports to Saint Domingue, however, French merchants were also capitalizing on another great war-driven export surge from Lower Guinea in West Africa, especially from the ports of Porto Novo and Whydah. The wars that led to the export of tens of thousands of people each year through Lower Guinea were quite different from those that drove the slave trade of the Angola region.

In late eighteenth century Lower Guinea, wars were interstate affairs rather than civil wars. Politically, there was a complex situation involving the expansion of two great powers, Dahomey and Oyo, their rivalries with each other, and the resistance of independent smaller states, both along the coast and farther in the interior, to their activities. We get an especially good picture of Dahomey's role in these various operations through a diary kept by Lionel Abson, the factor of Fort William, the English post at Whydah, from 1770 to 1803. Although his diary is no longer extant, it was used extensively by the Scottish sea captain Archibald Dalzel to write a detailed history of Dahomey in 1793.[18]

Dahomey is often seen as simply a slave-raiding state, conducting wars and terrorising its neighbours, while exporting people wholesale. Under such operations, the slaves exported through ports frequented by Dahomean merchants might well be simply peasants and not soldiers. In actual fact, however, Dahomey's military activities, undoubtedly like those of its neighbours, were motivated by other concerns than just capturing slaves, and moreover, her neighbours possessed their own military systems.[19] Dahomey lost many of its wars, and saw its own citizens enslaved by its would-be-victims, even as Dahomey also won wars. Moreover, smaller states, which probably had smaller armies, or at least smaller potential armies than Dahomey, often held their own as well as the larger ones might: in 1774, for example, Dahomey successfully attacked Little Popo, a small coastal state lying to its southwest and captured many slaves,[20] but a similar attack in 1775 on Serechi, Little Popo's eastern neighbour and an equally small state, was a military disaster.[21] Wars against the northern neighbours, the Mahi and Nagô country, often ended in defeats, as in a campaign of 1775 or 1776, but might also bring victory as in 1777.[22] Under these military circumstances it is not surprising that the motives for war were likely to be political or diplomatic, sometimes even to the detriment of the slave trade. Before going on campaign against Mahi in 1777, Kpengla, Dahomey's king, said, "I want heads, not slaves," and in fact few slaves were taken.[23]

The political and diplomatic situation made wars in the Slave Coast complicated. Far reaching alliances were sometimes assembled to conduct wars. In 1783 Dahomey joined Porto Novo and Sessu in an unsuccessful attack on Badagri, a state that lay east of Dahomey along the coast.[24] That attack failed, and in 1784, Dahomey joined a larger alliance led by the Empire of Oyo with Mahi, Port Novo, and the Nagô to attack Badagri.[25] During much of this time Dahomey was only semi-independent, having to share some of the spoils of war with Oyo.

In the last analysis, what was significant about this period was the frequency of wars—Abson's diary lists a war every year of his stay, and Dahomey was not necessarily involved in all the wars in the area. In 1787, for example, Oyo invaded Mahi, and although Dohamey was not involved in the operation, many feared that the Oyo army would eventually attack Dahomey.[26] The operation was immensely successful; according to reports received at the coast, by the start of the rainy season of 1788, the Oyo army had "ravaged no less than fourteen districts; and burning and destroying multitudes of towns and villages."[27] No doubt its casualties contributed to the peak of imports from this area in Saint Domingue in 1787–89. The accounts of these and other wars in Dalzel and occasionally in other sources make it clear that all operations of Dahomey faced resistance from well organized and disciplined military forces, and the ebb and flow of war was largely due to the generalship, hardiness or sometimes luck of the various armies. Here, as in central Africa, soldiers must have been among the many exported slaves.

These soldier, veterans of African wars, might well have had the military skills that made the revolution in Saint Domingue a success. The revolution was immensely complex, of course, with many episodes and differing histories in every region. In many areas, especially the revolutionary movements in the South and West Provinces, African military skills may not have been as important as elsewhere. For example, in the struggle between mulattos and various white factions in the South and West, both of these elite groups armed their slaves, formed them into military units and used them to reach their own goals. The military experience of these slaves might have been important, but perhaps not decisive, since most of the organizational skills and even the tactical programmes came from the European background of these who organized the slaves. In time, these slaves may have used their military experience from their service in the early stages of the revolution for their own ends, as Carolyn Fick, who has analysed the movements in the South province carefully, has argued.[28]

Where the African military background of the slaves counted for the most was in those areas, especially in the North, where slaves themselves led the revolution, both politically and militarily. But these areas, which eventually threw up the powerful armies of Toussaint Louverture and Dessalines, were the ones that eventually carried the revolution, and thus played an important role from a military standpoint. Even in the South and West, with its complex political manoeuvering between white and mulatto, there were slave-led movements, such as those of Romaine la Prophetesse, Hyacinthe, or Armand and Maréchal whose revolt led to the founding of the "Kingdom of Platons."[29] Although all these movements were smaller in scale than the explosion of the North, they still contributed to the shape of the revolution and its eventual outcome.

There can be little doubt that the early leaders of the northern revolt relied on the military skills of the slaves in the area to make the revolution's early success. Jean-François and Biassou, who had emerged as leaders in the North within a few weeks of the first outbreak of violence in August 1791, recognised the contribution of these slaves. In their correspondence with the Civil Commissioners,[30] the two leaders proposed ending the revolution and returning the rebel slaves to their plantations, in exchange for freedom for themselves and a number of their followers.[31] The only problem with the proposal was that Jean-François and Biassou did not really control the army that they led. They complained in one of their letters about "blacks in bands" who gave trouble,[32] and they specified their situation when they noted that any action they took was "entirely dependent on the general will" exercised by the rebels which they did not control. The makers of this "general will" were slaves, "a multitude of *nègres* from the coast [of Africa] who are scarcely able for the most part to say two words of French," but, and this was the important part," in their homelands, however, had been accustomed to war [*à guerroyer*]."[33]

It was not surprising that Jean-François and the other early leaders of the rebellion were captives of this general will, because they did not possess much military training themselves. They and many of their colleagues were creole slaves, born in the New World, who held skilled or managerial positions in the plantation economy of Saint Domingue. Many documents and inquests from the time show that these elite creole leaders arranged the conspiracy that led to the initial explosion in August 1791.[34] If they could organise a conspiracy, however, they could not necessarily do the fighting to make the revolt a success. Such fighting required the kind of skill and discipline that could be found in veteran soldiers, and it was these veterans, from wars in Africa, who made up the "general will" of the revolt.

We cannot know exactly what transpired in the conspiratorial meetings that started the revolt, but it is unlikely that they organized military movements, set up units and made tactical decisions, especially when the early destructive rage of the rebels gave way to serious fighting with the colonial militia and the regular troops from Le Cap François. Two American observers, Captain Bickford and Mr. Harrington, who were in Saint Domingue throughout the early months, noted a distinct evolution in the rebels' behaviour as the fighting developed between August and early November 1791, when they left for Boston. In the early stages, the attacks were irregular and often confused, and the rebels were equipped mostly with the "instruments of their labour," but as time went on, they began to come in "regular bodies" and were now bearing muskets and swords.[35]

The two Americans, probably repeating the theories of the colonial military leaders, believed that this newfound organization was attributable to the influence of mulattos with military experience, runaway white soldiers and Spanish instigators who provided the necessary training in the short time between late August and late October.[36] Certainly, such elements were found in the rebel bands, manning artillery, for example,[37] or among black and mulatto members of the elite who had served in colonial militias, and even overseas. M. Gros, who spent several months in the camps of the rebels, also noted occasionally that mulattos and free blacks held high office, although his account does not make it clear how important they were in organization of units or military tactics.[38] Given the very low opinion that the planter and governing class had of the slaves,[39] this theory seems to have been attractive and a good explanation for the surprising battlefield success that the slaves enjoyed.

In light of Jean François and Biassou's revelations, however, we should probably not place too much emphasis on the role of non-slaves in organizing the rebels or making their military success possible. In fact, the scattered documentation suggests that what contemporaries called "bands" formed quite spontaneously during August and perhaps September under individual leaders. Many of the band leaders were creoles, like Jean François, Jeannot or Biassou, but others, such as Sans Souci, mentioned as a leader by Gros, were slaves from Africa.[40] It was no doubt these bands, which were independently organized, that Jean François and Biassou complained could not be disciplined.[41]

To understand the nature of these bands, it might be appropriate to consider the way in which African armies were organized and fought, for their organizational and tactical principles were not identical to those of eighteenth century Europe, and seem to underlie those of the rebels. The art of war varied quite a bit in Angola or Kongo and in Lower Guinea, and we are much better informed about the manner of conducting war in Angola.

Portuguese soldiers who knew the African art of war in Angola often disparaged it, but as one militarily experienced observer, Elias Alexandre de Silva Corrêa, noted, it "had the same effect as that of Frederick the Great of Prussia." Indeed, Portuguese armies in Angola adopted most of the African tactical and organizational principles themselves, at least with their African troops.[42]

Kongolese armies, who probably contributed the most to Saint Domingue rebel bands, were generally recruited through fairly broad-based drafts that took in a considerable portion of the adult male population. Smaller bodies of professional soldiers who served as personal guards for various members of the nobility were also noticeable, as we learn from the account of Castello de Vide for 1781.[43] Soldiers were typically equipped with muskets; Castello de Vide believed that all 30,000 troops that stormed São Salvador in 1781 were armed with "musket and ball."[44] As a matter of some significance for those who eventually were to end up in Saint Domingue, Kongolese forces, especially after the 1780s, were typically equipped with French muskets.[45] A mid-eighteenth century illustration in a guide to missionaries shows the army of the Prince Antonio Baretto da Silva of Sonyo, the coastal ruler, fallen out to greet an arriving priest, in which all carry muskets, and include a small cannon among their equipment,[46] and another illustration in the same collection shows that even the personal guard of one of the lesser district rulers was so equipped.[47] On the other hand, archery skills were not entirely lost: the missionary guide also shows that their own escorts carried bows, and as late as 1790 both Portuguese and Kongolese forces engaged in a battle near Encoge had some archers among their musketeers.[48]

In addition to muskets, however, Kongolese soldiers also carried swords for close order combat. Kongolese, like other Africans, eschewed the use of the bayonet in close fighting, and appear to have preferred to use personal weapons, especially swords and battle axes, in close fighting, as well as shields. A Portuguese commander, who fought against troops in southern Kongo in 1790, noted that they used muskets very well, and all carried as "arme blanche" (*arma blanca* in Portuguese) swords, lances and axes as well as "good shields."[49] The missionary guide's illustrations also show these close order weapons, especially in one case where the priest is depicted blessing the swords and shields of combatants before they depart to fight. These swords were either straight bladed weapons closely resembling those of Europe, or were more like scimitars.[50]

Kongolese tactical organization was very different from that of Europe. The differences were especially important because Kongolese forces often confronted European-led armies in battle and in the years of war both sides had developed tactics that incorporated the two traditions. The Portuguese colony of Angola, located south of Kongo, had sought for many years to engross the trade of the area, and specifically to prevent northern Europeans from trading along the coast of Kongo or its northern neighbours. In 1759 they built a fort at Encoge in southern Kongo, and from time to time Portuguese forces based either at Encoge or at other points along the Kongo-Angolan frontier crossed into Kongo for shorter or longer campaigns.[51] These forces often engaged Kongolese armies, including those which would face each other in the battles of the civil wars around Sâo Salvador. The upper Mbrize valley, stronghold of the Kimulaza, bordered on Encoge, while the coastal regions where the Kimpanzu had their strength bordered on areas where the Portuguese struck up the coast from Luanda. These African forces had learned to deal successfully with Portuguese armies and tactics in the years of struggle, driving out invaders in 1788, invading Angola and nearly reaching Luanda in 1790 and giving a good account in the indecisive "North Coast" war of 1790–91.[52] No doubt these tactics could help those who found themselves in Saint Domingue on the eve of the revolution.

A detailed description of Kongolese arms and tactics can be found in the report of the "North Coast War" led by the Portuguese commander Paulo Martins Pinheiro de Lacerda against the Kongolese Marquisate of Musulu in 1790–91, and in the diary of another campaign that he led through the same region and then to Encoge in 1793, though they reflect the "art of war" of at least the previous half century as well. Kongolese armies seem to have been organized in fairly small units that operated independently, "irregular bodies dispersed like our platoons." They were probably identified by unit flags: Castello de Vide mentions numerous war flags [bandeiras de guerra] flying over the Kongolese army of 1781,[53] Portuguese accounts make note of capturing enemy colours in the wars of 1790.[54]

These plantoons struck at enemy advancing columns and sustained an engagement for a time before breaking off and retreating. In the 1793 campaign such engagements typically lasted from one to three hours.[55] In these encounters the Kongolese "fired without order" (probably meaning that they did not volley fire, but instead fired when ready), but with good effect. In the 1793 war it is clear they made use of cover, both from terrain and from woods and tall grass, in hiding their movements and directing their fire.[56] When they fled it was not possible to follow them.[57] The campaign diary of 1790 records numerous such sharp encounters between the Portuguese troops and the Kongolese: in the first three days of their advance the Portuguese force met four sharp and fairly sustained encounters with Kongolese forces,[58] in the entire campaign they fought nine "battles" of this sort, as well as three "shocks" [choques].

The "shocks" were much larger engagements involving massed Kongolese units. According to the Portuguese accounts, large bodies were assembled for shocks supported by artillery, sometimes they formed in extensive half-moon formations which apparently sought partial envelopment of opposing forces, in other cases in columns of great depth along fronts of 15–20 soldiers, presumably where penetration was desired. At the engagement at Quincolo (11 December 1791) six of these columns were deployed.[59] In similar engagements with forces formed in columns at Bingue on the 29th and 30th October 1790, Portuguese forces were compelled, in the words of the official report, to "reform, not retreat"; although the commander claimed victory, his forces evacuated the area the next day and fell back some distance.[60] Another action by the army of Nambuangongo, in which an estimated 6,000 troops were deployed, drove the Portuguese from that area in a sustained battle on 3 July 1793.[61] In another action on 6 May 1794 near Nambuangongo a wounded prisoner gave the strength of one such column at 1,230 muskets; given its source it was probably based on real muster counts, and is indicative of the typical size of such larger units.[62]

In summary, the organization of Kongolese armies probably favoured small commands (the platoons) that could operate independently. Junior commanders undoubtedly had considerable leeway for decision making, though units might be quite cohesive, as indicated by the attachment to unit flags. Their tactics showed a penchant for skirmishing attacks rather than the heavy assaults favoured by Europeans in the same era. On the other hand, Kongolese armies had a higher command structure that could mass troops quickly, and soldiers were also accustomed to forming effectively into larger units for major battles when the situation warranted it.

We possess a wealth of detailed information on the military culture of Kongo and its immediate neighbours in central Africa; unfortunately, we can say much less about the military systems of the Slave Coast. Only for Dahomey is there some information, and even there, military tactics and weapons are known from general descriptions, rather than from analysis of actual battlefield reports, as is possible in central Africa. Dahomey's armies included a fairly large professional force, recruited through a levy on male children who were then trained for war. This force was in turn supplemented in wartime by a general draft, although even in this case, it was the highly trained professional who did much of the fighting.[63] Much of the expense of maintaining military forces was born by titled nobles, who were called up for war, although the state provided central armouries in which necessary weapons and supplies were deposited.[64] Although travellers focused their attention on Dahomey, some information on the coastal region suggests that military organisation there resembled that of the near-by Gold Coast, in which larger militia armies, recruited, armed and equipped like those of Kongo, were more common outside of Dahomey.[65] In addition, however, mercenary armies raised from wealthier states like Great Popo might be added to the general levy in time of war.[66]

Certainly many seem to have been organized as the Dahomey army was: the same titles, for example, were born by general officers in the army of Badagry in 1783–4, and co-ordinated attacks by three divisions against Dahomey's invading army suggest higher level organization as well.[67] Allada's army seems to have had different titles, but still comprised regular military units.[68] In the Mahi country, the division of the region into many small states seems to have prevented the development of large forces, though Mahi states were capable of raising large unified armies to defend themselves, or even to attack: according to Dalzel, 100 "caboceros" of Mahi states joined the Dahomey army in an attack on Weme in 1786.[69] The small state of Ape, said to have had an army of 800 when Dahomey attacked it in 1778, managed a heroic resistance, first cutting up the army of Allada, Dahomey's ally for the moment, then gallantly resisting the whole of the Dahomean army for an extended period.[70]

Dahomey and the coastal states seem to have had muskets and swords as their principal weapons, the muskets as a long-range missile and the sword for close fighting. As elsewhere in Africa, people of the region were not interested in using bayonets and the tactics associated with them. The interior states, however, appear to have been less inclined to the use of muskets, perhaps because they lacked access to ready supplies.[71] Oyo in particular relied much more heavily on calvary forces to carry the day for them, and had relatively few foot soldiers.[72] If there was a shortage of muskets in the interior, however, it does not seem to have affected the capacities of these peoples in war, for throughout the eighteenth century it was Oyo, not Dahomey, that was the pre-eminent military power of the region.

The cavalry of Oyo may well have affected how Dahomey's infantry armies fared (horses could not survive well in the climate of Dahomey, although a few could be found, and one of the king's officials bore the title "Inspector of Cavalry"[73]). According to descriptions, Dahomey's troops, unlike those of central Africa, and even other parts of west Africa, fought in close order using fire discipline quite similar to that of Europe.[74] Such tactics make sense in battlefield situations involving cavalry, since tightly formed units can resist cavalry charges much better than the "open order" of Kongo. It also then makes sense to develop fire discipline so that this mass of soldiers can keep up the highest rate of fire possible, since manoeuvre and especially retreat are difficult in tightly formed units. This is perhaps the reason that Dahomey had a complicated mechanism to effect tactical withdrawals, always with an eye to maintaining order, since the type of rapid and dispersed retreat that was characteristic of the Angolan wars would be a disaster in situations with cavalry, as the horsemen could easily ride down fleeing infantry. In Dahomey, one of the principal functions of the ready reserve, in fact, was to prevent the flight of the soldiers by ensuring that unauthorized battlefield deserters were killed immediately by the comrades in rear areas.[75]

European visitors, who admired Dahomey's tactical structure and military drill for being similar to their own, thus gave Dahomey high marks for discipline and the capabilities of its army were typically rated very high, a feature which has often been repeated by modern scholars. But the historical record does not show that Dahomey had an decisive advantages over its enemies, drill notwithstanding. It was unable to resist the Oyo cavalry throughout the eighteenth century, and was often unable to have its way against its neighbours who did not possess horses, or fight in close order tactics. A number of times, opponents succeeded in ambushing advancing Dahomean armies, or took advantage of terrain features to resist and even to cut up their opponents, as the armies of Badagri did in 1773–4[76] or Croo-too-hoon-too in 1788.[77] Even so, some, like the king of Ape in 1778,[78] or the general of Agoonah in 1781,[79] could still stand up to Dahomean armies in sustained battle.

It was from these disparate "arts of war" that the revolutionary African soldier of Saint Domingue was trained. Certainly knowing this African background helps us make sense of some of the military action of the rebels in the opening months of the Revolution.

One can easily see, in the formation of the bands mentioned in the early descriptions of the war, the small platoons of the Kongolese armies, each under an independent commander and accustomed to considerable tactical decision making, or perhaps those small units characteristic of locally organized Dahomean units, the state armies of the Mahi country or the coastal forces of the Slave Coast. Often they were based in small camps, like the one that formed among the slave quarters of one planta-tion belonging to Monsieur Robillard within a week of the outbreak of violence.[80] These camps were defended by artillery in places, and became the base of operations for the units within them.[81] In addition the pattern of attacks, with small-scale harassing manoeuvers, short sustained battles and then rapid withdrawals are also reminiscent of the campaign diaries of the Portuguese field commanders in Angola. Félix Carteau, an early observer of the war in the north, noted that they harassed French forces "day and night." Usually, he commented, "they were repelled, but each time, they dispersed so quickly, so completely" in ditches, hedges and other areas of natural cover that real pursuit was impossible. However, rebel casualties were light in these attacks, so that "the next day they reappeared with great numbers of people."[82] "They never mass in the open," wrote another witness, or wait in line to charge, but advance dispersed, so that they appear to be "six times as numerous" as they really were. Yet they were disciplined, since they might advance with great clamour and then suddenly and simultaneously fall silent.[83]

Colonial troops who met these tactics sometimes reported at the time that they won all their engagements, as one enthusiastic French militia-man noted during the first week of fighting.[84] His diary reveals a number of these type of attacks, as for example one near Dondon on the 14th of September, 1791 where a strong body of rebels attacked the advancing French, but were repulsed, only to return shortly, reinforced for a renewed attack.[85] Another reaction to these tactics, reported by Captain Bickford and Mr. Harrington, noted that they began each engagement "with order and firmness, crying out 'Victory'" but they soon broke when hotly engaged, and once broken did not easily reform, at least according to the tactics of European trained soldiers.[86]

It was not long, however, before these observers also noted that the rebels had developed the sort of higher order tactics that was also characteristic of Kongolese forces, or those of the Slave Coast. Already on September 2, 1791, a very large force of rebels sought to take Le Cap François by storm. It was estimated at 4,000, although in such situations, these estimations might well be exaggerated.[87] A few days later, the plantation of Bréda was attacked by a force deployed in three columns,[88] a similar three column attack hit Port Marigot on September 14, while on September 19 the attacking force was now described as being in "three divisions" in an attack near Petit Anse.[89]

In addition to these tactical similarities to African wars, especially in Kongo, there were other indications of the African ethos of the fighters. Captain Bickford and Mr. Harrington, for example, noted that they marched, formed and attacked accompanied by the "music peculiar to negroes."[90] Religious preparation likewise hearkened back to Africa, for Pamphile Lacroix, using contemporary documents, noted that they began with the preparations of "wangas" or protective charms.[91] Another eyewitness noted that sometimes when rebel forces advanced there was complete silence, so that the only thing that could be heard was the "incantations of their sorcerers."[92] In this regard they resembled even the Christian Kongolese, for troops fighting in the "North Coast" campaign against Pinheiro de Lacerda in 1791 were also exhorted by a traditional priestess.[93]

The Saint Domingue rebels seem to have developed an effective artillery quite quickly, although the connections between African artillery use and that in Saint Domingue must be considered speculative. Dozens of guns and other field pieces were reported as being used by the rebels in the early engagements, and they seem to have been well served, as for example, in the action of one battery which successfully drove off an armed boat through well-aimed fire from 24-pounders.[94] Of the African armies, only the Kongolese seem to have made much use of artillery, though many of the slave coast states made use of artillery mounted on canoes[95] and apparently also in fortifications.[96] The Angolan campaign diary of 1793–94 shows not only a quite sophisticated use of guns, but considerable skill in fortifications employed by Africans, especially in the Marquisate of Kina.[97] But given the reports that various European deserters or mulattos with military experience served in rebel ranks, especially in artillery, it might be best to assume that they rather than the Africans among whom they fought were responsible for the action.

On the other hand, it is harder to explain the speed with which rebel forces developed an effective cavalry by invoking training of renegade white colonists, mulattos or Spaniards. A survey of rebel forces, probably exaggerated, suggested that they possessed six to eight hundred cavalry, "tolerably well armed" by August 27, 1791, less than a week after the outbreak of the rebellion.[98] These cavalry worked well with the infantry and gave them good support, as did a body of 150 in a hot engagement at Gallifet Plantation on 19 September.[99] Given that it is unlikely that many slaves would have learned equestrian skills as a part of their plantation labour, it seems likely that either all these horsemen were creoles and mulattos (but they are not so described) or they had acquired the skill in Africa. It would take longer than a few weeks to make plantation labourers into cavalry that could stand up against European horsemen. Since there was virtually no cavalry in Angola, one can speculate that rebels originating from Oyo might have provided at least some of the trained horsemen (Senegalese, though a minority, also came from an equestrian culture). However, the evidence cannot provide a definite answer to this question.

The importance of African trained soldiers, and the development of bands organized quickly from African plantation workers, posed something of a problem for the creole leadership of the revolution. Their dilemma is clearly revealed in the letters of Jean-François and Biassou, who saw this uncontrollable host of fighters as a barrier to their making the kind of political settlement they hoped for. Creole goals and those of their African fellow combatants were not always the same, as was revealed by the early attempts to stop the fighting. As early as September 13, 1791, the leader of the insurgents near Le Cap François wished to abandon his followers and surrender, no doubt in exchange for personal freedom, but he was "detained among them by main force."[100] Soon after, the division between the leadership, with its goal of modified restoration of the plantation system and personal freedom, and the mass of the insurgents was made clear throughout the negotiations that followed the arrival of the Civil Commissioners towards the end of the year. Gros, a witness from the rebel camp, reported on the suspicion with which the rank and file fighters viewed their leaders, even as it was reflected in the letters of Jean-François and Biassou.[101]

It is not surprising, therefore, that creoles began to form and train their own military forces, typically using Spanish assistance (offered from early in the revolt) or colon renegades to assist them, and copying European military organization. By 1793, Jean-François and Biassou had gathered considerable personal forces around themselves, but it was ultimately Toussaint Louverture who developed this strategy to its height. After his defection to the Republic in 1793, Toussaint actively allied his small personal army to that of the French general Étienne Laveaux and then used Laveaux's resources to develop a regular army, organized in regiments and half brigades and fighting in typically European drill.[102] By 1796 one could meet armies of several thousand under Toussaint's command that marched in close order, held their ground under fire, and charged with the bayonet, like those forces who sought to storm St. Marc in June of that year, but were repulsed with heavy losses.[103]

These forces were to provide the backbone for Toussaint's rise to power and the base which kept him in control in Haiti. They did not replace the older bands that had formed under African leadership and using African soldiers and tactics in the early months of the revolution; the older tactical arrangements continued to co-exist effectively along with the new armies of the creole and mulatto leadership.[104] In fact, increasingly these forces were opposed to Toussaint and the creole leadership. On one occasion, for example, he was required to attack a Nagô camp, while Macaya, one of his rivals and leader of a smaller band, raised his forces among Kongolese slaves, and by 1797 the forces loyal to creole generals (Toussaint and his southern rivals) were actively fighting the bands, no long subject, as Jean-François and Biassou had been, to their "general will."[105]

African soldiers may well have provided the key element of the early success of the revolution. They might have enabled its survival when it was threatened by reinforced armies from Europe. Looking at the rebel slaves of Haiti as African veterans rather than as Haitian plantation workers may well prove to be the key that unlocks the mystery of the success of the largest slave revolt in history.

NOTES

1 C.L.R. James, *The Black Jacobins: Toussaint L'Ouverture and the San Domingo Revolution* (London, 1938, 2d ed. New York, 1963), ix.

2 Prominent is James' classic study, *The Black Jacobins*.

3 For example, Thomas Ott, *The Haitian Revolution, 1789–1804* (Knoxville, 1972); David Geggus, *Slavery, War and Revolution: The British Occupation of Saint Domingue, 1793–1798* (Oxford, 1982).

4 Roger N. Buckley (ed.) *The Haitian Diary of Lieutenant Howard: York Hussars, 1796–1798* (Knoxville, 1985), 137–38, taking issue with statements in Geggus, 286–89.

5 David Geggus, "Sugar and Coffee Cultivation in Saint Domingue and the Shaping of the Slave Labor Force," in Ira Berlin and Philip Morgan (eds.) *Cultivation and Culture: Work Process and the Shaping of Afro-American Culture in the Americas* (forthcoming). My thanks to David Geggus for an advance copy of this article.

6 See the summaries of both plantation inventories and import statistics in David Geggus, "Sex Ratio, Age and Ethnicity in the Atlantic Slave Trade: data from French shipping and plantation records," *Journal of African History* 30 (1989): 23–44; David Richardson, "Slave Exports from West and West-Central Africa, 1700–1810: new estimates of volume and distribution," *Journal of African History* 30 (1989): 1–22.

7 Richardson, "New Estimates," 10–14. For another angle, based on shipping arriving in Saint Domingue, see Jean Fouchard, "The Slave Trade and the Peopling of Santo Domingo," in UNESCO, *The African Slave Trade from the Fifteenth to the Nineteenth Century* (Paris, 1979), 283–85.

8 For the background and early history of the civil wars, see John Thornton, *The Kingdom of Kongo: Civil War and Transition, 1641–1718* (Madison, 1983).

9 This process of alternating succession is described by an Italian priest, Cherubino da Savona, who resided in Kongo after 1760. It was probably not as neatly done or well kept as his retrospective account would have one believe: Cherubino da Savona, "Congo 1775. Breve ragguaglio del Regno di Congo e

sue Missioni," fol. 41 in Carlo Toso (ed.) "Relazioni inedite di P. Cherubino Cassinis da Savona sul 'Regno del Congo e sue Missioni'," *L'Italia Francescana* 75 (1974).

10 Da Savona, "Breve ragguaglio," fols. 41–41v.

11 The war and its aftermath are described by an eyewitness, Father Rafael de Castello de Vide, in Academia das Ciências de Lisboa, MS Vermelho 296, "Viagem do Congo do Missionario Fr. Raphael de Castello de Vide, hoje Bispo de S. Thomé," 118–22; MS of about 1800, recopying four letter reports of the period 1779–1788. The first of these reports survives in original form in the Arquivo Histórico Ultramarino (Lisbon), Angola, Caixa 64, doc. 62 [henceforward cited as AHU, Angola, Cx (Caixa), doc.] and was published in *Annes do Conselho Ultramarino*, ser, 11 (1859–61): 62–80. I have cited the MS pagination.

12 ACL, MS Vermelho 296, Castello de Vide, "Viagem," 260.

13 ACL MS Vermelho 296, Castello de Vide, "Viagem," 260–62; on the restoration of order by Henrique, see Raimondo da Dicomano, "Informação do Reino de Congo," fol. 108, MS of 1798 published from a Portuguese translation in the Biblioteca Nacional de Lisboa in António Brásio, "Informação do Reino do Congo de Frei Raimondo da Dicomano," *Studia* 34 (1972): 19–42. Analysis of the period, and publication of additional documents on the period 1792–4 can be found in the introduction and appendixes of Carlo Toso's Italian translation, *L'informazione sul regno del Congo di Raimondo da Dicomano* (Rome, 1977).

14 ACL, MS Vermelho 296, de Castello de Vide, "Viagem," 118–20.

15 For a general background, see Phyllis Martin, *The External Trade of the Loango Coast, 1576–1890* (Oxford, 1972). For an analysis of the slave trade and its impact on demography in this period, see John Thornton, "The Kongo Civil Wars, 1718–1844: Demography and History Revisited," Paper Presented at the Annual Convention of the Canadian African Studies Association, Montréal, 15–18 May 1992.

16 ACL MS Vermelho 296, Castello de Vide, "Viagem," 284–94 for the context of the attempts to end the slave trade with Vilis, and Castello de Vide's futile efforts to carry it out.

17 Richardson, "New Estimates," table 5, 12 and 6, 14. Note that Portuguese shipping exported over 154,000 slaves from Angola in the same time period, but it is likely that their source was not the same as those of England and France, though there was some overlap in southern Kongo.

18 Archibald Dalzel, *The History of Dahomey: an inland kingdom of Africa: compiled from authentic memoirs* (London, 1793, reprinted with introduction by J.D. Fage, London, 1967). Abson's memoirs begin with the year 1774, on pp. 156 et seq. Abson was an exceptionally well informed observer, not only speaking Fon, the local language, fluently, and having married several Dahomean women, but he had frequent interviews with the king and other high officials. For periods before 1774, Dalzel was dependent on Robert Norris, *Memoirs of the Reign of Bossa Ahâdee, King of Dahomey an inland country of Guiney* (London, 1789, reprinted London, 1968).

19 See, on this issue, especially Werner Peukert, *Der Atlantische Sklavenhandel von Dahomey, 1740–1797: Wirtschaftsanthropologie und Socialgeschichte* (Wiesbaden, 1978), a detailed critique of what he calls the "Atlantic model" of Dahomean history.

20 Norris, *Memoirs*, 130–32.

21 Dalzel, *History*, 163–65.

22 The attack is described on the basis of archival documentation by I.A. Akinjogbin, *Dahomey and its Neighbours, 1708–1818* (Cambridge, 1967), 165, as well as details in Dalzel, *History*, 165–67.

23 Dalzel, *History*, 166.

24 *Ibid*, 180.
25 *Ibid*, 182–90.
26 *Ibid*, 196.
27 Norris, *Memoirs*, 138–9.
28 Carolyn Fick, *The Making of Haiti: The Saint Domingue Revolution from Below, 1791–1804* (Knoxville, 1991), 133–34.
29 On these movements, see Fick, *Making of Haiti*, 127–29, 139–40, 141–53.
30 All this correspondence, 28 items in all, is found in Archives Nationales de France (henceforward AN), D-XXV, carton 1, dossier 4, [cited thus, AN D-XXV, 1, 4] "Lettres, addresses et pièces de correspondance des Commissaires Nationaux, avec les Chefs des Esclaves révoltés," December 1791.
31 For example, their plan as presented in AN D-XXV, 1, 4 no. 6, Jean-François and Biassou to Civil Commissioners, 12 October 1791; for a background on these events from the point of view of M. Gros, a European notary who served as their secretary, see M. Gros, *An Historick Recital of the Different Occurrences in the Camps of Grande-Riviere, Dondon, Sainte Suzanne and others from the 26th of October 1791 to the 24th of December of the Same Year* (Baltimore, n. d. [1793]; a French version was published the same year in Lille and then in Paris), 49–65.
32 AN D-XXV, 1, 4, no. 10, Jean-François and Biassou to Civil Commissioners, 17 December 1791.
33 AN D-XXV, 1, 4, no. 6, Jean-François and Biassou to the Civil Commissioners, 12 October 1791.
34 The original document is examined in detail in Fick, *Making of Haiti*, 260–66.
35 Their report was published in the Boston *Independent Chronicle and Universal Advertiser*, 23, 1201 (3 November 1791) and then in the Philadelphia *General Advertiser*, no. 351 (14 November 1791).
36 *Ibid*. This position was more or less firmly stated in the official published report of the revolution which made use of numerous documents, some still extant, others no longer so, J. Ph. Garran-Coulon, *Rapport sur les troubles de Saint Domingue* (4 vols., Paris, An V–VII [1797–99]) 2: 256.
37 Letter of James Perkins, printed in Boston *Independent Chronicle*, 23, 1199 (20 October 1791), entry of 11 September 1791; Gros, *Historick Recital*, 23.
38 Gros, *Historick Recital*, 21, 23, 32.
39 This attitude was well represented by Governor Blanchelande's reports, especially AN D-XXV, 46, 431 and 433
40 Gros, *Historick Recital*, 17–18.
41 AN D-XXV 1, 4, no. 10 Jean-François and Biassou to Civil Commissioners, 17 December 1791.
42 Elias Alexandre da Silva Corrêa, *Historia de Angola* ([1798], mod. ed. Manuel Múrias, 2 vols., Lisbon, 1937) 2: 57.
43 ACL MS Vermelho 296, Castello de Vide, "Viagem," 80, 93.
44 *Ibid*, 118.
45 AHU, Angola, Cx. 76, doc. 73, Letter to Manuel de Almada e Vasconcelos, 7 August 1791, fol. 1.
46 Biblioteca Civica di Torino, MS 457, published in full colour in Paolo Collo and Silvia Benso (eds.) *Sogno Bamba, Pemba Ovando e altre contrade dei Regni di Congo, Angola e adiacenti* (Milan, 1986), 144.
47 *Ibid*, 155.
48 AHU, Angola, Cx, 76, doc. 73, Letter to Manuel de Almeida e Vasconcellos, 7 August 1791, fol. iv.
49 "Noticia da campanha e paiz do Mosul, que conquistou o Sargento Mor Paulo Martins Pinheiro de Lacerda, 1790–91," printed in *Annaes Maritímos e Colonais* 3, 4 (1845): 129–30. Another detailed account of this campaign by the commander is found in his report in AHU, Angola, Caixa 76, doc. 28, 20 May 1791.

50 Collo and Benso (eds.) *Sogno*, 189.

51 For a general background to Portuguese policy, see Joseph C. Miller, *Way of Death: Merchant Capitalism and the Angolan Slave Trade, 1730–1830* (Madison, 1988), 581–630.

52 A summary is given in the account of the Barão de Mossamedes, AHU, Cx. 76, doc. 88, 20 September 1791, for details on the invasion of 1790, see doc. 73, letter to Manuel de Almeda e Vasconcelos, 7 August 1791, fol. 1. This document also describes a battle near Encoge at about the same time, fol. iv.

53 ACL, MS Vermelho 296, Castello de Vide, "Viagem," 93, 95.

54 AHU Angola, Cx. 76, doc. 34, Service Record of Felix Xavier Pinheiro de Lacerda, enclosure, report by Paulo Martins Pinheiro de Lacerda, n.d., early 1791.

55 Silva Corrêa, *História* 2: 182–83, which reproduces the diary, undoubtedly written by Paulo Martins Pinheiro de Lacerda.

56 *Ibid*, 181, 185, 188.

57 "Noticia da campanhia," 132.

58 AHU Angola, CX. 76, doc. 28, Paulo Martins Pinheiro de Lacerda report, 20 May 1791. See also note 54.

59 "Noticia da campanhia," 131; the date is given in AHU, Angola, Cx. 76, doc. 34.

60 See note 58.

61 Silva Corrêa, *História* 2: 183–4.

62 *Ibid*, 214.

63 Robin Law, *The Slave Coast of West Africa, 1550–1750* (Oxford, 1992), 97–101, 270–72. Although Law's focus is on the period prior to 1750, much of his evidence relates to the later periods as well.

64 Vicente Ferreira Pires, *Viagem de África em o Reino de Dahomé* (1800) (mod. ed. Clado Ribeiro de Lessa, São Paulo), 1957, 106.

65 On the Gold Coast, see Ray Kea, *Settlement, Trade and Polities on the Seventeenth Century Gold Coast* (Baltimore, 1982), 130–68; for the Slave Coast area, see Kea. "Firearms and Warfare on the Gold and Slave Coasts from the Sixteenth to the Nineteenth Centuries," *Journal of African History* 12 (1971).

66 Law, *Slave Coast*, 101, 229.

67 Dalzel, *History*, 180–2, 184–85.

68 *Ibid*, 168.

69 *Ibid*, 192.

70 *Ibid*, 167–69.

71 Ferreira Pires, *Viagem*, 105.

72 Robin Law, *The Oyo Empire, c. 1600–c. 1836: A West African Imperialism in the Era of the Atlantic Slave Trade* (Oxford, 1977), 193–98.

73 Ferreira Pires, *Viagem*, 46.

74 *Ibid*, 105; Law, *Slave Coast*, 269–72.

75 Ferreira Pires, *Viagem*, 101.

76 Dalzel, *History*, 184–5.

77 *Ibid*, 199.

78 *Ibid*, 167–68.

79 *Ibid*, 175–76.

80 AN D-XXV 78, 772, "Declaration que fait M. Robillard, habitant du Plaine du Nord . . . 29 September 1791.

81 AN D-XXV 78, 772. Anon report, Le Cap, 27 September 1791.

82 F. C.*** [Félix Carteau], *Soirées Bermudiennes, ou entretiens sur les événemens qui ont opéré la ruine de la partie française de l'île St. Domingue* (Bordeaux, An X [1802]), 100.

83 Étienne Descourtiltz, *Histoire des désastres de Saint Domingue* (Paris, An III [1795]), 192.

84 Diary of French militiaman, entry of 27 August 1791, printed in Philadelphia *General Advertiser* no. 321 (10 October 1791).

85 Diary, 14 September 1791 in Philadelphia *General Advertiser* no. 348 (10 November 1791).

86 "St. Domingo Disturbances," Boston *Independent Chronicle and Universal Advertiser* no. 1199 (20 October 1791).

87 Diary of militiaman, 2 September 1791 in Philadelphia *General Advertiser* no. 322 (11 October 1791).

88 Diary of militiaman, 10 September 1791, Philadelphia *General Advertiser* no. 322 (10 October 1791).

89 Diary of militiaman, 14 September and 19 September, Philadelphia *General Advertiser* no. 348 (10 November 1791).

90 "San Domingo Disturbances," Boston *Independent Chronicle and Universal Advertiser* 23, no. 1199 (20 October 1791).

91 Pamphile de Lacroix, *Mémoires pour servir à la revolution de Saint Domingue* (2 vols., Paris, 1819) 1: 94.

92 Descourtiltz, "Histoire des désastres," 192.

93 Pinheiro de Lacerda, "Noticia da campanha e paiz do Mosul," 131.

94 Diary of militiaman, 11 September 1791, Philadelphia *General Advertiser* no. 322 (11 October 1791).

95 Dalzel, *History*, 169.

96 *Ibid*, 225.

97 Silva Corrêa, *Historia* 2:

98 Diary of militiaman, 27 August 1791, Philadelphia *General Advertiser* no. 321 (10 October 1791).

99 Diary of militiaman, 19 September 1791, Philadelphia *General Advertiser* no. 349 (10 November 1791).

100 Diary of militiaman, 13 September 1791 Philadelphia *General Advertiser* no. 322 (11 October 1791).

101 Gros, *Historick Recital*, 51–63.

102 See Toussaint's ambitious plan in his letter to Laveaux, 3 Thermidor, An III [1794], in Gerard M. Laurent (ed.) *Toussaint Louverture à travers sa Correspondance 1794–1798* (Madrid, 1953), 206–212.

103 The action is described in the journal of Lieutenant Howard, (ed. Buckley), *Haitian Journal*, 91–93.

104 See a number of engagements described by Lieutenant Howard, *ibid*, 40, 48 and especially 80.

105 AN D-XXV, 1, 4, no. 6, Jean-François and Biassou to the Civil Commissioners, 12 October 1791.

9

SLAVE REBELLION IN BRAZIL

The Muslim Uprising of 1835 in Bahia

Chapter 5: The Sons of Allah in Bahia

João José Reis

Allah desires no injustice to His Creatures

—Koran, 3:108

Beyond a shadow of a doubt, Muslims played the central role in the 1835 rebellion. The rebels went into the streets wearing clothes peculiar to practicers of Islam. And the police found Muslim amulets and papers with prayers and passages from the *Koran* on the bodies of fallen rebels. These and other characteristics of the revolt led Chief of Police Gonçalves Martins to conclude the obvious: "What is certain," he wrote, "is that Religion played a part in the uprising." He continued: "The ringleaders persuaded the unfortunate wretches that pieces of paper would protect them from dying." Another Martins, the provincial president, said: "It seems to me that there was religious fanaticism mixed up in this conspiracy."[1] Everyone writing about this revolt could not avoid the religious factor, be it to exaggerate it, be it to diminish it. Both positions have their merits, but both are incomplete.

Before making a detailed examination of Muslim involvement in the 1835 rebellion, one should take stock of Islam's presence in the Afro-Bahian community of the time. Quite likely the first big contingent of Muslim Africans arrived in Bahia at the turn of nineteenth century. It is true that during the more than two hundred years of slave trade preceding that time, many slaves coming from West Africa were Mohammedans. Most of these were Malinkes, known in Bahia as *mandingos*. During the first three decades of the nineteenth century, of the some seven thousand slaves imported annually to Bahia the immense majority were Hausas, Yorubas (Nagôs), and neighboring peoples—victims as they were of the severe political and religious disturbances in their countries. It was a time of Islamic expansion in West Africa, especially in the western part of present-day Nigeria. Islam went its way peacefully, except when traditional leaders sought to block it; then it went to war. Such were the circumstances that led the Fulani Muslim leader Shehu Usuman Dan Fodio (or Sheik Dan Fodio) to begin a jihad, or holy war, in 1804 against the hostile government of King Yunfa of Gobir, considered by jihadists to be a wayward Muslim. This conflict produced thousands of slaves, mainly Hausas, who ended up stocking the slave-gathering outposts on the Bight of Benin, especially the up-and-coming port known as Eko or Onim, today Lagos. The leaders of that jihad were Fulanis, who ended up organizing the powerful Sokoto caliphate in Fulani and Hausa territory. As an expansionist caliphate, it was always involved in local conflicts, which continued to produce slaves for the Atlantic trade. Many African slaves interviewed in the late 1840s by Francis de Castelnau, the French consul in Bahia, had been soldiers captured during wars. Others had been taken prisoner in raids on villages or along the highways.[2]

Parallel events in Yoruba territory also explain the presence of Islamic slaves in Bahia. The end of the eighteenth century was the high point of the Yoruba Oyo empire, which exercised hegemony over Yoruba-speaking subgroups and satellite states surrounding it, such as Dahomey and the Nupe kingdom. The Oyo empire began to disintegrate starting with a series of civil wars begun by the revolt of Afonja (ca. 1797). The rebel leader was nothing less than the *are-ona-kakanfo* ("commander in chief") of the provincial armed forces, which included Oyo's powerful cavalry. He was also the ruler of the city of Ilorin, in the north, on the border with Sokoto. The revolt occurred during a decline in power suffered by the alafin (the king of Oyo), whose position Afonja had tried in vain to occupy. Support from provincial leaders had been to no avail in this endeavor. The next twenty years were a period of gradual disintegration in the center of the Oyo empire. This gradual disintegration accelerated beginning in 1817.

During that year a widespread slave revolt broke out in the territory still dominated by Oyo. Its instigator had been Afonja, and it was made up mainly of northern slaves: Fulanis, Bornus, Nupes, and especially Hausas. Hausas comprised the greater part of the Yoruba slave labor force. They were especially famous as ropemakers, cattle herders, and physicians and surgeons. They also had a reputation for being competent veterinarians, which the Yorubas sorely needed for their cavalry. Some of those slaves also worked in agriculture or as their masters' agents and commercial assistants. Even though Yorubas kept most of these skilled slaves, they traditionally sold some on the coast to Atlantic slave traders. But only with Afonja's revolt were their numbers to swell in the trading posts along the Bight of Benin.[3]

Those northern slaves became the backbone of Afonja's rebel forces. From the beginning, however, Muslim Yorubas, including some wealthy merchants, rallied around the commander in chief in reaction to pressure from the powerful alafin, whose power derived from the traditional Shango cult. (In Oyo the supreme deity, or orisha, was Shango, the mythical fourth alafin of the kingdom and the god of thunder.) With the help of these allies, Afonja's strictly political rebellion, according to Gbadomosi, "became mixed up with Islamic ferment and agitation of the time."[4] The slave revolt widened its field of operations and created Muslim strongholds in the north. Ilorin became a virtual Yoruba Mecca. There Muslims took possession of "pagan" slaves captured in battle. The Yoruba historian Babatunde Agiri ironically comments: "The slaves who successfully rebelled against the Oyo government in 1817 now owned slaves of their own."[5]

Between 1817 and 1820, Afonja, who was not himself a Muslim and who had even refused to be converted, tried to form his own *jama'a*, or band of Muslim militants. Soon, however, the imperial capital (Oyo) was attacked and partly destroyed. But the old empire was still able to defeat its attackers. At this time Afonja began to have problems with his Fulani and Hausa allies, who were leaning toward Sokoto. The commander in chief tried in vain to convince them to leave Ilorin and settle to the east of the city, but he was soon murdered. This was the end of Yorubas' control of Ilorin, which would become an emirate subject to the Fulani caliph in Sokoto. The Fulanis' advance over Yorubaland was slow but thorough. It lasted ten years, crushing one *oba* (Yoruba chief) after another and transforming the region into an inferno of minor wars that were more political than religious and that spread out like waves. Society became militarized with the formation of numerous independent armed bands fighting over the spoils of Oyo and capturing one another to supply slaves for the Atlantic trade. People from all over the region were caught up in civil wars, jihads, and rebellions of kingdoms formerly under the thumb of Oyo. Great numbers of Nupes (known as Tapas in Yorubaland as well as in Bahia), Bornus, and the peoples from Dahomey came ashore in the New World as slaves. Many of those slaves were Muslims.[6]

Islam played an ambiguous role in the political and religious movements of West Africa during the first half of the nineteenth century. On the one hand, for mainly expansionist states, it provided an ideology and inspired governments. Here it was an ally of power, often a military instrument at the service of slaveowners and merchants. On the other hand, it offered refuge for the poor—spiritual and moral strength as well as organization to free men subjugated to powerful groups supported by traditional religion. It also kept the hope of freedom alive for thousands of Muslim slaves. It was, then, an instrument of revolt as well. Concerning Yorubaland, Agiri sums up this contradictory movement nicely:

> Ilorin became the bridgehead for Muslim expansion to the south, but beyond its borders Islam played a far different role than it did in the emirate. In the independent Yoruba states, Islam was more often associated with slaves of Northern origin, and consequently this religion provided a potential rallying point for the

consolidation of a distinct slave subculture. Many Yoruba chiefs saw this danger.[7]

It was mainly this second Islamic tradition that the Muslim slaves, whose ranks now included Yorubas converted to Islam, tried to recreate within Bahian slave society.

Muslims Become Malês

In 1835 Muslim Africans were known as Malês in Bahia. The origin of this term has been the object of protracted debate. Braz do Amaral, for example, has made the ridiculous suggestion that it derives from the phrase *má lei* (a Portuguese phrase meaning "bad law"), which has been rejected even by Etienne Brazil, a Catholic priest and militant anti-Muslim. Perhaps Amaral wanted to attach a pejorative connotation to the name to suggest that Muslims would reject it. This was, however, wrong, since the term *Malê* did not seem negatively charged, at least at that time. With a firmer basis, R. K. Kent has linked *malé* with *malān*, a Hausa word taken from the Arabic *muʿallim*, which means "cleric," "teacher," or "preacher"—like *alfa* in several parts of West Africa, or its Yoruba variant *alufa*, which has come to be spelled *alufá* in Bahia. (In the 1835 police and trial records the Malê preachers, or alufás, are called *mestres*, a Portuguese word meaning "teacher," "spiritual guide," or "master" but not "*slave* master.")

On the other hand, Raymundo Nina Rodrigues, the first competent student of the Malês, suggested that the term is derived from *Mali*, the name of the once powerful Mandinka Muslim state on the Gold Coast. Still, the explanation that seems more sensible and direct has been presented by Pierre Verger, Vincent Monteil, and Vivaldo da Costa Lima, who link the term *Malê* with *imale*, a Yoruba term for Islam or for a Muslim, which may also have influenced the formation of the Fon term *malinou* or, even closer, *malé*. *Imale*, in turn, is held to be derived from the word *Mali*. Rodrigues, Brazil, Bastide, and others who point toward the Mandinka as originators of the term seem to have overlooked a closer word. *Mali* would perhaps be the starting point, producing *imale* and finally *Malê*, which is a plausible etymology.

Malê, imale, and similar expressions seem to have been in use in the eighteenth century to describe African Muslim merchants in the slave trading posts of the Bight of Benin, from where most Bahian slaves were coming in the years preceding the 1835 rebellion. In the 1720s, for example, Jean Baptiste Labat linked the term *mallais* specifically to Hausa slave traders, who probably called themselves by the Hausa term *musul-min*. In the nineteenth century the term *Malê* surfaced in Bahia, probably because of the then greater presence of Yorubas (Nagôs) and Aja-Fon (Jejes) peoples, who imposed a word from their languages on the others. Nonetheless, it should be clear that in 1835 Bahia *malê* did not refer to any

African ethnic group in particular, but to Africans who adopted the Islamic faith. And because of this there were Nagôs, Jejes, Hausas, Tapas, Bornus—that is, persons of various ethnicities—who were Malês.[8]

Islam was not the dominant religion among Africans in Bahia. Yet it is quite likely that it was a heavyweight contender in a cultural free-for-all that also included the Yoruba orisha cult, Aja-Fon Voodum, the Angolan ancestor spirit cult, among other African religious manifestations. Add to this a creole Catholicism, and you will have an idea of the religious plurality in the African and Afro-Bahian communities of the time. The only ethnic groups whose members seem to have wholeheartedly embraced Islam before coming to Brazil were the Hausas; their neighbors, the Nupes; and the Bornus. The majority of the Nagôs, the Bahian ethnic majority, continued to practice candomblé, the orisha religion. Even the Hausas, who were Islamicized, were still attached to their native spirit cult known as Bori, which is not to be confused with the candomblé ritual with the same name.[9]

Hausas were promptly identified with Islam in Bahia. Malê and Hausa became synonyms. In his report on the rebellion, the chief of police observed: "Generally almost all of them [the rebels] know how to read and write using unknown characters that look like Arabic and are used by the Hausas, who seem today to have combined with the Nagôs. The former nation was the one that rebelled quite often in this Province, but has been substituted by Nagôs."[10] And a slave named Marcelina, when asked about writings found in the house of an ex-slave, said: "The Malê prayer slips were made and written on by the others' elders, who go around preaching. These elders are from the Hausa Nation, because Nagôs do not know and are brought together by the mestres to learn, as well as by some from the Tapa Nation."[11] Among the Malê preachers in Bahia in 1835 were Dandará, the Hausa merchant whose Christian name was Elesbão do Carmo, and a Tapa slave named Sanim, whose Christian name was Luís. Both confessed to teaching Islamic doctrine in their homelands. Other Hausas admitted being familiar with Muslim writings. One of those, the slave Antônio, claimed to have attended a Koranic school in Africa.[12]

It is nonetheless incorrect to give the Hausas exclusivity in Islamic affairs in Bahia. As we have seen, Islam was a religion on the rise in Yoruba kingdoms, and most certainly hundreds of Islamicized Yorubas landed in Brazil as Nagô slaves. Around 1835, Malês in Bahia were probably for the most part Nagôs and not the offspring of minorities such as Hausas or the even rarer Tapas. At any rate, the Nagô Malês enjoyed power and prestige within the Muslim community. Ahuna and Pacífico Licutan, both slaves, were the two most important characters in the 1835 uprising, and both of them were alufás or preachers of Nagô origin. The alufá and rebel leader Manoel Calafate, a freedman in whose house the rebellion began, was also a Nagô. Several Nagôs confessed to having been initiated into Islam before crossing the Atlantic. A slave known as Gaspar to Bahians and Huguby to Africans declared he "knew how to read and write back in his homeland." During his arraignment, he even read some passages in Arabic for the justice of the peace, who wanted to know what a book the police had confiscated dealt with. But Huguby, according to the scribe, "was not able to or did not know how to tell it in our language." Another Nagô slave, Pedro, when asked about the contents of some papers and a book he had, answered that "the book contained prayers from his native land, and the papers contained doc- trines whose words and meaning he knew before leaving his country." Pompeu, a freedman, was more cautious. He claimed to "have learned [the Arabic writing] in his native land, as a small child, but now he remembered almost nothing." One can see that like the Hausas, the Nagôs had Muslims of long standing in their ranks whose prestige, influ- ence, and dominance cannot be underestimated.[13]

Malês of long standing tried to attract new Malês. Documents from the 1835 inquiry indicate vigorous proselytizing and conversion in Bahia during the 1830s. The label of passivity Bastide applied to the Malês is thus inapt. The slave community varied in its commitment to Islam. On a superficial level we find the adoption of external symbols of Islamic culture. Malê amulets and good-luck charms were especially popular. Students of African Islam are unanimous in recognizing Africans' esteem for these amulets, which prevail despite opposition from puritanical leaders, who throughout time have criticized them as elements of trad- itional, backward religion, as signs of pagan atavism. Though a pagan, Afonja put considerable trust in those magical amulets during his mili- tary campaigns. Even religions that had been unaffected by Islam acknow- ledged the virtues of those charms. The English traveler John McLeod, who visited Dahomey in 1803, wrote that Arab merchants "carried about with them scraps or sentences of the *Koran* which they distributed to the natives, who generally fastened them on the ends of sticks near their doors as charms against witchcraft."

In Bahia, because they were reputed to have strong protective powers, Malê charms were *de rigueur* adornments for Muslims and non-Muslims alike. And Rodrigues observed that at the end of the nineteenth century. Bahian blacks generally considered Malês to be "wizards familiar with high magical processes." Yorubas gave amulets the name *tira* (in Bahia, *tiá*, according to Etienne Brazil), and whites likened them to Catholic scapularies containing prayers, so they called them "briefs" (*breves*) in the 1835 proceedings. These amulets spread beyond the Malê group because they did not signify a strong commitment to Islam on the part of their wearer. They posed no threat whatsoever to the magical beliefs of "pagans" whose relationship with the supernatural was conceived largely in terms of solutions for immediate, day-to-day problems. Tiras promised protection for all and functioned well as a vehicle of Islamic propaganda in Bahia. From Bahia their influence spread to other ports in Brazil, especially Rio de Janeiro.[14]

The written word, which the Malês used, had a great seductive power over Africans whose roots belonged in oral cultures. The amulets consisted of pieces of paper containing passages from the *Koran* and powerful prayers. The paper was carefully folded in an operation that had its own magical dimension. It was then placed in a small leather pouch, which was sewn shut. In many cases, besides the paper, other ingredients appeared in those charms. A police scribe described the contents of one amulet as follows:

> Little bundles or leather pouches were opened at this time by cutting them at the seams with a penknife. Inside were found several pieces of insignificant things such as cotton wrapped in a little powder [*sic*], others with tiny scraps of garbage, and little sacks with some seashells inside. Inside one of the leather pouches was a piece of paper with Arabic letters written on it.[15]

The "insignificant" substances referred to here likely included sand moistened beforehand in some sort of holy water, perhaps water used by some renowned and pious alufá or water used to wash the tablets on which Malês wrote their religious texts. In the latter case, this water could also be drunk, since the ink was made of burnt rice; such a drink was believed to seal the body against outside harm. Some of the amulets were made of West African fabric; leather was used more often, since it provided better protection for both the sacred words and the other charms. There is a remarkable similarity between the Bahian Malê talismans and those still in use in black Africa, although the Bahian amulet seems to have had more "pagan" ingredients. According to Vincent Monteil, "In general the Islamic Talisman is a leather case, sewn together and containing a piece of stiff cardboard . . . and inside this is a folded piece of paper on which are written phrases in praise of God and cabalistic symbols— that is, Arabic letters, pentacles, and the like."[16] Kabbalistic drawings such as the ones mentioned here were found in several amulets confiscated in 1835.

The Magrebian Arabic in the Malê amulets found on the bodies of dead rebels or in Muslims' houses has been studied and translated by Vincent Monteil and Rolf Reichert.[17] Reichert took stock of twelve amulets some of which contained kabbalistic shapes. This is the description of what he found in one:

> (1) in the name of God the merciful the compassionate God praise be . . . later prophet. . . .

Next there is a rectangular magic figure divided into $11 \times 13 = 143$

squares filled with individual letters, to each of which one attributes a numerical value. Below the square:

(2) in the name of God the compassionate the (merciful) . . . God
(3) . . . God's help and imminent triumph gives the good news
(4) for believers God's help and imminent triumph gives the good news
(5) for believers God's help and imminent triumph gives the good news.
(6) for the believers

To the left there is a horizontal line:

They love us as God is loved but those who believe love God in a stronger way and. . . .

This is a sentence extracted from verse 13, sura 61, of the *Koran*. It seemed to have been tailored for the rebellion and repeated several times. Another example:

(1) in the name of God the compassionate the merciful
(2) God will protect you from all men
(3) God will not (guide) the infidel people God
(4) [He] will protect you from all men God will not (guide) the infidel
(5) people God will protect you from the
(6) All men God will not (guide) the infidel people
(7) if God wills and with God goes victory.

This text (verse 67, sura 5) is accompanied by several circles, each with the word "flight" (*fuga*) inside it. Besides that word Reichert found "master," "owner," and "alone." This could be a fugitive slave's magical passport. Other amulets scrimped on words:

(1) in the name of God the compassionate, the merciful

Next comes a magical rectangular figure, divided into sixteen square fields, each one filled with three, four, or five isolated letters.

(2) gabriel michael

This is a request for help from the archangels, who are also part of Islamic doctrine.[18]

The magic in the Islamic texts and drawings worked as protection against various threats. The Africans arrested in 1835 said little about their magic, and when they did say something, they avoided linking it to the revolt. However, besides their obvious political function, these amulets were especially designed to control daily life. A freedman named Silvestre José Antônio, a merchant, was arrested with five amulets in his case. He declared they "were prayers to save [him] from any unfortunate

Malês' spiritual arsenal: Koranic verses, Muslim "powerful" prayers, magic figures were used as amulets. Photographs courtesy of Arquivo do Estado da Bahia.

happenstance in his travels through the Recôncavo." Whether in Africa or in Brazil, a good Muslim merchant never traveled without a considerable number of protecting charms. A booklet of Islamic prayers could also work to protect its holder against evil spells. It was for that reason that a freedman named Pedro Pinto asked a literate Malê to make one for him, so he could "be free from wagging tongues." Pedro, by the way, was not a Malê.[19]

Besides protecting against human evildoers, these amulets helped their owners control the uncertain terrain of the spirit world. The *isköki*, for example, are Hausa spirits who, like all spirits, need to be cared for according to a specific protocol. Their essence is the air—*iska*, the singular of *isköki*, literally, the "wind." With the advent of Islam, these Hausa spirits dispersed and, as agents of good and evil, became confused with Muslims' jinns. These spirits, known as *anjonu* or *alijano* in Yoruba, are also formed from air when air is joined with fire. This helps explain why, in 1835, Lobão Maxado, a freedman, explained that several of the amulets found in his house were "to protect him from the wind." Likewise, José, a Nagô slave, said he bought his tira from an African negress "because she told him it was good for the wind." José had been living for ten years in white man's land but to a great extent still traveled his own cultural route. Interestingly, in popular wisdom wind still inspires fear. It is said to carry specific illnesses and to leave a body deformed should someone feign deformation either innocently or maliciously. Today it is the actual wind that does this, but the motivating force for these beliefs can be found embodied in the iska, jinns, anjonu, and other beings born by air.[20]

As a general rule, Muslim amulets were made and sold by alufás, whose mystic power, or *baraka*, was embodied in their product. In Africa the manufacture of talismans constituted (and still constitutes), in some cases, the main activity and an important source of income for literate Muslims. The belief that more amulets mean greater protection creates an ever-expanding market. (Of course it also creates an ever-expanding likelihood of fraud.) It is doubtful that in Bahian slave society the Malê preachers, especially those who were slaves, could live exclusively off the highly specialized occupation of manufacturing magic charms.

Even so, one Malê fisherman made a good living from amulet making. According to one witness, Antônio, a Hausa slave residing in Itapagipe, "wrote prayers in his language and sold them to his partners making 4 *patacas* [1,280 réis] a day doing that." When he was arrested, a writing quill was found in his room: "Asked . . . by the justice [of the peace] why he kept such a quill, the same slave answered that he kept it so as to write things having to do with his Nation. He was then asked to write and he made a few scribbles with the phoney quill and the justice asked . . . what he had written. He answered that what he had written was the name of the 'Hail Mary.' " This Islamic-Christian melding does not seem to have impressed the justice of the peace. Antônio calmly went on telling his questioners that "when he was a young boy in his homeland, he went to school," and there he had learned Arabic so as to write "prayers according to the schism of his homeland."[21]

A somewhat more innovative and daring amulet maker also melded Christianity and Islam. Consul Marcescheau reported having seen one document written half in Arabic and half in Latin, with the Latin section being a transcription of a passage from the "Song of Songs." This talisman may have been used in a lover's conquest rather than a military maneuver. Be that as it may, this is one more example of the Malês' scriptural sincretism, which challenges the notion that they were cultural separatists.[22]

Another sign of Islamic presence in the African community was the wearing of a totally white garment, a sort of long frock called an *abadá* in Bahia, an *aqbada* or *agbada* in Yorubaland. The abadá of Bahia was worn only in private so as not to attract attention or persecution from the officers of the law, who were always on the lookout for anything out of the ordinary among the blacks. It was only during the 1835 rebellion that the spectacle of hundreds of sons of Allah dressed in white first occurred in the streets of Salvador. For this reason police authorities called the abadás "war garments." As we have seen, the French consul observed early on that Nagôs wore their best clothing when they made war in Bahia, believing that if they died, they would reappear in their native land. During peacetime, Malês only wore white clothing at home, far from curious eyes, during their prayers and rituals. Thus, José, a slave from the Congo, belonging to a Nagô freedman, Gaspar da Silva Cunha, declared under questioning that his master only donned the "white petticoat" when "he went to talk in the attic" with fellow Muslims.[23]

Some Africans considered the abadá a symbol of social superiority. Bento, a Nagô slave, affirmed that "concerning those clothes, in his country important people, such as the King and his nobles, are draped in them." And the slave Higino said: "Those clothes come from the same place *pano da costa* [West African cloth] comes from, and whoever wears them is important and on the warpath."[24] These are curious affirmations, even if one takes into account that they might have been made in attempts to confuse the investigator. Could it be that Malês were seen as "important people" by the rest of the African community and that their clothing indicated their special status? This could also be a veiled allusion to the powerful Muslim warrior chiefs of Ilorin and other northern cities in the forefront of the conflict with Oyo. But any interpretation can only be tentative given the existing documentation. It is possible that both Bento and Higino belonged to a group of slaves who considered the Malês important because they were unaccustomed to Islamic ways. The Malês' need for secrecy helped maintain their image of importance, which they may have enjoyed, given their wishes for superiority. If the abadá only had (peacetime or wartime) ritualistic functions in Bahia, its use can be considered one more African cultural adaptation or shift in the face of restrictions established by a slaveholding society.

Since they could no longer wear traditional clothing in public, Bahian Malês had a special way of identifying each other on the streets. They wore rings of white metal, silver or iron, on their fingers. Similar rings, known as *kendé* in Africa, were worn by the Muslim allies of the rebel Afonja. According to Samuel Johnson, these rings were worn on the thumb and the third or fourth finger of the left hand. When rebels greeted one another, they struck their rings. Johnson maintained that this was "a sign of brotherhood." This custom appears to have crossed the Atlantic. In Bahia, according to the testimony of a Nagô freedman, João, "white rings . . . were the badge worn by members of Malê society to recognize each other." The police confiscated dozens of those objects after the uprising. It seems that with their defeat even that symbol disappeared because everyone now knew what it meant. One witness testified that "immediately, on the day after the blacks' insurrection, everyone took the rings off their fingers." Much later, at the beginning of the twentieth century, the pioneering ethnologist Manoel Querino wrote that Bahian Malês wore silver rings only as wedding rings.[25]

The Growth of Islam in Bahia

Salvador's urban environment in many ways facilitated Islamic activities. The relative independence of urban slaves, the presence of a large number of African freedmen, and the interaction between these two groups helped create a dynamic network and community for proselytizing and mobilizing. Whether slaves or freedmen, Malês who knew how to read and write Arabic passed their learning on to others. They gathered on street corners to offer their services, and while they waited for customers they concerned themselves with their religion and their rebellion. Besides reading, writing, and talking, they also sewed abadás and Malê skullcaps. One witness, a native-born black woman named Maria Clara da Costa Pinto, who lived on Mangueira Street, opposite one of those African gathering points, or *cantos*, claimed that Aprígio (a freedman living with Manoel Calafate), along with other Malês, "for a long time had been making notes of the sort that appeared or were found on the insurgents, using totally strange letters and characters, and bringing together at that place others of their Nation . . . to whom they taught to write with pointers dipped in ink they had in a bottle, as she had witnessed many times. They even taught them prayers in their language."[26] A second lieutenant and also a poet, Ladislau dos Santos Titara, when he was not busy writing patriotic verse, also kept an eye on the same gathering and acknowledged that "he had seen them, principally the latter [Aprígio], making huge shirts and skullcaps, which the insurgents donned as uniforms. He also heard that Aprígio taught others of the same nation how to read."[27]

The houses of African freedmen also provided space for Malê worship, meals, celebrations, and of course conspiracies. This was the case with Manoel Calafate's house, where, according to the testimony of the slave Ignácio, Malês frequently met, under the command of mestre Manoel. Another locale regularly frequented by Malês was the tobacco shop belonging to mestre Dandará, in the Santa Bárbara market. There, according to a confession made by the elder himself, he brought African young people together to teach them the word of Allah. One of the prosecution's witnesses declared that Dandará organized twice-daily prayer sessions (*salah*), which were a local adaptation of the five daily prayers of Islamic tradition. Such adaptations were necessary given the rigors of daily work under slavery. A Malê mestre named Luís Sanim in turn taught the faithful who gathered in the house of a Nagô freedman, Belchior da Silva Cunha. This house was located on Oração (meaning "prayer") Street, a short distance from Calafate's house.

In some cases slaves took advantage of their masters' largesse and met in their own quarters, where they received friends and spent time reading and writing. That went on in the house of an Englishman named Stuart. Another Englishman, Abraham, let his slaves James and Diogo construct a hut on his property. In 1835 this hut was perhaps the most important Malê community center in Bahia. Pacífico Licutan, the popular alufá, was not as lucky concerning his master, who was quite intransigent. Licutan and some other slaves pooled their money to rent a room where they could meet in peace. The majority of those "private mosques" (*machachalis* according to Etienne Brazil) were in downtown Salvador, except the one run by Dandará and the one in Vitória. Alufás Manoel, Sanim, and Licutan operated in a tiny area from Ladeira da Praça to Terreiro de Jesus.[28]

There is no detailed documentation concerning what went on behind those doors, but the little that exists is suggestive. The Malês met to pray, to learn to read and write Arabic, and to memorize verses from the *Koran*—all of which are important and indispensable tasks in Muslim education, regardless of time or place. Conversion through revelation in reading is expressed as follows in the *Koran*: "The unbelievers among the People of the Book [Jews and Christians] and the pagans did not desist from unbelief until the Proof was given them: an apostle from Allah reading sanctified pages from eternal scriptures" (98:1).[29]

It is quite impressive that the experience of reading and writing riveted the interest of slaves and freedmen, who always found time for these activities. During the searches begun after the revolt was put down the police confiscated dozens of writing slates used by Malês. These slates were wooden rectangles with a handle at one of the narrow ends. They were called *allo* by the Hausas and *wala* or *patako* by the Yorubas; *wala*, one more Yoruba word, displaced the others in Bahia. They wrote directly on the wood using ink made of burnt rice. Of course, they also used the slate as a desk for writing on paper, and their ink was sometimes black, sometimes red. Malês practiced their Arabic and religious lessons by copying prayers and passages from the *Koran*. Again, the water they used to erase the words was believed to have magical powers, especially if the words had been written by some prestigious Malê preacher.[30]

Not all the words were washed away, however. In spite of the high price of paper back then, Malês used it extensively to record matters of their faith. The police found many papers covered with Arabic writing and these papers made a deep impression at the time. In a society where even the dominant whites were largely illiterate, it was hard to accept that African slaves possessed such sophisticated means of communication. However, these papers revealed that among their slaves were people highly instructed in the language of the *Koran*, people who left their marks in perfect calligraphy and correct grammar. These were Africans who, even though they were slaves in Bahia, had certainly been members of an intelligentsia in Africa, if not members of the wealthy merchant classes. They had enjoyed social privileges that allowed them to spend much of their time in intellectual pursuits.

One of the flawless texts Reichert found is a copy of the *Koran*'s opening sura, the Exordium:

(1)   in the name of compassionate merciful God " praise
(2)   God master of the worlds " the compassionate the merciful
(3)   Lord of judgement day " we love thee
(4)   and from thee we ask for help " lead us in the path
(5)   of righteousness " in the path of those thou
(6)   didst favor and who are not the object of thy
(7)   wrath and not the wayward amen

But it was not just the hands of educated Malês that produced the famous "Arabic papers." Much of the writing came from inexperienced hands of students being initiated into Islam, or at least into its language. It is they who give witness to the dynamic pace of Muslim conversion and education in Bahia on the eve of the 1835 rebellion. Following is an example of a beginner's work:

(1)   in the name of compassionate merciful
(2)   god, may god protect thee
(3)   from evil, he will not tell them
(4)   all about . . .
(5)   . . . from them amen

Here, according to Reichert, "the author made obvious errors, omissions, clumsy letters, etc."[31]

All this writing was to help them memorize prayers and texts from the *Koran*. This was an important step toward Islamic integration, because it let the initiate participate fully in collective prayers, and it added his voice to the ritual drama. It signaled a deeper commitment to the Malê community and its projects. According to Gaspar da Silva Cunha, "he did not join the prayers because he was a beginner." Whoever did pray always had, in addition to a wala and the white abadá, pieces of paper and the Malê rosary *(tessubá)*, which Querino describes in the following manner: "50 centimeters long, with 90 crude wooden beads, ending in a ball instead of a cross." In 1835 a scribe described it as "a string of 98 coconut beads on a cotton ... cord." Whites and anti-Malê blacks maliciously called it a "pagan's rosary." Many of those rosaries were confiscated by the police during 1835.[32]

Women were conspicuously absent from Malê rituals. References to their role are rare in the inquiry. This is hardly remarkable; women's subservient role in the Muslim world is well known. In the words of Trimingham: "Women, seen as being in a constant state of ritual impurity, are not allowed to enter mosques." Although Islam does not formally forbid women to enter mosques, their inferior position is revealed in the *Koran:* "Women shall with justice have rights similar to those exercised against them, although men have a status above women" (2:228). Or: "Men have authority over women because Allah has made [men] superior to the others, and because they spend their wealth to maintain them. Good women are obedient" (4:34).

Doctrine is, of course, never carried out 100 percent in practice, and black Islam, both in Africa and perhaps mainly in Bahia, was obliged to make concessions to its feminine sector. In the 1835 goings-on alufá Dandara's companion, a slave by the name of Emereciana, handed out Malê rings like a general decorating meritorious recruits, an activity for which she was later sentenced to four hundred lashes. Emereciana was an exception, but as time went by, women became more and more integrated into Islamic rituals. Querino considered them to be totally incorporated into what he called "Malê masses." Also, in Rio de Janeiro at the end of the nineteenth century, women participated in funeral ceremonies; they ate and danced in an Islam of a more open variety.[33]

Even though the Malês of Brazil had to innovate with regard to Islam, they tried to maintain its basic characteristics. They tried to observe its food taboos and celebrate the most important dates on the Muslim calendar. Of course, it was not easy for the slaves to follow the Malê diet, since they could not always choose what they ate, even in the relatively flexible ambience of urban slavery. But matters pertaining to black Islam's eating practices appear throughout the inquiry. Malê suppers functioned as rituals of group solidarity. Communal dinners nourished dreams of independence and rebellion. Even if revolution itself is no banquet, as Mao Tse-tung wrote, the 1835 rebellion began with one at mestre Calafate's house.

Several witnesses saw Malês gather regularly to eat. One woman claimed that her neighbor, an ex-slave named Jacinto, "often had night meetings with dinner included at the house of his mistress Isabel, who lived on the Vitória road." (During the revolt Jacinto commanded a group of blacks who began their activities at Vitória Square [Largo da Vitória].) The slave sacristan at the Mercês Convent, Agostinho, invited Muslim companions to Christian quarters to, in his words, "just talk and eat." Ellena, a black woman, claimed that a slave known as Joaquim, who shared the rent of a room with alufá Licutan, "used to kill rams and have get-togethers during the day with his friends in his room, because at night they probably had to be in their masters' houses." Ellena was a Jeje ex-slave who lived in the same house. Further on, Ellena amended this and said the Malês "often came there to eat and have a party" only on Sundays and holidays, which was when slaves got time off.[34]

These suppers represented the Malês' effort to commit themselves to the Islamic precept of only eating food prepared by Muslim hands so as to avoid the danger of ritual pollution. They ate mutton frequently, which suggests ritual sacrifices. In Africa the ceremony in which a newly born child is given a name, on its eighth day of life, entails the sacrifice of a ram, which is then eaten. In some areas the same ritual is used when recently converted adults (newly born Muslims) receive their Islamic name. Quite likely these practices continued in Bahia. Querino also reports that males commemorated the end of Ramadan, the month of fasting, by sacrificing rams. Indeed, during 1835, at the request of a justice of the peace, a slave translated a text that was, according to the slave, "a sort of calender which the Malês use to keep track of their fasts and to know when to slaughter their rams." Querino also wrote: "When they sacrificed a lamb, they stuck the point of the knife into the sand and bled the animal saying the word *Bi-si-mi-lai*." (*Bismillah*, in its complete form *Bismika Allahumma*, opens all the suras of the *Koran* and means "In the name of Allah, the Compassionate, the Merciful.") This author also tells us that during Ramadan Bahian Malês lived on a diet of yams, bugloss (*efó*), rice, milk, and honey.[35]

It was also at the table that Malês celebrated their main religious holidays, including Lailat al-Miraj (Mohammed's ascension into Heaven), which in 1834 was celebrated at the end of November, less than two months before the uprising. In that year, the twenty-sixth day of Rajab (the seventh month in the Islamic calendar), the traditional date to celebrate Lailat al-Miraj, fell on 29 November. That day many people met in the hut behind Mr. Abraham's house on the Vitória road. In the words of the slave João, "There was a dinner where all the Nagô slaves belonging to Englishmen met, plus some boatsmen [*escravos de saveiro*] who came to town, as well as some belonging to Brazilians." This great meeting seems to have been the first time Muslims shed their traditional reticence, and for this they paid dearly.[36]

In the midst of the Malê celebrations, there came an unexpected visit from a well-known enemy, Inspector Antônio Marques. He had come to stop the "disturbance of the peace" on his block. He acted arrogantly, dispersing the celebrants and running them off. On the following day he informed the justice of the peace of Vitória Parish, Francisco José da Silva Machado, of the goings-on, and the justice of the peace then complained to Mr. Abraham. To avoid problems with the Brazilian authorities, the Englishman obliged the builders of the hut, Diogo and James, to destroy it. Later on James would say that this coerced gesture brought him resentment from the Nagôs: "The master made them take the same house down, which made some of his countrymen who used to meet there refuse to greet him." In another part of his testimony, the slave was to tell the building's history: "Built some five months earlier, it had been made . . . so that other partners and friends could enjoy themselves, getting together to eat, drink, play, and talk." The loss of the building, a veritable black mosque, was doubtless a sad event for the Malês.[37]

This incident in Vitória is not the only example of religious persecution to be found in the court records prior to 1835. If there were some masters who were tolerant of their slaves' religion, there were others who prohibited them from practicing Islam. From time to time some masters repented their past tolerance and began to prohibit slaves' religious ceremonies, as seems to have been the case with the English merchant Frederick Robelliard. At one point he had permitted his slaves to learn Arabic, but he later prohibited it, having concluded that their lessons kept them away from their work. Carlos, who learned to read with other slaves, said: "At one time the master did not stop them, but later, when he checked the boxes belonging to his teachers (mestres), he had the contents gathered and burnt, scolding them and intimating that because they had nothing better to do they spent their time learning and teaching the language of their land." A twenty-seven-year-old merchant, Teodoro Barros, reported that a Hausa slave, Antônio, used to teach "a slave belonging to José Vieira to write, and for that reason Vieira punished him because he did not want his slave learning that language." On the other hand, on the same occasion Antônio's master defended his slave's activities, "because such writing is pursuant to his prayers."[38]

The feast of Lailat al-Miraj was a sign of Islam's success in Bahia, an Islam on the rise and daring to be public. At that time Mohammedans were a well-defined segment of the Bahian black community; they had a charged identity and provided a strong point of reference for Africans living there. Slaves and freedmen flocked to Islam in search of spiritual comfort and hope. They needed it to establish some order and dignity in their lives. The *Koran*'s texts were especially appealing because of their sympathy for the discriminated, the exiled, the persecuted, and the enslaved. But if Allah is there to protect the weak, He also wants their fidelity and commitment to spread His word and the Islamic way of life. This militant aspect of Islam gave the Malês special distinction and attracted many Africans to them, but it also pushed others away.

Malês wove a web of complicity with other blacks using their amulets and their still incomplete rupture with the ethnic religions from Africa. This complicity aided the 1835 rebellion. There was, however, tension between the Malês and non-Muslim blacks who complained about the pride, the intolerance, and the orthodoxy of their Mohammedan brethren. A Yoruba-Ijebu slave by the name of Carlos made the following comment: "The Nagôs who can read, and who took part in the insurrection, would not shake hands with nor respect outsiders. They even called them *gaveré*." The word *gaveré* was the scribe's attempt at writing *kafiri* or *kafir* (plural *kafirai*), the Arabic word for "pagans." In the case in point, the word designated Africans still associated with traditional ethnic religions such as Candomblé. The Malês treated Catholics even worse. Marcelina, the slave of a nun living in the Desterro Convent, complained that they harassed her saying "she was going to Mass to worship a piece of wood on the altar, because images are not saints." In spite of the relative openness of black Islam in Bahia, the religious fervor of many Muslims and their moderate habits could seem excessively disciplined to Africans weary of discipline and more inclined to embrace the polar opposite movement toward worldly pleasure. Ezequiel, an African freedman, criticized the Malês for not eating pork and said of their life of self-denial: "They all want to be priests."[39]

One must regard these declarations with reservations, however. After all, it must not have been difficult for the authorities to hear arrested Africans utter words against the attitudes and customs of the Malês, since such utterances were means of saving one's skin. Still, those declarations cannot be considered bald-faced lies. In that context they are valuable insofar as they reveal tension and contention among Africans, but this animosity should not be blown out of proportion. Even Marcelina, the Catholic slave who complained about the Malês, did not let their behavior drive her from the room she rented from a well-known Islamic militant, Belchior da Silva Cunha, where she came into daily contact with many Muslims.

Bahian Muslims were in no way the fierce separatists many students of the 1835 rebellion have claimed them to be. They may have gone to some extremes in the defense of their religious point of view, but life had other facets for them, too. Besides religious communion, there were other forces of social solidarity and integration in Africans' lives: their Africanness, their ethnicity, their very situation as slaves and freedmen who were exploited and discriminated against. These forces were significant for all Africans without exception. Seen in this light, religious contention represented a dynamic element within the African community, which contained immense cultural variety and a plurality of world and otherworldly views. The Malês never posed a threat to that plurality, and there is no proof that a monopoly on religion was their principal objective in 1835, or at any other time.

NOTES

1 Francisco Gonçalves Martins, Relatório do chefe de policia Francisco Gonçalves Martins," in Etienne Ignace Brazil, "Os Malês," *Revista do Instituto Histórico e Geográfico Brasiliero* 72 (1909): 69–126, 115–123; President Martins to Minister of Justice, Salvador, 31 January 1835, Archivo do Estado da Bahia, Salvador (hereafter AEBa), *Correspondência*, livro 681, fol. 197.

2 M. G. Smith, "The Jihad of Shehu dan Fodio," in *Islam in Tropical Africa*, ed. I. M. Lewis (London: Oxford University Press, 1966), 296–315; J. S. Trimingham, *A History of Islam in West Africa* (London: Oxford University Press, 1970), 198ff.; H. A. S. Johnston, *The Fulani Empire of Sokoto* (Oxford: Oxford University Press, 1967), chaps. 4 and 5; Francis Castelnau, *Renseignments sur l'Afrique Centrale, etc.* (Paris: Bertrand, 1851), passim.

3 Ibid. See also Mahdi Adamu, "The Delivery of Slaves from the Central Sudan to the Bight of Benin," in *The Uncommon Market: Essays in the Economic History of the Atlantic Slave Trade*, ed. H. A. Gemery and J. S. Hogendom (New York: Academic Press, 1979), 176; and, in the same volume, Patrick Manning, "The Slave Trade in the Bight of Benin, 1640–1890," 127.

4 T. G. O. Gbadamosi, *The Growth of Islam among the Yoruba, 1841–1908* (Atlantic Highlands, N.J.: Humanities Press, 1978), 9.

5 Babatunde Agiri, "Slavery in Yoruba Society in the Nineteenth Century," in *The Ideology of Slavery in Africa*, ed. Paul E. Lovejoy (Beverly Hills: Sage, 1981), 136.

6 Allan G. B. Fisher and Humphrey J. Fisher, *Slavery and Muslim Society in Africa* (Garden City, N.Y.: Anchor, 1972), 36–37 and passim; Robert Smith, *The Kingdoms of the Yoruba* (London: Methuen, 1969), chaps. 10 and 11; Robin Law, *The Oyo Empire, c. 1600–c. 1836: A West African Imperialism in the Era of the Atlantic Slave Trade* (Oxford: Clarendon, 1977), pt. 3.

7 Agiri, "Slavery," 137.

8 Braz do Amaral's suggestion is quoted in Roger Bastide, *As religiões africanas do Brasil*, 2 vols. (São Paulo: Editora Pioneira and Editora da Universidade de São Paulo, 1971), 1:203 n. 3. See also Raymond K. Kent, "African Revolt in Bahia," *Journal of Social History* 3 (Summer 1970): 356; Rodrigues, *Os africanos*, 104; Pierre Verger, *Flux et reflux de la traite des nègres entre le golfe de Benin et Bahia de Todos os Santos* (Paris: Mouton, 1968), 352 n. 24; and Vincent Monteil, "Analyse de 25 documents árabes des Malês de Bahia (1835)," *Bulletin de l'Institut Fondamentale d'Afrique Noire*, ser. B, 29, nos. 1–2 (1967): 88. The best critical study is by Vivaldo da Costa Lima and is reproduced in Vânia M. C. de Alvim, "Movimentos proféticos, prepolíticos e contraculturais dos negros islamizados na Bahia do século 19" (Master's thesis, Universidade Federal da Bahia, 1975), 21–29. Lima discusses the term *muçurumim* or *musulmi*. The words come from Hausa and quite likely were used in Bahia during the early nineteenth century; however, they have not been documented in the written records of the period. Kathleen M. Stasik suggested the derivation of *imale* from *Mali* (see Stasik, "A Decisive Acquisition: The Development of Islam in Nineteenth-century Iwo, Southeast Oyo" [Master's thesis, University of Minnesota, 1975], 83). Bastide

confused *Malê* with *Malinke* or *Mandingo* in Brazil, and Manoel Querino, *A raça africana e seus costumes* (Salvador: Editora Progresso, 1955), 113, also errone-ously considered the Malês a specific ethnic group. On Labat's ethnic classifi-cation, see Manning, "Slave Trade in the Bight of Benin," 126–27.

9 Concerning black *irmandades* in Bahia see João José Reis, *A morte é uma festa: ritos fúnebres e revolta popular no Brasil do século XIX* (São Paulo: Companhia das Letras, 1991), chap. 2. For more information on traditional African religion, or Candomblé, in Bahia of the 1830s see João José Reis and Eduardo Silva, *Negociação e conflito* (São Paulo: Companhia das Letras, 1989), chap. 3. In Nagô candomblé, *bori* is the name of an initiation ritual (also known as "feeding the head") linked to religious initiation ritual (see Manoel Querino, *A raça Africana e seus costumes* (Salvador: Editora Progresso, 1955), 60–63: and esp. Roger Bastide, *Le Candomblé de Bahia [rite nagô]* [Paris: Mouton, 1958], 25–28, and Pierre Verger, "Bori, primeira cerimônia de iniciação ao culto dos Orisá nagô na Bahia, Brasil," in *Olóórisà*, ed. C. E. M. de Moura [São Paulo: Ágora, 1981], 33–56).

10 Martins, "Relatório," 121.

11 "Devassa do levante de escravos ocorrido em Salvador em 1835," *Anais do Arquivo do Estado de Bahia* 38 (1968): 1–142, 69–70.

12 The Trial of Antônio, a Hausa, slave of Bernardino José da Costa, AEBa, *Insurreições*, maço 2848, fol. 20.

13 The Trial of Gaspar, a Nagô, slave of Domingos Lopes Ribeiro, ibid., maço 2846, fol. 5; The Trial of Nécio, fol. 29; "Peças processuais do levante dos males," *Anais do Arquivo da Estado da Bahia* 40 (1971): 7–170.

14 Bastide, *As religiões africanas*, 1:217, speaks of Malê passivity. J. S. Trimingham, *Islam in West Africa* (Oxford: Oxford University Press, 1959), chaps. 2 and 5, discusses the interaction between Islam and ethnic religions; he mentions the generalized use of Islamic amulets by non-Muslims (35). See Law, *Oyo Empire*, 257, concerning the faith Afonja had in these amulets. For the citation in the previous paragraph see John McLeod, *A Voyage to Africa with some Account of the Manners and Customs of the Dahomian People* (London: John Murray, 1820), 94–95. Stasik also discusses the tradition of attributing power to Muslim amu-lets ("Decisive Acquisition," 10, 54). The quote from Rodrigues comes from his *O animismo fetichista dos negros baianos* (Rio de Janeiro: Civilização Brasileira, 1935), 29. There were an impressive number of Malê "sorcerers" around the turn of the twentieth century in Rio de Janeiro (see João do Rio's *As religiões do Rio* [Rio de Janeiro: Editora Nova Aguilar, 1976], esp. chap. 1). These amulets were used throughout Brazil during the eighteenth century, especially in Bahia. They were called *bolsas de mandinga* ("Mandingo purses") even when their magical contents included strong folk Catholic prayers rather than Islamic writings. Possession of these "purses" was a crime punishable by the Inquisition (see Laura de Mello et Souza, *O diabo e a Terra de Santa Cruz* (São Paulo: Brasiliense, 1986), 210–26, esp. 219–21, where she discusses Bahia. For more information on the use of Malê talismans in Rio de Janeiro see Mary Karasch, *Slave Life in Rio de Janeiro, 1808–1850* [Princeton: Princeton University Press, 1987], 263).

15 The Trial of Lobão Maxado, Nagô-Ibo, ex-slave, AEBa, *Insurreições*, maço 2847, fol. 4.

16 Vincent Monteil, "Marabouts," in *Islam in Africa*, ed. J. Kritzeck and W. H. Lewis (New York: Van Nostrand–Reinhold, 1969), 95.

17 Vincent Monteil, "Anályse de 25 documents árabes," 88–89; Rolf Reichert, *Os documentos árabes do Arquivo do Estado da Bahia* (Salvador: Centro de Estudos Afro-Orientais, Universidade Federal da Bahia, 1979); idem, "L'insurrection d'esclaves de 1835 à la lumière des documents arabes des archives publique de

l'Etat de Bahia (Brésil)," *Bulletin de l'Institut Fondamental d'Afrique Noire*, ser. B, 29, nos. 1–2 (1967): 99–104.

18 See Reichert, *Os documentos árabes*, nos. 29, 19, 21. The numbers in parentheses represent the lines in the original documents and are Reichert's.

19 The Trial of Silvestre José Antônio, a Hausa freedman, AEBa, *Insurreições*, maço 2849, fol. 6v; The Trial of José Gomes, a Hausa, and Pedro Pinto, Nagô, both freedmen, ibid., fol. 10.

20 For a good discussion on *isköki*, on their different types, nature, and power, as well as their relation to Islamic beliefs, see Joseph Greenberg, *The Influence of Islam on a Sudanese Religion* (Seattle: University of Washington Press, 1946), 27ff; see also J.S. Trimingham, *Islam in West Africa* (Oxford: Oxford University Press, 1970), 35–36, 54–55, 60, 63, 111, 155, and passim. For information on Yoruba counterparts of these spirits see Juana Elbein dos Santos, *Os nagô e a morte* (Petrópolis, Brazil: Vozes, 1976), 55ff. João do Rio identified the *aligenum* as "diabolical spirits to be evoked for both good and evil [and found] in a book of magic (*livro de sortes*) which was marked here and there with red ink" (*As religiões do Rio*, 23). Concerning the belief that the wind brought illness, a common belief among slaves in southern Brazil, see Emília Viotti da Costa, *Da senzala à colônia* (São Paulo: Difusão Européia do Livro, 1966), 254. The "wind" was an important element in African divination practices throughout Brazil (see Souza, *O diabo*, 27, 266, 353). The quotes from Africans come from the Trial of Lobão Maxado, fol. 4; and The Trial of José, a Nagô-Ibo, slave of Gey de Carter, AEBa, *Insurreições*, maço 2847, fol. 9.

21 For more information on the amulet trade in Africa see Monteil, "Marabouts," 95; and Trimingham, *Islam in West Africa*, 81. The quotes in this paragraph come from The Trial of Antônio, AEBa, *Insurreições*, maço 2848, fol. 6v.

22 Marcescheau to French Minister of Foreign Affairs, Salvador, 26 January 1835, AMRE, *CP/Brésil*, vol. 16, fol. 16v.

23 "Devassa," 75. Samuel Johnson claims the *aqbada* was always made from colored cloth, whereas the *suliya* was made of white cloth (see *The History of the Yorubas* [London: Routledge & Kegan Paul, 1921], III). However, the Yoruba pioneer historian seems to have been wrong: according to Stasik, "Decisive Acquisition," vi, an aqbada is a white Muslim garment.

24 The Trial of Higino; Transcript of the Trials at Conceição da Praia, fol. 26v.

25 Johnson, *History of the Yorubas*, 194; The Trial of Cornélio, a Nagô, slave of João Firmiano Caldeira, AEBa, *Insurreições*, maço 2847, fol. 15; Transcript of the Trials at Conceição da Praia, fol. 66; Querino, *A raça africana*, 108. Costa maintains that during the 1870s silver rings were worn by members of black secret societies in southern Brazil (*Da senzala*, 279).

26 "Peças processuais," 108.

27 Ibid., 107. In 1835 Titara wrote, perhaps not merely coincidentally, his famous poem "Paraguaçu," praising Bahian independence. I thank Luciano Diniz and Paulo César Souza for this reminder.

28 Concerning these Malês' activities see "Peças processuais," 15–16; Transcript of the Trials at Conceição da Praia, fols. 28v ff.; The Trial of Nécio, fol. 15v; "Devassa," 7–9, 74ff.; Brazil, "Os Malês," 85 (for *machachalis*).

29 Quotes from the *Koran* come from N. J. Dawood's translation (Harmondsworth: Penguin, 1974).

30 Trimingham, *Islam in West Africa*, passim; Brazil, "Os Malês," 77–88, Concerning the black and red ink see Manoel Joaquim de Almeida to President of the Province, Salvador, 29 January 1835, AEBa, *Juízes de Paz*, maço 2684; see also James Wetherell, *Stray Notes from Bahia, Being an Extract of Letters during Residence of Fifteen Years* (Liverpool: Webb & Hunt, 1860), 138.

31 Reichert, *Os documentos*, nos. 8 and 15 (Reichert's book has no page numbers).

32 The stages of initiation into Islam are discussed in Trimingham, *Islam in West Africa*, 34ff. Gaspar's citation comes from "Devassa," 35. See also Querino, *A raça africana*, 103; The Trial of José, slave of Gey de Carter, fol. 2; Transcript of the Trials at Conceição da Praia, fol. 14v. The scribe wrote: "a black rosary without a cross at the end and known as a pagan's rosary" (ibid., fol. 70).

33 Trimingham, *Islam in West Africa*, 73. Vincent Monteil (*L'Islam noir* [Paris: Seuil, 1971], 175–76) cites these suras from the *Koran*, but he argues that in black Africa Muslim women are independent and play important roles in some communities. Querino, *A raça africana*, 107. For information on Muslim women in Rio see Bastide, *As religiões africanas*, 1: 210–11.

34 The Trial of Nécio, fols. 35v, 61; "Devassa," 8.

35 Trimingham, *Islam in West Africa*, 75, 80, 174; "Devassa," 131; Querino, *A raça africana*, 110–11.

36 For the conversion of dates from Muslim to Christian calendars, I have used G. S. P. Freeman-Greenville, *The Muslim and Christian Calendars* (London: Oxford University Press, 1963); The Trial of Nécio, fol. 18.

37 The Trial of Nécio, fols. 16, 44–45.

38 Ibid., fol. 20v; The Trial of Antônio, fol. 9v.

39 "Peças processuais," 33; "Devassa," 131; The Trial of Cornélio, fol. 15.

10

SWEARING BY THE PAST, SWEARING TO THE FUTURE

Sacred Oaths, Alliances, and Treaties Among the Guianese and Jamaican Maroons

Kenneth Bilby

It was March 1994, and Queen Elizabeth II of England was scheduled to pay a rare visit to Jamaica. More than 250 years had gone by since the communities of escaped slaves known as Maroons had forced the British colonial government in that island to sue for peace. Little did the vacationing queen suspect that the descendants of these eighteenth-century rebels, still living in the hills of Jamaica, were eagerly awaiting her arrival. These present-day Maroons felt a special bond with the holder of the British crown; indeed, they expected nothing less than direct access to Her Majesty.

When their attempts to arrange a meeting with the British monarch were thwarted, the Maroons were quick to protest what they perceived to be a serious infringement of their rights by the Jamaican government. The incident was reported in the main Jamaican newspaper, the *Daily Gleaner*, as follows:

> The Maroons are disappointed and "very upset" that their request to have audience with Her Majesty Queen Elizabeth II, was turned down.
>
> According to chief of the Accompong, St. Elizabeth Maroons, Meredie Rowe, a group of government ministers, led by Minister of Foreign Affairs Dr. Paul Robertson, said they could not meet the Queen due to the lateness of their request. "If those men took the Maroons seriously, they would have allowed us at least five minutes with The Queen," chief Rowe complained.
>
> He added that the Maroons have long-standing "compelling issues" with the British monarchy. (Anonymous 1994)

To those acquainted with the recent political histories of the Jamaican

Maroon communities, it is easy to guess what some of the "compelling issues" the Maroons wished to discuss with Her Royal Highness might have been. High on the list would have been the two colonial treaties the Maroons' ancestors signed with emissaries of Queen Elizabeth's own great-great-great-great-great-great-grandfather, King George II, in 1739.

Why would the Maroons wish to discuss a centuries-old peace treaty with the symbolic head of the waning empire from which Jamaica had claimed its independence more than thirty years earlier? And why would they feel that the current British sovereign had any obligation to hear their thoughts on this subject?

While the Maroon treaties appear to the Jamaican government as anachronistic colonial documents with little or no binding force in the present, to the Maroons themselves they are phenomena of an entirely different order. As the anthropologist Barbara Kopytoff has clearly shown, present-day Maroons view their treaties as "sacred charters"—hallowed covenants that underpin and assure their very existence as separate peoples within the larger society of Jamaica (Kopytoff 1979; see also Adjaye 1994: 169, 177–79).

What makes these treaties sacrosanct is the manner in which they are said to have been concluded. According to Maroons, both of the treaties signed in 1739–one by Cudjoe in the Cockpit Country and the other by Quao in the Blue Mountains—were "blood treaties," backed by sacred oaths. In the Maroons' eyes, it is this historical act of oath taking, consecrated by both Maroon and British blood, that created a permanent bond between themselves and the British monarchy and that entitles them to a special audience with the current occupant of the royal throne.[1]

Whereas this notion of a "blood treaty" remains all-important to Maroons, its significance is easily overlooked from a British colonial perspective, and few historians have given more than passing consideration to it. This is hardly surprising, for a thorough grasp of the culturally specific meanings that underlie such sacred oaths, and of the ways in which they are embedded in the larger social and cultural contexts of which they are a part, requires a degree of ethnographic grounding that is seldom achieved by historians working solely with written documents.

In this article I attempt to enhance our understanding of the treaties made between Maroons and European colonial governments—not only in Jamaica but in the Guianas and elsewhere in the Americas—by viewing fragmentary historical data, both written and oral, alongside information on present-day Maroon life gathered both by myself and by other anthropologists who have carried out recent ethnographic fieldwork among Maroon peoples.[2] The data marshaled from these varied sources can best be understood, I believe, when interpreted with reference to what we know of oath-taking procedures (and related forms of politicoreligious conduct) in those African societies from which the Maroons' ancestors were drawn.

The ethnographically based approach I am advocating here promises to help us achieve a more balanced perspective on the significance of the treaties, and it may provide more general insights into the ways in which Maroon communities have relied, and continue to rely, on deeply rooted ideas about the combined moral and spiritual basis of human relationships to establish and legitimate political alliances. It might even be argued that such shared general concepts about the nature of the social universe were at the very heart of the process through which early Maroon groups were able, despite their diverse cultural origins, to construct new societies and identities.

In my view, the African-derived concepts of sacred bonding that underlie the Maroons' views of their treaties have serious implications for government policy in those countries where Maroons have survived as distinct populations until today. I close with a few brief remarks touching on some of these implications.

Maroon treaties: blood versus paper

Let us begin with the Jamaican case. In the primary sources on Jamaican Maroons, there exists, to my knowledge, only a single mention of an oath taken in conjunction with the 1739 treaties. This written account, however, reveals nothing specific about the manner in which the oath was administered. In a letter to the president of the Council of Jamaica, the British officer authorized to treat with the Leeward Maroons, one Colonel John Guthrie described the preparations for the treaty as follows: "Before I could bring it to bear in any Respect, I was obliged to tye myself up, by a Solemn Oath, not to Fight against them until he [Cudjoe, the Maroon chief] should Infringe the same" (Kopytoff 1979: 49; see also Schafer 1973: 126; Hart 1985: 104; Campbell 1988: 113). Perhaps because of this document's characterization of the oath as "solemn," a number of historians have been willing to accept this highly ambiguous fragment as evidence supporting the claim made by Accompong Maroons today that their treaty was consecrated by a "blood oath."[3]

Let us listen to one version of the Maroon oral tradition of a "blood oath," narrated to me by a well-known Accompong Maroon storyteller in 1991: "[The Englishmen] came out and shook hands with Kojo [Cudjoe], and offered the peace terms. And as a token of peace, they used white rum. [The Maroons] had a thing they called 'calabash'—or otherwise, 'gourdie.' That's what those people used to use. So they both cut their arms now, and drained the blood into the calabash, and threw white rum onto it and mixed it up. And both of them drank it. So they said that from that time on there would be a link between the Maroons and the white men."[4] This oral tradition, carried down from the ancestors, is very widely known in Accompong, where it has long served as a central symbol of Maroon identity. It much impressed the anthropologist Archibald Cooper, who carried out long-term fieldwork in Accompong more than fifty years ago (in 1938–39). Some years after returning from the field, Cooper (n.d.: 7) wrote:

> The signing of the treaty at [the] Peace Cave is an event that is well remembered to the present day. Captain Cudjoe "signed" for the Maroons, Col. Guthrie for the British. They each cut their arms with a knife and the blood was collected in a calabash cup. The mixture of the blood of the white man and the blood of the black was mixed with rum, and this is the ink with which the treaty was signed. Afterwards the mixture was drunk by both sides. Then Accompong [Cudjoe's brother] stepped forward and presented Col. Guthrie with a puzzle. First he called for a quart of strong coffee to which he added an equal amount of milk. Then he said to the Colonel, "Now you must divide the milk from the coffee." But Guthrie answered, "No, now that they have been mixed they can never be separated." And Accompong answered, "It is the same with us today. The white man is the milk, and the Maroon is the coffee. We have mixed our blood as the coffee and milk are mixed and they can never be separated." . . . This absolute quality of the treaty is stressed in all present day conversations concerning the treaty. The treaty is inviolable, they say, because it is a blood treaty.[5]

Another anthropologist, Werner Zips (in press), who worked in Accompong during the 1980s, has remarked on the importance of blood versus paper from a Maroon perspective:

> In the historical perspective of the Maroons, relevant for their present political identity, the Peace Treaty received its binding obligation by the exchange of blood between the representatives of the two parties. The signatures of the negotiators, John Guthrie and Francis Saddler for the British and Captain Kojo [Cudjoe] for the Maroons, are still not seen as the central symbolic act for the conclusion of peace. . . . the ritual mixing and drinking of blood seems to have been the only appropriate interaction to terminate the war according to the political practices known to the Maroons through their West African experience.

Over in the eastern part of the island, the descendants of those Maroons who found refuge in the Blue Mountains possess oral traditions concerning their treaty that are very similar to those of the Accompong Maroons. In their case, however, not a shred of contemporary written evidence has been found to support their description of the manner in which the treaty was concluded. Nonetheless, the present-day Maroons of Moore Town, Scot's Hall, and Charles Town (collectively known as the Windward Maroons) are unanimous in their conviction that their own treaty was consecrated with a blood oath. Since I first began recording oral traditions in Moore Town in 1977, I have collected dozens of narratives concerning this event, many of them told by Maroon ritual specialists. Despite variations in certain details, almost all accounts agree on the main points. Often they are told with remarkable vividness. Take, for example, the following two excerpts from longer narratives, recorded in Moore Town in 1991:

> [The white man] said, "peace." [Nanny, the Windward Maroon founding ancestress] said they had to take the *paki* [calabash], and cut the blood—her blood and the white blood—and mix it together, and let them drink it, for a peace treaty. And they agreed. And she threw it in there. And they mixed it up with what they were going to mix it with. And then the whites drank it. Bakra drank it. And the Maroons, and Nanny, drank it. And she was done. She took a johncrow feather—it was not a pen and ink; it was a johncrow feather she dipped in blood—and wrote the peace treaty, [saying] that the Maroons and whites were not to fight again. . . . so the treaty is in the Queen's house of business in England.[6]

> When the Maroons and Bakra were going to sign the treaty to make them abandon the foolish war, it was with blood and a feather . . . *adangka na mi blood! Adangka na mi blood* [a Kromanti expression]. They took the feather, and cut it like a pen—not these pens [of today]. These pens don't have any nibs now. But before-time pens had nibs. They cut the feather, picked the feather like a nib, and wrote in blood: "Maroon and Bakra . . . . We have fought war for so many years. So, we have come to a peace treaty now, which is done. And it is with blood. And it can't be abolished." It is *blood*! *Adangka na mi fren.* The Maroons signed the treaty with Bakra: "Bakra, Maroon, the time has come. We've killed out that fighting war, and both of us are friends." And they took the feather, and dipped it in blood, and wrote.[7]

Unlike the Accompong Maroons, those in Moore Town and the other Windward communities have not retained a paper copy of the 1739 treaty. Yet, as much as they would like to own one, in their estimation the binding force of their treaty is not in the least diminished by the absence of a paper document. During my fieldwork, Maroons often stressed to me the primacy of the blood oath over the paper on which the treaty was written, as in the following typical statement, made by a Moore Town Maroon in 1991: "The peace made there was a blood covenant peace. The white man drank the Maroon blood, and the Maroon drank the white man's blood. It was a blood covenant .... That was Grandy [Nanny's] treaty. ... It was a blood covenant. Kojo [Cudjoe] and the rest signed a treaty, but Grandy made a blood covenant."[8]

The overwhelming emphasis in Maroon accounts on the method by which the treaties were rendered sacred and eternal stands in stark contrast to the British preoccupation with legal instruments and the material artifacts that preserve them, without which contractual agreements lose all binding force over time. What matters, from a British legal standpoint, is the precise wording of the text inscribed on the treaty documents, as well as any subsequent legal actions or technicalities that might have a bearing on current interpretations of this text. From this perspective, the question of what the Maroons may actually have thought they were entering into when they agreed to the peace is immaterial. Some would argue, in fact, that, given the absence of unambiguous written evidence, we will never know for sure whether a blood oath was indeed sworn between the Maroons and the representatives of the British colonial government who treated with them.

In the Guianas, by contrast, where present-day descendants of eighteenth-century Maroons also possess memories of sacred oaths made with European colonial governments, archival evidence supporting these oral traditions is abundant. In some cases, in fact, the written descriptions we have are so firm and detailed, and so closely resemble the Jamaican Maroon accounts of their own treaties, that they would seem to lend credence to the latter, even though they concern events that occurred several decades later, more than a thousand miles away, in different colonial settings. Comparisons such as these, across such wide spans of space and time, are less outlandish than they may at first appear when we recognize that the Guianese and Jamaican Maroons' ancestors originated more or less from the same cross-section of African peoples (though, of course, demographic fluctuations created somewhat different ethnic balances in the two places) and from shared roots fashioned rather similar Afro-Creole cultures. As we shall see, their common African heritage included sacred oath-taking procedures such as those just described and related forms of political legitimation, some of which have remained important to Maroons in both Jamaica and the Guianas up until today.

The Guianese case on which I focus here is that of the Aluku or Boni Maroons of French Guiana and Surinam, since they are the Guianese Maroon people I know best. As opposed to the other Maroon groups that originated in the Dutch colony of Surinam, the Aluku never made a lasting peace with the Dutch during the eighteenth century, deciding in the 1770s to move across the Surinamese border into French territory, where the majority of them have remained ever since.

In 1780, soon after their arrival in French Guiana, the Aluku received a visit from a Frenchman named Cadet, who had been sent to them, along with a delegation from the coast, on a mission of peace. Apprehensive over the possibility of a hinterland insurrection similar to the one that had plagued their Dutch neighbors in Surinam, the French colonial authorities in Cayenne took the initiative of treating with the Surinamese Maroons who had recently penetrated their territory. The French emissary Cadet was received at first with much suspicion. After threatening him and accusing him of acting as a spy for the French, the Aluku finally accepted the offer of peace. Cadet and the Aluku paramount chief Boni swore an oath of friendship, sealed with blood drawn from both their arms and mixed together in a calabash, from which both men drank. Boni's parting words, while shaking Cadet's hand, were, "May every last Frenchman who breaks this treaty perish" (Hurault 1960: 92; my translation).

A short time later, in 1782, a French priest named Nicolas Jacquemin was sent to the interior of French Guiana on an information-gathering mission. The earlier peace between the French and the Aluku had not yet been finalized by the colonial government, and when the priest arrived in their territory, he was asked by the Aluku to renew the previous oath. Father Jacquemin's description of the pact he made in 1782 with the great Aluku warrior and leader Boni deserves quoting at length:

> They [the Maroons] said that it would be necessary to cement the alliance with an oath commonly used among them; as I knew what this oath consisted of, I showed repugnance, saying that it wasn't necessary. They noticed this and said that if I felt repugnance, the person who was with me would do it, which he did in the following way. A negro put some water in a calabash and then lightly pricked Jacquet [Father Jacquemin's companion] on his foot and on his hand with the point of a knife and drew a drop of blood, which he put in the calabash. After this he did the same thing to the negro captain, then put in the said calabash a bit of ashes and earth and mixed it all together. Then the chief spoke, saying that this ceremony, this mixing of our blood with theirs, signified that we had become brothers, that we must always be as one with them, and they with us, making a thousand curses against those who would violate this pledge, wishing that they be anathema. Then my companion and the first captain moved forward into the center, put one knee on the ground facing each other and crossed the toes of their other feet. Then, in a leaf shaped like a small chalice, a negro took a bit of the mixture that was in the calabash and poured it twice into their mouths; and during the ceremony the chief had me rest an arm on my companion's shoulder while he did the same thing on that of his first

captain, firmly shaking my hand. Having seen the seriousness, the care, and the religious silence that they brought to this ceremony, I do not believe that they will ever break this pledge.[9]

For various reasons, the formal treaty with the French government that was to have been concluded after the emissaries returned to Cayenne was abandoned, and the negotiations between the Aluku and the French came to a halt. Not until some five decades later, long after the death of the paramount chief Boni, were the Aluku approached by another Frenchman on an apparent mission of peace. In 1835, the explorer Leprieur stumbled on an Aluku settlement while searching for the source of the Maroni River. Fearing for his life, Leprieur pretended to be an emissary of the colonial government in Cayenne, which he claimed wished to treat with the Aluku. Before leaving the area, he was compelled to swear an oath, which he later described to the French authorities as follows: "While I went to examine the place, they [the Aluku] deliberated and consequently proposed, as an inviolable sign of friendship, to draw a bit of blood from me so that, mixed with water, it would serve us as a drink, and that by this means we would become sacred to one another. A long time before, I had become acquainted with this method among the peoples of West Africa and as I knew that I would be inviolable to them, I very gladly went along with this tacit promise to do them no harm."[10] Once again, this oath proved to be fruitless, for Leprieur had acted entirely without government authorization. On his return to Cayenne, he was harshly disciplined for having entered into diplomatic negotiations under false pretenses, and the French, no longer considering the Aluku a serious threat, did not pursue the peace process he had set in motion.[11]

Although these failed peace agreements, consecrated with blood oaths, appear not to have left any traces in Aluku oral tradition, accounts of the successful treaty that was finally negotiated jointly by the Dutch and the French in 1860—the watershed event that gave lasting recognition to the de facto freedom the Aluku had won long before—have been passed down by word of mouth. Given what we have learned from written eyewitness descriptions of earlier attempts to make peace with the Aluku, it would seem rash to rule out the veracity of the following excerpt from an oral narrative about these events, despite the fact that it appears to be contradicted by at least one archival document:[12]

He [the Dutch peacemaker] said, "Stretch out your arm. We are making peace today. If I come to kill the Aluku in the future, God above must kill me; I must die. And also if I come there [to the Aluku territory] and then the Aluku kill me, God above must know what to do with the Aluku – the curse will remain."
Then he said, "Stretch out your arm."
And he [Waide, the Aluku representative] stretched out his

arm. Then the *bakaa* [white man] cut his arm here, "tjírik," with a razor. And he licked the blood.

He then said, "Papa Waide, you lick it too."

And he [Waide] licked it. Then Waide moved the [white] man's own arm toward him. And he spoke. Then he cut it too. And the bakaa licked it.

He said, "Waide, you lick it."

And he licked it.

And so they made peace.[13]

The various attempts made by the Aluku to commit European colonial authorities to long-term alliances by swearing their envoys to sacred oaths of friendship were hardly isolated incidents (even though French peace overtures such as those that led to the abortive episodes described earlier were few and far between). In fact, throughout their history the Aluku relied on the same or similar procedures when treating with other peoples, including their Maroon neighbors and local Amerindians; indeed, they made use of the same methods when forging internal alliances between the *lo*, or initial bands of runaways, that later were to develop into corporate matriclans and become the building blocks of the Aluku nation.

Wim Hoogbergen, in an exhaustive historical study of the Boni Maroon Wars, mentions many archival references to this phenomenon, showing that these sacred blood oaths were repeatedly used to forge alliances between the Aluku and those with whom they came in contact during their treks through the forest.[14] According to one source cited by Hoogbergen (1990: 153), the Aluku leader Boni swore oaths of this kind with Ndjuka Maroon allies on at least eight separate occasions.

Nor is documentary evidence of such procedures lacking for the other Guianese Maroon peoples.[15] There exists, for instance, an archival document that gives a detailed eyewitness account of the sacred oath that was sworn in conjunction with the Ndjuka Maroon treaty of 1760, for which the two Dutch negotiators, much to their displeasure, were obliged to donate their own blood (Hoogbergen 1990: 27–29; Scholtens 1994: 21). Hoogbergen's (1990: 28) summary of these transactions as recorded in the archives (including portions of the eyewitness description mentioned above) is rich in detail:

> After the whole treaty had been reviewed to the satisfaction of the planters, the Ndjuka demanded that the peace treaty be confirmed in their way as well. They asked for a clean piece of white linen. When the linen arrived, a Maroon chief took a razor and cut the left arm of both the white negotiators and the Maroon chiefs to draw blood. "When this was done, someone else came up with the linen cloth. After examining the arm to see whether the blood

was dripping sufficiently, we had to wipe off our arms ourselves, and then a third man came with a gourd of clean water, in which the linen cloth was washed and rinsed, and he did the same and swore that peace had been settled with the white men, they would never ever bear grudge against nor do any harm to the white people. And that, if they ever did any such thing or if they did not comply with all that had been promised and signed, this mixture of blood would bring death and damnation upon them. Whereupon Arabie [the Ndjuka paramount chief] followed him and subsequently everyone who had signed and we did the same, every person for himself. When this was done, a man whom we believed to be their priest cried out: the earth cannot bear those who have sworn falsely and do not keep their promise. Thereupon, they all made an extraordinary noise and started to shout hooray."

Today, more than 230 years later, Ndjuka oral traditions concerning this treaty, like those of the Jamaican Maroons, continue to center on the blood oath to which the European envoys were sworn, as in the following account narrated by the Ndjuka paramount chief, Gaanman Gazon Matodja, in 1992: "When the whites [bakaa] were coming to make peace with us, they [the Ndjuka ancestors] put a calabash there. . . . they cut themselves and drew blood, and poured it in. The whites cut themselves and drew theirs and put it in [too], in order to drink the oath [diingi sweli], so that we wouldn't fight anymore. We made peace. . . . we made peace with the whites by drinking our blood together. And so there was no more war."[16]

Well over a hundred years ago, a comparable oral tradition was recorded in writing by a literate Matawai Maroon, Johannes King. King's (1995: 243) nineteenth-century account of a treaty made between his Matawai ancestors and the Dutch roughly a century earlier, in the 1760s, is similar to those still told by Maroons from various groups today:[17]

A short time after [the Dutch made the 1762 treaty with the Saramaka], the government once more sent other whites to the Matawai people to make peace with them. Now the Matawai people received the whites amicably, and they made the same conditions [as the Saramaka had] with the whites. They cut their arms slightly, and took the blood and put it in a glass. The whites cut themselves and drew blood first; then the blacks cut themselves and drew blood, too. And they took the blood of the whites and the blood of the blacks and put both in a glass. Then they poured red wine into it. Then the whites swore on the blood of the blacks, and the blacks swore on the blood of the whites. And the whites drank the blood, and the blacks drank the whites' blood, too. And they all swore on their blood and said they were completely done with the fighting.[18]

The Saramaka Maroons, too, frequently resorted to such spiritual sanctions in their ongoing negotiations with the Dutch. Richard Price (1990: 296–97) writes that in the period following their own 1762 treaty, distributions of Dutch tribute to the Saramaka were routinely accompanied by a ceremony that included a sacred oath in which Dutch officials were required to participate, "a 'blood oath' that had become a standard part of this transaction, and which whites as well as Saramakas, Christians as well as heathen, accepted as a central symbolic expression of their new political relationship." The same was also true of both the Matawai and the Ndjuka through the eighteenth and early nineteenth centuries. During the 1830s and 1840s, when he was a child, the same Matawai Maroon quoted above, Johannes King, witnessed two such distributions of Dutch tribute among his own people.[19] Many years later, he recalled these in his memoirs: "All the way up till my, Johannes King's, own time, when I was a little boy, the government used to send and distribute presents to all three Maroon areas, Ndjuka, Saramaka, and Matawai. But by the time of the second distribution of gifts that I saw, I was already an older boy; and they drank the oath [*dringi sweri*] again. That was the last time the whites [*bakra*] and the Maroons [*boesi ningre*] drank a blood oath [*broedoe sweri*]" (King 1995: 244).[20]

As Price (1990: 297) shrewdly suggests (in a statement that is applicable not just to the Saramaka, but to all the Surinamese Maroon peoples), "One might almost say that, just as the whites succeeded in symbolically possessing the Saramakas by means of writing, the Saramakas succeeded in possessing the whites by means of the blood oath and similar rituals to which they subjected them." Indeed, the willingness of Europeans to submit to such blood oaths, which they viewed as repugnant, is tantamount to an admission, if only a temporary one, that they did not necessarily have the upper hand in the negotiations taking place—which may help explain the near-total absence of references to such oaths in the British colonial correspondence concerning the Jamaican Maroon treaties.[21]

Maroon Oaths in Social Context

If one treats the oaths sworn in conjunction with Maroon treaties as isolated instances, then the matter ends there; if, however, one views these acts in a broader sociocultural and historical context, a new range of meanings and connections emerges. This was revealed to me with particular immediacy when I myself was sworn to a sacred oath in the Jamaican Maroon community of Moore Town for the first time in December 1977. I had been invited to a Maroon ceremony known as

Kromanti Play, held for the purpose of healing a sick person from outside the community. Normally, any Kromanti Play that includes spirit possession is closed to non-Maroons. Since this ceremony was expected to involve possession, I was allowed to remain only on the condition that I submit to an ordeal that would last most of the night.[22] At the end of this test, I was sworn to an oath as follows:

> The *granfa* [possessed dancer] grasped my hand and pulled me a ways outside of the booth; my protector sidled up alongside of us, prepared to act as interpreter for me. The *granfa* thrust the cutlass into my two hands, and showed me a particular way to hold it. He then ordered me to raise it high over my head. While [I was] stretched in this position, he asked me what I called the one who lives up there [where the machete was pointed]. I considered saying "Yankipong Assasi" [a secret Kromanti name for the Supreme Being that I had recently been taught], but on second thought[,] thought "God" would be a wiser reply. This satisfied him. He spoke to me in a mixture of deep patois and Kromanti.
>
> Next he told me to swing my body down and thrust the cutlass into the earth. This I did three times [as specified], whereupon he grabbed the weapon back .... he asked me if I would like to know where he is buried, where his grave is. I said, "that's up to you," and when this was translated to him he seemed satisfied .... he picked up his machete, and through the interpreter, told me to hold my head up straight. Several times he brought the sharp side of the blade to my throat. Then he commanded me to open my mouth; he gently placed the blade inside, sharp side in, and called for something – which turned out to be sugar and water, as far as my taste could tell. He told me to tip my head back, and with the cutlass still in my mouth, he poured the sweet fluid down my throat.
>
> After removing the blade, he ran me over to the drummers and took hold of a clump of my hair, severing it with the cutlass as he danced. Keeping this in hand, he sat me back down – that is, after taking hold of my left hand and twirling me in typical Maroon fashion, back and forth. He then told me that he liked me, that I was his friend.[23]

What I had experienced, as I soon came to realize, was an attenuated version of an oath of incorporation. I had been symbolically transformed by this rite from a categorical enemy into a conditional friend.[24] From then on, I was allowed to remain unmolested during possessions by the particular Maroon spirit that had sworn me; I was now asked to participate actively in Kromanti ceremonies and was entrusted with a wide variety of information not normally divulged to outsiders. This practice of swearing non-Maroons, which is still mandatory today whenever circumstances call for the presence of an outsider at a serious Kromanti Play, would seem to be closely related to, if not actually descended from, the oaths used in pretreaty times to induct new recruits into Jamaican Maroon communities. Fragmentary written evidence of such oaths of incorporation has been preserved in a 1733 document containing the testimony of a captured Maroon, who told his interrogators that "they [the Windward Maroons] give encouragement for all sorts of negroes to join them, and oblige the men to be true to them by an oath which is held very sacred among the negroes, and those who refuse to take that oath, whether they go to them of their own accord or are made prisoners, are instantly shot to death" (Kopytoff 1976: 44; see also Hart 1985: 65; Campbell 1988: 50). A similar oath of incorporation appears to have been used by Surinamese Maroons to initiate new recruits into their ranks. Hoogbergen (1990: 55) provides one documented example involving a group of runaways known as the Tesisi Maroons who, after the destruction of their villages in an attack, were incorporated into the Ndjuka nation by means of a sacred oath. The Dutch authorities tried for several years to retrieve the missing runaways from their Ndjuka allies, but the Ndjuka kept their part of the oath and never turned them in.

And what of the specific form taken by the present-day Windward Maroon oath to which I myself was sworn? What do its key components – the machete raised to the sky and then thrust into the earth three times, the invocation of a higher power, and the specially prepared potion – tell us about its origins? A reasonable place to look for answers would be among the Akan peoples of West Africa, whose culture is known to have contributed much to the Creole cultures developed by both the Jamaican and the Surinamese Maroons. Indeed, in the Jamaican case, the Akan influence appears to have been preponderant, though many contributions were made by people from other parts of the continent. In any case, we need look no farther than the Akan to begin to see very suggestive correspondences.

Consider the following brief description by R. S. Rattray (1911: 87) of the standard method by which an Ashanti (Asante) chief swears an oath to his councillors to observe the laws of the land: "Standing before them, he unsheathes the ceremonial sword, the point of which he raises first to the sky, then lowers until it touches the ground . . . [this motion implying the words] *Gye Nyame, gye Asase* (Save God and Mother Earth, I have no equal)." Interestingly enough, the Windward Maroons of Jamaica, like the Ashanti, link this same gesture with God and the earth, whom they invoke with their own Akan-derived expression, "Yankipong Asasi." Equally interesting is Rattray's (ibid.: 102–3) description of the oath of allegiance taken by the Ashanti *Amanhene*, or paramount chiefs, in the presence of the king, the *Asante Hene*:

The King sat in the courtyard known as *Premoso* (the place of the cannons) with all his *Nsafohene* [war captains] and attendants. The bearer of the sacred *afona* (ceremonial sword) called *Mponponsuo* was sent to call the *Nkwankwa Hene* [the unconfirmed paramount chief], who was awaiting the summons in the room in the palace known as *dandwanu*. ... [The paramount chief] approached the King, naked to the waist, and slipped his sandals before mounting the raised dais. He was supported round the waist by attendants. The sword-bearer of the *Mponponsuo* was seated on the left, the bearers of the *Bosommuru afona* (ceremonial sword) upon the right. He now unsheathed the former sword, leaving the sheath in the sword-carrier's hands, immediately raising the point to the sky, then lowering it to the earth. He then placed the hand holding the sword behind his back and bent his head, upon which the King, who remained seated, lightly placed the sole of his left foot, saying as he did so: *Wo ye dom da, abosom nku wo* ('If you ever become my enemy may the gods slay you'). ... Having finished, he handed back the sword. The King shook hands with him, thanking him, and addressing him according to his *ntoro*.[25]

As for the section of the present-day Windward Maroon oath that requires the initiate to drink a sweet liquid, this bears some resemblance to the Ashanti ceremony called *abosom nom*, which Rattray (1923: 110) translates as "drinking the gods":

A small bottle called *abosom toa* (the gods' phial), containing the liquid to be drunk, was produced. This water is generally made potent by having been poured either over a god or gods or possibly over a stool or some other article having special properties as being the shrine of some spirit, human or divine; in the former case to invoke the power of the god, in the latter the assistance of the spirit of the dead. A little rum was added to the contents of the bottle. The mixture was then poured into a cup made by twisting cleverly together leaves of a tree called *adwin*. The priest, who was to drink, now advanced his right foot and upon top of it the Mkwankwa chief placed his left foot. ... The Mkwankwa chief then raised the cup of leaves three times to the priest's lips, until he had drained all the contents. ... The chief who had administered the draught, said: *Se wanka nokware a, abosom yi nkum wo!* ("If you do not speak the truth may these gods slay you!").

This "drinking the gods" belongs to the category of oath the Ashanti call *nsedie*. The corresponding verb, *di nsew*, meaning "to swear an oath," is defined by Rattray (1927: 215) as "to call upon some supernatural power to witness what has been said and to impose a supernatural sanction should the statement be false" (see also Mensah-Brown 1975: 153–55). This corresponds roughly to the Jamaican (Windward) Maroon category of oath known as *swiri* and the Aluku Maroon category called *sweli*, both terms derived from the English verb *to swear*.[26]

The Jamaican Maroon concept of *swiri* embraces not only the kind of oath that I underwent but also any rite performed to establish whether an individual is telling the truth about a specific matter, as in an accusation or a denial of theft, sorcery, or some other crime. This jural technique, backed by powerful spiritual sanctions, was widely used in Jamaica during the slavery era, not just in Maroon communities but on the plantations; there are many accounts in the historical literature of such oaths among the slave population, often involving the ingestion of a potion, which sometimes caused those who refused to admit their guilt to swell up and die a painful death.[27]

The cognate Aluku term, *sweli*, covers an even broader range of practices, all of them tightly woven into the fabric of Aluku society. Although the term denotes several different kinds of procedures, all of them entail the public invocation of some higher power, which is usually called on to witness, and in some cases to confirm or act on, the truth of an assertion. The practice known as *faya sweli* (literally, "swearing by fire"), for instance, includes several distinct kinds of divination: one variety makes use of an oracle called *askadjan*, which consists of a piece of fiber stretched between two stakes planted in the ground, across which the red-hot blade of a machete is passed; another, known as *kangaa*, involves a sharpened splinter attached to a parrot feather, which is prepared with other materials over a fire and then is pressed against the tongue of an individual to see if it easily pierces it.[28] Both of these ordeals are intended to establish the truth of statements made by those who submit to them, and both are perceived as guided by spiritual forces. In fact, whenever the veracity of a serious allegation or accusation is in question, the parties involved may decide to *go a sweli*, that is, to swear an oath or consult one or another kind of oracle, with the gods or ancestors as witness, so as to reveal the truth.

Then there is *sweli gi wan sama* (swearing an oath against someone) or *seni gadu* (sending the gods). Though considered a moral offense, this practice is sometimes used as a last resort when an individual is accused of a serious crime such as sorcery or theft. Such a person may publicly invoke some nonhuman agent – perhaps an ancestor, a god, or even the Supreme Being – swearing his or her innocence and asking that anyone guilty of making unjust accusations be struck with disaster. A varied repertoire of gestures, most of which are probably African in origin, goes with this act. One of the most common is known as *sutu kini gi wan sama* (falling to one's knees while swearing an oath against someone). Other gestures include hitting a machete against the ground, holding one's hand up with open palm facing God, and throwing a gourd or some other object to the ground to break it, while uttering a curse. Such oaths are taken very seriously, and the resulting social tensions may call for collective measures, including complex divination and spiritual purification. At the same time, any appeal to higher powers via this form of *sweli* is bound to have an impact on public judgment of the case at hand.

Another kind of *sweli* is associated with the invocation and praise of one's deceased parents, or of ancestors belonging to one's own or one's father's matriclan. When an Aluku man ardently declares, for example, *mi sweli fu mi tata Bose, Kawina nenge paansu!* (I swear in the name of my father, Bose, of the Kawina clan!), he is both showing confidence in and drawing on the power of his father's spirit and the spirits of his father's matrilineal ancestors. Such a pronouncement might be made, for instance, when a man is threatened or challenged or simply when he wishes to underscore his pride, his courage, or his integrity by calling on these ancestors as witnesses.[29]

Finally, we return to what the Ashanti call "drinking the gods." The Aluku equivalent is known as *diingi sweli* (literally, "drinking an oath"). In the Aluku case, the god to whom this oath is normally drunk is Tata Odun, the most important and (after the Supreme Creator, Masa Gadu) the most powerful spiritual being recognized by the Aluku. Tata Odun is said to have come over from Africa along with the ancestors and to have led them safely through the forest to their present location. Today he remains the overarching tribal deity of the Aluku, as he watches over the entire nation and enforces a strict code of morality that must be obeyed by all who reside within the Aluku territory. So closely is Tata Odun associated with the oaths drunk to him that he is also known as the Sweli Gadu (the "swearing god").[30]

In recent times, *diingi sweli* has occurred most prominently in conjunction with antisorcery activity. Although the potion is rarely drunk today, the oath to the Sweli Gadu was once a regular feature of Aluku life. Until three decades ago or so, the *gaanman*, or paramount chief, would decide every few years to submit the entire Aluku population to a test of sorcery.[31] No member of the Aluku nation was exempted from this ceremony, which lasted several days; a day was set aside for each clan so that its members could be sworn all at once. The oath was administered in the form of an herbal concoction that each individual was required to drink. By swallowing this mixture, the oath takers swore their fidelity not only to the moral code enforced by Tata Odun, the Sweli Gadu, but to the Aluku paramount chief himself, who served as the principal custodian of Odun's shrines and oracles. Foremost among Tata Odun's laws is the prohibition against using spiritual or magical power to harm other human beings. It is said that those who had secretly been acting as *wisiman*, or sorcerers, would perish soon after consuming the potion, having been struck down by the wrath of Tata Odun.[32] Interestingly enough, the Ashanti once practiced a similar ordeal, known as *we odom*, or "chew *odom*" (referring to the bark of the tree known as *odom* or *odum*). Rather than being chewed, says Rattray (1927: 31), "the poison is really drunk, the bark being pounded and mixed in water. Should the person accused of being a witch vomit the poison and recover, the accuser would be fined such an amount as to ruin the whole family."[33] Even today, an Aluku person accused by another of working sorcery, or *wisi*, may defiantly offer to *go a sweli* and drink this oath to Tata Odun to prove his innocence.

A very similar Sweli Gadu once played a very important part in the religious life of the Ndjuka Maroons, whose territory borders that of the Aluku. The Ndjuka Sweli Gadu reached its peak during the eighteenth and nineteenth centuries but has since been superseded by other deities. According to H. U. E. Thoden van Velzen and Wilhelmina van Wetering (1988: 58–59): "Sweli Gadu was of concern to all. . . . Humans could enter into contact with the deity by drinking its sacred potion (diingi Sweli; diingi Gadu; nyan buulu: literally drinking of Sweli; drinking of God; eating of blood) while swearing an oath. . . . In the eighteenth century, all Ndjuka adults, male and female, were obliged to take the oath. Only by participating in this ritual could one become a member of the national community. Allegiance was sworn to the Ndjuka nation and to one's fellows." The last part of this statement makes a particularly important point: becoming a member of the Ndjuka community was contingent on participation in this rite, which was seen in part as an oath of political allegiance. By swearing to the Sweli Gadu in this manner, as they did through the nineteenth century, Ndjukas continued to rely on essentially the same method of forging and renewing sacred bonds as their ancestors had used during the early years to build a new society out of fragmentary elements.[34] As we have seen, the same method is well attested in the literature on the ancestors of the Aluku, who used blood oaths at every turn to create and cement political and military alliances with groups with whom they came in contact in the forest or to incorporate new members into their ranks.

The oath to the Aluku Sweli Gadu, Tata Odun, has retained a vestige of the latter function even today, for it is still used, under certain circumstances, to integrate individuals from other Maroon societies, such as the Ndjuka and Saramaka, into Aluku society – though their incorporation is only partial. This happens in the following way: After a Ndjuka or a Saramaka individual has lived in the Aluku territory for a certain time and has become intimately involved in local social relations (sometimes as the spouse of an Aluku man or woman), he or she may be ordered by the paramount chief to *diingi sweli*, to drink an oath of allegiance to Tata Odun and the Aluku nation. While assuring the *gaanman* that this person has no evil intentions and has abided by Odun's moral code, this oath also has the effect of partially incorporating the individual who swears it into the Aluku community; the person is said to have "become Aluku" (*toon Aluku*) and in most contexts is treated as if he or she *were* Aluku.[35]

This means, among other things, being allowed to be present at, and to participate in, secret divination sessions with the main Odun oracle—an activity closed to all others, whether whites, French Guianese or Surinamese Creoles, Maroons from other groups, or any other outsiders (*doosei sama*). The policy of excluding non-Aluku people from consultations of the Sweli Gadu oracle is strictly enforced; the fact that it is waived for outsiders who have drunk an oath of incorporation to Tata Odun is seen by the Aluku as an important indication of the extent to which such persons have become recognized as functioning members of the Aluku community.

There can be little doubt that the principle of creating and consecrating social and political bonds by means of sacred oaths is part of the African heritage of Maroons in both Jamaica and the Guianas. In the literature on the Akan of Africa, such oaths are mentioned in a wide variety of contexts and have been shown to play an important role in the political process at all levels of society, ranging from the humblest village to the most powerful kingdom. In fact, sacred oaths of allegiance resembling those employed by Maroons in the Americas appear to have been integral to Akan statecraft throughout the history of empire building in this region. To take a prime example, the political incorporation of newly conquered peoples and territories into the Ashanti state, on which the process of imperial expansion depended, was accomplished through sacred oaths of allegiance binding the conquered to the conqueror through hierarchical links. Less powerful Akan states relied on the same methods, sometimes even using them to break free of Ashanti hegemony by forming new alliances with neighboring peoples. D. J. E. Maier, in a study of religion and the politics of state building in nineteenth-century Ghana, provides ample evidence of this. Her account of the ever-shifting nineteenth-century alliance that became known as the Bron Confederation leaves little doubt as to the centrality of sacred oath taking in the political process among the Akan peoples: "The Bron Confederation was bound by an oath based on the Dente shrine and the ultimate sanction or retribution for a member betraying the alliance was the religious wrath of the god Dente" (Maier 1983: 106). The Aluku, who have their own Dente, known as Tata Odun, would be quick to grasp the religious foundations of the Bron Confederation, so similar to the sacred set of Sweli Gadu oracles that bind their own semiautonomous clans together into a unified polity under a single paramount chief.

By emphasizing Akan traditions of oath taking, I certainly do not wish to imply a simple, unilineal derivation from these; nor do I wish to minimize the importance and similarity of oath-taking procedures in other African societies. Akan traditions simply seem a good place to begin, given the many well-documented Akan contributions to the cultures of both Jamaican and Guianese Maroons, as well as the amount of attention that has been paid to oaths in the literature on Akan peoples.[36] But we can be sure that other African peoples contributed their own understandings to this area of Maroon culture, as they did in other spheres. That both Jamaican Maroon and Aluku oaths represent syncretic blends of specific features whose origins lie in several different parts of the African continent seems certain. Even a cursory glance at the literature on other African peoples shows that sacred oaths generally similar to those of the Akan are to be found across a wide cross-section of the continent. Broadly similar oath-taking traditions have been attested, for instance, among such widely separated peoples as the Bakongo of central Africa and the Wachagga of East Africa (see Jacobson-Widding 1979: 138–39; Moore 1978: 192–93). It was the shared, general concepts that underlie such widespread traditions—for instance, the understanding that social relationships, political alliances included, ultimately derive their moral legitimacy from a higher spiritual plane—that provided the Maroons' ancestors with common ground on which to build their societies. In the making of treaties between Maroons and Europeans, on the other hand, there may have been less common ground to build on than either side appreciated.[37]

Conclusion: The Spirit of the Treaties

In concluding treaties with European colonial powers in their own manner, Maroons were both swearing by the past – drawing on the legitimating power of their African gods and ancestors – and swearing to the future, by endorsing the new life of peace and prosperity that these pacts promised. From the Maroons' perspective, the sacred basis of the treaties has remained unchanged, partly because oath-taking procedures similar to those used during the eighteenth century remain embedded in Maroon religion and social practice. This is particularly true of Guianese Maroons, with their various Sweli Gadu (or in the Saramaka case, Sóói-Gádu) oracles and associated oaths. Thus it should come as no surprise that Guianese Maroons are every bit as vehement as Jamaican Maroons in their insistence on the immutability of their treaties. According to Richard Price (1990: 343): "Saramakas, like their Maroon counterparts in Jamaica . . . have continued to see the treaty as a sacred charter and have refused to believe that it could be fundamentally altered. The whitefolks' various ultimatums, sometimes couched in legalistic language, have never been understood by Saramakas as more than arbitrary and transitory words."

To postindependence governments, in contrast, the treaties often appear as little more than obsolete colonial documents whose only interest is historical. They are to be read, if at all, legalistically and literally, with the assumption that the understandings reached between Maroons and the colonial government in the distant past amount to what is seen on the page, nothing more and nothing less.[38] Given the many legal changes that have occurred in Surinam since the eighteenth century, some of them in apparent conflict with specific clauses of the treaty, it is assumed that the entire agreement represented by the document has long since been rendered invalid.[39] I again quote Richard Price (1995: 467) on the view from Surinam: "There is a long history of attempts by the colonial, and then national, elite in Paramaribo to abrogate *unilaterally* the understandings in the 18th-century treaties between the Dutch crown and the Maroons. Learned interpretations of various Surinam constitutions and the status of the treaties—all offered, of course, by non-Maroons—consistently minimized Maroon rights."

The evidence suggests that for Maroons, in both Jamaica and the Guianas, the spirit of their treaties has always been at least as important as the specific provisions spelled out in writing. Embodied in this spirit is a complex cluster of ideas concerning various facets of the Maroons' continuing right to self-determination, backed by the sacred guarantee of a sworn oath.[40] As we have seen, the sanctity of these original oaths has not diminished in recent years. Until the states with which Maroons share their territories show a willingness to come to terms with the *spirit* of the treaties, and not just the one-sided European language in which these treaties were recorded on paper by the colonizers against whom the Maroons' ancestors struggled, the potential for serious misunderstanding will remain. As Zips (in press), commenting on the legal ramifications of the Jamaican case, has recently warned, "The views of the Maroon administration and the Jamaican state on [the treaties] are highly perspectival, but should be both taken into consideration if peaceful relations are the overall aim" (in press). He goes on to note that, to date, "the Maroon perspective has not been seriously examined and [has been] constantly overlooked in legal and constitutional matters" (ibid.; see also Kopytoff 1973: 278–81).

Judging from recent events in Surinam, where the National Army spent a good part of the 1980s fighting Maroons from all groups in a brutal civil war (Thoden van Velzen 1990; Price 1995), or in Jamaica, where Maroons have recently demanded special representation in the Parliament and Senate and have raised their voices against their exclusion from the process of constitutional reform (Anonymous 1988; Anonymous 1991), the time may be ripe for a new round of sacred oaths.[41] The question is, With whom, if anyone, will Maroons be able to swear this time around?[42]

NOTES

1 Queen Elizabeth's visit to Jamaica in 1994 was not the first visit by British royalty to which Maroons reacted by requesting special involvement. On Tuesday, 3 November 1953, for example, the *Daily Gleaner* reported that "the Maroons of Accompong have sent a letter to the Colonial Secretary requesting Central Government to send them a train or diesel to convey them to Kingston on Thursday, November 26, so that they may join with the other people of the island in welcoming Her Majesty the Queen" (Anonymous 1953).

2 Unless otherwise noted, all the ethnographic data on present-day Jamaican Maroons presented in this article are derived from my field research among the Maroons of Moore Town, Scot's Hall, and Accompong, Jamaica (1977–78, 1991); the data on present-day Aluku Maroons were gathered during my subsequent fieldwork among the Aluku in both French Guiana and Surinam (1983–87, 1990, 1991).

3 For instance, on the basis of this archival fragment (and apparently no other contemporaneous written evidence), the foremost present-day historian of the Jamaican Maroons, Mavis Campbell (1988: 115), concludes that "the oath in question is the famous Ashanti oath – also performed during the Dutch treaties with their Maroons in Surinam later. It involved the drawing of blood from both the white officers and the Maroon leaders, into which rum was poured, and this mixture was drunk by both parties. It is for this reason that the Maroons to this day refer to their Treaty as the 'blood treaty.' " Reading between the lines of the same archival fragment, Richard Hart (1985: 104) comes to a similar conclusion: "Whilst making no direct reference to the min-gling of blood in the solemnisation of the treaty, a ritual which would no doubt have been regarded as too barbaric for the king's representative to have indulged in, Guthrie [the British negotiator] said enough to lend some credence to Maroon oral tradition."

4 Tape recording of interview with Thomas Rowe, Accompong, 7 January 1991. I have translated this passage, like all the excerpts from Jamaican oral narra-tives that follow, from Jamaican Creole into a register very close to standard English to make it comprehensible to a general readership.

5 A few years later, in 1943, Richard Hart encountered the same tradition dur-ing a visit to Accompong. As he later wrote, "Maroon tradition has it that the signatories [to the Leeward Maroon treaty] also took a solemn oath 'in the Cromanti fashion,' by the mingling of their blood" (Hart 1985: 104). See also Williams 1938: 389.

6 Tape recording of interview with Ruth Lindsay, Moore Town, 1 February 1991.

7 Tape recording of interview with Hardie Stanford, Moore Town, 7 February 1991.

8 Tape recording of interview with John Minott, Brownsfield, 6 February 1991. In fact, even the Accompong Maroons, who *do* possess a paper copy of their treaty, consider its importance secondary to that of the blood oath. As Mann Rowe, secretary of the Accompong Maroons, told a visiting journalist in 1972: "Our treaty is no scrap of paper. Ours was a blood treaty. Cudjoe made the white officers Guthrie and Ellis inject [*sic*] from the veins, blood, right here. . . . They catch it in an alabaster cup, put in some rum, and they drank it. So our treaty is in blood in the name of God the Father forever and ever AH-MEN. We not only signed our treaty, we drank it" (Dougherty 1972).

9 Nicolas Jacquemin, "Journal de mon voyage chez les Indiens et les Nègres Réfugiés sur nos terres, fait en décembre 1782," reproduced in Hurault 1960: 98–101 (my translation).

10 Leprieur, "Rapport de Leprieur, s. d. joint à une dépêche du gouverneur du le Octobre 1836," reproduced in Hurault 1954: 132–34 (my translation).

11 One more incident of this kind did take place in 1839, when the French biolo-gist and explorer Charles Couy swore a blood oath with a small group of Alukus and Amerindians he met in the forest, promising that he would try to persuade the authorities in Cayenne to conclude a peace treaty with the Aluku (Hurault 1960: 121; Hoogbergen 1990: 193).

12 According to one official report on the treaty concluded between the Dutch, the French, and the Aluku in the village of Pobiansi (Providence) on November 18,

1860, "a proposal by the Aluku to ratify the treaty by the drinking of the *soï* [*sweli*], or oath, in the traditional manner was rejected by the commission" (Scholtens 1994: 32; my translation). Even if this account is accurate, the possibility remains that one or more oaths were sworn by some of the parties involved at an earlier stage of the negotiations, perhaps days or weeks before the final treaty was concluded. I am unaware of any other evidence in the archives that might corroborate Aluku oral accounts describing a blood oath in connection with this 1860 treaty. In her detailed summary of the events surrounding the treaty, de Groot (1977: 68–81) mentions no such oath.

13 From a tape-recorded interview with Kapiten Tobu, Komontibo, French Guiana, 18 August 1990 (my translation from the Aluku). The fact that it is the European peacemaker in this account, and not the Aluku, who initiates and performs the first part of the blood oath may have to do with the complex history of relations between the Aluku and their more powerful Ndjuka Maroon neighbors, who annexed the Aluku territory in the 1790s. In the larger narrative of which this is a part, the Dutch protagonist has just gone against the wishes of the Ndjuka people (who consider the Aluku their subjects) by meeting with Waide, the Aluku envoy, in secret. Under the circumstances, the white man needs to impress on Waide in dramatic fashion his sincerity, since the success of the treaty will depend on the Europeans' readiness to stand up to the objections of the Ndjuka and their willingness to help the Aluku break free of Ndjuka rule. From an Aluku perspective, the leading role taken by the Dutch negotiator in this narrative, and his eagerness to perform the oath (with which he is already familiar from previous negotiations between the Dutch and the Ndjuka), fit this particular historical context.

14 For descriptions of several such instances of Aluku oath taking, see Hoogbergen 1990: 80, 113, 160–61, 165, 172. Additional examples can be found in Hoogbergen 1985: 186, 244, 298–99.

15 References to documents describing the swearing of sacred oaths as part of the final treaties made between the Ndjuka, the Saramaka, and the Matawai, on the one hand, and the Dutch, on the other, may be found, for example, in de Groot 1969: 8; 1977: 11; Scholtens 1994: 21, 23, 39; Price 1983a: 173; 1983b: 164, 186; 1990: 112, 306.

16 From a tape recording made at the Festival of American Folklife, Washington, D.C., 27 June 1992, during a narrative session that formed part of the program "Creativity and Resistance: Maroon Culture in the Americas" (my translation from the Ndjuka). This recording is archived at the Center for Folklife Programs and Cultural Studies, Smithsonian Institution, Washington, DC (cassette no. SI-FP-1992-CT-178).

17 Although King's account might refer to the renewal, among the Matawai in 1763, of the 1762 treaty originally made with the Saramaka tribe (of which the Matawai people were then still considered a part), it seems probable that it actually describes the final, separate peace concluded with the Matawai in 1769 (after they had split from the Saramaka), bringing to an end the hostilities that had broken out between them and the Dutch in the years immediately after the first two peace agreements. Yet another possibility, however, is that it refers to an earlier, less formal oath sworn with the Matawai in 1767 as part of the initial peace negotiations leading up to the definitive 1769 treaty; the drinking of this oath in 1767—in which Saramakas, Matawais, and a Dutch colonial official participated—is documented in the archives (Price 1990: 112). See de Beet and Sterman 1981: 10; Price 1990: 79–116; Scholtens 1994: 24.

18 My translation from the Sranan. King's (1995: 240–46) writings also include descriptions, based on oral tradition, of the colonial treaties earlier concluded

among the Ndjuka and Saramaka Maroons; in both cases, these descriptions mention blood oaths.

19 According to de Beet and Sterman (1981: 10), the Dutch government last distributed presents to the Matawai in 1849. This, as well as King's likely birth around 1830, allows us to date the events described in this account to the late 1830s or the 1840s.

20 My translation from the Sranan.

21 Equally interesting in this regard is the ritualistic test of good faith that the Dutch negotiators were required to undergo when they came to conclude the peace treaty with the Ndjuka Maroons in 1760. According to a contemporary writer, "Each of the [Dutch] delegates was obliged to sleep with one of the most prominent Negro women during their stay, in order to be more assured of the Peace, and because their confidence in the white men would thus be considerably increased" (Hartsinck 1770: 798; cited in de Groot 1969: 11). Such reports raise serious questions about the extent to which Europeans controlled the proceedings during peace negotiations with Maroons.

22 A portion of this ordeal is briefly described in Bilby 1981.

23 Kenneth Bilby, Field Journal, Moore Town, entry for 16 December 1977.

24 Daniel Schafer (1973: 232) describes a somewhat similar rite of "initiation" that he was made to undergo during a Kromanti ceremony in the Windward Maroon community of Scot's Hall in 1971.

25 It is worth noting that Jamaican Maroons refer to the machete that they use in swearing oaths (as well as in other contexts) with an Akan-derived word, *afana* (which Rattray writes as *afona*). This word belongs to the ritual language that Maroons call Kromanti. See Bilby 1981: 63, 94.

26 The Jamaican Maroon word *swiri* belongs to a distinct English-lexicon creole once spoken by Maroons and used today only by Windward Maroon *fete-man* (mediums) when they are possessed by Maroon ancestors. This is separate from the ritual language that Maroons call Kromanti. See Bilby 1983: 42, 77.

27 The historical literature is also full of references to the use of sacred blood oaths by the organizers of slave rebellions in Jamaica and other parts of the Caribbean in order to ensure the fidelity of participants (see, e.g., Schuler 1970: 383–84). After emancipation, such oaths continued to be used among the Jamaican peasantry for similar purposes (sometimes in forms influenced by Christianity). For instance, Paul Bogle, who led the Morant Bay rebellion in 1865, repeatedly swore his followers to oaths, performing ceremonies that sometimes combined kissing the Bible with the administering of "a dram of rum and gunpowder which they drank"; and an archival document reports that during the rebellion a "coloured man" suspected of disloyalty was asked to take part in a mutual tasting of blood "as a pledge" by one of Bogle's soldiers, who had found him in hiding and brought him in (Heuman 1994: 6, 19, 80–83). One of the most important "national legends" of the Haitian people— the "ceremony at Bois Caïman"—revolves around such a sacred oath (Hoffman 1990; Geggus 1991). According to one version of the story, only days before the Haitian Revolution broke out, a Jamaican-born slave leader named Boukman Dutty, together with an African-born slave priestess and a number of coconspirators, drank the blood of a sacrificial pig and swore an oath of vengeance against the whites. Although "there is absolutely no reliable historical basis for the story at all" (Mintz and Trouillot 1996: 138), its prominence in the Haitian collective imagination says much about the cultural weight still carried by the concept of sacred oaths in this African Caribbean society.

28 The *kangaa* ordeal, a version of which is also performed by Saramaka Maroons, appears to be traceable to the eighteenth-century kingdom of Benin. See Price 1990: 373–74.

29 Less frequently, an individual may also swear by his mother or his matriclan, as in, for example, *mi sweli fu mi mama Analia fu Dipelu paansu!* (I swear in the name of my mother, Analia, of the Dipelu clan).

30 For further background on Tata Odun, see Hurault 1961: 195–98. See also Bilby 1990: 200–203, 348–49, 359.

31 This collective antisorcery oath was discontinued during the latter days of Paramount Chief Difu's reign, in the 1960s. However, the current paramount chief, who took office in 1992, has publicly indicated that he plans to revive the practice.

32 A similar test of sorcery has been documented among Saramaka Maroons during the eighteenth century. Among them, when a person guilty of sorcery drank the potion, he would swell up and die (Price 1990: 374). For detailed discussions of sorcery/witchcraft among the Ndjuka Maroons, whose concepts are very similar to those of the Aluku, see Thoden van Velzen and van Wetering 1988 and van Wetering 1996.

33 The Akan name of this tree, *odum*, is most likely the source of the name of the Aluku "swearing god" known as [Tata] Odun.

34 The same was true of the ancestors of the Paramaka Maroons. According to the anthropologist John Lenoir: "To mark the formation of the fugitive community, all members had to drink an oath upon the Swelie. Breach of the oath through disloyalty to the group or betrayal of any other member would result in certain death by an act of God. . . . As a cult oracle of the Chief, it became a symbol of the origin and unity of the people and guarded against internal dissension" (cited in Thoden van Velzen and van Wetering 1988: 407).

35 A rather similar ceremony exists among the Maroons of Scot's Hall, Jamaica, where, according to Daniel Schafer (1973: 234), a certain "dance is held to initiate outsiders who have married Maroon women and wish to live within the village. . . . Today if an outside man marries a Maroon woman, moves into the village, and wishes to 'buy himself in,' he must pay a 'vooten' [fee] and go through an ordeal. . . . The purpose of the ordeal is to impress on the initiate: 'not to talk what you drink.' " Schafer (ibid.: 236) also claims to have been "made an honorary Maroon" himself, as part of a similar rite in the Jamaican Maroon village of Charles Town.

36 Aside from those sources on the Akan already cited, one might mention, for instance, Field 1960: 89. See also Debrunner 1959: 140.

37 It would be interesting to carry out a careful comparison of the Maroon case with others from different parts of the world. Roger Abrahams is currently at work on a study of the symbolic dimensions of treaty-making between American Indians and Europeans in North America. After reading the draft of this article, he commented that "the similarities are more striking than the differences, insofar as there is ceremonial elaboration in both areas, in which the vocabulary of continuing personal obligation is derived from both groups, but understood differently by each" (personal communication, 6 November 1996).

38 At least one historian, Carey Robinson, has admitted that the final versions of the Jamaican treaties that have come down to us on paper may not represent perfectly accurately what the British emissaries and the Maroons actually agreed to. Robinson's (1969: 51–52) astute observation deserves repeating here: "Guthrie [who signed for the British] and his witnesses had come well prepared to deceive and dissemble. What they put in spoken words to the tired Maroon chief under the cotton tree at Petty River Bottom on that first day of March in 1739 was probably quite different from what they eventually wrote on paper."

39 This tendency to judge entire treaties invalid on the basis of technicalities (such

as the fact that certain clauses may contain anachronisms) was manifested, for example, in the constitutional debates at the time of Surinamese independence in 1975. During one exchange, "Minister Hoost declared that the 18th-century treaties would henceforth lose their validity 'as they restricted both the Bush Negroes' and other Surinamers' movements.' And he proclaimed that since 'the Government had long ago ceased to restrict the movement of Bush Negroes out of their protected areas, it would not be in the Bush Negroes' interests to have the treaties enforced' " (Price 1995: 467). A strikingly similar position has been taken by some in Jamaica. One editorial in the leading newspaper there, for instance, offered the following snide commentary: "If the [Maroon] people of Scott's Hall [sic] make a practice of taking 'hogs, fowls, or any other kind of stock or provision' for sale outside the area, without some official pass, they are infringing the 'treaty.' That valuable document requires the Windward Maroons, on such occasions, to have 'a ticket from under the hand of one or more of the white men residing with them.' . . . If the inhabitants of Scott's Hall insist on what appears to us the barren privilege of not selling their produce without special permission, they will no doubt be able to make themselves popular figures in St. Mary [parish] by distinguishing themselves sharply in this way from everybody else" (Anonymous 1959). Another editorial had made a similar argument a few years earlier, asserting that the document signed by Cudjoe was "subject to modification despite the form 'forever hereafter' used in the actual Treaty. It was soon recognised . . . that the terms of the Treaty, which restricted the crops they might grow and the animals they might rear, threatened them with extinction and step by step [they] were granted other rights and privileges in an endeavour to assist them . . . Thus [because of this, as well as later legislation by the British government] the last lingering trace of the Treaty has long since disappeared forever" (Anonymous 1956). More recently, the Inter-American Court of Human Rights, in hearing a case brought by Saramaka Maroon plaintiffs against the government of Surinam, fell back on the same kind of reasoning. "The commission's argument that the Surinam military had violated Saramaka territory," writes Richard Price (1995: 461), "was ruled out on a peculiar technicality. Because, the court ruled, the 1762 treaty between the Saramakas and the Dutch crown, which granted Saramakas their freedom, included articles specifying the return of fugitive slaves, and since slavery is prohibited by every modern international human rights convention, 'an agreement of this kind cannot be invoked before an international court of human rights,' and all claims based on this sacred Saramaka document are moot before this court." "One might wonder," continues Price (ibid.) parenthetically, "whether such reasoning would not make the U.S. Constitution invalid, as it too discusses similar returns of fugitive slaves between states."

40 In recent times, the Maroons' right to self-determination has repeatedly been challenged, in both Surinam and Jamaica, with little consideration given by the government of either country to the question of whether the treaties were violated in the process. A very serious threat to Surinamese Maroon autonomy is currently being posed by multinational companies petitioning the central government for vast logging and mining concessions in the interior of the country, where the Maroons' traditional territories are located. Though they have inhabited these lands for more than two centuries, the Maroons themselves have been almost entirely excluded from the negotiations between these companies and the government (Colchester 1995; Lee 1995). Understandably, many Maroons fear that the economically strapped government, in violation of the treaties, intends to confiscate their lands for exploitation by these multinationals. In Jamaica, no such imminent threat of expropriation is apparent.

Yet the anthropologist Chris de Beet (1992: 192), who investigated land rights in Accompong in the 1980s, reports that "in the collective memory, questions of land rights in the past indicate that, at this point, one must remain on one's guard against the government, which has little interest in maintaining an enclave of Maroons" (my translation). The Maroons' wariness of the government continues to be fueled by occasional tirades against Maroon autonomy in the Jamaican press, such as the following: "I think the time has come—and many people with whom I have talked Maroons agree—when a hard look should be taken at the Maroons. Their lands should be taken under the Crown, surveyed and sold to those Maroons who wish to buy and to non-Maroons needing land. . . . Enough of Maroon mythology or Maroon lore" (Strong 1974).

41 The fact that the Maroon question was not dealt with in the constitution that took effect when Jamaica became independent in 1962 has since been used to argue against the validity of the treaties after independence. One opponent of Maroon autonomy, for instance, asserted that "the Maroons have no legal status in Independent Jamaica. Their treaties were signed with the British Government of long ago not with the Jamaican Government as now constituted. Those treaties, giving them lands and a degree of autonomy, were not ratified when Independence came—they were not even discussed when the Constitution was being drafted – and have not been renegotiated since. They are null and void, in my opinion. So the Maroons have become like any other Jamaican citizen, no more, no less, subject to the same laws and punishments, subject to the payment of taxes on the lands they occupy. Their autonomy, such as it was, is now a myth" (Strong 1974). In Parliament, Jamaican senator Dudley Thompson similarly argued that "there was no specific mention of the Maroon Treaty in the Constitution . . . [and] the Maroons did not make out any case for separate consideration as a minority group during the time the Constitution was being made up . . . [Thus] there was no difference or distinction whatever in the rights and obligations as defined by the law of the land between the persons residing in the former Maroon settlements and those of any other Jamaican subject" (Anonymous 1973). (One student of Jamaican law has since concluded that this position is "open to serious questioning" [Clarke 1974: 9–10].) Given such treatment in the past, it is hardly surprising that, as a recent article reported, "the Maroons feel that they were cheated out of their rights by not being recognised in the 1962 Constitution and are now seeking to correct that" (Anonymous 1991). Indeed, "so strong is their feeling on the matter that Lt. Oscar John Williams [an officer of the Scot's Hall Maroons] indicated their intention to 'stage demonstrations' and if necessary to draw 'international attention' to their cause if they are sidestepped this time around" (ibid.).

42 According to one source (Bakker et al. 1993: 157), the recent civil war in Surinam ended only after the two most important antagonists in the conflict—military dictator Desi Bouterse (a Creole) and Jungle Commando leader Ronnie Brunswijk (a Ndjuka Maroon)—had come together to perform a *sweri* ritual much like those described earlier in these pages. (*Sweri* is the Sranan-language term for the Creole [coastal Afro-Surinamese] equivalent of what Alukus and Ndjukas call *sweli*.) This ceremony of reconciliation is supposed to have taken place some time in 1991 (ibid.), whereas the formal peace treaty that "officially" ended the war—to which the Maroon paramount chiefs were signatories—did not go on paper until August 1992 (Price 1995: 459). In any case, an oath between Bouterse and Brunswijk would be considered binding only on themselves as individuals, since Brunswijk has never been recognized by traditional Ndjuka political and religious authorities as a legitimate representative of the Ndjuka people as a whole.

REFERENCES

Adjaye, Joseph K.
1994 Jamaican Maroons: Time and Historical Identity. *In* Time in the Black Experience. Joseph K. Adjaye, ed. Pp. 161–81. Westport, CT: Greenwood.
Anonymous
1953 Maroons Would Like to Welcome the Queen. Daily Gleaner, 3 November.
1956 The Maroons. Daily Gleaner, 16 March.
1959 Strange Privilege. Daily Gleaner, 14 September.
1973 Maroons Have No Special Rights under Jamaican Laws. Daily Gleaner, 10 February.
1988 Maroons Seek Voice in Parliament. Daily Gleaner, 19 March.
1991 Maroons on the 'Warpath' . . . over Constitution. Boulevard News (Kingston), 2–15 May.
1994 Maroons Upset over Not Meeting Queen. Daily Gleaner, 5 March.
Bakker, Eveline, Leo Dalhuisen, Maurits Hassankhan, and Frans Steegh
1993 Geschiedenis van Surinam: Van Stam tot Staat. Zutphen: Walburg Pers.
Bilby, Kenneth
1981 The Kromanti Dance of the Windward Maroons of Jamaica. Nieuwe West-Indische Gids 55: 52–101.
1983 How the "Older Heads" Talk: A Jamaican Maroon Spirit Possession Language and Its Relationship to the Creoles of Surinam and Sierra Leone. New West Indian Guide 57: 37–88.
1990 The Remaking of the Aluku: Culture, Politics, and Maroon Ethnicity in French South America. Ph.D. diss., Johns Hopkins University.
Campbell, Mavis
1988 The Maroons of Jamaica, 1655–1796: A History of Resistance, Collaboration, and Betrayal. Granby, MA: Bergin and Garvey.
Clarke, Michael B.
1974 The Maroons of Jamaica – A Socio-Legal Exposition. Unpublished MS, National Library of Jamaica, Kingston.
Colchester, Marcus
1995 Forest Politics in Surinam. Utrecht: International Books.
Cooper, Archibald
n.d. Econ. Ms. Accom. Seminar. Archibald Cooper MSS, West India Reference Library, University of the West Indies, Mona, Jamaica.
de Beet, Chris
1992 Een staat in een staat: Een vergelijking tussen de Surinaamse en Jamaicaanse Marrons. Oso 11: 186–93.
de Beet, Chris, and Miriam Sterman
1981 People in Between: The Matawai Maroons of Surinam. Meppel: Krips Repro.
Debrunner, Hans W.
1959 Witchcraft in Ghana: A Study on the Belief in Destructive Witches and Its Effects on the Akan Tribes. Kumasi: Presbyterian Book Depot.
de Groot, Silvia W.
1969 Djuka Society and Social Change. Assen: Van Gorcum.
1977 From Isolation towards Integration: The Surinam Maroons and Their Colonial Rulers. The Hague: Martinus Nijhoff.

Dougherty, Richard E.
1972   Sons of the Rebel Slaves. New York Times, 3 December.
Field, M. J.
1960   Search for Security: An Ethno-Psychiatric Study of Rural Ghana. London: Faber and Faber.
Geggus, David
1991   The Bois Caïman Ceremony. Journal of Caribbean History 25: 41–57.
Hart, Richard
1985   Blacks in Rebellion: Slaves Who Abolished Slavery. Kingston: University of the West Indies, Institute of Social and Economic Research.
Hartsinck, Jan Jacob
1770   Beschrijving van Guiana of de Wilde Kust in Zuid-Amerika. Amsterdam: Gerrit Tielenburg.
Heuman, Gad
1994   "The Killing Time": The Morant Bay Rebellion in Jamaica. London: Macmillan.
Hoffman, François
1990   Histoire, mythe et idéologie: La cérémonie du Bois-Caïman. Etudes créoles 13: 9–34.
Hoogbergen, Wim
1985   De Boni-Oorlogen, 1757–1860: Marronage en Guerilla in Oost-Surinam. (Bronnen voor de Studie van Afro-Amerikaanse Samenlevingen in de Guyana's 11.) Utrecht: University of Utrecht, Centrum voor Caraïbische Studies.
1990   The Boni Maroon Wars in Surinam. Leiden: E. J. Brill.
Hurault, Jean
1954   Documents pour servir à l'histoire des Noirs Réfugiés Bonis de la Guyane Française. Unpublished manuscript, Centre ORSTOM, Cayenne, French Guiana.
1960   Histoire des Noirs Réfugiés Boni de la Guyane Française (d'après les documents de sources françaises). Revue française d'histoire d'outremer 47: 76–137.
1961   Les Noirs Réfugiés Boni de la Guyane Française. Dakar: IFAN.
Jacobson-Widding, Anita
1979   Red-White-Black as a Mode of Thought: A Study of Triadic Classification by Colours in the Ritual Symbolism and Cognitive Thought of the Peoples of the Lower Congo. Uppsala: Almqvist and Wiksell.
King, Johannes
1995   Skrekiboekoe: Visioenen en Historische Overleveringen van Johannes King. Chris de Beet, ed. (Bronnen voor de Studie van Afro-Surinam 17.) Utrecht: University of Utrecht.
Kopytoff, Barbara Klamon
1973   The Maroons of Jamaica: An Ethnohistorical Study of Incomplete Polities, 1655–1905. Ph.D. diss., University of Pennsylvania.
1976   The Development of Jamaican Maroon Ethnicity. Caribbean Quarterly 22 (2–3): 33–50.
1979   Colonial Treaty as Sacred Charter of the Jamaican Maroons. Ethnohistory 26: 45–64.

Lee, Gary
  1995   Proposal to Log Suriname's Rain Forest Splits the Needy Nation. Wash-
         ington Post, 13 May.
Maier, D. J. E.
  1983   Priests and Power: The Case of the Dente Shrine in Nineteenth-Century
         Ghana. Bloomington: Indiana University Press.
Mensah-Brown, A. Kwodwo
  1975   The Nature of Akan Native Law: A Critical Analysis. Conch 7 (1–2): 137–
         64.
Mintz, Sidney, and Michel-Rolph Trouillot
  1995   The Social History of Haitian Vodou. In Sacred Arts of Haitian Vodou.
         Donald J. Cosentino, ed. Pp. 123–47. Los Angeles: UCLA, Fowler Museum
         of Cultural History.
Moore, Sally Falk
  1978   Law as Process: An Anthropological Approach. London: Routledge and
         Kegan Paul.
Price, Richard
  1983a First-Time: The Historical Vision of an Afro-American People. Baltimore,
         MD: Johns Hopkins University Press.
  1983b To Slay the Hydra: Dutch Colonial Perspectives on the Saramaka Wars.
         Ann Arbor, ML: Karoma.
  1990   Alabi's World. Baltimore, MD: Johns Hopkins University Press.
  1995   Executing Ethnicity: The Killings in Surinam. Cultural Anthropology
         10: 437–71.
Rattray, R. S.
  1911   Ashanti Law and Constitution. London: Constable.
  1923   Ashanti. Oxford: Clarendon.
  1927   Religion and Art in Ashanti. London: Oxford University Press.
Robinson, Carey
  1969   The Fighting Maroons of Jamaica. London: Collins and Sangster.
Schafer, Daniel Lee
  1973   The Maroons of Jamaica: African Slave Rebels in the Caribbean. Ph.D.
         diss., University of Minnesota.
Scholtens, Ben
  1994   Bosnegers en Overheid in Surinam: De Ontwikkeling van de Politieke
         Verhouding, 1651–1992. Paramaribo: Afdeling Cultuurstudies/Minov.
Schuler, Monica
  1970   Ethnic Slave Rebellions in the Caribbean and the Guianas. Journal of
         Social History 3: 374–85.
Strong, William
  1974   Maroons and Myth. Daily Gleaner, 25 January.
Thoden van Velzen, H. U. E.
  1990   The Maroon Insurgency: Anthropological Reflections on the Civil War in
         Surinam. In Resistance and Rebellion in Surinam: Old and New. Gary
         Brana-Shute, ed. Pp.159–88. Williamsburg, VA: College of William and
         Mary.
Thoden van Velzen, H. U. E., and Wilhelmina van Wetering
  1988   The Great Father and the Danger: Religious Cults, Material Forces, and
         Collective Fantasies in the World of the Surinamese Maroons. Dordrecht:
         Foris.

Wetering, Wilhelmina van

1996　Witchcraft among the Tapanahoni Djuka. *In* Maroon Societies: Rebel Slave Communities in the Americas, 3d ed. Richard Price, ed. Pp. 370–88. Baltimore, MD: Johns Hopkins University Press.

Williams, Joseph J.

1938　The Maroons of Jamaica. Anthropological Series of the Boston College Graduate School 3: 379–480.

Zips, Werner

in　　"Laws in Competition": Traditional Maroon Authorities within the
press　Context of Legal Pluralism in Jamaica. Journal of Legal Pluralism.

Part IV

INSURRECTION AND EMANCIPATION IN THE ATLANTIC

This final section collects pieces that provide an entry into four crucial moments in the nineteenth-century struggle for abolition that stretched from the wake of the Haitian Revolution to the Ten Years War in Cuba. Each of these essays focuses on the particular ways in which people of African descent, both free and enslaved, encountered and transformed the political worlds they inhabited. Here, we see imperial policies, social conflicts and conditions, and the impact of broader Atlantic economic and political developments come together to reshape the lives and perspectives of groups of people caught in the grip of slavery but imagining a way beyond it. The essays, taken as a group, showcase techniques of research and analysis that help us to reconstruct the political perspectives of the enslaved, as well as showing the close connections between local events and developments in other parts of the Atlantic. They also demonstrate the commonalities and echoes between different moments of emancipation in the Atlantic.

In the excerpts from Matthew Childs' book on the Aponte rebellion in Cuba, he uses the biographies of individuals involved in the rebellion to illuminate various features of the political and social life of the enslaved in Cuba. Childs emphasizes the role played by *cabildos*, religious organizations that provided a space for socialization, debate, and planning for this revolt. And, as Eric Williams and Steven Hahn do in their selections, he explores the way in which rumors of emancipation shaped the perspectives and hopes of the enslaved as they plotted in Cuba. Childs' work, the most recent presented here, builds on the insights and approaches of the earlier scholarship showcased in this collection. It provides a holistic and rigorously-researched accounting of how institutions, intellectual and religious practice, and events in nearby Haiti shaped the tactics and ideals of the Aponte rebellion.

Eric Williams' classic book *Capitalism and Slavery* generated decades of debate, much of it centered on his thesis that slavery drove the industrial revolution in England, and that abolition took place primarily because of the decline of the sugar economy. Here, however, we reproduce a short chapter that Williams placed at the end of his book in an effort to explore how the slaves themselves, the subject rather than the agents of the action in most of his book, viewed and participated in debates about abolition. The chapter centers around the presence of rumors of emancipation that circulated in the British Caribbean during the early nineteenth century, highlighting this important feature of slaves in politics. It represents an early attempt to grapple with the importance of rumor and revolt in the Caribbean.

Steven Hahn's analysis of a series of remarkable events that took place in 1865 also highlights the importance of rumor, which he defines compellingly in the article as "a field and form of political struggle" (p. 335). By focusing on one "insurrection scare" that took place at a pivotal moment in U.S. history, he shows us a world of political thought and political projects that shaped African-American life during this period. Hahn's essay, like his remarkable book *A Nation Under our Feet*, insists that rumor allows us to better understand the political vision that constituted African-American life during this period.[1]

Rebecca's Scott's essay, which takes us to the very end of the nineteenth century, represents perhaps the ultimate form of micro-history by telling the story not only of a family but more specifically of a hotly-contested mule. But through the story of this mule, Scott tells the story of the Cuban war of independence, of the impact of black military service in the wake of slavery, and of the ways in which national and indeed international war and political change shaped and were shaped by the ground-level struggle to control land and the animals necessary to farm it. The essay is a fitting conclusion to our collection, for it brings together many of the approaches taken by the historians presented here, and shows how a particular story can illuminate past, present and future in powerful ways.

NOTE

1 Stephen Hahn, *A Nation Under Our Feet: Black Political Struggles in the Rural South from Slavery to the Great Migration* (Cambridge, MA: Harvard University Press, 2003).

11

THE 1812 APONTE REBELLION AND THE STRUGGLE AGAINST SLAVERY IN CUBA (SELECTIONS)

Matt D. Childs

Excerpt from Chapter 3, "Organizing the Rebellion"

"*Cabildos de Nación*: African Ethnic Associations and Identity in Cuba"

Among the rebels crowded on the execution scaffold with José Antonio Aponte on the morning of 9 April 1812 stood the free black militiaman and director of the Mina Guagni fraternal society, Salvador Ternero. Judicial authorities learned that Ternero and his fellow rebels shared more than just the same punishment for insurrection. Reportedly, Aponte frequently came to Ternero's house as they resided in the same Havana neighborhood.[1] Like Aponte, Chacón, and others involved in the rebellion, Ternero served in the black militia and earned his living as an artisan. Authorities believed Ternero drew upon his militia connections to store ammunition in his house. Javier Pacheco reported that "Ternero was to have 300 to 400 armed men" at his command for the rebellion.[2] The crucial evidence of Ternero's involvement in the Aponte rebellion came from reports of secret meetings that took place on the roof of his home and his own admission of conversations about whether "there would or would not be a revolution."[3] Captain General Someruelos likely agreed with free black Melchor Chirinos's belief that Ternero represented "a demon with butchering thoughts," when he sentenced him to death by hanging.[4]

The Aponte Rebellion of 1812 was not the first time Spanish officials had come across the name Salvador Ternero. Four years earlier José Augustín Jurco arrested Ternero for a fight with a black Ganga slave named José Antonio. Ternero emphasized his militia service and *fuero* rights, resulting in his release due to his service as a soldier in the second company of the battalion.[5] One year later, authorities arrested Ternero again for involvement in a Havana riot targeting the French residents of

269

the city. Ternero recalled "being imprisoned" for what he described as the "revolution of the blacks when they attacked and robbed the French." For his role in the urban revolt, Ternero served one month of hard labor at La Cabaña military fortress. In the same year, authorities once again detained Ternero for a fight with a tailor immediately releasing him for unspecified reasons.[6] Ternero's record of individual fights and participation in an urban riot undoubtedly contributed to his guilt in the mind of colonial officials investigating the Aponte Rebellion.

In addition to criminal procedures, Ternero also attracted the attention of authorities from civil investigations. Salvador Ternero served as the leader of the Mina Guagni fraternal society that based its membership on a shared cultural and geographic heritage rooted in the Gold Coast of West Africa.[7] Prevalent in colonial society, these collective organizations became known as *cabildos de nación*, reflecting the voluntary grouping by common ethnic identity of the numerous African "nations" forcibly imported to Cuba. Cuban contemporaries as well as others from the plantation zones and port cities of the Atlantic world used the term "nation" for Kongos, Lucumies, Minas, and others to indicate African ethnic identity. To clarify, "nation" is here used to connote a group of individuals bound by a common language, culture, history, and geographic origin. In this context, "nation" is used as it was historically in the Afro-Atlantic world of the fifteenth to mid-nineteenth centuries to refer to African ethnicity, and not to project anachronistically backward the modern definition of "nation," linked primarily to the formation of political states.[8] Historian David Bell in discussing "nation" and "nationhood" for the early modern era offers the following operational definition that can be applied to Cuba: "As far as definitions go, I cannot do much more here than state that eighteenth-century authors most often used the 'nation' to mean a community that satisfied two loose conditions. First, it grouped together people who had enough in common— whether language, customs, beliefs, traditions, or some combination of these—to allow them to be considered a homogenous collective. Second, it had some sort of recognized political existence."[9] While discussions of African ethnicity and "nations" may conjure up ideas of "tribes" and "tribalism," Joseph Miller has emphasized that all too often scholars unsuspectedly (and sometimes intentionally) use the term "tribe" uncritically for African ethnicity and nationhood that echoes a procolonialist ideology.[10] It is not by coincidence these African associations became known as *cabildos de nación* in Cuba. The Spanish term *"cabildo"* represents the English language equivalent of a town council or a town government. Consequently, the labeling of these societies as *cabildos de nación* provides some indication of how they functioned as representative bodies for African "nations" by providing political and administrative services.[11]

On three separate occasions in the 1790s, several members of the *cabildo*

Mina Guagni challenged Salvador Ternero's authority as *capataz* (a term meaning steward or leader but also used for an overseer or foreman) to direct the financial affairs of the society. Unnamed members wrote to the captain general in 1794 complaining that *"capataz* Salvador Ternero . . . had sold the *cabildo"* house where the society regularly held reunions and bought a new house without consulting the members.[12] Three years later members of the Mina Guagni nation discovered that Ternero had purchased their new house in what amounted to a silent partnership with a free mulatta, Juana de Mesa, who demanded payment for revenues the *cabildo* generated by renting out rooms. The judge investigating the case ruled that Salvador Ternero as *capataz* of the Mina Guagni nation would have to pay 700 pesos to Juana de Mesa.[13] After selling the old *cabildo* house, purchasing a new one, and then being forced to pay 700 pesos, several members of the Mina Guagni nation petitioned to have Salvador Ternero removed as *capataz.*[14]

For some members, Ternero's actions recklessly jeopardized the existence of the *cabildo* Mina Guagni. The ownership of a house uniting slaves and free people of color by common ethnicity provided a sacred space for solidarity in a society increasingly divided along racial lines between slavery and freedom. Almost all the activities of the Mina Guagni nation revolved around the *cabildo* house that served numerous functions vital to the society: a home which rented rooms; a conference center for holding meetings and reunions; a school for education and training in the artisan trades; a bank through collection of membership dues, offering loans, and purchasing the freedom for slaves; a restaurant through food services such as the "plate of the day"; a theater for dances; and even a funeral parlor. As a consequence of the investigation into the divisions of the Mina Guagni nation, authorities prevented the *cabildo* house from carrying out its regular functions. Catarina Barrera and eight other members of the society pleaded with the captain general of Cuba to reopen the *cabildo* house "because it has been more than a year and a half since there has been amusement on the festival days."[15]

Ternero's abuse of authority and violation of the members' trust represent a story of graft and corruption common to many organizations, *cabildos* or otherwise. Ternero, in fact, never specifically denied the accusations nor felt compelled to elaborate on his purchases. Upon learning of the charges brought against him by fellow *cabildo* members, he requested the investigation be taken over by a military court, where he hoped to find a more sympathetic jury as a militia member.[16] Ternero turned to the highest-ranking militia officer, Antonio Seidel, who oversaw and supervised the operation of the black militia in Havana, to intervene on his behalf and have the case moved to a military court.[17] Seidel confirmed "Salvador Ternero as a soldier of the 5th company," which entitled him to the military jurisdiction of the *fuero* court. Ternero provided a copy of the letter authorizing him as the elected *capataz* to administer the financial, legal, and material affairs of the *cabildo*, to demonstrate he had not exceeded his authority.[18] He then proceeded to direct the investigation away from his purchases by focusing on the issue of identity and membership rights as criteria for challenging his leadership.

Ternero defended his position as *capataz* of the *cabildo* on the basis of his birth in Africa. According to Ternero, it was "the intention of some black Creoles that endeavor to destroy" the *cabildo* that created the division.[19] He dismissed the complaints as irrelevant because they were made by "Creoles who are not members of the national body [*no son miembros del cuerpo nacional*]." Ternero further argued that "the Creoles and slaves do not have a voice or a vote in *cabildo*" functions.[20] Ternero explained that slaves of Mina Guagni ethnicity could be members and take part in the functions of the society. However, the rules and regulations of the Mina Guagni society did not grant them the right to vote, because the "touch of slavery" prevented them from always "attending *cabildo*" functions, according to Ternero. Only upon becoming free did they enjoy full membership rights.

As for the free Creoles who challenged Ternero, he argued that "according to the constitution of the *cabildo*, and according to general custom they are prohibited representation . . . even if they are the children of black members of the nation." Creole Manuel Vásquez raised the loudest voice calling for Ternero's removal as *capataz*. "Ultimately," Ternero reasoned, "the defects (speaking with reservation) of being a black Creole" rendered Manuel Vásquez's complaints illegitimate because he was not born in Africa of the Mina Guagni nation.[21] Ternero reversed the standard explanation of colonial society that structured hierarchical privileges by place of birth from the white Spaniard at top of the hierarchy followed by the white Cuban, mulatto Cuban, black Cuban, and then the "pure-blooded" African on the bottom. Puzzled as to how to respond to Ternero's argument of legitimate African identity based on place of birth and full membership in the Mina Guagni nation, Captain General Luis de las Casas ordered officials to investigate other *cabildos* to determine if Creoles also participated and received voting rights.[22]

After receiving the order, Francisco Faveda and notary José Díaz Velásquez visited several *cabildo* houses and knocked on their doors to inquire if they had Creole members. According to Juan de la Torre and José de Jesús, the *capataces* of the Kongo Masinga nation, Creoles "were not represented in the *cabildo*." Upon inquiring at the *cabildos* Kongo and Karabali Osso, Faveda and Velásquez learned that Creoles were members but "did not have votes" for deciding the societies' functions.[23] Believing that the organizations drew their membership only from the African-born sectors of Cuba's population, the presence of Creoles in *cabildos* perplexed authorities and revealed how little they knew about the societies. Behind closed doors, *cabildos* provided relative autonomy and distance from master and government supervision that could shelter the planning of the rebellion.

Ternero keenly observed that Cuban officials disapproved of Creole participation in *cabildos* and expressed shock upon learning that they joined African societies. Masters and colonial officials believed the African and Creole populations did not socialize and would not make common cause in rebellion. Consequently, Ternero deftly emphasized Creole participation in the Mina Guagnination to discredit their challenge to his leadership. Ternero acknowledged that "it is true [Creoles] dance and amuse themselves in the *cabildos*, but it is not by a right that they have, but by permission."[24] For Cuban authorities, *cabildo* dances represented the clearest indication of the cultural differences between Africans and Europeans. Black Creoles who voluntarily participated in the ethnic-based *cabildos* contradicted the ideological justification for slavery that supposedly saved Africans from "heathenism" and "backwardness" with the benefits of Western culture. It further called into question the comforting belief of slaveowners that the African-born and Cuban-born populations remained culturally distinct and would not make common cause. Despite the evidence of financial mismanagement, the captain general dismissed the charges against Ternero and allowed him to retain the title of *capataz*. He ruled that "black Creoles should not vote," according to "the custom of such communities," and therefore had no grounds for a complaint.[25]

Outraged over the ruling, Manuel Vásquez protested that Ternero had denied Creoles and slaves their "rights to vote" within the *cabildo* for his own benefit. Realizing Cuban authorities discouraged fraternization between *bozales* and Creoles, Vásquez dropped the complaint on behalf of Cuban-born blacks, but continued to protest Ternero's leadership for denying slaves the right to vote. Vásquez emphasized that "Augustín Morales, being legitimate of the nation" should not be "excluded for his servile condition."[26] Further, since slaves contributed financially to the *cabildo* without enjoying voting rights, Vásquez compared their treatment by Ternero with that of the "extensive violence" committed by their masters who also did not recognize their rights.[27] Despite prohibiting slaves from voting, fifteen members supported Ternero by pointing out that "Augustín Morales who is of the nation . . . is the only slave who follows the band of Vásquez."[28] Overall, the investigation into the financial affairs of the Mina Guagni nation revealed that the vast majority of both free and enslaved members continued to regard Ternero as the rightful leader of the *cabildo*.

The dispute among members of the Mina Guagni nation provides crucial insights into both the process of identifying others and self-identification in early nineteenth-century Cuba. Spanish authorities sought to separate the African and Cuban-born populations and, therefore, discouraged Creole participation in *cabildos*. In the same vein of preventing a broad racial identity, government officials encouraged the formation of *cabildos* because they emphasized distinct African ethnicities. Despite official discouragement and even limited political rights, some Creoles joined *cabildos* and continued to identify with the nation of their parents and ancestors. Although Cuban society at large tended to privilege Cuban-born blacks over Africans, within *cabildos, bozales* exerted more authority by claiming "legitimate" ethnicity as members of the nation. Social identity for Africans in Cuba showed a great degree of variation in the processes by which certain groups became identified legally and culturally by others and in the way people self-identified individually and collectively; *cabildos* provided opportunities to build solidarity that transcended the boundaries of birth, ethnicity, gender, and legal status.

"Kings and Queens to Watch Over Their Interests"

The formation of ethnic groups based upon African nations represented a common feature of slave societies in the Americas. Masters throughout the New World recognized that Africans did not represent an undifferentiated mass of laborers but brought with them forms of social organization and cultural differences that they perpetuated and refashioned in the Americas as survival strategies. Robert Jameson, a British observer in Cuba, recognized how both master and slaves identified Africans by nations in the early nineteenth century: "The different nations to which the negroes belonged in Africa are marked out in the colonies both by the master and the slaves; the former considering them variously characterized in the desired qualities, and the latter joining together with a true national spirit in such union as their lords allow."[29] Masters often stereotyped certain nations for possessing distinguishing characteristics that some historians regard as offering a few "glimmers of truth" about African cultural traits.[30] Regardless of what masters' stereotypes can tell us specifically about African identity in the New World, it is clear that profits depended on an awareness of cultural differences. Historian David Eltis has soundly observed that "[w]hile the planters' basic requirement was slave labor from anywhere in Africa, no one can read the transatlantic correspondence of the early modern slave systems without recognizing the importance of African nationhood in the shaping of the plantation regimes."[31] African ethnic categories that came to be known as "nations" in the diaspora provide an analytic lens to examine how slaves and free people of color defined themselves and were defined by Europeans.

Depending on the nature of the documentation and the quality of reporting, the existence of societies based upon African nationhood can be found throughout the Americas for the whole period of slavery. Scholars have begun to revise the emphasis placed on the heterogeneity of the slave population that was once described as a "crowd" of diverse African ethnicities and have pointed toward specific cultural groups that can be tracked in the diaspora.[32] For the slave societies of Anglo-America, the action of Africans grouping themselves by nations normally became known in the context of a rebellion, often among Gold Coast slaves known as Coromantees.[33] The Iberian slave societies have left a particularly rich documentation related to African ethnicity, compared to the Anglo colonies in the New World. The Portuguese colonies in Brazil and Africa often recognized African nations through religious ceremonies.[34] The common appearance of Angolan and Kongolese ethnicity among African and Afro-Brazilian Catholic brotherhoods likely indicates religious traditions slaves took with them and transformed when they crossed the Atlantic.[35] For example, "Angolan Kings and Queens" received payments for directing the brotherhood of Our Lady of the Rosary in Recife.[36] According to Tomás Treolar, who worked at a Brazilian gold mine, Africans chose "kings and queens to watch over the interests and welfare of their respective nations."[37] Throughout the Americas, Africans created associations, relationships, and networks by looking back across the Atlantic to their cultures of origin to create survival strategies in the New World.

Spanish America appears to follow the same general pattern as Portugal of recognizing national differences among Africans through the church. At least a century before the conquest of the New World, municipal authorities in Seville appointed a steward to settle disputes between slaves and masters, and the African population formed religious brotherhoods that gathered on feast days to perform their own dances and songs.[38] These practices were then carried to the Americas and expanded when introduced to a larger African slave population. Sodalities in Lima, Peru, often reflected African ethnicity, such as the Dominican brotherhood for the "negros Congos," and the brotherhood of Nuestra Señora del Socorro for Angolans.[39] In addition, organizations formed along lines of African ethnicity expressed their desire to separate from church control. In Buenos Aires, for example, Africans in the nineteenth century regularly petitioned the police department for permission to form societies based upon their common national backgrounds to better serve their spiritual, cultural, and financial needs.[40] Whether through the church, informal organizations on plantations and mines, or state-sanctioned societies, Africans in Latin America grouped themselves along lines of African ethnicity and culture.

In Cuba, Catholic brotherhoods included Africans as early as the sixteenth century. In 1573, the town council of Havana reported that Africans took part in the procession of Corpus Christi, and wills indicate they regularly made donations to sodalities.[41] The Mandinga, Karabali, Lucumi, Arara, Ganga, and Congo nations proliferated in Havana and organized important brotherhoods. Most of the organizations selected a patron saint that they honored on his or her feast day with elaborate festivals and ceremonies.[42] In 1755, Bishop Morell de Santa Cruz wrote with shock at the lack of interest in Christianizing "these miserables [slaves and free people of color who] have been left totally abandoned as if they were not Christians and incapable of salvation."[43] In particular, the bishop's report emphasized the "scandalous and grave disorders" created by the "cabildos ... when they congregate on festival days."[44] Apparently, during the span of the sixteenth and seventeenth centuries some *cabildos* had separated from the brotherhoods and taken on a social role independent of the church. The bishop planned to bring the "lost sheep of the flock to the Good Shepherd [by] ... administering to the *cabildos* the sacrament of confirmation, reciting the Holy rosary," and appointing lay religious officials to instruct and supervise the societies.[45] Despite the bishop's protest, it does not appear the nations became "converted to temples of the living God," as he optimistically predicted.[46] For example, although the *cabildo* Karabali Induri affiliated itself with the Catholic Church Nuestra Señora del Buen Viaje, it does not appear as if any religious officials oversaw their activities or intervened to settle disputes among members in 1800.[47] By the mid-eighteenth century, if not earlier, *cabildos* likely outnumbered brotherhoods.[48]

Various scholars have traced the origins of the *cabildos* to religious holidays and Catholic brotherhoods of Spanish origin, but Philip Howard pointed out that analogous societies were common to West and Central Africa.[49] At the port of Old Calabar and surrounding regions in the Bight of Biafra, an all-male secret society known as Ekpe formed as early as the second half of the seventeenth century. Identified with the leopard, Ekpe members paid dues assessed by their rank in the organization. According to historians Paul Lovejoy and David Richardson, Ekpe society created an "interlocking grid of secret associations [that] served to regulate the behavior of members."[50] The secret organization crossed the Atlantic and resurfaced in nineteenth-century Cuba through an altered form with a different purpose as the Abakuá society.[51] In the Yoruba kingdom of Oyo there existed a semisecret organization known as the Ogboni society that advised the king on religious and political matters. Scholars disagree about the founding date of the Ogboni society and the extent of its influence. However, it is almost certain that because the war-torn region of Yorubaland funneled thousands of Africans to Cuba in the nineteenth century, some knowledge of the organization likely crossed the Atlantic and influenced the Yoruba-based *cabildos*.[52] Associations, organizations, and secret societies in West and Central Africa provided an institutional framework that enslaved and free Africans could mold to their New World surroundings in Cuba.

Various other societies could be found in West and Central Africa that performed charitable, recreational, political, and economic functions for members who often shared the same language, ethnicity, and nationality.

The collective and communal organizing principles of these organizations often translated into mutual aid societies in the Americas. The African-born and American-born populations of African descent displayed a strong tendency to socialize and meet with those who shared a similar ethnicity, and to form some sort of organization, formally or informally, to keep in touch with and look out for each other. In Cuba and elsewhere in the Americas, the association of Africans who shared a common language, culture, history, and identity often functioned as a mutual aid society that linked the more fortunate and well-placed members with their poorer and severely exploited members through patron-client networks.[53] The Yoruba in West Africa, for example, operated mutual aid societies as early as the eighteenth century through the Ajo and Esusu saving institutions. Each member paid dues into a collective fund that would then be made available for individual loans. When Yoruba slaves began to be exported across the Atlantic, the Esusu savings association emerged in the Caribbean.[54] Spanish colonial administrators and Catholic priests regarded African *cabildos* in Cuba as a natural and safe extension of their own religious sodalities. The organizations for Africans, however, surely did not represent something entirely of Spanish or Cuban origin, but an Old World institution modified in a New World setting.

"Those From Ethiopia Who Want to Join Today": The Growth of *Cabildos*

Over the last forty years a great expansion has occurred in the knowledge of the forced migratory process linking the Americas and Africa. As a result of collaborative efforts, computer assistance, and the construction of data sets, it has become easier for scholars to eschew the generic non-descriptive terms "Africa" and "African" and identify more precisely the origins of slaves and their New World destinations. David Eltis, David Richardson, Stephen D. Behrendt, and Herbert S. Klein have compiled an easily accessible database of more than 27,000 slaving voyages that now makes it possible to trace the Old World origins and American destination of Africans with greater precision than ever before.[55] For example, two out of every three slaves imported into the British Caribbean from roughly 1650 to 1710 left from a 200-mile stretch of territory on the Gold/ Slave Coast of Africa.[56] Despite the greater precision in specifying African origins and New World destinations, at least two salient problems face the scholar studying African ethnicity and the Atlantic slave trade. First, most records reveal only the ports where ships left from, not the origin of slaves brought to the African coast. And second, Europeans who authored the documents, while cognizant of ethnic differences, often confused one group with another.[57]

Unlike other slave-importing regions of the Americas, tracing a particular dominant African culture in Cuba through census data from the Atlantic slave trade remains difficult because no single exporting region provided more than 31 percent of the migrants. The most recent scholarship has shown that "[o]f all the receiving areas in the Americas, Cuba received the greatest mix of African peoples."[58] For reasons that remain unclear, slave purchasers in Spanish America showed less concern for regional preferences than their counterparts elsewhere in the Americas.[59] Examining *cabildos* in the era of the Atlantic slave trade provides an opportunity to study how African ethnicity in Cuba was a product of the middle passage, but from an angle other than migration records. As Africans formed *cabildos* and defined their own ethnicity, these sources provide a rare view into how they identified themselves. Salvador Ternero, for example, did not need to know the percentage of Mina Guagni slaves imported to Cuba to understand how the slave trade shaped ethnic identities in his *cabildo*. He simply recognized that "when they founded the *cabildo* in 1731 there had not come those from Ethiopia who want to join today."[60] The increase in the slave trade and the spread of sugar plantations across Cuba strengthened the importance of Mina Guagni ethnicity within the *cabildo* and made African fraternal associations all the more important in daily interactions.

The same process occurred in the *cabildo* of Lucumies, as the population of Yoruba ancestry was known in Cuba. As the war-torn region of Yorubaland began to funnel slaves to Cuba at the end of the eighteenth century, a "confederation of Black Creoles" formed within the *cabildo*, representing the sons and daughters of the original founding members, Creole Manuel Blanco attempted to prevent the sale of the *cabildo* house that his parents had helped purchase. The marked increase of *bozal* Lucumi members, however, resulted in the Africans winning the case by their numerical superiority.[61] Cuba (along with Brazil) represents something of an anomaly for African identity transformation in the Americas during the late eighteenth and nineteenth centuries. In other parts of the New World, a broad-based racial identity began to eclipse African ethnicities with the ending of the slave trade, the growth of a Creole slave population, and the gradual abolition of slavery. In Cuba, however, African ethnic identity remained strong due to the dramatic increase in slave imports.

Charting the overall growth of the number of *cabildos* and the membership in each society proves difficult because no single governmental institution supervised the associations for the early nineteenth century, further revealing the relative autonomy these societies enjoyed. As a result, historians have yet to find a concentrated corpus of records on the societies. While quantifying the growth of *cabildos* remains difficult, qualitative sources indicate a noticeable increase in these societies from 1750 to 1820. In 1753, the Cuban bishop complained of the "noisy shouting of males mixed with females amusing themselves in extremely clumsy and provocative dances . . . that sanctify the festivals in this city." The bishop counted twenty-one *cabildo* houses that he emphasized "served the devil": the Karabalies owned five; the Minas, three; the Lucumies, two; the Araras, two; the Kongos, two; the Mondongos, two; the Gangas, two; the Mandingas, one; the Luangos, one; and the Suangos, one.[62] Scattered references to more than thirty *cabildos* found in civil disputes for the years spanning 1790 to 1820, along with frequent mentions of associations in official correspondence and criminal proceedings, suggest the number of Havana societies increased to at least fifty by 1812.[63]

The division of several *cabildos* provides a qualitative indication of the growth of the societies as a result of what Ternero described in the 1790s as the "arrival of those from Ethiopia who want to join today." In the 1780s, a dispute surfaced within the Lucumi *cabildo* between the diverse ethnicities that claimed membership. One member recalled that "the *cabildo* was erected by the Lucumi nations, specifically the Nangas and the Barbaes," but also included members from the Chabas and Bambaras.[64] By the seventeenth century Yoruban culture and language had become a lingua franca along the Western African coast, promoting what John Thornton has described as "cultural intercommunication."[65] In Cuba, this process apparently expanded the cultural boundaries of inclusion that facilitated the collaboration of several nations under a broad Lucumi identity. Near the end of the eighteenth century, however, with the increase of slaves from the Yoruba region, the society divided into separate *cabildos* represented by the Nangas and Barbaes in one house and the Chabas and Bambaras in another. A similar division emerged in the *cabildo* Kongo Musolongo in 1806 as indicated by their request to Cuban authorities to separate into two different societies.[66] Likewise, as a result of a contested election Juan Gavilan and a group identifying themselves as the Karabali Osso desired to separate from the Karabali Umugini *cabildo* despite "fourteen years more or less of unity."[67] The ability to incorporate members from different nations at one moment and then at another draw lines of exclusion corresponding to fluctuations in populations among West Africans in Havana demonstrates the flexibility of African ethnicity and culture in the New World and the ever-changing ways Africans viewed each other.

Cuban slaveowners clearly understood the important functions of *cabildos* in a slave society dependent on the Atlantic slave trade. The existence of societies sharing a common language and culture served to mitigate slightly the horrific experience of the middle passage through collective solidarity even as they also prepared slaves for their new lives as unpaid laborers. As discussed in chapter 1, in 1789 the king of Spain issued a slave code that sought to protect slave marriage, limit work hours, specify food and clothing rations, and prohibit excessive punishment. In addition, the code held implications for the activities of the *cabildos* by emphasizing the need for slaves "on holidays to . . . be instructed in the Christian doctrine" and prevent the "uniting with others . . . in simple and natural diversions [and] to avoid excessive drinking."[68] Cuban slaveowners immediately protested all the provisions that curtailed their authority as masters, yet these same slaveowners surprisingly defended the rights of slaves and free people of color to form *cabildos* and perform their dances. Diego Miguel de Moya authored a petition signed by "all of the masters of sugar plantations in this jurisdiction" that argued by "taking away now the slaves' right to holidays that they count on to leave their enslavement (*salir de su esclavitud*), would for certain be an infallible principle of their resentment."[69] Cuban slaveowners, obviously, did not mean that all the slaves who participated in *cabildos* became free. Rather, they recognized that some slaves survived the brutal daily life of slavery with the hope that participation in a *cabildo* could lead to liberation.

Masters also revealed more than they realized. Participation in *cabildo* functions allowed slaves, however briefly, to "leave slavery" and the confines of master dominion. Further, when masters emphasized that the "inclined diversion of the Blacks is to dance in the barbarous style of their countries," they recognized "that if this [right] is denied them, it will cause an irresistible pain and produce bad consequences."[70] Cuban masters convinced themselves that by providing slaves and free people of color with a limited sense of autonomy, they would not rise in rebellion. Indeed, the town council of Havana reasoned that French slaveowners destroyed by the Haitian Revolution had only encouraged insurrection by "making slaves work on holidays."[71] In a society fueled by the forceful importation of thousands of Africans every year, slaveowners quickly realized the benefits of allowing organizations that fostered African ethnic solidarity to round off the sharp edges of the master-slave relationship.

"Children of the Same Nation": The Diversity of *Cabildo* Membership

Cabildo membership served to strengthen networks and resources weakened by living in a slave society that showed little hesitation in destroying kin relations. The common practice of referring to fellow *cabildo* members by words with familial connotations reveals how the organizations served as a surrogate for an incomplete family structure.[72] Francisco Alas, the "emperor" of a Mina and Mandinga *cabildo* in Bayamo, described a meeting attended by his "*parientes* (relatives), free Blas Tamayo, slave Mateo and his wife, and the slave Candelaria Dolores."[73] One member of a *cabildo* reported that while he "was sick, all of his relatives had come to visit him."[74] José Caridad Perrera, a free black of Karabali ethnicity, ate dinner during festival days in "the house of Antonio José Barraga the Captain General" of the *cabildo* together with "various other relatives."[75] Other *cabildos* simply referred to members as part of one family. Cristóbal Govín, the second captain of the *cabildo* Karabali Oquella, complained of the new discord caused by an election "between a family that has always carried on with the utmost peace and harmony."[76] Still others described their fellow *cabildo* members with the more general "*compañero*" (companion) that conveyed a sense of the shared camaraderie that developed from being part of a community.[77] Whether described as "family" members, "relatives," or "companions," *cabildos* provided a widened network of associations that fostered collective solidarity.

Rebel leader Salvador Ternero's dispute with the Cuban-born Creoles in the Mina Guagni *cabildo* indicates that within a nation, the rights and benefits accorded to "family" members, "relatives," or "companions" could vary widely. While African ethnic identification tended to define who could be counted on *cabildo* membership lists, evidence from various societies suggests that the treatment of mulattos, Cuban-born Creoles, and slaves depended on the regulations and customs of each society. Contemporary documents leave little indication that mulattos participated in *cabildos*. Given that nations in Cuba based their membership on a shared African ethnicity, *cabildos* may have excluded mulattos. Cuban officials may have also prohibited them from joining *cabildos*, as they sought to prevent blacks and mulattos from making common cause. Despite the tendencies that worked to exclude mulattos, some may have participated in the *cabildos* or visited houses during festival days. On 25 February 1811, authorities arrested José Montero, Felipe Santiago, and Rafael Rodríguez, all soldiers in the free mulatto militia, for attending a meeting at a "*cabildo* of Blacks."[78] Other than this brief reference, there is not enough evidence to conclude that mulattos regularly participated in *cabildo* functions, just as there is no evidence to argue that the nations specified their exclusion.

Ample evidence suggests that Cuban-born blacks regularly participated in the nations. For example, the free Creole Juan Bautista Valiente, appropriately known as "el Cubano" to reflect his place of birth among Africans members of the society, participated in the Mina *cabildo*.[79] The *cabildo* Musolongo allowed Creole participation and recognized Juan Ruíz as a member, "even though he is a Creole, son of a father and a mother of the nation, and married to a free black of the nation."[80] Regardless of Salvador Ternero's bitter dispute with Manuel Vásquez over Creole voting rights, he recognized Creoles as members and described them as "children of the same" nation, and never proposed their expulsion.[81] While the differences between African-born and Cuban-born members could lead to rivalries within organizations, colonial officials appeared more alarmed than the *cabildos* that the two groups fraternized. Judicial authorities chastised rebel leader and free black Clemente

Chacón for allowing his son Juan Bautista, "a free black Creole, to play the drums with the Kongo nation" during what they suspected were meetings to coordinate the uprising.[82]

While some Creoles actively participated in ethnic associations, others began to separate themselves from the African-born population. Leaders of the Lucumi *cabildo* complained of the formation of a Creole group that opposed the interest of the *bozales*. As Cuban authorities settled disputes within *cabildos* and became cognizant of Creole participation in the associations, they came to suspect that "there had formed a *cabildo* of black Creoles." The free black José Herrera denied any association with the society and insisted that he had no knowledge that his "sister-in-law Manuela González had been elected Queen of the Creole *cabildo*." Further, Herrera elaborated that "should one [*cabildo*] form, he would not join, because he was not a man of *cabildos* . . . and could not make the movements of the *bozales*." Rather, Herrera emphasized, he was somebody who "danced the minuet, as is the custom of Creoles."[83] Herrera's contrast between the minuet and *cabildo* performances drew a clear distinction between African and Creole dances. He also revealed, perhaps simplistically, the degree to which some Creoles defined themselves in contrast to *bozales*, and the complexity of racial and ethnic identity in Cuba.

Slaves and Creoles alike, in contrast to *bozales*, had limited rights and privileges in *cabildos*. The *cabildo* Karabali prevented slaves from voting for leaders; the organization's electoral roster listed only free members.[84] Likewise, other societies prevented slaves from participating in elections and deciding the financial expenditures of the nations.[85] Given that the distinction between free and slave represented the primary division of Cuban society, and given the prevalence of slavery in Africa, it should not be surprising that *cabildos* defined membership rights based upon legal status.

A few *cabildo* members even owned slaves. In 1807, Antonio Ribero, a member of the Lucumi Llane nation, purchased a slave for 500 pesos. The transaction caught the attention of the *cabildo* not because they opposed the purchase on moral grounds but because they suspected Ribero had bought the slave with money stolen from the society.[86] In 1804 Cristóbal Govín, *capataz* of the Karabali Oquella nation, opposed remodeling several dilapidated rooms of the *cabildo* house, because he "would have to transfer my habitation during the construction" to the one of "Rafaela, slave of Teresa Barreto who lives in another room of the same house."[87] When Salvador Ternero assumed the title of *capataz* of the Mina Guagni *cabildo*, the nation authorized him to administer "whatever quantities of maravedíes, gold pesos, silver pesos, jewelry, slaves, merchandise, agricultural products, and other goods."[88] Although nations fostered ethnic identification and a community beyond the immediate supervision of white masters, the ownership of slaves by some *cabildo* members and the limited voting rights extended to human chattel illustrated how slavery pervaded every aspect of Cuban society.

Whereas some nations limited the participation of slaves in *cabildo* functions because of their enslaved condition, others attempted to overcome the barriers that blocked active participation. Festival days represented crucial events that allowed for a collective solidarity to be expressed through ceremony and dance. While masters might grant their slaves permission to participate in a *cabildo* as a reward, they also benefited from such participation. The nation Karabali Osso recognized the important participation of slaves in *cabildo* functions. In 1803 their account book recorded this entry: "payment for slaves' daily wages of our nation" to masters in order to secure their participation at *cabildo* events.[89] The Karabali Osso nation, in effect, hired the attendance of its enslaved members by paying wages to their masters. As slavery represented obstacles to full participation, generated additional expenses through payment of wages to masters, and undermined collective strength, *cabildos* often provided loans to emancipate members.[90] The *cabildo* Kongo, for example, reported that Cayetano García owed "80 pesos of the 200 that he was given for his freedom."[91] Free members could not only participate more actively in *cabildos* than slaves, but as the rightful owners of their own labor, they could contribute more generously to the nation's financial resources.

Some societies accepted members from other nations. Authorities assumed the free black Antonio from Bayamo was Karabali because he participated in the nation's festival days and "lived among them," but he described his ethnicity as Kongo.[92] Although the Mina and Mandinga could trace their nations to the distinct geographic areas of the Gold Coast and the upper Niger Valley respectively, they formed a joint *cabildo* that extended membership to both groups.[93] Members of different nations could even gain considerable authority within a *cabildo* with which they did not share a common ethnicity. In 1803 the *cabildo* Karabali Induri elected Juan Echevarría to the position of second *capataz* by an overwhelming majority. Jesús Sollazo, the leader of the *cabildo*, immediately declared Echevarría's election "null . . . because he is not of the nation Induri." The captain general sided with Echevarría because he had won the election outright and because of "the fact that he had been admitted to the *cabildo*" long before the election took place.[94] Although not an African-born member of the Karabali Induri nation, he apparently had enough supporters within the *cabildo* who did not define leadership qualities exclusively by ethnicity. For the leader of the nation, however, it was precisely his lack of ethnicity that made him unsuitable to serve as an elected officer. Echevarría's election pointedly reveals both the contested nature and flexibility of identity defined by African ethnicity in Cuba.

Cabildos routinely extended membership to people of diverse ethnicities, but as with Creoles and slaves, tended to restrict their voting rights. Salvador Ternero had dismissed Manuel Vásquez's complaint as "not having legitimate representation of the nation" because he was a Creole and had the support of only one slave. In addition, Ternero emphasized that among Vázquez's supporters was "María de la Luz Romero who is of a different nation."[95] The Karabali Apapa, like other nations, did not limit membership to only one ethnic group. When a dispute divided the *cabildo* over buying a new house, however, only those members of Karabali Apapa ethnicity and those who had been extended voting rights could debate the purchase. The leaders of the *cabildo* explained that members of other ethnicities "do not have representation in the *cabildo* according to the resolutions of this government, *without obtaining the right and permission from us*, and the others who make up the nation."[96] Voting rights in *cabildos* appear to have been universally granted to free African-born members who represented the ethnicity of the *cabildo*. For Creoles, slaves, and *cabildo* members of other ethnicities from the dominant group, generalizations prove elusive because the practices and customs of each society tended to differ, illustrating the diverse experiences of people of African ancestry in Cuba.

Although *cabildos* often restricted participation in their associations along ethnic lines, they also recognized commonalties with larger cultural groups common to areas of the slave trade. Manuel Blanco explained to authorities that the division of the Lucumies into separate nations reflected the different homelands of the members while recognizing their common Yoruban culture. According to Blanco, "the truth is that among the blacks who call themselves Lucumies, some are Chabes, others Barbaes, Bambaras and Nangas . . . all of them take the name Lucumi, but some are from one homeland and the others from another." The same recognition of a larger shared culture can be observed among the different groups of Kongolese in Cuba. Blanco observed that "there are many Blacks who call themselves members of the Kongo nation, but as they are from diverse homelands they have in this city diverse *cabildos*."[97] The Karabali also identified themselves as part of a larger cultural group, but divided their *cabildos* to reflect a specific homeland of the members. In addition to choosing leaders for each Karabali *cabildo*, they also elected "José Aróstegui as the *capataz* of the five Karabali nations" to coordinate activities among the organizations.[98] The Lucumies, Kongoleses, and Karabalies formed associations based on a broadly shared cultural identity rooted in Africa. They then limited *cabildo* membership to build close solidarity among those of their same nation and homeland, whom they affectionately described as their "paisanos" (countrymen).[99]

"Who Moves All of These Machinations?":
The Leadership of *Cabildos*

Within each *cabildo*, several members held administrative positions that strengthened the *capataz*'s leadership. The *cabildo* Karabali, located in the city of Matanzas, elected Rafael as their new leader in 1814. They then decided upon a general staff that resembled a king's court. They agreed that Rafael's wife would serve as queen mother; María Rosario Domínguez as princess; Diego as first minister, Nicario as second minister; Bernardo as first captain; Miguel de la Cruz as second lieutenant; Manuel del Portillo and Felipe as musicians; and Francisco as treasurer.[100] In addition to these titles, other *cabildos* created positions such as governor, emperor, sergeant-at-arms, queen of war, and captain of war.[101] Although denied voting rights within *cabildos*, slaves often attained leadership roles. The slave Patricio served as "captain of the Karabali slaves" and Alonzo Santa Cruz held the position of "King of the Kongo slaves."[102] The captain general of Cuba attempted to prevent the establishment of an elaborate leadership structure and recommended that "there should not be positions other than first, second, and third *capataz*."[103] The captain general attempted to restrict the *cabildos*' ability to provide members with titles because of the dangers of allowing slaves and free people of color to create their own hierarchical structures.

Cuban authorities remained torn over how to deal with the leadership organization created by *cabildos*. They recognized the important role of *cabildos* for a rapidly expanding slave society, as they provided crucial cultural adjustment for slaves recently imported from Africa. Further, a single leader provided the important function of serving as an intermediary between colonial officials and African laborers. Nonetheless, the Cuban government continually voiced concerns over the power that came with being a *capataz* of a *cabildo*. In 1759, the captain general of Cuba informed Spanish officials that, "as a precaution for certain disorders, it has been established by this government to name for each [*cabildo*] a Captain to watch and supervise their functions and meetings, who is of the same nation, and of old and mature age."[104] By the late eighteenth and early nineteenth centuries, the previous policy of the colonial government appointing leaders had been replaced by the *cabildos* electing their own leaders. *Cabildo* elections ultimately required approval by the colonial government which, in turn, shaped who would and would not be an acceptable candidate. However, there are not any known extant examples of authorities overturning an election. The change in policy from government-appointed to *cabildo*-elected leaders reflected the ability of nations to create a leadership structure acceptable to colonial officials. *Cabildos* expanded their restricted autonomy to determine the internal affairs of their societies by selecting leaders who did not attract the government's close scrutiny.

While government officials referred to *cabildo* leaders as *capataz* or captain, some nations came up with their own titles. The free black José Caridad Herrera described Antonio José Barraga, the leader of the Karabali *cabildo*, as "Captain General."[105] Authorities learned that "inside the house" of the Kongo nation, members called the *capataz* Joaquín "the Kongo King."[106] The difference between the government-given title of *capataz* and the chosen title, by some *cabildo* leaders, of captain general or king probably did not represent any vast difference in the function of nations. Nonetheless, the distinction does reveal the tension that informed the process of identification and self-identification. The decision by the Kongolese to give their leader the title of king might be considered as something more than a generic reference to monarchical authority. Throughout the eighteenth century one of the central claims to legitimate rule in the Kongo region was made by asserting "I am the King of the Kongos."[107] Civil wars split the Kingdom of Kongo into various camps that claimed adherence to a military king or a blacksmith king, which may have informed who became selected as a leader of a *cabildo* in Cuba. Some *cabildos* eschewed the leadership titles of *capataz* and captain provided by the colonial government. Perhaps they did so in reaction to how colonial society disproportionately shaped the discourse of identity, from stripping Africans of their birth names to deciding what titles could be given to *cabildo* leaders.

Many of the leaders of the *cabildos* earned their elected position by distinguishing themselves as militia soldiers. Manuel Blanco rose to a leadership role within the black militia by commanding a 100 man company that fought in the American Revolution. He also served as a leading force in directing the financial affairs of the *cabildo* Lucumi.[108] Retired militia soldiers of the black battalion of Havana, Tomás Poveda and Clemente Andrade, served as the elected leaders of the *cabildo* Karabali.[109] Juan Gavilan, also a retired soldier, emphasized his military service when he wrote to the captain general to resolve a dispute within the *cabildo* Karabali Umugini.[110] Military distinction and service helped to single out these soldiers as leaders among people of color and within their own communities.[111] For many soldiers, the militia represented an opportunity for social advancement and a steppingstone toward achieving what some scholars have regarded as "social whiteness" through the acquisition of legal rights denied to blacks and mulattos.[112] The acquisition of rights and special privileges accorded to soldiers, however, did not necessarily preclude identification with slaves and free people of color. The common appearance of militiamen as elected *cabildo* leaders likely indicates their military status did not automatically separate them from slaves and free people of color, but rather could elevate them to leadership roles.

Cabildo leaders tied to the militia would often have their *fuero* rights extended to the associations. Domingo Acosta, the *capataz* of the Karabali Apapa nation, drew upon his connections as a retired militia soldier to request that a military court settle a dispute within the *cabildo*.[113] Captain General Someruelos recommended that a "military tribunal" investigate the financial affairs of the Mina Guagni nation after Esteban Torres and Salvador Ternero emphasized their militia service.[114] When Manuel Blanco became involved in a property dispute with the *cabildo* Lucumi over selling the nation's house, he hoped to win the case by mentioning his volunteer militia service and stressing that he did it "without receiving a salary or any gratification."[115] The selection of *cabildo* leaders from the ranks of the colored militia served to present colonial authorities with individuals they regarded as loyal subjects of the Spanish Crown. By electing leaders acceptable to government officials, the *cabildos* would suffer less scrutiny and supervision.[116]

An examination of the electoral process indicates that female members often guided the affairs of the nation, not the elected *capataz* as Cuban officials believed. Because of their numerical superiority among the *cabildo*'s voting members, women often decided the selection of new leaders. For example, of the forty-two eligible voters who participated in the *cabildo* Karabali Oquella elections of 1804, thirty-one were women.[117] Although the majority of males cast their votes for Cayetano García as the new *capataz* for the *cabildo* Kongo Macamba in 1807, Antonio Diepa won the election because of six females votes.[118] Of the forty-seven votes cast in favor of Juan Echevarría for the position of second *capataz* of the *cabildo* Karabali Induri, thirty-two came from women, guaranteeing his margin of victory by a ratio of two to one. The *capataz* of the *cabildo* Jesús Sollazo attempted to overturn Echevarría's election on the basis that he was not of Karabali Induri ethnicity, "but also because the general customs observed in the *cabildos* of this city for the elections of *capataz* do not admit the votes of women."[119] The captain general ruled against Sollazo's motion to not accept the women's votes for *capataz* because it was "contrary to what is daily observed."[120] The *capataz* of the Karabali Oquella, Cristobal Govin, shared Jesús Sollazo's opinion that female participation in *cabildos* should be limited because Lázaro Rodríguez won the election with "only the assistance of Teresa Barreto's supporters."[121] As women actively participated in the urban economy and made up a noticeable percentage of the urban free population of color, they played a decisive role in determining who led the *cabildos*.

While some *cabildo* leaders felt threatened by the authority women could exert in shaping the leadership of African societies, others recognized their important role in maintaining the unity of nations. In 1805 José Arostegui of the *cabildo* Karabali Osso informed the captain general of the death of Rita Castellanos who held the leadership position among the female members of the nation. Shortly thereafter, Barbara de Mesa "occupied her place with all the support of the nation for her recommendable" characteristics. Arostegui requested that the captain general "give his recognition to Barbara de Mesa as *capataza*" so that she could "govern the women of said *cabildo* with authority" to insure "perfect peace and harmony."[122] Other *cabildos* not only recognized the important role of women in governing female members but acknowledged their crucial role in promoting a unified organization. When the queen of the Kongo Macamaba nation, Rafaela Armentaras, died, the *cabildo* recognized that without her leadership "the disorder has increased," and they could no longer resolve disputes by themselves but required government intervention.[123]

Not only did females in *cabildos* exhibit considerable authority in determining leaders, they also influenced financial expenditures. Through membership dues, renting rooms, collecting alms, and hosting festivals, *cabildos* normally held savings in cash that varied from 300 to 1,000 pesos. These savings represented a significant amount given that the prices for slaves in Havana newspapers usually ranged from 300 to 500 pesos.[124] The important duty of guarding the safe that contained the *cabildo's* money usually fell upon the queen. When the *cabildo* Karabali Osso became involved in a dispute that required paying a legal fine, Barbara de Mesa would not turn over the safe to the neighborhood commissioner José Castillo "until she had been threatened with prison."[125] When members of the *cabildo* Karabali Oquella challenged the financial expenses of the *capataz*, the whole nation went "to the house of Teresa Barreto, queen of said *cabildo*," to count the money in the safe. The *cabildo* leaders pulled from the safe "a bag full of money and in the presence of the nation . . . counted 946 pesos."[126] Most *cabildos* entrusted the queen of the nation with guarding their money, but they took precautions to insure that it would take more than one person to open the safe.

Cabildos used a safe modeled on the Spanish coffer that required three different keys to prevent one person from making a withdrawal.[127] The *cabildo* Karabali Induri distributed its "three different keys" to the "First *Capataz*," the "Second *Capataz*" and "an elected person in consultation with all the nation." The three key holders could only open the safe in the presence of "twenty people, men or women, of the nation" to explain the purpose of withdrawals.[128] Likewise, the *cabildo* Kongo Macamba also required its safe to be opened in the presence of its members to "avoid future disputes, objections, and suspicions of the *capataz*."[129] Female leaders of *cabildos* guarded the safe, but they did not hold the keys to open it. The Kongo Macamba nation stated very clearly that whoever "takes on the task of treasury" would have to be a "black male."[130] The leader of the *cabildo* Karabali Oquella, Cristóbal Govín, feared that "the funds of the *cabildo* held by Teresa Barreto, a rebellious women with bad ideas," would jeopardize the stability of the nation.[131] Govín feared she could get a hold of "the common money of the nation," which would empower her to "move all of these machinations."[132] Whether through deciding elections or guarding the safe, females decisively shaped *cabildo* functions.[133]

"Entertainment, Food, and Drink": Unity Through Collective Identity

The *cabildos* showed remarkable flexibility in maintaining an overall sense of unity despite their divisions. While it is important to emphasize distinctions of ethnicity, place of birth, legal status, and gender, given that the members of the nations themselves made these distinctions, it is just as important to recognize that *cabildos* continued to support the collective efforts of the nation as a whole. Moreover, the documentary record is biased to show divisions because the archival sources were created when the colonial state intervened to settle disputes. As with many organizations representing lower-class interests in a society controlled by a powerful elite, the tension between the specific needs of individual members and the unity of the *cabildos* created friction within the associations. *Cabildos* could recognize and address dissent within their own ranks without causing the complete dissolution of their societies, indicating that collective needs often superseded individual interests. The organizations represented the only institutions that permitted voluntary grouping along ethnic lines by Africans and Creoles, men and women, and slaves and freedpersons in Cuba. For a colony rigidly divided between white European masters and black African slaves, *cabildos* stood in contrast to the racial slave-free paradigm that defined the circles of inclusion and exclusion for most of Cuban society.

Cabildos also broke down the division between rural and urban society. Although the urban *cabildo* house provided the center for the nations' activities, members represented both the city and countryside. When the *cabildo* Kongo Musolongo elected Augustín Pedroso to the position of *capataz* in 1806, the rural members of the nation could not travel to Havana to participate in the election. Before Pedroso could assume leadership of the *cabildo*, however, the nation recognized—in something akin to an absentee ballot—that the members "absent in the countryside agreed with the election of Pedroso."[134] Not only could *cabildos* break down rural and urban division by both groups participating in elections, but housing could also link the two distinct geographic areas. The free black María Francisca Duarte lived in the *cabildo* house of the Karabali Apapa located outside the city walls of Havana. She shared the room on weekends with her husband who worked in the countryside. "On the first day of the month," according to María Francisca, she paid five pesos in rent to the *capataz* of the *cabildo* when, "as customary, [her] husband came from the countryside."[135] Temporary housing on weekends served to unite rural and urban members of the nation and likely facilitated their attendance at *cabildo* functions in the city. In addition, and perhaps more importantly for María Francisca and her husband, the *cabildo* house offered temporary marital unity. The geographically gendered division of labor often separated spouses. Females most commonly found employment as market vendors and domestic servants in urban areas, whereas male laborers tended to dominate rural plantations.

The *cabildos'* cooperative methods of raising revenues and deciding expenditures revealed an emphasis on collective rather than individual goals. During three months in 1801, the *cabildo* Karabali Osso raised 576 pesos from membership donations. Apparently, the *cabildo* did not require a specific amount for all members to pay. Domingo Alcántra made the largest donation of 72 pesos, while Trinidad de Medina contributed the smallest amount of 29 pesos. Given that only fourteen members (six women and eight men) made donations to the *cabildo*'s safe, it is likely that participation in a nation did not require paying dues. According to Manuel de Jesús, who participated in an unnamed *cabildo* in Puerto Príncipe, slaves "were poor blacks who could contribute [only] one coin for the festivities."[136] The *cabildos* Karabali Induri and Karabali Oquella realized some members could not contribute from their own pockets but could provide money to the nation by begging for alms.[137] *Cabildos* represented diverse economic backgrounds such as free landowners, artisans, market vendors, and unpaid slave laborers. Consequently, a universal membership fee of any substantial amount for joining a nation would have been difficult to collect.

Cabildos often redistributed their money back to members. The society would hold a special meeting, and the members who had voting rights would then decide the financial affairs of the *cabildo*. Nations commonly provided loans to members and even purchased freedom for slaves who participated in the *cabildo*.[138] The account books of the *cabildo* Karabali Umugini recorded loans to José María Rebollo, María Dolores Méndez, and Josefa for unspecified reasons in December 1801.[139] In addition, *cabildos* offered medical and financial assistance to sick members. The Karabali Osso paid ten pesos to rent a "carriage to take a sick [member] of the nation to the village of Guanabacoa" located on the eastern side of Havana harbor.[140] Tomás, the king of Karabali Induri nation, recorded that the *cabildo* gave four pesos to "Matías Billalta who was sick."[141] The *cabildos* also paid for burial services that normally fell upon the lay brotherhoods of the Catholic Church.[142] Loans, medical assistance during periods of illness, or a solemn burial, brought the nation together by pooling their limited financial resources.

Festivals, more than any other activity, served to unite the nation. Almost all *cabildos* held elaborate celebrations on 6 January, the Day of the Kings. In addition, on other religious holidays, Sundays, and to transfer power to a newly elected leader or commemorate the death of a past one, *cabildos* hosted reunions at which they performed music and danced. During the festival days of San Blas in Bayamo in early February, all the *cabildos* of the city held gatherings and parades.[143] According to British traveler Robert Jameson, *cabildo* performances on Sunday could be observed throughout the city of Havana. "At these courtly festivals (usually held every Sunday and feast day) numbers of free and enslaved negroes assemble to do homage with a sort of grave merriment that one would doubt whether it was done in ridicule or memory of their former condition. The gong-gong—(christianized by the name of diablito), cows-horns, and every kind of inharmonious instrument, are flourished on by a gasping band assisted by clapping of hands, howling and the striking of every sounding material within reach, while the whole assemblage dance with maniac eagerness till their strength fails."[144] Jameson's musical preferences led him to describe the performances as played on nothing more than crudely fashioned instruments that revealed neither musical talent or purpose. It is likely that colonial authorities held the same opinion, and therefore, saw nothing threatening in the collective gatherings.

The view of *cabildos* as Africans engaged in simplistic savage dances depended, of course, on who witnessed them. When asked why a *cabildo* member from Bayamo participated in the festivals held by his nation, he told authorities that he had "entered for entertainment, food, and drink."[145] Juan José Moroto of the Lucumi nation, who grew up in Philadelphia, explained his participation in *cabildos* as an opportunity to express a collective ethnic solidarity not permitted in North America. Moroto told colonial officials that he "had been raised in North America where the blacks do not dance in *cabildos* and are not permitted to have dances, on the days of work they are working and on Sundays they are in the church praying."[146] In order to hold a dance, the *capataz* of the *cabildo* had to notify the neighborhood military officer and purchase a license; otherwise, they could be fined. For example, in 1796 military commissioner Juan García fined the Karabali Apapa nation eight pesos for "dancing in the *cabildo*" without a license.[147] Although *cabildo* festivals ultimately required approval from colonial authorities, they allowed Africans to identify themselves as members of ethnic-based organizations by performing rituals and customs they had brought across the Atlantic and transformed in Cuba.

Cabildo dances served to bring the members of the nation together to express a collective identity and solidarity and, at the same time, raise money for the nation. During festival days *cabildos* often opened their doors to nonmembers. For a small entrance fee, nonmembers of the *cabildos* could become spectators to the dances and ceremonies and purchase food and drink. *Cabildos* attracted a wide audience that included not only members of their own ethnic groups, but other Africans, people of African ancestry born in Cuba, and even curious white observers, according to European travelers.[148] Depending on the size of the festival, the *cabildos* could raise a substantial sum. In 1808 the *cabildo* Lucumi Llane collected fifty-seven pesos from entrance fees for a fiesta held in March.[149] The *cabildo* Karabali Osso raised 240 pesos over several religious holidays celebrated during Christmas in 1805.[150] The revenues, derived from selling tickets for *cabildo* performances, provided financial resources to fund the nation's other activities. Further, the attendance by members of different nations at *cabildo* houses during festival days provided the opportunity for the diverse African populations in Cuba to share the cultures they held in common. At the same time, the festivals also demonstrated what made the nations different from one another based on their place of origin. As the next chapter will analyze, *cabildo* members involved in the Aponte Rebellion would employ the shelter of festival days around Christmas in 1811 to collectively meet, plan, and organize the rebellion.

*

Members of *cabildos* chose to join associations to define themselves in cooperation with others who shared a similar ethnicity. In this sense, they show the importance of understanding that Africans in the Americas did not immediately or exclusively adopt a racialized identity of blackness. While *cabildos* above all emphasized ethnic identity, they did not ignore that whites were not slaves and that the ruling class of Cuba was not Africa. At meetings inside *cabildo* houses when nations discussed the needs of their members, they surely addressed the problems their organization faced of existing in a society based upon a racial hierarchy that privileged the European over the African. As a result, African ethnic identity was not necessarily in conflict with a New World racial identity of blackness. By providing a network of alliances and an institutional structure that offered a limited sense of familiarity for Africans in Cuba, *cabildos* helped their members to survive in a society based upon racial oppression.[151]

The process by which *cabildos* and the free people of color militia could address the specific needs of their own nations and fellow soldiers, and also serve the common interests of all people of African ancestry, became apparent in the Aponte Rebellion of 1812. Militia member and *cabildo* leader Salvador Ternero drew on his experiences as a soldier to gather arms, and he discussed and organized the rebellion in the security of Mina Guagni *cabildo* house.[152] Cuban authorities encouraged free people of color to participate in the militia and provide armed assistance for the colonial state, as this tied individuals to the Spanish Crown. Likewise, Cuban officials allowed the formation of *cabildos* because they believed African ethnic identification would prevent the formation of a broad-based racial movement. The Aponte Rebellion, however, revealed the flexibility and innovative nature of African identity in Cuba. Africans in Cuba could define themselves by simultaneously emphasizing both their Old World ethnicity and their New World racial identity, revealing the strength—not the weaknesses colonial officials assumed and some present-day observers fear—of cultural diversity.

Excerpt from Chapter 5, "Vanquish the Arrogance of Our Enemies"

"Emancipation Rumors and Rebellious Royalism"

And the executions continued for months. The hangman's list did not end with the leader José Antonio Aponte, the Frenchman Juan Barbier, the slave Tiburcio Peñalver, the free black Juan Bautista Lisundia, the black militiaman Clemente Chacón, the *cabildo* leader Salvador Ternero, and the mulatto Estanislao Aguilar. The executioner added free black Francisco Javier Pacheco's name to his deadly list. A Creole born in Havana who lived in the Salud neighborhood outside the city walls, Pacheco earned his living by working as a carpenter specializing in the repair of carriages. He also served as a volunteer militiaman in the black battalion of Havana.[153] Pacheco had been on the plantations at the time of the rebellions in March but eluded arrest until military authorities finally captured him on 7 May when he recklessly returned to Havana.[154]

After several days of questioning during May and June, Rendón sentenced Pacheco to death by hanging.[155] As with the slave Tiburcio Peñalver, mentioned in chapter 2, colonial officials postponed Pacheco's sentence until October to stage a collective execution of several conspirators. Early in the morning at 6:20 A.M. on 23 October 1812, an armed regiment of professional soldiers and volunteer militiamen escorted Pacheco and three others to La Punta military fort on the western side of Havana Bay. Captain General Apodaca reported that the crowd "applauded the gesticulations" of Pacheco and the other rebels during their last earthly moments as they dangled from the end of ropes.[156] The bodies were left hanging for nearly nine hours until at three in the afternoon, the Brotherhood of Charity removed them.[157] Afterward, the executioner severed Pacheco's head, affixed it to a pike, and placed it at the entrance to his neighborhood outside the city walls to serve as a grim warning for all to see.[158]

Pacheco had close associations with many of his fellow rebels. He informed authorities that he had "known Aponte ever since he was a small boy because he learned his [carpentry] trade with him as an apprentice."[159] Pacheco often visited Aponte's house and like many others had seen Aponte's book of drawings.[160] He also knew Clemente Chacón, testifying he visited "his house three times to eat lunch."[161] Authorities believed Pacheco and Juan Barbier organized the insurrection during several meetings at Chacón's tavern.[162] The slave Antonio Cao from Peñas-Altas informed officials that he met Pacheco at Aponte's house when they planned the rebellion.[163] Pacheco's connections with the important leaders of the Aponte Rebellion only further contributed to his guilt in the minds of colonial officials investigating the movement.

The crucial evidence for Pacheco's role as a leader of the movement related to a political manifesto tacked to the captain general's home on 15 March 1812, proclaiming independence, and attributed to his handwriting.

Several people stated Pacheco had transcribed the proclamation from dictation by Aponte. The powerful message of the declaration stated in no uncertain terms that the revolution was on: "At the sound of a drum and a trumpet you will find us ready and fearless to end this empire of tyranny, and in this manner we will vanquish the arrogance of our enemies."[164] The bold action of nailing the manifesto to the captain general's house offered not merely an explicit warning to the colonial state of their intentions but a call to arms for their followers. Although not a formal political document composed by a congress or a junta, it should be regarded as a declaration for Cuban independence (if not Cuba's first). As explained in the previous chapter, slaves and free people of color denounced the movement in Havana on 10 March. Placing the declaration of independence on the residence of the highest-ranking Spanish official in Cuba sent a clear message to their partisans of a steadfast conviction to follow through with their plans for insurrection.

The Havana town council petitioned Someruelos to conduct an immediate investigation when they met two days later in the exact same building where the rebels had posted their insurrectionary declaration. The town council recognized that "the revolution," as they referred to the movement, was well planned, as seen "by what happened to the door of this house on the fifteenth." According to the Havana town council, the manifesto indicated an intent to repeat the same events as the "windward island," in reference to Haiti.[165] Aponte later confessed that he "dictated the manifesto to Pacheco, who transcribed it and assumed the responsibility for posting it."[166] Authorities found a draft of the proclamation at Clemente Chacón's house, which he reportedly planned to circulate prior to the rebellion.[167] The declaration posted on the captain general's residence, the draft found in Chacón's home, and knowledge of the document among rebels, caused authorities to believe the insurgents circulated the manifesto during the planning and organization of the rebellion. Despite Pacheco's claims of ignorance about the declaration, authorities concluded "Aponte dictated the seditious manifesto transcribed by Pacheco, who assumed the responsibility for placing it on the house of government."[168] For colonial officials investigating the rebellion, the political intentions behind the document that called slaves and free people of color to arms for what they regarded as a revolution required swift and severe punishments.

This chapter explores the rebels' motivations, hopes, aspirations, goals, and ideas that inspired the bold action of drafting a declaration of independence to announce courageously the beginning of their movement. Two political and ideological currents represented by royalism and racial revolution converged in the Aponte Rebellion. A series of rumors circulated throughout the island that a distant king had declared the slaves free, but their masters would not promulgate the decree. Emancipation rumors by royal decree became intertwined with stories and sightings of black military leaders from the Haitian Revolution. Reportedly, the Haitians came to Cuba to assist slaves and free people of color in their insurrection. Aponte and other leaders aligned their movement with these stories and rumors, circulated them, and refashioned them as a basis for legitimizing their cause and catalyzing the insurrection. In conjuring royalist approval for the insurrection and Haitian military and political power, they crafted a complex and seemingly contradictory political culture. Monarchical authority had the power to end slavery by decree, and the Haitian Revolution showed slaves how to claim their freedom with their own hands.

Royalist Emancipation Decrees Crisscrossing the Atlantic World

The reports of slaves being declared free circulated widely throughout the island at the end of 1811 and during the first months of 1812. As a result of the limited privileges slaves had to visit and socialize with friends beyond the confines of their own plantations, word began to spread rapidly among them about declarations of freedom during the Christmas holiday season. In the town of Puerto Principe, the slave Manuel de Jesús reported that during the Christmas "celebrations attended by the blacks" from various plantations, they talked of their freedom.[169] The twenty-five-year-old Mandinga slave named Francisco Xavier testified that during Christmas he and other slaves had "conversations about being given their freedom."[170] An unnamed slave reported that they had conversations discussing that "the King had given them their freedom but the Caballeros [in reference to the Cuban elite]" would not recognize the decree.[171] In the eastern town of Bayamo, slaves congregated on the festival days of La Candelaria, San Blas, and San Blas Chiquito, from 2 to 4 February, when they socialized and heard rumors of their possible freedom. According to a slave owned by Teresa Barreta, slaves and free people of color in Bayamo discussed that in Puerto Principe "the blacks had revolted" because "their freedom had been denied to them."[172] Through Christmas and other holidays that allowed slaves to temporarily step outside the bounds of master supervision, word of a reported decree of freedom began to spread rapidly across the island.

In Havana, authorities began to investigate the widespread talk about a slave emancipation decree before insurrections erupted on the plantations in mid-March. According to Pablo José, owned by Don Melchor Valdés, in February slaves began to discuss being declared free but denied the right by their masters.[173] The administrator of a coffee plantation outside of Havana reported to officials that an unknown black man spread news among slaves that a decree of freedom "had been hidden by the Governor and the [town] council and that he had come to call together all the people to go to Havana to obtain their liberty."[174]

According to the slave driver on a coffee plantation owned by Santiago Malagamba, an unknown black man asked him to assemble the slaves so that "they could go to Havana to ask for their letters of freedom."[175] After insurrections erupted on several nearby plantations, authorities arrested Francisco Galano for inciting slaves to rise in revolt and march on Havana to claim their freedom.[176]

Emancipation rumors that circulated widely across the island traced some of their roots to the turbulent politics in Spain during the Napoleonic Wars. As a result of the French occupation of the Iberian Peninsula, the weakened regency had conceded parliamentary representation to the colonies. On 26 March 1811, a Mexican representative to the Cortes at Cádiz proposed that "slavery as a violation of natural law, already outlawed by the laws of civilized countries ... should be abolished forever."[177] The shocking suggestion quickly crossed the Atlantic. Cuban captain general Someruelos wrote the Cortes urging them "to treat the issue with all the reserve, detailed attention, and thought that its grave nature requires in order to not lose this important island." News of the debate over slavery circulated in Havana and other cities through the *Diario de sesiones de Cortes*, causing "a significant sensation among the inhabitants of the capital, and a very sad series of grumblings ... throughout the island," according to Someruelos.[178] The Cuban representative to the Cortes, Andrés de Jáuregui, wrote to the Havana town council informing them of the debate in Spain that "conjures up a storm so threatening to my country ... it could degenerate into horrific conclusions."[179] Jáuregui recommended that if the Cortes had to debate the issue of slavery and the slave trade, it be done in "secret and with moderation ... [to] not excite any murmuring in our servants."[180] The Havana town council concluded that the discussions in the Cortes resulted in "exciting the slaves' aspirations to obtain their freedom with the confidence that it had already been given to them."[181] When word of the debate in the Cortes reached Puerto Principe in June, the council decided to increase the number and frequency of slave patrols in the countryside to guard against their "domestic enemies."[182]

Cuban slaveowners correctly concluded that any actions to end the slave trade and slavery threatened their economic prosperity and could result in financial ruin. The town council of Santiago emphatically protested that any discussion of abolition would result in slaves "emancipating themselves by their own hands and repeating in the island of Cuba the same catastrophe that covered in blood and ashes the largest and most opulent colony of the Antilles," an allusion to French Saint Domingue.[183] William Shaler, an American commercial agent in Havana, wrote to the United States government that the prospect of abolition moved Cuban planters to suggest to him that the "Island of Cuba ought to become part of the United States."[184] The question of the abolition of slavery attracted the attention of a wide and varied audience: masters concerned about their property; Spanish officials seeking to maintain the colonial status of Cuba; and pre-Monroe doctrine Americans eager to expand their power in the hemisphere. Perhaps nobody, however, showed as much interest as the slaves, who had the most to gain.

Cuban fears that the ongoing discussion of abolition in the Spanish Cortes could result in slaves making their own conclusions about the debate came to fruition during the first months of 1812. Captain General Someruelos claimed that the "contagion . . . of false and attractive news and promises that the Cortes had decreed the slaves free, and [that] the government of this island had concealed from them this extremely important point," resulted in "the slaves becoming involved in the criminal project."[185] Slaves such as Maria Candelaria explained their participation in the revolt "because in spite of having granted the slaves their freedom, it had been denied to them" by their masters.[186] Free black Juan Bautista Vaillant, who had been born in Jamaica and later moved to Cuba, reported that it was not the Cortes but the king who "decreed that all the blacks are free, but the whites . . . did not want to give them their freedom."[187] Slaves deftly crafted a response that stated their reasons for rising in rebellion centered on loyalty to misunderstood directives of the Spanish Cortes and king.

The repeated references to a declaration of freedom resulted in judicial officials recommending lighter punishments for slaves, since false rumors had motivated their actions. Lawyers Francisco Maria Agüero and José Maria Ortega reasoned that the slaves should not receive harsh punishments for believing their "owners had usurped the sovereign disposition of the Cortes," and that the Cortes "acted in their favor" with an emancipation decree.[188] Perhaps better than anybody, slaves understood the asymmetrical patron–client relations that defined Cuban political culture. By claiming royalist approval for rising in rebellion, slaves provided a recognized justification to explain their actions in a colony governed by a monarchical paradigm for political and social organization. Cuban officials increasingly narrowed their questions on why slaves rose in revolt to the Cortes decree because it explained the insurrection as simply a "misunderstanding" rather than a strike for freedom. Not all slaves, however, explained their participation as a result of a decree that originated in Spain.

Several slaves and free people of color arrested for their involvement in the rebellion explained that the king of England had declared them free. Free black Francisco Javier Pacheco, for example, reported that at the time of the rebellion a rumor spread throughout the plantation districts that the "King of England" had called for freeing all the slaves in Cuba. Pacheco elaborated that the "English had seized ships filled with slaves that came to Cuba because they did not want slavery . . . sending them [instead] to Santo Domingo [Haiti] because there they were ruled by a black King."[189] The African-born Kongo slave Francisco González repeated a similar story of England's role as an emancipating force on the island.

During the planning of the insurrection, Francisco had been told "Havana was in rebellion because there had arrived an English General ordering the Captain General" of Cuba to provide "freedom for all the slaves." Similar to the story of the declaration of freedom by the Spanish Cortes, slaves emphasized that the "Captain General hid the decree." As a result, Francisco and other slaves planned "to join together and go to Havana to look for the letter."[190] Captain General Someruelos later suggested that the idea of England interceding on the slaves' behalf resulted from the widespread circulation of an article originally published in London in October 1811 critical of Cuban slavery that could be found in the "hands of everybody" on the island.[191]

Whether through overhearing masters talk about British abolitionist activities or through their own forms of information, slaves and free people of color came to learn of emancipation activities in other parts of the Atlantic world. As they planned their own rebellion, they connected their struggles for freedom to stories and rumors that an English king had declared them free. Slaves from the British Caribbean imported to Cuba through legal and contraband trade may have spread stories about an English king taking on a liberating role in the Aponte Rebellion. As plantation agriculture expanded across Cuba and the actions of the British Parliament led Jamaican masters to fear an immediate abolition by decree, an illicit slave trade from Jamaica to Cuba flourished. Colonial officials reported periodically on the illegal importation of slaves from Jamaica and emphasized the need to take "all the proper precautions to not permit the landing of any slaves until they have been classified as pure *bozales*" direct from Africa.[192] Despite such precautions, transactions of individual slave sales reveal that Jamaica remained an important source for laborers in the eastern portion of the island throughout the first half of the nineteenth century.[193] Several plantations had large populations of Jamaican slaves that required English-speaking overseers to direct the laborers who understood little Spanish.[194] The large presence of Jamaican slaves was poignantly revealed in the 1805 Bayamo Conspiracy when an English-speaking slave took on the role of official court translator because no free person white or black could be found to perform the task.[195] In the 1840s, British abolitionists discovered that "so large is the number of British subjects held in slavery in one district in the island of Cuba that the English language is almost exclusively spoken among them."[196] As the slave population from the British Caribbean increased in Cuba, it appears that some slaves transformed the rumor from the Cortes declaring them free to one that reflected their own cultural background, represented by an English king.

The rumors and stories of emancipating monarchs aiding the Aponte Rebellion in the form of the kings of Spain and England also included the king of the Kongo. Among slaves of Kongo ethnicity in the town of Puerto Príncipe, word spread that the "King of the Kongo" had declared them free and was sending troops to aid the rebellion. According to the twelve-year-old female slave María Belen, slaves she identified as members of her same "nation" discussed the emancipation rumor during the Christmas holiday. María learned of the rumor from fellow Kongo slave José María while working in her master's kitchen. In a conversation that likely occurred in their native African language, María reported that José told the slaves that the "King of the Kongos had sent letters here to order freedom for the blacks." The blacks, however, remained enslaved because "*el mundo* [the world]," the term used by slaves to "designate white people," did not, according to María, want to grant them their freedom. As a result, the king of the Kongos "would send many Blacks to kill all the whites and give land to the slaves." María reported that she had heard similar stories from the slaves Francisco and Domingo, indicating that the rumor had apparently been discussed widely.[197]

Judicial officials then proceeded to question the slaves who had reportedly spread the rumor of Kongo assistance. José María did not deny that he told María Belen "while they were in the kitchen that the King had ordered the freedom of the blacks and that the whites here opposed" the decree.[198] María Belen even told her mistress, Ana Rita Coronado, about the decree for fear that she could get in trouble for having simply participated in the conversations. Upon learning of the discussion among the slaves about the king of the Kongo, Coronado decided to disregard the rumor because she claimed "nobody believed it," as it came from the mouths that others regarded as "liars."[199] Slaves from the Kongo region decisively influenced Cuban society through their culture, social organizations, and political ideas that they brought with them that survived the horrific middle passage. Of the slaves and free people of color questioned for their involvement in the Aponte Rebellion who specified their African ethnicity in testimony, 40 percent, 56 out of 139, claimed a Kongo identity among various other West African groups such as Mandinga, Lucumi, Mina, Carabali, Ganga, Arara, and others.[200] This figure of 40 percent corresponds with the latest data that estimates west-central Africans represented 41 percent of the overall Cuban slave imports for the period 1806–20.[201] Only after the insurrections erupted on the plantations and Kongo slaves had been arrested for participating in the rebellion did authorities recognize that the stories they regarded as harmless conversations about the wishful assistance of the king of the Kongo could have influenced slaves to revolt.

The reference to the king of the Kongo and his role in aiding the Aponte Rebellion was not unique to Cuba. Historian John Thornton has argued that the civil wars in the eighteenth-century Kingdom of Kongo that funneled thousands of slaves across the Atlantic resulted in Africans bringing with them clearly defined notions of monarchical authority. Slaves' allegiance to the Kingdom of Kongo and explicit references to define themselves as subjects of the "King of Kongo," played an important role in the Haitian Revolution. Kongolese political ideology decisively shaped how some participants in the Haitian Revolution defined monarchial authority and served as a point of reference for slaves to legitimate their cause.[202] Similarly, on the nearby island of Martinique, rumors circulated in the 1760s and 1789 that the king of Angola would come with a powerful army to free the slaves and take them back to their country.[203] As many Cuban slaves had their primary political and cultural ideas formed by their experiences in Africa and not just the New World, we should not be surprised to find references to the "King of the Kongo" as a likely source for an emancipation decree and to the aid he would provide for the Aponte Rebellion.

"The Black King José Antonio Aponte Had Painted"

A similar story of Cuban slaves being liberated by an order from a king with aid of military generals also found inspiration from the nearby island of Haiti. Several slaves reported that it was not the Spanish Cortes, the English king, or the ruler of Kongo that had declared them free, but the king of Haiti. At the time of the rebellion, some of the arrested were found in possession of proclamation from Saint Domingue that had reportedly been shown to others.[204] "Havana was very agitated," slave José Antonio had heard, "because some black generals from Haiti had come with an order from the black King to tell the governor of Havana to give the slaves freedom."[205] Another bondsman reported one or two black captains from Haiti had ordered the Governor to free the slaves in the name of the King of Haiti."[206] Slave Joaquin Belaguer had reportedly "talked in his excessive inebriation" about the elaborate" "coronation of [Henri] Christophe," only recently crowned emperor of Haiti in 1811, which resulted in slaves regarding him as the liberating king.[207] Cuban authorities who suppressed the insurrection remained convinced that Haitian agents planned to aid the rebellion. Captain General Someruelos told the successor to his office that "he believed without a doubt . . . there had been here several hardened black warriors that had served in Saint Domingue with military rank."[208] Planters reported to the town council of Havana that "external enemies" had been conducted to Cuba by an "emissary" from the "neighboring and close island of Santo Domingo [Hispaniola]."[209] Havana's representatives to the Spanish Cortes at Cádiz stated that "it was believed, and rumors circulated, that for the planned [revolt] the black Henri Christophe . . . would play a part with boats and arms."[210] In Puerto Rico, similar reports of Henri Christophe as a liberating monarch circulated throughout the island in 1812, which prompted Governor Meléndez to form slave patrols to monitor the plantations.[211] As the only nation to abolish slavery in the Americas, Haiti seemed to many Cuban slaves, a logical point of origin for an emancipation decree.

Singled out among the presumed revolutionary generals from Haiti as one who would order the Cuban captain general to free the slaves was Jean François known in Spanish-speaking Cuba as Juan Francisco. Several of the arrested rebels testified to seeing and talking with Juan Francisco at the time of the rebellion. Free mulatto Estanislao Aguilar told authorities that he had attended a "meeting in a tavern" near the "road that leads to the sugar plantations, accompanied by Juan Francisco, or Juan Fransura."[212] Juan Lisundia, a free black arrested for his involvement in a revolt on a sugar plantation outside Havana, had heard that "the black Juan Francisco . . . had arrived at the village of Guanabacoa."[213] Javier Pacheco reported that he "had dinner with other blacks and Juan Francisco, who brought two bottles of wine to toast their good success."[214] According to free black Clemente Chacón, José Antonio Aponte had told him that Juan Francisco "was an Admiral that served at the orders of the black king Christophe of Santo Domingo and came with his dispatches to seduce the free blacks and slaves of this island."[215] The "Admiral" was the title Jean François called himself while fighting with the Spanish against the French during the early years of the Haitian Revolution. Knowledge of his title may reveal the detailed information received by blacks in Cuba regarding events in Saint Domingue.[216]

Untangling the stories of who had seen, talked with, and talked about "Juan Francisco" and other revolutionaries from Haiti remains difficult. The life-or-death threat of imminent punishment greatly influenced how participants recounted the events of the past. Authorities later concluded from the testimony of other rebels, who knew him as "Juan Francisco," that Juan Barbier, a free black who had traveled to Charleston, South Carolina, and spent considerable time in Saint Domingue where he learned how to read, write, and speak French, assumed the identity of the famous agent to galvanize support for the insurrection.

Judicial officials at first assumed Juan Barbier was the Haitian agent "Juan Francisco" when they arrested him in March 1812. They quickly questioned him about his involvement in the rebellion and attempted to swear him into the criminal proceedings with the name "Juan Francisco." Juan Barbier stubbornly refused to answer any questions until he was sworn in as "Juan Barbier" and not "Juan Francisco." He emphatically asserted that his "true name is Juan Barbier" and "because he has his own true name he will not be called" Juan Francisco. Dumbfounded by Barbier's assertion and with no evidence but hearsay from other slaves and free people of color to prove otherwise, judicial officials followed Barbier's request and he was sworn in as "Juan Barbier," not "Juan Francisco."[217] What requires further exploration is placing within a Cuban context the numerous references by slaves and free people of color to an emancipation decree from Haiti and its association with Henri Christophe and Juan Francisco, to understand how it resonated with the rebels' own experience.[218]

"Juan Francisco" became intimately associated with the Aponte

Rebellion for reasons stemming from his historical presence in Cuba. "Jean François" the historical figure had been an early leader of the Haitian Revolution who had allied with Spanish forces against the French. His inability to develop a strategy of slave emancipation or identify with the French National Convention's declaration of abolition, as had Toussaint Louverture, resulted in his declining influence. In July 1795, Spain and the Directory of the French Republic signed a peace treaty ceding western Hispaniola to France, leaving Jean François and his troops without a country. "In the year 1796," Captain General Someruelos later recalled, "Juan Francisco, *caudillo* of the blacks from Santo Domingo, with other military chiefs of his," namely Georges Biassou and Gil Narciso, attempted to settle in Cuba.[219] Havana's town council barred Jean François from living in Cuba because "several blacks had prepared functions to celebrate the arrival of Juan Francisco to show their affection toward him and his officials without ever meeting them."[220] Cuban governor Luis de Las Casas wrote to Madrid in December 1795 protesting Jean François' plans to settle in Cuba because "his name rings in the ears of the mob as an invincible hero, redeemer of the slaves . . . and [one who] germinates the seeds of insurrection."[221] The exiled troops from Saint Domingue stayed only a brief time in Cuba, prohibited by officials from disembarking while docked for several weeks on the other side of the harbor to minimize their interaction with free people of color and slaves.[222] After a short stay in Havana, Jean François left for Cádiz, Spain; Georges Biassou, for Saint Augustine, Florida; Gil Narciso, for Guatemala; and other troops scattered throughout the Spanish Caribbean.[223]

Jean François' association with Cuba did not end with his brief Havana stay in 1796. Over the next fifteen years, there would be several reports of Jean François' soldiers visiting Havana or attempting to settle on the island.[224] In 1805, for example, authorities in Bayamo investigated a reported conspiracy among slaves who had talked about the Haitian Revolution. The slave Juan Bautista stated he would be "Captain" of the movement and "kill his master," just as "Juan Fransura" would have done.[225] Such stories may have served to transform Jean François, the reluctant slave emancipator of Saint Domingue defeated by Toussaint Louverture's rise to power, into "Juan Francisco," an admiral that served at the orders of the black "King Christophe." "Juan Francisco" may have even represented the black King. Free black Salvador Ternero claimed that Aponte "assured" him "that he knew the black King, and had seen him in Havana many years ago."[226] Aponte may have been referring to the "many years ago" when Jean François had briefly stayed in Havana. Reports of aid from "Juan Francisco" to execute the orders of Haitian king Henri Christophe literally took on a life of their own. Jean François had died in Cádiz, Spain, in 1805. His resurrection, however, as "Juan Francisco" in the minds of Cuba's slave and free people of color population provided another life for the revolutionary from Haiti.[227]

The arrival in Havana and subsequent arrest of several soldiers who had more than ten years earlier served under Jean François provided further credibility to the reports of Haitian assistance for the Aponte Rebellion. At the end of December 1811, "twenty blacks from the island of Santo Domingo with six heads of family" arrived in Havana. Captain General Someruelos housed the blacks from Saint Domingue at the military fort Casa Blanca, provided a "ration in specie of silver" to buy goods and supplies owing to their previous service to the Spanish Crown, and allowed them to stay in Havana while they prepared to return to Hispaniola.[228] During their stay at Casa Blanca, Gil Narciso and others made several requests to cross the harbor to hear mass, wash clothes, and receive medical treatment in Havana.[229] Sometime before 24 March 1812, colonial officials detained Gil Narciso and three of his aides, Juan Luis Santillán, José Gaston, and Isidro Plutton, for suspected involvement in the rebellions. Santillán explained that it was not the first time he and the others had been to Havana: "We came in a boat from Bayajá [Fort Dauphin] when Juan Francisco had also come, and after staying awhile, we went with Gil Narciso to the Kingdom of Guatemala."[230] Narciso told authorities that while in Guatemala, he had learned of a royal order from Cádiz "for all of the migrants of said island [Hispaniola] to return to their origin." Jean François' former soldiers explained that they had only stopped in Havana en route to Santo Domingo.[231]

Cuban authorities did not ask questions specifically related to their possible involvement in the rebellion but only whether they had contact with blacks from Havana. Narciso admitted he had visited the free people of color and slave neighborhoods located outside the city walls of Havana. Greeted by various people of color, mulattos as well as blacks, Narciso had been "asked from where he had come and where he was headed."[232] José Gaston told authorities that several blacks and mulattos "on various occasions, asked if it was true that among him and his companions there was a Brigadier." Gaston noted that he was asked by slaves that the brigadier "be shown in a uniform."[233] The interest expressed in seeing the "brigadier" may refer to Gil Narciso's military rank while fighting under Jean François in the service of the Spanish Crown.[234] Likewise, the "people of color in the neighborhoods outside the city walls," showed an interest in the military uniform of Isidro Plutton.[235] Just one day after questioning Narciso, Santillán, Gaston, and Plutton for the first time, Captain General Someruelos ordered that "the blacks who are imprisoned at Casa Blanca should leave today for Santo Domingo," and they left the island.[236]

The brief questioning, prompt release, and unspecified dates of detention in Havana, make it difficult to establish the relationship of Jean François' former soldiers to the Aponte Rebellion. Someruelos may have decided to release the prisoners in the belief that Gil Narciso and those under his command intended to aid the rebellion; thus, by sending them to Santo Domingo, he followed the familiar policy of isolating Cuba from the contagion of radical insurgents. On the other hand, the captain general may have believed that while unconnected to the rebellion, the soldiers' presence in Havana and the interest shown by people of color in their uniforms fanned the flames of an already insurrectionary situation by legitimizing the rumors of Haitian assistance. It is also possible that Narciso and the others had intended to join the rebellion but, after learning of its quick suppression, opted to continue on to Santo Domingo. Gil Narciso may have been a man in search of a revolution. The same year Narciso arrived in Santo Domingo, he participated in a slave revolt.[237] At the very least, the presence of Gil Narciso and his troops served to substantiate rumors of "Juan Francisco's" participation in the revolt, if not provide the inspiration for such reports.

While it is unclear if Jean François' former soldiers planned to participate in the rebellion, several free people of color and slaves sought them out to ask them why they had come to Havana. Isidro Plutton noted—as had Gil Narciso and José Fantacia Gaston—that several people "had come to visit him and his companions.[238] Among those who wanted to see and talk with the troops of Gil Narciso was Salvador Ternero. He testified that he crossed Havana's harbor and went to the small military fort of Casa Blanca that quartered the former soldiers of Jean François "to see them and ask if they were Brigadiers as it had been said."[239] Ternero reported that there he spoke with three of the soldiers but did "not see the French general that Aponte told him" about.[240] The free black Juan Barbier also went to Casa Blanca to see the soldiers.[241] According to Clemente Chacón, Barbier told several at a meeting at Aponte's house that "the blacks at Casa Blanca are his people and they have come to conquer this land for the people of color as they had done numerous times."[242] The leaders of the Aponte Rebellion seized upon the opportunity provided by the presence of former soldiers of Jean François to build support and enthusiasm for their own movement. As an artist accustomed to working with images and representations, Aponte used the medium of Haiti to craft a powerful movement supported by the only independent black country in the Western Hemisphere born from the liberating destruction of a slave revolution.

In addition to stories of Haitian assistance and the presence of Saint Domingue veterans in Cuba, the rebels creatively invoked the military uniforms of the Haitian Revolution as a recruitment strategy in planning the insurrection. After the military quashed the rebellion, a slave named Joaquín owned by José Domingo Pérez told the mayor of San Antonio Abad that, at the time of the revolt, he had seen a "black with a uniform from Guarico [Haiti]."[243] Unless Joaquín was from Haiti, somebody must have influenced his ideas of what a "uniform from Guarico" looked like. Clemente Chacón reported to authorities that he had been introduced to Juan Francisco, who was "dressed in a blue military jacket demonstrating he was a great subject, indicated by his line of gold buttons on his jacket, some with the image of an anchor and an eagle."[244] Gold buttons may have caught the attention of Chacón because they were often included in wills of free people of color.[245] Further, French traveler Julian Mellet reported that "buttons of gold" served as a form of currency in Cuba.[246]

For Juan Barbier to convincingly assume the identity of Juan Francisco as an admiral that served at the orders of Haitian emperor Henri Christophe required an elaborate uniform to project status and authority. Estanislao Aguilar testified that when he traveled to the plantations to recruit slaves for the rebellion, "Juan Francisco . . . entered a slave hut and returned dressed in a blue military jacket and military pants, taking off the clothes he had worn."[247] Several other rebels questioned about the revolts provided similar descriptions of soldiers in uniform.[248] Soldiers in the free men of color militia could have obtained military uniforms relatively easily. When authorities searched Aponte's house, they found his "blue military jacket" in a closet.[249] The success of the Haitian Revolution added new meaning to the familiar sight of people of African ancestry in military uniforms throughout the Caribbean. In recruiting others to their cause, the leaders of the Aponte Rebellion refashioned their own military experience in Cuba to wed it with the imagery of the Haitian Revolution.[250]

In addition to emancipation decrees by Henri Christophe, the arrival of Jean François' former troops, and the wearing of military uniforms, Aponte's drawings of Haitian revolutionary leaders added yet another layer of Haitian connections to the Aponte Rebellion. The most fascinating document to emerge from the Aponte Rebellion was Aponte's book of drawings. As mentioned in the introduction, the book of drawings has yet to be found by scholars, but what does exist is the testimony in which for three days Aponte explained the significance of the book to authorities.[251] Colonial officials demanded that Aponte elaborate on where he obtained the images of the black revolutionaries that once filled the pages of his book. Aponte explained that the portraits of Louverture, Dessalines, and Jean François "were copied by myself from many other engravings acquired when the Campaign of Ballajá came to Havana."[252] The "campaign of Ballajá" refers to the exodus of the Spanish-allied black Saint Domingue troops from the city of Fort Dauphin in 1795. Aponte told judicial officials that he "had copied the portrait of Enrique the First [Henri Christophe] from another owned by a black who worked on the docks." Melchor Chirinos, one of the many suspected conspirators, told authorities that Aponte had drawn the portrait from a copy owned by black militia captain Fernando Núñez.[253] When asked about the portraits' location, Aponte explained that "he had burnt them for having heard . . . they were banned illustrations."[254] Apparently, Aponte and Núñez were not the only people who owned portraits of Haitian revolutionary figures. After the colonial government suppressed the rebellion and captured the principal leaders, another portrait surfaced when soldier Domingo Calderón "found in the street a portrait of the king Enrique."[255]

Many of the captured rebels stated that Aponte had shown them drawings of Haitian leaders in what probably amounted to lessons in the history of the Haitian Revolution. Melchor Chirinos told officials that "many asked" to see "the black King José Antonio Aponte had painted."[256] Salvador Ternero reported that Aponte "showed [him] a book that had three figures painted . . . one a black King and two generals of the same color."[257] Free black militiamen Francisco Javier Pacheco and José del Carmen Peñalver stated that "Aponte showed them the portrait of the black king of Haiti named Henrique Cristóval, informing us of his coronation and recognition by the King of England and the King of Spain."[258] According to the testimony of accused rebel Clemente Chacón, Aponte's portrait of "Cristóval Henriques" contained the inscription. "Execute what is ordered."[259] Authorities concluded that "following the examples and events of those of the same class in the neighboring colony of Haiti, Aponte kept a portrait of Enrique Cristóbal, the first king of Haiti, to show the slaves."[260] Aponte and other people involved in the rebellion were not unique in displaying a fascination with Haiti. People of African ancestry throughout the Americas held great admiration for revolutionary leaders from Haiti. Only a year after Haitian independence, slaves as far away as Rio de Janeiro wore necklaces bearing the image of Dessalines.[261] The Haitian Revolution provided powerful images of a black king and military generals that inspired Aponte and others. The rebels' particular fascination with Haiti perhaps had as much to do with its successful example of slave revolution as with its status as an independent black country. While there is no documentation or reported pronouncements that Aponte and other excluded mulattos or other races from their movement, of the known racial characteristics among the arrested rebels, 96 percent were black.[262] In crafting their own ideology of insurrection, they interwove emancipation decrees and powerful black Haitian imagery to create a political and cultural tapestry to resist their subordinate position demanded by a society based upon racial hierarchy.

Rebellious Royalism

The widespread circulation of emancipation rumors stemming from diverse monarchical figures in 1812 Cuba confirms the important role of royalist ideology, or what other scholars have labeled "naïve monarchism," in shaping movements of resistance by slaves, peasants, and other subaltern groups. Only by the end of the eighteenth century and throughout the nineteenth century did a concerted action to limit and eventually abolish monarchical forms of governments sweep through the Atlantic world. Similar to serfs in nineteenth century Russia, slaves utilized the rhetoric of the benevolent monarch that would deliver them from bondage. As scholar James Scott has observed, it was common for peasants to rebel "on behalf of reforms in serfdom, or its abolition, which had been decreed by the czar but concealed from them by cruel officials." In what Scott describes as a "symbolic jujitsu," slaves and peasants could transform an apparently conservative myth counseling loyalty to the king into a legitimizing basis for violent insurrection.[263]

As part of the legitimizing process in planning the insurrection, Cuban slaves made constant references to edicts that king-given rights had been denied them.[264] Several slaves reported that the order issued by the king had been hidden in an effort to usurp their rights. In response, they planned to go to Havana to demand its promulgation.[265] Similarly, twenty years earlier in Saint Domingue, slaves reported that the king and National Assembly in Paris issued decrees abolishing the whip and providing three free days a week to work on their own. Their masters, however, would not enact the new laws.[266] Roughly occurring at the same time as the Aponte Rebellion of 1812, but in a different context, historian Eric Van Young noted that during the War for Mexican Independence, the use of documents or references to edicts "were often seen as essential to legitimate community collective action."[267] Undoubtedly, the three centuries of employing written documentation in dealing with the Spanish colonial state served to reinforce the centrality of edicts, papers, and orders in shaping protest behaviors. The importance of documentation may have acquired additional importance in slave societies such as Cuba in legitimating struggles for freedom because ultimately it was a written document that reduced individuals to enslavement and a written document that could free them.[268]

The Aponte Rebellion of 1812 shares certain similarities with other protest movements by slaves and peasants in its appeal to royalist ideology or "naïve monarchism," but the divergent discourses of the emancipating ruler in the form of the kings of Spain, England, Haiti, and the Kongo powerfully illustrate the different cultural and political influences in Cuba. In Mexico or Russia, for example, Native Americans and serfs constructed their "naïve monarchism" around the authority of a single and apparently widely recognized monarch. In Cuba, however, the divergent backgrounds of slaves and free people of color, coupled with the changing politics of the era that began to question slavery as an institution for the first time, often determined which monarch the rebels ascribed with emancipatory powers. The competing ideologies of monarchical authority in Cuba testified to how rebels and slaves could transform rumors to resonate with their own concepts of legitimate authority, which were not constructed through the Spanish colonial context alone. The appeal to royalist authority in the form of the kings of Spain, Britain, Haiti, and Kongo represented a political counterweight that Cuban rebels attempted to swing against their masters and the institutions they controlled.

Situating the Aponte Rebellion in its multiple Caribbean, Latin American, African, and Atlantic contexts, the different monarchial decrees from the kings of Spain, England, Haiti, and the Kongo offered a reflection of the diverse backgrounds and experiences of the population of African descent on the island. Consequently, applying Van Young's suggestion for Mexico, it is enlightening to think of the Aponte Rebellion not as an appeal to "naïve monarchism" in terms of "false consciousness," where slaves and free people of color could only construct a movement through the hegemonic authority of monarchical power, but rather as a ritualized aspect of planning the insurrection. The repeated references to monarchical authority indicate a widely recognized and widely shared political script. The rebel leaders incorporated references to royalist authority to catalyze their movement. Slaves and free people of color involved in the Aponte Rebellion legitimated their actions through royalist power that would aid them in their battle against the colonial elite.[269]

The ideology of a benevolent king interceding on behalf of loyal subjects did not prevent rebellion by slaves in early nineteenth-century Cuba. Just the opposite occurred. References to Cuban masters and government officials usurping monarchical authority served to frame and justify the argument for insurrection in the widely recognized political idiom of the day. That this rebellious royalism operating in Cuba could be bent, twisted, and refashioned to include the kings of Spain, England, Haiti, and the Kongo to sanctify insurrection testifies to the effectiveness of slaves and free people of color in crafting their own ideology of liberation to reflect their own specific circumstances.

NOTES

1 ANC-AP, leg. 12, no. 14, fol. 75.
2 ANC-AP, leg. 12, no 18, fol. 28, leg. 13, no. 1, fol. 44v.
3 ANC-AP, leg. 12, no.14, fols. 4–4v, 90.
4 Ibid., leg. 13, no. 1, fol.167; "Bando del Capitán General de la Isla," Havana, 7 Apr. 1812, ANC-AP, leg. 12, no. 24; ANC-AP, leg. 13, no. 38, fol. 3v.
5 José Augustino Jurco to Someruelos, San Lázaro, Havana, 21 Nov. 1808, AGI-PC, leg. 1680.
6 ANC-AP, leg. 12, no. 18, fol. 32.
7 I have relied on the following sources for identifying African ethnicity: Benjamin Nuñez, *Dictionary of Afro-Latin American Civilization* (Westport, Conn.: Greenwood, 1980); John Thornton, *Africa and Africans in the Making of the Atlantic World, 1400–1800*, 2nd ed. (Cambridge: Cambridge University Press, 1998), x–xxvi; Philip D. Curtin, *The Atlantic Slave Trade: A Census* (Madison: University of Wisconsin Press, 1969), esp. 291–298; Jorge Castellanos and Isabel Castellanos, *Cultura afrocubana: (El negro en Cuba, 1492–1844)*, 4 vols (Miami: Ediciones Universal, 1988–1994), 1:28–43 and "The Geographic, Ethnologic, and Linguistic Roots of Cuban Blacks," *Cuban Studies* 17 (1987), 95–110; Fernando Ortiz, *Los negros brujos* (Reprint: Havana, Editorial de Ciencias Sociales, 1995 [1906]), 22–26 and *Los negros esclavos* (Reprint: Havana, Editorial

de Ciencias Sociales, 1975 [1916]), 40–59; Pedro Deschamps Chapeaux, *El negro en la economía habanera del siglo XIX* (Havana: Unión de Escritores y Artistas de Cuba, 1971), 31–46, "Cabildos: Solo para esclavos," *Cuba 7*, no. 69 (Jan. 1968): 50–51, and *Los cimarrones urbanos* (Havana: Editorial de Ciencias Sociales, 1983), 42–47; George Reid Andrews, *The Afro-Argentines of Buenos Aires, 1800–1900* (Madison: University of Wisconsin Press, 1980), 233–34; Frederick P. Bowser, *The African Slave in Colonial Peru, 1524–1650* (Stanford: Stanford University Press, 1974), 346.

8 For a discussion of the terms "nation" and "ethnicity" as they apply to identity in the early modern world and the African Diaspora in particular, see David Eltis, *The Rise of African Slavery in the Americas* (Cambridge: Cambridge University Press, 2000), 244–57; Michael Gómez, *Exchanging Our Country Marks: The Transformation of African Identities in the Colonial and Antebellum South* (Chapel Hill: University of North Carolina Press, 1998), 2–8 and "African Identity and Slavery in the Americas," *Radical History Review* 75 (1999): 111–20; Robin Law, "Ethnicity and the African Slave Trade: 'Lucumi' and 'Nagô' as Ethnonyms in West Africa," *History in Africa* 24 (1997): 205–19; Paul E. Lovejoy, "Identifying Enslaved Africans in the African Diaspora," in *Identity in the Shadow of Slavery*, edited by Paul E. Lovejoy (London: Continuum, 2000), 1–29; John K. Thornton, "The Coromantees: An African Cultural Group in Colonial North America and the Caribbean," *Journal of Caribbean History* 32, no. 1–2 (1998): 161–78 and *Africa and Africans*, 183–205.

9 David Bell, "The Unbearable Lightness of Being French: Law, Republicanism and National Identity at the End of the Old Regime," *American Historical Review* 106, no. 4 (Oct. 2001): 1215–35, pp. 1218–19.

10 Joseph C. Miller, "History and Africa/Africa and History," *American Historical Review* 104, no. 1 (Feb. 1999): 1–32, pp. 14–16.

11 In his pioneering study of the *cabildos* historian Philip A. Howard states the societies were "known as *cabildos de naciones de afrocubanos.*" *Changing History: Afro-Cuban Cabildos and Societies of Color in the Nineteenth Century* (Baton Rouge: Louisiana State University Press, 1998), xiv. I only found the societies described as "*cabildos de nación*" in documents from the 1790s to 1820s.

12 Mina Guagni to Capitán General, Havana, 29 Apr. 1794, "La nación mina guagni contra Salvador Ternero sobre que de cuentas del producido del *cabildo* de la misma nación," 1794, ANC, fondo Escribanía Ortega, (ANC-EO), leg. 65, no. 11, fols. 1–iv.

13 "La nación mina contra Juana de Mesa," 1797, ANC, fondo Escribanía Antonio D'aumy (ANC-ED), leg. 673, no. 9.

14 "La nación mina guagni contra Salvador Ternero sobre cuentas," 1794–97, ANC-ED, leg. 893, no. 4, fol. [?]. (It is not possible to cite all the specific folios of this document and others in the fondo Escribania because the pagination has been destroyed by deterioration.)

15 Francisco Ferrer to Capitán General, Havana, 24 Jan. 1794, ANC-EO, leg. 65, no. 11, fol. 5.

16 ANC-ED, leg. 893, no. 4; ANC-EO, leg. 65, no. 11, fol. 55.

17 Entry for "Dn. Antonio Seidel" in "Libro de los veteranos que componen la plana mayor de blancos agregada por S. M. al batallón de Morenos libres de la Havana, arreglados hasta fin de diciembre de 1795," Archivo General de Simancas, fondo Guerra Moderna, leg. 7262. (Microfilm copy consulted at Howard-Tilton Memorial Library, Tulane University.) The 1795 Havana city index listed Antonio Seidel as the highest-ranking official supervising the black battalion. See *Calendario manual y guía de forasteros de la isla de Cuba par el año de 1795*, 119, P. K. Yonge Library, Special Collections, University of Florida, Gainesville.

18 ANC-ED, leg. 893, no. 4.

19 Salvador Ternero to Capitán General, Havana, 4 June 1794, ANC-EO, leg. 65, no. 11, fol. 40.

20 ANC-EO, leg. 65, no. 11, fols. 65v, 123v.

21 ANC-ED, leg. 893, no. 4, fols. 143–44 (parentheses in original).

22 Ibid., fol. 51v.

23 Ibid., fol. 52–53.

24 Ibid., fol. [?].

25 Ibid., fol. [?]. Scholar Stephan Palmié hastily concluded, with only consulting a handful of published sources, that for Ternero "we will, of course, never know what precisely these ostensibly ethnic identity referents mean in the historical context in which these men deployed them." Historians interested in Ternero's own words, however, can certainly gain critical insights into his own ideas behind such terms, how he created degrees of Mina Guagni ethnicity depending on African or Cuban birth, and the historical setting in which he used these terms by consulting the sources. Stephan Palmié, *Wizards and Scientists: Explorations in Afro-Cuban Modernity and Tradition* (Durham: Duke University Press, 2002).

26 ANC-EO, leg, 65, no. 11, fol. 72.

27 ANC-ED, leg. 893, no. 4, fol. 61v.

28 Ibid., fol. [?]. Morales may have sided with Vásquez in the hope that, should Ternero be removed as *capataz*, he would be rewarded by the new leader buying his freedom.

29 Robert Francis Jameson, *Letters from the Havana during the Year 1820* (London, J. Miller, 1821), 21.

30 See Gómez, "African Identity and Slavery," 118; and Thornton, "Coromantees," 161.

31 Eltis, *Rise of African Slavery*, 244.

32 For the emphasis on the heterogeneity of the slave population see in particular, Sidney Mintz, "The Caribbean as a Socio-Cultural Area," *Cahiers d'Histoire Mondiale*, no. 4 (1966): 912–937; Sidney Mintz and Richard Price, *The Birth of African-American Culture: An Anthropological Perspective* (Boston: Beacon, 1992); and Philip Morgan, "The Cultural Implications of the Atlantic Slave Trade: African Regional Origins, American Destinations and New World Developments," *Slavery and Abolition* 18, no. 1 (April 1997): 122–145. For the revisionist emphasis on African ethnicity and culture, see Lovejoy, "Identifying Enslaved," 1–29; Thornton, *Africa and Africans*, 183–205; Eltis, *Rise of African Slavery*, 224–57; and Gómez, "African Identity and Slavery," 111–20.

33 For references to African "nations" in Anglo-America, see Richard Ligon, *A True and Exact History of the Island of Barbadoes* (Reprint, London: Frank Cass, 1970 [1657]), 55; Eltis, *Rise of African Slavery*, 230; Thornton, *Africa and Africans*, 195; Thornton, "Coromantees," 161, 173; Peter Linebaugh and Marcus Rediker, *The Many-Headed Hydra: Sailors, Slaves, Commoners and the Hidden History of the Revolutionary Atlantic* (Boston: Beacon, 2000), 152; Michael Craton, *Testing the Chains: Resistance to Slavery in the British West Indies* (Ithaca: Cornell University Press, 1982), 108–10, 125–39; David Barry Gaspar, *Bondsmen and Rebels: A Study of Master–Slave Relations in Antigua* (Baltimore: Johns Hopkins University Press, 1985); Richard Sheridan, "The Jamaican Slave Insurrection Scare of 1776 and the American Revolution," *Journal of Negro History* 61(3) (1976), 290–308, p. 303. While scholars continue to debate whether there actually was a slave conspiracy led by Denmark Vesey in 1822 Charleston, South Carolina, contemporaries believed it was quite plausible that an ethnically organized Igbo column led by Monday Gell from the Bight of Biafra played a leading role in planning the rebellion: see "Trial of Peter, 21 June 1822," in Edward A. Pearson, *Designs against Charleston: The Trial Record of the Denmark Vesey*

Slave Conspiracy of 1822 (Chapel Hill: University of North Carolina Press, 1999), 176; Douglas Egerton, *He Shall Go Out Free: The Lives of Denmark Vesey* (Madison: Madison House, 1999), 133; and Gómez, *Exchanging Our Country Marks*, 3. For the debate on the veracity of the Vesey Conspiracy, see Michael P. Johnson, "Denmark Vesey and his Co-Conspirators," *William and Mary Quarterly* 58, no. 4 (October 2001): 915–76; the responses by various authors in the forum titled "Making of a Slave Conspiracy," *William and Mary Quarterly* 59, no. 1 (January 2002), 135–202; Robert Paquette and Douglas Egerton, "Of Facts and Fables: New Light on the Denmark Vesey Affair," *South Carolina Historical Magazine* 105, no. 1 (January 2004), 8–48; and Paquette, "From Rebellion to Revisionism: The Continuing Debate about the Denmark Vesey Affair," *Journal of the Historical Society* 4, no. 3 (Fall 2004): 291–334.

34 As historian Linda M. Heywood has argued, "African folk Christianity" thrived among Lisbon's black population of the sixteenth century and in the Portuguese colonies of Africa and Brazil because, in part, the church honored petitions to establish ethnic-based confraternities. "The Angolan-Afro-Brazilian Cultural Connections," *Slavery and Abolition* 20, no. 1 (April 1999): 9–23, p. 10.

35 Heywood, "Angolan-Afro-Brazilian Cultural Connections," 19; Elizabeth W. Kiddy, "Ethnic and Racial Identity in the Brotherhoods of the Rosary of Minas Gerais, 1700–1830," *Americas* 56, no. 2 (Oct. 1999): 221–252, pp. 238–43; João José Reis, *Slave Rebellion in Brazil: The Muslim Uprising of 1835 in Bahia* (Baltimore: Johns Hopkins University Press, 1993), 149–51, 153 and "Différences et resistances: Les noirs à Bahia sous l'esclavage," *Cahiers d'etudes africaines* 32, no. 1 (1992): 15–34, 19, 21; Patricia A. Mulvey, "Slave Confraternities in Brazil: Their Role in Colonial Society," *Americas* 39, no. 1 (July 1982): 39–68; A.J.R. Russell-Wood. "Black and Mulatto Brotherhoods in Colonial Brazil," *Hispanic American Historical Review* 54, no. 4 (Nov., 1974): 567–602, pp. 582–83; Mary C. Karasch, *Slave Life in Rio de Janeiro, 1808–1850* (Princeton: Princeton University Press, 1987), 84–85, 358–59; Mariza de Carvalho Soares, *Devotos da cor: Identidade étnica, religiosidade e escravidao no Rio de Janeiro, século XVIII* (Rio de Janeiro: Civilização Brasiliera, 2000); Marina de Mello e Souza, *Reis negros no Brasil escravista: história da festa de coroação de rei congo* (Belo Horizonte: Editora de UFMG, 2002).

36 See the numerous documents on an Angolan brotherhood reprinted in Robert C. Smith, "Manuscritos da igreja de Nossa Senhora do Rosario dos homens pretos do Recife," and "Décados do Rosario dos pretos: documentos da irmandade," in *Arquivos* (Recife) 4–10, nos. 7–20 (Dec. 1951): 53–120 and 143–170.

37 St. John d'el Rey Mining Company, *Circular to the Proprietors*, 39, in St. John d'el Rey Mining Company Archive, Nettie Lee Benson Latin American Collection, University of Texas at Austin. In 1849 the superintendent of the same gold mine told the House of Lords that masters grouped Africans by nations "for the purpose of preserving peace on the establishment. [Otherwise t]hcy would be able to league together." Great Britain, House of Lords, "Report from the Select Committee," vol. 9, par. 2493, p. 171.

38 Ruth Pike, "Sevillan Society in the Sixteenth Century: Slaves and Freedmen," *Hispanic American Historical Review* 47, no. 3 (Aug. 1967): 344–59, pp. 344–46.

39 Bowser, *African Slave in Colonial Peru*, 249–50, 339.

40 See the numerous petitions in *Indice del Archivo del Departmento General de Policía*. For a broader discussion see Oscar Chamosa, " 'To Honor the Ashes of Their Forebears': The Rise and Crisis of African Nations in the Post-Independence State of Buenos Aires, 1820–1869," *Americas* 59, no. 3 (Jan. 2003): 347–78; and Andrews, *Afro-Argentines of Buenos-Aires*, 142–51.

41 Fernando Ortiz, *Los cabildos y la fiesta afrocubanos des Dia de Reyes* (Reprint: Havana, Editorial de Ciencias Sociales, 1992 [1921]), 6; Carmen Victoria Montejo–Arrechea, *Sociedades de instrucción y recrea de pardos y morenos que existieron en Cuba colonial: 1878–1898* (Veracruz: Instituto Veracruzano de Cultura, 1993), 14–16.

42 Jane G. Landers, *Black Society in Spanish Florida* (Urbana: University of Illinois Press, 1999), 109.

43 Morell de Santa Cruz, "El Obispo Morell de Santa Cruz oficializa los *cabildos* africanos donde nació la Santería, conveirtiéndolos en ermitas,' Havana, 6 Dec 1755. In *Cuba: Economie y sociodad, del monopolio hacia la libertad commercial (1701–1763)*, edited by Levi Marrero (Madrid: Editorial Playor, 1980), 8: 159–61.

44 Ibid.

45 Ibid., 159–60.

46 Ibid., 159.

47 "Diligencias sobre cuentos del *cabildo* de la nación Induri pos su capataz Nicolas Veitia," 1800, ANC-ED, leg. 398, no. 23, fols. 1–5.

48 This date is earlier than Howard's, who argues that by "the beginning of the nineteenth century, *cabildos* . . . outnumber[ed] cofradías." *Changing History*, 26–7.

49 Antonio Bachiller y Morales, *Los Negros* (Barcelona: Gorgas y compaña, 1887), 114–115. Ortiz, *Los cabildos*, 4–6; Montejo-Arrechea, *Sociedades*, 12–13; Deschamps Chapeaux, "*Cabildos*," 51; Pedro Deschamps Chapeaux, "Sociedades: la integración de pardos y morenos," *Cuba* 7, no. 71 (Mar. 1968): 54–55; Howard, *Changing History*, 21–25.

50 Paul E. Lovejoy and David Richardson, "Trust, Pawnship, and Atlantic History: The Institutional Foundations of the Old Calabar Slave Trade," *American Historical Review* 104, no. 2 (April 1999): 333–55, 347–49; also see the discussion in Randy J. Sparks, *The Two Princes of Calabar: An Eighteenth Century Atlantic Odyssey* (Cambridge, MA: Harvard University Press, 2004).

51 Lovejoy, "Identifying Enslaved Africans," 8; Howard, *Changing History*, 48, 53, 68–69, 109–10. The classic treatment of the Abakuá in Cuba remains Lydia Cabrera, *La Sociedad Secreta Abakua, narrada por viejos adeptos* (Havana: Ediciones, C.R., 1959).

52 Peter Morton-Williams, "The Yoruba Ogboni Cult in Oyo," *Africa* 30 (1960): 362–74; J.A. Atanda, "The Yoruba Ogboni Cult: Did it Exist in Old Oyo?," *Journal of the Historical Society of Nigeria* 6, no. 4 (1973): 365–72; Robin Law, *The Oyo Empire, c. 1600–c. 1836: A West African Imperialism in the Era of the Atlantic Slave Trade* (Oxford: Clarendon, 1977), 61. For Yoruba imports into Cuba, see David Eltis, "The Diaspora of Yoruba Speakers, 1650–1865: Dimensions and Implications," in Toyin Falola and Matt D. Childs, eds., *The Yoruba Diaspora in the Atlantic World* (Bloomington: Indiana University Press, 2004), 17–39.

53 Thornton, "Coromantees," 163, 169.

54 Toyin Falola and Adebayo Akanmu, *Culture, Politics, and Money Among the Yoruba* (New Brunswick: Transaction, 2000), 131–39.

55 David Eltis, David Richardson, and Stephen D. Behrendt, and Herbert S. Klein, eds., *The Trans-Atlantic Slave Trade: A Database on CD-ROM* (Cambridge: Cambridge University Press, 1999).

56 Eltis, *Rise of African Slavery*, 251–54. A growing body of scholarship is linking specific ports of exporation in Africa with specific ports of importation in the Americas. For historiographical and methodological approaches, see Kristin Mann, "Shifting Paradigms in the Study of the African Diaspora and of Atlantic History and Culture," *Slavery and Abolition* 22, no. 1 (Jan. 2002): 135–202; Linda Heywood, "Introduction," in Linda M. Heywood, ed., *Central Africans*

and Cultural Transformations in the American Diaspora (Cambridge: Cambridge University Press, 2002), 1–18, 2–8 and Childs and Falola, "Yoruba Diaspora," 1–14.

57 For an emphasis on the methodological problems, see Mervyn C. Alleyne, "Linguistics in the Oral Tradition," in Barry Higman, ed., *Methodology and Historiography of the Caribbean*, Vol. 6 of *General History of the Caribbean* (London: UNESCO, 1999), 19–45, and Morgan, "Cultural Implications," 122–45.

58 David Eltis, David Richardson, and Stephen D. Behrendt, "Patterns in the Transatlantic Slave Trade, 1662–1867: New Indications of African Origins of Slaves Arriving in the Americas," in Maria Diedrich, Henry Louis Gates, Jr., and Carl Pedersen, eds., *Black Imagination in the Middle Passage* (Oxford: Oxford University Press, 1999), 21–32.

59 Eltis, *Rise of African Slavery*, 253 n. 104

60 ANC-ED, leg. 893, no. 4, fol. [?].

61 "La nación lucumi contra Dn. Manuel Blanco y otros sobre propiedad del terreno en que se halla fundado el cavildo de nación," 1777–81, ANC-EC, leg. 147, no. 1, fols. 50–53v.

62 Bishop of Cuba to His Majesty, Havana, 6 Dec. 1753, in Ortiz, *Los negros curros*, 212–13.

63 Estimate derived from documentation found in the following: ANC-EC, leg. 6, no. 6, leg. 47, no. 1; ANC-ED, leg. 336, no. 1, leg. 398, no. 23, leg. 439, no. 16, leg. 548, no. 11, leg. 583, no. 5, leg. 610, no. 15, leg. 660, no. 8, leg. 673, no. 9, leg. 893, no. 4; ANC-Escribanía de Gobierno (hereafter ANC-EG), leg. 28, no. 4, leg. 123, no. 15, leg. 123, no. 15-A, leg. 125, no. 3, leg. 277, no. 5; ANC-EO, leg. 3, no. 8, leg. 6, no. 1, leg. 65, no. 11, leg. 494, no. 2; ANC-Escribania de Valerio (ANC-EVal), leg. 671, no. 9873; ANC-Escribanía de Varios (ANC-EVar), leg. 211, no. 3114; ANC-AP, leg. 11, no. 37, leg. 12, nos. 9, 14, 17, 27, leg. 13, no. 1, leg. 14, no. 1; ANC-Donativos y Remisiones (ANC-DR), leg. 542, no. 29; AGI-PC, leg. 1433-B, 1667. There is no documentation in various secondary sources or primary sources that would support Fannie Theresa Rushing's very conservative estimate that in "1801, there were thirteen *cabildos de nación* in Havana" or her statement that by 1827 "there were twenty-one *cabildos de nación* in Havana." Fannie Theresa Rushing. "Afro-Cuban Social Organization and Identity in a Colonial Slave Society, 1800–1888," *Colonial Latin American Historical Review* 11, no. 2 (Spring 2002): 177–201. For the city of Matanzas alone, historian Israel Moliner Castañeda has identified seventeen *cabildo* houses in 1816. *Los Cabildos Afrocubanos en Matanzas* (Matanzas: Ediciones Matanzas, 2002), 83–84.

64 ANC-EC, leg. 147, no. 1, fol. 53v.

65 Thorton, *Africa and Africans*, 190; also see Law, "Ethnicity and the Slave Trade," 207, 209.

66 "Pedro José Santa Cruz solicitando nombramiento de Capataz al *Cabildo* de la nación Congos Musolongos," 1806, ANC-ED, leg. 660, no. 8, fols. 1–4.

67 "La nación Caravali Umugini sobre división con la Osso y con la misma Umugini, y liquidación de cuentas con el capitán Pedro Nolasco Eligió," 1805 6, ANC-EG, leg. 123, no. 15-A, fol. 9.

68 "Real cédula de su magestad sobre la educación, trato y ocupaciones de los esclavos, en todos sus dominios de indias, e islas filipinas baxo las reglas que expresan," Aranjuez, 31 May 1789, BNJM-Morales, leg. 79, no. 3, fol. 7.

69 Diego Miguel de Moya to His Majesty, Havana, 19 Jan. 1790, ANC-RCJF, leg. 150, no. 7405, fol. 11.

70 Ibid., fol. 18v.

71 AOHCH-AC, leg. 76, Cabildo Minutes, Havana, 2 Mar. 1809, fol. 73v.

72 For a detailed discussion of the slave family and the role of *cabildos* related

to family structure, see Maria de Carmen Barcia Zequeira, *La otra familia: Parientes, redes ye descendencia de los esclavos en Cuba* (Havana: Fondo Editorial Casa de la Américas, 2003), 121–136.

73 ANC-AP, leg, 12, no. 9, fol. 9v.

74 Ibid., fol. 22v.

75 Ibid., fol. 30v. In Brazil, Africans who shared a similar ethnic bond also used the Portuguese term for relative, "parente," to refer to each other. See João José Reis and Beatriz Gallotti Momigonian, "Nagô and Mina: The Yoruba Diaspora in Brazil" in Falola and Childs, eds., *Yoruba Diaspora*, 77–110.

76 "Expediente seguido por Cristoval Govin, capataz de la nación Oquella contra Lázaro Rodríguez, capataz del la Agro, sobre cuentas," 1799, ANC-EO, leg. 6, no. I, fol. 62.

77 ANC-AP, leg. 12, no. 9, fol. 23v.

78 Francisco Alonzo de Morazan to Someruelos, Havana, 28 June 1811, AGI-PC, leg. 1667.

79 ANC-AP, leg. 12, no. 9, fols. 86–87.

80 "Cabildo musolongo sobre nombramientos de Capataz," 1806, ANC-ED, leg. 548, no. II, fols. 15v–16.

81 ANC-ED, leg. 893, no. 4, fol. [?].

82 ANC-AP, leg. 12. no. 14, fol. 12.

83 ANC-AP, leg. 14, no. I, fols. 182v–83v. According to contemporary J. M. Pérez, the minuet was the most popular dance in 1800. "Siglo XIX: Costumbres de Cuba en 1800 por J. M. Pérez," AOHCH-JLF, leg. 214, no. 31.

84 ANC-AP, leg. 12, no. 9. fol. 109.

85 ANC-ED, leg. 893, no. 4, fol. 46; "La nación Caravali Induri sobre nombramiento de capataz del cavildo del Santo Cristo de Buen Viaje," 1802–6, ANC-EG, leg. 125, no. 3, fol. [?]; ANC-EO, leg. 65, no. 11, fol. 72.

86 "Juan Nepomuceno Montiel y Rafael Arostegui como apoderados en la nación Lucumi Llane contra Agustina Zaraza y Antonio Ribero sobre la extracción de pesos que hicieron de la caja de la nación," 1807–10, ANC-EC, leg. 64, no. 6, fols. 13–15.

87 ANC-EO, leg. 6, no. 1, fol. 59.

88 ANC-ED, leg. 893, no. 4, fol. [?].

89 ANC-EG, leg. 123, no. 15-A, fol. 21.

90 Howard, *Changing History*, 48.

91 "José Antonio Diepa, capataz del cabildo nación Congo, sobre que se recojía los memoriales que promovió Cayetano García y socios para despojarlo del encargo de capataz del cabildo nación Congo Macamba," 1808–9, ANC-ED, leg. 439, no. 16, fol. 51v.

92 ANC-AP, leg. 12, no. 9, fols. 68v–69v.

93 Ibid., fols. 13, 44v.

94 ANC-EG, leg. 125, no. 3, fols. 106–15.

95 ANC-ED, leg. 893, no. 4, fol. 47.

96 "José Xavier Mirabal y consortes contra Domingo Acosta y socios sobre pesos, trata del cabildo de Apapa," 1808–30, ANC-ED, leg. 583, no. 5, fols. 82–82v (emphasis in original).

97 ANC-EC, leg. 147, no. 1, fol. 54v.

98 "Tomás Poveda, Clemente Andrade, Antonio de Prucia, Joaquín de Soto y Antonio María Lisundia contra el moreno José Arostegui sobre que cuentas de caja del cavildo," 1805, ANC-ED, leg. 336, no. 1, fol. 40. Joao José Reis has identified a similar process of how the Yoruba in Bahia, Brazil, began to forge a common Nagô identity: "The Yoruba of the Oyo, Ehba, Ijebu, Ilesha and Ketu kingdoms became Nagôs in Bahia through complex exchanges and convergences of cultural signs with the help of a common language, similar

divinities (Orishas), the unification of many under Islam, long experience as subjects of the Oyo *alafins* (kings), Yoruba urban traditions and, obviously a life of slavery in Bahia." " 'The Revolution of the Ganhadores': Urban Labour, Ethnicity and the African Strike of 1857 in Bahia, Brazil," *Journal of Latin American Studies* 29, no. 2 (May 1997): 355–93.

99 ANC-EO, leg. 6, no. 1, fol. 60v.

100 "Expediente relativo a la renovación de cargos de un cabildo de nación ante las autoridades en la ciudad de Matanzas," ANC-DR, leg, 542, no. 29, fol. 1. Some of the documentation for the Matanzas Karabali cabildo is published in "Constitución de un cabildo Carabali en 1814."

101 ANC-AP, leg. 12, no. 9, fols. 45, 68v, 73.

102 Ibid., fols. 36v, leg. 13, no. 1, fol. 101.

103 ANC-EG, leg. 125, no. 3, fol. 115–15v.

104 Pedro Alonso to [?], Havana, 10 Oct. 1759, published in Fernando Ortiz, *Los negros curros* (Reprint: Havana, Editorial de Ciencias Sociales, 1986 [1909]), 214.

105 ANC-AP, leg. 12, no. 9, fol. 30v.

106 Ibid., no. 27, fol. 12v.

107 John Thornton, " 'I Am the Subject of the King of Congo': African Political Ideology and the Haitian Revolution," *Journal of World History* 4, no. 2 (Fall 1993): 181–214.

108 ANC-EC, leg. 147, no. 1, fols. 41–42.

109 "Tomás Poveda, capataz de los cabildos Carabali Osso solicitando nombramiento de otra capataz," 1806, ANC-ED, leg. 610, no. 15.

110 "La nación Caravali Umugini sobre división con la Oso y con la misma Umugini, y liquidación de cuentas con el capitán Pedro Nolasco Eligio," 1805–6, ANC-EG, leg. 123, no. 15A.

111 "Salvador Flores y demás individuos de la nación Carabali Ibo sobre que se suspenda capataz a José Maria Pimenta y que de cuentas," 1814, ANC-EG, leg. 123, no. 15; "Cabildo musolongo sobre nombramientos de Capataz," 1806, ANC-ED, leg. 548, no. 11; "La nación mina guagni contra Salvador Temero sobre que de cuentas del producido del cabildo de la misma nación," 1794, ANC-EO, leg. 65, no. 11; "La nación mina contra Juana de Mesa," 1797, ANC-ED, leg. 673, no. 9; "La nación mina guagni contra Salvador Ternero sobre cuentas," 1794–97, ANC-ED, leg. 893, no. 4; also see Howard's detailed treatment in *Changing History*, 31–36.

112 Allan J. Kuethe, "The Status of the Free Pardo in the Disciplined Militia of New Granada," *Journal of Negro History* 56, no. 2 (Apr. 1971): 105–17, 109.

113 ANC-ED, leg. 583, no. 5, fol. 24.

114 ANC-EO, leg. 65, no. 11, fol. 55.

115 ANC-EC, leg. 147, no. 1, fol. 41; also see Howard for the link between militia soldiers and *cabildo* activities, *Changing History*, 31–36.

116 Kimberly S. Hanger discovered that in New Orleans the town council often rejected petitions by blacks to hold dances, "but when the free black militia, represented by four officers, submitted its request in 1800," authorities approved it. *Bounded Lives, Bounded Places: Free Black Society in Colonial New Orleans, 1769–1803* (Durham: Duke University Press, 1997), 132.

117 "Expediente seguido por los de la nación Caravali Oquella sobre nombramiento de segundo y tercero capataces," 1804, ANC-EV, leg. 211, no. 3114, fols. 9v–12.

118 ANC-ED, leg. 439, no. 16, fol. [?].

119 ANC-EG, leg. 125, no. 3, fol. 108v.

120 Ibid., fol. 115.

121 ANC-EO, leg. 6, no. 1, fol. 60v–61.

122 ANC-ED. leg. 336, no. 1, fol. [?].

123 ANC-ED, leg. 439, no. 16, fol. [?].

124 See for example *Diario de la Habana*, 3 Feb. 1812, 3; for an analysis of newspaper slave sales, see Antonio Nuñez Jimenez, *Los esclavos negros* (Cuba: Fundación de la Naturaleza y el Hombre, 1998), 79–148.

125 ANC-ED, leg. 336, no. 1, fol. 38v.

126 "Expendiente de cuentas que produce Tomás Betancourt de las cantidades que han entrado en su poder del cavildo Caravali Oquella," 1804, ANC-EO, leg. 3, no. 8, fol. 7v.

127 Ibid., fol. 6v; ANC-EO, leg. 6. no. 1, fol. 8v; for a discussion of the Spanish coffer, see Amy Bushnell, *The King's Coffer: Proprietors of the Spanish Florida Treasury, 1565–1702* (Gainesville: University Presses of Florida, 1981).

128 ANC-ED, leg. 398, no. 23, fol. 3.

129 ANC-ED, leg. 439, no. 16, fol. [?].

130 Ibid., no. 16, fol.[?].

131 ANC-EO, leg. 6, no. 1, fol. 33.

132 Ibid., fol. 30v.

133 Howard, *Changing History*, 40–42.

134 ANC-ED, leg. 660, no. 8, fol. 4.

135 ANC-ED, leg. 583, no. 5, fol. 100.

136 "Sobre la conspiración intentada por los negros esclavos para invadir la villa a resultas de la libertad que suponen estarles declaradas por las Cortes Generales y estraordinarias del Retno de Puerto Principe," Jan. 1812, ANC-AP, leg. 11, no. 37, fol. 58.

137 ANC-ED, leg. 398, no. 23, fol. 1; ANC-EO, leg. 6, no. 1, fol. iv.

138 ANC-EO leg. 3, no. 8, fol. 3v; ANC-EC, leg. 64, no. 6, fol. 60; ANC-ED, leg. 439, no. 16, fol. 51v.

139 ANC-EG, leg. 123, no. 15A, fol. 6.

140 ANC-ED, leg. 336, no. 1, fol. 22v.

141 ANC-EG, leg. 125, no. 3, fol. 167.

142 ANC-ED, leg. 336, no. 1 fol. 22, leg. 610, no. 15, fol. 2; ANC-EO, leg, 3, no. 8, fol. 7.

143 ANC-AP, leg. 12, no. 9, fols. 68v–69.

144 Jameson, *Letters from the Havana*, 21–22; Daniel E. Walker, *No More, No More: Slavery and Cultural Resistance in Havana and New Orleans* (Minneapolis: University of Minnesota Press, 2004), 1–18.

145 ANC-AP, leg. 12, no. 9, fol. 23.

146 ANC, fondo Comisión Militar, leg. 11, no. 1, fols. 456v–458. I would like to thank Gloria García for directing me to this source.

147 ANC-ED, leg. 893, no. 5, fols. 51–51v.

148 Jameson, *Letters from the Havana*, 21–22; Frederika Bremmer, *The Homes of the New World: Impressions of America*, 2 vols., translated by Mary Howitt (Reprint, New York: Johnson Reprint, 1968 [1853]) 2: 379–383.

149 ANC-EC, leg. 64, no. 6, fol. 60.

150 "Tomás Povea, capataz de los cabildos Carabali Osso solicitando nombramiento de otra capataz," 1806, ANC-ED, leg. 610, no. 15, fol. 2.

151 Howard identifies the same process whereby "members of these organizations manifested a 'consciousness of kind': an identity that mitigated, to a certain degree, differences of language, ethnicity, and customs, an identity that allowed them to discern the common problems all people of color confronted on a daily basis." *Changing History*, xvii.

152 ANC-AP, leg. 12, no. 14, fols. 4–4v, 90.

153 ANC-AP, leg. 12, no. 25, fol. 48, leg. 13, no. 1, fols. 42, 314, leg. 13, no. 38, fol. 4.

154 ANC-AP, leg. 12, no. 25, fols. 5v, 36–37; Hernández to Rendón, Havana, 7 May

1812, ANC-AP, leg. 12, no. 25, fol. 47; Apodaca to Pezuela, Havana, 19 July 1812, AGI-SD, leg. 1284, no. 21.

155 ANC-AP, leg, 13, no. 18, fols. 5v–6; Apodaca to Antonio Caro Manuel, Havana, 3 Sept. 1812, AGI-SD, leg. 1284, no. 39.

156 Apodaca to Antonio Caro Manuel, Havana, 28 Oct. 1812, AGI-SD, leg. 1284, no. 60; the same letter can be found in Apodaca to Antonio Caro Manuel, Havana, 28 Oct. 1812, AGI-SD, leg. 1286.

157 Juan de Dios Corona to [Apodaca], Havana, 23 Oct. 1812, ANC-AP, leg. 13, no. 1, fols. 329v–30.

158 ANC-AP, leg. 13, no. 1, fols. 438–38v.

159 ANC-AP, leg. 13, no. 15, fol. 73v, leg. 12, no. 25, fol. 53v.

160 ANC-AP, leg. 12, no. 17, fols. 13v, 70v.

161 ANC-AP, leg. 12, no. 25, fols. 54–55v, leg. 13, no. 15, fol. 73v.

162 ANC-AP, leg. 12, no. 25, fols. 68v, 75v.

163 Ibid., fols. 89–90.

164 The original proclamation nailed to the captain general's residence can be found in ANC-AP, leg. 12, no. 14, fol. 35. For reasons that remain unclear, Stephan Palmié did not consult Franco's more widely known book on the Aponte Rebellion that would have qualified some of his conclusions about the historiography. Instead, Palmié consulted Franco's *Las conspiraciones de 1810 y 1812* (Havana: Editorial de Ciencias Sociales, 1977), a very brief twenty-four-page introduction to the document collection that only has two footnotes, as it was intended for a general and not a scholarly audience. Palmié writes: "Franco makes rather vague references to what he thinks may have been prior seditious activities on the part of Aponte. He thus claims that Aponte dictated an inflammatory proclamation that was posted in Havana in early March 1812 but fails to cite any evidence." *Wizards and Scientists*, 80–81. Had Palmié consulted the more detailed 1963 study, he would have found that not only did Franco cite evidence of the proclamation for the rebellion, he also provided a facsimile of the document that Aponte dictated. See Franco, *La conspiración de Aponte* (Havana: Publicaciones del Archivo Nacional, 1963), between pp. 20–21.

165 Cabildo Minutes, Havana, 18 Mar. 1812, AOHCH-AC, leg. 83, fols. 65–65v.

166 ANC-AP, leg. 12, no. 14. fol. 77. Reportedly, Aponte repeated the same statement in his last confession, which is not included in the extant trial record. ANC-AP, leg. 13, no. 1, fol. 49.

167 ANC-AP, leg. 13, no. 1, fol. 49, leg. 12, no. 14, fol. 82.

168 ANC-AP, leg. 13, no. 1, fol. 48.

169 ANC-AP, leg. 11, no. 37, fol. 58.

170 Ibid., fol. 59v.

171 Ibid., fols. 63v–64.

172 ANC-AP, leg, 12, no. 9, fol. 7v.

173 Ibid., no. 13, fol. 18.

174 Ibid., no. 21, fol. 8.

175 Ibid., fol. 13.

176 Ibid., fol. 26.

177 "Proposiciones del Sr. don José Miguel Guridi Alcocer," Cádiz, 26 March 1811, in Spain, Cortes, *Documentos de que hasta ahora se compone el expediente que principiaron las Cortes Extraordinarias sobre el trafico y esclavitud de los negros* (Madrid: Imprenta de Repulles, 1814), 87. For an account of the issue of slavery in the Cortes debates, see James F. King. "The Colored Castes and American Representation in the Cortes of Cádiz," *Hispanic American Historical Review* 33, no. 1 (Feb. 1953): 33–64; Franco, *Las conspiraciones de 1810 y 1812*, 15–16; Toronto, *Crecimiento económico* 80–89; and Alain Yacou

"La conspiración de Aponte (1812)," *Historia y sociedad* (Puerto Rico) 1 (1988): 39–58.

178 "Representación que el Capitán General de la isla de Cuba, Marques de Someruelos, elevó a las Cortes," Havana, 27 May 1811, in Spain, Cortes, *Documentos*, 102–3.

179 Andres de Jáuregui to Ayuntamiento de la Ciudad de la Habana, Cádiz, 2 Apr. 1811, ANC-DR, leg. 561, no. 8, fol. 1.

180 "Correspondencia del Sor. Don Andrés de Jáuregui diputado á Cortes con el Ayuntamiento de esta ciudad, 1811 a 1813," ANC-GSC, leg. 11000, no. 40589.

181 "Copias de la Junta del Real Consulado y Sociedad Patriótica, sobre las proposiciones relativas la manumisión de los esclavos y los graves peligros que podrian resultar a esta Isla," Habana, 23 May 1811, HL-EC, box 19, no. 18, fol. 13.

182 Cabildo Minutes, Puerto Principe, 18 June 1811, AHPC-AC, no. 26, fol. 314v.

183 "Documentos que se refiere al acta del cabildo celebrado por el Ayuntamiento, fecha Santiago de Cuba 25 de Junio de 1811, en que se trató del proyecto presentado a las Cortes sobre la abolición de la esclavitud," ANC–AP, leg. 213, no. 81, fol. 8.

184 Shaler to Smith, Havana, 14 June 1811, USNA-RG, 59.

185 "Bando del Capitán General de la Isla D. Salvador José de Muro y Salazar, fecha Habana 7 de Abril de 1812, acera de las medidas acordadas con motivo de la alternación del orden . . ." ANC-AP, leg. 12, no. 24.

186 ANC-AP, leg. 12, no. 9. fol. 7v; also see ANC-AP, leg. 13, no. 15, fols. 42–43; and AHPC-AC, no. 27, fol. 35, for additional comments.

187 ANC-AP, leg. 12, no. 9. fol. 110.

188 ANC-AP, leg. 13, no. 15, fol. 43v.

189 Ibid., no. 1, fols. 315–16.

190 ANC-AP, leg. 12, no. 21, fol. 15v–16.

191 Someruelos to Ignacio de la Pezuela, Havana, 5 Mar. 1812, AGI-UM, leg. 84, no. 348.

192 Francisco Sánchez to Juan Baptista Valliant, 16 May and 29 Oct. 1795, Bayamo, ANC-GG, leg. 540, no. 27096; for Jamaican slaves in Cuba see Alfred Clarke to José de Ezpuleta (*sic*), 9 March 1789, Jamaica, PRO-CO, 137/88, fols. 23–24; "Testimonio de las diligencias obradas sobre la profugación de los seis negros venidos de esta Ciudad de la Colonia Bretanica en solicitud de la Cristiandad como de ellos mas bien consta," 1789, in PRO-CO, 137/89, fols. 55v–56v; Julian Mellet, *Viajes por el interior de la América meridional* (Reprint, Santiago de Chile: Imprenta Universitaria, 1908 [1824]), 386; Kindleman to Corral, Santiago de Cuba, 9 May 1810, ANC-AP, leg. 212, no. 26.

193 AHPG-Protocolos, leg. 4, libro 1, fols, 6v, 7v, 10, libro 2, fols. 15, 20, 30, 60v, 73, 122, 163, 179, 206, 211, 228, leg. 11, libro 3, fol. 13; Cabildo Minutes, Puerto Principe, 26 Aug. 1808, AHPC-AC, leg. 25, fols. 81–85.

194 ANC-AP, leg. 12, no. 9, fol. 54.

195 Sarah Louise Franklin, "Gender and Slave Rebellion in Colonial Cuba: The Bayamo Conspiracy of 1805," Master's thesis, Florida State University, 2003), 107–11.

196 James Thompson, "Narrative of James Thompson, a British Subject, Twenty-One Years a Cuban Slave," *The Anti-Slavery Reporter* 4, no. 9 (3 May 1843): 71–72.

197 "Quaderno sobre la denuncia que hiso la Negra María Antonio Atola contra el Negro José Wilson eslavo de Rafael Wilson," Puerto Principe, 1812, AGI-PC, leg. 1865A, fol. 4.

198 Ibid. fol. 5.

199 Ibid. fol. 7v.

200 African ethnicity through self-identification by slaves and free people of color (as opposed to identification by masters and government officials, who often incorrectly labeled African origins and ethnicity, as evidenced in census and notarial records) among those questioned for involvement in the Aponte Rebellion is taken from testimony found in ANC-AP, leg. 11, no. 37, leg. 12, nos. 9, 11, 13, 14, 16, 17, 18, 20, 21, 23, 25, 26, 27, leg. 13, nos. 1, 15, 18, 38, leg. 14, no. 1, leg. 15, no. 22; AGI-PC, leg. 1640, 1778-A, 1780, 1864, 1865A.

201 Oscar Grandío Moráguez, "The African Origins of Slaves Arriving in Cuba, 1789–1867," in David Eltis and David Richardson, eds., *Transatlantic Connections: The Repeopling of the Americas and the New Slave Trade Database* (Cambridge: Cambridge University Press, forthcoming).

202 Thornton, " 'I Am the Subject,' " 181–214.

203 David Geggus, "The Slaves and Free Coloreds of Martinique during the Age of the French and Haitian Revolutions: Three Moments of Resistance," in *The Lesser Antilles in the Age of European Expansion*, edited by Robert Paquette and Stanley Engerman (Gainesville: University Press of Florida, 1996), 280–301, 284.

204 ANC-AP, leg. 12, no. 14, fols. 9, 19–24, 34, 70.

205 ANC-AP, leg. 12, no. 26, fol. 34.

206 Ibid., fol. 36.

207 ANC-AP, leg. 12, no. 27, fols. 13v–14v.

208 Apodaca to Ministro de Guerra, Havana, 29 Oct. 1812, AGI-PC, leg. 1849, no. 184.

209 "Informe presentado al cabildo los Sres. D. Joaquín Herrera, D. Luis Hidalgo Gato y Dor. D. José María Saenz, sindico procurado general relativo a la moción de la Cortes para abolir al trafico de negros," Havana, 23 Mar. 1812, BNJM-Morales, leg. 78, no. 8, fol. 90.

210 Andres de Jáuregui and Juan Bernardo O'Gavan, "Memorial de los diputados de la Habana sobre una insurreción de esclavos en el ingenio de Peñas-Altas," Cádiz, 23 May 1812, BNJM-Morales, leg. 79, no. 72, fol. 292.

211 Salvador Meléndez to Secretario de Estado, Puerto Rico, 30 Jan. 1812, in Artura Morales Carrión, comp., *El proceso abolicionista en Puerto Rico: Documentos para su studio*, 2 vols. (San Juan: Instituto de cultura puertorriqueña, 1974), 1:117; Guillermo A. Baralt, *Esclavos rebeldes: Conspiraciones y sublevaciones de esclavos en Puerto Rico (1795–1873)* (Rio Pedras: Ediciones Huracán, 1982), 27.

212 ANC-AP, leg. 12, no. 18, fol. 6.

213 Ibid., no. 16, fol. 12.

214 ANC-AP, leg. 13, no. 1, fol. 49.

215 Ibid., fol. 70. Aponte denied Chacón's assertion that Juan Francisco was his confidant and that he told others the Haitian admiral was on the island to serve at the orders of Henri Christophe. Instead, he countered that "one morning Chacón and Juan Lisundia appeared at his [Aponte's] house." According to Aponte, Chacón told him that "Juan Francisco had gone to the countryside . . . to carry out . . . the orders of his King." ANC-AP, leg. 12, no. 18, fol. 29v–30.

216 C.L.R. James, *The Black Jacobins: Toussaint L'Ouverture and the San Domingo Revolution*, 2nd ed. (New York: Vintage, 1963), 94.

217 ANC-AP, leg. 12, no. 16, fol. 13.

218 ANC-AP, leg. 12, no. 14, fol. 73, no. 16, fols. 4–5, 13–14, no. 18, fols. 8–9, 34v, leg. 13, no. 1, fols, 83v–84, no. 15, fol. 18v. Invoking the Haitian Revolution through assuming the name of revolutionary figures also occurred in the Curaçao rebellion of 1795. Among the leaders executed by Dutch authorities,

one called himself Toussaint, and another was known by the nickname Rigaud. Julius Scott, "The Common Wind: Currents of Afro-American Communication in the Era of the Haitian Revolution" (Ph.D. diss., Duke University, 1986), 264.

219 Someruelos to Ministro de Estado, Havana, 1 Sept. 1800, AHN-Estado, leg. 6366, caja 1, exp. 20, no. 1, fols. 2v–3; Luis de Las Casas to [?], Havana, 13 Jan. 1796, AGI-Estado, leg. 5-A, no. 28.

220 AOHCH-AC, 4 Dec. 1795, fols. 204v–5; García to Príncipe de la Paz, Santo Domingo, 3 Mar. 1796, no. 48, in Emilio Rodríguez Demorizi, ed., *Césion de Santo Domingo a Francia: Correspondencia de Godoy, García, Roume, Hedouville, Louverture, Rigaud y otros, 1795–1802* (Trujillo: Impresora Dominicana, 1958), 75.

221 Luis de Las Casas to Paz, Havana, 16 Dec. 1795. AGI-Estado, leg. 5, no. 176. I would like to thank David Geggus for directing me to this source. According to Cuban historian José Luciano Franco, Aponte's *cabildo* planned to participate in the festivities welcoming Jean François. I could find no sources to confirm this statement. Franco, *La conspiración de Aponte*, 9.

222 Matthew D. Childs, " 'A Black French General Arrived to Conquer the Island': Images of the Haitian Revolution in Cuba's 1812 Aponte Rebellion," in David Geggus, ed., *The Impact of the Haitian Revolution in the Atlantic World* (Columbia: University of South Carolina Press, 2001), 135–56, 144–148.

223 Nicholas Rey, "Les Garifunas: Entre 'mémoire de la résistance' aux Antilles et transmission des terres en Amérique centrale," *Cahiers d'etudes Africaines* 177 (2005); 131–163; Jorge Victoria Ojeda, "Jean François: de la revolución haitiana a su exilio en España," *Secuencia* 58 (2004): 26–48; David Patrick Geggus, *Haitian Revolutionary Studies* (Bloomington: Indiana University Press, 2002), 179–203; Jane Landers, "Rebellion and Royalism in Spanish Florida: The French Revolution on Spain's Northern Colonial Frontier," in David Barry Gaspar and David Patrick Geggus, eds. *A Turbulent Time: The French Revolution and the Greater Caribbean* (Bloomington: Indiana University Press, 2002), 156–177, 163–70; Jacques Houdaille, "Negros franceses en América Central a fines del siglo xviii," *Antropologia e historia de Guatemala* 6, no. 1 (1954): 65–67; Francisco Fernández Repetto and Genny Negroe Sierre, *Una población perdida en la memoria: Los negros de Yucatán* (Mérida, Yucatán: Universidad Autonoma de Yucatán, 1995), , 55; Ben Vinson, "Race and Badge: Free-Colored Soldiers in the Colonial Mexican Militia," *Americas* no. 4 (Apr. 2000): 471–96, 491; Rina Cáceres Gómez, "Los esclaves del rey: Omoa, Honduras y la historia afrocentroamericana." Paper presented at the XXIV Latin American Studies Association International Congress, Dallas, Tex., March 27–29, 2003.

224 Someruelos to [?], Havana, 27 Jan. 1800, AHN-Estado, leg. 6366, caja 1, exp. 2; Someruelos to [?], Havana, 31 July 1804, AGI-PC, leg. 1778-B; Someruelos to Bardari y Azara, Havana, 10 Feb. 1811, AGI-SD, leg. 2210.

225 "Testimonio de la criminalidad seguida de oficios contra el negro Miguel, Juan Bautista, y José Antonio, sobre la conjuración que intentaban contra el Pueblo, y sus moradores, Juez, El Sor Teniente Gobernador," Bayamo, 25 Aug. 1805, AGI-PC, leg. 1649, fol. 46.

226 ANC-AP, leg. 12, no. 14, fol. 93.

227 Geggus, *Haitian Revolutionary Studies*, 199–200, esp. note 103.

228 ANC-AP, leg. 214, no. 28, fols. 2–3v.

229 Gil Narciso, Josef Fantacia, Juan Luis Santillan, and Ysidro Pluton to Someruelos, Casablanca, Habana, 10 Jan. 1812, Joseph Antonio de la Ossa to Someruelos, Havana, 21 Jan. 1812, ANC-CCG, leg. 93, no. 8; Juan Antonio Lopez to [Someruelos?], Havana, 28 Dec. 1811, ANC-CCG, leg. 93, no. 13; Aguilar to Cristóbal Solas, Havana, 2 Mar. 1812, ANC-CCG, leg. 94, no. 8.

230 ANC-AP, leg. 12, no. 16, fol. 6.
231 Ibid., fol. 4.
232 Ibid., fol. 4.
233 Ibid., fol. 8v.
234 Luis de Las Casas to [?], Havana, 13 Jan. 1796, AGI-Estado, leg. 5-A, no. 28.
235 ANC-AP, leg. 12, no. 16, fol. 10.
236 Ibid., fol. 22.
237 Franco, *La conspiración de Aponte*, 33; David Patrick Geggus, "Slavery, War, and Revolution in the Greater Caribbean, 1789–1815," in Gaspar and Geggus, eds., *Turbulent Times*, 1–50, 15; Renée Méndez Capote, *4 conspiraciones* (Havana: Institute Cubano del libro, 1972), 38.
238 ANC-AP, leg. 12, no. 16, fol. 10.
239 ANC-AP, leg. 12, no. 14, fol. 91. The military fort Casa Blanca would later provide the name for the neighborhood that grew around the building.
240 ANC-AP, leg. 12, no. 14, fol. 92.
241 Ibid., fol. 88.
242 ANC-AP, leg. 12, no. 16, fol. 18.
243 Ibid., no. 26, fol. 30.
244 Ibid., no. 14, fol. 73.
245 AHPSC-Protocolos, leg. 63, fol. 26v, leg. 64, fol. 156, leg. 243, fol. 118; AHPG-Protocolos, leg. 11, libro 3, fol. 52.
246 Julian Mellet, *Viajes por el interior de la América meridional* (Reprint: Santiago de Chile: Imprenta Universitaria, 1908 [1824]).
247 ANC-AP, leg. 12, no. 18, fols. 9, 34v.
248 Ibid., no. 13, fols. 21v–23v, 31, 36–37, no. 17, fol. 72.
249 Ibid., no. 26, fols. 7–14. For a description of Cuban militia uniforms in 1809, see *Calendario manual y guía de forasteros de la isla de Cuba par el año de 1809*, 177, 179, P.K. Yonge Library Special Collections, University of Florida, Gainesville, Florida.
250 In attempting to make sense of the proliferation of Haitian imagery, and in particular the widely reported role of Juan Barbier assuming the identity of "Juan Francisco," Stephan Palmié writes that it "is tempting to rationalize Barbier's posing as a Haitian revolutionary hero as a strategy to mobilize popular support," but he dismisses such interpretations because they "will necessarily remain guesswork of a dangerously teleological character." In terms of critiquing historical teleologies of radical revolution, Juan Barbier posing as "Juan Francisco" most accurately illustrates the antiteleological vision Aponte and others had of history. If historians are to use revolutionary teleological terminology, "Jean François," the historical figure, was a "reactionary royalist" of the Haitian Revolution who did not embrace full emancipation for all the slaves or the conversion of them into "revolutionary citizens" of the French Republic. The proclamations, statements, and actions by the Aponte rebels make it clear that they manipulated Haitian imagery and converted the historical figure of "Jean François" into "Juan Francisco" for their own political goals. To dismiss such actions as merely latter day inventions of historians caught in teleological traps reveals a condescending academic understanding of the past. Palmié, *Wizards and Scientists*, 133, 135.
251 Most, but not all, of Aponte's testimony discussing the book of drawings with authorities is found in "Expediente sobre declara José Antonio Aponte el sentido de las pinturas que se hallan en el libro que se le aprehendido en su casa," ANC-AP, leg. 12, no. 17.
252 ANC-AP, leg. 12, no. 17, fol. 78v. Stephan Palmié incorrectly states that the images "were not of Aponte's making." *Wizards and Scientists*, 99.
253 ANC-AP, leg. 12, no. 18, fols. 27–28.

254 Ibid., no. 17, fol. 80.
255 Ibid., no. 18, fol. 41.
256 Ibid., fol. 25.
257 ANC-AP, leg. 12, no. 14, fol. 92.
258 ANC-AP, leg. 13, no. 1, fol. 316.
259 ANC-AP, leg. 12, no. 17, fol. 16.
260 ANC-AP, leg. 13, no. 15, fol. 18v. Guarico was used in Spanish to refer to the city of Le Cap François, but also generically to Saint Domingue and Haiti.
261 Reis, *Slave Rebellion in Brazil*, 48.
262 Data taken from ANC-AP, leg. 11, no. 37, leg. 12, nos. 9, 11, 13, 14, 16, 17, 18, 20, 21, 23, 25, 26, 27, leg. 13, nos. 1, 15, 18, 38, leg. 14, no. 1, leg. 15, no. 22; ANC-GG, leg. 545, no, 27103; AGI-PC, leg. 1640, 1649, 1778A, 1780, 1864, 1865A; AGI-UM, leg. 84; AHPC-AC, leg. 27.
263 James C. Scott, *Domination and the Arts of Resistance: Hidden Transcripts* (New Haven: Yale University Press, 1990), 98.
264 See the discussion of the important role of these edicts for shaping slave identity in Díaz, *Virgin*, 303–4.
265 ANC-AP, leg. 11, no. 37, fols. 63v–64, leg. 12, no. 9, fols. 7v, 110, leg. 12, no. 13, fol. 18, leg. 12, no. 21, fols. 8, 15v–16, leg. 12, no. 26, fol. 44, leg. 13, no. 1 fols. 315–16; AGI-PC, leg. 1865A, fol. 4.
266 Laurent Dubois, " 'Our Three Colors,': The King, the Republic and the Political Culture of Slave Revolution in Saint-Domingue," *Historical Reflections* 29, no. 1 (2003): 83–102, 87, 92.
267 Eric Van Young, *The Other Rebellion: Popular Violence, Ideology, and the Mexican Struggle for Independence, 1810–1821* (Stanford: Stanford University Press, 2001), 488.
268 Henry Louis Gates, Jr., *Figures in Black: Words, Signs and the 'Racial' Self* (New York: Oxford University Press, 1987), 3–28. For the cultural importance of literacy and written documents in slave insurrection, see James Sibury, *Ploughshares into Swords: Race, Rebellion, and Identity in Gabriel's Virginia, 1730–1810* (Cambridge: Cambridge University Press, 1997), 73–82; Reis, *Slave Rebellion in Brazil*, 96–104; and Jack Goody, "Writing, Religion and Revolt in Bahia," *Visible Language* 20 (1986): 318–43.
269 Van Young, *Other Rebellion*, 464–65.

12

THE SLAVES AND SLAVERY

Eric Williams

We have considered the different attitudes to slavery of the British Government, the British capitalists, the absentee British West Indian planters, and the British humanitarians. We have followed the battle of slavery in the home country. It would be a grave mistake, however, to treat the question as if it were merely a metropolitan struggle. The fate of the colonies was at stake, and the colonists themselves were in a ferment which indicated, reflected, and reacted upon the great events in Britain.

First, there were the white planters, who had to deal not only with the British Parliament but with the slaves. Secondly, there were the free people of color. And, thirdly, there were the slaves themselves. Most writers on this period have ignored them. Modern historical writers are gradually awaking to the distortion which is the result of this.[1] In correcting this deficiency they correct an error which the planters and the British officials and politicians of the time never made.

First, the planters. In 1823 the British government adopted a new policy of reform towards West Indian slavery. The policy was to be enforced, by orders in council, in the Crown Colonies of Trinidad and British Guiana; its success, it was hoped, would encourage the self-governing colonies to emulate it spontaneously. The reforms included: abolition of the whip; abolition of the Negro Sunday market, by giving the slaves another day off, to permit them time for religious instruction; prohibition of the flogging of female slaves; compulsory manumission of field and domestic slaves; freedom of female children born after 1823; admissibility of evidence of slaves in courts of law; establishment of savings banks for slaves; a nine-hour day; and the appointment of a Protector of Slaves whose duty it was, among other things, to keep an official record of the punishments inflicted on the slaves. It was not emancipation but amelioration, not revolution but evolution. Slavery would be killed by kindness.

The reply of the planters, in the Crown Colonies as well as in the self-governing islands, was an emphatic refusal to pass what they considered "a mere catalogue of indulgencies to the Blacks."[1a] They knew that all such concessions meant only further concessions.

Not one single recommendation received the unanimous approval of the West Indian planters. They were roused to fury especially by the proposals for the prohibition of the flogging of female slaves and the abolition of the Negro Sunday market.

From the planters' standpoint, it was necessary to punish women. Even in civilized societies, they argued, women were flogged, as in the houses of correction in England. "Our black ladies," said Mr. Hamden in the Barbados legislature, "have rather a tendency to the Amazonian cast of character; and I believe that their husbands would be very sorry to hear that they were placed beyond the reach of chastisement."[2]

On the question of the abolition of the Negro Sunday market, Barbados refused to surrender one-sixth of its already reduced income.[3] Jamaica replied that the "pretence of having time for religious duties" would merely encourage idleness among the slaves.[4] So great was the opposition of the planters that the governor deemed any attempt at alteration highly imprudent and could see no alternative but leaving it "to the operation of time and that change of circumstances and opinions which is slowly but surely leading to the improvement of the habits and manners of the slaves."[5] It was a true and important fact that, with time, mere contact with civilization improved the slave, but the slave was in no mood for the inevitability of gradualism.

The whip, argued the planters, was necessary if discipline was to be maintained. Abolish it, "and then adieu to all peace and comfort on plantations."[6] A Trinidad planter called it "a most unjust and oppressive invasion of property" to insist on a nine-hour day for full-grown slaves in the West Indies, while the English factory owner could exact twelve hours' labor from children in a heated and sickly atmosphere.[7] In Jamaica the bill for admitting slave evidence aroused a great and violent clamor, and it was rejected on the second reading by a majority of thirty-six to one.[8] The Assembly of the island postponed the savings banks clause to a future session,[9] and the governor dared not even mention the question of the freedom of female children.[10] The legislature of British Guiana decided that "if the principle of manumission *invito domino* is to be adopted, it is more for their consistency and for the interests of their constituents that it should be done *for* them than *by* them."[11] In Trinidad the number of manumissions declined considerably,[12] while appraisals for manumission increased suddenly:[13] "the possibility of sworn appraisers pronouncing an unjust decision," Stephen confessed, "was not contemplated and is not provided against."[14] One manager in Trinidad talked of "the silly orders in council," and in recording punishments resorted to language unbefitting his responsibility and insulting to the framers of the legislation.[15] The office of Protector of Slaves in British Guiana was a "delusion": "There is no protection for the Slave Population," wrote the incumbent in 1832, "I am desperately unpopular. . . ."[16]

Not only did the West Indian planters question the specific proposals of the British Government, they also challenged the right of the imperial parliament to legislate on their internal affairs and issue "arbitrary mandates . . . so positive and unqualified in point of matter, and so precise and peremptory in point of time."[17] From Barbados the governor reported that any attempt at dictation gave rise to instant irritation and opposition.[18] The inconsistency of slave owners talking of rights and liberties was dismissed as "the clamour of ignorance." Look to history, expostulated Hamden, "you will there find that no nations in the world have been more jealous of their liberties than those amongst whom the institution of slavery existed."[19]

In Jamaica the excitement reached fever pitch. The Assembly vowed that it would "never make a deliberate surrender of their undoubted and acknowledged rights" by legislating in the manner prescribed[20] "upon a subject of mere municipal regulation and internal police."[21] If the British Parliament was to make laws for Jamaica, it must exercise that prerogative without a partner.[22] The doctrine of the transcendental power of the imperial parliament was declared to be subversive of their rights and dangerous to their lives and properties.[23] According to the governor, "the undoubted rights of the British Parliament have been wantonly and repeatedly denied, (and) unless the arrogance of such pretensions is effectually curbed, His Majesty's authority in this colony will exist only in name."[24] Two Jamaican deputies, sent to England in 1832 to lay their grievances before the home authorities, pointedly uncovered the *arcana imperii*: "We owe no more allegiance to the inhabitants of Great Britain than we owe to our brother colonists in Canada . . . . we do not for a moment acknowledge that Jamaica can be cited to the bar of English opinion to defend her laws and customs."[25] One member of the island assembly went further: "as for the King of England," he asked, "what right I should be glad to know has he to Jamaica except that he stole it from Spain?"[26] A West Indian in Parliament reminded the British people that "by persisting in the question of right we lost America."[27] Talk of secession was rife. The home government was warned that there was constant communication in Jamaica with individuals in the United States,[28] and that feelers had been put out by some planters to the United States Government.[29] The cabinet took the matter sufficiently seriously to question the governor about the matter.[30] Had not Saint Domingue, in similar circumstances, offered itself to Britain?

This was more than the language of desperate men or an insane flouting of the "temperate but authoritative admonition"[31] of the imperial authorities. It was a lesson not so much to the public of Great Britain as to the slaves of the West Indies. If the governor of Jamaica found in the planters "a greater reluctance to part with power over the slave than might have been expected in the present age,"[32] it is obvious how the recalcitrance of the plantocracy appeared to the slaves. The Negroes, least of all people, were likely to forget that, in the words of the governor of Barbados, "*the love of power of* these planters over the poor Negroes, each in his little sugar dominion, has found as great an obstacle to freedom as *the love of their labor.*"[33] Emancipation would come not from the planters but despite the planters.

Whilst the whites were plotting treason and talking of secession, the free people of color were steadfastly loyal. They deprecated "a dissolution of the ties which bind us to the Mother Country as the greatest calamity that could possibly befall ourselves and our posterity."[34] To their great credit, the governor of Trinidad reported, they had not participated in those meetings "whereat so much pains have been taken to sow the seeds of discontent in the colony both among the free and the slave population."[35] Whilst the whites were refusing to hold office, the mulattos were insisting on their right to public service.[36] They were loyal not from inherent virtue but because they were too weak to gain their rights on their own behalf and could see no prospect of their own emancipation except through the British government. Furthermore, the local governments, in so far as they were trying to carry out the policy of the anti-monopolists, had to lean on them. In Barbados, wrote the governor, the balance of refinement, morals, education, and energy was on the side of the mulattos, whilst the whites had nothing but old rights and prejudices to maintain their illiberal position. "You will see," he advised the home government, "a large policy in present circumstances in bringing these castes forward. They are a sober, active, energetic and loyal race; and I could equally depend on them if need came, against either slaves or white militia."[37]

Contrary to popular and even learned belief, however, as the political crisis deepened in Britain, the most dynamic and powerful social force in the colonies was the slave himself. This aspect of the West Indian problem has been studiously ignored, as if the slaves, when they became instruments of production, passed for men only in the catalogue. The planter looked upon slavery as eternal, ordained by God, and went to great lengths to justify it by scriptural quotations. There was no reason why the slave should think the same. He took the same scriptures and adapted them to his own purposes. To coercion and punishment he responded with indolence, sabotage and revolt. Most of the time he merely was as idle as possible. That was his usual form of resistance—passive. The docility of the Negro slave is a myth. The Maroons of Jamaica and the Bush Negroes of British Guiana were runaway slaves who had extracted treaties from the British Government and lived independently in their mountain fastnesses or jungle retreats. They were standing examples to the slaves of the British West Indies of one road to freedom. The successful slave revolt in Saint Domingue was a landmark in the history of slavery in the New World, and after 1804, when the independent republic of Haiti was established, every white slave-owner, in Jamaica, Cuba, or Texas, lived in dread of another Toussaint L'Ouverture. It is inconceivable a priori that the economic dislocation and the vast agitations which shook millions in Britain could have passed without effect on the slaves themselves and the relation of the planters to the slaves. Pressure on the sugar planter from the capitalists in Britain was aggravated by pressure from the slaves in the colonies. In communities like the West Indies, as the governor of Barbados wrote, "the public mind is ever tremblingly alive to the dangers of insurrection."[38]

Not nearly as stupid as his master thought him and later historians have pictured him, the slave was alert to his surroundings and keenly interested in discussions about his fate. "Nothing," wrote the governor of British Guiana in 1830, "can be more keenly observant than the slaves are of all that affects their interests."[39] The planters openly discussed the question of slavery in the presence of the very people whose future was under consideration. "If the turbulent meetings which are held here among the proprietors," wrote the governor of Trinidad in 1832, "are countenanced, nothing that may occur need be matter of surprise. . . ."[40] The local press added to the inflammable material. A Trinidad paper called the order in council "villainous,"[41] another spoke of "the *ridiculous* provisions of the ruinous Code Noir."[42] One judge refused to sit on any trial arising out of the order in council and walked out of court.[43] The planters have been blamed for this reckless attitude. But they could not help it. It is a feature of all deep social crises. Before the French Revolution the French court and aristocracy discussed Voltaire and Rousseau not only freely but, in certain spheres, with real intellectual appreciation. The arrogant behavior and intemperate language of the planters, however, served only to inflame the minds of the already restless slaves.

The consensus of opinion among the slaves, whenever each new discussion arose or each new policy was announced, was that emancipation had been passed in England but was withheld by their masters. The governor of Jamaica reported in 1807 that abolition of the slave trade was construed by the slaves as "nothing less than their general emancipation."[44] In 1816 the British Parliament passed an act making compulsory the registration of all slaves, to prevent smuggling in violation of the abolition law. The slaves in Jamaica were of the impression that the bill "contemplates some dispositions in their favour which the Assembly here supported by the inhabitants generally are desirous to withhold,"[45] and the planters had to recommend a parliamentary declaration that emancipation was never contemplated.[46] A similar misunderstanding prevailed among the slaves in Trinidad[47] and Barbados.[48] All over the West Indies the slaves were asking "why Bacchra no do that King bid him?"[49] So deeply was the idea imbedded in the minds of the slaves that some great benefit was intended for them by the home government in opposition to their masters that they eagerly seized upon every trifling circumstance in confirmation.[50] Every change of governor was interpreted by them as emancipation. The arrival of D'Urban in British Guiana in 1824 was construed by the slaves as involving "something interesting to their prospects."[51] The governor of Trinidad went on leave in 1831; the Negroes had it that he "was to bring out emancipation for all the slaves."[52] Mulgrave's arrival in Jamaica in 1832 created great excitement. At a review near Kingston he was followed around by a greater number of slaves than had ever assembled before in the island, all with one idea in their minds, that he had "come out with emancipation in his pocket."[53] The appointment of Smith as governor of Barbados in 1833 was understood by the slaves as meaning general emancipation. His arrival in the island gave rise to a considerable number of desertions from distant plantations to Bridgetown "to ascertain if the Governor had brought out freedom or not."[54]

The slaves, however, were not prepared to wait for freedom to come to them as a dispensation from above. The frequency and intensity of slave revolts after 1800 reflect the growing tensions which reverberated in the stately halls of Westminster.

In 1808 a slave revolt broke out in British Guiana. The revolt was betrayed and the ringleaders arrested. They consisted of "the drivers, tradesmen, and other most sensible slaves on the estates,"[55] that is, not the field hands but the slaves who were more comfortably off and better treated. In the same way a rebel in Jamaica in 1824, who committed suicide, openly admitted that his master was kind and indulgent, but defended his action on the ground that freedom during his lifetime had been withheld only by his master.[56] It was a danger signal. Toussaint L'Ouverture in Saint Domingue had been a trusted slave coachman.

In 1816 came the turn of Barbados. It was a rude shock for the Barbadian planters who flattered themselves that the good treatment of the slaves would "have prevented their resorting to violence to establish a claim of natural right which by long custom sanctioned by law has been hitherto refused to be acknowledged."[57] The rebels, when questioned, explicitly denied that ill treatment was the cause. "They stoutly maintained however," so the commander of the troops wrote to the governor, "that the island belonged to them, and not to white men, whom they proposed to destroy, reserving the females."[58] The revolt caught the planters off their guard, and only its premature breaking out, as a result of the intoxication of one of the rebels, prevented it from engulfing the entire island.[59] The Jamaican planters could see in the revolt nothing but "the first fruits of the visionary schemes of a few hot-headed philanthropic theorists, ignorant declaimers, and bigotted fanatics."[60] All they could think of was urgent representations to the governor to recall a detachment that had sailed a few days before to England and to detain the remainder of the regiment in Jamaica.[61]

But the tension was rapidly mounting. British Guiana in 1808, Barbados in 1816. In 1823 British Guiana went up in flames, for the second time. Fifty plantations revolted, embracing a population of 12,000. Here again the revolt was so carefully and secretly planned that it took the planters unawares. The slaves demanded unconditional emancipation. The governor expostulated with them—they must go gradually and not be precipitate. The slaves listened coldly. "These things they said were no comfort to them, God had made them of the same flesh and blood as the whites, that they were tired of being slaves to them, that they should be free and they would not work any more." The governor assured them that "if by peaceful conduct they deserved His Majesty's favor they would find their lot substantially though gradually improved, but they declared they would be free."[62] The usual severities followed, the revolt was quelled, the planters celebrated and went their way, unheeding. Their sole solicitude was the continuation of the martial law that had been declared.[63]

"Now the ball has begun to roll," wrote the governor of Barbados confidentially to the Secretary of State for the Colonies when he heard the news of the Guiana revolt, "nobody can say when or where it is to stop."[64] The next year the slaves on two plantations in the parish of Hanover in Jamaica revolted. The revolt was localized and suppressed by a large military force and the ringleaders executed. The slaves as a group, however, could only with difficulty be restrained from interfering with the execution. In addition, the executed men, wrote the governor, "were fully impressed with the belief that they were entitled to their freedom and that the cause they had embraced was just and in vindication of their own rights." According to one of the leaders, the revolt had not been subdued, "the war had only begun."[65]

Outward calm was restored in British Guiana and in Jamaica, but the Negroes continued restless. "The spirit of discontent is anything but extinct," wrote the governor of British Guiana, "it is alive as it were under its ashes, and the negro mind although giving forth no marked indication of mischief to those not accustomed to observe it, is still agitated, jealous and suspicious."[66] The governor cautioned against further delay, not only for the sake of the intrinsic humanity and policy of the measure, but that expectation and conjecture might cease and the Negroes be released from that feverish anxiety which would continue to agitate them, until the question was set definitely at rest.[67] No state of the Negro mind was so dangerous as one of undefined and vague expectation.[68]

This was in 1824. Seven years later the same discussions about property and compensation and vested rights were still going on. In 1831 the slaves took the matter into their own hands. An insurrectionary movement developed in Antigua. The governor of Barbados had to send reinforcements.[69] In Barbados itself the idea prevailed that the King had granted emancipation but the governor was withholding the boon, while a rumor spread that, in the event of insurrection, the King's troops had received positive orders not to fire upon the slaves.[70]

The climax came with a revolt in Jamaica during the Christmas holidays. Jamaica was the largest and most important British West Indian colony, and had more than half the slaves in the entire British West Indies. With Jamaica on fire, nothing could stop the flames from spreading. An "extensive and destructive insurrection" broke out among the slaves in the western district.[71] The insurrection, reported the governor, "was not occasioned by any sudden grievance or immediate cause of discontent, it had been long concerted and at different periods deferred." The leaders were slaves employed in situations of the greatest confidence, who were consequently exempted from all hard labor. "In their position motives no less strong than those which appear to have actuated them—a desire of effecting their freedom, and in some cases of possessing themselves of the property belonging to their masters—could have influenced their conduct."[72]

The West Indian planters, however, saw in these slave revolts nothing but an opportunity of embarrassing the mother country and the humanitarians. From Trinidad the governor wrote as follows in 1832: ". . . the island, as far as the slaves are concerned, is quite tranquil and very easily could be kept so if such was the desire of those who ought to guide their endeavours in this way. . . . It would almost appear to be the actuating motives of some leading people here to drive the Government to abandon its principles, even at the risk of exciting the slaves to insurrection."[73] The governor of Jamaica encountered the same situation: "There is no doubt that there would be those short sighted enough to enjoy at the moment any disturbance on the part of the Negroes arising from disappointment which these persons despairing of their own prospects would consider as some consolation from its entailing embarrassment on the British Government."[74] The West Indian planter, in the words of Daniel O'Connell, continued to sit, "dirty and begrimed over a powder magazine, from which he would not go away, and he was hourly afraid that the slave would apply a torch to it."[75]

But the conflict had left the stage of abstract political discussion about slaves as property and political measures. It had become translated into the passionate desires of people. "The question," wrote a Jamaican to the governor, "will not be left to the arbitrament of a long angry discussion between the Government and the planter. The slave himself has been taught that there is a third party, and that party himself. He knows his strength, and will assert his claim to freedom. Even at this moment, unawed by the late failure, he discusses the question with a fixed determination."[76] From Barbados the governor emphasized the "double cruelty" of suspense—it paralyzed the efforts of the planters, and drove the slaves, who had been kept in years of hope and expectation, to sullen despair.[77] Nothing could be more mischievous, he warned, than holding out to the slaves from session to session that their freedom was coming.[78] It was most desirable, he wrote a fortnight later, that "the state of this unhappy people should be early considered and decided on by the Home Authorities, for the state of delusion they are labouring under renders them obnoxious to their owners and in some instances encreases the unavoidable misery of their condition."[79]

In 1833, therefore, the alternatives were clear: emancipation from above, or emancipation from below. But EMANCIPATION. Economic change, the decline of the monopolists, the development of capitalism, the humanitarian agitation in British churches, contending perorations in the halls of Parliament, had now reached their completion in the determination of the slaves themselves to be free. The Negroes had been stimulated to freedom by the development of the very wealth which their labor had created.

NOTES

1 See C. L. R. James, *The Black Jacobins* (London, 1938) for the slave revolution in Saint Domingue. H. Aptheker, *Negro Slave Revolt in the United States* (New York, 1943), should also be consulted. An admirable short summary, for the entire Western Hemisphere, is to be found in Herskovits, *op. cit.*, 86–109.

1a Colonial Office (hereafter C. O.). 28/95. House of Assembly, Barbados, Nov. 15, 1825.

2 C. O. 28/92. Report of a Debate in Council on a despatch from Lord Bathurst to Sir H. Warde, Sept. 3, 1823. Mr. Hamden, pp. 21–22. See also C. O. 295/59, where the governor of Trinidad argued that this concession to the female slaves would be considered an injustice by the men. Woodford to Bathurst, Aug. 6, 1823; C. O. 295/60. Mr. Burnley, one of the leading planters of Trinidad: "I confess the idea appears to me so monstrous and extraordinary that I hardly know how to approach the subject."

3 C. O. 28/92. Report of a Debate in Council. . . . Mr. Hamden, p. 5.

4 C. O. 137/145. Shand to Bathurst, Nov. 26, 1817.

5 C. O. 137/148. Manchester to Bathrust, July 10, 1819.

6 C. O. 28/92. Report of a Debate in Council. . . . Mr. Hamden, p. 24.

7 C. O. 295/92. Edward Jackson to Governor Grant, Dec. 31, 1831.

8 C. O. 137/156. Manchester to Bathurst, Dec. 24, 1824.

9 C. O. 137/163. Manchester to Bathurst, Nov. 13, 1826.

10 C. O. 137/154. Manchester to Bathurst, Oct. 13, 1823.

11 C. O. 111/55. D'Urban to Bathurst, July 4, 1826.

12 C. O. 295/85. Oct. 29, 1830. The following is the number of manumissions, 1825–1830:

Year	Number Manumitted	Manumissions Paid for	Field Slaves	Domestic Slaves
1825	162	98	38	124
1826	167	108	46	121
1827	167	129	49	118
1828	128	84	33	95
1829	87	41	15	72
1830 (to Oct. 29.)	32	22	6	26

13 C. O. 295/72. Woodford to Bathurst, Aug. 8, 1826.

14 C. O. 295/73. Stephen to Horton, Oct. 5, 1826.

15 C. O. 295/67. Henry Gloster, Protector of Slaves, to Governor Woodford, July 7,

1825. Fitzgerald's returns are as follows: Slave John Philip—"7 stripes on that part where if the foot be hostilely applied is considered in all civilized countries an act of the vilest indignity"; Slave Philip—"23 stripes on that part which my Lord Chesterfield strongly recommends to be the last to enter and the first to retire on all presentations at levies and to name which in the presence of ladies is considered a great breach in the laws of politeness"; Slave Simon Mind—"23 stripes on that particular part of the body corporate which is rarely guilty of a crime but which pays for transgressions committed by other members."

16 Bell and Morrell, *op. cit.*, p. 382.
17 C. O. 28/99. Carrington, Agent for Barbados, to Bathurst, March 2, 1826.
18 C. O. 28/93. Warde to Bathurst, Oct. 21, 1824.
19 C. O. 28/92. Report of a Debate in Council. . . ., p. 33.
20 C. O. 137/165. Message of House of Assembly, Dec. 1827.
21 C. O. 137/143. Oct. 31, 1815.
22 Bell and Morrell, *op. cit.*, 405. Protest of Assembly of Jamaica, June, 1838.
23 C. O. 137/183. Manchester to Goderich, Nov. 13, 1832.
24 *Ibid.* Manchester to Goderich, Dec. 16, 1832.
25 C. O. 137/186. Memorial of the Jamaica deputies to Britain, Nov. 29, 1832.
26 C. O. 137/183. Manchester to Goderich, secret and confidential, Dec. 16, 1832.
27 *Hansard*, XXXI, 781–782. Marryat, June 13, 1815.
28 C. O. 137/183. Manchester to Goderich, secret and confidential, Dec. 16, 1832.
29 C. O. 137/187. Z. Jones to Goderich, Feb. 22, 1832.
30 C. O. 137/187. Goderich to Manchester, secret, March 5, 1832.
31 The phrase is Canning's.
32 C. O. 137/154. Manchester to Bathurst, Dec. 24, 1823.
33 C. O. 28/111. Smith to Stanley, July 13, 1833.
34 C. O. 295/92. Memorial for ourselves and in behalf of all our fellow subjects of African descent (enclosed in Governor Grant's despatch to Goderich, March 26, 1832).
35 *Ibid.* Grant to Goderich, March 26, 1832.
36 *Ibid.* William Clunes to Goderich, Jan. 27, 1832.
37 C. O. 28/111. Smith to Stanley, May 23, 1833.
38 C. O. 28/88. Combermere to Bathurst, Jan. 15, 1819.
39 C. O. 111/69. D'Urban to Murray, April 20, 1830. See also C. O. 295/87. Smith to Goderich from Trinidad, July 13, 1831: "The slaves have an unaccountable facility in obtaining partial, and generally distorted, information whenever a public document is about to be received which can in any way affect their condition or station."
40 C. O. 295/92. Grant to Goderich, March 26, 1832.
41 *Ibid. Gazette Extraordinary*, March 25, 1832.
42 C. O. 295/93. Extract from a Trinidad paper, n.d.
43 C. O. 295/92. Grant to Howick, April 30, 1832.
44 C. O. 137/119. Coote to Castlereagh, June 27, 1807; C. O. 137/120. Edmund Lyon, Agent for Jamaica, to Castlereagh, July 17, 1807.
45 C. O. 137/142. Manchester to Bathurst, Jan. 26, 1816.
46 C. O. 137/143. Extract of a letter from Jamaica, May 11, 1816.
47 C. O. 295/39. John Spooner, of Barbados, to Governor Woodford, April 18, 1816.
48 C. O. 28/85. Col. Codd to Governor Leith, April 25, 1816; *Ibid.*, Rear Admiral Harvey to J. W. Croker, April 30, 1816.
49 C. O. 295/60. A commandant of Trinidad to Governor Woodford, Aug. 30, 1823.
50 C. O. 137/145. Shand to Bathurst, Nov. 26, 1817.
51 C. O. 111/44. D'Urban to Bathurst, May 5, 1824.
52 C. O. 295/89. Grant to Howick, Dec. 10, 1831.

53 C. O. 137/183. Mulgrave to Howick, Aug. 6, 1832.
54 C. O. 28/111. Smith to Stanley, May 23, 1833.
55 C. O. 111/8. Nicholson to Castlereagh, June 6, 1808.
56 C. O. 137/156. Manchester to Bathurst, July 31, 1824.
57 C. O. 28/85. Leith to Bathurst, April 30, 1816.
58 *Ibid.* Codd to Leith, April 25, 1816.
59 *Ibid.* Leith to Bathrust, April 30, 1816.
60 C. O. 137/143. Alexander Aikman, Jr. to Bathurst, May 2, 1816.
61 C. O. 137/142. Manchester to Bathurst, May 4, 1816.
62 C. O. 111/39. Murray to Bathurst, Aug. 24, 1823.
63 *Ibid.* Murray to Bathurst, Sept. 27, 1823.
64 C. O. 28/92. Warde to Bathurst, Aug. 27, 1823.
65 C. O. 137/156. Manchester to Bathurst, July 31, 1824.
66 C. O. 111/44. D'Urban to Bathurst, May 5, 1824.
67 *Ibid.* D'Urban to Bathurst, May 5, 1824. (This was the second letter in one day.)
68 *Ibid.* D'Urban to Bathurst, May 15, 1824.
69 C. O. 28/107. Lyon to Goderich, March 28, 1831.
70 *Ibid.* Lyon to Goderich, April 2, 1831.
71 C. O. 137/181. Belmore to Goderich, Jan. 6, 1832.
72 C. O. 137/182. Belmore to Goderich, May 2, 1832.
73 C. O. 295/92. Grant to Howick, April 30, 1832.
74 C. O. 137/188. Mulgrave to Goderich, April 26, 1833.
75 *Hansard, Third Series*, XIII, 77. May 24, 1832.
76 C. O. 137/191. F. B. Zuicke to Governor Belmore, May 23, 1832.
77 C. O. 28/111. Smith to Goderich, May 7, 1833.
78 *Ibid.*
79 *Ibid.* Smith to Stanley, May 23, 1833.

13

"EXTRAVAGANT EXPECTATIONS" OF FREEDOM

Rumour, Political Struggle, and the Christmas Insurrection Scare of 1865 in the American South

Steven Hahn

During the summer and fall of 1865, in the tense and uncertain aftermath of the Civil War and slave emancipation, rumours spread through the former Confederate states of an impending moment when, by federal government fiat or armed black insurrection, the already shattered world of the Old South might be turned fully upside down. Some thought, or feared, that the day of reckoning could arrive at any time; most looked to the Christmas season, and particularly to Christmas or New Year's Day. Expectations varied as to what would, in fact, occur. A good many freed-people seemed to hold the rather vague belief that there would be "some great change in the condition of affairs", that "something very important is going to happen", or that there would be "some great enhancement of their condition".[1] Growing numbers of whites, on the other hand, warned of a race war, "a negroe Jubilee insurection (*sic*)", when ex-slaves, re-enacting the "horrors of Jamaica and St. Domingo", would attempt to murder or drive off their former masters.[2] Of widest currency, however, was the idea that "the Government is going to take the Planters land and other property from them and give it to the colored people", or, failing that, that the blacks would carry out such a "general division of property" themselves.[3]

As it happened, the holidays passed without major disturbance. There was neither retribution from armed and vengeful blacks nor redistribution of white-owned property. Thus, what is called the "Christmas insurrection scare of 1865" has come to be understood chiefly as a "drama of the white imagination", of "fevered minds [fanning] . . . the flames of conflagration they had largely created themselves", of white "schizophrenia" and "paranoia", and as a further example of the racial panics that sporadically gripped the white South. In so far as the rumours of black violence that circulated among whites are treated as the principal narrative or as separable from the rumours of land redistribution that circulated among freed blacks, such an interpretation may seem plausible, if not compelling.[4] But if, instead, the various currents of rumour are treated together and, in certain regards, as mutually reinforcing, then the rumours become something more than psychological projections, and the interpretive possibilities become more complex and intriguing.

Most importantly, the rumours may be imagined as a field and form of political struggle. This is not, of course, readily apparent, for rumours often seem to indicate either disruptions in communication or perhaps haphazard and rearguard interventions. At all events, they seem easily distinguishable from "news" and scarcely illustrative of serious political engagement.[5] Yet, scholars in a number of disciplines have of late begun to interrogate the distinction between "rumour" and "news", and to find in rumours social dynamics and collective aspects that lend them substantial political bearing. And they have suggested that for subordinate groups in societies marked by great disparities of wealth and high levels of repression, rumours can be essential means of conducting cultural and political affairs: of establishing identities, interpreting information and actions, and entering the terrain of public discourse. Rumour surely has much to offer subalterns as a discursive and political practice. Its source is cloaked in anonymity; it normally flows through the channels of everyday life; and it is open to continuous improvisation and embellishment. Indeed, where events of vital importance are taking place among social groups historically subjected to direct personal domination and excluded from the official arenas of politics, rumour may be critical to popular communication and resistance. In the words of the political scientist and ethnographer, James C. Scott, "rumor . . . is not only an opportunity for anonymous protected communication, but also serves as a vehicle for anxieties and aspirations that may not be openly expressed".[6]

So considered, the Christmas insurrection scare of 1865 may emerge as a significant episode, less in the collective psychology of the white South than in the grass-roots politics of early Reconstruction. The ex-slaves, to be sure, had not been invested with official political standing, but in a more general sense the South of 1865 was very much a liminal political world. The foundation of social relations (slavery) and the most recent structure of governance (the Confederacy) had almost simultaneously been destroyed, but no new social or political system had either quickly emerged or been imposed to replace them. Only the Union army of occupation held official political authority in most areas, and even then local commanders had much latitude in carrying out their still-ambiguous assignments. Thus, with so much at stake in so explosive an environment, resolution of the great issues of land, labour, power and authority often involved, at least initially, the elaboration and intensification of customary political practices.

The insurrection scare thereby revealed and embodied much of the tenor of political engagement in the immediate post-war South, and illuminated many of the nascent dynamics of Reconstruction. It exposed the gnawing apprehensions, the confusion and disarray, and the enduring sources of power that the old master class brought out of military defeat and economic debilitation. It gave expression and direction to the tensions, ambiguities and developing trajectory of federal policy. And, above all else, it dramatized the political sensibilities and resources that ex-slaves possessed and built upon in the aftermath of emancipation. For them, the rumours of land redistribution not only resonated with widely shared aspirations; they also served as instruments for political debate and mobilization well before the granting of the franchise, and provided important leverage in contests for local power. In the end, the Christmas insurrection scare of 1865 may too have helped to propel the wheels of Reconstruction in a more radical political direction and advanced the cause of enfranchisement itself.[7]

I

Like rumours of slave or peasant rebellions and emancipations that erupted intermittently in many rural societies, those associated with the Christmas insurrection scare have murky and mysterious features. It is not entirely clear when and where the rumours first surfaced, how widely they circulated, or whether some of them ever had much substance. If the reports of alarmed southern whites and concerned federal officials together provide clues, word of general property division and black-inspired violence began to circulate along the coast of North and South Carolina by the early summer of 1865, and then spread quite rapidly, especially through those areas of the South where freedpeople could be found in largest numbers. By November, both the expectations of blacks and the apprehensions of whites had been raised in the plantation districts of Virginia, North Carolina, Georgia, Alabama and Texas, and more widely still in South Carolina and the Mississippi Valley states of Louisiana, Mississippi, Arkansas and Tennessee. One Freedmen's Bureau official familiar with Mississippi, Arkansas, Tennessee and Alabama reckoned that "a majority of the colored population positively believed that the government would take the plantations, with their old masters who had been in rebel service, cut them up into forty acre parcels, and give them to the colored people".[8]

Ex-slaves as well as ex-slaveowners had good cause to lend such rumours more than a little credibility.[9] By the time the Civil War ended – owing to congressional legislation, military field orders and wartime planter flight – the federal government controlled nearly 900,000 acres of southern land and had authority to set it apart for eventual acquisition by "loyal refugees and freedmen". Much of that land lay in the fertile areas of the south-eastern seaboard and the lower Mississippi Valley, and a good bit of it, chiefly in the low-country of South Carolina and Georgia, was already occupied by freedpeople who expected to obtain formal title. Although President Andrew Johnson, in his Amnesty Proclamation of 29 May 1865, made provision for the restoration of most of this property to its former owners, the "land question", like the more general issues of social and economic reorganization, remained very much alive. "We are but at the beginning of the war", a worried North Carolina conservative could write that July.[10]

Indeed, the rumours of federally sponsored property redistribution thrived, as rumours often do, on the mix of hopes and fears that the war had unleashed and on the great contention that characterized the making of federal policies. Observers pointed, not only to the influence of sympathetic Union soldiers and government agents who wished to break the slaveocracy even in the face of executive resistance, but also to the dire warnings of Confederate planters who had tried to rally support against the Yankee invaders. General Rufus Saxton, briefly the Freedmen's Bureau Assistant Commissioner for South Carolina, Georgia and Florida, summarized the situation:

> Previous to the termination of the war the negroes had heard from those in rebellion that it was the purpose of our government to divide up the southern plantations among them, and that was one of the reasons the rebels urged among their own people to excite them to greater activity .. Our own acts of Congress and particularly the one creating the Freedmen's Bureau, which was extensively circulated among them, further strengthened them in this dearest wish of their heart – that they were to have homesteads.[11]

The rapidity and scope with which rumours about federal policies, with attendant embellishments, circulated among southern blacks astonished some northern officials. "It was a wonder to me", Lt. George O. Sanderson, who served in North Carolina, remarked: "It seemed to pass, as intelligence will, in the strangest manner, from one to another quickly . . . with unaccountable speed".[12] The slaves had called their networks of communication, built out of years of struggle, experience and accumulated trust, the "grapevine way", or "grapevine telegraph". House servants, coachmen, artisans and hired slaves, some of whom had gained the rudiments of literacy, carried news from the big house, the courthouse, the tavern and the market-place back into the quarters where it was discussed, interpreted and then further disseminated, when slaves visited kinfolk on other plantations and farms, met each other on the back roads, or held brush-arbour religious meetings. In these ways the slaves, in many different locales, learned of the antislavery movement in the North, the sectional conflict and other "great events". So it was that "when the war came", as Virginia ex-slave Horace Muse recalled, "de news spread like a whirlwin". We heard it whispered 'roun' dat a war come fer to set de niggers free".[13]

The Civil War and early Reconstruction not only brought the slaves' communication networks to more public light, but also helped to extend, deepen and institutionalize them. The combination of Confederate mobilization and Union invasion pushed and pulled thousands of slaves to social sites where rumours, news and debate proliferated in a manner impossible to control: to Confederate fortifications and war industries; to Union and Confederate army posts; to federal contraband camps; and to newly formed black Union regiments. William I. Johnson, taken by his master into General Robert E. Lee's Army of Northern Virginia in 1863, first "learned from another slave that Lincoln had freed all of us". A year later, in camp near Fredricksburg, he seized an opportunity to talk with some recently captured Yankee prisoners, who "explained to us about slavery and freedom . . . and told us if we got a chance to steal away from camp and got over to the Yankee side we would be free". Along with four other slaves, Johnson soon fled and ended up in a Union quartermaster's corps.[14]

Such runaways who joined federal military outfits could then have met the likes of George H. Hepworth, a white, commissioned officer in the black, Fourth Louisiana Native Guards. Seeing "large numbers of blacks . . . crowding within our lines", Hepworth believed that "the *best* thing to do was to enlist all able-bodied men, confiscate every plantation in the department, and dividing the land into twenty acre lots, give each black family one such lot, and let them try the experiment of free labour for themselves". On the home front, both relaxed discipline and shifting troop movements created further openings for the transmission of information. "My first job in the fight for the rights of my people", recalled George Washington Albright, a Mississippi slave who later served in the state senate, was "to tell the slaves that they were free, to keep them informed and in readiness to assist Union armies".[15]

At the war's end, swelling streams of black migration and the organizational activities linked to the initial phases of Presidential Reconstruction together multiplied and amplified these lines of communication. Indeed, as federal policy makers and their subordinates increasingly locked horns over the questions of land, labour and political rights, they appear to have fuelled, rather than stifled, the freedpeople's expectations. When thousands of ex-slaves who had remained on plantations and farms until the surrender flocked, at least temporarily, to towns and cities, they could have joined urban blacks at processions and mass meetings and heard the speeches of federal representatives and local black leaders as to their rights and prospects. In Savannah, Georgia, they could have heard General Rufus Saxton promise to "aid you in getting 40 acre farms as homes". In Pulaski, Tennessee, they might have heard what was derisively described as an "impudent [and] . . . incendiary speech of a Capt. Redford", which lent some in the black audience "an idea that they are to be vested with a sort of proprietary interest in the lands and houses of the white people from whom they contract to work". And in Hampton, Virginia, they would have been assured by the fiery lawyer and Union League activist, Calvin Pepper, that "they could *all* have lands, and their rights should be secured to them". Near the South Carolina capital of Columbia, the planter, E. B. Heyward, thus grumbled about the "extravagant expectations" that members of the "radical party of the north" had nourished.[16]

As many of the black migrants departed from urban areas, they opened only some of the increasing number of channels through which these "extravagant expectations" could move across the countryside. Returning refugees, especially from districts where wartime labour experiments hinted at more general land reform, opened additional ones. Union army officers in the interior of South Carolina, noting the "general discontent . . . on the part of the negroes" around their posts, attributed it to the arrival of "many freedmen" who had been "absent on the coast", where early federal occupation and Sherman's Field Order No. 15 had begun to reorganize the plantation system. "They lead them to believe that they are to have land, on the first of January", Lt.-Col. F. H. Whittier wrote from Sumter, and although he did "all in my power to do away with the expectation . . . I no sooner get back than there is another story started".[17]

More important in disseminating ideas about the freedpeople's prospects and in raising their expectations were black Union soldiers. Nearly 85,000 of them served in the army of occupation (accounting for more than one-third of the total federal occupying force), and over half of their numbers were to be found in the states of Mississippi, Louisiana, Tennessee and Kentucky, from which many of the reports regarding land redistribution and possible insurrection emanated. Planters and other white southern leaders came to groan incessantly about what they viewed as the "demoralizing" influence exerted by the "colored troops" on the freed black labour force, particularly by encouraging belief in property division. "The Negro Soldiery here", a Panola, Mississippi, landowner complained, "are constantly telling our negroes that for the next year, the Government will give them land, provisions, Stock and all things necessary to carry on business for themselves". "Strange to say", he added with evident befuddlement, "the negroes believe such stories in spite of facts to the contrary told them by their employers". Even Carl Schurz, who reported to President Johnson on conditions in the South and generally praised the discipline and demeanour of the black troops, none the less acknowledged that they "are sometimes found to put queer notions into the heads of negroes working on the plantations".[18]

The presence of black troops and of black veterans mustered out of service helped advance the local organization of freed communities. The Revd Horace James, federal Superintendent of Negro Affairs in North Carolina, marvelled in January 1865 that blacks "form societies, leagues, combinations, meetings, with little of routine or record, but much of speech making and sage counsel". Within months, countless meetings, some large and some small, had assembled elsewhere — in rural churches, county seats, camp-grounds, plantations, and less accessible locations — where discussion ranged widely and, at times, promoted and validated rumours of land redistribution. In June, the Freedmen's Bureau Superintendent of the Eastern District of Arkansas expressed irritation at black preachers who spent their "time teaching the people that they should, *of right*, own every foot of soil" instead of instructing them in "sound practical truths". At the end of September, twenty members of the Wilkes County, Georgia, grand jury told a Freedmen's Bureau official that a recent meeting of nearly three thousand blacks, "of which much the larger proportion were Males . . . [and] sworn to secrecy", supplied many with the belief "that there will be a general division among the lands and property of the county". And in early November, a series of meetings in Terrebone Parish, Louisiana, from which whites were excluded, appeared to raise the idea that "some great change in the condition of affairs was expected to take place before the 1st of January".[19]

For growing numbers of freedpeople, these incipient fora of mobilization framed the issues of early Reconstruction, led to more public debate, and, in the words of a Union officer in Georgetown, South Carolina, "strengthened . . . the impression that lands are to be given". When, for example, two candidates vied for selection to the North Carolina freedmen's convention before a late September gathering of blacks in Tarrboro, one "took the ground that there would be no division of Land, and that they only would get land who made money to buy it". "He did not receive a single vote out of an assembly of probably 1,500 persons", the local Freedmen's Bureau agent recorded "as another sign of the times". But "the other took the opposite ground and was unanimously elected". Small wonder that federal authorities often had difficulty trying to convince rural blacks that no property division would occur. One such emissary in Amite County, Mississippi, who provided the freedpeople with "all the necessary instructions and advice they needed" and thought "they seemed at the time to be very well satisfied", later learned "that a great many of them said they did not believe what I told them . . . They are still hopeful that something is going to turn up about Christmas".[20]

The planters were, of course, quick to see any non-submissive behaviour on the part of the freedpeople, or any interventions on the part of federal agents, as harbingers of grander and more insidious designs; and the blacks themselves, at mass meetings and conventions, frequently took pains to dispute any suggestion that they planned an armed rising.[21] Yet the rumours of land redistribution, which formed so important a part of the Christmas insurrection scare, must not be dismissed as mere "illusions" entertained by ex-slaves or as mere creations of frightened white imaginations. They derived powerful credibility from federal actions, spread widely among African–Americans in the southern countryside, and, despite (or, better, because of) reversals in federal policy, percolated through a myriad of meetings and encounters. Indeed, given the freedpeople's exclusion from the official arenas of political negotiation and the risks they faced in publicly expressing their aspirations and wills, the rumours could have served them as vital points of political contact, conversation and identification; as safer ways in which to introduce themselves as political actors; and as potent means for shaping — and advancing — the terrain of political debate. Rumour, one student of politics notes, is a "distinctive form of political learning — in the sense both of what is learnt and how it is learnt". And, as the historian Anand A. Yang writes, "The presence of rumours in society does not necessarily signal a breakdown of communication but an attempt at collective conversation by people who wish to enter their sentiments into the public discourse".[22] The rumours, the "extravagant expectations" of what freedom might bring, that is, played a significant role in defining the political communities of rural blacks newly emerged from bondage.

II

Whatever many planters preferred to believe, the freedpeople did not need tutors or outside agitators to nurture their desire for, or sense of entitlement to, the land. They neither had to be apprised of the advantages that proprietorship would hold nor reminded that their long-endured and uncompensated toil and suffering had built both the South's great fortunes and the nation's prosperity. Yet, the expectations of property division also revealed complex aspirations and sets of beliefs. And they shed considerable light on the ways that African–Americans drew upon the political sensibilities and rituals they had forged under slavery to give shape and substance to the course of emancipation and early Reconstruction: on shared understandings of power and process that the general social relations of slavery had encouraged; on the discrete, and often very different, settings and circumstances in which those relations took hold; and on the new formulations and projects that the military destruction of slavery made possible.

The expectations of land redistribution expressed an almost universally held notion of just compensation for the travails of slavery, of what was rightfully due those who tilled the soil, and of what could provide meaningful security in a post-emancipation world. In this, the ex-slaves closely resembled subject rural folk in many societies, for in one form or another the "land question" charged social struggles in all servile and semi-servile labour systems and surfaced in connection with most servile emancipations.[23] But the expectations reflected, as well, the African-Americans' intensely personal and spiritual conception of the world and the logic of the deliverance narratives that many had heard and embellished as slaves. It is not surprising, therefore, that as their masters' claims to sovereignty were eroded and then undermined by invading Union armies, many slaves could see at work the hands of a powerful protector, one experienced in very immediate terms. More than a few, for example, later remembered learning of their liberation when "Marse Linkum" came riding through their locales.[24]

Although such imaginings could be seen as evidence of the painful and potentially debilitating legacy of enforced dependency, they more likely exemplified one of the ways in which ex-slaves chose recognized and available appellations of authority and respect to interpret the great events sweeping the South (and, not incidentally, to rebuke their former owners). Significantly, they also chose others which assimilated Lincoln into their own leadership and struggles. "The 'rice people' always spoke of the President as 'Uncle Sam' and 'Papa' Linkum", the sensitive northern teacher, Elizabeth Hyde Botume, wrote from the coast of South Carolina, hinting at his association with the elders and preachers of the slave community: "They gave him credit for all the wonderful things that had been done since the world began".[25]

Such personified representations of the coming of freedom melded with, and were reinforced by, the millennial strains that ran through a developing Afro-Christianity. For years the slaves, linking the figures of Moses and Jesus in a manner that some white observers deemed "curious", "crude", or "ignorant of the scriptures", had prayed for deliverance from their collective suffering; when it came, the linkage seemed to be embodied in God's new earthly agents.[26] "[The negroes] almost adore the persons who have brought them deliverance", Revd Horace James noted, "but Abraham Lincoln is to them the chiefest among ten thousand ... They mingle his name with their prayers and their praises evermore. They have great reverence for the 'head men' and for all in authority". A South Carolina freedman, after learning of Lincoln's death, told Philadelphian Laura M. Towne that "Lincoln died for we, Christ died for we, and me believe him de same mans". "Talk of Linkum; no man seen Linkum; Linkum walk as Jesus walk", another somewhat mystically informed a federal army captain who later remarked on "what ideas they get from the Bible". Others conflated the figures of Abraham Lincoln, William T. Sherman and Rufus Saxton with those of Moses and Jesus.[27]

The rumours of land redistribution resonated powerfully with the millennial meanings the slaves attached to their deliverance from bondage. After all, they called emancipation the "day of Jubilo" and sang of it in many parts of the South:

Old master's gone away and the darkies stayed at home;
Must be now that the kingdom's come and the year for jubilee.

Rich in the stories, characters, images and allegories of the Bible as their community religious experiences came to be, could they not have known too that the Biblical "jubilee" joined freedom with the restitution of the land to its rightful claimants?[28]

Freedpeople in south Georgia may well have been signifying such an understanding when they proclaimed "that 'Head man' will come before next Christmas and will make them 'more free' and 'distribute the lands' to them". Others in Mississippi heard ("from the voice of the Angels probably", as a local agent chortled, perhaps acknowledging echoes of the millennial Book of Revelation) "that a Great Document has been received by the 'Freedmens Bureau' sealed with four seals . . . to be broken on the 1st day of January 1866", the third anniversary of the Emancipation Proclamation. "This wonderful paper [is believed] to contain [the freedmen's] final orders from the Yankee Government which they believe is omnipotent". The abolitionist, Thomas Wentworth Higginson, who commanded black troops in wartime South Carolina and listened carefully to their spirituals, thus tellingly insisted that "the Apocalypse . . . with the books of Moses constituted their Bible; all that lay between, even the narratives of the life of Jesus, they hardly cared to read or hear".[29]

The mythic and millennial aspects of these expectations had both deep symbolic meanings and concrete political uses. For by investing the government, often in the person of the president, with the authority and intent to carry out the injunctions of the "jubilee", the freedpeople not only rejected their former owners' pretensions to absolute power, but also provided a standard of justice and equity against which the policies and actions of federal officials were to be judged. A Mississippi planter conceded as much when he wrote Andrew Johnson, with considerable exasperation, that local blacks thought "that they will own all and we will have to emigrate elsewhere . . . [and] all will come by you and from you". Efforts to dissuade them simply failed, because "some of the negroes dont believe a word of it — and say the *President* will do more for us".[30]

A Freedmen's Bureau agent in northern Louisiana made a related point in trying to explain, with more equanimity and some amusement, why "the illusion . . . [of] a general division of property . . . [was] very natural for their simple minds": "inasmuch as the Government has made them free, they consider that a share of the property which their past services have acquired justly belongs to them; and imagining that the Government regards the subject in the same light, they adhere to the fallacy very tenaciously". So tenaciously, in fact, that the freedpeople might suspect the motives and veracity of federal authorities who sought to disabuse them of such a "fallacy". In the tradition of invoking the just and good ruler

343

disobeyed by unfaithful subordinates (what some scholars have called "naïve monarchism"), "a large number of Freedmen" in southern Mississippi could therefore announce "that the late President Lincoln intended . . . to divide the lands of their former owners among them; that in some way his intention has been defeated and that they are being cheated out of their rights".[31]

It was not by accident, then, that many of the ex-slaves looked to the Christmas season for the dispensation of their just rewards, for at no other time of the year had the slaveowners' claims to authority been more ritualistically displayed and contested. Following long-established custom, slaveholders had taken the occasion of Christmas to demonstrate their wealth and patriarchal benevolence by distributing gifts and sponsoring barbecues, suppers and parties for their black, as well as their white, "families". Playing grateful servants to the master's Lord Bountiful, the slaves, in their turn, had serenaded the big house with joyful cries of "Christmas gif, Christmas gif". But if the masters could congratulate themselves on their generosity and imagine that the loyalties and labours of their charges would be suitably encouraged, they wrote only part of the script. Among the slaves, the gifts and festivities provided for them were a much less important feature of the holidays than the accompanying opportunities to provide for themselves. With work largely suspended and the reins of supervision loosened on the days between Christmas and New Year's, they moved relatively freely to visit family and friends on neighbouring plantations and farms. There they staged their own rites of community, held their own dances and celebrations, and partook of the spirit and the spirits of the season.[32]

So unruly could the frolicking appear that slaveowners nervously warned of the need for greater vigilance. Not surprisingly, a substantial portion of the ante-bellum slave insurrection panics fixed on the Christmas interlude; all the more so after Jamaican slaves launched a massive rebellion on 27 December 1831. When the Civil War broke out, these apprehensions only intensified. "As far as the memory of man can go, there has existed among the negro population a tradition which has caused us many sleepless nights", a planter in St Charles Parish, Louisiana, wrote in December 1862. "They imagine they are to be freed by Christmas. Vague reports are spread about that they intend . . . to come in vast numbers and force the federal government to give them their freedom".[33]

In their preoccupation with the potential consequences of revelry in the quarters, worried planters tacitly admitted the limits of their paternalist sway while supplying lurid visions of social inversion that the slaves preferred to enact symbolically and metaphorically, eventually lending further substance to rumours of a momentous change in the making. Like dependent classes in other pre-industrial societies, the slaves used holidays such as Christmas not only to strengthen the threads binding their communities, but also to ridicule the pretensions of their betters and conjure up a world in which relations of subordination might be negated or inverted.[34]

The most ritualized manifestations of these symbolic inversions and appropriations of white prerogatives were to be found in eastern North Carolina and southern Virginia, where Yuletide brought what was variously called "Jonkonnu", "John Canoe", "John Kuner", or "John Canno", replete with threateningly costumed slaves, cacophonous serenades, "extraordinary" dances and highly choreographed exchanges.[35] Elsewhere in the South, though less elaborately and agonistically, the slaves also took satirical jabs at their masters, simultaneously mocked and challenged the structure of plantation authority, transgressed the customary spatial boundaries of slave life and enacted rites of reciprocity rather than submission. The slaveholders may well have been amused, and the festivities undoubtedly provided a relatively safe release for accumulated social tensions, not to mention a chance for the slaves to engage in rivalries of their own. Yet in these special ways, the slaves also nourished collective sensibilities of their self-worth, of their masters' false claims to rule and of the possibilities of organizing the world in an altogether different fashion.

If the freedpeople could see in the rumours of a Christmas property division the hand of a truly just and sovereign authority acting against the pretenders and usurpers, they imagined in the results less a wholesale inversion — when masters would become slaves and slaves masters — than a rearrangement or reconstitution of social relations. And although representations of the process could be rather vague, expectations and claims derived from the concrete experiences of enslavement. Many African-Americans in plantation districts, and especially in areas long-settled and relatively stable, therefore anticipated obtaining control, not just of any land, but of the estates on which they lived and laboured. Their attachment to their "old homes" or the "old range" was, as white observers widely commented, deep and powerful. It expressed not only a sense of place and of "right to the cattle and hogs that they have raised and taken care of, and the [crops] they have raised", but also a commitment to maintaining and reinforcing the networks of kinship, friendship and customary practice that had sustained them under slavery and informed the sense of right itself. Indeed, along the coast of South Carolina, where slave communities had especially extended generational roots, the freedpeople might even reject opportunities to pre-empt or take title to tracts of land if doing so necessitated relocation.[36]

The interrelation of land, kinship and years of community labour helps to explain why expectations of land redistribution were far less common in regions of the South where farms and small plantations predominated. There the slaves were more closely tied to the organization and rhythms of white households. It was more likely that they had to work in the fields alongside their owners; it was less likely that they could live with all members of their immediate families, tend customary garden plots and engage in the day-to-day activities that made for the dense culture of the quarters and encouraged identification with the parcels of land on which they resided. For them, the immediate post-emancipation period was given over chiefly to the tasks of reuniting and reconstituting their own households and kinship groups, which had been scattered over the neighbouring countryside, if not over greater distances.[37]

As one moved from non-plantation or small plantation regions back into the plantation belt, rumours of an impending property division could be heard once again. But in the more recently settled or socially volatile plantation districts, and in those where few holdings had been abandoned by owners during the war, the rumours may well have been interpreted as a government promise, less to partition particular estates, than to provide opportunities for the acquisition of homesteads, farm implements and draft animals under favourable terms. Asking "what is the good of freedom if one has nothing to go on?", some freedpeople searched for the chance to set up on small tracts or patches where they could "become householders themselves". And, according to one disgruntled white North Carolinian, "they believe that the Government will wink at their attempt to assert ... their ideas, and will maintain them in their claim of equality".[38]

Other freedpeople began to pool resources accumulated by years of extra work, hiring out, and selling the eggs, poultry and vegetables raised on their provision grounds in hopes of buying or leasing land that was or would be confiscated. In July 1865, Thomas W. Conway, the sympathetic Freedmen's Bureau Assistant Commissioner in Louisiana, reported receiving "many applications from freedmen, some who have $10–15,000, some $3–5,000, and some who have nothing but are anxious to work and give a share of the crop for advances". A month later, "a portion of the freedmen of Lenoir County [North Carolina] ... being desirous of embracing every facility which the US government offers to provide for ourselves the comforts of a permanent home", formed "a society to purchase homes by joint stock", pledging to raise $10,000 in monthly instalments by 1 January 1868. In this, they and other ex-slaves may have been influenced by black soldiers who, in squads, companies and even regiments, took their savings and applied "for such portions of land as they consider themselves able to purchase and cultivate". Thus, when an "intelligent" Mississippi freedman, exemplifying the "great eagerness of the blacks ... [to] have homes of their own", was told that "the whites intend to compel you to hire out to them", he shot back, "what if we should compel them to lease us lands?"[39]

The agitation and rumours about land redistribution were, as might be expected, principally rural affairs. In the cities and towns of the South, where black political mobilization was most advanced in 1865, mass meetings and freedmen's conventions, dominated as they were by men who had been free before the war, focused on demands for suffrage and civil rights. To that end they invoked the Declaration of Independence, the treasonous behaviour of the slaveholders, the long-standing loyalty of black Americans, and the crucial role of black troops in saving the Union. But as like-minded federal officials, black leaders and black soldiers made their way into the countryside, assembling the freedpeople and apprising them of their rights and prospects, they provided them with a new language and new categories in which aspirations for land could be expressed.[40]

Already, such voices as the *New Orleans Tribune*, run by well-educated, politically experienced mulattos, and arguably one of the most radical newspapers to be published in nineteenth-century America, had outlined the arguments in terms familiar to national politics and political discourse. Proclaiming that "we must come out of the revolution not only as emancipationists, but as true Republicans", the *Tribune* excoriated wartime federal policies that served to restore the plantation system and called for the confiscation and redistribution of rebel-owned property. "Our basis for labor", the *Tribune* imagined, "may now be put on a democratic footing".[41]

The editors of the *Tribune*, by the autumn of 1865, thought that some, "and especially the most active", of the freedmen in the "country parishes" had read at least a few issues of the paper.[42] Early political lessons were to be received, as well, from white and black allies – those whom the planters and conservative federal agents deemed "malicious", "evil" and "designing" persons – who aided the ex-slaves in defending claims to the lands they occupied, resisting the coercion of their former masters and finding avenues to secure independence. Albeit slowly and unevenly, rural freedpeople learned how to compose and frame petitions, to best articulate their expectations, and to represent their goals in relation to the larger political struggles sweeping the South and the nation.

Among the most extraordinary of the students were Henry Bram, Ishmael Moultrie and Yates Simpson, constituted as a "committee in behalf of the people" of Edisto Island, South Carolina. In late October 1865, having learned "with deep sorrow and Painful hearts" that the lands they cultivated under the provisions of Sherman's Field Order No. 15 would soon be restored to the white owners, they wrote to President Andrew Johnson and Freedmen's Bureau Commissioner O. O. Howard to ask that the decision be reconsidered. They began by attributing their emancipatory jubilee to divine authority carried "through our Late and Beloved President [Lincoln] proclamation and the war", and prayed that Johnson's decisions might be guided by "that wisdom that Cometh from above to settle these great and Important Questions". Echoing peasant appeals to a sovereign, they then suggested that the new president's policy reversals must be the result, not of motives they believed unjust, but of "the many perplexing and trying questions that burden your mind".

The committee rested its claims to the land, in part, on the traditional ground of unrequited labour performed by a kin-based community over many generations: "we are at the mercy of those who are combined to prevent us from getting land enough to lay our Fathers bones upon. . . . Here is w[h]ere we have toiled nearly all our lives as slaves and were treated like dumb Driven cattle. This is our home, we have made These lands what they are". Yet, significantly, the committee members also couched their grievances in language and constructions that spoke both to their direct experiences and to what the president might find compelling. Indeed, they took their understandings of the war and its results, and of the political predilections of Johnson, whose hostility to the Confederacy and the southern landed aristocracy was well known, and used them to make their case:

> Here is where secession was born and Nurtured . . . we were the only true and Loyal people that were found in possession of these Lands. we have always been ready to strike for Liberty and humanity yea to fight if needs be To preserve this glorious union. Shall not we who Are freedman and have always been true to this union have the same rights as are enjoyed by Others? Have we forfieted our rights of property In land? – If not then! are not our rights as A free people and good citizens of these United States To be considered before the rights of those who were Found in rebellion against this good and just Government . . . are these rebellious Spirits to be reinstated in their *possessions* And we who have been abused and oppressed For many long years not to be allowed the Privilige of purchasing land But to be subject To the will of these large Land owners? God fobid, Land monopoly is injurious to the advancement of the course of freedom, and if Government Does not make some provision by which we as Freedmen can obtain obtain A Homestead, We have Not bettered our condition.[43]

The Edisto Islanders may well have been hitching their particular aspirations for land to the national project then being devised and advanced by Radical Republicans and their black allies, still chiefly to be found in southern and northern cities. But it may equally have been the case that there, as elsewhere in the plantation South, they were seeking to protect and consecrate their own project of community-building by placing it under the jurisdiction of an earthly sovereign power that they themselves had helped to sustain. At all events, the black struggle to define the meaning of freedom took place in an explosive and ill-defined political environment still very much influenced by the world of enslavement.

III

By the fall of 1865, white southerners had good cause to doubt that the federal government would continue to spearhead a program of property confiscation and redistribution. For despite the determined efforts of some Radical Republicans in the Congress, the bureaucracy and the military, President Andrew Johnson – without much other effectual opposition – spent his first months in office simultaneously hastening the restoration of rebel-owned estates and reprimanding, overriding or dismissing those who sought to stand in the way.[44] What southern whites increasingly claimed to fear was a move by disappointed freedpeople to take matters into their own hands by the only means left available: concerted violence.

This was the insurrectionary scare, and its resemblance to earlier slave insurrection panics (not to mention similar panics in other highly oppressive societies) was not fortuitous. It came at a time of heightened tensions and anxieties, of political division and social unrest; it inflated episodic resistance and discontent into full-blown conspiracies; it implicated outsiders; and it served to inspire greater vigilance among whites and even harsher repression against blacks. Indeed, it suggested how much the social relations and expectations of slavery continued to govern the perspectives and behaviours of former masters.[45]

But the 1865 scare had distinctive features which must not be overlooked. Compared with its predecessors, it proved more protracted and certainly more extended in scope. Of even greater significance, it occurred in the aftermath of a sweeping emancipation that involved the military defeat and political marginalization of slaveowners, and created something of a power vacuum in the plantation districts, while opening new channels of negotiation to ex-slaves through the presence of the Union Army and Freedmen's Bureau. In the end, therefore, together with rumours of property redistribution that circulated among freedpeople, the insurrectionary scare came to be a weapon of direct struggle over the balances of power in the countryside.

An episode in the Alabama black belt revealed how quickly, and under what circumstances, the dynamic could be set in motion. In the early fall of 1865 a freedman came into the office of Freedmen's Bureau agent Andrew Geddes in Tuskegee, wishing "to get a few arms and permission for himself and 2 or 3 others" to go "down to Pike County" and give "aid to their friends and relatives" who "were being treated very cruelly and unjustly by the white citizens". Geddes denied the request and threatened the freedman with arrest, whereupon the freedman "seemed to go off satisfied". Soon thereafter, however, "a committee of citizens" told Geddes that it had "been *reported* to them than an 'insurrection' was on foot among the negroes and that application had been made for arms &c". Despite Geddes's denials, the committee remained "quite excited and appeared to seriously apprehend an immediate rising of the negroes armed and equipped and crying for *vengeance*". They decided to alert Lewis Parsons, the native Alabamian who had been appointed the state's provisional governor by President Johnson.[46]

With their own political status and social power still unsettled, growing numbers of planters and other white landowners brought their fears of insurrection to the attention of federal officials and, especially, the governors appointed or elected under the auspices of Presidential Reconstruction. They were most likely to do so in states where blacks formed clear or near population majorities, and where some federal officials, together with newly installed post-Confederate officeholders, were regarded as sympathetic to their concerns — Mississippi, Louisiana, Alabama, Georgia and South Carolina being the prime examples. They called for the withdrawal of black troops, who were represented as the chief instigators, and for authority to raise local militia companies so as to maintain order and generally "overawe the colored population". A group of "white citizens of Caddo and Bossier parishes, many of whom are planters", thus wrote to Louisiana Governor J. Madison Wells in October of "a prevailing idea among the colored people that after January 1 there is to be a general distribution of property . . . [instilled] principally by the colored troops, who have been for some months stationed among us". They insisted that "great apprehension pervades the countryside" and asked Wells for such help as arms, ammunition and permission to organize the militia "under officers of our selection".[47]

The governors, in turn, contacted the commanders of military departments, the assistant commissioners of the Freedmen's Bureau, and, if necessary, President Johnson, to win official support for the suppression of a potential outbreak. In this, the governors served less as the president's state representatives than as the planters' national brokers, testing the boundaries of federal policy while presenting the planters' case in a way the president might view as a demonstration of public responsibility. Most vocal and persuasive among them was Mississippi's William L. Sharkey, a former member of the Whig party who had opposed secession but was closely identified with the planting interest. As early as August, Sharkey wrote Johnson that "the negroes are bold in their threats" and "there is a . . . widespread opinion amongst the people . . . that about Christmas they intend a general rising for the purpose of taking the property". To "begin preparation for such an emergency and to suppress crime", he thereby "called for volunteer companies of militia in each county" and asked for control of the "state arms" and the power "to organize the whole of the militia". Sharkey later warned Freedmen's Bureau Commissioner Howard that black troops were expected to lead a revolt in the winter if the distribution of property was not carried out and suggested that they be expeditiously removed from the state. Other governors added their voices, including Governor Parsons of Alabama who forwarded a resolution of the state constitutional convention recommending the formation of "one or more companies of militia, in each county, as soon as practicable".[48]

Federal officials in the former Confederate states generally responded to these alarms with studied scepticism. Nevertheless, by November the Bureau began to send agents into the rural districts with instructions to "disabuse" the freedpeople of "the false impression that the lands of their former owners are to be divided out among them on or about Christmas next" and "urge them at once to make contracts for 1866". In the less "extravagant" political economy of freedom that most federal authorities had come to preach, the blacks heard that "you must labor for what you get like other people", that "idleness and vagrancy" would not be tolerated, that property had to be purchased, and that any attempt "to take property from anyone . . . would be punished with utmost severity".[49]

Initially, however, army commanders blocked the mobilization of the militias, and Johnson was given good reason to sustain their actions. In Louisiana, General E. R. S. Canby found that local militia companies "indulged in the gratification of private vengeance and worked against the policy of the Government", while from Mississippi Carl Schurz pleaded that "General Slocum's order . . . prohibiting the organization of the militia in this state . . . be openly approved". Schurz had met Governor Sharkey, and although he believed Sharkey to be "a good, clever gentleman, and probably a first class lawyer", he doubted whether Sharkey could be trusted: "He is continually surrounded by a set of old secessionists whom he considers it his duty to conciliate". Johnson thus stunned many federal officials in the South, and aroused suspicion and mistrust in much of the North, by agreeing to countenance — and then by welcoming — what proved to be the rearming of ex-Confederates and the revitalization of slave patrols. Indeed, shortly after approving Sharkey's actions, Johnson advised neighbouring Provisional Governor Parsons to raise "in each county an armed mounted *posse comitatus* organized under your militia law", noting that "a similar organization by me in Tennessee when military governor worked well".[50]

Johnson's decision followed from a more general aim to restore self-government quickly in the South through policies that might stimulate a show of loyalty, moderation and proper conduct. But as with other concessions to what has been termed "self-reconstruction", the organization of militia companies only stimulated white defiance toward the federal government and retribution against the freedpeople. If anything, it blurred the lines between legal and extra-legal coercion, and gave the go-ahead to vigilantes who, like the "Black patroles" around Tuskegee, Alabama, traversed the countryside "whipping and otherwise male (*sic*) treating the Freedmen".[51] Using the threat of insurrection as shield and sword, the planters and their allies launched a campaign to disarm, disperse and intimidate rural blacks, intending to reassign them to the "tender mercies" of white landowners. Any black assembly, any sign of economic independence, any attempt to ignore or reject the conventions of racial subordination became invitations to harassment or summary punishment. Away from their posts, even black soldiers fell vulnerable to confrontations, ritual humiliations and physical violence. As a "party" of whites in Sumter County, Georgia, proclaimed, "they would make their own laws ... and if the negroes failed to hire and contract upon their terms before Christmas, or at that time, they would make the woods stink with their carcasses". "Our negroes have ... a tall fall ahead of them", a white Mississippian, who looked on with approbation, predicted: "They will learn that freedom and independence are different things".[52]

Federal authorities and other northern observers largely mocked reports of freedmen secreting arms, holding nightly meetings and drilling in military fashion, and usually discovered upon investigation that such "stories" were "not worthy of consideration".[53] Yet, exaggerated as they normally were, these false alarms also spotlighted the early political activities of black communities and the developing contests for power that emancipation unleashed. For just as white landowners turned rumours of land redistribution into harbingers of insurrection so as to reassert their local prerogatives, the freedpeople used the rumours to bolster their own bargaining positions.

When, during the summer of 1865, a planter in north-eastern Mississippi "broached the matter of hiring to his negroes [by proposing] to give something to eat and keep some till Christmas", they showed their "exalted ideas" by rebuffing him and demanding "in addition a part of the crop". In mid-September, the overseer on William Alexander Graham's Leper plantation in York District, South Carolina, finding it difficult to maintain order, charged that "your hands say they will git one half of your crop let them work or not and you cant drive them off for this land dont Bee long to you". A group of Arkansas landowners wrestling with black labourers on their estates later that autumn could see "an unusual stir ... to exist among the negroes and a great deal of passing to and fro at night and congregating at certain out of the way places". In this, they "apprehended" a "great danger and considerable probability of an outbreak", since the labourers had "an idea amongst them that they are to have homes and farms of their own allotted to them after the present year", and "many are known to have firearms in their possession". While travelling through east-central North Carolina, the journalist, Sidney Andrews, who discounted the "charge that the blacks are pretty generally organizing and ... drilling semi-weekly", none the less learned "that negroes hold weekly meetings in some neighborhoods".[54]

More widely, freedpeople refused to enter into labour agreements for 1866 despite the prodding of landowners and Freedmen's Bureau agents alike. Some, associating the terms of contracts with the compulsions of servitude, feared "that if they hire to their former masters for the coming year, they will be held for 5 years and if they attempt to leave they will be punished". Many others saw no reason to accept the small remuneration, open-ended responsibilities and close supervision commonly offered when the new year might bring the opportunity to farm on their own account. The "Negroes . . . are not inclined to make any contracts until after Christmas", a landowner in Madison County, Tennessee, recorded in October 1865, in a typical complaint: "They seem to expect something to take place about that time, a division of lands or something of the kind". An army officer in Columbus, Mississippi, discovered that "the freedmen give various reasons for not entering into contracts", either they believed "they will be visited by some horrible punishment . . . for hiring to the 'Rebs' without orders", or they expected "to receive a donation of land from the Government", or they hoped to "rent land somewhere and thus 'work for themselves' ". "Still others", he scowled, "have so little sense or judgement that they . . . are waiting for the coming of Christmas for something to happen which will relieve them from work".[55]

Whether or not they genuinely anticipated a federally sponsored division of property, the freedpeople often sought to utilize the breathing space and manoeuvring room that such a rumour afforded. This is what John Dennett came to recognize as he conversed with a group of blacks on a large estate near Marion Village, South Carolina, in late October. Inquiring about their work, Dennett learned that they "didn' plan" cotton . . . jus' don broke corn' and did not know if they would "make cotton this next year". "We's waiting till Jenewerry come. Den we kin know", one of the men asserted. "We heares dis an' dat, dis an' dat", an older freedman added, "an" we told [Major G—] we'd hol' on tell Jenewerry". As "several men and women" came "out of the neighboring cabins or were standing in the door-ways", Dennett remarked "that Major G—had made you a very fair offer" and asked "why not sign the agreement now?" "I ain't agwine to bin' myself", a "young fellow" answered, "not till I kin see better". Dennett then brought up "the subject of a division of lands' since "such an opinion is universally prevalent in the lower districts of the state", and although the freedpeople "seemed disinclined to speak plainly", they finally said, "with some hesitation", that "they'd been told so". Dennett replied that "it was very unlikely that any land would be given away by the Government", but while they listened to what he said, they "appeared to receive it with dissatisfaction and incredulity": "We's agwine to wait anyhow", a freedman interjected. "We dunno whar we'll be next year, nor what they'll do with us. They tell what they'll do at Columby, and they tell another thing over to headquarters, and I goes for waitin' anyhow".[56]

IV

The wait eventually ended. When "Jenewerry" arrived, the freedpeople on Major G—'s estate probably accepted terms to work there or reached agreement with a neighbouring planter, and soon commenced planting cotton as well as corn. In so doing, they joined the great mass of rural blacks who, during the first two months of 1866, reluctantly but steadily signed contracts to cultivate the land as agricultural labourers. They had few alternatives. All that the Christmas season had brought them were further rounds of harassment, floggings, late-night searches and land evictions. Little wonder that a federal agent on inspection in Lowndes County, Alabama, just after the new year found, not simmering rebelliousness, but "a great deal of timidity on the part of the freedmen". No gift of land had been offered and no black insurrectionary plot had been hatched, on either a small or grand scale.[57]

It appears, therefore, that southern whites who urged defiance instead of conciliation as the best means to combat an even more revolutionary settlement of the Civil War, and who circulated rumours of upheaval in their battles for local power, were vindicated by the tumultuous course of the Christmas insurrection scare. For rather than provoking the strong fist of the federal government, the strategy seemed to bring many of the desired results. President Johnson redoubled his efforts to restore confiscated and abandoned lands; military commanders removed black troops from trouble spots, to some extent for the soldiers' own safety; Freedmen's Bureau officials went to considerable lengths to dispel rumours of impending property division and pressure freedpeople into contracting for the coming year; southern constitutional conventions and legislatures elected under the auspices of Johnsonian Reconstruction began to restrict black opportunities for either economic independence or civic equality, most flagrantly in states like South Carolina and Mississippi, by enacting draconian "Black Codes"; and in many black, belt districts, planters used the atmosphere created by the rumours of insurrection and by Johnson's "self-reconstruction" policies to set about enforcing contracts, punishing "vagrants", limiting competition for labourers, prohibiting the rental or sale of land to blacks and providing for regular policing.[58]

Yet, if it then seems that ex-Confederates were regaining on the field of peace much of what they had lost on the field of battle, appearances could be deceiving. President Johnson's Reconstruction policies, which initially enjoyed wide support in the northern states even among Republicans, were in fact in disarray and subject to growing doubts. And perhaps nothing troubled and incensed more northerners or pushed more moderate and conservative Republicans into opposing Johnson than did the epidemic of violence against blacks and white unionists that exploded amid rumours of federal land reform and Christmas insurrection. Reported extensively in the antislavery and Republican press, and on lecture circuits that drew large audiences, the violence seemed most directly to threaten the results of the war and to exceed the boundaries of northern tolerance.[59] Thus, when the newly selected southern congressional delegation, which included prominent ex-Confederates, arrived in Washington for the Thirty-Ninth Congress that December, the dominant Republicans rejected Johnson's advice and were able to act with dispatch: they refused to seat the southern claimants, established the Joint Committee on Reconstruction, and began in earnest to contest the President's policies and authority. Had they done otherwise, Reconstruction would have been at an end; now a more radical road was being paved.[60]

The expectations and struggles that the rumours of land redistribution promoted may have had an equally notable effect in the southern countryside. For they led freedpeople in many areas — often as a consequence of collective decision-making, as on Major G—'s estate — to hold off from signing contracts until the new year, creating a temporary labour shortage and thereby weakening the landowners' attempts to tie them down and dictate the terms. The freedpeople began "changing homes", seeking better arrangements. Some, as on the Virginia peninsula, "were willing to work for fair wages for a certain length of time, but were unwilling to hire themselves for one year".[61] Most others yielded to annual agreements while pressing for higher monthly pay or larger shares of the crop, and for greater control over their labour time. Even in Lowndes County, Alabama, where blacks initially showed "a great deal of timidity" and "planters made a strong combination to hire no negroes away from home", it was discovered that "the freedmen stood it out until the planters gave way and they finally hired at random, at a little higher wages than were generally paid elsewhere". Delay in contracting, observed an army officer in Orangeburg, South Carolina, "proved to be beneficial to many because planters anxious to secure their services gave them better pay after New Years than they would have given before Christmas".[62]

The land question was by no means laid to rest. For another few years it received an occasional hearing in Congress. With the advent of Radical Reconstruction in 1867, it mobilized the energies of some black delegates at ensuing southern constitutional conventions and then of some black representatives in subsequent southern state legislatures.[63] Rumours of property redistribution and attendant insurrectionary panics would also continue to erupt, especially at moments of intense political agitation as the customary, subterranean practices of grass-roots politics born in the slave South still lent shape and resonance to the public and electoral practices that would emerge in the post-emancipation South: during the early registration of black voters, during state and local election campaigns, and during heated labour conflicts. And in those areas of the South in which tentative claims to land had been established during and immediately after the war, the freedpeople battled tenaciously — and with some success — to fend off restorations and dispossessions. Small, black, truck farms were to be found where wealthy rice and sea-island cotton planters once ruled, and a handful of landed black communities were carved out in the midst of other plantation districts.[64]

The failure of general land reform in 1865, of course, dramatized the limits of the post-emancipation settlement devised by the federal government and made it likely that ex-slaves would struggle on principally as rural workers rather than as yeoman or peasant proprietors. The eager, millennial anticipations of the first months of freedom gave way to daily, monthly and yearly skirmishes: over rights to the growing crop and the raising of livestock, obligations to cut wood and repair fences, the allocation of family labour, common rights to hunt, fish and graze, the nature of remuneration and the cultivation of garden plots, the organization and rhythms of field work, the sources of provisions and the disposition of surpluses, and over many other details of life and labour.[65]

Still, the expectations of land and the accompanying contests over the social relations of freedom that swirled through much of the southern countryside during the Christmas insurrection scare of 1865 must be regarded as events of genuine political importance and as evidence of the complex ways in which politics were conducted in a South making the transition out of slavery. Far more, perhaps, than the pressure of Congressional Radicals and urban-based black leaders, they undermined Presidential Reconstruction, rendered untenable a southern world as the ex-slaveholders would have made it, and opened the way for wholly different possibilities. The expectations and contests also suggest that the land question unfolded, not as a parallel episode, but as an integral part of rural labour struggles and, more generally, that the politicization of black communities both had deep roots in slavery and underwent intensification well in advance of the federal government's granting of the franchise to black men. Thus, when Union League and Republican party activists arrived in 1867 to build a new electoral arena in the southern states, the freedpeople in many locales had already laid a substantial foundation for the work ahead. And they undoubtedly suspected already that the realization of their dreams would, in good measure, need to be an achievement of their own making.

NOTES

1 Capt. Thos Kanady to Lt. Z. K. Wood, New Orleans, La, 23 Dec. 1865: National Archives, Washington, DC (hereafter NA), RG 393, pt 1, Department of the Gulf, Letters Received, L-896 1865 [C-655] (bracketed notations refer to document file numbers at the Freedmen and Southern Society Project, University of Maryland); Carl Schurz to Andrew Johnson, Macon, Ga, 13 Aug. 1865, in *Advice after Appomattox, Letters to Andrew Johnson, 1865–66*, ed. Brooks D. Sumpson et al. (Knoxville, 1987), 95; John J. Robertson *et al.*, to Maj.-Gen. James B. Steedman, Wilkes County, Ga, 27 Sept. 1865; NA, Bureau of Refugees, Freedmen and Abandoned Lands (hereafter BRFAL), RG 105, Georgia Assistant Commissioner, Affidavits and Petitions [A-5166]; Robert Cartmell Diaries, 30 Oct. 1865: Tennessee State Library and Archives, Nashville, Tenn., vol. III; *Senate Executive Documents*, no. 2 (39th Congress, 1st sess., Washington, DC, 1866), 31.

2 Samuel A. Agnew Diary, 3 Nov. 1865: Southern Historical Collection, Chapel Hill, NC; William S. Thomson to W. A. Thomson, Marietta, Ga, 7 Dec. 1865:

Emory Univ. Archives, Atlanta, Ga, William S. Thomson Papers, box 1, folder 8; C. C. Emerson to Gov. William W. Holden, Wilmington, NC, 3 June 1865, North Carolina Department of Archives and History, Raleigh, NC, Governors' Papers, box 185.

3 See, for example, Lt. D. H. Reese to Lt. D. G. Fenno, Shreveport, La, 31 Oct. 1865: NA, BRFAL, Louisiana Assistant Commissioner, Letters Received [A-8589]; Chaplain Thos Smith to Lt. S. D. Barnes, Macon, Miss., 2 Oct. 1865: NA, BRFAL, Acting Assistant Commissioner for Northern District of Mississippi, Register of Letters Received [A-9317]; H. M. Spofford to Maj.-Gen. R. W. Johnson, Pulaski, Tenn., 10 July 1865: NA, BRFAL, Tennessee Assistant Commissioner, Register of Letters Received [A-6194]; Andrew J Hamilton to Andrew Johnson, Austin, Tex., 21 Oct. 1865, in *The Papers of Andrew Johnson*, ed. Paul H. Bergeron, 11 vols. (Knoxville, 1991), ix, 263–4; H. H. Montgomery to Gov. Sharkey, Sharon, Miss., 16 Aug. 1865. Mississippi Department of Archives and History, Jackson, Miss., Gov. Records, RG 27, box 62; *Report of the Joint Committee on Reconstruction*, 3 pts (39th Congress, 1st sess., Washington, DC, 1866), pt iii, 31, 160.

4 Historians have, in fact, devoted relatively little close attention to the insurrection scare. The one detailed account is Dan T. Carter, "The Anatomy of Fear: The Christmas Insurrection Scare of 1865", *Jl. Southern Hist.*, xlii (1976). But briefer discussions and assessments can be found in Edward Magdol, *A Right to the Land: Essays on the Freedmen's Community* (Westport, 1977), 140–3; Leon F. Litwack, *Been in the Storm so Long: The Aftermath of Slavery* (New York, 1979), 399–408, 425–30; Eric Foner, *Reconstruction: America's Unfinished Revolution, 1863–1877* (New York, 1988), 104–6; George C. Rable, *But There Was No Peace: The Role of Violence in the Politics of Reconstruction* (Athens, Ga, 1984), 25–8.

5 Pioneering and influential early research on rumour was undertaken during and immediately after World War II, and published by Gordon W. Allport and Leo Postman. They tended to view rumour as something of a relic of a world in which channels of official (and, by extension, rational) communication were not well developed, as well as a form of psychological and emotional adaptation: Gordon W. Allport and Leo Postman, *The Psychology of Rumor* (New York, 1947).

6 James C Scott, *Domination and the Arts of Resistance: Hidden Transcripts* (New Haven, 1990), 144–8. See, too, Ranajit Guha, *Elementary Aspects of Peasant Insurgency in Colonial India* (Delhi, 1983); Anand A. Yang, "A Conversation of Rumors: The Language of Popular *Mentalités* in Late Nineteenth-Century Colonial India", *Jl Social Hist.*, xx (1987); Arlette Farge and Jacques Revel, *The Vanishing Children of Paris; Rumor and Politics before the French Revolution*, trans. Claudia Mieville (Cambridge, Mass., 1991); Clay Ramsay, *The Ideology of the Great Fear: The Soissonais in 1789* (Baltimore, 1992). For important work that considers rumour in more contemporary settings, see Tamotsu Shibutani, *Improvised News: A Sociological Study of Rumor* (Indianapolis, 1966); Jean-Noel Kapferer, *Rumors: Uses, Interpretations, Images* (New Brunswick, 1990); Gary Alan Fine and Ralph Rosnow, *Rumor and Gossip: The Social Psychology of Hearsay* (New York, 1976); Patricia A. Turner, *I Heard It Through the Grapevine. Rumor in African-American Culture* (Berkeley, 1993). One of the earliest historical works remains an essential starting point for any serious research in this area: Georges Lefebvre, *The Great Fear of 1789: Rural Panic in Revolutionary France*, trans, Joan White (1932; New York, 1973).

7 It is tempting, and it has been common, to regard rumours, panics and other such forms of struggle and confrontation as being "pre-" or "proto-" political in their character, as opposed to the more organized, institutionalized and officially sanctioned activities that we have come to call "political" in the

modern sense. But these are just the sort of categories and oppositions I wish to break down, suggesting instead that the notion of "political" be more broadly encompassing and socially and historically contextualized.

8 *Report of the Joint Committee on Reconstruction*, pt iii, 31. Also see C. C Emerson to Gov. William W. Holden, Wilmington, NC, 3 June 1865: North Carolina Department of Archives and History, Governors' Papers, box 185; A. M. Waddell to Gov. William W. Holden, 18 June 1865: North Carolina Department of Archives and History, Governors' Papers, box 185; *New Orleans Tribune*, 21 Oct. 1865; *Senate Executive Documents*, no. 27 (39th Congress, 1st sess., Washington, DC, 1866), 83–4; Carter, "Anatomy of Fear", 346–8.

9 On the importance of credibility in the circulation of rumours, see Ramsay, *Ideology of the Great Fear*, xxvii, 123–7.

10 David L. Swain to William A. Graham, Chapel Hill, NC, 4 July 1865, in *The Papers of William A. Graham*, ed. Max R. Williams, 6 vols (Raleigh, 1976), vi, 324. The most important enabling acts were the Second Confiscation Act of 1862, General William T. Sherman's Field Orders No. 15 of January 1865, and the Freedmen's Bureau Bill of March 1865. On federal land and confiscation policy during this period, see James M. McPherson, *The Struggle for Equality. Abolitionists and the Negro in the Civil War and Reconstruction* (Princeton, 1964); Magdol, *Right to the Land*; Claude F. Oubre, *Forty Acres and a Mule: The Freedmen's Bureau and Black Landownership* (Baton Rouge, 1978); William S. McFeely, *Yankee Stepfather. O. O Howard and the Freedmen* (New Haven, 1968); Foner, *Reconstruction*, 158–9, 183–4.

11 *Report of the Joint Committee on Reconstruction*, pt ii, 221; T. William Lewis to Maj.-Gen. Devens, Charleston, SC, 26 Dec. 1865: NA, RG 393, pt 1, Department of the South, Letters Received; W. J. Minor *et al.*, to Maj.-Gen. Banks, 14 Jan. 1863, in Ira Berlin *et al.* (eds.), *Freedom: A Documentary History of Emancipation, 1861–67*, iii, *The Genesis of Free Labor: The Lower South* (1st ser., Cambridge, 1990), 408–9. On the more general conditions promoting the circulation of rumours, see Scott, *Domination and the Arts of Resistance*, 144–8; Allport and Postman, *Psychology of Rumour*, whose argument on this matter is still widely embraced among scholars.

12 *Report of the Joint Committee on Reconstruction*, pt ii, 177.

13 Charles L. Perdue *et al.* (eds.), *Weevils in the Wheat: Interviews with Virginia Ex-Slaves* (Bloomington, 1976), 216. On communication networks among slaves and free blacks in the Atlantic world of the late eighteenth century, see Julius Scott III, "The Common Wind: Currents of Afro-American Communication in the Age of the Haitian Revolution" (Duke Univ Ph.D. thesis, 1986). For broader comparisons, see Lefebvre, *Great Fear*, 67–74, 148–55; Guha, *Elementary Aspects of Peasant Insurgency*.

14 Perdue *et al.* (eds), *Weevils in the Wheat*, 167–8; W. E. B. DuBois, *Black Reconstruction in America, 1860–1880* (New York, 1935); Ira Berlin *et al.* (eds.), *Freedom: A Documentary History of Emancipation, 1861–1867*, i, *The Destruction of Slavery* (1st ser., Cambridge, 1985); Litwack, *Been in the Storm so Long*; Clarence L. Mohr, *On the Threshold of Freedom: Masters and Slaves in Civil War Georgia* (Athens, Ga, 1986); Armstead L. Robinson, "Day of Jubilo: Civil War and the Demise of Slavery in the Mississippi Valley, 1861–1865" (Univ. of Rochester Ph.D thesis, 1977); Stephen V. Ash, *Middle Tennessee Society Transformed: War and Peace in the Upper South* (Baton Rouge, 1988).

15 George H. Hepworth, *The Whip, Hoe, and Sword; or, The Gulf Department in '63* (Boston, 1864), 25–6; George P. Rawick (ed.), *The American Slave: A Composite Autobiography*, 12 vols. (1st suppl. ser., Westport, 1977), vi, 12.

16 *Savannah Republican*, 5 Feb. 1865, enclosed in Mansfield French to Samuel Breck, Savannah, Ga, 28 Feb. 1865; NA, RG 94, Letters Received, F-174 1865

[K-504]; H. M. Spofford to Maj.-Gen. R. W. Johnson, Pulaski, Tenn., 10 July 1865; NA, BRFAL, Tennessee Assistant Commissioner, Register of Letters Received [A-6194]; Capt. C. B. Wilder to Col. Orlando Brown, Ft Monroe, Va, 17 Nov. 1865: NA, BRFAL, Virginia Assistant Commissioner, Unregistered Telegrams and Letters Received [A-7521]; E. B. Heyward to Gen. Wade Hampton, Charleston, SC, 15 Nov. 1865, enclosed in Heyward to Gen. D. E. Sickles, Charleston, SC, 13 Dec. 1865: NA, RG 393, pt 1, Department of South Carolina, Letters Received, H-147 1865 [C-1383].

17 Lt.-Col. F. H. Whittier to Lt. C. B. Fillebrown, Sumter, SC, 4 Nov. 1865: NA, RG 393, pt 1, ser. 4112, Department of South Carolina, Letters Received, box 1; Capt. J. J. Upham to Lt. J. W. Clous, Lawtonville, SC, 4 Sept. 1865: RG 393, pt 1, ser. 2383, Subdistrict of Coosawatchie, Letters Sent [C-1595], Sherman's Special Field Orders No 15, issued on 16 January 1865, set apart and reserved for exclusive black settlement the sea islands "from Charleston south, the abandoned rice-fields along the rivers for thirty miles back from the sea, and the country bordering the Saint John's River, Florida", to be subdivided "so that each family shall have a plot of not more than forty acres of tillable ground": *Official Records of the War of the Rebellion*, 55 vols., ser. i (Washington, DC, 1895), xlvii, pt 2, 60–2.

18 E. G. Baker to Messrs Irby, Ellis and Mosely, Panola, Miss., 22 Oct. 1865, in Ira Berlin *et al.* (eds.), *Freedom: A Documentary History of Emancipation, 1861–1867: The Black Military Experience* (2nd ser., Cambridge, 1982), 747–8; Carl Schurz to Andrew Johnson, Vicksburg, Miss., 29 Aug. 1865, in *Advice after Appomattox*, ed. Simpson *et al.*, 113–14. More generally on blacks in the army of occupation, see Berlin *et al.* (eds.), above; Joseph T. Glatthaar, *Forged in Battle; The Civil War Alliance of Black Soldiers and White Officers* (New York, 1990).

19 Revd Horace James, *Annual Report of the Superintendent of Negro Affairs in North Carolina, 1864* (Boston, n.d.); Capt. Henry Sweeney to Col. Levering, Helena, Ark., 30 June 1865; NA, RG 393, pt 1, Department of Arkansas and 7th Army Corps, Letters Received, S-119 1865 [C-232]; John J. Robertson to Maj.-Gen. James B, Steedman, Wilkes County, Ga, 27 Sept. 1865: NA, BRFAL, Georgia Assistant Commissioner, Affidavits and Petitions [A–5166]; Capt. Thos Kanady to Lt, Z. K. Wood, New Orleans, La, 23 Dec. 1865: NA, RG 393, pt 1, Department of the Gulf, Letters Received, L-896 1865 [C-655].

20 Lt.-Col. A. J. Willard to Capt. G. W. Hooker, Georgetown, SC, 19 Nov. 1865; NA, Department of South Carolina, Letters and Reports Received, box 1; F. M. Garrett to Col. Whittlesey, Enfield, NC, 25 Sept. 1865: NA, BRFAL, North Carolina Assistant Commissioner, Unregistered Letters Received [A-645]; Capt W. L. Cadle to Maj.-Gen. D. Reynolds, Woodville, Miss., 10 Dec. 1865: NA, BRFAL, Records of the Subassistant Commissioner for the Southern District of Mississippi, Register of Letters Received, C-14 1865 [A-9446].

21 See, for example, *Proceedings of the Colored People's Convention of the State of South Carolina, Held in Zion Church, Charleston, South Carolina, November 1865* (Charleston, 1865), 17; "We the colorde people to the govencr of Mississippi", Claiborne County, Miss., 3 Dec. 1865: NA, Mississippi Assistant Commissioner, Register of Letters Received [A-9035]; *Report of the Joint Committee on Reconstruction*, pt ii, 62.

22 Colin Seymour-Ure, "Rumour and Politics", *Politics*, xvii (1982), 1; Yang, "Conversation of Rumors", 485.

23 See, for example, Michael Craton, "Proto-Peasant Revolts? The Late Slave Rebellions in the British West Indies, 1816–1832", *Past and Present*, no. 85 (Nov. 1979); Thomas C. Holt, *The Problem of Freedom: Race, Labor, and Politics in Jamaica and Britain, 1832–1938* (Baltimore, 1992); Eric Foner, *Nothing but Freedom: Emancipation and its Legacy* (Baton Rouge, 1983); Jerome Blum, *The End*

of the Old Order in Rural Europe (Princeton, 1978); Sidney Mintz, Caribbean Transformations (1974, New York, 1989)

24 See George P. Rawick (ed.), The American Slave: A Composite Autobiography, 19 vols. (orig. ser., Westport, 1972), vii, 38, Testimony of Elizabeth Rose Hite [1930s] Louisiana State Univ. Archives, Works Progress Administration, Ex-Slave Narrative Project.

25 Elizabeth Hyde Botume, First Days amongst the Contrabands (Boston, 1893), 174. On the debilitating legacy of slavery in this regard, see Eugene D. Genovese, Roll, Jordan, Roll; The World the Slaves Made (New York, 1974). On the use of kinship titles as designations of respect and community leadership among slaves, see Herbert G. Gutman, The Black Family in Slavery and Freedom, 1750– 1925 (New York, 1976); Margaret Washington Creel, "A Peculiar People": Slave Religion and Community Culture among the Gullahs (New York, 1988), 280–6.

26 In his influential account of slave religion, Eugene Genovese discounts the millennial thrust But the intermingling of Moses and Jesus, their conflation with a number of earthly figures in positions of social and political authority, and the vision of worldly collective deliverance in the slaves' prayers, preaching and spirituals, before, and especially during, the Civil War together offer powerful evidence for a millennialist (and perhaps pre-millennialist) orientation with a vague messianic aspect that inspired and informed political struggle. See Genovese, Roll, Jordan, Roll; Albert J. Raboteau, Slave Religion: The "Invisible Institution" in the Antebellum South (New York, 1978). On millennial sensibilities, see Katharine L. Dvorak, "After the Apocalypse, Moses", in John B. Boles (ed.), Masters and Slaves in the House of the Lord: Race and Religion in the American South, 1740–1870 (Lexington, 1988), 173–80.

27 James, Annual Report of the Superintendent of Negro Affairs in North Carolina, 1864, 45; Botume, First Days amongst the Contrabands, 102; Laura M. Towne, Letters and Diary of Laura M. Towne: Written from the Sea Islands of South Carolina, 1862–1884, ed Rupert S. Holland (1912; New York, 1969), 162.

28 Lev. 25: 10–12. On the jubilee, see Lawrence W. Levine, Black Culture and Black Consciousness Afro-American Folk Thought from Slavery to Freedom (New York, 1977), 137–8; Peter Linebaugh, "Jubilating: or, How the Atlantic Working Class Used the Bible Jubilee against Capitalism, with Some Success", Radical Hist. Rev., no. 50 (1991); Dvorak, "After the Apocalypse, Moses", 180; Robinson, "Day of Jubilo".

29 Capt. C. C. Richardson to Capt. W. W. Deane, Thomasville, Ga, 28 Nov. 1865: NA, BRFAL, Georgia Assistant Commissioner, Unregistered Letters Received [A-5256]; Lt. S. D. Barnes to Lt. E. Bamberger, Columbus, Miss., 30 Dec. 1865: NA, BRFAL, Acting Assistant Commissioner of Northern District of Mississippi, Register of Letters Received, B-23 1866 [A-9292]; Thomas Wentworth Higginson, Army Life in a Black Regiment, notes and intro.; John Hope Franklin (1869; Boston, 1962), 205. I am greatly indebted to Harold S. Forsythe of Fairfield University for a number of interpretive suggestions.

30 F. Marion Shields to Andrew Johnson, Macon, Miss., 25 Oct. 1865: NA, BRFAL, Mississippi Assistant Commissioner, Letters Received [A-9065].

31 Lt. D. H. Reese to Lt. D. G. Fenno, Shreveport, La, 31 Oct. 1865: NA, BRFAL, Louisiana Assistant Commissioner, Letters Received, R-233 1865 [A-8589]; Circular by G. D. Reynolds, Natchez, Miss., 22 Nov. 1865: NA, BRFAL, Assistant Commissioner for Southern District of Mississippi, Letters Sent [A-9475]. On versions of "naive monarchism" and their role in sparking peasant and slave unrest, see Yves-Marie Bercé, History of Peasant Revolts, trans. Amanda Whitmore (1986; Ithaca, 1990); Blum, End of the Old Order, 333–5, 346; Mary Turner, Slaves and Missionaries: The Disintegration of Jamaican Slave Society, 1787–1834 (Urbana, 1982), 150–1; Emilia Viotti da Costa, Crowns of Glory, Tears

of Blood: The Demerara Slave Rebellion of 1823 (New York, 1994), 78–9, 174–8; Scott, *Domination and Arts of Resistance*, 96–103, see esp. Daniel Field, *Rebels in the Name of the Tsar* (1975; Boston, 1989). There was, of course, nothing terribly naive about "naive monarchism" It was, rather, an important way of practising politics for those traditionally excluded from a society's official political arenas.

32 On Christmas rites, see Genovese, *Roll, Jordan, Roll*, 573–84; Raboteau, *Slave Religion*, 224; Roger D. Abrahams, *Singing the Master: The Emergence of African-American Culture in the Plantation South* (New York, 1992), 30–2; Charles Joyner, *Down by the Riverside: A South Carolina Slave Community* (Urbana, 1984), 134–40.

33 Thos D. Hailes to Col. Richard D. Irwin, New Orleans, La, 20 Dec. 1862: NA, Department of the Gulf, Field Records — Banks' Expedition, Letters Received, H-65 1862 [C-824]; Carter, "Anatomy of Fear", 358; Herbert Aptheker, *American Negro Slave Revolts* (1943, New York, 1974), 345–8; Michael Craton, *Testing the Chains: Resistance to Slavery in the British West Indies* (Ithaca, 1982). Also see Robert Dirks, *Black Saturnalia. Conflict and its Ritual Expression on British West Indian Slave Plantations* (Gainesville, 1987), 167–8, who notes that in the British West Indies between 1649 and 1833 nearly one-third of the slave revolts occurred during the month of December.

34 See, for example, Peter Burke, *Popular Culture in Early Modern Europe* (New York, 1978); Natalie Zemon Davis, *Society and Culture in Early Modern France* (Stanford, 1975).

35 With roots in West Africa and the early contact between West Africans and Europeans, Jonkonnu appears to have developed in Jamaica and spread to a number of other British possessions in the Caribbean. But there are still many questions to be answered about the origins and geographical boundaries of Jonkonnu on the North American mainland. For the most complex and pro-vocative treatments, see Elizabeth A. Fenn, " 'A Perfect Equality Seemed to Reign': Slave Society and Jonkonnu", *North Carolina Hist. Rev.*, lxv (1988); Michael Craton, "Decoding Pitchy-Patchy. The Roots, Branches, and Essence of Junkanoo", *Slavery and Abolition*, xvi (1995), Dirks, *Black Saturnalia*. But also see Sterling Stuckey, *Slave Culture: Nationalist Theory and the Foundations of Black America* (New York, 1987), 67–73; Levine, *Black Culture and Black Consciousness*, 13.

36 See, especially, Julie Saville, *The Work of Reconstruction: From Slave to Wage Laborer in South Carolina, 1860–1870* (Cambridge, 1994), 72–101; John R. Dennett, *The South As It Is, 1865–1866*, ed. and intro, Henry M. Christman (London, 1965), 229; *Report of the Joint Committee on Reconstruction*, pt i, 108, pt ii, 185, 248; pt iii, 122; Lygon N. Low to Wm E. Whiting, Beaufort, SC, 20 Sept. 1865: American Missionary Association Records, South Carolina, Amistad Research Center, New Orleans, roll 2. The planter, E. B. Heyward, whose family owned several plantations in the South Carolina Low Country thus could write "we find . . a general expectation among them of land being given by the govern-ment and that this land is to be that which they now occupy": E. B. Heyward to Gen. Wade Hampton, Charleston, SC, 15 Nov. 1865, enclosed in Heyward to Gen. D. E. Sickles, Charleston, SC, 13 Dec. 1865: NA, RG 393, pt 1, Department of South Carolina, Letters Received, H-147 1865 [C-1383].

37 Saville, *Work of Reconstruction*, 102–10; Cartmell Diaries, 1 Jan, 1866, vol. iii: Tennessee State Library and Archives. On slavery in non-plantation areas, see Ash, *Middle Tennessee Society Transformed*, 53–4; Steven Hahn, *The Roots of Southern Populism: Yeoman Farmers and the Transformation of the Georgia Upcoun-try, 1850–1890* (New York, 1983), 29–32, 56–7; John Inscoe, *Mountain Masters, Slavery, and the Sectional Crisis in Western North Carolina* (Knoxville, 1989).

38 Chaplain Thos Smith to Lt. S. D. Barnes, Macon, Miss., 2 Oct. 1865: NA,

BRFAL, Acting Assistant Commissioner of Northern District of Mississippi, Register of Letters Received [A-9317]; *Report of the Joint Committee on Reconstruction*, pt iii, 174; James, *Annual Report of the Superintendent of Negro Affairs in North Carolina, 1864*, 45; *New York Tribune*, 22 July 1865.

39 Thomas W. Conway, *The Freedmen of Louisiana. Final Report of the Bureau of Free Labor, Department of the Gulf* (New Orleans, 1865), 16–17; Anthony Blunt et al., to Commissioner of Freedmen, Lenour County, NC, 7 Aug. 1865: NA, BRFAL, North Carolina Assistant Commissioner, Letters Received, B-15 1865 [A-509]; J. T. Trowbridge, *The South: A Tour of its Battlefields and Ruined Cities* (Hartford, 1866), 362. On other associations formed by freedpeople to lease or purchase land, see Magdol, *Right to the Land*.

40 Thomas Holt, *Black over White. Negro Political Leadership in South Carolina during Reconstruction* (Urbana, 1977); Foner, *Reconstruction*, 110–19; Roberta Sue Alexander, *North Carolina Faces the Freedmen: Race Relations during Presidential Reconstruction, 1865–1867* (Durham, NC, 1985); "Proceedings of the Convention of the Colored People of Virginia Held in the City of Alexandria, August 2–5, 1865", in *Proceedings of the Black State Conventions, 1840–1865*, ed. Philip S. Foner and George E. Walker, 2 vols. (Philadelphia, 1980), ii.

41 *New Orleans Tribune*, 15 Nov., 24 Sept. 1864; 6 May, 19 Apr., 1 Mar. 1865.

42 *Ibid.*, 14 Oct. 1865.

43 Henry Bram *et al.*, to Maj.-Gen, O, O, Howard, Edisto Island, SC [28? Oct, 1865]: NA, BRFAL, Washington Headquarters, Letters Received, B-53 1865; Henry Bram *et al.* to the President of these United States, Edisto Island, SC, 28 Oct 1865 NA, BRFAL, Washington Headquarters, Letters Received, P-27 1865. The petitions appear to have gone through several drafts and to have benefited from the advice and editorial assistance of a local Freedmen's Bureau agent. Howard, who had gone to Edisto Island on Johnson's orders and informed the black settlers that their old masters had received pardons and would have their property restored, responded quickly to the committee but could only urge that "the people had better enter into contracts, leasing or for wages or purchase when possible for next year". Johnson simply forwarded the committee's petition to Howard without comment. Excerpts from an earlier draft are presented in Mary Ames, *From a New England Woman's Diary in Dixie in 1865* (1906; New York, 1969), 99–103. For a close and insightful treatment of the episode, see Saville, *Work of Reconstruction*, 90–8.

44 See, for example, Circular No. 15, 12 Sept, 1865: NA, BRFAL, Washington Headquarters, Printed Circulars and Circular Letters Issued by the Bureau [A-10711]; Eric Foner, *Politics and Ideology in the Age of the Civil War* (New York, 1980), 138; McFeely, *Yankee Stepfather*; Oubre, *Forty Acres and a Mule*; C. Vann Woodward, *The Future of the Past* (New York, 1990), 190–1.

45 See, for example, Laurence Shore, "Making Mississippi Safe for Slavery: The Insurrectionary Panic of 1835", in Orville Vernon Burton and Robert C. McMath (eds), *Class, Conflict, and Consensus. Antebellum Southern Community Studies* (Westport, 1982); John Scott Strickland, "The Great Revival and Insurrectionary Fears in North Carolina: An Examination of Antebellum Southern Society and Slave Revolt Panics", *ibid.*; Charles B. Dew, "Black Ironworkers and the Slave Insurrection Panic of 1856", *Fl Southern Hist.*, xli (1975); Shula Marks, *Reluctant Rebels: The 1906–08 Disturbances in Natal* (Oxford, 1970).

46 Capt. Andrew Geddes to Col. C. Cadle, Jr, Tuskegee, Ala., 6 Oct. 1865: NA, BRFAL, Alabama Assistant Commissioner, reel 18.

47 *New Orleans Tribune*, 21 Oct. 1865. Also see H. H. Montgomery to Gov. William Sharkey, Sharon, Miss., 16 Aug, 1865: Mississippi Department of Archives and History, Gov, Records, RG 27, box 62; Carl Schurz to Andrew Johnson, Vicksburg, Miss., 29 Aug 1865, in *Advice after Appomattox*, ed. Simpson *et al.*,

113–14; Richard Jones *et al.*, to Gov. Lewis Parsons, Lawrence County, Ala., 26 Sept. 1865; Alabama Department of Archives and History, Montgomery, Ala., Governor Lewis Parsons Papers; Thomas W Holloway to Gov. James L. Orr, Pomaria, SC, 18 Dec. 1865: South Carolina Department of Archives and History, Columbia, SC, Governor Orr Papers, Letters Received, box 1.

48 Gov. William L. Sharkey to Andrew Johnson, Jackson, Miss., 20, 28 Aug, 1865, in *Papers of Andrew Johnson*, ed. Bergeron, viii, 627–8, 666–7; Gov. William L. Sharkey to Maj.-Gen. O. O. Howard, Jackson, Miss., 10 Oct. 1865: NA, BRFAL, Mississippi Assistant Commissioner, Letters Received [A-9062]; Gov. Lewis Parsons to Andrew Johnson, Montgomery, Ala., 2 Oct. 1865, in *Papers of Andrew Johnson*, ed. Bergeron, ix, 171; Resolution of the Constitutional Convention, 20 Sept. 1865, Alabama Department of Archives and History, Governor Parsons Papers; *New Orleans Tribune*, 27 Aug. 1865

49 Col. Samuel Thomas to Maj.-Gen. O. O. Howard, Vicksburg, Miss., 2 Nov. 1865: NA, BRFAL, Washington Headquarters, Letters Received [A-9219]; *Report of the Joint Committee on Reconstruction*, pt ii, 128; Circular No. 2, 3 Oct. 1865: NA, BRFAL, Georgia Assistant Commissioner, General Orders, xxvi, 325–6 [A-480]; Circular No. 5, 19 Oct. 1865: South Caroliniana Library, Columbia, SC, South Carolina Assistant Commissioner, Reconstruction Scrapbook; General Orders No. 13, 31 Oct. 1865: NA, BRFAL, Mississippi Assistant Commissioner, General Orders and Circulars [A-9536]; *Athens Southern Banner*, 15 Nov. 1865; Dennett, *South As It Is*, 250; *Senate Executive Documents*, no. 27, 36, 82.

50 Carl Schurz to Andrew Johnson, Vicksburg, Miss., 29 Aug., 2 Sept. 1865, in *Advice after Appomattox*, ed. Simpson *et al.*, 105, 109, 112, 119; Gov. William L. Sharkey to Andrew Johnson, Jackson, Miss., 30 Aug 1865, and Johnson to Sharkey, Washington, DC, 21 Aug. 1865, in *Papers of Andrew Johnson*, ed. Bergeron, viii, 635, 685; Andrew Johnson to Gov. Lewis Parsons, 1 Sept 1865, *ibid.*, ix, 12; McPherson, *Struggle for Equality*, 332–3; Michael Perman, *Reunion without Compromise; The South and Reconstruction, 1865–1868* (Cambridge, 1973), 134–6.

51 Lt. Spencer Smith to Col. C. Cadle, Tuskegee, Ala., 25 Nov. 1865: NA, BRFAL, Alabama Assistant Commissioner, Reports of Operations from Subdistricts [A-1608]. On Johnson's policies, see Perman, *Reunion without Compromise*; Foner, *Reconstruction*; Dan T. Carter, *When the War was Over: The Failure of Self-Reconstruction in the South, 1865–1867* (Baton Rouge, 1985).

52 Capt J. H. Mathews to Lt. Stuart Eldridge, Magnolia, Miss., 12 Jan. 1866: NA, BRFAL, Mississippi Assistant Commissioner, Register of Letters Received, M-6 1866 [A-9124]; Capt Warren Peck to Lt.-Col. R. S. Donaldson, Copiah County, Miss., 16 Dec. 1865: NA, BRFAL, Acting Assistant Commissioner of Northern District of Mississippi, Register of Letters Received, P-24 1865 [A-9312]; Capt. A. C. Bardwell to Col. H. F. Sickles, 14 Dec. 1865: NA, BRFAL, Subassistant Commissioner in Savannah, Unregistered Letters Received [A-5022]; Agnew Diary, 15 Dec. 1865: Southern Historical Collection; *Hinds County Gaz.*, 25 Nov. 1865.

53 See, for example, Dennett, *South As It Is*, 240–1; L. M Hobbs to Col. T. W. Osborn, Tallahassee, Fla, 26 Dec. 1865: NA, BRFAL, Florida Assistant Commissioner, Letters Received, H-33 1865 [A-1116]; Trowbridge, *The South*, 374; *Report of the Joint Committee on Reconstruction*, pt iii, 30, 72.

54 Agnew Diary, 31 July, 25 Dec, 1865: Southern Historical Collection, *Papers of William A. Graham*, ed. Williams, vi, 363; Earl C. Branaugh *et al.*, to Gov. Isaac Murphy, Cleburne, Ark., 31 Oct. 1865: NA, BRFAL, Arkansas Assistant Commissioner, Letters Received [A-2409], Andrews, *South since the War*, 179.

55 Lt. O. B. Foster to Capt. J. H. Weber, Skipwith's Landing, Miss., 30 Nov, 1865: NA, BRFAL, Assistant Commissioner for Western District of Mississippi, Register of Letters Received [A-9251]; Cartmell Diaries, iii, 30 Oct. 1865:

Tennessee State Library and Archives; Lt. S. D. Barnes to Lt. E. Bamberger, Columbus, Miss., 28 Nov. 1865: NA, BRFAL, Acting Assistant Commissioner for Northern District of Mississippi, Register of Letters Received [A-9291].

56 Dennett, *South As It Is*, 187–9.

57 *Senate Executive Documents*, no 27, 64–5; Capt. J. H. Mathews to Lt. Stuart Eldridge, Magnolia, Miss., 12 Jan. 1866; NA, BRFAL, Mississippi Assistant Commissioner, Register of Letters Received, M-6 1866 [A-9124]; Dennett, *South As It Is*, 275. The only armed movements among freedpeople, mainly along the coast of South Carolina, came in the form of scattered resistance to being dispossessed of property restored to its original owners.

58 Foner, *Reconstruction*; Perman, *Reunion without Compromise*, 78–81; *South Carolina Leader*, 16 Dec. 1865; *Planters' Banner* [Franklin, La], quoted in *New Orleans Tribune*, 19 Dec. 1865; Oubre, *Forty Acres and a Mule*, 37. In the fall of 1865, the War Department decided to disband all black regiments raised in the North (that is, those with the longest experience of freedom), and by January 1866, the black representation in the army of occupation had already shrunk by about 20 percent. As of October 1866, only 13,000 black troops remained in the South, and the last departed by October 1867. See James Sefton, *The Army and Reconstruction, 1865–77* (Baton Rouge, 1967), 50–3; Berlin *et al.* (eds.), *Freedom: Black Military Experience*, 733–6.

59 See, for example, *Report of the Joint Committee on Reconstruction, 1*, xv, *Cincinnati Daily Gaz.*, 2 Dec. 1865; J. Michael Quill, *Prelude to the Radicals: The North and Reconstruction during 1865* (Washington, DC, 1980); Georges Clemenceau, *American Reconstruction, 1865–1870*, ed. with intro. Fernand Baldensperger, trans. Margaret MacVeagh (1928; New York, 1969), 35–6; Foner, *Reconstruction*, 193–7; McPherson, *Struggle for Equality*, 329–40.

60 In his message to Congress on 4 December, Johnson recommended that the southern states "resume their places in the two branches of the National Legislature" once the Thirteenth Amendment was ratified, which occurred on 18 December; see "Message to Congress", 4 Dec 1865, in *Papers of Andrew Johnson*, ed. Bergeron, ix, 472.

61 Capt. Buel C. Carter to Lt.-Col. H. B. Scott, Richmond, Va, 7 Nov. 1865; NA, BRFAL, Virginia Assistant Commissioner, Unregistered Letters and Telegrams Received [A-7489].

62 Brig.-Gen. Wager Swayne to Maj.-Gen. O. O. Howard, Montgomery, Ala., 2 Jan. 1866: NA, BRFAL, Alabama Assistant Commissioner, Weekly Reports, reel 2; Col. E. A. Koylay to Maj. W. H. Smith, Orangeburg, SC, 29 Jan. 1866: NA, BRFAL, Acting Subassistant Commissioner in Orangeburg, Letters Sent, ccl, 3–4 [A-7274].

63 Holt, *Black over White*, Foner, *Reconstruction*.

64 Magdol, *Right to the Land*; Gerald D. Jaynes, *Branches without Roots: Genesis of the Black Working Class in the American South, 1862–1882* (New York, 1986); Vernon L. Wharton, *The Negro in Mississippi, 1865–1890* (Chapel Hill, 1947), 41–3; Sydney Nathans, "Fortress without Walls: A Black Community after Slavery", in Robert L. Hall and Carol B. Stack (eds.), *Holding onto the Land and the Lord: Kinship, Ritual, Land Tenure, and Social Policy in the Rural South* (Athens, Ga, 1982), 55–65; Janet Hermann, *Pursuit of a Dream* (New York, 1981); Elizabeth R. Bethel, *Promiseland: A Century of Life in a Negro Community* (Philadelphia, 1981).

65 See, for example, Steven Hahn, "Hunting, Fishing, and Foraging: Common Rights and Class Relations in the Postbellum South", *Radical Hist. Rev.*, no 26 (1982); Joseph P. Reidy, *From Slavery to Agrarian Capitalism in the Cotton Plantation South Central Georgia, 1800–1880* (Chapel Hill, 1992); Jaynes, *Branches without Roots*; Foner, *Nothing but Freedom*; Saville, Work of Reconstruction.

14

RECLAIMING GREGORIA'S MULE

The Meanings of Freedom in the Arimao and Caunao Valleys, Cienfuegos, Cuba, 1880–1899

Rebecca J. Scott

... and as for Ciriaco even though he has possession of the mule you should charge him for the grass if only because he didn't inform you, and give notice to [the town of] Arimao; Carlos says the mule is three years old and has been eating on the estate those years; and as far as Antonio's [mules] are concerned, if he comes I will tell him that without an order from you I won't give them to him and you are the one who should give me orders, not the Mayor...[1]

With these angry words, on 19 August 1899, Constantino Pérez, the manager of the Santa Rosalía sugar estate in central Cuba, admitted defeat in his contest of wills with the former slave Ciriaco Quesada. Pérez's letter to the agent of the plantation's owner, Manuel Blanco, identified the formal problem as one of misplaced authority. Instead of respectfully awaiting the judgement of his former master, Ciriaco Quesada had taken a claim of rights directly to the neighbouring town of Arimao, registered proprietorship of the mule in his name, and enlisted the mayor's support to send a rural guardsman to Santa Rosalía and take possession of the animal. Now the plantation manager could only rail against this impudence, try to collect a recompense for the grass the mule had eaten during its three years on the estate, and vow to resist more strongly if a claimant named Antonio took this as an opening to try to recover *his* mules.

Scholars of post-emancipation societies who have traced in detail the struggles over productive resources that characteristically follow the end of slavery can quickly recognize a familiar dynamic to the conflict between Constantino Pérez and Ciriaco Quesada. Slavery had come to a legislated end in Cuba in 1886, as the Spanish government sought to reorder labour relations with the aim of maintaining both colonial rule and sugar plantation production. A former slave might attempt to

365

undertake small-scale farming on his or her own account, and thereby avoid the need to perform year-round wage labour on a plantation. But to do this he or she needed resources. A mule was both an immediate asset of the farm itself, and a potential bargaining chip in negotiating a share-cropping or rental arrangement. Precisely because so much was at stake such struggles were very hard for former slaves to win.[2]

To understand how Ciriaco Quesada succeeded in wresting control over this mule from Constantino Pérez in 1899, one needs to work backward to the 1880 slave register of the Santa Rosalía plantation on which the name Ciriaco appears, and then forward again through the halting process of slave emancipation as it unfolded in this corner of the Cuban countryside in the 1880s. As one approaches the summer of 1899, and the struggle that seems to have begun in June, when a former slave named Gregoria began making inquiries about the mule, the most important gap to fill may be the one just prior to the confrontation: where had Ciriaco and Gregoria Quesada been during the three years that the mule was eating the green grass on Santa Rosalía?

The years 1895–8 were, of course, a time of bitter war between Cuban separatists and the Spanish forces trying to maintain colonial rule. Indeed, these years were the last stage in a thirty-year process of insurrection against Spain that had reshaped Cuban society even as it failed to achieve political independence. The rebel army of 1895, the *Ejército Libertador*, was drawn from all regions and classes. Although it reproduced some of the hierarchies of Cuban society, it had nonetheless emerged as a remarkable experiment in interracial democracy. Moreover, the war itself had raised expectations – many of them ambiguous or contradictory – and the presence of black and mulatto officers in command of white troops had altered social relations.[3] 1899 was the first season of formal peace after the long war of independence, a time when many of these new social relations would be tried on for size, and these expectations would be voiced or negotiated, met or frustrated.

In the war, as in the process of slave emancipation, something called freedom was the prize. But the freedom from slavery that all descendants of Africans could claim after formal abolition in 1886, and the freedom from Spanish rule that Cuban separatists had called upon Cubans to seek in 1895, were quite different things. They were linked, and we may correctly say that it was in part because former slaves found their legal freedom within a colonial context to be incomplete that they became candidates for recruitment to a rebellion that seemed to promise a new beginning. But such a generalization blurs the enormous difference between individual, familial and community autonomy on the one hand, and national independence on the other. It raises without answering the question of how the two goals might be related to each other in a single life.

This essay tries to grapple with the interlinking and overlapping of these two fields of action – the achievement of freedom from chattel bondage, and the struggle for freedom from colonial rule. It explores the possibility that being a former slave helped to determine when and with whom one might participate in the insurgency, and asks how the experience of fighting shaped subsequent patterns of alliances, rights and obligations. My approach is microhistorical, focused on a single rural neighbourhood defined by the valleys of the Arimao and Caunao rivers, to the east of Cienfuegos in central Cuba.[4] This exceptionally beautiful expanse of land, known as the *partido* of Cumanayagua, encompassed in 1877 nearly as many free black and mulatto residents as enslaved, and the majority of its population were categorized as white. Its varied social geography shaped both emancipation in the 1880s and the mobilization of insurgency in 1895.[5]

The relatively flat terrain of the valleys was suitable for growing cane. By 1860 the region held almost a dozen plantations that shipped their sugar down the rivers to the burgeoning port city of Cienfuegos, and about half of them used relatively modern sugar-refining technology. Those grinding with steam-powered mills included the Ingenio Santa Rosalía, owned by José Quesada, and the Ingenio Soledad, owned by the Albis/Sarría family. But the land was also ribbed with limestone ridges that were less suitable for cane, and often served for grazing cattle. Though it produced a substantial sugar crop, this was not a zone of endless cane fields, nor of monoculture. In addition to sugar plantations, the region held *potreros* (livestock farms), as well as *sitios de labor* and *estancias* (small farms) devoted to cultivating food crops.[6]

Eastward and to the south, the land rises to the foothills of the Trinidad mountains. These hills beckoned not so much for the quality of the soil – though it was not bad – but as a refuge for small cultivators and others who wished to keep their distance from the world of sugar and slavery. Plantation owners came to see these hills as a source of danger – home to bandits, runaways and uncontrollable elements of various kinds. The inland riverside town of Arimao, looking toward the *sierra*, was thus a world away from the rich, even elegant, sugar port of Cienfuegos. When, after the outbreak of war in 1895, Spanish authorities stationed some 350 troops on a line between the towns of Arimao and Cumanayagua, they were attempting not only to protect the sugar estates from a rebel attack from Oriente, but to insulate the *llano* (lowlands) more generally from the *monte* (hills).[7]

One great value of microhistory is the possibility it presents for layering information from disparate sources in order to capture multiple perspectives on the life histories of individuals and groups. If one has luck with the records, it is sometimes possible to build up a dynamic picture of choices, affiliations and local collective action, revealing something new about the larger social movements under examination.[8] Fortunately, through accidents of historical preservation, several remarkable bodies of

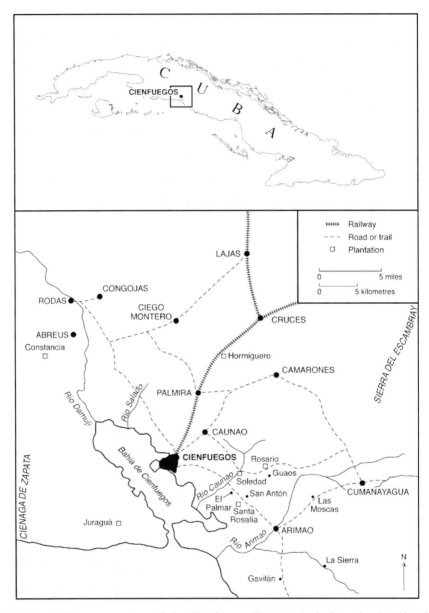

The South-Eastern portion of the Cienfuegos District, including the *Partido* of Cumanayagua.

documents have survived from Santa Rosalía and the neighbouring Soledad sugar estate, along with records reflecting life in adjacent communities. One can thus capture some sense of this neighbourhood as a living space, and sketch a few of its networks of friendship, rivalry and exchange, in order to understand how emancipation unfolded in the 1880s, and how insurgency took shape in these hills and valleys in the mid-1890s.

Microhistory has a further virtue. It lends itself to being learnt from and shared with the descendants of the protagonists, the current dwellers of the region. Shortly after I first began to piece together the story of Ciriaco Quesada and the mule, I met Tomás Pérez y Pérez, aged ninety-six, son of a former slave, and a long-time workman and cane farmer on the Soledad plantation. Did he, I asked, remember Ciriaco Quesada? Sure, he remembered Ciriaco, as well as his close friend Cayetano Quesada. Ciriaco was a light-skinned man of colour, tall and thin and forceful. Cayetano was younger, darker skinned, and a superb *"desmochador de palmiche"*, known for his ability to go up palm trees to bring down the small fruits used as fodder. Tomás Pérez y Pérez had never heard the story of the showdown over the mule, which took place three years before he was born. But after talking with Tomás Pérez and with his former co-worker Leonardo Alomá I realized that not only had Ciriaco won that struggle, but he had also lived on in memory as a *personaje*, a person of importance in the neighbourhood.[9] Exploring his story might provide a glimpse of the complex, halting and often thwarted processes by which former slaves constructed their rights and gave meaning to their freedom.

I

The Santa Rosalía sugar plantation, situated between the Caunao and the Arimao rivers, was founded around 1840 by José Quesada, an immigrant from the Canary Islands who had made his way up in the world to become a landowner.[10] Much of the estate's land was hilly and stony, but it included flat fields, suitable for growing cane, near the mill and down by the Caunao river. Local legend held – somewhat implausibly – that José Quesada intended that the estate lands be divided among his slaves upon his death, but that his wily manager Manuel Blanco manoeuvred his way into ownership.[11] Blanco, himself a crusty Spanish immigrant entrepreneur who had worked as a cooper and then as a *mayordomo* for Quesada, took possession of the estate in the mid-1870s, when it comprised at least 15 *caballerías* of cane land (500 acres), worked by some 150 slaves, and produced roughly 32,000 pesos' worth of sugar per year. Among the names listed in an 1876 inventory of the slaves and freed children on Santa Rosalía are Ciriaco, a Creole, age twelve, and his brother, Paulino, age eight.[12] Manuel Blanco lived in the city of Cienfuegos, where he attended to his multiple commercial activities, served as a municipal councillor, and joined the *Casino Español*, a group resolutely hostile to the abolition of slavery and opposed to autonomy for the island of Cuba.[13]

Edwin F. Atkins, owner of the neighbouring Soledad plantation, was equally crusty in his own way. A Yankee from Boston, he had been trained in accounting and through apprenticeship to his merchant father, Elisha Atkins, and to his father's Spanish and Cuban associates in Cienfuegos. The firm of E. Atkins and Co. participated in the early 1880s in a foreclosure on the properties of the Sarría family, and subsequently bought out a portion of the claim of their Cuban partner Joaquin Torriente, thus becoming proprietors of the Ingenio Soledad, an extensive plantation operated with somewhat outmoded equipment. In the late 1870s, Soledad had cultivated 27 *caballerías* in cane (approximately 900 acres), worked by some 180 slaves. It shipped its 52,000 pesos' worth of sugar down the Caunao river, past Santa Rosalía, to the port of Cienfuegos.[14]

Manuel Blanco and Edwin Atkins appear to have distrusted – and perhaps politely detested – each other. An awkward divided claim between the Sarría family and Manuel Blanco to the intermediate property called San Mateo stalled the final transfer of Soledad to E. Atkins and Co., and the Soledad general manager fumed about Blanco's obstructionism.[15] Oral tradition has it that Atkins at some point suggested to Manuel Blanco that he sell the Santa Rosalía estate to its expanding neighbour, Soledad. Blanco is said to have replied angrily that perhaps Atkins should instead sell Soledad to Santa Rosalía.[16]

The Spanish government had eliminated the juridical category of slave in 1880, through a law establishing the *patronato*, under which former slaves, henceforth denominated *patrocinados* (apprentices), were bound to work for a token stipend for several years for their former owners. In letters to his mother in Massachusetts, the good Unitarian Edwin Atkins was relatively discreet about this state of affairs. Though he shared with her the image of himself at "the centre of a crowd of over two hundred negroes, each one of whom kneeled down on passing me, saying 'Your blessing, Master'", he refrained from openly acknowledging that in taking possession of Soledad plantation he became, like his neighbour Manuel Blanco, an owner of bound labourers.[17] An 1880 assessment of the estate had estimated the value of Soledad's "*dotación de negros*" (black workforce) at $26,200, a considerable sum, and an 1881 inventory listed 136 men and 93 women.[18]

In 1883 Manuel Blanco registered his *patrocinados* with the mayor of the town of Arimao, seat of the local judicial district, formalizing his continued authority over them. The administrator of Santa Rosalía kept a careful account book in 1885–6 that listed each *patrocinado* by name, and logged his or her stipend, purchases at the store and date of emancipation. Candidly, however, his entries often referred to the *patrocinados* as *esclavos* (slaves) until they purchased or won their full legal freedom. Many were listed with the surname Quesada, that of the previous owner. Others' first names were followed by an African ethnonym, such as

Congo, Gangá, Lucumí or Mandinga, and some with the denomination "Criollo" (Creole). Some *patrocinados* carried the surnames of proprietors in the district, including Apezteguía, Capote, and Zulueta, presumably because they had been held as slaves on these nearby estates. A few men were identified by terms such as *Emancipado* (Freedman) or *Maquinista* (Machinist), or simply *Grande* (Big). Only two had the surname Blanco, after the new proprietor.[19]

Most of the *patrocinados* on Santa Rosalía seem to have achieved their full legal freedom one at a time, at dates scattered through 1885 and 1886. The law of 1880 fixed progressively diminishing prices at which *patrocinados* could purchase their freedom, a process construed as the "indemnification" of the master for remaining services owed. Some of the *patrocinados* on Santa Rosalía apparently followed this path and obtained a *cédula*, a certificate attesting to their freedom. Others were freed under the provision of the 1880 law that called for a fraction of each owner's *patrocinados* to be liberated by lottery each year after 1884, in descending order of age.[20]

Ciriaco Criollo (he had not yet taken the surname Quesada), son of Francisca, was probably about twenty-three years old in 1885.[21] In February 1885 he used part of his stipend to purchase thread from the plantation store, and in the following months he bought four kinds of coarse fabric (*crehuela*, *silesta*, *dril* and *rusia*). He gave charity to the victims of cholera, purchased *un calzoncillo* (underpants) in December, and then, in January 1886, achieved his freedom and spent several days in town. (If his mother was a good seamstress, he may have looked quite trim by the time he reached Cienfuegos.)[22] He returned to work at 10 pesos a month, and in the autumn of 1886, Ciriaco and his brother Paulino each deposited 1 peso per month with the estate owner, apparently to support their ageing mother Francisca.[23]

Francisca Quesada, *la vieja* (the old one), is mentioned in the logbook in connection with the lives of a number of Santa Rosalía's black residents. In April 1885 she collected Donato Lucumí's 3-peso monthly stipend in the form of a length of *rusia* fabric. Donato Lucumí was in his forties, and perhaps a somewhat less active labourer — his wage was often 6 pesos a month, rather than the 10 common among younger freedmen. In December 1885 he did buy a jacket for 3.60 pesos, ordered from town. But a year later he seems to have been hungry or short of funds: he was apparently caught stealing *bonatos* (sweet potatoes).[24] Antonio Apezteguía, a 37-year-old man born in Africa, was still under the *patronato* at Santa Rosalía in 1885. He earned 3 pesos a month, with 10 cents deducted for each of his many sick days. Out of the balance, he paid for three pairs of shoes: one for Francisca *la vieja*, one for Liborio and one for himself. He became free on 8 September 1886, just a month before final abolition.[25]

The purchases made by *patrocinados* on Santa Rosalía reflected both their family ties and their initial consumption priorities – including fabric, shoes, tobacco and oil (*petróleo*). Some were distinctly ambitious. Felipe Criollo, who was in his mid-thirties in 1885, achieved his freedom on 8 July 1885, and henceforth earned 10 pesos a month. He too bought shoes that his mother (who is unnamed) collected, and he began spending time in town as soon as he was free. He seems quickly to have saved for major purchases: a cape (*capote*) at 3.50 pesos, and a saddle (*albarda*) at 9 pesos. He paid for some soap and rice for his mother, took a large cash loan, cleared the debt, took additional wages in cash and continued to make visits to town.[26]

As they moved into formal freedom, the labourers of Santa Rosalía marked their new status both with a change in their footwear and dress, and with a change in their work rhythm, expanding their effective range of action to encompass the nearby towns. The month before Rita Quesada was recorded as having achieved her freedom, the administrator noted several deductions from her pay: "For 6 days in town and 2 without working: .80 [deducted]". The next year her wage rose from 3 pesos a month to 8, but she did not work at all on the estate from June to December 1886, in contrast to the year before.[27] Ciriaco and Paulino appear again on the payroll at Santa Rosalía three years after the end of slavery. In April 1889, Ciriaco – now using the surname Quesada – earned 13.78 pesos for twenty-six days' work. However, whether by choice or involuntarily, neither of them was working at Santa Rosalía six months later, in the low season of October.[28]

At the adjacent Soledad plantation, the new management of E. Atkins and Co. was busy investing in machinery to expand the grinding capacity of the mill. The recently arrived general manager, J. S. Murray, occupied himself during 1884–5 with renewing contracts with various *colonos* (farmers who supplied cane to the mill) and hiring new labourers at about $15 a month during the grinding season, $10 to $12 in the "dead time". Murray also struggled to assert effective control over the ninety-five *patrocinados* who constituted an important portion of the labour force.[29]

Murray found that many were eager to purchase their full freedom, and his accounts recorded their payments — including a total of $578 from six *patrocinados* in June 1884. Murray candidly wrote to Atkins that three of them — Victor Gangá, whose age was listed as fifty-two, Benicia Criolla, listed as forty-nine, and Eduvijes, fifty-one — were "in reality over 60 years of age, therefore free according to law". The previous owner had apparently falsified the *patrocinados'* ages in order to prevent their coming under the terms of the 1870 Moret Law, which freed all slaves at the age of sixty. Murray was content to continue the fiction and extract unwarranted payment along the way — the money apparently derived from the *patrocinados'* sale of hogs.[30]

In addition to those formally under the *patronato*, Soledad employed *libertos* (freedpeople), including young men and women covered by the provision of the Moret Law that had freed children born to slave mothers after 1868. Murray commented on a group of *libertos* who had been driven away by the disgruntled previous manager: "I have taken all the able ones back, they work better, cost less and are much easier to manage than white men and they all more or less have fathers, mothers, sisters and aunts that attach them to the estate". His optimism, however, was short-lived. He soon began to complain that "allmost every negro on the estate owns a horse and they are a source of constant trouble in some way".[31] Murray hated those horses, and his letters reflect a continuing campaign to force their owners to get rid of them.

By May 1885 he had decided to crack down across the board on the ownership of animals: "I have given order to negros to sell all their hogs, prohibiting in the future the raising of hogs". He offered to increase their monthly salary by 50 cents as a recompense, but he then went on to order them to sell their horses as well. Murray's new regime appears to have been counter-productive: there was an immediate work stoppage, and a few days later "all the libertos rebeled". When they refused Murray's terms he ordered them off the estate, grumbling "we are better without them as they are now only working when they feel like it, and keeping up a constant loafing during the day in the ranchos".[32]

Murray's references to hogs, horses and "loafing" in the *ranchos* (shacks, sometimes with attached garden plots) make it clear that an internal economy, the lineal descendant of the old system of *conucos* (slave provision plots), was alive and well at Soledad. Murray tried to trim it down, but in doing so he encountered the point of maximum resistance of the estate's former slaves. Murray had the upper hand, because he controlled lodging and wage income, and could win the first round: "All the libertos have come to terms and all beged to stay, I sent off only the two head men, They know how they stand with the estate and I don't intend to loose control of them in the future".[33]

But Murray's resolution did not stand. By August 1885 his relationship with the remaining *patrocinados* had degenerated still further, and he had taken the strictly illegal step of putting several of them in the stocks. His methods reflected the increasing hopelessness of maintaining strict control over the behaviour of men and women who could see the imminent ending of their own bondage. He proposed to Atkins that they cut a deal with the remaining *patrocinados*: "give all the negros their liberty at the price established by the government, fixing a salary of from $8 to $10 deducting 50% each month". It was hardly a generous proposition, but Atkins was unwilling to assent to it, for he did not wish to lose "the bal[ance] of Patrocinado a/c [account] as it stands in your ledger". Atkins proposed holding on to the *cédulas* (freedom papers) while each *patrocinado* worked off his or her price as it appeared in the company account books.[34]

Finally, in May 1886, Murray came to the conclusion about to be reached by masters throughout the island: continued legal bondage, carrying a special, invidious, and hence resented role for *patrocinados*, was no longer worth whatever financial benefits it may have entailed. Murray offered the remaining *patrocinados* their freedom for a payment of $20, or $5 a month deducted from their wages for those who did not have the cash. He anticipated that he would be able to "organize them better when all of one class". Besides, he reasoned, "we will have to give them their liberty in a short time". A capitalist initiative in favour of ending slavery, posited by free labour ideologists but rarely seen among Cuban planters, thus arrived at Soledad eighteen years after the beginning of slave emancipation. Less than five months later the Spanish government would decree the final abolition of the *patronato* across the island.[35]

Murray kept up his campaign against the ownership of horses, reporting that he had sent off one group of workers and would rehire them only when they got rid of their horses. "Of course some will let them loose in the potreros [pastures] others will hide them in the woods for a few days". It is not clear whether Murray's greatest concern was the mobility and status that having a horse gave to a workman, or the attention and grass the horses would consume. But he resolved that "I will get rid of them all in the end and do not intend they shall have them back".[36]

The issue of access to horses also appeared, by implication, in the register of slaves and *patrocinados* on Santa Rosalía. When Felipe Criollo succeeded in 1886 in earning enough to purchase a cape and a saddle — having presumably got access to a horse to go under it — he joined the category of "negros who have horses", achieving the autonomy and distinction that Murray was trying to prevent among the former slaves at the more prosperous Soledad. With a horse, one could go overland to Cienfuegos, about ten miles away, or ride a few hours in the opposite direction to the ford on the Arimao river, cross to the town of Arimao, and continue up to the foothills hamlet of La Sierra. Alternatively, one could cross the river and carry on directly to the mountains.[37]

Once slavery was gone for good in late 1886, both Soledad and Santa Rosalía had to reorient their patterns of employment and production. The two estates followed quite different paths. Edwin Atkins was enthusiastic about his enterprise, and poured money into upgrading its equipment, expanding its holdings, signing contracts with new tenants to provide cane to the mill, and recruiting new workers. Soledad was well positioned to respond to the boom in demand occasioned by the provisions of the 1891 Foster-Cánovas Treaty and to attract seasonal and long-term immigrant workers from Spain and the Canary Islands. By the mid-1890s Atkins could speak confidently of the estate as covering some 12,000 acres, with up to 5,000 acres of standing cane and 22 miles of private railroad. "There are living upon the property during the season of active operations, some 1,200 people." He reported that a large proportion of the labourers at Soledad were Spaniards.[38]

A few miles away, Santa Rosalía was in much less impressive condition. Though he had weathered the financial crisis of 1884 and continued to accumulate capital, Manuel Blanco seems to have let the plantation stumble along with a reduced work force and without adequate new investment in equipment. The eminent Bostonian Charles Francis Adams II paid a brief visit to Santa Rosalía in the winter of 1890, while spending some weeks at Soledad. His letters home portray Santa Rosalía as a model of backwardness, noting that the engine at the mill was dated 1859, and claiming that "the purging process, through which the molasses is drained from the sugar, at Blanco's mill, takes 30 days; under the process Atkins has in use it takes four minutes".[39] The daybooks of Santa Rosalía for the 1890s show a modest influx of Spanish workers, many of whom departed entirely after the end of the harvest. Former slaves, often bearing the surname Quesada, laboured year-round or seasonally, with most of the women working for wages only during the months of the harvest. Ciriaco Quesada appeared on the payroll from October 1893 to February 1894.[40]

Gregoria Quesada, who had been registered among Manuel Blanco's apprentices in 1883, apparently left Santa Rosalía after emancipation and moved to the town of Cienfuegos. Her name figures in an 1891 court case there, when she testified in support of a female neighbour named Francisca Sarría, who had accused a companion of assault and battery. Both women, and another named Juana Quesada, lived in the neighbourhood of the Calle del Castillo, near the public fountain alongside the city aqueduct, on the outskirts of town in the direction of Santa Rosalía.[41]

II

The general North American financial panic of 1893 devastated investors — including Charles Francis Adams II — from Boston to Cienfuegos and beyond. By 1894 the island of Cuba had entered a deep crisis. Edwin Atkins was distressed at the drop in sugar prices and rise in the cost of supplies that followed the collapse of trade negotiations between Spain and the United States, though he was nonetheless able to bring in and grind a large crop at Soledad. Manuel Blanco bowed to necessity, and Santa Rosalía began to ship its cane over Soledad's railway to be ground in the Atkins mill. Santa Rosalía's need for workers thus declined. Throughout the region, unemployment rose. At Soledad the cold and damp of winter were accompanied by an epidemic that may have been influenza. It was a miserable time for those who were laid off and hungry.[42]

Then, in February and March 1895, came rumours of war. At first Edwin Atkins was confident and a bit sarcastic: "in these parts the trouble seems confined to a bunch of bandits in vicinity of Sn Lino, . . . I do not think there will be any fighting outside of N York Herald".[43] But in the East the rebellion took hold, and Spain had once again to fight to defend its sovereignty in Cuba. The rebel leadership, including José Martí, son of a Spaniard, and Máximo Gómez, a veteran from Santo Domingo, made explicit its goals of ending Spanish control and fighting against racial discrimination. The much-admired Antonio Maceo, a mulatto rebel general with a long record of anti-racism, landed from abroad and began to raise troops throughout the East. Juan Gualberto Gómez, a man of colour and leader of the battle for civil rights for Cubans of African descent, was conspicuously affiliated with the campaign in the western portion of the island — and was promptly arrested by the Spanish authorities.

In the province of Santa Clara (Las Villas) as a whole, the separatist rebellion was initially suppressed. But by the summer of 1895 regional insurgent leaders succeeded in gathering together supporters, and there were risings in several towns. In late June work was still proceeding smoothly at Soledad, though Spanish forces were said to be "chasing a party of a dozen or so in the vicinity of Cumanayagua", to the east toward the mountains. In late July, an exile rebel expeditionary force led by Serafín Sánchez landed, and the insurrection began to gather strength in the region. In the hills and valleys around Soledad and Santa Rosalía, something recognizable as a local rebel force began to coalesce.[44]

From the vantage point of the management on Soledad, these were more or less lawless men appearing in scattered small groups. Edwin Atkins associated the recruitment with growing unemployment, and asserted that "many men, particularly negroes, joined the insurgents or took to the woods to live by pillage". His manager wrote that small parties were "seen in various places, one in this vicinity, but they are all hurrying up country. Yesterday our carpenter met a party of four back of Vaquería, like most of them armed with revolvers and machetes". Then came word in August of "some fighting beyond Arimao", and of an encounter between Spanish forces and rebels just half an hour east of Soledad. By September, insurgent bands were said to be operating under "a chief named Rego", a white officer known within the rebel forces as Colonel Alfredo Rego.[45]

In late 1895 the insurgent high command, aiming to defeat Spain by destroying the export economy, ordered sugar estates not to mill their cane. Soon, any estate that continued to prepare for grinding was vulnerable to armed attack and to the torching of cane fields. On 20 November, a rebel party of "eight negroes" appeared at Soledad with the order to burn cane, and had a confrontation with the management. Fires began in and around Soledad in earnest in late November, and the manager again reported that "a small party of negroes" had set them, under the supervision of a larger group of rebels. Atkins promptly lobbied the Spanish authorities to obtain protection, and soon a detachment of Spanish soldiers was stationed on the estate.[46]

A key figure in the rebellion around Soledad was Claudio Sarría, born a slave on the Soledad sugar plantation. J. S. Murray had rarely referred by name to those with whom he argued over horses, pigs and freedom, but many of them were undoubtedly Sarrías, former slaves using the surname of the family that had previously owned Soledad. Virtually all of the Sarrías would have witnessed the moments of exceptional callousness on Murray's part, including the placing of former slaves in stocks, the disregard of their property ("The removing of old wall left negros pig styes without protection so they will have to sell or have them stolen it is imeterial to us which"), and the generally hostile and dismissive treatment of their interests: "Some of the negros give as an excuse that they have no body to cook for them as I have sent off a number of negro women that would not work nor pay rent for their rooms. They want all the privileges of both freedmen and patrocinados, but none of the responsibilities and it will take some time before they can understand their possition".[47] We cannot know precisely how grievances against Soledad might have combined with the promises of the new rebellion to bring Claudio Sarría to take up arms. But his interests almost certainly cut in several directions at once. Soledad was the home of most of his kin, and therefore a place to which he would return again and again. But it was also the symbol of a very recent slavery and of a continuing foreign presence. An order to burn its fields might elicit mixed feelings.

At first, letters from Soledad portrayed Sarría simply as a vengeful individual with a gang of bandits. But by late December J. N. S. Williams, who had replaced Murray as manager, linked Sarría to a larger network of "sitio negroes" who had been living at Soledad, presumably working a *sitio* (provision farm) on estate property. Williams expelled most of them, but initially allowed an older man named Aniceto to remain on the *batey* (millyard), near the heart of the estate. He soon repented, writing to Atkins on 12 December 1895: "Regarding Aniceto and his family, I have made up my mind that the next time Claudio comes around that house to pull it down and send the negro and his family off the place. They are spies, I am pretty sure, and it is only consideration for your personal wishes respecting the old man that he has been kept on".[48]

That very week full-scale war reached the Arimao Valley. At the end of 1895 the main body of the rebel army from the eastern end of the island, under the leadership of Máximo Gómez and Antonio Maceo, had broken out of Oriente and begun an audacious invasion westward. Local insurgent units joined them along the way, and the combined force reached the rich heartland of Santa Clara province in early December. Skirting the heavily fortified town of Cumanayagua, the invading rebel army pushed through the countryside north-east of Cienfuegos, inland and north of Soledad and Santa Rosalía. The major confrontation with Spanish forces came on 15 December 1895, at Mal Tiempo, just north of Camarones and east of Cruces. The rebel forces defeated the Spaniards in a ferocious battle, and continued their march westward.[49] To the southeast, near the town of Trinidad, stationed behind to guard their flank, was Quintín Bandera, a black rebel general famed for his bravery and independence of mind, in command of a formidable group of soldiers from Oriente.[50]

By January 1896 there was no denying that Claudio Sarría and his followers were part of a larger structure: Williams reported a "uniting of [the] small parties into one large party of rebels", comprising some three hundred men. Equally alarming to planters were reports that "Quentin Bandera was this side of the Arimao River a couple of days ago looking the ground over".[51] Elías Ponvert, the owner of the Hormiguero estate some fifteen miles north of Soledad, emphasized that the insurgent bands were generally mounted, and continually moving.[52] Formal distinctions between infantry and cavalry units seem to have been moot in the organization of local raids; many men were on horseback.

On 17 January 1896, a Soledad manager reported that "All the rebel forces from the eastern departments seem to be en route for here", and 150 cavalry and infantry from Quintín Bandera's command paid a formal visit to Soledad. For the moment, relations were courteous: "They were here under trying circumstances, hungry, barefooted and half naked, yet not one of them appropriated the smallest thing to himself without permission. . . . With exception of the officers, they were all colored". The next day, local insurgents visited, seeking sweet potatoes, and were reported to have "behaved very well indeed".[53]

In early February the rebel high command ordered Higinio Esquerra, a white officer, to gather the scattered local bands formally included in the Fourth Corps, and bring them together as an infantry under the black general Quintín Bandera.[54] On 21 February Claudio Sarría and Ta-Ta Monte, another former slave from the area, apparently burned buildings at San Esteban. P. M. Beal reported to Atkins from Cienfuegos that "we are now passing the most critical time since the beginning". Flying squadrons of pro-Spanish guerrillas were apparently forming to "operate against the smaller roving bands".[55]

In March Atkins returned to Soledad to find it an armed garrison. He wrote to his wife that 50 to 80 percent of the rebels were black, and that "I hear from various sources that with the leaders are a few negroes supposed to have come from Haiti or Santo Domingo who wear rings in both their ears and noses". From the repetition of racialized rumours he moved on to a more specific and bitter indictment: "Most of our losses have been caused by negroes, and the lowest class of people, but *all* duly commissioned officers in the 'Army of Liberty,' carrying out general orders of their chiefs". Atkins did succeed in fortifying the *batey*, the core of the estate, and ground some cane in March and April.[56]

A surviving insurgent enlistment record, dated November 1896, from the Infantry Regiment of the Cienfuegos Brigade, Second Division of the Fourth Corps, conveys something of the internal structure of the local "bands". The administrator at Soledad had long suspected that Claudio Sarría had "all the negros bearing the name of Sarría at his service". The roll of soldiers is more precise: Claudio Sarría, age twenty-five, married, gave his date of enlistment as August 1895 and was, by November 1896, captain of Company 3 of the First Battalion. One of his sergeants was José Sarría.[57] In all, there were five men named Sarría in the company: Claudio, José, Lorenzo, Rufino and Anastasio, as well as three more in Company 2: Felipe, Félix and Ambrosio. They were accompanied by others with planter surnames like Stuart, Tartabull, Ponvert, Acea and Moré, who are likely to have been former slaves, as well as one Rafael Iznaga from Arimao. A few of the rebels had been born in Spain. Dozens of others had names that provide no clue about race or status, such as Mendoza, Díaz, López and González.[58]

The name of one soldier leaps out of the register of Company 3: Ciriaco Quesada, age thirty-four, single, almost certainly the former slave from Santa Rosalía, son of Francisca. Like his neighbour Claudio Sarría, Ciriaco Quesada gave his date of enlistment as August 1895. He had thus been in rebellion for four months before the troops of Maceo and Gómez arrived from the East. Cayetano Quesada, also from Santa Rosalía, was a foot soldier in Company 2, having enlisted in October 1895 at the age of sixteen or seventeen.[59]

Another black man named Quesada apparently collaborated with the local rebel Sixto Roque, but the vagaries of memory make it difficult to pin this down. The owner of the Colonia Angelita, Juan Piñol, later testified, "This Quesada was found hanging about 2 years ago, after the war ended, what was that devil Quesada's name, I have forgotten his name, my memory is very poor for names. It was said that they did this burning, I don't know whether it was so or not, I wasn't there".[60] Piñol may have been exaggerating his distance from the events — he was in fact a former officer in the Spanish army who served in the pro-Spanish *guerrilla* that was stationed on Santa Rosalía in 1896.[61]

In addition to Ciriaco and Cayetano Quesada, at least four other recruits to the Cienfuegos Brigade seem to have been from the families of former slaves on Santa Rosalía. Victoriano Quesada signed up at what must have been nearly the earliest opportunity, in June 1895. Felipe Quesada y Rodriguez, son of Felipe and Francisca, also joined the Cienfuegos Brigade. (I suspect that he was the younger of the two freedmen on Santa Rosalía named Felipe, the one who bought the cape and saddle, but the record is unclear.) Ramón Quesada y Quesada joined up in September 1895, and Manuel Quesada in February 1896.[62]

Little documentation has survived that would enable us to scrutinize directly the motives of each of the recruits named Quesada and Sarría. (One observer's claim that Claudio Sarría had simply been "naturally bad from his childhood" can take us only so far.[63]) It is possible, however, to trace some of the webs of communication that helped to make mobilization thinkable. Santa Rosalía and Soledad were just two miles apart, linked by rail and river as well as footpaths. Former slaves employed on each estate met in the course of work and in the *tiendas* (country stores) where they spent their pay. Friendships and the exchange of information presumably developed as well during journeys back and forth between each estate and the city of Cienfuegos, and to the smaller communities like San Antón, Guaos and Arimao. There was plenty to talk about as word of the insurgency in the East spread to the countryside of Cumanayagua. The earlier anti-colonial struggles, in 1868–78 and 1879–80, had attracted black supporters named Sarría and Quesada; these men would by now have been old-timers who could recall the cat-and-mouse tactics of gangs in the woods raiding estates for cattle and recruits.[64] There were, moreover, examples close to hand of Spanish intransigence, including Manuel Blanco himself, a temperamental anti-reformist Spaniard and long-time supporter of slavery, and Juan Piñol, commander of the pro-Spanish partisan force at Santa Rosalía.[65]

In these conversations, the memories and observations of locals could be supplemented by collective discussion of news from the press. In Arimao, for example, Bárbara Pérez, a former slave who had learnt to read from her owner's niece, customarily read the newspaper aloud to the entire town. Her son Tomás Pérez recalled hearing her explain that the neighbours would each bring a chair, and seat themselves in front of their houses to listen to her. (Family tradition also holds that when Barbara Pérez, who worked as a laundress, washed the uniforms of Spanish soldiers, she would retrieve any loose ammunition she found, and smuggle it to the rebels in the nearby hills under the guise of collecting wood to heat the washwater.)[66]

There was, however, nothing automatic about the decision to join the rebellion. One former *liberto* resident on Santa Rosalía, Ramos Quesada, remained on the estate throughout the war to guard Manuel Blanco's cattle — and perhaps to secure his own future and that of his kin.[67] Indeed, after the death of the revered insurgent general Antonio Maceo at the end of 1896, and through the months of pitiless repression of civilians by the Spanish general Valeriano Weyler, the process of recruitment to the rebel army in the Cienfuegos region stalled. In some cases it even reversed itself, with surrenders and desertions exceeding new recruits in 1897.[68] In the eyes of one white officer of the *Ejército Libertador*, the insurrection was in terrible disarray, and the rebel "bands" in the neighbourhood were again out of control. "Pequeños grupos, incoherentes e inconexos, merodeaban como diluidos" ("Small groups, incoherent and unconnected, wandered about weakened and scattered").[69]

The insurgency regained some strength in the region as Higinio Esquerra became chief of the rebel Cienfuegos Brigade and worked to pull things together. With Spanish losses mounting as well, it seemed possible by early 1898 that the rebels' next summer campaign might extend their power from the countryside into the cities. Máximo Gómez began, for the first time, to predict an imminent victory.[70]

International politics were soon to make the question moot. In the spring of 1898 the United States declared war on Spain, invaded the island of Cuba, attacked the Spanish fleet in the Philippines, and brought the war to a prompt and controlled end. Spain was defeated, but the Cuban rebel government-in-arms was allowed no part in the treaty negotiations, and formal authority passed to a US military government established for the island. Edwin Atkins could report with pleasure that when he started grinding at Soledad on 8 January 1899, there was "an American flag floating from a staff in the batey and another one over the house".[71]

Flags did not necessarily reflect relations of power in the countryside, however. When Atkins toured the area around Soledad with a captain in the US forces in January, "we found the insurgents in control under negro officers" in Guaos and Arimao. Atkins saw this as proof positive of the need to maintain an armed guard at Soledad, and the captain seems to have agreed.[72] A significant gap nonetheless persisted between the formal structures of foreign military rule, on the one hand, and the contest for day-to-day power in villages and on estates, on the other. Although the US military governor of Cuba was busy appointing Cubans to municipal offices during 1899, he did not get around to naming anyone to so minor a post as *alcalde de barrio* (mayor) of Arimao. According to Brigadier-General James H. Wilson, US military governor of the central region, Spanish military commanders, between the cessation of hostilities and the arrival of US forces, had named temporary municipal authorities, chosen from among the moderate Autonomists and other *pacíficos* (non-combatants). But once Spanish troops withdrew, and Cuban soldiers in the *Ejército Libertador* were discharged, there was another shift, as some veterans "were at once engaged as municipal, rural and private police" and others became candidates for office.[73] Neither US forces stationed at Cienfuegos nor armed guards lodged at Soledad could easily project their effective authority to the inland town of Arimao, for example, where rebel troops were restlessly waiting to see what the outcome of their long struggle would be.

III

By the summer of 1899 Soledad was again in expansion, and Edwin Atkins was a man of influence with the occupying US forces. Things were otherwise at Santa Rosalía, where the end of the war brought a renewed but ineffectual effort to make the estate profitable, with attention to the dairy and to food production as well as cane. The workforce was very much diminished, and the daily reports from the manager, Constantino Pérez, convey a sense of an irritable man struggling to get labour from ill-paid and ill-fed employees, and being thwarted at every turn. Many of the former slaves with the surname Quesada seem to have departed during the war or afterwards; others were dismissed by Pérez for talking back to him or defying orders.[74] Caridad Quesada, whose mother lived through the war, recalls that when some of the women returned after the war, having been interned in one of General Weyler's "reconcentration" camps, they found that Manuel Blanco had permitted other people to settle on Santa Rosalía, and there was no place for them.[75]

Some former residents of Santa Rosalía moved toward the mountains, to the upper part of the valley of the Arimao river, where the main activities were cattle-raising and the production of coffee, tobacco and vegetables for family consumption.[76] Included among these migrants was a veteran of the war, Fermin Quesada. A routine report filed some years later by the Military Information Division of the US Army of Cuban Pacification sketched a hostile portrait: "QUESADA, FERMIN. Negro. Liberal. Age: About 35 years. A farmer by occupation. Lives near Arimao . . . Served in the Cuban Army during the 95–98 war reaching the grade of sergeant . . . Has a very bad reputation. Is said to be a cattle thief operating in the vicinity of Arimao and La Sierra . . . Has but little influence, and that among the negro farmers in the country. Is considered a dangerous man in case of trouble".[77] Even years later, folks in and around Arimao were apparently well aware of each other's wartime service.

In the hungry, drought-ridden summer of 1899 the tumultuous events of 1895–8 were still very vivid. There was particular bitterness among veterans toward those Cubans who had served in the pro-Spanish *guerrilla*, and scores were sometimes settled with violence.[78] At other times, people just taunted and grumbled. Constantino Pérez, the manager at Santa Rosalía, was uneasy about the groups that clustered around Felix's *tienda*, the country store at San Antón, just down the hill from Santa Rosalía. The manager reported back to Manuel García that one of the estate's employees had got into a fight with "un ciudadano de esos Bandidos" ("a citizen from among those bandits") who congregated around Felix's. The employee had been taunted that anyone who would take care of Manuel Blanco's cattle "had no shame". Pérez wrote that these "rateros" (petty thieves) were around every day, looking to steal something, and moreover that they said that Manuel Blanco's employees were not going to last long. Asunción, one of the workers on Santa Rosalía, had repeated this to Pérez, who was not sure quite what was meant by it.[79] As scholars of gossip have pointed out, this kind of talk around the well or the corner store constitutes an important part of what used to be called in Latin *publica fama* (common knowledge), and helps determine whose power or property is seen as legitimate — or at least secure — and whose can be challenged.[80]

All of which brings us back to the showdown over the mule at Santa Rosalía, in August 1899. We know from the manager's correspondence that there had been earlier discussion about what was characterized at first as "el mulo del hijo de Gregoria", Gregoria's son's mule. Back in June, it seems, someone — presumably Gregoria Quesada herself — had made an initial claim with Manuel Blanco, or with his nephew and agent Manuel García Blanco, down in the city of Cienfuegos. Constantino Pérez had looked into the matter, checking with the cattle-handler named Carlos, who confirmed that there was such a mule, with a brand "like three tubes", and that it had been on the estate for three years. Carlos said he had raised the question with "Don Manuel", who told him not to give the mule to anyone without express permission.[81]

Then, on 17 August, Constantino Pérez reported that Ciriaco and Paulino Quesada, sons of *la vieja Francisca*, had come to see him about

Receipt for a mule turned over to Ciriaco Quesada, signed by Sergeant Francisco A. Oliva.

(*Document courtesy of Orlando García Martínez*)

"that mule you told me about, Gregoria's". In this initial encounter, the administrator stood on ceremony: he would not give up the mule without a written order from Manuel García Blanco. Indeed, he seemed rather pleased with himself for turning away the request.

At 7 a.m. the next morning, however, a sergeant in the local Rural Guard, Francisco Oliva, appeared on the estate and called for the manager. Oliva presented Pérez with an order from the mayor of Arimao to turn over the disputed mule to Ciriaco Quesada. Pérez initially refused, but the guardsman told him that Ciriaco Quesada had entered the mule in the property register at Arimao. The guardsman made it clear that he would, if necessary, go get the mule himself. Pérez seems to have become a bit disconcerted, and blustered that Ciriaco Quesada could just as easily register all the cattle on the estate, that would not change anything. But he did send for Carlos to bring the mule. The guardsman proffered a receipt, in case Manuel Blanco wanted to collect for the grass the mule had eaten in the meanwhile. Pérez fumed in his letter to Manuel García that any day now Antonio would turn up to look for *his* two mules, since he had been around earlier to get them. By the next day, Pérez was advising the owner to try to collect from Ciriaco Quesada for the three years the mule had been eating on the estate, if only to make the point that he should not have gone to the mayor.[82]

Scattered clues make it possible to imagine what had happened. The mule had been at least three years on the estate, perhaps since Ciriaco Quesada's enlistment in the *Ejército Libertador* in August 1895, or since the time that the *columna invasora* swept across the countryside around Soledad and Santa Rosalía in December 1895, and residents of the plantation left for safety elsewhere. Now the war was over, and Ciriaco and Paulino Quesada had come to make a claim on the mule, on behalf of Gregoria. They were initially treated with customary high-handedness by Constantino Pérez.

The passing phrase in Constantino Pérez's letter, noting that Ciriaco Quesada had entered the mule in the property register in Arimao, suggests a precedent for the strategy Ciriaco Quesada was following. In June 1899, US military governor John R. Brooke had issued an order that former soldiers of the *Ejército Libertador* could gain title to horses they had acquired during the war by entering them in the municipal registers of livestock.[83] Ciriaco Quesada may have had such a horse, and might thus have travelled to Arimao to go through this formality early in the summer of 1899. When, a few months later, the ownership of the mule came into contention, Gregoria Quesada seems to have sought his assistance, and it could have occurred to him to use the same mechanism. In each case, these were procedures instituted to regularize property titles under an occupation government. Ciriaco Quesada was employing them, however, to legitimate property whose acquisition had its roots in wartime and pre-war claims of a quite different sort.

Although the initial claim to the mule was made in her name, Gregoria herself remains off-stage. She apparently lived on the outskirts of Cienfuegos, but stayed in close touch with events on the plantation. Though other women from Santa Rosalía had ended up in the "reconcentration" camps during the war, Gregoria seems to have escaped that fate. We catch a glimpse of the activities of a Gregoria Quesada, *morena* (black woman), age forty-one, in a brief notarial record registered in 1897 in the city of Cienfuegos. She appears as the purchaser of a plot of land located in the small community of La Sierra, in the foothills beyond Arimao. Perhaps job opportunities in the garrisoned city of Cienfuegos had enabled her to accumulate a bit of capital, and depressed wartime land values had brought the price of a small farm in the contested countryside within reach.[84] With the end of fighting and the return of some of Gregoria's male family members, small-scale cultivation of food and market crops would have begun to seem feasible. The mule left at Santa Rosalía would at that moment become an important step toward greater self-sufficiency, either for herself if she planned to resettle in the countryside, or for her son or other kin. It was time to get it back.

What is striking is how quickly Ciriaco Quesada enlisted the mayor and the Rural Guard of Arimao on behalf of the claim that he, Paulino and Gregoria were making. Manuel Blanco and the management of Santa Rosalía, an estate that had served as the base for a pro-Spanish *guerrilla*, seem to have been distinctly unpopular among many of the Cuban country people who were their neighbours. If power was still held in Arimao by the insurgents whom Atkins had reported as being in control seven months earlier, there was little reason to think that Blanco's priorities as a planter would necessarily hold sway. And although in future years the Rural Guard would come to be seen as an agent of elite power, in the early months after the Spanish defeat it was a cross-racial force composed in part of Cuban veterans of the recent war.

Equally important, when Ciriaco Quesada arrived in Arimao on 17 August, after his first unsatisfactory exchange with Constantino Pérez about the mule, he arrived not as a supplicant but as a citizen. In the same town where his name would have appeared twenty years earlier in official records of the slave property of Manuel Blanco, he now came as a former comrade-in-arms of the veterans who probably made up the Rural Guard, if not of the mayor himself. Although questions of suffrage and citizenship were still very much in debate, and the future status of the island was entirely in dispute, relations of power on the ground in this little riverside town could favour the claim of a former slave with a network of kin and comrades behind him.

IV

Nearly one hundred years after Ciriaco Quesada made his journey from Santa Rosalía to Arimao, Leonardo Alomá accompanied three historians eastward along the same trail, the old Camino Real. One thing quickly became clear: to have got to Arimao and back so quickly, Ciriaco Quesada must have had a horse. The hills above Arimao are easily visible, but they are not close. On foot, we were not going to make it there and back in an afternoon. But we could see the lie of the land, with the mill at Soledad and the Caunao River behind us, and Santa Rosalía over a hill to our right. A few kilometres from the Soledad mill we arrived at the crossroads at San Antón. The tile-roofed house on the corner belonged to an uncle of Leonardo Alomá's, and we chatted with him, asking whether anyone with the surname Quesada, descended from slaves at Santa Rosalía, lived in the neighbourhood. Yes, down the new road that crosses the old Camino Real lived Ramona, Humberto, Francisco and Gerardo Quesada — this last identified as a "marvellous first baseman" in his day.

Hesitant to barge in, three of us waited outside Ramona Quesada's entryway while Leonardo Alomá went ahead to explain — I am not sure quite how — about the unexpected visitors and their collective curiosity about the Quesadas of Santa Rosalía. Ramona Quesada was welcoming, and pleased to talk about her father and his service in the 1895–8 war. Her father was Cayetano Quesada, the young man who had enlisted in 1895 as a teenager, and joined Company 2. Cayetano and Ciriaco Quesada, she recalled, had been close friends during the war and afterwards — the younger and the older veteran, both from the community of former slaves and *libertos* on Santa Rosalía.

The written evidence suggests that Ciriaco Quesada's assertiveness had been honed in wartime service, and that his network of friends and fellow veterans probably helped him to hold his ground against the representative of his former master. But where did he establish himself as a citizen after the 1895–8 war? I asked Ramona Quesada: did she have any idea where Ciriaco Quesada had settled?

She replied immediately: "Ahí cerca, ahí, ahí en la parte esa del potrero" ("Right over there, close by, there, in that part of the pasture"). She pointed to the field that began at the edge of the patio on which we were sitting. Ciriaco Quesada and Cayetano Quesada had settled side by side, on land adjacent to the cane fields of Soledad. Cayetano Quesada planted his *sitio* (small farm) in maize, plantains, peanuts and root crops like *boniato*, while in the adjacent pasture Ciriaco tended livestock.

Through the recollections of Ramona Quesada and her husband Evelio Castillo, as well as those of her brothers Gerardo and Francisco, the space of freedom that Ciriaco Quesada had sought took on a topography. In San Antón, Ciriaco Quesada was out of reach of Manuel Blanco and Constantino Pérez, though his precarious holding might be menaced by the expansion of Soledad's cane land. On horseback, he could reach Cienfuegos in a few hours, or Arimao and La Sierra in a few more. On foot, he could visit kin and companions at Santa Rosalía or El Palmar, and socialize at Félix's store. Within the boundary of his *potrero* he could raise horses and cattle undisturbed — and, perhaps, even the occasional mule.[85]

V

CONCLUSION

Examining slave emancipation and anti-colonial insurgency through the unfolding of events in the Arimao and Caunao Valleys enables us to see these as overlapping fields of action that involved complex networks of kin and comrades. Freedom in the world of cane rested on reciprocities between Ciriaco and Francisca Quesada as *patrocinados* and between Cayetano and Ciriaco Quesada as neighbours, and it involved a progression of strategies for acquiring rights to mobility, productive resources, and respect. Ciriaco Quesada's enlistment in the rebellion and Gregoria Quesada's purchase of land in the nearby foothills thus come into focus together, as Ciriaco's right as a veteran to keep a horse overlaps with Gregoria's claim to retrieve a mule under some form of customary right. Moreover, the authority that Ciriaco had established as a veteran seems to have strengthened his hand vis-à-vis his former owner, and to have strengthened as well his ability to provide leadership within the community of former slaves from Santa Rosalía. Viewed through this high-magnification lens, property rights and citizenship rights appear as hard-won, intertwined, and tenaciously held, even by those who had relatively few resources with which to enforce them.

This microhistorical approach also focuses attention on the very smallest units of the rebel *Ejército Libertador*, the groups of armed men Edwin Atkins would call gangs and the enlistment registers would call companies. After the war was over, these "bands" seem to have functioned as a cluster of potential allies, linked by a set of shared memories and loyalties. At moments of challenge, they may have provided an alternative grounding for one's political and moral identity as a citizen — even in so simple an act as entering an animal in the property register. The actions and conversations of these veterans and their companions also helped to define a very Cuban countryside in 1899, despite the presence and ostensible hegemony of occupying US forces.

The history of Ciriaco, Gregoria and Cayetano Quesada gives us a glimpse of the exercise of liberty in the everyday, and some clues as to where we can look to "catch the vision of freedom".[86] The picture turns out to encompass, among other things, the image J. S. Murray of Soledad so detested, that of former slaves with horses. But it need not necessarily dissolve into the classic icon of the rebel *mambí* fighter galloping into battle against the Spanish army. Instead, it may also look like a horseman loping along, on his way to Arimao, to persuade an old comrade to come back with him, so that he can assert proprietorship under the rule of law, stand his ground in the face of a familiar and high-handed figure of authority, and successfully reclaim Gregoria's mule.

NOTES

1 The text of this letter is not easy to parse, given its syntactic idiosyncrasies, and my translation is necessarily somewhat approximate. "Y de Ciriaco aunque mismamente tenga la propiedad de la mula V deberia cobrarle el piso tan solo por no haberle avisado a V. y dar parte Arimao pues Carlos dice que tiene tres años en la mula y son los que lleba comiendo en la finca y de las de Antonio ya si biniesen ya le diré que sin orden de V. no se las entrega que V. es quien tiene que darme a mi la orden y no el Alcalde' The word *propiedad* here is ambiguous between "possession" and "title". Constantino Pérez to Manuel García, 19 Aug. 1899, in the file "Correspondencia Santa Rosalía", personal collection of Orlando García Martínez, Cienfuegos (hereafter OGM, CSR).

2 The literature on post-emancipation societies is now abundant. For studies that call particular attention to the struggle over productive resources, see the volumes of Ira Berlin et al. (eds.), *Freedom: A Documentary History of Emancipation* (Cambridge, 1982–93); Julie Saville, *The Work of Reconstruction: From Slave to Wage Laborer in South Carolina, 1860–1870* (Cambridge, 1994); Barbara J. Fields, *Slavery and Freedom on the Middle Ground: Maryland during the Nineteenth Century* (New Haven, 1985); Thomas C. Holt, *The Problem of Freedom: Race, Labor and Politics in Jamaica and Britain, 1832–1938* (Baltimore, 1992); Frederick Cooper, *From Slaves to Squatters: Plantation Labor and Agriculture in Zanzibar and Coastal Kenya, 1890–1925* (New Haven, 1980). The classic study emphasizing citizenship and politics is Eric Foner, *Reconstruction: America's Unfinished Revolution, 1863–1877* (New York, 1988). For an overview that links struggles over resources to the search for political voice, see Frederick Cooper, Thomas Holt and Rebecca Scott, *Beyond Slavery: Explorations of Race, Labor, and Citizenship in Postemancipation Societies* (Chapel Hill, 2000).

3 On this question, see Ada Ferrer, *Insurgent Cuba: Race, Nation, and Revolution, 1868–1898* (Chapel Hill, 1999), esp. ch. 6; Rebecca J. Scott, *Slave Emancipation in Cuba: The Transition to Free Labor, 1860–1899* (Princeton, 1985), 287–93; Aline Helg, *Our Rightful Share: The Afro-Cuban Struggle for Equality, 1886–1912* (Chapel Hill, 1995), ch 2.

4 In the design of this project, I owe a methodological debt to my colleague John Shy, whose essay, "Hearts and Minds in the American Revolution: The Case of 'Long Bill' Scott and Peterborough, New Hampshire", in his *A People Numerous and Armed: Reflections on the Military Struggle for American Independence*, rev. edn (Ann Arbor, 1990), is a source of continuing inspiration.

5 Of the *partido*'s 5,148 inhabitants in 1877, 3,218 were categorized as white, hence free; 949 were *de color* and enslaved (521 males and 428 females), 936 were *de color* and free (455 males and 481 females, including all children under the age of ten, legally free under the terms of the 1870 Moret Law); 37 were indentured Chinese workers, and another 8 were free Chinese, Enrique Edo, *Memoria histórica de Cienfuegos y su jurisdicción*, 3rd edn (Havana, 1943), 487–9.

6 See Carlos Rebello, *Estados relativos a la producción azucarera de la Isla de Cuba* (Havana, 1860). The other mills in Cumanayagua operating with steam power were Buena Vista, owned by Antonio Abreu; Caledonia, owned by Diego Julián Sánchez; Conchita, owned by Juan Iznaga; Rosarío, owned by Domingo Sarría;

and Santa Bárbara, owned by Félix Iznaga. (The surnames of these owners often reappear as surnames among former slaves.) The most detailed study of the genesis of the sugar industry in the Cienfuegos region is Orlando García Martínez, "Estudio de la economia cienfueguera desde la fundación de la colonia Fernandina de Jagua hasta mediados del siglo XIX", *Islas*, lv–lvi (1976–7). A good recent discussion can be found in Laird Bergad, Fe Iglesias García and María del Carmen Barcia, *The Cuban Slave Market, 1790–1880* (Cambridge, 1995).

7 See Edwin F. Atkins, *Sixty Years in Cuba* (Cambridge, Mass, 1926, repr. New York, 1980), 167.

8 Giovanni Levi has posited this as the defining feature of microhistory, as opposed to simple local history The choice of a scale, he suggests, is a means rather than an end "The unifying principle of all microhistorical research is the belief that microscopic observation will reveal factors previously unobserved". Giovanni Levi, "On Microhistory", in Peter Burke (ed.), *New Perspectives on Historical Writing* (Cambridge, 1991). Jacques Revel provides a subtle discussion of the question of scale in Revel (ed.), *Jeux d'échelles: la micro-analyse à l'expérience* (Paris, 1996). James Amelang synthesizes the discussion nicely in "Microhistory and its Discontents: The View from Spain", in Carlos Barros (ed.), *Historia a debate: actas del Congreso Internacional "Historia a Debate" celebrado el 7–11 de Julio de 1993 en Santiago de Compostela*, 3 vols. (Santiago de Compostela, 1995), ii.

9 Interviews with Tomás Pérez y Pérez and Leonardo Alomá, Mar. and June 1998, Cienfuegos. Alomá, who was born in Vega Vieja, between Soledad and Arimao, and has worked most of his life on Soledad (now Pepito Tey), is the one to whom I owe the use of the term *personaje* to describe Ciriaco Quesada. I also thank Modesto Hernández and Sebastián Asla Cires, formerly of Santa Rosalia; José M. Iznaga, Araceli Quesada y Quesada, Caridad Quesada, Jesús Manuel Rodríguez, Félix Tellería and Fermin Tellería, in Cienfuegos; Domingo Cruz Díaz at La Campana, Marciano Alomá, Ramona Quesada de Castillo, Evelio Castillo, Francisco Quesada, Gerardo Quesada and Humberto Quesada in San Antón, and Julio Vargas in Havana, for their valuable oral historical testimony. Orlando García Martínez, Aims McGuinness and I collaborated in several of the oral history interviews, and Evelyn Baltodano worked with dedication to produce accurate transcriptions.

10 José Quesada appears as owner of the estate in 1860 in Rebello, *Estados*, 14. See also Atkins, *Sixty Years in Cuba*, 59–60. Atkins mistakenly refers to Felipe Quesada, rather than José Quesada, as owner of the estate. David Sartorius, who has studied the early records of Santa Rosalía, tells me that Felipe Quesada was a kinsman of José Quesada who carried out some business dealings with Atkins: Sartorius, personal communication, Jan. 1998. See also David Sartorius, "Slavery, *Conucos*, and the Local Economy: Ingenio Santa Rosalía, Cienfuegos, Cuba, 1860–1886" (Univ. of North Carolina at Chapel Hill MA thesis, 1997).

11 This story was conveyed to me by Sebastián Asla Cires, a former *montero* (horseman) on Santa Rosalía, in an interview in May 1997. Other memories recall an intent by Quesada to leave the estate to his young widow. See Atkins, *Sixty Years in Cuba*, 60. After the initial publication of this article, Orlando García Martínez uncovered the record of a lawsuit that was probably the basis for the story of the misappropriated inheritance. I have analyzed the suit in chapter eight of Rebecca J. Scott, *Degrees of Freedom: Louisiana and Cuba after Slavery* (Cambridge, Mass., 2005).

12 Biblioteca Nacional de Cuba, Havana, Colección Cubana, Colección Manuscrita Julio Lobo (hereafter BNC, CC, CMJL), no. 118, "Relación jurada".

13 See *Revista económica*, 7 June 1878, "Noticia de las fincas azucareras en producción que existían en toda la isla de Cuba al comenzar el presupuesto de 1877–78", 7–24. The figure of 150 slaves probably does not include children under the age of ten. On Blanco's activities in Cienfuegos, see Edo, *Memoria histórica*, 454–5; Sartorius, "Slavery, *Conucos*, and the Local Economy".

14 See *Revista económica*, 7 June 1878, "Noticia de las fincas", for estimates of expanse and production in 1877.

15 See J. S. Murray to Edwin F. Atkins, 22 Apr. 1884, in Massachusetts Historical Society, Boston, Atkins Family Papers (hereafter MHS, AFP), series IV (Soledad Sugar Co. records).

16 This story was recounted by Sebastián Asla Cires, interview, May 1997.

17 See Atkins, *Sixty Years in Cuba*, 75.

18 The valuation, which Atkins's partner Esteban Torriente thought inflated, appears in Esteban Torriente to Edwin F. Atkins, 28 Oct 1880, in MHS, AFP, ser. II (Edwin F. Atkins papers, 1875–1919). The inventory appears in Archivo Provincial de Cienfuegos, Cienfuegos (hereafter APC), Protocolos Hernández Castiñeiras, Escritura #200, Año 1881, "Venta de fincas por el Señor Juez de Primera Instancia de esta ciudad a favor de la Sociedad de Torriente y Hermanos", fos. 840ff.

19 This remarkable document is titled "Libro no. I de los negros, Santa Rosalía", and is held in the APC. Emilio Blanco appears on fo. 201, and Ramón Blanco on fo. 223. Fos. 176 and 210 contain lists of twenty-eight or twenty-nine additional individuals, apparently children, titled "Criollos y los que ganan al mes".

20 APC, "Libro no. 1".

21 *Ibid.*, fo. 17. There is only one Ciriaco in the 1880 slave list from Santa Rosalía, and he is listed as eighteen years old. There is one Francisca, age fifty-four, who is presumably his mother, one Francisca who is fifteen; and a free child named Francisca who is one year old. See BNC, CC, CMJL, no. 173, "Lista de la Dotación del Ing. Santa Rosalía [18 Aug 1880]"; no. 158, "Cédulas de Patrocinado, 10 de marzo de 1883".

22 See APC, "Libro no 1", fo. 17. On fo. 15 there appears a Ciriaco Sabanilla, who had a son, but his relationships were with individuals named Crecencio and Macario, and I expect that he was a member of a different family.

23 *Ibid*, fo. 16.

24 Donato appears as forty years old and Creole on the list of the *dotación* of the estate compiled on 18 Aug. 1880, in BNC, CC, CMJL, no. 173, "Lista". His purchases appear in APC, "Libro no. 1", fo. 41.

25 See APC, "Libro no. 1", fo. 11. He appears simply as Mo[reno] Antonio, age thirty-five, born in Africa, in BNC, CC, CMJL, no 158, "Cédulas".

26 There are two men named Felipe in the 1880 list of the *dotación* on Santa Rosalía, one age fifty and the other age thirty. See BNC, CC, CMJL, no. 173, "Lista". A certificate of *patronato* for Felipe, *criollo*, age 36, appears in BNC, CC, CMJL, no. 158, "Cédulas". There are also two Felipes in the 1885–6 record book; one named Felipe Congo, who I assume is the elder of the two, and the other named Felipe Criollo. See APC, "Libro no, 1", fos 55, 57.

27 The entry for Rita Quesada appears in APC, "Libro no. 1", fo. 171. On the workforce in the 1890s, see APC, "Libro mayor no. 3 perteneciente al Ingenio Sta Rosalía propiedad de Dn Manuel Blanco y Ramos".

28 BNC, CC, CMJL, no. 159, vol. 1, "Individuos y los días que tienen trabajados en el transcurso del finado mes de Abril de 1889", and "Individuos y los días que tienen trabajados en el transcurso del presente mes de Otobre del 1889".

29 I have derived the figure of ninety-five by adding Murray's tally of the number of *patrocinados* who had been freed by 26 May 1885 (forty) to the number he reported as held by the plantation two months later (fifty-five). He does not

include children, who were technically *libertos* (freedpeople) if born after 1868. See J. S. Murray to Edwin F. Atkins, 23 June 1884, 4 Dec. 1884, 26 May 1885, 6 Aug 1885, in MHS, AFP, ser. IV, box 1.

30 The discussion of the six self-purchases is in the letter of J. S. Murray to Edwin F. Atkins, 19 June 1884, in MHS, AFP, ser IV, box 1.

31 J. S. Murray to Edwin F. Atkins, 1 July 1884, 21 Oct 1884, in MHS, AFP, ser. IV, box 1.

32 See J. S. Murray to Edwin F. Atkins, 26 May 1885, 2 June 1885, in MHS, AFP, ser. IV, box 1. The *patronato* as a system of control was breaking down at the same time. Murray reported on 26 May 1885: "Thirty one (31) patrocinados obtained their liberty through the government and of our best men and women have bought theirs 40 in all, and no doubt more will buy their liberty as soon as all the hogs are sold".

33 J. S. Murray to Edwin F. Atkins, 26 May 1885, 2 June 1885, 4 June 1885, in MHS, AFP, ser. IV, box 1. A key work on what is sometimes termed "the slaves" economy' is Ira Berlin and Philip D. Morgan (eds.), *Cultivation and Culture: Labor and the Shaping of Slave Life in the Americas* (Charlottesville, 1993).

34 See J. S. Murray to Edwin F. Atkins, 6 Aug. 1885, in MHS, AFP, ser. IV, box 1; Edwin F. Atkins to J. S. Murray, 18 Aug. 1885, in MHS, AFP, ser. IV, vol 2. Atkins's letter seems to betray both a relentless concern for the paper value of the estate, and something of a bad conscience: "Regarding the negroes I shall be glad when they are all free, but we do not want to lose the bal of Patrocinado a/c as it stands in your ledger; can you arrange to retain their cedulars until you get their value crediting them $8–$10 per month until they work it out? Any arrangement which would secure the value of the a/c would meet our approval and I much prefer to finish entirely with the old system as soon as we can safely do so without loss, in this as in other matters you can use your judgement knowing what our views are".

35 On the general decline of the *patronato*, see Scott, *Slave Emancipation in Cuba*, chs. 6–8. On Soledad, see J. S. Murray to Edwin F. Atkins, 27 May 1886, in MHS, AFP, ser. IV, box 2. The language is not altogether clear: "I have arranged with the fiew [*sic*] patrocinados that remain to pay each $20 those that have not the money to pay $5 per month out of their wages".

36 J. S. Murray to Edwin F. Atkins, 24 May 1886, in MHS, AFP, ser, IV, box 2.

37 On Felipe Criollo, see APC, "Libro no. 1", fo. 57, Some years later, an employee described Soledad's location in terms of these routes: "The Government road from Cienfuegos to Los Guaos passes along the northern boundary and that from Cienfuegos to Arimao passes through the center of the estate and alongside of the batey". United States National Archives, Washington, DC, Record Group 76 (hereafter USNA, RG 76), US/Spain Treaty Claims, claim 387 (Atkins), pt I, deposition of L. F. Hughes.

38 Edwin F. Atkins to Alvey A. Adee, Acting Secretary of State, 3 Sept. 1895, in MHS, AFP, ser. II, vol. 39. See also USNA, RG 76, US/Spain Treaty Claims, claim 387 (Atkins), pt I, deposition of Edwin F. Atkins, pp. 118–29, 207.

39 Charles Francis Adams II to John Quincy Adams II, 3–5 Feb. 1890, in MHS, Adams Family Papers, box 35. The letter is judgemental in tone, and filled with stereotypes, but the overall contrast between the machinery of the two mills appears accurate.

40 For the 1890s, see APC, "Libro mayor no. 3, Santa Rosalía"; Ciriaco Quesada appears on fo. 261. On Manuel Blanco's finances, and his continuing relationship with E. Atkins and Co., see Atkins, *Sixty Years in Cuba*, 60.

41 See APC, Juzgado Municipal de Cienfuegos, Año 1891, "Juicio de faltas contra el moreno Marcos Rodriguez por golpes y amenazas a la idem Francisca Sarría". Gregoria Quesada appears in the 1883 register of apprentices with an

age of twenty. Juana appears in the 1880 slave list with an age of eight. See BNC, CC, CMJL, no. 173, "Lista"; no. 158, "Cédulas".

42 Atkins refers to the grinding of cane from Santa Rosalía in 1895. See his letter of 4 Mar. 1895, in MHS, AFP, ser. II, vol. 14, p. 66. On the epidemic, see Atkins, *Sixty Years in Cuba*, 152–4.

43 See Edwin F. Atkins to Brooks, 7 Mar. 1895, in MHS, AFP, ser. II, vol. 14, p. 82.

44 On Soledad, see Atkins, *Sixty Years in Cuba*, 161. On the rebellion in Las Villas see José S. Llorens y Maceo, *Con Maceo en la invasión* (Havana, 1928), 39.

45 See Atkins, *Sixty Years in Cuba*, 162, 163, 167.

46 *Ibid.*, ch. 13, recounts these events.

47 J. S. Murray to Edwin F. Atkins, 23 June 1885, 6 Aug. 1885, 14 Sept. 1886, in MHS, AFP, ser. IV, boxes 1 and 2.

48 See Atkins, *Sixty Years in Cuba*, 184–8. A comment by Murray in 1885 reveals the genesis of one of the settlements of former slaves: "I have given several lots of land to old and useless negros in place indicated in plan, this is a lot of waste land on a hill and is far enough from batey to keep them away", J. S. Murray to Edwin F. Atkins, 16 June 1885, in MHS, AFP, ser. IV, box 1. Conversations with former residents suggest that the "sitio negroes" may have been those who lived on a provision farm closer to the *batey*, perhaps near what is now called the Callejón del Palmar.

49 A useful analysis of the war in Cienfuegos is Orlando García Martínez, "La Brigada de Cienfuegos: un análisis social de su formación", in Fernando Martínez Heredia, Rebecca J. Scott and Orlando García Martínez (eds), *Espacios, silencios y los sentidos de la libertad: Cuba, 1878–1912* (Havana, 2001).

50 See Ada Ferrer, "Rustic Men, Civilized Nation. Race, Culture, and Contention on the Eve of Cuban Independence", *Hispanic Amer. Hist. Rev.*, lxxviii (1998).

51 Atkins, *Sixty Years in Cuba*, 192–3.

52 See USNA, RG 76, US/Spain Treaty Claims, claim 293 (Hormiguero), pt 1, deposition of Elias Ponvert, 25 Jan. 1904.

53 P. M. Beal to Edwin F. Atkins, 17 Jan. 1896, printed in Atkins, *Sixty Years in Cuba*, 196. The texts of the letters from Soledad that Atkins printed in his published memoir do not always match the manuscript letters, and I generally cite the manuscript letter when available. Most of the letters from Soledad in 1896, however, have not yet appeared in the Atkins Family Papers at the MHS, so I have relied on the memoir.

54 See José Rogelio Castillo, *Autobiografía del General José Rogelio Castillo* (Havana, 1973), 149. Castillo also noted that "el ciudadano Claudio Sarría" ("the citizen Claudio Sarría") had been charged with "hechos punibles" ("punishable offences"), but he seems not to have been punished: *ibid.*, 134–5.

55 Atkins, *Sixty Years in Cuba*, 202, 203.

56 *Ibid.*, 227–33. On the circulation and significance of rumours of nose-rings, see Ferrer, *Insurgent Cuba*, 147–9.

57 Atkins, *Sixty Years in Cuba*, 202. The enlistment list is in Archivo Provincial de Santa Clara, Santa Clara, Cuba, Colección de documentos del Ejército Libertador Cubano (hereafter APSC, EL), expediente 60, inventario 1, "Documentos relativos a la Inspección General del Ejército. Expediente que contiene la relación de jefes, oficiales, clases y soldados y el estado de las armas y animales de la Brigada de Cienfuegos. 27 de Noviembre de 1896". I am grateful to Michael Zeuske and Orlando García for sharing their photocopies of these documents.

58 APSC, EL, "Documentos".

59 *Ibid.* My initial information on Cayetano Quesada came from interviews in Cienfuegos with his grand-niece, Araceli Quesada Quesada, and his niece, Caridad Quesada, in May 1997 and Mar. 1998. Cayetano Quesada's roots on

Santa Rosalía are confirmed in the lists of slaves and free workers on Santa Rosalía, where his age in 1880 is listed as one year. See BNC, CC, CMJL, no. 173, "Lista". Further evidence of Cayetano Quesada's service in the *Ejército Libertador* is in his pension request of 1936, filed in APC, Juzgado de Primera Instancia de Cienfuegos, legajo 477.

60 USNA, RG 76, US/Spain Treaty Claims, claim 387 (Atkins), pt 2, deposition of Juan Piñol, 26 May 1906.

61 See USNA, RG 76, US/Spain Treaty Claims, claim 387 (Atkins), pt 1, deposition of L. F. Hughes. See also BNC, CC, CMJL, no. 99. (This last reference to Piñol was conveyed to me by David Sartorius.)

62 Victoriano Quesada appears in the enlistment register of 27 Nov. 1896, APSC, EL, "Documentos", Felipe Quesada y Rodríguez is listed as a soldier with the Gómez infantry in Andrés Soto Pulgarón, *Corazones cubanos* (Havana, 1950), 201. (One Felipe Quesada appears in the Cienfuegos cavalry regiment in Carlos Roloff y Mialofsky, *Indice alfabético y defunciones del Ejército Libertador de Cuba* (Havana, 1901), 735, with an unusually late enlistment date of 14 Feb. 1898, and Felipe Quesada Rodríguez appears on the same page as a member of the Gómez infantry (I think this index may reflect a duplicate record, since each man is listed as the son of Felipe and Francisca.) Ramón Quesada and Manuel Quesada both appear in Soto Pulgarón, *Corazones cubanos*, 201. Each of these names more or less matches information from Santa Rosalía: identity papers for Victoriano (age nineteen) and Felipe (age thirty-six) appear among the sixty *cédulas de patrocinado* registered by Manuel Blanco in Arimao in 1883. Three black men named Ramón were registered on Santa Rosalía, including a carpenter who would have been forty years old in 1895, and a domestic servant. See BNC, CC, CMJL, no 158, "Cédulas". A Manuel Ganga and a Manuel Emancipado appear in APC, "Libro no. 1", fos. 100, 101.

63 See USNA, RG 76, US/Spain Treaty Claims, claim 250 (Beal), deposition of Peter M. Beal, 26–28 Apr. 1906.

64 Slaves belonging to Manuel Blanco were reported as having joined the insurrections of the late 1870s. See BNC, CC, CMJL, nos. 229, 46. An African named Sebastián Sarría was deported from Cienfuegos as a political prisoner, and later appealed for amnesty in the 1880s. See Archivo Histórico Nacional, Madrid, Sección de Ultramar, legalo 4805, expediente 56.

65 For evidence on the rebellion around Soledad and Santa Rosalía during the earlier conflicts, see the correspondence in BNC, CC, CMJL. I infer Manuel Blanco's temperament from the general tone of Atkins's reminiscences combined with the surviving correspondence of Santa Rosalía, and his antiabolitionism from his prominent role in the *Casino Español* of Cienfuegos. See Atkins, *Sixty Years in Cuba*, 59–60.

66 Interviews with Tomás Pérez y Pérez, Mar. and June 1998, Cienfuegos.

67 See David Sartorius, "Conucos y subsistencia: el caso de Santa Rosalía", in Martínez, Scott and García (eds), *Espacios, silencios y los sentidos de la libertad*. Louis A. Pérez, Jr, has pointed out that if we assume an automatic predisposition on the part of former slaves to join the rebellion we may also obscure the enlistment of some of them in the anti-insurgent *guerrillas* that supported the Spanish struggle. Pérez, personal communication, Jan. 1998.

68 I owe this picture of the war in Cienfuegos in 1897 largely to Orlando García Martínez, personal communications, 1997. See also García, "La Brigada de Cienfuegos", in Martínez, Scott and García (eds.), *Espacios, silencios y los sentidos de la libertad*.

69 Carlos Trujillo, *De la guerra y de la paz* (Havana, 1943), 52.

70 See Louis A. Pérez, *The War of 1898: The United States and Cuba in History and Historiography* (Chapel Hill, 1998), 10–12.

71 On the end of the war, see Louis A. Pérez's classic *Cuba between Empires,*
1878–1902 (Pittsburgh, 1983). See also Pérez's provocative essay, "Approaching
Martí: Text and Context", in José Amor y Vázquez (ed.), *Imagining a Free Cuba:*
Carlos Manuel de Céspedes and José Martí (Thomas J. Watson, Jr, Inst. for Internat
Studies, Brown University, occasional papers, xxiv, Providence, 1996). On the
flags, see Atkins, *Sixty Years in Cuba*, 294.

72 Atkins, *Sixty Years in Cuba*, 294–6.

73 See *Civil Report of Major-General John R. Brooke, US Army, Military Governor,*
Island of Cuba (Washington, DC, 1900), 329–38.

74 See the letters of Constantino Pérez to Manuel García, 1899, OGM, CSR.

75 Interview with Caridad Quesada, Mar. 1998, Cienfuegos.

76 See USNA, Record Group 395, Military Information Division, Army of Cuban
Pacification, Correspondence, entry 1008, file 74, item 3, report of 29 Nov. 1906.

77 See USNA, Record Group 395, Military Information Division, Army of
Cuban Pacification, Correspondence, entry 1008, file 79, item 107, report of
13 Apr. 1907.

78 Evidence of such violence can be found in the judicial records held in the APC.
For a general description of the drought that summer, see *Civil Report of*
Major-General John R. Brooke, 12, 13.

79 Constantino Pérez to Manuel García, 27 Dec. 1899, OGM, CSR. The original
text, which is not easy to construe, reads as follows: "Me dijo Carlos también
que hoy Andrés Simeon tubiera una agarrada con un ciudadano de esos
Bandidos, este estaba en la portada de San Anton en la tienda de Felis y que le
dijo que no tenía verguenza el hombre que le cuidaba el ganado à Manuel
Blanco y por ahi empezaron y en esa tienda todos los días hay algunos de estos
rateros dice que vicen por los guaús [Guaos?] y que si pueden pescar algo de
aqui lo llevan para allá y también dicen que los encargados de aqui no vamos
durar mucho tiempo eso también me lo dijo asuncion no se con que sentido
sera".

80 See, for example, Chris Wickham, "Gossip and Resistance among the
Medieval Peasantry", *Past and Present*, no. 160 (Aug. 1998).

81 See Constantino Pérez to Manuel García, 28 June 1899, OGM, CSR. In this
letter, Pérez writes to Manuel García in Cienfuegos, and refers to "Dn Manuel",
evidently the estate owner, Manuel Blanco: "de lo que me dice del mulo del hijo
de Gregoria, estube con Carlos y le pregunte con disimulo y me dijo que si, que
aqui habia una mula con el hierro especie de trés tubos, pero que nacio aqui y
aqui está que Carlos mismo le hablo a Dn Manuel de esa mula y le contestó que
sin orden de el no la entregara a nadie asi es que si vuelbe ya Vd. está enterado"
("concerning what [your letter] says about Gregoria's son's mule, I was with
Carlos and inquired discreetly and he said yes, that there was a mule here with
a brand like three tubes, but that it was born here and is still here, that Carlos
himself spoke to Don Manuel about this mule and he told him that without an
order from him it shouldn't be given to anybody so if [he/she] comes back you
now know").

82 See the letters of Constantino Pérez to Manuel García, 28 June, 17, 18 and
19 Aug. 1899, OGM, CSR.

83 See *Civil Report of Major-General John R. Brooke*, 55, 70.

84 I am enormously grateful to Orlando García Martínez for using his vast knowledge of the Cienfuegos *protocolos* to locate this fleeting reference to Gregoria
Quesada. See APC, Protocolos Verdaguer, Escritura #617, fo. 3504, "Venta de
finca rústica por la Sra Doña Lutgarda Díaz y Nodal viuda de Rosés, a favor
de la morena Da Gregoria Quesada", 23 Oct. 1897. The age does not quite
match that given for Gregoria on the 1883 list of *patrocinados* (twenty), but
inconsistencies of this kind are fairly common, as in the acknowledged

disparities in the ages attributed to *patrocinados* at both Soledad and Santa Rosalía.

85 The group conversing on the patio in June 1998 included Leonardo Alomá, Orlando García, Aims McGuinness and myself, visiting Ramona Quesada de Castillo, her husband Evelio Castillo, her brothers Gerardo Quesada and Francisco Quesada, and her daughter Carmen Castillo.

86 This lovely phrase is Elsa Barkley Brown's. See her "To Catch the Vision of Freedom: Reconstructing Southern Black Women's Political History, 1865–1880", in Ann D. Gordon et al. (eds), *African American Women and the Vote, 1837–1965* (Amherst, 1997).

PERMISSION ACKNOWLEDGEMENTS

Every effort has been made to cite completely the original source material for each work compiled in this collection. These selections appear here as they did in their original form, with a few exceptions. In the Gaspar and Rebecca Scott essays, we have incorporated some corrections at the request of the authors, and in the selections from the books by Childs, Reis, Julius Scott and Williams, whose footnotes sometimes made use of abbreviations listed elsewhere in the book, of references in previous chapters, or of bibliographies, we have added complete references to footnotes to allow readers to find the materials referred to there. In the event that something has been inadvertently been used or cited incorrectly, every effort will be made in subsequent editions to rectify the error. We offer our sincere thanks to all of the sources that were courteous enough to help us reproduce the contents of this volume.

David Barry Gaspar, "'A Dangerous Spirit of Liberty': Slave Rebellion in the West Indies in the 1730s," *Cimarrons* 1 (1981): 79–91. Courtesy of the author.

Richard Sheridan, "The Jamaican Slave Insurrection Scare of 1776 and the American Revolution," *Journal of Negro History* 61(3) (1976), 290–308. Courtesy of the Association for the Study of African American Life & History.

Neville A.T. Hall, "Maritime Maroons: *Grand Marronage* from the Danish West Indies," *William and Mary Quarterly* 42, no. 4 (1985): 476–498. Courtesy of WMQ.

Julius S. Scott, "'Negroes in Foreign Bottoms': Sailors, Slaves, and Communication," pp. 59–113 in *The Common Wind: Currents of Afro-American Communication in the Era of the Haitian Revolution*. Courtesy of the author.

Richard Gray, "The Papacy and the Atlantic Slave Trade: Lourenço da Silva, the Capuchins, and the Decisions of the Holy Office," *Past and*

Present 115 (May 1987): 52–68. Courtesy of the editors of *Past and Present* and Oxford University Press.

Ira Berlin, "From Creole to African: Atlantic Creoles and the Origins of African-American Society in Mainland North America," *William and Mary Quarterly*, 3rd ser., vol. 53 (April 1996): 251–288. Courtesy of WMQ.

Emily Clark and Virginia Meacham Gould, "The Feminine Face of Afro-Catholicism in New Orleans, 1727–1852," *William and Mary Quarterly*, 3rd ser., vol. 59, no. 2 (April 2002): 409–448. Courtesy of WMQ.

John K. Thornton, "African Soldiers in the Haitian Revolution," *Journal of Caribbean History* 25: 1 and 2 (1991), 58–80. Courtesy of Alvin Thompson and John Thornton.

João José Reis, *Slave Rebellion in Brazil: The Muslim Uprising of 1835 in Bahia* (Baltimore, MD: Johns Hopkins University Press, 1993), Chapter 5: "The Sons of Allah in Bahia." Courtesy of John Hopkins University Press.

Kenneth Bilby, "Swearing by the Past, Swearing to the Future: Sacred Oaths, Alliances, and Treaties Among the Guianese and Jamaican Maroons," *Ethnohistory* 44: 4 (1997), 655–689. Courtesy of Duke University Press.

Matt D. Childs, *The 1812 Aponte Rebellion and the Struggle Against Slavery in Cuba* (Chapel Hill, NC: University of North Carolina Press, 2006), excerpt from Chapter 3: "Organizing the Rebellion," 95–119, and Chapter 5: "Vanquish the Arrogance of Our Enemies". Courtesy of University of North Carolina Press.

Eric Williams, *Capitalism and Slavery* (Chapel Hill, NC: University of North Carolina Press, 1994 [1945]), selections from "The Slaves and Slavery." Courtesy of University of North Carolina Press.

Steven Hahn, "'Extravagant Expectations' of Freedom: Rumour, Political Struggle, and the Christmas Insurrection Scare of 1865 in the American South," *Past and Present* 157 (November 1997): 122–158. Courtesy of the editors of *Past and Present* and Oxford University Press.

Rebecca J. Scott, "Reclaiming Gregoria's Mule: The Meanings of Freedom in the Arimao and Caunao Valleys, Cienfuegos, Cuba, 1880–1889," *Past and Present* 170 (February 2001): 181–216. Courtesy of the editors of *Past and Present* and Oxford University Press.

INDEX

399